A New American Scripture

*How and Why the Real Illuminati®
Created the Book of Mormon*

This is the second of three volumes:

*The True History of Religion—How Religion Destroys the Human Race and
    What the Real Illuminati® Has Attempted to do Through Religion to Save
    the Human Race*

*A New American Scripture—How and Why the Real Illuminati® Created
    the Book of Mormon*

One People, One World, One Government

A New American Scripture

*How and Why the Real Illuminati® Created
The Book of Mormon*

The Real Illuminati

Worldwide United Publishing
Melba, Idaho

A New American Scripture—How and Why the Real Illuminati® Created the Book of Mormon

Text and cover design copyright © 2020 by Worldwide United Publishing.

All rights reserved. No part of this book may be used or reproduced in any manner whatsoever without written permission of the author or publisher, except by a reviewer who may quote brief passages.

July 4, 2021
First Edition

HARDBACK ISBN 978-1-937390-20-4
SOFTCOVER ISBN 978-1-937390-21-1

Library of Congress Control Number: 2019957208

Worldwide United Publishing
an imprint of Pearl Publishing, LLC
2587 Southside Blvd., Melba, ID 83641
www.pearlpublishing.net—1.888.499.9666

———————————

This book is a trial of our authority to make valid claims that can change our world. In writing this book, we present a strong case against the secret combinations of political, religious, and business powers that control and deceive humanity.

If one takes the time to *only* read Chapter 1 (**our opening statement**) and Chapter 20 (**our closing argument**), one will have an overall and clear understanding of the crucial points of our case. This book contains substantial evidence that proves our case. We call upon humanity to be our judge and jury.

We are the Real Illuminati®. We wrote a new American scripture (which consists of the *Book of Mormon* and *The Sealed Portion*) that we know could change our world, if our writings are considered for their true intent and purpose.

This book offers the reader the opportunity to put our claims on trial.

—The Real Illuminati®

———————————

CONTENTS

PROLOGUE ix

FOREWORD xxix

INTRODUCTION 1

1   The Real Illuminati®—Authors' Note
    (Our Opening Statement) 23

2   Author and Proprietor 35

3   The Greatest Human Deception 65

4   Exposing Secret Combinations 84

5   According to the Portion of His Word 105

6   The Plates of Gold 129

7   Looking Beyond the Mark 159

8   The 116-page Lost Manuscript 199

9   The Forced Revision 214

10 The Atonement—A Christian Delusion 240

11 Transfiguring the Holy Word of God 276

12 Pride and Vanity—Destroyers of Civilization 311

13 The Family of Pride 341

14 Wars and Rumors of Wars 371

15 True Messengers 398

16 Humanity's Salvation—The Fullness of the
    Everlasting Gospel 442

17 The Great White Nation of the United States 485

18 Other Books, Other Peoples 509

19	A Marvelous Work and a Wonder®—A Promise of Peace and Life Eternal	525
20	The Great Apocalypse—A Message to the Youth of Planet Earth **(Our Closing Argument)**	557
APPENDIX I	*The Sealed Portion*—How Money and Secret Combinations Began	607
APPENDIX II	*The Sealed Portion*—Adam Teaches the Fullness of the Everlasting Gospel	631

FREQUENT REFERENCE	685
ABBREVIATIONS USED IN FOOTNOTES	686
WORKS CITED	689

PROLOGUE

*(Note: The following facts and events can be investigated and verified by any credible and honest examiner. Each and every one is true. The names of those involved have not been changed. The dates in some cases are approximated, but very close to the actual dates when each of the facts or events occurred. Although a prologue is usually used in the presentation of a fictitious novel—in order to reveal information that is not necessarily consistent with the book's storyline—this book is **not** a work of fiction.* **This book is a documentary of fact.** *Therefore, in order for a full disclosure and clear understanding of this book's intent, which is to bring out of obscurity the Real Truth™ about our Book of Mormon,* **it is vital that the following facts and events be considered and researched before one reads the rest of this book.***)*

On October 2, 2016, during the 186th Semiannual General Conference of the Church of Jesus Christ of Latter-day Saints (LDS/Mormon Church), one of this church's members of the Quorum of the Twelve Apostles, Elder Gary E. Stevenson, gave a conference address titled, "Look to the Book, Look to the Lord." Apostle Stevenson told the members of his church:

> Each of you can also receive a personal witness of this book! Do you realize the Book of Mormon was written for you—and for your day? This book is one of the blessings of living in what we call the dispensation of the fulness of times.[1]

Stevenson emotionally and emphatically told the members how important and blessed they were for having the *Book of Mormon*:

---

[1] Elder Gary E. Stevenson, "Look to the Book, Look to the Lord," Oct. 2016 General Conference, The Church of Jesus Christ of Latter-day Saints, churchofjesuschrist.org/study/general-conference/2016/10/look-to-the-book-look-to-the-lord.

You have the benefit of holding in your hands the complete Book of Mormon. Interestingly, one of the Book of Mormon prophets, Moroni, saw our day—YOUR day. He even saw YOU, in vision, many hundreds of years ago! Moroni wrote: "Behold, the Lord hath shown unto me great and marvelous things concerning that day when these things," meaning the Book of Mormon, "shall come forth among you. Behold, I speak unto you as if ye were present, and yet ye are not. But behold, Jesus Christ hath shown you unto me, and I know your doing."[2]

It would appear that the overall purpose of Stevenson's conference address was to tell the members how important gaining a personal witness of the *Book of Mormon* is to their faith. He challenged the Mormon youth to set aside at least 10 minutes each day for reading the *Book of Mormon* instead of spending "an average of seven hours a day looking at TV, computer, and smartphone screens."

The members of the LDS church revere their Twelve Apostles and other General Authorities as "special witnesses of Jesus Christ." Most members are of the belief that these special men have actually met Jesus and received verbal instruction directly from Christ himself. The members of this church hold their leaders in the highest esteem and in great reverence. They believe that Jesus Christ himself is guiding them and giving them direction through their priesthood leaders.

LDS people listen intently and carefully to their leaders' words. Their leaders deliver their words to the members (at least in public) with the *appearance* of great humility and passion. The same is true in the case above with Apostle Stevenson as he explained to the Mormon people that Jesus Christ was aware of them "many hundreds of years ago." Stevenson delivered the above quoted part of his sermon with a level of emotion that brought him near to tears. The spiritual sensations that the faithful

---

[2] Video of Stevenson's address found at "Look to the Book, Look to the Lord," YouTube, 1 Oct. 2016, youtube.com/watch?v=LHxUcozPcfg. (The relevant part starts 9 minutes in).

members feel from the words delivered by their leaders in public, increase the members' testimonies. The members have no reason to doubt or question their leaders. In this church, the members are counseled to not question their leaders. If any member does, the member is chastised. Questioning a leader can also lead to a person's excommunication.[3]

Regardless of the emotional effect his words had on his followers, on October 2, 2016, this supposed Apostle of Jesus Christ blatantly lied to the members of his church. Apostle Stevenson "transfigured the holy word of God." Ironically, if Apostle Stevenson had read *all* of the *Book of Mormon* verses in complete context, both the verses before and those after the quote he used, the following is what the members of this church would have heard him say:

> O ye wicked and perverse and stiffnecked people, why have ye built up churches unto yourselves to get gain? Why have ye **transfigured the holy word of God**, that ye might bring damnation upon your souls? Behold, look ye unto the revelations of God; for behold, the time cometh at that day when all these things must be fulfilled.
>
> Behold, the Lord hath shown unto me great and marvelous things concerning that which must shortly come, at that day when these things shall come forth among you.
>
> Behold, I speak unto you as if ye were present, and yet ye are not. But behold, Jesus Christ hath shown you unto me, and I know your doing.
>
> And I know that ye do walk in the pride of your hearts; and there are none save a few only who do not lift themselves up in the pride of their hearts, unto the wearing of very fine apparel, unto

---

[3] *See* "Latter-day Saints," in "Apostasy," *Wikipedia*, Wikimedia Foundation, 14 May 2021, en.wikipedia.org/wiki/Apostasy#Latter-day_Saints.

envying, and strifes, and malice, and persecutions, and all manner of iniquities; and your churches, yea, even every one, have become polluted because of the pride of your hearts.

For behold, ye do love money, and your substance, and your fine apparel, and the adorning of your churches, more than ye love the poor and the needy, the sick and the afflicted.

O ye pollutions, ye hypocrites, ye teachers, who sell yourselves for that which will canker, why have ye polluted the holy church of God? Why are ye ashamed to take upon you the name of Christ? Why do ye not think that greater is the value of an endless happiness than that misery which never dies—because of the praise of the world?

Why do ye adorn yourselves with that which hath no life, and yet suffer the hungry, and the needy, and the naked, and the sick and the afflicted to pass by you, and notice them not?

Yea, why do ye build up your secret abominations to get gain, and cause that widows should mourn before the Lord, and also orphans to mourn before the Lord, and also the blood of their fathers and their husbands to cry unto the Lord from the ground, for vengeance upon your heads?

Behold, the sword of vengeance hangeth over you; and the time soon cometh that he avengeth the blood of the saints upon you, for he will not suffer their cries any longer.[4]

What is a young Latter-day Saint/Mormon person, reading the *Book of Mormon* for ten minutes each day, supposed to think when they hear Stevenson's uplifting and flattering quotes, and then read the same quote in

---

[4] *BOM*, Mormon 8:33–41, emphasis added.

context with the other surrounding verses? A member of this church believes that the *Book of Mormon* is one of the most important "revelations of God," as mentioned in the above quoted passages from our new American scripture. In context, the prophecy clearly states that the *ancient Book of Mormon prophet* is speaking about "that day when all *these things* must be fulfilled." According to the true text of our new American scripture, "these things" are the *wicked* "doing[s]" of the people, as the full context describes.

Elder Stevenson did not limit his deception and "transfiguration of the holy word of God" to this blatant duplicity (obvious deception) only. Stevenson also lied when he told the members of his church that what they had in their homes, from which they were supposed to read just ten minutes each day, was the "whole book ... the complete Book of Mormon."

Stevenson knew that the "whole ... complete" book was not translated by Joseph Smith, Jr. Only a portion of it was. Honest and transparent LDS/Mormon history reports correctly that Joseph Smith published the *Book of Mormon* to the world in 1830 as its "Author and Proprietor."[5] Any honest reader has no choice but to admit that the 1830 *Book of Mormon* is the "lesser portion of the word," according to the book's narrative, and that the *sealed part of the gold plates* is "the greater portion of the word."[6]

The *Book of Mormon* explains very clearly that the "sealed portion" is the most important part of our new American scripture. Its narrative specifically states that those who possess *only* the **unsealed** part of the gold plates (i.e., what Joseph was allowed to publish in 1830 as the *Book of Mormon*), which is the "lesser portion of the word ... are taken captive

---

[5] *See* Joseph Smith Jr., Author and Proprietor, *The Book of Mormon—An Account Written by the Hand of Mormon, Upon Plates Taken from the Plates of Nephi* (Palmyra: E. B. Grandin, 1830), found online at realilluminati.org/the-book-of-mormon; and
"Book of Mormon, 1830," The Joseph Smith Papers – Church Historian's Press, josephsmithpapers.org/paper-summary/book-of-mormon-1830/7.

[6] *BOM*, Alma 12:10.

by the devil, and led by his will down to destruction. Now this is what is meant by the chains of hell."[7]

Our new American scripture is clear that the *unsealed* part of what was presented to the world as the "gold plates," is a

> lesser part ... which is expedient that they should have first, to try their faith, and if it so be that they shall believe these things [the *unsealed*, 1830 *Book of Mormon*,] then shall the greater things be made manifest unto them. And if it so be that they will not believe these things, then shall the greater things be withheld from them, unto their condemnation.[8]

The members of the LDS Church look to their prophets and apostles with unwavering and unquestioning faith. They would never believe that one of their leaders would intentionally mislead them; and their leaders *know* this. These leaders are also aware that most members do not read the *Book of Mormon* regularly, and, of those who do, few understand its true meaning. All scripture was written by "dead prophets." However, the members of this church are told that,

> The living prophet is more important to us than a dead prophet. ... Beware of those who would pit the dead prophets against the living prophets, for the living prophets always take precedence.[9]

If Apostle Stevenson would have been honest with members of his church about what this "dead prophet" of the *Book of Mormon* had prophesied about them and their "doing," he would have told the members that they, and the church to which they belong, were under grave

---

[7] *See BOM*, Alma 12:9–11.
[8] *BOM*, 3 Nephi 26:8–10.
[9] *See* Ezra Taft Benson, "Fourteen Fundamentals in Following the Prophet," 26 Feb. 1980, found online at speeches.byu.edu/talks/ezra-taft-benson/fourteen-fundamentals-following-prophet.

condemnation. Further, Stevenson would have properly disclosed that the *unsealed* part of the gold plates (the *Book of Mormon*), which the LDS Church accepts as another "word of God," is NOT "whole ... and complete." He would have referred to what the book's main author, "the dead prophet" Mormon, said about what he was writing:

> And these things which I have written, which are a lesser part of the things which [Jesus] taught the people ... they should have first, to try their faith, and if it shall so be that they shall believe these things then shall the greater things be made manifest unto them. And if it so be that they will not believe these things [the *Book of Mormon*], then shall the greater things be withheld from them, unto their condemnation.[10]

The members and leaders of the Church of Jesus Christ of Latter-day Saints, regardless of the sincere and seemingly humble testimonies they give to the rest of the world about our *Book of Mormon*, "*do not believe these things.*" In fact, this church has rejected "the greater things" contained in *The Sealed Portion—The Final Testament of Jesus Christ*, finally published in 2004.

We wrote our *Book of Mormon* for the intent to do good—to influence the early European-American Christians to consider a different way of looking at the "fulness of the Gospel of Jesus Christ"[11]—especially how Christianity *should* relate to the native American people of the Western Hemisphere. Regardless of the lessons we tried to teach in the lesser part of our new American scripture, Mormons are led to believe that their leaders' words take precedence over any scripture. The Mormons believe that their leaders' words *are scripture*—the words of God given to the people living on the earth, by God's chosen leaders.

---

[10] *BOM*, 3 Nephi 26:6–11.
[11] *D&C*, 20:9; *compare* JSH 1:33–5.

In spite of the LDS Church proclaiming to the world that the *Book of Mormon* is "the most correct of any book on earth, and the keystone of [their] religion, and a man would get nearer to God by abiding by its precepts, than by any other book,"[12] it was written by "dead prophets." VERY LITTLE of what our new American scripture teaches is incorporated into the modern curriculum and teachings of the LDS Church.

We will prove in this book, *A New American Scripture*, that the *Book of Mormon* is a work of fiction. The LDS/Mormons see it as an actual history. In spite of the prevailing LDS/Mormon view and proclamations about the *Book of Mormon*, we will prove that it is *not* an actual historical account. We will prove that it was NOT our intent, in writing a new American scripture, to establish a new church and religion that would disregard every single one of our book's teachings and eventually evolve into one of the wealthiest churches in the history of the world.[13]

What Apostle Stevenson left out of his address about the "complete Book of Mormon," was any mention of the "greater portion." We anticipated there would be transfiguration and deceit when we first wrote our new American scripture. We knew this might happen if the people who read our book disregarded its basic teachings and tenets (which they have and do), and only listened to their deceptive leaders. Our inclusion in the storyline of the important subplot about the "greater portion"—the *sealed portion* of the gold plates—was the *failsafe* that we intended for the narrative of our book.

We needed a failsafe in case our original message and intent were ignored. A *failsafe* is a system or plan that comes into operation in the event of something going wrong, or is there to prevent such an occurrence from

---

[12] *See* B.H. Roberts, *History of the Church of Jesus Christ of Latter-day Saints*, 7 vols. (Salt Lake City: Published by the Church and Deseret Book Co., 1902–12), 4:461. (Hereafter cited as *History of the Church*).

[13] *See* "Religious organizations," in "List of wealthiest organizations." *Wikipedia*, 24 May 2021, en.wikipedia.org/wiki/List_of_wealthiest_organizations#Religious_organizations.

happening. (Again, for clarification, and to inform those unfamiliar with the LDS/Mormon religion, the lesser portion of our new American scripture, the *Book of Mormon*, was published in 1830, and the rest of it, the greater portion, *The Sealed Portion—The Final Testament of Jesus Christ*, was published in 2004.)

We will present indisputable and unequivocal (unmistakable) evidence that, since the time of Joseph Smith, the European-American Christians who have read and embraced our new American scripture have completely ignored, disregarded, and often *transfigured* our message. They have done and currently do this to receive praise from the world, to uphold and support their love of money and success, and to justify the wearing of very fine apparel. The context left out by Stevenson clearly and perfectly describes these modern "doing[s]" of the church that resulted from people ignoring and transfiguring the message of our book.

If the world knew what the members of the LDS Church *really* believe, in spite of what they say to their non-member friends and associates, the world would stand amazed and perplexed at the profound arrogance of it all.

We will provide the evidence of how a prophet, seer, and revelator of this religion (named Wilford Woodruff) gave testimony that all of the United States Founding Fathers "and fifty other eminent men, making one hundred in all" (including John Wesley, Christopher Columbus, and George Washington), appeared to him in one of the LDS temples.[14] At that time, this *living* prophet reported that these notable men asked to be baptized into the LDS Church and receive the "holy saving ordinances" vicariously. This is another of the many evidences of the way this church deceives its members and misleads the world to believe that it is God's *only true and living* church, and that without their church, humanity cannot be saved. (Again, this church refers to itself as God's *ONLY TRUE AND LIVING CHURCH* because it claims to be the only church with *living* prophets who communicate directly with Jesus

---

[14] "Eminent Spirits Appear to Wilford Woodruff," *Joseph Smith Foundation*, 4 Nov. 2020, josephsmithfoundation.org/wiki/eminent-spirits-appear-to-wilford-woodruff.

Christ, and receive direction from Christ, in spite of the direction that the "dead prophets" wrote in the scriptures.)

Joseph Smith never made such an arrogant claim about baptism being a necessity for people to gain a remission of their sins. In fact, his elder brother Alvin had died before the Church was organized and the priesthood power restored to the LDS leaders, as they supposed. In their own scripture, Joseph recounts how he had a vision in which he saw

> Father Adam and Abraham; and my father and my mother; my brother Alvin, that has long since slept; And marveled how it was that [Alvin] had obtained an inheritance in [the celestial kingdom of God], seeing that he had departed this life before the Lord had set his hand to gather Israel the second time, and had not been baptized for the remission of sins.[15]

Joseph reported that his brother didn't need baptism, because "the Lord, will judge all men according to their works, according to the desire of their hearts."[16]

Throughout this book, we will provide substantial (clear and solid) evidence of how Joseph Smith was forced to deal with his followers, who often disregarded the lessons of the *Book of Mormon* and "sought for things that they could not understand." We instructed Joseph to deliver "unto them many things which they cannot understand, because they desired it." And because they desired it, Joseph gave his followers what they wanted "that they may stumble."[17] We will explain how Joseph did what he had to do according to the direction that we gave him concerning our new American scripture. We will also explain how and why many of his original followers left Joseph Smith and called him a fallen prophet.

---

[15] *D&C*, 137:5–6.
[16] *D&C*, 137:9.
[17] *BOM*, Jacob 4:14.

Prologue

With patience, we waited as long as we could—hoping that one day the members of the Church of Jesus Christ of Latter-day Saints would actually read our book, pay attention to its teachings, and give heed to its prophecies and warnings. We waited patiently, to no avail. The religion that touts our book as its own has gotten progressively and exponentially worse as time has passed.

We could wait no longer.

In 2004 we put our *failsafe* into operation. We wrote and published *The Sealed Portion—The Final Testament of Jesus Christ* (the *sealed* part of our new American scripture). It is the "greater" and "sealed" 2/3 part of what we allowed to be presented as the gold plates. The *unsealed* 1/3 of the plates was written by a character in our story named Mormon, and his son, Moroni (pronounced Mō-rō´nī). The *sealed* 2/3 was written by Moroni, as we presented these characters appropriately throughout our storyline.

There have been many faithful Mormons who have *actually* read and studied our *Book of Mormon* and realized that they must have the "greater portion of the word," otherwise, they would "know nothing," and would remain under condemnation. Those members who were and are looking for the *sealed portion* of the gold plates to come forth, once they read ours, "with a sincere heart with real intent," were and will be convinced beyond any doubt that our sealed portion IS the promised "greater portion."

Our *Book of Mormon*'s storyline presents various times when the people were righteous and established the proper form of a church. Our narrative also presents many times when the Church became corrupt and unrighteous. Each time that the "church of God" became corrupt, the Church's leaders did not recognize the wickedness, because they were the ones perpetuating it.

The narrative of our new American scripture presents subplots that show that a non- or former member of the wicked church was the one sent each

A New American Scripture

time to call the Church, its leaders, and its people to repentance. When we published *The Sealed Portion—The Final Testament of Jesus Christ* in 2004, we chose to do so with a man whom the LDS Church views as an "apostate," or rather, as a former member who no longer conforms to or follows that particular religion.

The LDS Church teaches that God will not allow its leaders to mislead the people. It teaches that if God has something important to tell the people of the world, God will do so through the established priesthood leadership and proper ecclesiastical (religious) authority and divine power of *their* church only. It teaches that God will only speak through its *living* prophets, again, regardless of what any "dead prophet" might have written or prophesied.

In each instance in the storyline of our new American scripture when the church became corrupt, we introduced a character who was *outside* of the Church—even one who would be viewed as an apostate. In our story, only these "apostates" were called of God to confront the Church and its leaders and call them to repentance.

Our original storyline started out with two prophets who did not belong to the church at Jerusalem. These two prophets were not recognized by the Church as "prophets, seers, or revelators." We called these two prophets, *Zenos* and *Zenock*. However, the *Book of Mormon* does not mention from where these two prophets originated. We will explain later how we were forced to change the initial way that we presented our story. This change was necessary because the people to whom Joseph Smith shared our work (as a *peer review group*) were unable to accept its original beginning. We will detail how and why this happened. The LDS/Mormon people would recognize our original storyline as the *Book of Lehi—The Lost 116-Page Manuscript*.[18] However, this original storyline was never

---

[18] Read for free at realilluminati.org/the-book-of-lehi.

actually "lost." It was *purposefully* replaced with a new presentation of what we intended as our new American scripture's initial subplot.

In our original story, one of our main characters—Lehi—was one of the rich and popular High Priests in the church at Jerusalem. Lehi believed what the prophets Zenos and Zenock said about the corrupt nature of Gods' holy church. When Lehi tried to stand up for these two prophets, he was ridiculed, rebuked, and cast out of the Church as an apostate. This was the first scenario that we presented to show that God would not, and could not, choose an appointed True Messenger from among church priesthood leadership, when the major source of corruption *was* the leadership of the Church.

The next scenario was presented in the subplot about the prophet Abinadi. The third subplot that presented this protocol for calling a *true prophet* to confront a wicked church was in the story of Samuel the Lamanite. Each of these *true prophets* was cast out of the Church. Each was called by God to go back to the Church and call the members and the leaders to repentance. Whereas the subplot describing what Zenos and Zenock did was in our *original* narrative, the two scenarios about Abinadi and Samuel the Lamanite are in the *Book of Mormon* as it is currently circulated and accepted by the LDS/Mormons.

To be reflective and consistent with Hebrew theology concerning the necessity of three witnesses, we wrote three subplots to our narrative. We provided three witnesses of the fact that God will not, and cannot, choose a *True Messenger* from among wicked church leaders to confront a wicked church. The man whom we chose as our True Messenger to publish our *sealed portion* to the world in 2004 was chosen, recruited, and instructed in a very similar way to the way we chose, recruited, and instructed Joseph Smith to publish our *unsealed* 1/3 *portion* of the gold plates to the world in 1830.

In both cases, the words "translated" (or rather "transcribed" from the gold plates, as it will be explained later in this book) were *our words*, not theirs. Neither of these modern-day True Messengers deserves the credit nor the persecution that each has endured in assisting us to perform our work. We presented our work in the storyline of our new American scripture as a "great and marvelous work" (a Marvelous Work and a Wonder®). We call it this in fulfillment of ancient prophets' writings.[19] Of course, this causes a problem when we present our work in this way. This is because the Mormons discount anything that a "dead prophet" said or wrote. Consequently, the LDS/Mormon people reject the lessons about the proper protocol in calling a *True Messenger* as we presented in the subplot scenarios that we included in our storyline. Instead, the LDS members believe *only* what their own *living* leaders say or write. Their leaders teach them that God will not call anyone to do His will outside of the official and authorized lines of priesthood authority found only in God's *True and Living Church*.

In 2007, Ida Smith, the great, great granddaughter of Hyrum Smith (and great, great grandniece of Joseph Smith, Jr.), found and read our book: *The Sealed Portion—The Final Testament of Jesus Christ.* Ida was profoundly connected to many of the LDS Church General Authorities at that time, as well as to some of the politicians with whom this church secretly combined its power to become one of the wealthiest churches in the world.

Ida Smith hand delivered *The Sealed Portion—The Final Testament of Jesus Christ* to many of the authorities and popular leaders with whom she had been intimately associated throughout her life. Some accepted her gift. Others refused to receive it. None of them read it with a sincere heart and real intent. Ida made the book available to two of her former bosses, under whom she was employed at Brigham Young University: LDS Church Apostles Dallin H. Oaks and Jeffrey R. Holland. Ida offered the book to her cousin, Apostle M. Russell Ballard, as well as to other of her lifelong friends who were not quite as prominent in the LDS Church's hierarchy.[20] Ida boldly and without reservation gave a copy of our book to two of her best

---

[19] *See BOM*, 1 Nephi 14:7; *BOM*, 2 Nephi 27:26; OT, Isaiah 29:14.
[20] *See letter* written to Ida Smith on August 23, 2008, from several prominent LDS women at "Ida Smith and The Man From Joe's Bar and Grill," The Real Illuminati®, realilluminati.org/the-man-from-joe-s-bar-and-grill.

friends—former United States Senators Orrin Hatch and Robert ("Bob") Bennett. She encouraged them to read it with a sincere heart and real intent, as she had. These powerful men refused to read it.

Concerned for Ida's safety and eternal salvation (as they perceived it from within the LDS Church), these powerful men used their positions of authority to investigate the man whom we had chosen as our True Messenger. As we have presented in our *Book of Mormon*, those in authority attempt to put True Messengers in prison, if they can, in order to silence them and disparage their character. However, in spite of their strong efforts and their religious and political power, *combined in secret*, nothing these leaders found could be legally used against our chosen True Messenger to charge him with a crime or to put him in prison.

Interestingly, Ida Smith knew these men for many, many years. She was able to meet our True Messenger and us before her death in 2015. She spent a great amount of time in the presence of our chosen True Messenger—*but she had spent a lot more time in her life around the men* we have listed above. Having been in the presence of both, Ida could clearly see the difference between the personalities and characteristics of the revered men of religion and politics, contrasted to that of our simple and ordinary True Messenger.

Ida Smith never married. Although Ida rubbed shoulders daily with some of the world's most notable and popular men, she would report to her family and friends that she never found a man quite suitable enough to warrant her constant companionship. After comparing these prominent LDS/Mormon men to our unknown and very unpopular True Messenger, Ida determined from her own experience that none of her former associates could hold a candle to our chosen messenger when it came to being a *good* man worthy of her companionship. Ida Smith loved our True Messenger with all of her heart, might, mind, and soul.

Ida Smith did everything in her power to get these powerful men to meet with our True Messenger in her presence. She tried, hoping that she could experience both in the same room, and demonstrate to them (and to anyone else present) that these prominent men who were popular in the eyes of the world, were nothing like Zenos, Zenock, Abinadi, and Samuel the Lamanite of the *Book of Mormon*. It was Ida's personal involvement with our True Messenger that solidified her testimony that the LDS Church was as unrighteous as our *Book of Mormon* explains it to be.

One of the things that Ida Smith discussed with her prominent LDS Church friends was the fact that the LDS Church was not as concerned about the poor and the needy as it was about (1) doing genealogy work and redeeming the dead, (2) "perfecting the Saints" (making members of the Church "perfect"), and (3) preaching the "gospel" (according to the Church) to the rest of the world. These three doctrines and practices *were* the Church's Three-Fold Mission[21] before Ida Smith began to point out the Church's great hypocrisy concerning what our *Book of Mormon* taught.

After Ida made her appearance and confronted the prominent men listed above, the LDS Church leadership "miraculously" (not coincidentally) received a "revelation from God" in 2009. The Church changed its Three-Fold Mission to a Four-Fold Mission, which finally included caring for the poor. Ida Smith was entirely responsible for this change.[22]

Mocked and ridiculed by her family and friends, and having known many popular and powerful people throughout her over eighty-three years of life, Ida Smith never wavered. Shortly before her death, we had the opportunity to meet with Ida. Seldom do tears manifest in our eyes, except for the "sins of the world."[23] In this case, along with our chosen True Messenger, we said goodbye

---

[21] *See* Spencer W. Kimball, "A Report of My Stewardship," *Ensign*, May 1981. Found online at churchofjesuschrist.org/study/ensign/1981/05/a-report-of-my-stewardship?lang=eng.

[22] *See* Peggy Fletcher Stack, "New LDS emphasis: Care for the needy," *The Salt Lake Tribune*, 9 Dec. 2009, archive.sltrib.com/story.php?ref=/lds/ci_13965607.

[23] *BOM*, 3 Nephi 28:38.

to one of the most courageous and significant women among those who have ever called themselves a Latter-day *Saint.*

We published *The Sealed Portion—The Final Testament of Jesus Christ* (the sealed part of our new American scripture) in 2004. Its publication led faithful members to leave the LDS Church. After these faithful members confronted their local leaders and left the Church, the leadership of the Church instructed missionaries and church teachers throughout the world to discontinue discussing the *sealed portion* of the gold plates. The Internet provides people throughout the world with the opportunity to investigate anything of their choosing. This is how most people find *The Sealed Portion—The Final Testament of Jesus Christ*. Upon reading the *Book of Mormon*, if read with sincerity and real intent, the reader wonders about the "greater portion" mentioned. A simple Internet search takes the researcher directly to our Marvelous Work and a Wonder®.

In order to mitigate (lessen) the amount of people finding our work by doing such a simple search, the LDS Church needed to take action in order to limit a person's curiosity of the *sealed portion* of our "gold plates" mentioned in the *Book of Mormon*. The Church has various depictions and facsimiles of the gold plates that it presents to the world. Before Ida Smith confronted her friends, these pictures and similes of the gold plates included bands around two-thirds (2/3) of the plates, to show that part of it was sealed and not translated by Joseph Smith in 1830. In every way possible, the LDS Church leaders have mandated (ordered) that the *sealed portion* of the gold plates no longer be discussed, nor the gold plates be depicted as having any part that was sealed. For this very reason, Apostle Stevenson lied and told the members that the *Book of Mormon* was "whole ... and complete."[24]

---

[24] Elder W. Mark Bassett of the Seventy also gave a talk at the same General Conference mentioned. Bassett's talk's purpose appears to be to dissuade members from wanting this greater portion. *See* Bassett, "For Our Spiritual Development and Learning," churchofjesuschrist.org/study/general-conference/2016/10/for-our-spiritual-development-and-learning?lang=eng.

In 2018, the LDS Church prophet and president, Russell M. Nelson, received another "revelation" for the members of this church. They were told to no longer refer to themselves as "Mormons," but rather as members of the "Church of Jesus Christ."[25] This was a significant change that is not generally accepted by the rest of the world. The world views the members of the religions that embrace the *Book of Mormon* as "Mormons." LDS/Mormons present their church as a positive outcome of the *Book of Mormon*. They falsely claim that the *Book of Mormon* is the "keystone" of their church. These claims justify the way that the rest of the world views them as "the Mormons."

However, we applaud the LDS Church leadership for doing everything possible to distance this church from our new American scripture. Indeed, if the ancient prophet Mormon were a real person, and he visited the modern LDS/Mormon Church, we have no doubt that Mormon would see the "doing" of this church as fulfillment of his son's ancient prophecy. Mormon would be relieved that this church no longer wants to use his name in vain.

Our new American scripture couldn't be further removed from being the "keystone" of this church. The LDS Church couldn't be any further away from being a positive reflection of our *Book of Mormon*. Except for caring for the poor, none of the other three main tenets of the Mormon Church's mission statement are taught in our *Book of Mormon*. In fact, our book CONDEMNS the first three parts of that religion's original mission statement, as well as almost everything else this church teaches as its gospel and doctrine.

The LDS Church is full of hypocrisy (pretending to have qualities or beliefs that it does not really have). In 2011, many in the world finally caught on to this pretended righteousness, which the world sees correctly as

---

[25] *See* Sarah Jane Weaver, "'Mormon' Is Out: Church Releases Statement on How to Refer to the Organization," *Church News*, Intellectual Reserve, Inc., 16 Aug. 2018, churchofjesuschrist.org/church/news/mormon-is-out-church-releases-statement-on-how-to-refer-to-the-organization?lang=eng.

hypocrisy. A couple of popular playwrights recognized the deception of this church and the way that it uses our *Book of Mormon* in its missionary efforts to convert people throughout the world. They were especially frustrated by the way that the LDS Church treats the poor. The Church's missionaries promise the poor people a better life, if they convert to Mormonism—a promise that is never delivered. These playwrights wrote and produced a Tony Award-winning musical comedy—*The Book of Mormon*. The play presents how most of the world views our book. The play honestly portrays how the LDS Church uses our book to gain converts. Nevertheless, in spite of how well the New York Broadway musical presents LDS/Mormon missionary efforts, it does NOT correctly reflect the true meaning, teachings, doctrine, and intent of our new American scripture.

We do not blame the world for viewing our *Book of Mormon* the way that it does. We blame the LDS Church. The facts behind how and why we wrote the *Book of Mormon* will finally dispel the erroneous (incorrect) ways in which the world views our new American scripture. Through this book (*A New American Scripture—How and Why the Real Illuminati® Created the Book of Mormon*), we hope to mitigate (reduce the harmful effects of) the hypocritical things that the LDS Church does in misusing, misrepresenting, and transfiguring the beauty of the *Book of Mormon* teachings. We hope the world will give our book a second chance when it understands the intent to do good that we had in mind when we wrote a new American scripture.

The leaders of the LDS Church will continue to do everything in their power to distract their members from the "greater portion of the word," even from the *Book of Mormon* itself. In spite of what this church says about our book, it has no right to claim our book as its own. It has no right to present our work as part of its gospel. <u>The "gospel" presented to the rest of the world by the LDS/Mormon Church has nothing whatsoever to do with what is taught in our book.</u>

A New American Scripture

To protect the integrity of our work and the way that we presented the intended lessons in the original narrative of our new American scripture, the *Book of Mormon*, we proudly and purposefully proclaim that our work, alone, is the Marvelous Work and a Wonder® that is introduced and prophesied of in our book.[26]

The facts and events presented in this Prologue, together with the rest of this book, will leave the reader with little doubt that we, who are now recognized throughout the world as the Real Illuminati®, wrote both the *Book of Mormon* (the unsealed portion of the gold plates from which the book was transcribed) and *The Sealed Portion—The Final Testament of Jesus Christ* (the *sealed portion* transcribed from the same gold plates).

We introduced ourselves in the *Book of Mormon* according to the Christian-based narrative that we presented in our new American scripture, as follows:

> [We] will be among the Gentiles, and the Gentiles shall know [us] not. [We] will also be among the Jews, and the Jews shall know [us] not.
>
> ... Therefore, great and marvelous works shall be wrought by [us], before the great and coming day when all people must surely stand before the judgment-seat of Christ;
>
> Yea even among the Gentiles shall there be a great and marvelous work wrought by [us], before that judgment day.[27]

This book, *A New American Scripture—How and Why the Real Illuminati® Created the Book of Mormon*, is part of our great and marvelous work, even a Marvelous Work and a Wonder®.

---

[26] *See BOM*, 1 Nephi 14:7; BOM, 2 Nephi 27:26; OT, Isaiah 29:14.
[27] *BOM*, 3 Nephi 28:27–8, 31–2.

FOREWORD

The Real Illuminati® have asked me to write a foreword for this second book of their important Trilogy. I'm to introduce their work because I am the world's foremost expert on them and on their work. Furthermore, they have asked me to help them perform the final edits of this book. My help was required so that I could use my limited vocabulary and education to make this book more readable for the general public. If left unchanged in the original words of the Real Illuminati®, few would easily follow their writing style.

Their work is called a "Marvelous Work and a Wonder®," which is a legally registered trademark held by the publisher who owns and publishes their writings. Their work also includes The Humanity Party®, a legally registered U.S. political organization. Personally, I make no income for anything that I do for them. Owning nothing of any value, I rely on the care and generosity of a very few who support what they do and how they do it.

I became the foremost expert on the Real Illuminati® through being involved with them and their work for well over thirty years. The Real Illuminati® is a group of the most intelligent humans on Earth. Their existence is presented allegorically in their new American scripture by the introduction of the characters known as the *Three Nephites* and *John the Beloved*. They now refer to themselves as the *Real Illuminati®* because they claim to be *illuminated* with a fullness of the Real Truth™.

(NOTE: This book's authors are taking the necessary steps through their publisher to legally trademark this term—"Real Truth"—for their specific use. Joseph Smith once explained the Real Truth™ as knowledge of things as they [really] are, and as they [really] were, and as they [really] are to come; And whatsoever is more or less than [Real Truth™] is the spirit of that wicked one who was a liar from the beginning.[1] In this book we explain the difference between what the world sees as truth and what is *really* occurring. Our claim is that we understand the Real Truth™ of all things. We claim that the world, with all of its wisdom and pride, knows nothing about how things *really* are. And because of this great ignorance, humanity is going to fall, and "the fall thereof [will be] exceedingly great." [2])

My name is Christopher. This is my true birth name given to me by my mother. (My last name is not important and will not be given here, nor do I desire to be associated with those who share this family surname.) The name "Christopher" means *Bearer of Christ*. Although I neither claim to be Christian, nor do I believe or support Christianity or any of the other world religions, I understand what the *true* meaning of "Christ" represents, according to what I have been taught in my associations with the Real Illuminati®. After being involved with this book's authors for many years, I came to understand what *their* definition of a "Christ" actually means. When they use the word "Christ" in their writings, the inference, in each and every instance, could be properly interchanged with the term "Real Truth™." In regards to Christianity—the religion upon which they focused most of their writings—Jesus, the Christ, is described as

> even the Spirit of truth; whom the world cannot receive, … Howbeit when he, the Spirit of truth, is come, he will guide you into all truth … and he will shew you things to come.[3]

I am the Real Illuminati®'s contemporary (modern-day) True Messenger, as they refer to me. I say nothing about the Real Truth™ unless I am repeating exactly what they have taught me. Therefore, I am a *bearer* of the truths that *they* want to share with the world.

---

[1] *D&C*, 93:24–5.
[2] *See BOM*, 1 Nephi 11:36.
[3] NT, John 14:17; 16:13.

Before me, there was another. His name was Joseph Smith, Jr. Using our names and help, respectively, the Real Illuminati® published their *Book of Mormon* (the unsealed portion of the "gold plates" from which the book was "translated") in 1830, and *The Sealed Portion—The Final Testament of Jesus Christ* (the *sealed portion* of the so-called "gold plates") in 2004. The misguided religions that claim the *Book of Mormon* as their official scripture often refer to the Real Illuminati® as the "Three Nephites" and "John the Beloved." Yet, in spite of the clear way in which they introduced themselves in their new American scripture, none of these false religions can explain who these people are and what they are doing.

The so-called *Three Nephites* were introduced in the *Book of Mormon* as "those who were never to taste of death"—the three who "were caught up into heaven, and saw and heard unspeakable things."[4] The so-called *John the Beloved* is introduced in the *Book of Mormon* as "a man, and he was dressed in a white robe … one of the twelve apostles of the Lamb" who wrote the Bible's book of Revelation.[5]

The publication of the first book of the Real Illuminati®'s Trilogy was in 2019: *The True History of Religion—How Religion Destroys the Human Race and What the Real Illuminati® Has Attempted to do Through Religion to Save the Human Race*. In that book it is revealed that, as a group, the Real Illuminati® has been around since the dawn of humanity. This group's greatest accomplishment in modern history was influencing the development of a new religion—Christianity—that saved the Great Roman Empire from complete destruction. Saved by this new religion, the Eastern Roman Empire survived and was responsible for the development and prosperity of the European world. (Some of what this group did for the Roman Empire is disclosed in that first book of their Trilogy.)

This book, *A New American Scripture—How and Why the Real Illuminati® Created the Book of Mormon*, is the second book of their Trilogy.

---

[4] *BOM*, 3 Nephi 28:25, 13.
[5] *See BOM*, 1 Nephi 14:19–27.

A New American Scripture

Both Joseph Smith, Jr. ("Joe") and I were recruited by the Real Illuminati® after we had each experienced our own *illumination*. When Joe was fourteen years old (April 1820), he became distraught and disillusioned with the religions of his day. Seeking for guidance from a god that he did not know, but from whom he had been taught since his early childhood that he could approach and request an answer, Joe prayed for direction. It was while praying that Joe's mind was *illuminated*, or *transfigured*—as this enlightenment process is explained in the *Book of Mormon* concerning the *Three Nephites*.[6]

In June of 1987, I too became distraught and disillusioned with the religion in which I had participated for twenty-five years. I also prayed for guidance. What happened to Joe, happened to me … the EXACT same thing! Although Joe's experience has been referred to by his religious followers as the *First Vision*, it was not any type of a vision. Like mine, it was actually an *enlightenment*.

Later in his life, as a religion grew from Joe's introduction of the *Book of Mormon*, Joe often referred to the visions that he experienced, not as actual visitations, but as "the eyes of our understanding [being] opened."[7] Referring to a "vision" that Joe shared with Oliver Cowdery (the man who acted as his main scribe in producing the *Book of Mormon*), Joe wrote: "The veil was taken from our minds, and the eyes of our understanding were opened." In this particular *vision of understanding*, Joe and Oliver Cowdery "saw the Lord standing upon the breastwork of the pulpit, before us."[8] They also saw *Moses*, *Elias*, and *Elijah*,[9] not with their physical eyes, but with the "eyes of [their] understanding" *through the veil*.

---

[6] *See BOM*, 3 Nephi 28:15.
[7] *D&C*, 110:1.
[8] *D&C*, 110:2.
[9] *D&C*, 110:11–14.

A few years before this very important "vision" in Mormon history, Joe shared another "vision" with Sydney Rigdon (another important figure in Mormon history). Of this "vision" Joe wrote:

> By the power of the Spirit our eyes were opened and our understandings were enlightened, so as to see and understand the things of God.[10]

There was never a time during the lives of Oliver Cowdery or Sydney Rigdon when either man testified that he *actually* saw something with his physical eyes. Rather, each man would relate the experience as an enlightenment of his "understandings." In spite of these supposed supernatural and heavenly experiences, Cowdery would later become one of Joe's most vociferous (vocal and insistent) critics and enemies. Logic and reason would clearly suppose that if Cowdery had *actually* seen Jesus, Moses, Elias, and Elijah with his physical eyes, there is no way that he could have ever turned against Joe; but he did—vehemently (strongly). (To clarify, neither Cowdery nor Rigdon saw and understood the same things that Joe and I did during our personal enlightenment/transfiguration.)

At the time Cowdery and Joe had the "eyes of [their] understanding" opened, Joe had not yet explained exactly what had happened to him when he was fourteen years old. He had not fully disclosed what would later be referred to as the *First Vision*. An honest review of Mormon history would reveal a few different versions of what Joe reported happened to him as a young boy. It wasn't until 1838 that Joe was mandated by the Real Illuminati® to publish what became the LDS/Mormon religion's official narrative of Joe's first "vision."[11]

---

[10] *D&C*, 76:12.
[11] *See* Joel B. Groat, "Joseph Smith's Changing First Vision Accounts," 15 July 2011, Mormons In Transition - Institute for Religious Research, mit.irr.org/joseph-smiths-changing-first-vision-accounts.

A New American Scripture

The LDS Church presents its own version of the events that led to the alienation of Oliver Cowdery, David Whitmer, and Martin Harris (the Three Witnesses of the *Book of Mormon*), as well as several others who were known in Mormon history as the Eight Witnesses to the *Book of Mormon*. These men left Joseph around the same time that he released his official story about the *First Vision*. The dishonest, "official" version of its history, reported by the Church of Jesus Christ of Latter-day Saints after Brigham Young took over the reins of this church, gives excuses that are not the Real Truth™.

The Three Witnesses, as well as other prominent and important historical figures in Mormon history, distanced themselves from Joseph Smith primarily because of the "official" version of the *First Vision* that Joe was mandated to present to the world. Although later LDS/Mormon leaders (Brigham Young, etc.) used their power and authority to remove the facts and present a fictitious account of why these important men left, logic and reason override the deception. These three men (the Three Witnesses) loved the *Book of Mormon* more than they loved Joe or the organized Church and its priesthood authority—an authority of which David Whitmer had a lot of issues.[12]

In Joe's official and final version of what happened to him as a young teenager, Joe presented that he saw God the Father, and His Son, Jesus Christ, as two *separate* beings, in the flesh and in person. This directly contradicted the *Book of Mormon*'s description of the "Father and the Son." The *Book of Mormon*'s definition and description are very clear that both God and Jesus are the exact same person.[13]

At no time in the *Book of Mormon* narrative do both God and Jesus physically appear as separate, individual beings—nor are they presented as such. The witnesses of the *Book of Mormon* knew this. Cowdery also knew that neither he nor Joe ever *actually* saw the Lord, Moses, Elias, or

---

[12] *See* David Whitmer, "An Address to All Believers In Christ," (Richmond, MO: 1887), found online at "An Address to All Believers in Christ," *Wikisource*, Wikimedia Foundation, 19 Jan. 2014, en.wikisource.org/wiki/An_Address_to_All_Believers_in_Christ.

[13] *See BOM*, Mosiah 15:1–4.

Elijah with their physical eyes. Therefore, when Joe presented the final and official version of the *First Vision*, Cowdery saw through Joe's deception. From that time forward, Cowdery distanced himself from Joe and his *new* doctrines and revelations.

Joe often told his followers that he was not revealing all that he knew about the "mysteries of God"—that if he did, they would rise up and kill him.[14] At the time, the people had rejected the *Book of Mormon* for the intent and purpose for which it had been written. This rejection led its authors (the Real Illuminati®) to give the mandate to Joe—as was written in their *Book of Mormon*:

> [to] take away his plainness from them, and deliver unto them many things which they cannot understand, because they desired it. And because they desired it God hath done it, that they may stumble.[15]

In the same way that the Real Illuminati® had mandated Joe, they also mandated me. I was to present a false account about what happened in the Salt Lake City LDS Temple on June 16, 1987, when I had my own *first vision*.[16] In other words, Joe and I were told to lie to the people about how our enlightenment took place. We lied to the people because this is what the people wanted to hear. But neither Joe nor I would have lied had we not been instructed by our recruiters, the Real Illuminati®. Joe did not see God the Father nor His Son, Jesus Christ. Neither did I see the resurrected Joseph Smith during my own *first vision*, and of whom I reported had shown me the *gold plates* so that I could "translate" the plates' *sealed portion*.

---

[14] *See* Robert Horne, "Reminiscences of the Church in Nauvoo," *Millennial Star*, vol. 55 no. 36, 4 Sept 1893, 585; also found online at contentdm.lib.byu.edu/digital/collection/MStar/id/19227. (Download the PDF to view all the pages.)

[15] *BOM*, Jacob 4:14.

[16] *See* Christopher, *The Sealed Portion*, "How I Received The Gold Plates of Mormon," 582–8. Read for free at realilluminati.org/the-sealed-portion.

There *were* actual plates that the Real Illuminati® had constructed with the "appearance of gold." However, like Joe, I did not see the plates until about four years *after* I had experienced my *enlightenment*, or better, four years after *the veil was taken from my mind and the eyes of my understanding were opened*. This *enlightenment* actually meant that Joe and I knew the Real Truth™ about what had *really* happened on Earth in the past, what was *really* happening currently, and what was *really* about to happen, none of which had anything to do with what was being taught religiously or secularly. This *enlightenment* took place instantaneously, without Joe or me having to do anything. Our critics would claim that it was at that moment that both Joe and I lost our minds.

Joe received his enlightenment in April 1820. It wasn't until September 1823, almost four years later, that Joe met the Real Illuminati® and was shown the plates for the first time. I received my enlightenment in June 1987. It wasn't until the early spring of 1991 that I was approached and recruited by the Real Illuminati® and shown their gold plates for the first time.

Joe was a very young man (not yet eighteen years old) at the time when he first met the Real Illuminati®. He met with them periodically for almost another four years before he was ready to do what they recruited him to do: produce the *unsealed part* of their gold plates as the *Book of Mormon*. Being young, without wife or children, and excited to be involved in such an endeavor, Joe was malleable and motivated for the task before him.

I was not.

After my own *first vision* in 1987, I completely changed my lifestyle because of the enlightenment that I had experienced. I no longer viewed life upon Earth, or the value placed upon anything associated with it, like I did before I experienced this "transfiguration" of my brain. I was married at the time to a wonderful woman. She followed me as we moved around, and helped me with my two oldest children from a former marriage, of whom I had been given full custody. Later, we had two more wonderful boys before I met the Real Illuminati®. I loved being a father and husband. I loved my new lifestyle. I was happier than I had ever been in my life. About these specific details, I have been instructed by the Real Illuminati® to write my autobiography. One day I will reveal all the details of my association with this group of enlightened ones.[17]

After our enlightenments, what were Joe and I supposed to do with our new understanding of the Real Truth™? No one would believe us. How were we supposed to explain what we now knew: that all mortals upon Earth were actually dream characters; that we were playing out life upon Earth in the advanced, eternal mind of each of our True Selves? How were we supposed to explain that there was no god outside of our own mind; that there was no such thing as a devil; that the good or bad that each person does is a direct result of their own free will and desires?

How were we supposed to explain that each person has lived various incarnations (multiple lives) before, and that this particular one is the most important ... for now ... until we die? How were we supposed to explain that death is nothing more than an awakening in our *advanced world* where we have always existed as advanced human beings, in the same world as the same person we were before being born, and who we will be after we die? These were things that we found almost impossible to describe and explain.

Our recruiters, the Real Illuminati®, explained their own enlightenment the best way that they could. They explained that:

> the heavens were opened, and they were caught up into heaven, and saw and heard unspeakable things. And it was forbidden them that they should utter; neither was it given unto them power that they could utter the things which they saw and heard; And whether

---

[17] *See* "The Man From Joe's Bar and Grill," The Real Illuminati®, realilluminati.org/the-man-from-joe-s-bar-and-grill.

they were in the body or out of the body, they could not tell; for it did seem unto them like a transfiguration of them, that they were changed from this body of flesh into an immortal state, that they could behold the things of God.[18]

Neither Joe nor I had the power or ability to utter or explain the things that we both saw and heard in our enlightenments, which we didn't see or hear with our physical eyes and ears, but only through the "eyes of our understanding." We can also humbly admit that we were not and are not immortal. Joe was killed. And many now would like to see me killed.

Unlike my experience with them, Joe was never allowed to specifically name the Real Illuminati® or give them the credit for their "great and marvelous work." It was their desire to "bring the souls of men unto Jesus, while the world shall stand"[19] by allowing people their free will to act and be acted upon, according to the people's desires of righteousness. If the people's free will required a religion, they would get their religion, regardless of how wicked it might become. Not since the publishing of the *Book of Mormon* has there existed a religion that has properly helped the Real Illuminati® in their "great and marvelous work." The Church of Jesus Christ of Latter-day Saints could not be more diametrically opposed to their work. This church has greatly abused, misused, and misrepresented their new American scripture.

One of this church's senior Twelve Apostles, Jeffery R. Holland, was secretly recorded discounting the existence of the *Three Nephites*. In a recorded conversation he had with his longtime friend, Ida Smith, Holland also claimed that the *sealed portion* of the gold plates would not come through anyone "from Joe's Bar and Grill."[20] Holland said the following

---

[18] *BOM*, 3 Nephi 28:13–15.
[19] Compare *BOM*, 3 Nephi 28:9.
[20] *See* "Ida Smith and The Man From Joe's Bar and Grill," The Real Illuminati®, realilluminati.org/the-man-from-joe-s-bar-and-grill.

about me, as the guy chosen by the Real Illuminati® to publish the *sealed part* of their plates:

> He got this notion about the 116 pages of the Book of Mormon that were missing, and then it ... began to be the sealed portion of the plates that were missing, and then he ... sorta started to walk and talk with Timothy, the Disciple in the Book of Mormon who was raised from the dead. ... I don't want to impugn the man personally ... but his behavior, and his track record into polygamy, and the moving with Nephite disciples, who were raised from the dead; you know, that just kinda hasta have you raise your eyebrows. So that's where I am.[21]

Ida Smith sincerely explained to Holland how important the *sealed portion* of the gold plates was to her, to which Holland responded,

> Be wonderful! Yeah. Well, I'd like it, yeah there's nothing I'd be more excited about. But you've also gotta know, Ida, that when that happens, it's not gonna happen to, it's not gonna come to, somebody down at Joe's Bar and Grill.

The Real Illuminati® have instructed me to write my autobiography under the title *The Man From Joe's Bar and Grill.* As I said above, my autobiography will give specific details about my involvement with the Real Illuminati® over the last thirty years. And as is the case with EVERYTHING associated with them and their work, my autobiography will be available free of any charge and found through a search of my name on the Internet.

---

[21] View the transcript of Holland's conversation with Ida Smith here: "Transcription Telephone Call – 10:50 am, 12 June 2007, Ida Smith & Jeffrey (Jeff) Holland," *Pearl Publishing, LLC,* pearlpublishing.net/bom/download/HollandTelephoneTranscript.pdf.

Listen to the audio here: "Ida-Holland Audio," *Pearl Publishing, LLC,* pearlpublishing.net/bom/download/Ida-Holland-audio.mp3.

If I could meet with the LDS leaders, my comments and questions to them would be sincere:

First of all, the *Three Nephites* and *John the Beloved* are *not* resurrected from the dead. You have no idea who these people are and what they are doing. What do you Brethren believe these men are doing today, because none of you have ever mentioned anything about them? They are certainly not doing anything with your church. Have you met any of them?
Have you ever sat down with me, looked me in the eyes, and asked me about who they are and how I got involved with them? You have no right to give an authoritative statement on me without hearing my own words. So stop making things up and deceiving the members of your church.

In my expert opinion as one who has been enlightened, and as the former official spokesperson of the Real Illuminati® and their proclaimed only True Messenger on Earth, I can emphatically and without reservation proclaim that none of the Real Illuminati®'s "great and marvelous works" has yet exceeded the incredible Real Truth™s that they have presented in this book, the second book of their Trilogy …

A New American Scripture—How and Why the Real Illuminati® Created the Book of Mormon.

—Christopher, *Bearer of Truth*

INTRODUCTION

In the early nineteenth (19th) century, the European Americans were migrating to and settling in the Western Hemisphere. *Why* we wrote a new scripture for them is very important to understand. It will be much easier to explain *why* we wrote the *Book of Mormon* (and with fewer words and detail) than *how* we wrote it.

We wrote our new scripture to confront and hopefully control the pride and egos of the people responsible for establishing and developing the United States of America. We were especially concerned about the pride that leads to racism. The early European Americans were very racist.[1] Racism divides humanity and disenfranchises a particular group of humans solely based on the color of their skin. The Eastern Hemisphere had long been divided into areas of power and control, specifically based on race.

At the time European explorers began to travel outside of the Eastern Hemisphere, their nations (Spain, Portugal, France, and England) held great power and dominion over all other societies. The white-skinned nations were able to advance in technology and innovation much faster and more efficiently than the darker-skinned nations of the Orient, of the Middle East, and of Africa.

Some might argue that Oriental and Middle Eastern cultures, as well as the ancient Egyptians, had made great advancements in their particular societies. This is true to some extent, but none of these other nations of the Eastern Hemisphere survived long enough to become a great, modern power of influence and control. Conversely, the white-skinned European nations *would* eventually dominate the entire world. The white-skinned nations would

---

[1] *See* Meilan Solly, "Historical Context," in "158 Resources to Understand Racism In America," *Smithsonian Magazine*, 4 June 2020, smithsonianmag.com/history/158-resources-understanding-systemic-racism-america-180975029/#sectionOne.

go on to discover the greatest power that exists: nuclear energy. With this new technology and understanding, nothing stood in the way of the human race eventually controlling and dominating all of nature's laws.

European pride was responsible for the European religions that were invented and used to control the lighter-skinned masses. Bible believers reasoned that if God's people were white, and if God started the human race with two white people (Adam and Eve), as they were taught, then God intended for all humans to be white. They believed that if God intended for all humans to be light-skinned, then there must be a good reason why the darker-skinned races existed. Therefore, because the white God controlled everything on Earth, then the white God must have done something to allow the darker-skinned people to appear.

During the great power and dominance of the Greek and Roman Empires (mostly white societies), the stories about the supernatural gods began to show up.[2] However, systemic racism was not as prevalent and divisive in the ancient Greek and Roman societies as it would become in the later European nations. Darker-skinned people were more equal, but different than the lighter-skinned Greco Romans. In fact, the beauty of the Egyptian queen, Cleopatra, whose ancestry was both white and black, inspired the idea that the mixture of the races could create the most beautiful humans.

In the ancient Babylonian Empire, there were two main centers of commerce and government: Babylon in the north, and Ur in the south. The people of Babylon were more affluent than their neighbors to the south, and were prideful of their economic successes. Ur had financial problems. The pride of each city caused a considerable amount of discontent and divisiveness.

---

[2] *See* "Greek mythology," *Wikipedia*, Wikimedia Foundation, 20 Apr. 2021, en.wikipedia.org/wiki/Greek_mythology; and
"Roman mythology," *Wikipedia*, Wikimedia Foundation, 5 May 2021, en.wikipedia.org/wiki/Roman_mythology.

This eventually led to the Babylonian Empire's (of which the cities of Babylon and Ur were two of its largest cities) downfall (*circa* 600 B.C.E.).

During the Persian takeover of that area of the world, many Babylonians fled. There was a particular family of great wealth and influence residing in the ancient city of Ur. This family fled into the Arabian desert and wandered aimlessly in the wilderness for many years. Destitute and on the brink of starvation, the family eventually made its way to Egypt where there was plenty of food and water. The family offered to become Egyptian slaves in exchange for help and a place to live. The Egyptians (a dark-skinned race of a mixed black and white heritage) gave the family some land east of Egypt, which is modernly known as the State of Israel.

It wasn't until this small group of white-skinned people became separated from their ancient Babylonian roots that the color of one's skin became important. The lighter-skinned slaves saw themselves at least equal to their darker-skinned Egyptian masters; but their condition as slaves caused an emotional problem with their pride. The oral stories that were passed on through generations of this particular family (mentioned above) were based on the pride and ego of the family patriarchs. They could not easily justify to their posterity how they ended up the way that they did—in slavery and under the control of a darker-skinned race.

Alexander the Great, a white-skinned relation to the ancestors of this family, eventually freed this family from their obligation and contract with the Egyptian government. Feeling a sense of salvation and victory over the darker-skinned Egyptians, this family began to invent stories that made their family the most important family on Earth—"God's chosen people." From these oral histories, the Hebrew *Pentateuch* (*Torah*, the five books of Moses[3]) was eventually created by Greek writers. This written history became more relevant and popular shortly after the Macedonians (Greeks) and Alexander the Great were conquered in that part of the world.

---

[3] *See* "Judaism: The Written Law – Torah," *Jewish Virtual Library*, jewishvirtuallibrary.org/the-written-law-torah.

This family, once uncertain about its value to the rest of the world, finally found its place of worth in the Middle East. Once incorporated into and protected by the powerful white people of the Greek and Roman governments, this family became known as the *Hebrews*[4] (Greek: Ἑβραῖος; Latin: Hebraeus). This name was given to them by the Romans. Largely left alone, as long as they paid their taxes to Rome and obeyed Roman law, the Hebrews began to flourish in their land—a land that the Romans called the *Levant*.[5]

Hebrew stories were the epitome of pride, ego, and especially racism. It is from the Hebrew stories that the idea originated of God being white, and creating the white-skinned Adam and Eve as the parents of the human race. If their stories were true, Hebrew leaders could prove their worth and value to the rest of the world. Instead of being wanderers, who had begged to be saved by the Egyptians and eventually *did* become Egyptian slaves, the Hebrews touted their worth as the "chosen people of the only one true God."[6]

It was the pride and ego of the people, inspired by the few who wielded power and control over them, that created all forms of their religious beliefs. No religious belief has caused more problems for humanity than what became of the Hebrew's religion. When the three main Hebrew-rooted religious systems (Judaism, Christianity, and Islam) are considered honestly and transparently, <u>these are the main sources of most systemic racism that exists on Earth today</u>.

In writing our new American scripture, we wanted to counter this racism and present a new idea: <u>that the entire human race, regardless of skin color, belonged to the same family unit</u>. In order to do so, we had no

---

[4] *See* "Hebrews," *Wikipedia*, Wikimedia Foundation, 6 May 2021, en.wikipedia.org/wiki/Hebrews.
[5] *See* "Levant," *Wikipedia*, Wikimedia Foundation, 23 May 2021, en.wikipedia.org/wiki/Levant.
[6] *See* "Jews as the Chosen People." *Wikipedia*, Wikimedia Foundation, 18 May 2021, en.wikipedia.org/wiki/Jews_as_the_chosen_people.

choice but to work behind the scenes and come up with a logical narrative that the powers that controlled the masses would believe and accept.

The Hebrew stories evolved into Christian stories, and then into Islamic stories. Later, white European nations embraced Christianity (a belief system based on the Bible's New Testament's Jesus Christ) as their power and authority. Knowing all of this, we concentrated our efforts entirely on the Hebrew stories of the Bible that created racism in the first place.

Dovetailing and combining the Hebrew idea that God was white and that this god created two white people to populate the earth, we had to present a storyline that contained the proper nuances and plots that supported this racist idea. Therefore, we used the most popular form of the Hebrew scripture accepted by the most powerful European nations: the King James Version of the Bible.[7] We had to present a logical storyline that proved that ALL dark-skinned peoples came from Adam and Eve, through the lineage of the most important character in Hebrew mythology: Abraham.

Here's an interesting fact: The Greek authors were helping the ancient Hebrews put their oral histories on paper in a way that made sense. At the same time, the Hebrew priests responsible for telling the stories were having a problem explaining *how* the genealogy of their family unit could be traced back so far into the past. How could their family line reach the time when the Hebrews claimed that God had created the Earth and placed Adam and Eve on it? There were too many ancestors missing from their oral histories.

The Greek writers couldn't have cared less whether or not the Hebrew stories were true. They were just happy to be paid good money to write the oral stories for their employers. To the relief and amusement of the Greek writers, who were listening to the oral stories given to them in order to write

---

[7] *See* "King James Version." *Wikipedia*, Wikimedia Foundation, 24 May 2021, en.wikipedia.org/wiki/Authorized_King_James_Version.

this people's history, the Hebrew authorities simply applied various years of age to their ancient ancestry in order to make their genealogy fit with more modern time frames. For example, Methuselah was the oldest at 969 years. The six generations back to Adam all had patriarchs that lived close to 900 years each. Enoch was the only exception. Enoch, according to Hebrew mythology, was taken by God at about 365 years old. As the characters of their oral stories started to fit in with the more modern written histories of other cultures, the Hebrews' great men started dying at the age that everyone else in the world was dying.

There should be no doubt to an honest and rational mind that the Hebrew stories that constitute the Bible are far from a realistic account of history. Even so, we had to come up with the proper storylines that fit the Hebrew narrative accepted by the powerful Christian European nations that we were trying to influence. Again, it was our intent to prove to the Christian people that all races, regardless of skin color, were from the same "house."

We first envisioned our idea to help the early Americans see the darker-skinned native Americans as belonging to the chosen house of God (the house of Israel). Because of this, we started with a story about the native Americans' ancestry. We tied their existence into a Bible narrative that was widely accepted as a historical "fact": the rise and power of the Babylonian Empire, just before the house of Israel was destroyed. In every way possible, we tied the Hebrew myths to contemporary historical events that many accepted as a true history.

It is important to note here that NO annotated and recorded history is the Real Truth™—events as they *really* occurred in the past. All of recorded history is taken from the prejudice of the recorder. However, regardless of the lack of veracity (accuracy) of any reported historical event, the Bible has been accepted by billions of people as the ultimate "truth." It was because of people's belief in the Bible that we were forced to confront the pride that created racism in the Bible narrative.

We took the Bible story of the darker-skinned grandchildren of Jacob (Israel), whose names were *Manasseh*[8] and *Ephraim*,[9] and we started our new American scripture there. (Jacob's name was later changed to "Israel." This is where the "House of Israel" and the "Twelve Tribes of Israel" came from.[10]) One of Jacob's twelve sons was named Joseph.[11] Joseph was white. The Egyptians were of a darker-skinned ancestry, a mix of the darker skin of the subregions of Africa and the lighter-skinned northerners who traded with Egypt for many years. Joseph's wife was Egyptian.[12] Therefore, Joseph's only two sons were of black heritage.

According to the Hebrew stories, no one with the blood from black heritage could receive the same priesthood blessings as the "pure blood" of the house of Israel. Joseph's wife's blood was "cursed" with the blood of the ancient son of Adam and Eve—Cain, who slew his brother Abel. (In other words, their skin was supposedly changed to a darker skin tone because of Cain's rebellion against the Hebrew god.)

To present and offer empirical evidence that the native Americans were *actual* descendants of the house of Israel, yet possessed a darker tone of skin color, we chose our storyline's characters from one of the tribes of Israel that had darker skin in their DNA. In our first attempt at presenting our original storyline, we had our main character's family be descendants of Joseph's son, Ephraim. (This is the same Joseph mentioned above, one of the sons of Jacob/"Israel.")

Ephraim was younger than Joseph's firstborn son, *Manasseh*. According to the Bible story, because Joseph's sons both had the "bad blood"

---

[8] *See* "Manasseh (Tribal Patriarch)." *Wikipedia*, 26 Nov. 2020, en.wikipedia.org/wiki/Manasseh_(tribal_patriarch).
[9] *See* "Ephraim." *Wikipedia*, 21 Apr. 2021, en.wikipedia.org/wiki/Ephraim.
[10] *See* "Jacob," *Wikipedia*, 26 May 2021, en.wikipedia.org/wiki/Jacob.
[11] *See* "Joseph (Genesis)," *Wikipedia*, 24 May 2021, en.wikipedia.org/wiki/Joseph_(Genesis).
[12] *See* "Asenath," *Wikipedia*, 9 May 2021, en.wikipedia.org/wiki/Asenath.

of the dark-skinned races, Joseph asked his father, Israel, to bless his two boys and officially adopt them into the house of Israel. Joseph wanted his eldest son to be granted the birthright blessing, which was always the customary practice. Israel refused and placed his right hand on the younger Ephraim's head, telling Joseph that Ephraim "shall be greater than [Manasseh], and his [descendants] shall become a multitude of nations."[13]

The Bible story places the younger Ephraim above the elder Manasseh, but is perfectly clear that both have the "cursed blood." If these two boys did not have the "cursed blood," they would not have had to be *adopted* into the "pure blood" of the house of Israel. (It is believed by the LDS/Mormons that people who are of "non-Israelite" lineage are *adopted* into the house of Israel through the ordinances of their church.)

We allowed our chosen messenger (Joseph Smith, Jr.) to present the first part of our original storyline to his family, friends, and peers, once it had been transcribed. We did this in order to monitor their reaction to the way we wanted to present the beginning of our story. We learned that using Ephraim in the genealogical lineage of the main character in our story caused some concern for a few Bible scholars. They valued their personal heritage as having the pure blood of the "non-tainted," white-skinned part of the house of Israel. They were also confused by Israel's prophecy that the descendants of Ephraim would become a "multitude of nations" (explained below). The native American peoples were not considered a "multitude of nations" to the few early American Christians who peer-reviewed our original storyline.

We had properly satisfied, so we assumed, the probability that the native American people could have darker skin because of their lineage back to the darker-skinned sons of Joseph (son of Jacob/"Israel"). But we were surprised by the attack on and resistance to our narrative in regards to the sparse (meager) tribal associations of the native Americans compared to Israel's prophecy that Ephraim's house would become a "multitude of nations."

---

[13] OT, Genesis 48:19.

It was to our chagrin (disappointment) that these few of the peer review group had a problem with the association we made with our character, Lehi, to Ephraim. Because of this, and other problems that some of the first peer review group had with our original storyline, we were forced to change the narrative. We had to allow *Manasseh* to be the ancestor of our native American genealogical line. Unfortunately, we had to do whatever it took to make our story more believable and palatable for racist American Christians.

We did not expect the issue of ancestry to become a further problem once we removed our initial *Book of Lehi* and replaced the narrative of our story's beginning with the book of Nephi, our character Lehi's son. However, we underestimated the pride and racism of the American people who would continue to peer review our book. Even so, few (if any) of the past or present readers of our new American scripture (the *Book of Mormon*) realize that the characters of our story possessed the supposed "bad blood." Christians do not want to believe that *any* of the Twelve Tribes of Israel were tainted with a cursed lineage.

Our mission in remaining and working behind the scenes of history has always been to oppose superstition (false ideas), especially excessive credulous (naïve) belief in and reverence for supernatural beings that give believers reason to treat other human beings poorly and unequally. We try to bring to light the facts or full details of what is really happening behind the scenes of the powerful institutions that control and shape human life upon the earth. We fight religious influence over public life—supporting, promoting, and perpetuating a strict separation of church (religion) and state (government). We work to influence for good, the plots or schemes of the powers that control society. We attempt to control these institutions without dominating them.[14]

---

[14] *See* "About Us – The Real Illuminati®," The Real Illuminati®, realilluminati.org/about-us.

Individual free will is the most important part of being human. No human should attempt to dominate the free will of another, in any way. We fully respect free will and do everything that we can to protect it. People often use their free will to establish and support institutions of power that they allow to control their lives (religions and governments). When this happens, we make every effort and attempt any means possible to infiltrate these institutions. We try to introduce ideas that are not easily discernable (noticed) from those already embraced by the free will of the people. In so doing, it is our desire and the design of our work to influence a different perspective. We hope to possibly change the minds and hearts of the people without them knowing that we disagree with and detest what their free will has already established.

Most people on Earth do not have free will to act and allow themselves to be acted upon without force. Being forced to go to work at a job that you do not want to do—which brings you misery—violates individual free will. You either work doing whatever you have to do to survive (whether you would freely choose to work at the available jobs or not), or you die. Besides being forced to work at a job, there are many other forces against free will. Some of these are obvious, such as being restrained, threatened, punished, tortured, or physically forced to do something. But the force against one's free will to *think* what one chooses to think is much subtler and less detectable. It is a different kind of non-physical force.

The majority of people do not use their own free will to think. They do not consider that the ideas that come to their minds are *not* chosen freely, but induced by deception. Therefore, many of the beliefs that have resulted from their thinking are not their own. Their beliefs were created by the free will of *someone else* from whom they learned these beliefs. These beliefs are a result of thoughts being placed in their heads as they grew up. People believe what they have been taught since birth (inculcated) to think and believe. Their parents, teachers, and peers have taught them these ideas. They have also been taught what to think by the institutions that they support in society (government, business, and religion). People *think* that these institutions are important because they have been taught and are convinced that they *are* important.

In our world, few people have the time or energy left over from a hard day's work to think for themselves. At that point, people want to leave the daily drudgery (unpleasant work) that is forced upon them behind, and relax and be entertained. In being entertained, a person is finally able to exercise unconditional and unforced free will. One chooses by what means one allows oneself to be entertained. By being allowed a few moments in one's life to choose their own acts, or to choose the way that they are acted upon, this *seems* to be enough for each person to feel empowered and in control of their life.

All humans start out the same, with unconditional and uncontrollable free will. They are little children first. Little children do whatever their free will encourages them to do. As they grow, the only thing that stands in the way of them thinking what they want and doing what they want, is the free will of those who wield power and control over their lives.

Humans are born into a world (society) of previously and firmly established institutional powers (government and religion) that control their free will and shape them into "productive members of society." However, it is the institution, not the individual, that chooses what kind of thoughts and actions the aged child (adult) experiences, and what it means to be a "productive member of society." Being forced to do someone else's bidding, or having our thoughts controlled by what *someone else* chooses for us to think, greatly impedes our own individuality. Our pride and ego constitute (form) our individuality. Therefore, being proud of one's own individual, free-willed (unforced) accomplishments brings a person joy (the feeling of happiness).

Here we would like to give you an example of how we undetectably (unnoticed) introduced a new idea about free will into the thoughts of the reader. We will explain how we used our new American scripture to infiltrate early American Christianity, and subtly (carefully) convinced readers "to act [for themselves and not] be acted upon."[15] Acting for yourself is exercising your own free will to do and think what *you* choose to think, not being forced in any other way or by any other means.

If we had tried to convince the early American Christians that the Bible was not a true history, no one would have paid attention to us. They did not want to know that the Bible was no different or less influential than the great ancient Greek myths that controlled people and helped create the great Greek and Roman empires. We needed to introduce new ideas into hardened hearts and closed minds that were already shaped by the Hebrew and Christian Bible. (In the case of early America, the King James Version of the Bible was the most significant and widely accepted.)

How could we possibly tell the American Christians that their accepted Bible was "blinding the eyes and hardening the hearts of the children of men … causing them to stumble, yea, insomuch that Satan hath great power over them,"[16] and in a way that they would accept it and believe it?

Before a person opens their mind to anything, the first thing that must be penetrated is the person's pride and ego. People must be convinced to believe that they are in control of their own thoughts, and that someone is not trying to convince them that they are wrong. Early American Christians were convinced that Jesus was the great Messiah of the world, and that he was going to reappear to put the world in the proper order, according to *his* law and authority. There was no way that we could have convinced them that they were wrong and that they must save the world themselves—a world they had shaped and corrupted with their own free-willed choices. Our subtle manipulation had to remain completely focused and established on the Jesus Christ presented in the King James Bible.

---

[15] *BOM*, 2 Nephi 2:14.
[16] *Compare BOM*, 1 Nephi 13:27–9.

To boost their egos, we presented the idea at the beginning of our storyline that the Western Hemisphere, especially the United States of America, was another "promised land." Appeasing the ego is a way that a person is manipulated to open their mind to a new idea.

By the beginning of the nineteenth (19th) century, the Europeans had already overrun most of the Western Hemisphere and subjected the native Americans (both in North and South America) to European ideas and beliefs. The native Americans, who were once exercising their own form of free will, had been forced to accept someone else's.

In America, an idea existed called *Manifest Destiny*.[17] This was a widely held political and religious belief supporting the idea that Christianity was divinely destined to spread throughout the world. The people claimed that the expansion of European ideas and lifestyle throughout the American continent had been prophesied. They believed it was Christian-inspired, Christian-justified, and that a Christian belief system was the inevitable fate of the entire Western Hemisphere, as well as the rest of the world. In our new American scripture's narrative, we presented the idea that Jesus Christ was behind the discovery and settling of the Western Hemisphere. This boosted the pride and ego of the early European-American Christians.

In our storyline, we presented the development of the area where the United States of America was established as one of God's "promised lands." Europeans (called "Gentiles" throughout the story) poured across the "many waters" (Atlantic Ocean). We supported their egotistical idea of *Manifest Destiny* by explaining that "the wrath of God is upon the native Americans."[18]

All native Americans had darker skin. Therefore, we were forced to support the insidious (false) and dangerous Bible-based belief that dark skin was the "curse" of Cain. This was a belief that was justified in the minds of

---

[17] *See* "Manifest Destiny," *Wikipedia*, 12 May 2021, en.wikipedia.org/wiki/Manifest_destiny.
[18] *Compare BOM*, 1 Nephi 13:11, 14.

the Christian Americans (as we explained above). This is because they believed that the Bible's Adam and Eve were white-skinned. According to this belief, *all* of Adam and Eve's posterity (*all* people on Earth) should be white-skinned as well.

Once we had penetrated the readers' hearts and opened their minds (imperceptibly, but cleverly, by stroking their pride and ego and presenting firm Christian beliefs in our storyline), we were able to introduce into our new American scripture the idea that the King James Bible was corrupt. This is how we did it:

> And after [the eyewitness accounts of Jesus' mission written in the New Testament gospels] go forth by the hand of the twelve apostles of the Lamb, from the Jews unto the Gentiles, thou seest the formation of that great and abominable church, which is most abominable above all other churches; for behold, they have taken away from the gospel of the Lamb many parts which are plain and most precious; and also many covenants of the Lord have they taken away.
>
> And all this have they done that they might pervert the right ways of the Lord, that they might blind the eyes and harden the hearts of the children of men.
>
> Wherefore, thou seest that after the book hath gone forth through the hands of the great and abominable church, that there are many plain and precious things taken away from the book, which is the book of the Lamb of God.
>
> And after these plain and precious things were taken away it goeth forth unto all the nations of the Gentiles; and after it goeth forth unto all the nations of the Gentiles, yea, even across the many waters which thou hast seen with the Gentiles which have gone forth out of captivity, thou seest—because of the many plain and

precious things which have been taken out of the book, which were plain unto the understanding of the children of men, according to the plainness which is in the Lamb of God—because of these things which are taken away out of the gospel of the Lamb, an exceedingly great many do stumble, yea, insomuch that Satan hath great power over them.[19]

At this point, we were able to sow a seed of doubt in the mind of a person reading our new American scripture about the correctness and authenticity of the King James Bible. When religious people *feel* the "Holy Spirit" speaking to them as they are considering a new thought, this *feeling* becomes a powerful testimony to them that what they are reading is from God.

Before the publication of the book that you are currently reading, we released a book that we titled, *Pentateuch Illuminated: A Five Part Series Introducing A New American Scripture—How and Why the Real Illuminati® Created the Book of Mormon.*[20] (This is not the first book of our Trilogy, but an introduction to this, the second book of our Trilogy). On pages 213–16 of that book (large print edition), we explained the Real Truth™ about "spiritual feelings." We explained about the

> ability of the brain to produce *feelings* that *cause* the *spiritual feeling.* ... It's about *how* the story is told. It's about what the brain sees, hears, smells, tastes, and touches.

Because there is nothing that is heard, smelled, tasted, or touched when one reads a story, it is important that an author presents a plot that influences the reader's imagination, so that a "spiritual" sensation is *physically* experienced (felt).

We would encourage one to read the *Pentateuch Illuminated* book before proceeding with this book (*A New American Scripture*).

---

[19] *BOM*, 1 Nephi 13:26–9.
[20] Read for free at realilluminati.org/pentateuch-illuminated.

Again, it was our intent to penetrate established (conventional) beliefs that had been forced upon people all of their lives. We did this to open people's minds to another way of thinking, and then try to compel them to act upon their new way of thinking. Although compelling (forcing) a person to think a certain way appears to be counterproductive and hypocritical in our desire to get people to exercise their free will and think for themselves, our intent was to remove those established beliefs that control people to behave contrary to their true humanity.

Once the plot of our story succeeded at getting the reader to accept that the Bible might be corrupt, and would allow the devil to have "great power over them," we were able to introduce our own version of Jesus Christ and his uncorrupted "plain and precious" teachings. Below is one way (of the many) that we presented the idea of protecting and supporting free will, while actually manipulating the Christian mind. We wanted the Christian reader to accept our Messiah "and hearken unto his great commandments; and be faithful unto his words":

> Adam fell that men might be; and men are, that they might have joy.
>
> And the Messiah cometh in the fulness of time, that he may redeem the children of men from the fall. And because that they are redeemed from the fall they have become free forever, knowing good from evil; to act for themselves and not to be acted upon, save it be by the punishment of the law at the great and last day, according to the commandments which God hath given.
>
> Wherefore, men are free according to the flesh; and all things are given them which are expedient unto man. And they are free to choose liberty and eternal life, through the great Mediator of all men, or to choose captivity and death, according to the captivity and power of the devil; for he seeketh that all men might be miserable like unto himself.

> And now, my sons, I would that ye should look to the great Mediator, and hearken unto his great commandments; and be faithful unto his words, and choose eternal life, according to the will of his Holy Spirit;
>
> And not choose eternal death, according to the will of the flesh and the evil which is therein, which giveth the spirit of the devil power to captivate, to bring you down to hell, that he may reign over you in his own kingdom.[21]

Our intent was to get the American people to accept *our* Jesus over the one that was presented in the King James Version of the New Testament. Our intent was to convince the reader that our Jesus was real, that our Jesus was no different than the one in which they believed, and that our stories about Jesus were more credible and reliable than the Bible's. By the time we presented the subplot of Jesus actually teaching the people upon Earth, for a second time as a resurrected being, the reader's mind and heart were fully penetrated, opened, and ready to be influenced. We made the reader feel an actual emotional and physical feeling that a Christian Bible-believer would credit to originating from the "Spirit of God." The "Holy Spirit" would testify to the reader that our version of Jesus Christ was true.

The gospel we wanted Christians to accept and follow was a much different gospel than that in which the early American Christians believed. Therefore, in our story, when the Jesus Christ of the New Testament returned to Earth a second time, as the resurrected Messiah, we wanted to get their full attention. Before we had Jesus teach the "fulness of the everlasting gospel," we had our resurrected Jesus tell a person that they had to "become as a little child." He repeated it twice to reiterate its importance:

---

[21] *BOM*, 2 Nephi 2:25–9.

And again I say unto you, ye must repent, and become as a little child, and be baptized in my name, or ye can in nowise receive these things. And again I say unto you, ye must repent, and be baptized in my name, and become as a little child, or ye can in nowise inherit the kingdom of God.

We had our Jesus tell the people that what he was about to deliver to them would be "my doctrine, and whoso buildeth upon this buildeth upon my rock, and the gates of hell shall not prevail against them."[22]

Unfortunately, we had very little success at getting early American Christians to accept our new scripture for the purpose for which it was intended. The few who did accept it, completely ignored all the teachings and doctrines we had presented. At the time, a new American religion was formed by those who read our book and were convinced that it was from God. Because they were the only ones who accepted our new American scripture as "Another Testament of Jesus Christ,"[23] they were convinced that they were the "chosen ones," the "elect," the "righteous ones."

We had known there was a high probability that the early Christians who were convinced of the truthfulness of our book would "look beyond the mark" and desire a religion. In an effort to prevent this, and mitigate (reduce) the outcome of yet another religion that impeded the free will of people, we incorporated various clues, warnings, and easy-to-understand prophecies into our storyline.

In the Prologue of this book (*A New American Scripture*), the reader was introduced to the great lengths that have been taken by the LDS/Mormon Church that touts our book as the "keystone of [their] religion." We gave unquestionable proof of how this church has corrupted

---

[22] *BOM*, 3 Nephi 11:37–9.
[23] This subtitle was added to the *Book of Mormon* for the 1982 edition from the LDS Church. *See* the announcement in Boyd K. Packer, "Scriptures," *Ensign*, Nov. 1982, found online at churchofjesuschrist.org/study/general-conference/1982/10/scriptures?lang=eng.

our message yet continues to use our book deceptively to catch an unsuspecting investigator. This church allows our book to cause a person to "feel the Spirit of God," convincing the person that because this church is the only church that has our book, then this church *must be* God's "only true and living church"[24] upon Earth.

We explained how this great deception warranted (justified) our coming forth as the Real Illuminati® and providing the evidence that we wrote the unsealed *Book of Mormon*. We needed to clarify our purpose for writing it, which had nothing to do with establishing a new religion and church.

Through the books that we are now writing, we are offering the people of this world easy-to-read explanations about the origins of religion, how we used religion to try to help society, and what *should* be done by the human race to establish peace on Earth and goodwill towards **all** of Earth's inhabitants (people).

The first book of our Trilogy, *The True History of Religion*, presents the Real Truth™ about how all religions first started.

Our second book (this one, *A New American Scripture*), dovetails (fits with) the first and gives empirical (factual) evidence of *How Religion Destroys the Human Race and What the Real Illuminati® Has Attempted to do Through Religion to Save the Human Race*.

The third book of our Trilogy will present a blueprint for the perfect human government and what laws are necessary to impose in order to protect and support individual free will.

Today, there are race wars occurring (large-scale conflicts between different races). There are also many wars over religion. All of these wars must

---

[24] Elder Dallin H. Oaks, "The Only True and Living Church," *The Church of Jesus Christ of Latter-Day Saints*, churchofjesuschrist.org/study/new-era/2011/08/the-only-true-and-living-church?lang=eng.

end before the right form of government can exist upon Earth. We ended the first book of our Trilogy by explaining that we cannot help save humanity unless we can convince people that religion is the problem, not the solution.

We must first deal with the race wars that are about to explode all across the globe, largely based on religious identification and belief. In the first book of our Trilogy, we asked who was going to be the first to step forward and finally admit the falsity of their religious beliefs. Will the Jews? Will the Christians? Will the Muslims?[25]

When will the lighter-skinned race (the white race) acknowledge their prejudice (the way that they perceive darker-skinned people) and admit that they possess a natural displeasure in seeing a person of a different skin color? When and how will this type of prejudice end? This prejudice, taught and influenced by the Bible, has created human inequality, and is responsible for the past suffering of the darker-skinned people, a suffering that continues unabated in today's world.

"African American" is one of many phrases used in the United States of America to define why a person's skin shade is different. Traditionally, this choice of words refers to those who have darker skin. But who will be the first African American who will acknowledge and respect their white heritage? The white side of their DNA gives them beautiful features that many African Americans desire: straight hair, thinner lips and nose, fairer skin. These are all features that are inherited from their white ancestors. Who is going to acknowledge that they are partially black and partially white, instead of exploiting their black heritage in order to become, for example, President of the United States (a nation of the greatest and most powerful group of humans in modern history)? Who is going to stand up and proclaim that humans should be only ONE race—the Human Race?

---

[25] *THOR*, iv. This can be read free at realilluminati.org/the-true-history-of-religion.

Focusing on race-based ideologies, problems, suffering, and division leads to hate. Hate leads to fear and mistrust. When will the hate of each group end? Little children look at each other with unwavering respect and acceptance.[26] When will one person look at another as little children look at each other, regardless of skin color or belief?

There is only one thing that can change the hard hearts and closed minds that cause racism, ethnic cleansing, and religious hatred: the Real Truth™ about how things *really* are and *really* were in the past. People must be taught things that they should have been taught from the time that they started to learn as a little child. They must be taught how the religions started that introduced prejudice, especially regarding race, which resulted in the divisions that are destroying humanity today.

This book will provide some very important empirical evidence of how easily people are duped by others who claim to know, when these others don't know anything. These *others* claim to know God and then invent a god to bring value to themselves. Their invented gods determine which race is God's *chosen one* and which races are not. In order to counter racial profiling, the gods that created a profile for how a human being should look and act must be confronted and destroyed. This can only be done by the "sharp two-edged sword" of Real Truth™.

The "Marvelous Work and a Wonder®" is a legally registered trademark under which we disseminate (share) the Real Truth™ to the people of the world, without charge or obligation. The religion that misuses our new American scripture has no right to claim this term as its own. We own it. We wrote the *Book of Mormon* and *The Sealed Portion* for the purpose of opening up the reader's mind to the Real Truth™ about "the great and marvelous things which have been hid up from the foundation of the world,"[27] which are the things that can save humanity.

---

[26] *See* "Toddler Besties Share Huge Hug on Sidewalk." Inside Edition, YouTube, 11 Sept. 2019, youtu.be/nDQezECAxtQ.
[27] *BOM*, Ether 4:15.

We can teach the world how all different colors of skin came into existence. The Real Truth™ about the origination of the different races of the same human family is far from what the world teaches from its supposed wisdom and pride. ALL religious and secular authorities' teachings about race are not only false, but are causing all of the negative ramifications of differing skin tones, which are negative feelings that no little child possesses until taught.

Again, to help the people of Earth learn how they have been and are being deceived, we have written this book. We will provide actual proof of the deceptive ways that religion—and the governments that are inspired and supported by religion—cause most of humanity's problems.

Above we have tried to explain *why* we wrote the *Book of Mormon*. The following chapters will provide specific details on *how* we wrote it. Again, we strongly recommend reading the book we published as an introduction to this book, *Pentateuch Illuminated: A Five Part Series Introducing A New American Scripture—How and Why the Real Illuminati® Created the Book of Mormon.*

We are confident that if the world will consider what we present in the following chapters, the pride that is responsible for poverty, inequality, and racism will slowly dissolve away, as humanity begins to drink from the cup we offer. Within the cup is a new wine that provides the reader with a taste of why we, the Real Illuminati®, created a new American scripture.

Chapter 1
The Real Illuminati®—Authors' Note
(Our Opening Statement)

We have little doubt that many people will become disturbed, uncomfortable, and some very angry, if and when they read this book. This book will prove, beyond any reasonable doubt, that the Bible is a collection of stories and accounts that are *not* true. This book will prove that the world's three major religions that use the Bible as their standard scripture—Judaism, Christianity, and Islam—are not only false, but are the cause of most of humanity's current problems.

This book will prove that most people do not think rationally or logically. The evidence in this book will show that most humans depend on their emotions to guide their thoughts and actions. The evidence is overwhelming that, because of this emotional dependency, when confronted with details that make complete sense, and with information that can be proven to be empirical and sound, anger and frustration result. As a result of this anger and frustration, the problems that face humanity are getting worse ... much worse.

Many books have been written by unbelievers and skeptics of religion in an attempt to open the closed minds of believers. Many of these books contain very logical and reasonable arguments against religion. Nevertheless, very few of these books have been able to breach the thick filters of prejudice and belief that can hold a person in emotional chains of ignorance. These filters must be penetrated in order to open a person's mind—a mind that is convinced beyond any reasonable doubt that God is real, aware of human life, and that God interacts with humans living on the earth.

Very few religious skeptics (no matter how sound their logic and no matter how clear their arguments) have been able to dissuade people (convince them to believe differently) who believe they have felt the presence of and a connection with God. Few, if any, spiritually-minded people can be convinced that this transcendent (supernatural) and divine feeling—which embodies the foundation of faith—does *not* prove that any god, of any nature, exists. Unbelievers who have never personally experienced these spiritual feelings cannot explain this *feeling of faith*; nor can these skeptics present any reasonable arguments that can thoroughly convince a *spiritual* person of their error in judgment.

Marketing researchers, who are employed to figure out the best way to sell things to people, have discovered that human emotion compels their decisions more than logic does.[1] This research is highly valued by the business world. However, this research does not discount the necessity of logic:

> Logic provides the foundation to make ideas stick long after the emotional high is gone, so both are necessary. However, logic has a much better chance of being accepted and remembered, if it is preceded by a receptive emotional state.[2]

We understood what these researchers have discovered about how to sell products to the human race. We utilized this same understanding to write our new American scripture. We wrote the scripture for a purpose. We wanted to teach certain lessons. We hoped that these lessons would result in helping the human race to open their minds and consider logical Real Truth™s that would "stick long after the emotional high [was] gone." To do this, we first had to create the "emotional high." We reveal in this book the way that we used our understanding of this sales

---

[1] For one of many examples, *see* Peter Noel Murray, "How Emotions Influence What We Buy," 26 Feb. 2013, *Psychology Today*, Sussex Publishers, psychologytoday.com/us/blog/inside-the-consumer-mind/201302/how-emotions-influence-what-we-buy.

[2] *See* LiveseySolar, "Head Versus Heart: Why Emotion Is More Powerful than Logic." *LiveseySolar Cataract & Laser Eye Surgery Marketing*, LiveseySolar, 6 Nov. 2013, liveseysolar.com/head-versus-heart-why-emotion-is-more-powerful-than-logic.

technique to *sell* humanity the things we hoped that they would *buy*: things that would help humanity in the long run.

Consider how easy it *should* be to convince a reasonably intelligent person that it is impossible that the Bible stories could be real. If the Bible were true, the human race started around 6000 years ago. This biblical "fact" is supposedly indisputable because of the ages of the early patriarchs given in the Bible. From Moses, who lived about 120 years, back to Adam, who lived 930 years, the math of the Bible fills in the "correct" amount of time when the first humans lived upon the earth … at least according to the Bible.[3]

Throughout our writings, we have revealed how the Bible was actually put together. We have explained how the Hebrew scholars and priests were able to create a believable storyline of oral tales that were passed down in their culture over hundreds of years. We explained how they made up whatever age was necessary for all of the characters in their oral stories who supposedly lived before King David. After King David, the characters in their history usually died at a more normal and acceptable age (70 to 100 years). Hebrew storytellers were forced to present a more normal life span for their later Bible characters because other cultures' histories were also being written that could logically counter their myths. Few other cultures claim that their ancestors lived for hundreds of years. Furthermore, there was no contemporary person of Hebrew ancestry who lived beyond the normal age of mortality.

Genealogy (the family line) is very important to the Hebrew/Jewish people. Hebrew mythology presented a narrative that God created the first humans as male and female (Adam and Eve). The biblical narrative claims that these two humans started the *entire* human race. Because of this, and because Hebrew genealogy *must be* proven as factual, Jewish lineage *must be* traced back to Adam. The storytellers had to fill in the years between when they were telling their stories to the rest of the world (around the sixth [6th] century B.C.E.) and when Adam was first created, according to their oral histories and traditions. We

---

[3] *See* "Biblical Literalist Chronology." *Wikipedia*, Wikimedia Foundation, 24 May 2021, en.wikipedia.org/wiki/Biblical_literalist_chronology.

have shown how the Hebrew scholars gave hundreds of years of life to the various characters of their stories. This was done so that their actual lineage could be mathematically proven and traced according to the presentation of their accepted myths.

Our writings have explained how the Hebrew priests and scholars, who were responsible for the oral history of the Jews, commissioned and paid Greek writers to turn their *oral* history into a *written* history circa (around) the sixth (6th) century B.C.E.[4] The Greek writers didn't have a problem writing fantastical tales of myth. They had been doing it for many years to entertain Greeks and to help their *own* priests keep their own people in line and subjected to mythical *Greek* gods. This was done through the teachings of the leaders of their own religions.

Besides the extraordinary and supernatural ages of the Bible's early patriarchs, the idea that ALL races (skin colors) came from just two white people during the course of a few millennia, simply doesn't make any sense. If the Bible were true, then ALL of the dark-skinned races and ALL of the other inhabitants of the earth must be accounted for and their histories and cultures explained. This includes ALL of the descendants of the millions of Earth's citizens who existed in other families at the time when Abraham's family and descendants were supposedly picked as "God's chosen house."

The many different human skin tones (colors) that exist on Earth today is another logical fact that cannot be explained within the Bible's narrative. If the question of race was answered *honestly* by Bible believers, according to an honest interpretation of their scriptures, these would have no choice but to

---

[4] *See THOR*, 121, 126;
see also The Real Illuminati®, *Pentateuch Illuminated: A Five Part Series Introducing A New American Scripture—How and Why the Real Illuminati® Created the Book of Mormon* (Melba: Worldwide United Publishing, 2020), found online at realilluminati.org/pentateuch-illuminated, 200–2. Hereafter *Pentateuch Illuminated*.

answer that God "cursed" the skin color of some of Adam's posterity who upset Him. There is simply no other explanation.

Irrationally, many Bible apologists (people who defend the Bible) will argue that God isn't racist and didn't curse any of Adam's children. But these supporters of the Bible cannot give any reasonable explanation as to where all the different skin colors originated, if all humans are direct descendants of the white-skinned Adam and Eve. These apologists simply do not want to appear to be racist. And yet their personal and emotional beliefs cause them *cognitive* dissonance, which is a natural, emotional, cognitive (mental) response when their beliefs are challenged with logic and reason. (*Cognitive dissonance* occurs in people's minds when new information makes sense, but conflicts with their already-established *truths*.)

If honestly considered without involving the emotions responsible for biases, prejudices, and preconceived notions from cultural tradition, there should be no doubt in anyone's mind that the Bible's narrative is responsible for ALL of the racist, ethnic, and religious prejudices and divisions that exist in modern times. A further honest consideration and review would reveal that most, if not ALL, of the problems that humanity faces today can be traced to racism, ethnicity, and religion. No logical or reasonable person can deny this Real Truth™. It is the way things *really* are upon Earth today.

The Bible's story of Noah and the ark, of Moses and his miracles, even the rise of kings David and Solomon, and all the stories in between, simply do not make any sense. And they certainly cannot be proven by any honest scientific review of impartial historical accounts. Although honesty, transparency, and scientific exploration can rationally and reasonably <u>dis</u>prove the Bible's stories, billions of people remain convinced that the Bible is God's one and only truth. Outside of those who believe in the Bible, a great majority of the rest of humanity believes in some kind of supernatural entity and force. These staunch believers remain convinced, beyond logic and reason, because of their personal experiences with what they perceive to be some kind of supernatural entity. These feelings are actual, physical *feelings* that the believers would never and could never honestly deny due to their own personal experiences. No one has the power, or the right, to tell another person what that individual has personally experienced or not. Each human is naturally and equally endowed with a special, uniquely human cognitive force: the power of free will to believe.

What if there was a way to show the people that their *feelings and emotions* had been manipulated? What if there was a way to convince them that they had been deceived and misled? How would they respond if they were allowed a choice to *believe* or *not to believe*? What if this choice was based on their own physical sensations, which are very real to them and cannot be disputed by a skeptic?

The only way to properly do this would be to replicate (recreate) and cause these feelings to manifest in the mind and body *without* affecting a person's dignity and free will to choose. Science has already proven that this can be done,[5] but only for those who have *allowed* themselves to be subjected to scientific observation and experimentation. Once a person has submitted to such testing, that one has already been convinced to doubt what she or he has previously experienced as spiritual manifestations. Therefore, these types of experiments are easily disputable. On the other hand, believers can pull up evidence that a non-believer can be similarly susceptible to spiritual manifestations, *if* the atheist allows the same unbiased and impartial experimentation.[6]

We do not dispute that the feelings that occur in a person's mind are accepted as *real* and *undeniable* experiences. However, what if it could be proven empirically, beyond any reasonable doubt, that the source of these

---

[5] Watch Neuroscientist Dr. Michael Persinger use "The God Helmet" to create a "God Experience" in this 8-minute video hosted by Morgan Freeman "The God Helmet, Through the Wormhole, Uncut": vimeo.com/144332709.

[6] To watch mentalist Derren Brown cause an atheist to have a strong conversion experience, with a detailed commentary on the methods he is using, *see* Derren Brown, "Do You Believe In GOD? | Faith and Fear | Derren Brown," YouTube, 16 Jan. 2021, youtube.com/watch?v=6-xBFjQjFG4. The most relevant part starts around 7 minutes 30 seconds in.

feelings is *not* actually real? What if it could be proven that the source was made up by someone who wanted to replicate these feelings for a certain purpose? *If* this could happen, only then might the people consider that perhaps ALL of the sources that made them feel the exact same spiritual manifestations could have also have been a deception.

The evidence given in this book will show that the Bible has deceived billions of people because of the spiritual manifestations that the people experience upon reading it. The evidence we present will show how a few people, usually men, wrote scripture that supported their own agenda and pride. We will prove that their agenda was to keep their followers divided and alienated from other groups of people that did not choose to follow these few deceptive and unprincipled leaders. Logical and reasonable evidence will be presented to prove that the Bible continues to be the chief and principal source of most racism, ethnic cleansing, and the religious wars that have existed and continue to exist throughout the world, ALL of which are destroying humanity.

In order to prove what the Bible has done, to open the minds of the billions deceived thereby, and to provide them with an opportunity to choose logic and reason over their spiritual emotions, we created a new American scripture. In creating our new scripture to counter the deceptions of the past that continue to threaten peace and sanity upon the earth, we wrote the *Book of Mormon* and its "greater portion of the word," *The Sealed Portion*.

This book will prove *how* and *why* we have done what we have. This book will prove how easily the human race is susceptible to deception by the devious few who wanted to control and manage humanity for their own personal gain. We wrote this book to expose, not only the naïveté of the human mind, but also its vulnerability to deception. In explaining what we did to replicate the same spiritual feelings that Bible-believers experience upon reading the Bible, we will reveal the methods that have been used in the past to make people do things that harm themselves and harm the rest of humanity.

This book is not about hate and vengeance. This book is about love—an overwhelming emotion that can unite humanity as one race and one people and result in peace on Earth and goodwill towards all humans. We present this type of love in the *unsealed portion* of our new American scripture as the

> tree of life ... a representation of the love of God; ... which sheddeth itself abroad in the hearts of the children of men; wherefore, it is the most desirable above all things ... and the most joyous to the soul.[7]

It was out of our love for humanity that we wrote this book. It was out of our love for humanity that we wrote our new American scripture (the *Book of Mormon* and *The Sealed Portion*). The reader of this book might find that at times our written words are harsh, unrelenting, and appear to be cruel, especially in regards to organized religion. More particularly, at times, our words are directed specifically towards the LDS/Mormon people who make an effort to spread our new American scripture throughout the world. But if our words and intent are taken in context and considered with sincerity and real intent, our love for humanity will shine through what might appear to be bitterness and hostility.

We do not hate any person. We love ALL people the same, regardless of how wrong their actions might appear to us. If there were any religious belief or spirituality, of any kind, from any source, that would rid this world of racism, ethnic cleansing, and war, we would embrace and support such a system of belief and faith. However, we know that there is no such religion or spiritual persuasion that has this power. The best we can do is to utilize our *faith* in humanity and attempt to effectuate a change of heart and mind that will not allow prejudice, division, and strife of any kind.

We are part of YOU. You are part of US. Often this realization of our mutual humanity causes us to mourn for all of us. We invented the concept

---

[7] *BOM*, 1 Nephi 11:25, 22–3.

of the "tree of life" as a symbolic representation of our unity as a human race. The "tree of life" is a representation of the love that we are capable of feeling one towards another. It is a tree that bears a fruit that, if tasted and consumed, can heal ALL the nations upon Earth.

We have provided substantial evidence that our group was also responsible for the Bible's book of Revelation.[8] In Revelation, as we also did in our new American scripture, we presented the "tree of life" as that which "yielded her fruit … and the leaves of the tree were for the healing of the nations."[9] There should be no dispute of what love can do to heal this world. It is our hope that by revealing what we have done in creating a new American scripture, we can present the fruit of our "tree of life" and give humanity the choice of whether to eat it or not.

We are the Real Illuminati®. We are the authors of this book. We are confident that if the reader sincerely and with real intent reads our book, the reader will also be convinced that human love is possible. Being convinced, we hope that the reader will finally have some *faith* and *hope* in humanity. For this purpose, we present this book about *How and Why the Real Illuminati® Created the Book of Mormon*. We wrote this book as clearly as possible. We instructed the editors of our words to present our words so that all people could easily understand them.

We know that many people pick and choose parts of a non-fiction book that they would usually otherwise have no interest in reading. Because of this, we constructed each chapter of the book you are reading to stand on its own and teach the core principles and main points that we presented in our new American scripture.

---

[8] *See* Christopher, *666, The Mark of America—Seat of the Beast: The Apostle John's New Testament Revelation Unfolded*, Worldwide United Pub., 2006. This book is free to read at realilluminati.org/666-mark-of-america. Hereafter referred to as *666 America*.

[9] NT, Revelation 22:2. *See also* NT, Revelation 2:7, all of chapter 22; and *BOM*, 1 Nephi, chapters 8 and 11.

If one opens this book to any of its chapters and reads just one, we are confident that the content of the chosen chapter will inspire further reading. Because of the repetition and redundancy of the core principles and main points that we present in each and every chapter, a more well-read person might become irritable with our manner of writing. To these, who in their pride might condemn us for how we write, we repeat what we wrote in the *unsealed part* of our new American scripture:

> And I said unto him: Lord, the Gentiles will mock at these things, because of our weakness in writing; for Lord thou hast made us mighty in word by faith, but thou hast not made us mighty in writing; for thou hast made all this people that they could speak much, because of the Holy Ghost which thou hast given them;
>
> And thou hast made us that we could write but little, because of the awkwardness of our hands. Behold, thou hast not made us mighty in writing like unto the brother of Jared, for thou madest him that the things which he wrote were mighty even as thou art, unto the overpowering of man to read them.
>
> Thou hast also made our words powerful and great, even that we cannot write them; wherefore, when we write we behold our weakness, and stumble because of the placing of our words; and I fear lest the Gentiles shall mock at our words.
>
> And when I had said this, the Lord spake unto me, saying: Fools mock, but they shall mourn; and my grace is sufficient for the meek, that they shall take no advantage of your weakness;
>
> And if men come unto me I will show unto them their weakness. I give unto men weakness that they may be humble; and my grace is sufficient for all men that humble themselves before me; for if they humble themselves before me, and have faith in me, then will I make weak things become strong unto them.

> Behold, I will show unto the Gentiles their weakness, and I will show unto them that faith, hope and charity bringeth unto me—the fountain of all righteousness.[10]

It is our hope that one so inclined to consider her or himself above the literary application of our words in this book checks her or his pride and does not become a fool. We can assure such a one so imposed by her or his own sense of an elevated education, which in turn produces a grandiose sense of self-worth and pretentiousness, that we could compose a treatise of the magnitude and consequence of your exalted expectations. But here, we warn those readers who pretend to this illustrious rationale: YOU are the fools. YOU are those who, in the pride of your hearts, are contributing to the fall of humanity. We provide evidence of this throughout this book.

Do not neglect the chance to review and consider the evidence that we present in this book just because you think it was written below your level of education and reading ability. If you are not a fool, and you value your intelligence worthy of your own self-imposed accolades, then so endowed and empowered, we challenge you to find error and discrepancy in the case we present in this book.

In the scripture above, we mentioned one of the characters in our new American scripture called ***the brother of Jared***. One might reasonably question why this character has no name except that of being the brother of another. For the same reason we gave no specific name to this character, we do not reveal our true names. The story of *the brother of Jared* will be explained. Our story and reasoning in hiding our true names is simple: we want neither accolade, nor persecution, for our intelligence. We will provide evidence in this book of what has happened throughout history when those like us stand up against the powers that control this world. It has not ended well for us. And it certainly has not ended well for humanity.

---

[10] *BOM*, Ether 12:23–8.

We are the Real Illuminati®. There are no others who are *illuminated* with Real Truth™ as we have been. What we know can lead humanity to peace and life eternal upon this earth. With great love and a sincere hope for all of humanity, we offer some of the fruit from the "tree of life." This book provides some of this fruit, which we offer freely to you for your pleasure and consumption.

May you eat of this fruit and clearly understand:

A New American Scripture—How and Why the Real Illuminati® Created the Book of Mormon.

Chapter 2
Author and Proprietor

In the first book of our Trilogy, *The True History of Religion—How Religion Destroys the Human Race and What the Real Illuminati® Has Attempted to do Through Religion to Save the Human Race*, we revealed many historical facts. One of these facts was that none of our previous chosen True Messengers (a few of whom we disclosed as Socrates, Inpendius, and Mohammed) left any of their own handwritten documents. We also explained *why*:

> We had cautioned Socrates about leaving any teachings in written form, knowing that if something is written, then it can be rewritten. According to our counsel, Socrates left no writings.
>
> Unfortunately, some of Socrates' students misinterpreted his teachings in the presentation of their own. His few students found that they received value, prestige, and money in the community when they presented information that was politically and socially correct. So, they simply took some of Socrates' information that wasn't politically and socially correct and made it so. Whatever they learned from our True Messenger, they changed it to conform to what their community wanted to hear, for which they were compensated handsomely (received a very good payment).[1]

We intended for our new American scripture to be another "word of God" that was a companion to the Christian King James Bible. Early American Christians believed that their Bible was the perfect and ultimate "word of God." Therefore, when it was announced that Joseph Smith had

---
[1] *THOR*, 110–11.

published a "gold bible" (referring to the gold plates) as another "word of God," one can only imagine how the Christian world responded.

According to Christian belief, God gave all the words that he intended for humankind through the Bible. The Jews also believe this about the parts of the Old Testament that they accept as *their* "god's word," given through God's chosen messengers. Muslims believe that the Quran is God's infallible, unchangeable, and complete "word" for humanity, given through Allah's (the Muslim god) final messenger, Mohammed.

In each case, a reasonable and honest person must conclude that the words written in all religious texts were *not* actually written by any god, but by a person who could write. Religious people anchor their faith and hope in their scriptures on the belief that their chosen leaders (mostly men) were *inspired* by their particular god to write what this god wanted.

As we explained in the first book of our Trilogy, Inpendius is the actual person upon whose life the stories of Jesus were based. The people believed that Jesus was a holy prophet, even the literal son of God. If Inpendius had left any actual handwritten documents, then whatever of his writings were passed on, the people would have believed were most sacred and unchangeable. However, the only way to verify that the written words were actually his, would be if we had a verifiable copy of his personal handwriting that lasted over the centuries. If not, anyone could have written anything pretending to be Inpendius, or change what he had written.

The only possible way to prove that a document has not been changed from its original form is to have a verified copy of the original document that can be independently and objectively studied. However, outside of what we (the Real Illuminati®) possess, there are no original documents on Earth that contain what modern religions claim is the infallible "word of God."

We have explained and logically shown (in the first book of our Trilogy) that the *Pauline Letters* (all of the New Testament books attributed to Paul) were incorporated *after* the original testimonies of the Gospels were published. We revealed that these letters were written in order to appease the people who lived in Rome, Corinth, Galatia, Ephesus, Philippi, Colossae, and Thessalonica, whose pride was hurt because Jesus never personally visited their communities. If the New Testament apostle Paul had actually existed, it would be very easy for the Catholic Church to prove that Paul was a real person. It could show the world his original letters. The Catholic Church cannot produce Paul's letters, because these letters do not exist; neither did Paul. But even if the Catholic Church *did* have any evidence of the existence of Paul, it would be very easy for a forgery to be created, if Paul's original handwriting could not be verified.

We have the original Greek drafts of the New Testament gospels, as well as a few other New Testament inclusions. Of course, we also have the original draft, preserved meticulously, of our book of Revelation. But one can just imagine the uproar and fallout if we revealed these documents to the world at this time (circa 2020). In *secret*, the religious leaders of this world would *combine* their power and authority with that of the politicians, who believe in these religious leaders, and ensure that these authentic documents never saw the light of day. Nothing threatens Real Truth™, honesty, and transparency more than the *secret combinations* of political, religious, and business powers.

Someday, the time might be right for us to reveal ourselves to the world and bring out the original and authentic documents in our possession. If and when this happens, we will provide indisputable scientific evidence that ALL religious scripture on Earth is far from what it claims to be. In our new American scripture, we gave a clue that we might be able to one day "minister unto all … nations, kindreds, tongues and people."[2] But for this to

---

[2] *BOM*, 3 Nephi 28:29.

happen, we would need the support of the masses. Otherwise, the secret combinations that hold the power on Earth will seek our destruction.

Our book of Revelation presents symbolism that is only understood by its authors (us). The idea of Christ coming to Earth *in glory*, presented symbolically as a man with a "sharp two-edged sword" coming "out of his mouth," can be properly understood when one understands what we, the original authors of Revelation, meant by the "glory of God." In some of his teachings, Joseph Smith Jr. touched upon this important clue:

> And truth is knowledge of things as they are, and as they were, and as they are to come; And whatsoever is more or less than this is the spirit of that wicked one who was a liar from the beginning. The Spirit of truth is of God. I am the Spirit of truth, and John bore record of me, saying: He received a fulness of truth, yea, even of all truth; ... The glory of God is intelligence, or, in other words, light and truth.[3]

The *true Christ*, or better—the *true Spirit of Christ*—is nothing more or less than the Real Truth™ that is logically and reasonably understood by a mortal person's mind. We present things as they *really* are today, and as they *really* were in the past.

Regarding ALL religious scripture, a few honest questions can be asked: what happened when this scripture was created, who created it, and why was it created?

The True Messenger whom we symbolically presented in our book of Revelation is simply a person from whose mouth the Real Truth™ is given. <u>When the Real Truth™ is given, it is more reasonable, more logical, and makes more sense</u> than what is given by the philosophies of men mingled with their scriptures. <u>Nothing that religious leaders teach can be</u>

---

[3] *D&C*, 93:24–6, 36.

proven with common sense and honesty. Most of what these leaders do is done in secret. When possible, religious leaders *combine* the power that they hold over their followers' minds, with the power of the laws of the land held by the government officials who support the lies of the religion in which these officials believe.

When a True Messenger confronts the lies of religion and exposes the *secret combinations* in which the leaders of religion, government, and business engage, these deceptive men use the power of their institutions to do everything in their power to silence the "sharp two-edged sword" of Real Truth™ coming out of the messenger's mouth.

A True Messenger can confound any lie of any person or of any institution, regardless of the person's power over the minds and hearts of the masses. If there comes a time when a True Messenger is protected by the laws of the land, and these laws protect the messenger from the threats of the institutions to which the masses have submitted their minds and hearts, then that True Messenger will be safe to explain things as they are, as they were, and as they are to come. What such a True Messenger says ... what comes out of his mouth ... silences these powers and proves to the masses that their leaders and institutions are liars, and have been from the beginning.

What a True Messenger says makes sense. Regardless of whether or not the masses listen, the Real Truth™ will always make more sense than a lie. This is what angers the masses and their leaders. If a True Messenger's message or teachings did not make sense, then the powers on Earth that hold the minds of the masses in captivity would not become angry and seek to destroy such a True Messenger. Such a messenger would be ignored or laughed off as being insane. Something that doesn't make sense does not threaten the pride of those who know not, and know not that they know not, but who have convinced others that they know.

The information that Joseph Smith received for our new American scripture came through the "*Urim and Thummim.*" This was a device we named based on the Bible's presentation of a method that the Hebrew God used to allegedly communicate with High Priests and give "God's word" to the people. The terms have been loosely interpreted as *Lights and Perfections*.

The glory of any god is the intelligence that the god has that mere mortals do not. Mortals expect a god to have more intelligence than they do. Mortals should expect that their god can answer any question, and that this god's answers are perfect. In other words, a god's intelligence can be said to be *Light and Truth Unto Perfection* ... or the PERFECT REAL TRUTH™.

The first part of our new American scripture was published as the *Book of Mormon* in March of 1830. There was only one legal author and proprietor (writer and owner)—Joseph Smith, Jr. The copyright was his alone. He owned it. When our new American Christian scripture was first published and announced, and it claimed to support the Bible, the Christian leaders living in America were livid.

Joseph's publication actually led to the U.S. Congress addressing copyright laws and amending its Copyright Act of 1790. Incorrectly reported by history, the revision of the Copyright Act (1831)[4] was a result of a simple man's desire to exercise freedom of speech and religion. This man had little means and no special standing in society. His last name was the most common American surname—Smith. The established Christian leaders were upset because this simple young man made the same claim that was made by Bible authors—that he had received and written the word of God. These leaders were upset because "Joe's Gold Bible" caused the exact same spiritual manifestations and feelings to occur in a reader's mind that the Bible does.

There are always two sides to every story. There are those who believe in our new American scripture—published as the *Book of Mormon*—and those who do not. A *truth* is established by each side, not necessarily according to Real Truth™ (i.e., things as they *really* happened), but, more often

---

[4] *See* "Copyright Act of 1831," *Wikipedia*, Wikimedia Foundation, 17 Apr. 2021, en.wikipedia.org/wiki/Copyright_Act_of_1831.

than not, according to the emotional slant and bias taken by each. Each side can find supporting evidence, documentation, and "facts" that support its own truth. If one side's truth counters or conflicts with the other's, it is difficult for a neutral party to find the Real Truth™.

We have coined the statement, "Everyone is right. Which makes everyone wrong®." When a person is curious about something and makes an honest effort to find out the truth, objective neutrality (being unbiased so as not to support either side) can be threatened by the strong emotional fight in which each side engages to defend its *own* truth.

So, how does one find Real Truth™?

Humans have a special set of tools that are unique to our species and can help us figure out the truth. We have logic and reason. *Logic* deals with the principles and criteria of what one might consider to be true based on <u>actual</u> events that support the accepted truth. *Reason* is the ability to determine if the events were *actual.*

Joseph Smith Jr. was murdered on June 27, 1844. Brigham Young and the apostles did not return to Nauvoo until August 6, 1844. Shortly after that, Brigham Young and Heber C. Kimball showed up at Joseph's widow's home in order to give their condolences. Let us use *reason* and *logic* to deduce the Real Truth™ about what happened when Young and Kimball showed up at Emma Smith's house. We can logically assume that it is correct this event actually took place, because it would be a reasonable act that the highest leaders of the early Mormon church would visit their prophet's widow to offer their condolences.

Those who believe that Joseph Smith was a true prophet of God might present their "facts" about Young's and Kimball's visit to the Smith home differently than those who do not believe that he was a prophet of God. Therefore, the Real Truth™ about this event cannot be outrightly confirmed by listening to the biases of either side.

However, there is an event that *is* confirmed by both sides. Joseph Smith's wife, Emma Hale Smith; his mother, Lucy Mack Smith; his brother, William Smith; and many of his closest friends did *not* follow Brigham Young out West. They did *not* continue Young's version of the religion that had developed among the early Mormons before the death of their prophet, seer, and revelator. Shortly after Joseph Smith's murder, his intimates (closest friends and family) reorganized the early LDS/Mormon Church (which was in *logical* and *reasonable* disarray and confusion). They called this reorganization the *Reorganized Church of Jesus Christ of Latter-day Saints*.

Sidney Rigdon had been Joseph's trusted Counselor in the First Presidency since almost the beginning of what the world calls "Mormonism" as a legal church (first known as the Church of Christ, established April 6, 1830). Rigdon was still Joseph's Counselor on the day of Joseph's murder. This logically and reasonably gives some validity to Rigdon's opposition to Brigham Young's desire to take over the Church, and Rigdon's claim of ascension to take Joseph's place. It is hard to determine what the *real* reason was why Rigdon chose not to follow Young. This is because both sides (those who followed Brigham Young versus those who didn't) have their own "facts."

Both sides report that when Young and Kimball showed up at Emma's home, her mother-in-law, Lucy Mack, was there consoling her. This seems *logical* and *reasonable*. Only one side reports that Emma kicked Young and Kimball out of her house, yelling, "You licentious Fein! Then why not take her sister Mercy?"—a statement heard and reported by others.

Once many of the Apostles, who had been away on missions, returned to Nauvoo, it is *logical* and *reasonable* to assume it correct that many of Joseph's faithful followers were outside of Emma's house wanting to go in and offer their condolences too. People from this group later reported what Emma said as she was kicking Young and Kimball out of her house. However, the "facts" presented by the side that believe that Young and Kimball were "called by God" to replace Joseph and Hyrum Smith exclude this event. They do not report what Emma yelled at Brigham Young and Heber C. Kimball as they were kicked out of the door. (Hyrum Smith was Joseph Smith's older brother. He had been the Assistant President in the First Presidency and had died by his brother's side.)

It is *logical* and *reasonable* that the Mormons who believe that Young and Kimball were called of God to take over the Church (which was in direct opposition to what Joseph's wife, mother, brother, and closest companions believed) would *not* offer these facts in their history if the presentation thereof showed Young and Kimball in a bad light. Regardless, modern-day supporters of Brigham Young cannot deny that Joseph's close intimates did *not* follow Young. Instead, Joseph's closest associates, of whom Brigham was *not* one, reorganized the church in a completely different way than Young did out West in Utah.

Why would Emma Smith call Brigham Young or Heber C. Kimball a "licentious Fein" and include the name of her sister-in-law, Mercy? Which man was Emma addressing? This cannot be determined by honest reflection alone. Keep in mind what logic and reason are:

Logic deals with the principles and criteria of what one might consider to be true based on actual events that support what is considered to be true. Reason is the ability to determine if the events were actual.

Kimball married Hyrum Smith's widow, Mary Fielding Smith, on September 14, 1844—not even three months after Hyrum's murder. There is no argument over this fact. Hyrum had three wives at the time of his death, one of whom was Mary Fielding, and one of whom was her sister, Mercy. What could be the *logical* and *reasonable* reason why Emma became so upset, that she kicked the men out of her house, yelling, *"You licentious Fein! Then why not take her sister Mercy?"*

Both sides agree that Brigham Young made Heber C. Kimball his right-hand man (First Counselor) in Young's new church in Utah. Both sides agree that both Mary Fielding's son and her grandsons eventually became head prophets of Young's Utah church, and that Joseph Smith's descendants had no part of that church. Alternately, Joseph's son and grandsons became the prophets, seers, and revelators of the *Reorganized Church*.

We (the Real Illuminati®) had no part in either organized church. But we do know what happened during the event that took place at Emma's home shortly after the murder of our True Messenger. (He had been counseled by us to *not disclose his true identity* during his tenure as prophet, seer, and revelator of a religion that we had no part in organizing or perpetuating.)

A few days before the Smith brothers' murders at Carthage, Illinois, two of Joseph's most trusted friends (Dan Jones and Stephen Markham) visited the jail where Joseph was incarcerated. While they were there, Joseph lamented that he was about to be killed. During their discussions, Jones mentioned a prophecy that Joseph had given about the "sealed portion" of the gold plates (from which plates the *Book of Mormon* was published). Joseph had said that if anything ever happened to him, his brother, Hyrum, would assure that the "kingdom of God would roll forth until the Lord accomplished his purposes." These "purposes" included bringing forth the *sealed portion* when the Saints were ready for it. (For this reason, Joseph made his brother an equal to him as the "Assistant President" of the Church in 1841, shortly before both were murdered.)

At the jail, Jones asked about this and sought instruction about how Hyrum would proceed if Joseph were to be killed. Hyrum took issue with it and said he would give his life for his brother. Nothing else was said about it until just moments before Hyrum was killed. As bullets flew through the jail cell's door, Hyrum shielded his brother and again reiterated his (Hyrum's) desire to protect Joseph. John Taylor later reported what Joseph said to Hyrum prior to that moment:

One day it shall be you who will finish the mission that I could not during my lifetime. ... May the Lord's work be cut short in the righteousness of what you will do for our eternal Father in heaven. I love you my brother, my friend.[5]

A few moments later, a bullet entered Hyrum's face and killed him instantly. Joseph was killed a few moments after that.

After Brigham Young was notified of Joseph's and Hyrum's murders, he called a meeting of those who were at the jail and asked about the details. Taylor and Jones reported what Joseph had said, which had left both of them confused. How could Hyrum fulfill the prophecy that Joseph had given about Hyrum leading the Church, if Hyrum was now dead?

These concerns had been voiced to Emma and Lucy Mack before they were known by Young. Jones had visited both Emma and Mary Fielding together after he left their husbands at Carthage a few days before. Jones told the women the details about what he knew. The information that Jones told Emma made sense to her at that time because of a blessing that Joseph had recently given to their son, Joseph Smith III. Joseph had blessed their son to follow in his father's (Joseph Smith, Jr.'s) footsteps when he was old enough. Until then, Joseph explained that if anything were to ever happen to him, Hyrum would tutor and mentor Joseph Smith III until he came of age.

It didn't take Young too long to invent a solution to the issue at hand—that Hyrum was no longer living to fulfill the expectations placed upon him by the prophecy given by Joseph while at the Carthage Jail. Young announced that it wasn't necessary that Hyrum fulfill the prophecy as long as one of Hyrum's *sons* was able to. While visiting with Joseph's wife and mother, Young announced that the Lord had revealed to him that he was to take care of Emma, a very beautiful and well-endowed woman, and that Heber Kimball was to take care of Mary Fielding. This meant that Emma

---

[5] See *JS Bio*, 15–17.

would become one of Young's plural wives, and that her son would no longer receive her murdered husband's mantle.

Logic and *reason* can easily guess Emma's response. Emma Smith had been very close to Hyrum's first love and wife, Jerusha. While he was married to the love of his life, Hyrum wanted nothing to do with plural marriage (unlike so many other early Mormon men did at the time). After Jerusha's untimely death, Hyrum was a single father of five children. Joseph introduced Mary Fielding to Hyrum and asked her to help take care of Jerusha's children.

Hyrum could never love Mary like he did Jerusha. Mary could feel this. She knew how special Jerusha's children were to Hyrum. Hyrum married Mary Fielding in December of 1837. For the first while, Hyrum could not have sex with Mary because of his strong love for Jerusha. Logically, Mary would have been affected by this.

Emma and Jerusha had been best friends. It was hard enough on Mary to take care of Jerusha's kids. However, it was even harder to establish a relationship with her very popular and prominent (in the Church) sister-in-law. These two women had many problems. The mutual death of their husbands brought them together ... but only temporarily. Brigham Young destroyed their sisterhood and bond.

When Young asked Heber Kimball to step in for Hyrum, take Hyrum's wife Mary, and raise Hyrum's kids as his own, Kimball was not shy in telling Young that he was not attracted to Mercy, one of Hyrum's other wives. Emma could feel these things, which led to what she yelled at Kimball as she kicked them out of her house.

We have included the above historical relation to show how both sides of Mormonism (those who claim to believe in the *Book of Mormon*) present their own history.

It is important for the reader to keep in mind that most history we have today is the <u>opinion</u> of those who wrote it. It is very easy to *logically* and *reasonably* conclude that written history cannot be trusted to be the Real Truth™. Human leaders are very capable of using deception to present themselves in a false *light* (this is far from *perfect*). For this reason, we used the term *Urim and Thummim* (*lights* and *perfections*) to express the source from which our chosen **True** Messengers receive their information (which is very opposite of how *false* messengers get their information).

In the next chapter, we will explain how the Bible is one of the greatest human deceptions of all time. If the Bible didn't exist, then the three major religions (Judaism, Christianity, and Islam) that control the most powerful nations on Earth would not exist. If the Bible didn't exist, we would not have written our new American scripture. We would not have needed to.

The Old Testament was a deception created by Hebrew leaders to control their people. The New Testament was a necessary deception to control the people who believed in the story of the Old Testament—who believed that God had chosen only one human family as His chosen people. The Holy Quran was a deception to convince the Arab people that they were just as important to God as the Jews and the Christians. Our new American scripture was a deception to open up the readers' minds to all of these great deceptions.

It has always been our goal to stop the destruction of human society. With the knowledge that we have, we invented stories about the demise of society that can be easily understood. Most importantly, we wrote these stories in a way that our intended audience would consider and accept them as true, based on the spiritual manifestations that the readers experience, as we've explained above. Our new American scripture is all about the development of great societies, starting with just a few people, and what ultimately caused their demise. We incorporated into our storyline various examples of how a human society can develop and how it can easily destroy itself.

All of our stories are fictitious, but based on the Real Truth™ that we know about past civilizations. It was our hope that in presenting stories based on what our intended audience already believed and accepted as truth, the moral behind each story would be understood, and that the readers would "*liken all scriptures unto [them], that it might be for [their] profit and learning.*"[6] We had hoped that the early American Christian people would read our new American scripture and "profit" from it. We hoped that they would "learn" what to do and what not to do in developing one of the greatest societies in modern history.

We needed to write a story that people would believe and want to read. *Wanting* to read the story was just as important to us as *believing* the story. We knew we could convince early American Christians to *believe* our story, if it was based on the Bible's stories. Although not one story in the Bible is actual Real Truth™, billions of people believe the stories that are told in its narrative. Basing our stories on Bible stories would ensure that our story was believable to our targeted audience. But how could we write a story that people *wanted* to read?

In the following chapters, we will explain that although the Bible is *one* of the greatest deceptions of all time, *spiritual energy* is the *greatest* of all human deceptions. This is the *feeling* that a person gets upon reading something in which the person is taught to believe, that seems to confirm to the person that what is being read is true. This confirmation is accepted by religious believers as feelings associated with the "Spirit of God" or the "Holy Ghost." Without this affirming feeling, it would be hard to convince a person to *want* to read a story. Being taught and accepting that a story is true is not enough incentive for most to want to *read* the story.

Therefore, we created the stories included in our new American scripture to manipulate the reader's mind so that the reader experiences this confirming "Spirit of God" *feeling*. Our desire was to lead the reader to

---

[6] *BOM*, 1 Nephi 19:23.

believe and accept our words, but also to experience the actual *feeling*. This feeling would convince them that the "Holy Spirit" can teach them the truth of all things. We wrote:

> And when ye shall receive these things [read our *Book of Mormon*], I would exhort you that ye would ask God, the Eternal Father, in the name of Christ, if these things are not true; and if ye shall ask with a sincere heart, with real intent, having faith in Christ, he will manifest the truth of it unto you, by the power of the Holy Ghost. **And by the power of the Holy Ghost ye may know the truth of all things.**[7]

To make a person *want* to read our story, we formulated each part of it to be relatable to the reader's personal experience. And nothing is more important to most humans than their family unit. We used this filial (devoted to one's family) importance and emotional codependence to start our new American scripture's narrative.

Each part (subplot) of our story makes complete sense to the reader because of how we incorporated real emotions that might be reasonably associated with the reader's personal life. This included ensuring that the accepted "facts" (including "facts" from the Bible) about the events and explanations given in the story made sense and could be verified if the reader wanted to research what they already accepted as *truth*. To illustrate this, we share the following example.

Many of our critics reject the presentation of the ancient language that we introduced in our story when we described the characters that were engraved on the "plates." We referred to these characters as "reformed Egyptian." We had one of our authors, Nephi, first introduce the form of engraving that was on the "plates" that we provided to our chosen messenger:

---

[7] *BOM*, Moroni 10:4–5, emphasis added.

> Yea, I make a record in the language of my father, which consists of the learning of the Jews and the language of the Egyptians.[8]

Our character, **Mormon**, who is also our story's main author and responsible for the bulk of the "unsealed" part of the plates that we made, reiterated this particular new language later in the storyline:

> And now, behold, we have written this record according to our knowledge, in the characters which are called among us the reformed Egyptian, being handed down and altered by us, according to our manner of speech.[9]

We were forced to introduce this "reformed Egyptian" that described the characters engraved on the "plates" because the early American Christians that peer-reviewed the book had a hard time relating to hieroglyphic characters that were not Hebrew in nature. When we allowed our chosen messenger (Joseph Smith, Jr.) to show the plates to others, they saw hieroglyphics (little pictures) instead of actual words.

Christians believe that the Bible was written in Hebrew, with words that came out of the Hebrew god's mouth. The few who were shown our plates, as evidence that Joseph Smith did not write the story himself, had a hard time accepting what was engraved. In their minds, if God was Hebrew, then why wouldn't God give his "word" in Hebrew and have it written ONLY in Hebrew, and not in a pagan language (reformed Egyptian)?

To counter their resistant and emotional response to our story, we had our story's main author, Mormon (of the "unsealed part of the plates"), repeat his mention of "reformed Egyptian." Mormon gave the following explanation:

> And if our plates had been sufficiently large we should have written in Hebrew; but the Hebrew hath been altered by us also;

---

[8] *BOM*, 1 Nephi 1:2.
[9] *BOM*, Mormon 9:32.

Chapter 2: Author and Proprietor

and if we could have written in Hebrew, behold, ye would have had no imperfection in our record. But the Lord knoweth the things which we have written, and also that none other people knoweth our language; and because that none other people knoweth our language, therefore he hath prepared means for the interpretation thereof.[10]

This explanation appears to be something that we came up with ... or rather critics of our book believe that Joseph Smith came up with this *reasonable* explanation. Many Bible-believing peer reviewers have taken issue with our new American scripture not being written in Hebrew "like their Bible was." The Real Truth™ is that the Bible was NOT originally written in Hebrew; it was actually written in Greek. This fact was not really of any importance to our Christian audience; therefore, a solid connection to the Bible had to be made. Here's how we did it:

The connection was made in our original storyline (the *Book of Lehi*), as well as implied throughout the "unsealed" part of the plates (the abridged story that was eventually published in 1830 as the *Book of Mormon*). One of our story's strong connections to the Bible was established upon a prophecy given in the book of Ezekiel concerning the "stick of Joseph, which is in the hand of Ephraim" and "the stick of Judah."[11] In ancient times, the scrolls upon which scribes wrote were called "sticks" because the scroll was rolled onto a piece of wood.

Bible scholars teach that the Torah (the first five books of Moses and the history of the Jews) was written and kept by the "tribe of Judah." Judah was one of the twelve sons of Israel; thus, the "tribe of Judah" was, by birth, part of the house of Israel. These writings of the Bible, as well as the poetic writings of the Jews and the words of the prophets, were written on the "stick of Judah."

---

[10] *BOM*, Mormon 9:33–4.
[11] *See* OT, Ezekiel 37:19.

Ezekiel's prophecy mentioned above tells that there was a "stick of Joseph" separate from the "stick of Judah" (separate from the Bible), and that the Lord God was going to "make them one stick, and they shall be one in mine hand." Biblical scholars of the past had no idea what the "stick of Joseph" was or where it was. These scholars only recognized, studied, and accepted the "stick of Judah," whose tribe had the right from birth to account for and record Jewish history.

The Jews never acknowledged anything written by anyone outside of the "tribe of Judah." Throughout Jewish history, various attempts were made by Jewish authorities to explain what the prophet Ezekiel meant. None of their explanations made any sense.

We made it make sense.

We invented our own "stick of Joseph, which is in the hand of Ephraim." In other words, Joseph's son, Ephraim, wrote the history of his own people (tribe/house) upon his own "stick." We justified and connected our new American scripture to the Bible's narrative by making our *Book of Mormon* story the "stick of Joseph, which is in the hand of Ephraim."

Simply put, our new American scripture was a history of the descendants of Joseph (one of the Twelve Tribes of Israel), through his two sons, Manasseh and Ephraim, who were also two of Jacob/"Israel's" grandsons. As we have already explained, these two grandsons could NOT become natural members of the "house of Israel" because of the dark ("cursed") skin that they received from their Egyptian mother. We explained how they were adopted into the house of Israel in the Introduction of this book.

Logically, as the story was portrayed, Ephraim and Manasseh's dark-skinned mother could have taught them the Egyptian language. They would have learned Hebrew from their father. As a result of this learning, Ephraim's and Manasseh's descendants could have developed a "reformed Egyptian" style of writing that was consistent with the Hebrew language.

Chapter 2: Author and Proprietor

According to our *original* story (the 116-page lost manuscript, the *Book of Lehi*), the native American people had the "curse" of the dark skin, not from what they did, but from their ancient grandmother's Egyptian heritage and DNA. Our first version (of the history of the native Americans) implied that the color of their skin was passed on to them through their lineage. Lehi's genealogy was presented to support the connection that our story made with the Bible, as the "stick of Joseph, which is in the hand of Ephraim."

According to our story, Lehi wrote on his own "stick," which we turned into "plates" to reflect how we *engraved* characters in "reformed Egyptian." Lehi then commanded his children and posterity to continue to write their history—as the Bible's prophesied "stick of Joseph, which is in the hand of Ephraim." Lehi's genealogy had to include a connection to Joseph (one of the twelve sons of Israel), through Ephraim. Lehi couldn't have been a descendent of Manasseh, because Manasseh was the ancient Joseph's other dark-skinned son and <u>wasn't the one mentioned in Ezekiel's prophecy</u>.

This is where an error was made in the publication of the "unsealed" part of our plates. Oliver Cowdery, Joseph Smith's scribe at the time, committed the error before he delivered the final draft to the printer. In the 1830 publication, one of the subplots presented Lehi as a descendant of Manasseh, NOT of Ephraim. This subplot also introduced another character named Aminadi. This subplot of our story was printed in the 1830 edition as follows:

> And Aminadi was a descendant of Nephi, who was the son of Lehi, who came out of the land of Jerusalem, who was a descendant of Manasseh, who was the son of Joseph who was sold into Egypt by the hands of his brethren.[12]

IF Lehi and his posterity were the ones responsible for writing the "stick of Joseph, which is in the hand of Ephraim," then this passage in the 1830 *Book of Mormon* contradicted our desired connection to the Bible's prophecy.

---

[12] *BOM*, Alma 10:3.

A New American Scripture

Martin Harris had been Joseph's original scribe. He had written for Joseph as Joseph read the words that he transcribed ("translated") from our plates through the *Urim and Thummim*. Harris wrote Lehi's original genealogy (in the *Book of Lehi*) this way:

And Saresh was the son of Judah, who was the son of Ephraim, who was the son of Joseph [who was sold into Egypt and was one the twelve sons of Jacob/"Israel"].[13]

This original genealogy in the *Book of Lehi* was correct. This connection with Ephraim completed the logic of our storyline with Ezekiel's prophecy about what God had said: "Behold I will take the stick of Joseph, which is in the hand of Ephraim ... even with the stick of Judah, and make them one stick, and they shall be one in mine hand."

The later mistake (of presenting Lehi as a descendant of *Manasseh* and NOT of Ephraim) was made by Oliver Cowdery, who took over for Harris when our original storyline was replaced with a different narrative. (In a following chapter, we will explain the replacement of our storyline in detail, and why it was necessary.) Joseph Smith did not catch Cowdery's mistake until it was pointed out to him by Harris AFTER the book had already been published and printed. Joseph brought the mistake to our attention. This was not the only mistake that had occurred in the transcription by Cowdery of Joseph's spoken words. There were other errors in how Cowdery wrote what he thought he heard from Joseph's mouth.

Critics of our *Book of Mormon* take issue with the 1830 publication and some changes that were eventually made to it, not by Joseph Smith, but by later dishonest Mormon leaders. The modern version of the accepted *Book of Mormon*, as published by the LDS Church, was made as

---

[13] *TSP*, Lehi 1:11.

Chapter 2: Author and Proprietor

an attempt to rectify these imperfections.[14] However, these ignorant leaders and scholars did *not* need to correct these imperfections. We had anticipated that there would be some "imperfections" in what Joseph actually said versus what his scribes thought they heard him say. We accounted for these "imperfections" in our storyline:

> And if our plates had been sufficiently large we should have written in Hebrew; but the Hebrew hath been altered by us also; and if we could have written in Hebrew, **behold, ye would have had no imperfection in our record**. But the Lord knoweth the things which we have written, and also that none other people knoweth our language; and because that none other people knoweth our language, therefore he hath prepared means for the interpretation thereof. ... And I said unto him: Lord, the Gentiles will mock at these things, because of our weakness in writing; ... And thou hast made us that we could write but little, because of the awkwardness of our hands.[15]

Joseph was unsettled and somewhat concerned that the mistake made by Cowdery and the printer (about Lehi's lineage being associated with Manasseh instead of Ephraim). Joseph was concerned that the discrepancy would somehow shed a negative light on our work. He asked our permission to have the printer change the errors that had been made. We explained that this was not necessary, and was actually beneficial to providing evidence of the truthfulness of our original storyline, if one day we again brought forth the "lost" 116-page manuscript.

In 2004, after we had published the "sealed" part of our story (*The Sealed Portion*), we also published the original *Book of Lehi* that properly

---

[14] To compare references between various English language editions of the *Book of Mormon*, see "Corresponding Chapters in Editions of the Book of Mormon," The Joseph Smith Papers – Church Historian's Press, josephsmithpapers.org/back/corresponding-chapters-in-editions-of-the-book-of-mormon.

[15] *BOM*, Mormon 9:33–4, emphasis added; Ether 12:23–4.

A New American Scripture

accounted for our story's connection to Ezekiel's prophecy. We had to make sure that every part of our story was logical and could be proven true through the accepted history and "truths" believed by most Christian scholars. The mistake that Cowdery made could have easily been made by Mormon in his original abridgment of the history of the native American peoples, as we presented them as belonging to the "tribe of Joseph."

In the presentation of our story, **Mormon** is our main character and author (the engraver of "reformed Egyptian" on metal plates). In the part where the mistake was made about Lehi's ancestry being *Manasseh* instead of *Ephraim*, it could be reasoned that Mormon engraved a summary of what he read from what Alma had engraved. Alma engraved what he heard his partner, Amulek, say about his (Amulek's) heritage. These are a lot of second- and third-hand accounts that would not be considered very reliable, allowing for mistakes. We created it this way, anticipating some "imperfections" in the "translation" as mentioned above.

Making the connection between the native American people and the "tribe of Joseph" wasn't the only or the most important link we made to the Bible's narrative. The strongest tie to the Bible that we intended for our new American scripture, was through the Old Testament book of Isaiah. In our story, we included ALL of the words from Isaiah, chapter 1 through chapter 14, verbatim (word for word). We incorporated a few more chapters of Isaiah when necessary.

Isaiah's words sarcastically, but prophetically, condemned two issues. First, they addressed the concern the early American Christians had about the mistake made in our book about Mormon's heritage (Mormon being the author according to our storyline). Second, Isaiah's words handled the problems the Jews had with dark-skinned people being adopted into their *precious* house. Of the problems that Jews have with the adoption of Joseph's dark-skinned sons into the "chosen house" of

Israel, Isaiah writes: "Manasseh, Ephraim; and Ephraim, Manasseh; and they together shall be against Judah."[16]

As in all of Isaiah's writings, he condemned the pride of the Jewish people regarding their ancestry and genealogy. Nothing creates more pride and is more responsible for the downfall of human society than a person's concentration and value on one's own family and genealogy. We made this perfectly clear in our new American scripture after our original storyline was rejected. The early Christians who were peer reviewing our book argued about genealogy and the "cursed" blood issue. Later, we will explain why we had to change our original storyline to make our book more palatable and acceptable to our intended Christian audience, all of whom were full of American Christian pride.

We clearly stated that arguments about someone being a descendant of Manasseh or Ephraim didn't matter in the slightest to the purpose of our writing the "stick of Joseph, in the hand of Ephraim." We wrote, referring to any and all genealogy:

> For it sufficeth me to say that we are descendants of Joseph. ... Wherefore, I shall give commandment unto my seed, that they shall not occupy these plates with things which are not of worth unto the children of men.[17]

Our story is about the fall and demise of societies because of the pride associated with family, community, and nations that put one people above another. They do this because of these societal divisions, which are usually caused by heritage, the color of one's skin, or economic classifications. Our storyline, along with every subplot, character, event, war, and situation that we invented for our narrative, was intended as a lesson. We hoped to teach people <u>what causes human misery and is responsible for the destruction of great societies</u>, as well as <u>what humanity can do to save itself.</u>

---

[16] OT, Isaiah 9:21; *see also BOM*, 2 Nephi 19:21.
[17] *BOM*, 1 Nephi 6:2, 6.

Each detail in our storyline coincides with historical events and traditions, especially as presented in the Bible.

The reader should pay close attention to the details that we explain throughout this book, *A New American Scripture*, about how we presented our stories in order to maintain a sure connection with what the world already accepted as truth at the time we wrote it.

One profound example of how we made our story consistent with what the world accepts as historical and secular *truth* is how we used two names in our narrative that are associated with a small, obscure group of islands off the southeast coast of Africa. These obscure islands were named long ago—long before we invented our storyline. This group of islands is called the *Comoros Islands (*also called the *Comoro Islands)*.[18] Their capital city is called *Moroni*.[19]

Compare the names of this group of islands and its capital city with our story's "Hill Cumorah," *where* the gold plates were allegedly hidden, and with our character "Moroni," *who* supposedly hid these plates. An honest study of how we purposefully used these names in our storyline will help the reader understand how and why we made these kinds of verifiable connections in order to protect the integrity of our book.

The Bible contains stories that are easily confronted and disproved with scientific analysis and accepted historical accounts. Unlike the Bible, we wanted our new American scripture's narrative to not only make sense, but to be able to be proven as *probable* and a likely outcome of recorded and accepted history.

We were careful to not introduce a part of our story that we could not explain as something that *could* have happened. For example, there is no way that any reasonable person would believe that ancient men, who lived

---

[18] *See* "Comoro Islands," *Wikipedia*, 21 Feb. 2021, en.wikipedia.org/wiki/Comoro_Islands.
[19] *See* "Moroni, Comoros," *Wikipedia*, 6 Apr. 2021, en.wikipedia.org/wiki/Moroni,_Comoros.

Chapter 2: Author and Proprietor

just a few thousand years ago, could have lived for hundreds of years (e.g., Adam living 930 years, and Methuselah living 969 years). No reasonable person would believe that Noah saved all species of animals, including insects and birds, among all others, on a big boat.

But more glaring of the Bible's deception is what it presents as actual history. There is no verifiable and scholarly accepted record that proves that Solomon was who and what Bible myth claims this important king to be. In fact, the very existence of Solomon is questioned because the only historical reference of him is in the Bible. Some Bible apologists quote the Hebrew/Roman historian, Josephus, as giving verifiable proof of Solomon's existence. These apologists quickly lose their argument upon conceding that Josephus was a Hebrew who believed in the Bible.

Honest scholars question the existence of Jesus with the same criteria they use to dismiss the existence of Solomon. Christian apologists also use a couple of spurious (questionable) and suspicious mentions of Jesus by Josephus as the basis of their proof.[20] More honest scholars simply refer to Josephus' original, handwritten manuscript to correctly prove that the few mentions of Jesus were added by unscrupulous (shifty) Christian authorities.[21]

One need only study original manuscripts to find out the Real Truth™. However, as we have explained, many original manuscripts were destroyed by those in power who derived their authority over the masses because the people were taught to believe in these records. These authorities and powers would have fallen had science been given the opportunity to study the original manuscripts. We did not want to make the same mistake as the Bible writers made. We wanted to present stories that not only were believable, but that we could argue as *probable*.

---

[20] *See* "Josephus on Jesus," *Wikipedia*, 11 May 2021, en.wikipedia.org/wiki/Josephus_on_Jesus.
[21] *See* "Arguments for presence of Christian interpolations," in "Josephus on Jesus," *Wikipedia*, 11 May 2021,
en.wikipedia.org/wiki/Josephus_on_Jesus#Arguments_for_presence_of_Christian_interpolations.

A New American Scripture

In the example we mentioned above, by including the names of the group of *Comoros Islands* and its capital city, *Moroni*, we knew we were establishing a *probability* in our story that we could prove. The following is how we could have proven the probability that the ancient people described in our *Book of Mormon*, who were living in the Western Hemisphere, were also responsible for naming the group of *Comoros Islands* and its capital city *Moroni*.

Our story ends with the character Moroni hiding the gold plates (upon which our story was presented as written) in the ground in upstate New York, U.S.A. Before he hid the plates, Moroni reported that most of the white-skinned people were hunted down and killed by the darker-skinned, ancient native Americans. After writing the *sealed parts of the plates* mentioned in our story, Moroni writes that

> after the great and tremendous battle at Cumorah *[compare: Comoros, Comoro]*, behold, the Nephites who had escaped into the country southward were hunted by the Lamanites, until they were all destroyed. … and I have not friends nor whither to go; and how long the Lord will suffer that I may live I know not.[22]

Had our new American scripture accomplished what we had intended, we would have had the *resurrected* "angel Moroni" explain what happened to him after he hid the gold plates in the ground in upstate New York. We would have had this "angel of God" appear to our chosen True Messenger and relate the rest of his story, somewhat as follows:

> And it came to pass that after I, Moroni, was commanded by the Lord to hide up the records in the earth, by the grace of God, I made mine escape from the Lamanites. And I did remember my friends and kinsfolk who did flee southward before the Lamanites, and did follow the selfsame course.

---

[22] *See BOM*, Mormon 8:2, 5.

And behold, to my astonishment and great joy, I encountered a group of my brethren who were still alive. And my brethren and their families were constructing a ship to flee the promised land, and the persecution and sure death at the hands of the Lamanites.

And I joined my brethren on their journey. And it came to pass that we set sail from the land southward, putting our lives and souls in the hands of the Lord, praying without ceasing that God would safely guide us and save us from destruction.

And for many days we were upon the great waters, not knowing where the winds of the Lord would carry our ship. And it came to pass that we arrived at a land that was unfamiliar to us. And this land was also inhabited by a dark people like unto those who had sought our destruction in the promised land. And it came to pass that the inhabitants of this land also sought our destruction; but we fled from them eastward on the land upon which the Lord had delivered us from the great waters.

And after many days of wandering in the wilderness, we arrived again at the great waters; and being pursued by the inhabitants of this land, we were again caused to construct another ship by which to flee for our safety.

And it came to pass that we sailed eastward on the great waters for a short time; and, by the hand of the Lord, we reached land again. And it came to pass that this land was also inhabited by a people who had the dark skin. But behold, now it came to pass that the people who we encountered on these islands of this sea were a peaceful people, who, many years before, had fled their motherland for safety from their own brothers who had sworn to take their lives.

And it came to pass that these peaceful people welcomed us with open arms. And to our astonishment, these people had kept a history of their ancestors; and this history included a visitation of Jesus Christ to their ancestors, fulfilling the word that our Savior spoke in the land of Bountiful: I have other sheep which are not of this land, neither of the land of Jerusalem, neither in any parts of that land round about whither I have been to minister. I have received a commandment of the Father that I shall go unto them, and that they shall hear my voice.

And it came to pass that I remembered that our fathers had written the words of Isaiah in their records concerning the people living upon the isles of the sea: Hearken unto me, my people; and give ear unto me, O my nation; for a law shall proceed from me, and I will make my judgment to rest for a light for the people. My righteousness is near; my salvation is gone forth, and mine arms shall judge the people. The isles shall wait upon me, and on mine arm shall they trust.

There is much more that we could have written to prove that the native Americans' ancestors had migrated from North America to the ancient *Comoros Islands*. Nevertheless, the above is just an example of an excerpt of how we *could* have continued the story of Moroni. Another verifiable probability is the inclusion of a city in our storyline named Angola.[23] If considered, it is easy to believe that when Moroni and his friends fled the Western Hemisphere and traveled to the African continent, at some point during their travels, the name "Angola" stuck with the African people.

If not for the way that our new American scripture was treated by those who received and accepted it as another "word of God" along with the Bible, we would have continued the story of how Moroni and his friends found the ancient people of the Comoros Islands. We would have made an account of how these people were also visited by Jesus Christ, and that Jesus taught the

---

[23] *See BOM*, Mormon 2:4.

people the same words that he taught the Jews, which were the same words that Jesus taught the ancient native American people.

The things that Jesus taught were intended to be the most important part of our book's lessons. If the Americans ("Gentiles") had not ignored this important part, if they had not set up a religion based on doctrines and tenets that have no part of the words spoken by Jesus—doctrines and tenets which are actually condemned in our book—we would have given the world many more of the things that "Jesus truly taught the people." In our 1830 *Book of Mormon*, we explained that not "even a hundredth part of the things which Jesus did truly teach unto the people"[24] was included in its narrative.

Our continuation of Moroni's history would have provided indisputable empirical evidence of why these islands were called "Comoros" [Cumorah], and further, why these ancient people named their most important city after one of our story's most notable and popular characters, *Moroni*. Because the "Gentiles" (Americans) who accepted our *Book of Mormon* transfigured, abused, and largely ignored it, we found it unnecessary, even futile, to further the storyline. If we had, these proud Christians would have ignored it anyway.

We can explain perfectly and logically how every story and subplot in our new American scripture was created, and what we intended to teach in the lessons presented in each subplot. We made sure that all of our stories connected emotionally with the Bible-believing readership. We knew that making this connection would cause a person who had been deceived by the Bible to FEEL the power of the "Spirit of God" witnessing to the reader. We promised the reader that after reading our book, "by the power of the Holy Ghost ye may know the truth of all things."[25]

---

[24] *BOM*, 3 Nephi 26:6.
[25] *BOM*, Moroni 10:5.

Unfortunately, the missionaries of the modern LDS Church use the power that the sincere investigator feels while reading our new American scripture to convince the reader that their church is the only true church on the earth. As we mentioned, this great deception motivated us to write this book and reveal the Real Truth™ about the *Book of Mormon*.

We were and are masters at using this same power to make a person *want* to read our new American scripture, believe it, and ignore whoever its *Author and Proprietor* was. More often than not, regardless of how powerful and wonderful a book's contents might be, if its author is not believed to be credible, the reader's mind becomes prematurely biased. However, when read with "a sincere heart, with real intent,"[26] the power of our writings gives ample proof of our book's integrity.

We wrote our new American scripture in any way necessary to add to our story's integrity, regardless of what the world feels about its *Author and Proprietor*.

---

[26] *BOM*, Moroni 10:4.

Chapter 3
The Greatest Human Deception

The Bible is one of the greatest human deceptions of all time. When we refer to the Bible, we mean the writings that are presented as its Old and New Testaments.

It is not necessary to the purpose of this book to provide strong evidence of the Bible's deceptions and falsehoods. If one is so disposed and willing, one can research what has been provided by the world's scholars on the subject of the Bible. Although if one is so disposed to pursue this course of study honestly and sincerely, one will soon learn that most scholars disagree on almost every "fact" that each uses to support his or her own opinion.

For the intention of this book, it is important for the reader to know which parts of the Bible we actually wrote, or over which we had a strong influence. By revealing which parts of the Bible we had direct association with, the reader will gain a greater appreciation and understanding of our ability to write scripture, especially in regards to our new American scripture: the *Book of Mormon* and *The Sealed Portion*. In our new American scripture, we mentioned most of the Bible books that we wrote or influenced: *Isaiah*, *Malachi*, and *Revelation*. We gave the most attention to the references of these books that we felt would have the greatest impact on the reader. And again, our targeted readership was the Christians of European ancestry who were establishing and developing the United States of America.

We were entirely responsible for writing the New Testament's *Apocalypse* (Disclosure), which is more commonly known as the book of Revelation. Originally written in Greek, the Greek word we used as its title was "*Apokálypsi.*" This word is generally understood as "an unveiling or unfolding of things not previously known and which could not be known apart from the unveiling." Our first mention in the *Book of Mormon* of the New

A New American Scripture

Testament's *Revelation* was in a futuristic vision that one of our storyline's main characters (Nephi, the son of Lehi) had. This vision was about the Western Hemisphere, and especially about the United States of America.

We wrote our new American scripture in the early nineteenth (19th) century. By this time, we already knew what had happened to form the United States—or rather, we knew what the world had been *told* about the establishment of the United States. We understood what people accepted as its true history in that day. Therefore, it was a simple feat to base our character's (Nephi's) vision of the future on the events that had *already occurred* before we wrote the narrative of our storyline.

We based the narrative of Nephi's vision on the form of Christianity that had developed in the Eastern Hemisphere and was practiced throughout Europe and the other countries of the Eastern Hemisphere influenced by European control. We then continued the narrative by introducing the importance of the Western Hemisphere as "*the land of promise.*"[1] At this point, we gave the following brief explanation about the native American peoples whom European explorers had discovered in the Western Hemisphere. (Keep in mind that this was written according to what the Christians could—and most importantly, *would*—accept about them.)

> I beheld, after they had dwindled in unbelief they became a dark, and loathsome, and a filthy people, full of idleness and all manner of abominations.[2]

The native Americans were far from a "loathsome, and a filthy people" when they were discovered. However, it was *necessary* to maintain this falsehood in order to draw in the Christian reader. We had to use a description of the native Americans that was a typical Christian's *perception* of these people during that time period.

---

[1] *See e.g.*, *BOM*, 1 Nephi 4:14.
[2] *BOM*, 1 Nephi 12:23.

Chapter 3: The Greatest Human Deception

Nephi's vision goes on to explain why the Europeans in the Eastern Hemisphere ("the nations and kingdoms of the Gentiles") wanted out of Europe. Poverty and inequality became an extensive social problem in Europe, especially after the foundation of European Capitalism. We described this particular *economic foundation* in Nephi's vision, as:

> the formation of a church which is most abominable above all other churches, which slayeth the saints of God, yea, and tortureth them and bindeth them down, and yoketh them with a yoke of iron, and bringeth them down in captivity. ... And I also saw gold, and silver, and silks, and scarlets, and fine-twined linen, and all manner of precious clothing; and I saw many harlots. And the angel spake unto me, saying: Behold the gold, and the silver, and the silks, and the scarlets, and the fine-twined linen, and the precious clothing, and the harlots, are the desires of this great and abominable church.[3]

In the Bible's book of *Revelation*, we referred to the same type of capitalistic economy that had formed during the Great Roman Empire as a

> beast; saying to them that dwell on earth, that they should make an image to the beast ... and cause that as many as would not worship the image of the beast should be killed. And [the beast] causeth all, both small and great, rich and poor, free and bond, to receive a mark ... or the name of the beast, or the number of his name [i.e., money].[4]

Nephi's vision introduced how European Christians used their Bible to justify and support a capitalistic ideology (a political set of ideas that controls the economy). The great European religions were secretly combined with

---
[3] *See BOM*, 1 Nephi 13:5–8.
[4] NT, Revelation 13:14–17.

their political authorities. We presented this *combination* of power later in our story as a "secret combination … which combination is most abominable and wicked above all, in the sight of God."[5] Nephi's vision warned the developing United States (the "Gentiles") of these secret combinations.

Before we wrote our new American scripture, we were doing everything in our power (behind the scenes) to influence the minds and hearts of the American Founding Fathers to keep a strict separation (no *combination*) of church and state in governing the people. Our desire in confronting this important separation motivated us to include a warning about it in our new American scripture.

The economic policies of the European nations controlled the masses and created great wealth for the minority ("the few") by using the power of religious belief. In this way, the poor were "yoked" to the control of wealthy government officials and business leaders in the form of taxes and obligations of employment (i.e., you either work for a paycheck and pay your taxes, or you die or become incarcerated). This created the backbone of Capitalism ("the formation of a great and abominable church"[6]). The people were *captivated* by the promises of wealth that a capitalistic society offers, ostensibly to everyone equally. With the promise of establishing a private company and becoming wealthy, the people were drawn in and held captive by the *image* (what people imagine) that economic success would bring.

We had our character Nephi see the future and report how religious leaders—who were among the wealthiest citizens—used the Bible to maintain and support the image, mark, and desires of a capitalist society. The "plain and precious" message that Christianity's Jesus taught (the *Sermon on the Mount* found in Matthew 5, 6, and 7) was transfigured and misinterpreted by this "great and abominable church of the devil"—as we portrayed Capitalism in Nephi's vision. We wrote,

---

[5] *BOM*, Ether 8:18.
[6] See *BOM*, 1 Nephi 13:4–6.

> because of these things which are taken away out of the gospel of the Lamb, an exceedingly great many do stumble, yea, insomuch that Satan hath great power over them.[7]

In this way, we explained how the most popular European version of the Bible—the King James Bible—became corrupted.

We subtly introduced the Bible's susceptibility to corruption by the *secret combinations* of religious, political, and business powers (i.e., we showed how easily the Bible could be influenced by them). By doing this, we were able to introduce our book as another "word of God" that would *help* the "Gentiles." This became important so they would not "forever remain in that awful state of blindness."[8]

In our Nephi's vision, we explained how the people of the United States of America (the "Gentiles") became the greatest nation on Earth, and how they could continue to be the greatest—but only

> **if** the Gentiles shall hearken unto the Lamb of God in that day that he shall manifest himself unto them in word [referring to the gospel that Jesus taught the people].[9]

In our book of *Revelation*, we explained what happened to the Great Roman Empire's "great and abominable" capitalistic society. We wrote that one of the "beast's heads" (heads: the Western and Eastern parts) was "as it were wounded to death; and his deadly wound was healed: and all the world wondered after the beast."[10]

---

[7] *BOM*, 1 Nephi 13:29.
[8] *BOM*, 1 Nephi 13:32.
[9] *BOM*, 1 Nephi 14:1, emphasis added.
[10] NT, Revelation 13:3.

The Western part of the Great Roman Empire was one of the "heads" that was completely destroyed and *not* healed. The Eastern Roman Empire, although *wounded* by the fall of the Great Roman Empire, healed and became the great and powerful Byzantine Empire, where Capitalism continued to flourish and grow. This expansion and growth was something that made "all the rest of the world wonder after the beast."[11] The Byzantine Empire was largely Christian and centered its government institutions primarily on the Bible.

When we wrote Revelation, we knew the course that Capitalism had taken in every society in which this great beast had carried humanity upon its back. When Capitalism flourishes uncontrolled, it becomes like unto a

> great and abominable church ... which slayeth the saints of God, yea, and tortureth them and bindeth them down, and yoketh them with a yoke of iron, and bringeth them down into captivity.[12]

We referred to this economic system as a "church" because of its power over humans in the way they congregate around it, submit to it, and *worship* it, allowing Capitalism to dominate and completely control their lives. We have seen the demise of any civilization that joins this great church that "causeth the earth and them which dwell therein to worship [this] beast."[13]

In Revelation, we prophesied that eventually the Great Roman Empire would fail. We also knew that other nations would "*come up out of the earth*" and bridle and ride the beast, or rather, join this "*great and abominable church.*" From the fall of the Western Roman part of this great empire and the rise of the Eastern part, Capitalism helped the Byzantine Empire flourish. This economic system was eventually also responsible for the establishment of the United States of America. Truly

---

[11] *Compare* NT, Revelation 13:3.
[12] *BOM*, 1 Nephi 13:6, 5.
[13] NT, Revelation 13:12.

one of his heads was as it were wounded to death; and his deadly wound was healed: and all the world wondered after the beast. Truly all the world wonders after the [United States of America]. Who is like unto [the United States of America]? Who is able to make war with it? [14]

It was our intent to warn humanity of the consequences of Capitalism's unbridled power. We used our new American "word of God" to establish a permanent and important segue (link) to the Bible's book of Revelation, which we had also written to warn humanity.

As we explained above, our character Nephi had a vision about the future of the United States of America. He saw its establishment and rise to power and greatness. The angel who guided him through this vision ended it by introducing Jesus' most beloved apostle, John. It was this character from the Jesus stories whom we represented as the author of our book of *Revelation*. Our new American scripture's angel would say to Nephi:

Behold one of the twelve apostles of the Lamb. Behold, he shall see and write the remainder of these things; yea, and also many things which have been. And he shall also write concerning the end of the world.[15]

In our Nephi's vision, we tied the introduction of the Bible's book of Revelation and its importance to the introduction and importance of the "sealed portion" of our book. In other words, both the "unfolding" of the meaning of Revelation and *The Sealed Portion* would be presented to the world at around the same time. We also stated the importance of these two significant scriptures in helping to explain the Real Truth™ about what *really* happened in the past, and what would *really* happen in the future *if* humanity didn't repent and change the way that it allowed Capitalism to exist unbridled and out of control.

---

[14] *Compare* NT, Revelation 13:3–4.
[15] *BOM*, 1 Nephi 14:20–2.

A New American Scripture

Our Nephi's vision was the *first* time that we made this connection between the "sealed portion" of our new American scripture and our book of *Revelation*. Later in the *Book of Mormon*, we introduced a fictitious nation of the earliest white-skinned settlers of the Western Hemisphere: the Great Jaredite Nation. This nation was meant to represent the American people and the Great United States of America. The narrative of the Jaredite subplot presented the Jaredite people becoming vast, populous, and extremely powerful. This nation met its end because of the secret combinations of religious, political, and business powers—the very same combinations that threaten the demise (destruction) of the United States of America today—that use Capitalism to control human life and free will.

Our new American scripture is called the *Book of Mormon* because our character **Mormon** was the author of the "unsealed portion" of our gold plates. As the story goes, his son **Moroni** would go on to author the "sealed portion" of our story. Moroni explains the importance of his *sealed portion*, as

> the very things which the brother of Jared [after whom the Jaredite Nation was named] saw; and there never were greater things made manifest than those which were made manifest unto the brother of Jared.[16]

In the beginning of the Jaredite subplot, we made a connection for a *second* time (Nephi having made it first) between our *The Sealed Portion* and our book of *Revelation*:

> then shall my **revelations** which I have caused to be **written by my servant John** be unfolded in the eyes of all the people.[17]

The character in the Jaredite subplot, ***the brother of Jared***, had the same vision that Nephi had. The brother of Jared is one of the "others" to whom we referred in what we presented in Nephi's vision as

---

[16] *BOM*, Ether 4:4.
[17] *BOM*, Ether 4:16, emphasis added.

others who have been, to them hath he shown all things, and they have written them; and they are **sealed up** to come forth in their purity.[18]

In order for us to be convincing, we knew that when we brought forth the *sealed portion* of our story, we would also "unfold in the eyes of all the people" the *purity*, or pure meaning, of our book of Revelation. To accomplish our goal of persuasion, we published *The Sealed Portion—The Final Testament of Jesus Christ* in 2004. Shortly thereafter, we published a complete and detailed *apocalypse* (i.e., unfolding) of our book of Revelation.[19]

In our previous book (*Pentateuch Illuminated*), meant as an introduction to this one, we explained in some detail how we introduced one of the books of the Christian Bible that we had actually written—the book of Isaiah.[20] As one reads the rest of the chapters of this book (*A New American Scripture*), one will become familiar with

> other books, which came forth by the power of the Lamb [which we wrote], from the Gentiles unto them, unto the convincing of the Gentiles … that the records of the prophets and the twelve apostles of the Lamb are true.[21]

In our new American scripture, we included as many books as we felt necessary to convince Christians of the error of their misguided ways. We mentioned Isaiah many times throughout our new American scripture. To accentuate its importance, we had our story's resurrected Jesus say of Isaiah:

> And now, behold, I say unto you, that ye ought to search these things. Yea, a commandment I give unto you that ye search these things diligently; for great are the words of Isaiah.[22]

---

[18] *BOM*, 1 Nephi 14:26, emphasis added.
[19] See *666 America*. Read for free at realilluminati.org/666-mark-of-america.
[20] *Pentateuch Illuminated*, 199–204.
[21] *BOM*, 1 Nephi 13:39.
[22] *BOM*, 3 Nephi 23:1.

A New American Scripture

We wrote both Isaiah and Revelation with symbolism and allegory (a story of imagery) that *only* we could properly explain in their *purity*. We knew that our ability to provide a proper explanation of each would provide concrete evidence that, not only had we written both, but that the religious scholars and leaders who could *not* explain their meanings were false teachers. We also wrote the book attributed to the prophet Malachi, and used our subtle influence to have it included as the final book of the Old Testament.

Although we also influenced the writing of the Gospel of John and a few epistles (letters) attributed to him, we felt there was no need to include these New Testament additions in our new American scripture. We felt it was sufficient to leave the New Testament reader wondering about John's immortality, according to Jesus' words:

> If I will that he tarry till I come, what is that to thee? ... Then went this saying abroad among the brethren, that that disciple should not die.[23]

When the first gospels were given to the ancient Christian world, there was no mention of a person being immortal and living until the Christian Christ returned. We chose to present this idea ourselves. We knew that it would eventually assist us in introducing whatever new scripture needed to be created in order to penetrate the hard hearts and closed minds of the deceived believers in scripture.

If history were honest, it would be known that the book of Revelation was not written until many years after the original New Testament was first published. And, if *John the Beloved* was believed to be immortal, there would be no problem with us assigning him as the author of some of our writings.

---

[23] NT, John 21:22–3.

People believe in the Bible, and millions believe in our new American scripture, because of the *spiritual energy* (feelings) that they receive upon reading the words. One would be very hard-pressed to convince a believer that these books, as well as every other religious book on Earth, are deceptions. People's personal testimonies of these books are solidified by the actual physical feelings that they experience upon reading these books, or when they listen to religious leaders pretending to be oracles chosen by God. People believe these feelings are given to them through the Holy Spirit of God. **It is this *spiritual energy* that is the greatest of all human deceptions.**

It is this *spiritual energy* that we understand. With this understanding, we were able to write our new American scripture to replicate and cause this spiritual energy as one reads our story. This spiritual energy is the single human-based ideology (idea) that is responsible for the majority of humanity's problems. It is a power that holds the most influence over human action.

It is a mental process, uniquely human, that stimulates a person to do or feel something. It endows absolute power on a single person. It has crowned kings and queens and exalted and deified popes, priests, and saints (i.e., raised ordinary people to the status of a god). This spiritual energy causes a belief that the greatest power in the universe (God) gives authority to mere mortals to use God's power on Earth. This belief is able to stimulate a simple man's mind (the mind of one who would otherwise just be viewed as common and ordinary) to believe that he has been given this power—i.e., priesthood authority.

Again, and this Real Truth™ is worthy of repeating, this spiritual energy causes a mental process that is the greatest deception of humankind. It causes personal revelation (*inspiration*), where a person's brain is stimulated to feel or think things that the person is convinced did *not* originate in his or her own brain. The idea that thoughts or feelings come from a source of good (God, Allah, etc.) or a source of evil (the devil) outside of one's own brain, is *the greatest human deception* of any and all.

However, this spiritual energy has also provided hope to the masses in their impoverished and inequitable (unfair) life experiences. On the other hand, it has also provided justification for the few to accept their standing apart from the majority and view themselves as successful, special, or blessed above others.

The human perception caused by this spiritual energy is a problem that none of the world's greatest thinkers has been able to mitigate (lessen) or moderate (manage). How do you convince a person that there is no source of inspiration, feeling, or energy outside of that which originates in one's own brain? How do you convince the masses that their emotional feelings and ideas come from the mental conditioning that each of them has experienced since being born as a new member of Earth's population?

You don't. You can't.

It's very difficult to convince people that their own brain—and only their own brain—is the source of everything that they experience. Human pride and stubbornness make it impossible to convince the masses of this important Real Truth™.

<u>*Personal mental processes* create the feelings and thoughts that people have been convinced come from a higher source or power.</u>

Although we (the Real Illuminati®) know some information that *can* convince a person of this *Real* Truth™ (versus the *truth* that humans accept concerning "personal revelation"), we have only been able to convince a few. Therefore, in this book (*A New American Scripture*), we will refrain from providing the information that can convince you that there is no such power or influence outside of that generated by your own brain.

This book is not about convincing the reader that they are being deceived by the ideology (belief) of personal revelation. This book is about what we felt was necessary to do in order to control and inspire the deceived

Chapter 3: The Greatest Human Deception

to use their feelings and thoughts for the good of humanity. In writing our new American scripture, we hoped to provide another source ... and unfortunately, another deception ... that supported the unwavering belief in an outside higher power that could stop the inevitable destruction of the human race. This deception has been going on as long as humans have been conscious upon Earth and looking for the answers and reasons for their existence.

A little child is not born with the answers. It is not natural for a little child to believe that there exists an outside source of thought and feeling, except for what is cognitively experienced in the child's own brain. No little child is born with a belief in a higher power. The greatest power that influences a little child's thoughts and feelings is the little child's *own* thoughts and feelings. There is no other power known or experienced by a little child, except that with which ALL little children have been mutually, equally, and naturally endowed.

This is why we reiterated throughout our new American scripture that "becoming like a little child" is the most important aspect of learning Real Truth™.[24] We included "becoming like a little child" in our new American scripture because of its importance in helping people be able to uncover deceptions that they have previously been convinced of throughout their life. We used "become like a little child" as a foundation. In other words, ignore what you have been taught since you were a little child. We hoped by introducing the concept of "becoming like a little child" that it would set the correct course for the establishment and growth of the greatest nation the modern human race had yet to know: the United States of America.

Before the United States was discovered and formed in the Western Hemisphere, the most significant power and control among humans was European Christianity in the Eastern Hemisphere. This Christianity was based on "personal revelation." The story of Jesus Christ came from the New Testament of the Bible. The Bible is accepted by billions of people as

---

[24] *See BOM*, Mosiah 15:25; and *BOM*, 3 Nephi 9:22; 11:37–8.

"God's word." "God's word" implies that there is a higher power that speaks (the "word") to mere mortal people. And when a little child asks who wrote the Bible, or who speaks for God, there is only one answer that can be given—God chooses some *people* to whom God speaks so that they can tell the rest of us what God wants us to hear.

To a little child, that answer seems reasonable. This is because the innocent and honest child knows through their own life experience that God isn't speaking to them. They do not see God. They do not hear God. Trusting those upon whom they depend to teach them about life on Earth, little children are easily deceived. Yet, in their innocent state, little children are smart, perceptive, assertive, and resourceful.

However, little children eventually become *aged children* and are eventually accepted by society as "adults." As people gain life experiences, they learn what they need to know in order to survive and be valued by society. They soon start to reason and ask themselves, "If God speaks to another human, who is just like me, then why wouldn't, why couldn't, God speak directly to me?" They wonder, "Why does that person get to tell me what to do and how to live *my* life? Why does God tell him what *I* need to do? How do I know that God is actually speaking through him? If I ask God, why wouldn't God tell me, personally, what God wants me to do?"

The idea that there is a god that will answer a person's questions is the substance, reasoning, and imagined validation of *personal revelation*. Personal revelation wouldn't be such a bad thing, if a person kept it *personal*. But in order to gain value and acceptance from others, *personal* revelation—the thoughts and feelings of the mind that belong to one particular person rather than to anyone else—can start a new religious movement.

The person who does not feel important and valuable to society finds no purpose or worth in existing as a self-aware entity. Instead, an impersonal force that others already accept as valuable ("God") can provide a person with that which is emotionally needed in order to be valued by others: a divine calling to speak for God.

No other group of people on Earth invokes the name of God (Heavenly Father) as much as members of the LDS Church. Unfortunately, and to our chagrin, this religion was deceptively spawned from our attempts to inspire early Americans to do the right thing in developing a new nation. The members of this church are also widely known as the Mormons—a title inspired by their ostensible (supposed) acceptance of part of our new American scripture, the *Book of Mormon*.

The Mormons claim to accept our *new American scripture* as another "word of God," and even call it "Another Testament of Jesus Christ." But, instead of heeding the simple lessons and counsel written in our book, this church completely ignores them. Our book was created in an effort to influence those who read it to help make the United States of America the greatest, most righteous nation on Earth. This was intended so that the United States could help those who were undervalued and marginalized. Instead, the LDS Church became part of the "great and abominable church"—as we described it above—and has used our work to become one of the wealthiest institutions in the world.

Members of the LDS Church speak of their "Heavenly Father," of the "Holy Ghost (Spirit)," and of "Christ," with a frequency and dependency that creates the implication that each member must be personally guided, observed, valued, and known by any one member of their accepted Christian Godhead.

No other religion on Earth teaches *personal revelation* like the LDS Church does. Mormons believe that whatever action they take is "inspired"—either by God or by the devil. Whatever feeling comes into their head, they do not recognize that it is actually coming from their own head, *personally*. The LDS religion has been very successful because of the control that this church has over its members' hearts and minds, especially in regards to its teachings that people can have an actual *personal* relationship with Christ, in which relationship Christ is continually with them, leading, guiding, and walking beside them, helping them find the way back to their Heavenly Father.

LDS belief in *personal revelation* can inspire a Mormon in their daily activities—however mundane and ordinary, major or significant. However, this church teaches that *personal revelation* must be in line with revelation given by its leaders. Any *personal revelation* received that is *not* compatible with the teachings of this church is considered to be evil inspiration. In our *Prologue*, we explained how these members are taught that the words of their *living* prophets take precedence over the words of *dead* prophets who wrote their scriptures. This deceptive doctrine completely obliterates the meaning, purpose, and lessons of our new American scripture.

The forces of good and evil inspire every Mormon thought and action. Unlike any other religion, Mormons believe that God has given His power to ordinary men. They call this power the Holy Priesthood. (Melchizedek Priesthood is the higher, and Aaronic Priesthood is the lower). A Latter-day Saint male child is given this priesthood when the child is the most capable of being shaped or influenced mentally and emotionally: at the age of about twelve (12).[25] This is the time when the child is very open to things that create self-worth and value. A male child is taught that he possesses the "actual power of God to act for God upon Earth."[26]

From that time forward, these very young boys "holding" this Priesthood feel a sense of worth and power that benefits their pride and ego in a world that might not recognize their individual worth. Most disturbing,

---

[25] *See* "Age Changes for Youth Progression and Ordination Announced," Contributed by Camille West, 14 Dec. 2018, *Church News*, Intellectual Reserve, Inc., https://www.churchofjesuschrist.org/church/news/age-changes-for-youth-progression-and-ordination-announced?lang=eng.

[26] *See* "Priesthood," *True to the Faith: A Gospel Reference* (Salt Lake City: The Church of Jesus Christ of Latter-day Saints, 2004), found online at abn.churchofjesuschrist.org/study/manual/true-to-the-faith/priesthood?lang=eng.

believing one has priesthood power and authority increases both the power and instances of one's own *personal revelation*. If a man or boy believes that he has been given the power of God through the priesthood, then when that man/boy has a thought form in his head, the possibility exists (and is very real to the man/boy) that it could be God inspiring the priesthood holder to think or to act.

Both past and modern LDS/Mormon history accounts for many *evil* things that were and are done by LDS/Mormon males believing they were and are receiving inspiration from God to act in God's name.[27] Even modern Mormon women are susceptible of justifying evil works when they believe inspiration is felt.[28]

In this book, we will explain every important detail of how we used the greatest deception of humankind (belief in personal revelation/inspiration coming from an outside source) in writing our *new American scripture*—yet only to *inspire* good. Every story, every event, every character, and every plot in our book was meant to inspire good. Each was meant for the "intent to do good."[29]

Our story uses Christianity (the belief in Jesus Christ) as its base. Jesus is its center. The overpowering culmination of our invented narrative centers around the *Second Coming of Jesus Christ*, which we had occur among the ancient inhabitants of the Western Hemisphere in our narrative. Our *Book of Mormon* Jesus comes in his glory as a resurrected being. When we presented Jesus appearing, we dovetailed the New Testament story and had our American Jesus deliver "the fulness of [his] everlasting Gospel"[30] to the people, just like he did to the Jews in the Bible stories.

---

[27] For one of many examples, *see* "Utah v. Lafferty," *Wikipedia*, Wikimedia Foundation, 3 Apr. 2021, en.wikipedia.org/wiki/Utah_v._Lafferty.

[28] For one example, *see* "Deaths of Tylee Ryan and J. J. Vallow." *Wikipedia*, Wikimedia Foundation, 23 May 2021, en.wikipedia.org/wiki/Deaths_of_Tylee_Ryan_and_J._J._Vallow.

[29] *BOM*, Jacob 2:19.

[30] JSH 1:34

We tried to present our story as profoundly, clearly, and simply as we could. Unfortunately, the LDS Church used humanity's greatest deception (spiritual feelings of personal and priesthood/leader revelation) to transfigure our words. This has caused those who believe in our book to do things that are not good for society, when they think they are doing something good because they have the Holy Priesthood or receive direct revelation.

As we have explained, and will reiterate throughout this book, the LDS Church teaches a Gospel that is completely different from what Jesus taught in our *Book of Mormon* storyline. LDS/Mormon "gospel and teachings" couldn't be **more** different from the simple teachings of Jesus. Modern-day and personal revelation have deceived those who have read our book. They ignore it and have replaced its teachings with whatever comes into their heads, or especially, into their leaders' heads.

Before our Jesus delivered the "fulness of [his] everlasting Gospel" to the ancient American people, we had him say:

> ye must repent, and become as a little child, and be baptized in my name, or ye can in nowise receive these things [i.e., the things he was about to teach them].[31]

As explained above, little children are not born into this world deceived by the power and influence of any revelation (personal or otherwise) from any outside source. They only listen to their own mind and thoughts. Except YOU become *as* a little child, you will not understand what this book presents, and you might believe that it came from the devil, or that it simply is not true.

As you read this book, *A New American Scripture—How and Why [We] Created the Book of Mormon*, we are confident that you will begin to understand how and why we (the Real Illuminati®) created a new scripture the way that we did and for the purpose for which we did. As you read this

---

[31] *BOM*, 3 Nephi 11:37.

book, use your own mind. Use the power of your naturally endowed *logic* and *reason*. Think on your own, apart from any other inspiration that your mind has been conditioned through deception to believe.

If you open your mind and use the power with which you were endowed as a little child, you will begin to see why we were forced to use *the greatest human deception* (personal inspiration) in order to counter *the greatest human deception*: personal inspiration that can be turned into "God's word" and authority to do bad things for the rest of humanity.

Chapter 4
Exposing Secret Combinations

There were all kinds of Christian sects in early America claiming to be God's ONLY true religion. When people believe that their church is God's "only true religion," then there is only one way that they can view other churches—from the devil. If there is only "one true religion" on Earth, then whatever the god of that religion mandates and expects of the people is the right way, the only way. Everyone who doesn't belong to this religion is wrong. And if you are wrong and not following God, then whatever happens to you, is God's punishment for not doing what is right.

This attitude is the reason why poverty and inequality are justified and rampant throughout the world. It is this uniquely human attitude and prejudice, not found in any other lifeform, that proves that humans, not the devil, are completely responsible for most things that cause human misery. Much human misery is directly caused by the actions, or inactions, of those who are trying to punish the *sinners*.

Religious belief can cause a government to turn a blind eye to human misery. This is because the religious powers that control *church* and *state* believe in a god who gives commandments about how humans *should* live and what humans *should* do. These leaders teach that those who suffer in this world are *sinners* who are being punished by the leaders' god for disrespecting Him.[1] Wars are waged in defense of "this *only true* god." Economies are devastated in support of the "just punishments" of this god. Poverty is usually the result of a religious majority punishing a minority of supposed *sinners*.

A good contemporary example of this is the Israeli-Palestinian conflict currently occurring in the Middle East (circa 2020). Jews believe that their

---

[1] For one of many examples, *see* "Hurricane Katrina: Wrath of God?" 5 Oct. 2005, *NBC News*, NBC Universal, nbcnews.com/id/wbna9600878.

god gave their ancestors the disputed land. The Bible justifies any action that the Jews need to take in order to ensure that non-believers do not inhabit their "promised land." The Israeli state has no problem allowing the Palestinian people to suffer for trying to usurp their god's commandments and promises. If a Palestinian lives in the State of Israel, it is the Israeli government that enforces the laws by which a Palestinian must live.

On the other hand, the Palestinian god appears to hate the Jews and gives mandates and decrees that the Jews should be hated and destroyed by any means. Unfortunately for the Palestinian people, the powerful western Christian nations do not believe in the Holy Quran. Christians believe in the Bible and in the god that chose the Jewish people as the Christian god's "chosen people." The Israeli people live in economic security. The Palestinian people live in abject poverty. The actions of the people, regardless of their faith, are directly responsible for this great inequality and misery.

However, when it comes to the Real Truth™ about why Palestinians are evicted from their homes, it has nothing to do with Israeli evils. It is not any different than if an American citizen is removed from their home for not obeying the laws of the State in which the American citizen lives. If a Palestinian family is living within the State of Israel and this family refuses to abide by and obey Israeli law, the family will be removed. Palestinian pride is responsible for the eviction. If the Palestinian family would simply abide by Israeli law and order, the family would be left alone to live in peace.

It is the pride instilled in the Palestinian and Israeli people that keeps them in constant conflict with each other. It is this pride that is causing most of humanity's problems. (We will cover "pride" extensively in upcoming chapters.)

Unfortunately for the human race, without religion, the greatest nations and empires that have existed throughout history would not have become so great and vast, so quickly. The masses needed to be controlled in order to help build these great nations and empires. Kings needed to be seen as divine, chosen by the gods in whom the people believed, so that the people viewed the breaking of the king's law as being sacrilegious against God. The people needed to believe that breaking these laws would be punishable both temporally and spiritually for eternity. Furthermore, convinced that their leaders were also chosen by their gods, the people did whatever they were commanded to do. This always included making sure their leaders lived comfortably and with great riches as a reward for being God's chosen leaders.

Historically, in order for any group of free-willed humans to survive and thrive, especially to become one of the greatest and strongest nations on Earth, the individual free will of each citizen had to be controlled. Regardless of what an individual thought and wanted for himself or herself, if the thought or action did not benefit the governing powers that existed (most of which were established according to religious belief), there was a law against the free-willed act.

Most great societies became powerful, populous, and successful because of the laws that governed the people. The societies that lasted the longest were established by similar laws, codes, and ordinances. When one of these societies failed, a later one would study what caused the failure and attempt to learn from the mistakes. It would seem beneficial to humanity for the more modern societies to learn these important lessons and change the laws that led to the downfall of past societies. But if humanity is not told the Real Truth™ about what happened in the past, modern people will continue to make the same mistakes over and over again.

In most ancient communities, religious leaders were able to convince people that an omnipotent (all-powerful) god existed and that they (the leaders) were that god's representatives. This made it easy for the leaders to give laws, mandates, codes, and edicts (statements enforced by law) that *they* wanted for the group. Before the group was served and supported, the leaders were always supported first. The paying of religious offerings to the leaders spared the people from hell, fire, and damnation (a punishment for not paying their tithing to God).

Chapter 4: Exposing Secret Combinations

These spiritual mandates and punishments were the first form of taxation. This taxation (as religiously mandated donations) placed great wealth in the hands of the rulers. The people believed that paying tithes and making their rulers great were also pleasing and honoring God. However, the people being controlled would not have known the god and that god's mandates and punishments without first receiving this knowledge from the preaching of their religious leaders.

It was a much easier life for one of the leaders who controlled the group than it was for the people *being* controlled. Without law and order, there would have been anarchy. As for the laws that were written out, that constituted "God's will" for the people, they were "set in stone" and guaranteed the success of the group. This was true as long as the people followed these constituted laws, which the people were convinced were given by the god who "set them in stone" (but which laws were actually created by unscrupulous [deceitful] leaders bent on controlling the people).

One of the first known state constitutions was the *Code of Hammurabi*[2] (Hammurabi was an ancient Babylonian king[3]). The laws of Moses were very similar to the *Code of Hammurabi*. The Jewish scholars may or may not like this, but they cannot present any solid evidence that Moses, Abraham, or Israel actually existed. This is because there is no known ancient record of their existence outside of Hebrew history.

One need only to study both the *Code of Hammurabi* and the *Law of Moses* to recognize the similarities.[4] In fact, an honest review of King Hammurabi's code would present some evidence of the foundation of the

---

[2] *See* "Code of Hammurabi." *Wikipedia*, Wikimedia Foundation, 19 May 2021, en.wikipedia.org/wiki/Code_of_Hammurabi.
[3] *See* "Hammurabi." *Wikipedia*, Wikimedia Foundation, 15 May 2021, en.wikipedia.org/wiki/Hammurabi.
[4] *See* John R. Sampey, "The Code of Hammurabi and the Laws of Moses," *Baptist Review and Expositor* (1904) vol. 1 issue 2, 233–43; also found online at *SAGE Journals*, journals.sagepub.com/doi/abs/10.1177/003463730400100207?journalCode=raea.

Christian *Royal Law:* Do unto others as you would have them do unto you (love thy neighbor as thyself).

All of the world's greatest societies had powerful religions that controlled the people's hearts and minds. These religions were vital to the success of the government because there were a lot more people that needed to be governed and controlled than there were the VERY FEW controllers. In fact, because of the emotional hold and control (the captivity over the mind) that religion held, a small boy could be presented to the people as "God's divine ruler" in order to keep the people under control.[5] It wasn't the boy who actually ruled the people. It was those who ruled the boy who ruled the people.

In modern times, a short, physically weak, mildly unattractive man named Adolf Hitler was able to control millions of people. Hitler got his people to do anything that he wanted. The religion that gave him this ability was the very same religion that gave the few American Founding Fathers the ability to control the people of their new nation. This religion was European Christianity. It was easy for Hitler (an Austrian who gained German citizenship) to condone the destruction and displacement of the Jews. This was because the German people (mainly Christian) believed that the Jews had killed their Savior and had corrupted and rejected Jesus' law.

Most of the American Founding Fathers were wealthy Christian businessmen. They met in *secret* and discussed how they could create a new government that would be successful and, of course, benefit themselves as well as control the people.

The American founders relied on their employees, which included a majority of unpaid slaves and indentured servants, to make them wealthy. They realized that they could *combine* the economic power they acquired (because of their wealth) with the religious power that controlled the hearts and minds of the people. This would ensure a government that would benefit

---

[5] *See* "Kings & Queens - by Age of Accession to the Throne," *Britroyals*, britroyals.com/ascend.asp.

them and their families to a much greater degree than it would benefit their employees and slaves. These corrupt and selfish leaders formed a government around a capitalistic economy that forced the masses to work for the few in order for the employed to acquire the basic necessities of life. There is nothing more corrupt, and nothing that has caused the downfall of humanity more than an individual being forced to do something in order to survive that the individual would not otherwise choose to do.

The United States Founding Fathers are the perfect example of those who were part of the *secret combinations* about which we warned the "Gentiles" in our *Book of Mormon*. We warned the early American Christians, who were the targeted audience of our new American scripture, about the "secret plans … oaths and their covenants"[6] of these secret combinations of political, economic, and religious powers.

We presented a subplot of our story in which some government leaders were considering overthrowing the current political structure that controlled them. This is because these leaders had set their "heart[s] upon the kingdom and upon the glory of the world." We related the story of a king who lost a battle to his brothers. We presented the idea that this king who lost the battle searched the "account concerning them of old [i.e., recorded history], that they by their secret plans did obtain kingdoms and great glory."[7]

The American Founding Fathers likewise searched through the recorded histories of the world that were available for their review and study. They looked for the "account concerning" the Great Roman Empire and its successor, the Great Byzantine Empire. They learned the "secret plans" by which these great governments obtained their kingdoms and great glory.

---

[6] *BOM*, Alma 37:29.
[7] *BOM*, Ether 8:7–9.

The subplot that we used to introduce these secret *combinations* of government, religious, and economic powers was included in the history that we invented to represent the great white nation—the Jaredites, a nation specifically meant to represent the United States of America.[8] The story tells of kings that used religion to control the people. One of the great kings, "did execute a law throughout all the land, which gave power unto the prophets that they should go whithersoever they would."[9] These prophets were supposed to keep the people in line with the laws of the state—laws that the people believed were constituted by God (brought about and accepted by Him). When the people "did repent of their iniquities and idolatries the Lord did spare them, and they began to prosper again in the land."[10]

In our invented history of the Great Jaredite Nation, we explained how politicians gained popularity and power in their government. The way that we presented a politician's success at deceiving and convincing the masses was the exact same way that politicians did it in the ancient great societies: "They did flatter many people, because of their cunning words, until they had gained half of the kingdom."[11]

In the most recent election (2020)—one of the most controversial modern-day elections for the United States Presidency (Donald J. Trump vs. Joseph R. Biden)—both candidates "did flatter many people, because of their cunning words, until each had gained half of the popular vote of the people." Not to our surprise, during his presidency, Donald Trump held a press conference in front of a church near the White House. During the staged press conference, Trump held up a Bible to promote the idea that the decisions that he made for the American people were based on the Bible.[12]

---

[8] *See* the Book of Ether in the *BOM*.
[9] *BOM*, Ether 7:25.
[10] *BOM*, Ether 7:25–6.
[11] *Compare BOM*, Ether 8:2.
[12] *See* Zach Montague, "Holding It Aloft, He Incited a Backlash. What Does the Bible Mean to Trump?" *The New York Times*, The New York Times, 2 June 2020, nytimes.com/2020/06/02/us/politics/trump-bible-st-johns.html.

Chapter 4: Exposing Secret Combinations

Politicians have always used flattery to gain power and control over the people. Leaders are able to further their own interests through excessive and insincere praise (flattery). This is how the American Founding Fathers were able to convince at least half of the early Americans to rise up against Britain in war. We had our Jaredite kings do similar things to what the American Founding Fathers had done. We based what our Jaredite kings did on what we knew was going on behind the scenes, in secret, in the doings of the early American politicians.

Most of the American Founding Fathers were Freemasons.[13] Freemasons belonged to a secret society—a *secret combination* of the wealthiest men in politics, religion, and business. Freemasons met in secret in their Masonic Temples that none other could enter except those properly endowed with specific permission.[14] They made covenants in these temples, swearing by an oath that they would

> be faithful in the thing which shall be desired of them. They all swore to him who was administering the oaths, by the God of heaven, and also by the heavens, and also by the earth, and by their heads, that whoso should vary from that which they swore to should lose his life.[15]

Each *endowed* Freemason bowed his head and said "Yes" to the person who administered the oaths of Freemasonry. We put this into our story in this particular way to show the connection between these secret oaths and the religious beliefs of those who take them, especially in regards to the powerful early American politicians.

---

[13] *See* Ron Blue, "MASONIC TOPICS," 19 Jan. 1993, Edited by George S. Robinson, Jr. *A Page About Masonry*, web.mit.edu/dryfoo/www/Masonry/Misc/more-usa-faq.html.
[14] *See* Tom Garlinghouse, "Freemasons: Behind the veil of secrecy," July 2020, *Live Science*, Future US, livescience.com/freemasons.html.
[15] *Compare BOM*, Ether 8:13–14.

These secret oaths were used during the development of what would become the greatest nation in modern times—the United States of America. These oaths were also used in business, an example of which is the "Oath of a Freeman."[16] This particular oath was taken to ensure that anyone who worked for a particular business vowed obedience to the company's rules and regulations and covenanted not to conspire against the business. (These were similar to modern-day non-disclosure agreements [NDAs] that are enforceable by law today.)

These oaths were administered when political, religious, and business leaders met in secret to make their plans on how to control the people. These oaths were used to keep the people in darkness so that the people did not know what was going on behind the closed doors of political committees, of religious solemn assemblies, or of corporate board meetings. The oaths "helped such as sought power to gain power." In our new American scripture, we presented these

> secret combination[s], even as they of old; which combination [of such powers over the people behind their backs] is most abominable and wicked above all, in the sight of God.[17]

We knew how the American Founding Fathers acted and what they did in secret to establish the U.S. Constitution. This constitution would become the law and authority that controlled the people and guaranteed the success of what would become the most powerful nation on Earth. We knew of the evil and selfish intentions of the founders of this nation. We knew that the American politicians, along with the religions and businesses that supported them, had used the same oaths of the secret combinations of old that had contributed to the establishment of the great nations of the past. Our warnings about these *secret combinations* were meant to help the Americans establish a righteous, open, transparent government, the

---

[16] *See* "Oath of a Freeman," *Wikipedia*, Wikimedia Foundation, 18 May 2021, en.wikipedia.org/wiki/Oath_of_a_Freeman.

[17] *See BOM*, Ether 8:16, 18.

powers of which were not to be established through combining powers in secrecy. Every nation of the past that used combinations of political, economic, and religious powers in secret failed ... EVERY SINGLE ONE.

Ironically, one of the main aspects that caused these great societies to fail was the same thing that made them successful—SLAVERY (taking away the free will of the masses to serve the interests of "the few"). It took slaves to build the great pyramids of the Egyptian Empire, the incredible structures of the Roman Empire, and the grand churches of the Byzantine Empire. Slaves and indentured servants (those who work to pay off a debt to a wealthy person) are not paid. If the primary labor source that established the foundation of these great societies was completely controlled and didn't cost the founders any money, the personal success and rise of the leaders was almost guaranteed.

SLAVERY was the basis for the rise and foundation of the great economic success and establishment of the United States of America. As they contemplated forming a new government and writing a new Constitution of laws, not one Founding Father mentioned the plight or the rights of the unpaid slaves, or of the indentured servants who worked for nothing. These people were controlled by the few, for the sake of the few.

An example of how these early American leaders used secret combinations to maintain their power and control over the people is seen in the original U.S. Constitution. This Constitution specifically discriminated against slaves and indentured servants (society's labor base), as well as all women, and any who didn't own land. It expressly prohibited all of these people from voting and exercising the same rights and powers that were guaranteed by the Constitution to the rest of the people, especially to the wealthy.

In modern times, the American people continue to be held in the dark and unaware that slavery still exists and controls all aspects of American society. Of this we wrote in our unfolding of our book of *Revelation*, which we appropriately named *666, The Mark of America—Seat of the Beast*:

> For every **one** person who can claim success in reaching the standard of accepted self-awareness and prosperity, **ninety-nine** others suffer from the means used to achieve this prosperity without the ability to attain it for themselves. In the race to be counted of worth in a world of values and standards set to benefit those who set them, no notice is given to the devastating effects of the contest.
>
> "Freedom" is an abstract idea perpetuated by those in power over others. Evident forced slavery has simply been replaced with tacit [silent, unspoken] slavery. Rising to the sound of a rooster's crow to harness the mule to the plow has been replaced with the obtrusive sound of an alarm clock that signals the beginning of another enslaved day. In both types of slavery, the *wise ones* are forced to work or they will die. The former was provided food, clothing, and shelter; the latter is given a piece of paper that must be exchanged for commodities owned by another slave owner.
>
> The slave's desire to live enriches the landowner for whom he or she works, and also the merchant from whom he or she must purchase life. The former was forced into chains if work and rules were not completed as established by the master; the latter is locked in a jail cell for the same reasons. Neither chose to be born into slavery; each would have *rather* been born the child of a slave owner: one who never saw the butt end of a mule pulling a harrow [a farm tool used for preparing the soil for crops], or the other who will never hear the sound of a time punch-clock.
>
> Though modern owners do not outwardly display their employees as personal human property, the slave trade has transformed itself into a shared commodity of the corporations

and wealthy of the world. Within the commercial organizations that buy and sell goods, make products, and provide services, there exists a proprietary implication [ownership that is unspoken] that if a slave refuses to work for one business, in order to remain alive, the rebellious runaway must submit to another. By running away from one plantation, the need to eat, and be clothed and housed necessitates the acceptance of another.[18]

The economic and social inequality that slavery promotes and sustains, and which religious belief justifies, is the one thing that all fallen great human societies have in common. <u>It is slavery, both obvious and implied, that must first be eliminated in order for any human group to succeed and continue to prosper.</u>

The laws of the Hebrews (written in stone as the "Hebrew Constitution" and named in their scriptures as the "law of Moses") made slaves out of non-believers who didn't believe in the Jewish god. Hebrew Constitution and law justified the murder of ALL non-believers. Their god commanded them to take

> all the cities and utterly destroy the men, and the women, and the little ones, of every city full of non-believers, and leave none to remain.[19]

Similarly, early American "murderous combinations" utterly destroyed the men, women, and little ones, of every city and tribe of the native Americans because they would not accept Jesus Christ.[20] In more

---

[18] "*666 America*, 38–9.
[19] *Compare* OT, Deuteronomy 2:34.
[20] *See* Donald L. Fixico, "When Native Americans Were Slaughtered in the Name of 'Civilization'." *History.com*, A&E Television Networks, 2 Mar. 2018, history.com/news/native-americans-genocide-united-states.
See also "Category: Massacres of Native Americans." *Wikipedia*, Wikimedia Foundation, 23 Feb. 2021, en.wikipedia.org/wiki/Category:Massacres_of_Native_Americans.

modern times, these same *secret combinations* destroy any nation that rises up against the United States of America.

Again and again—and this explanation of *why* we wrote our new American scripture the way that we did is worth repeating—we wanted to warn the Americans (both early and modern) of these secret combinations. That was one of the purposes of our book. Therefore, we demonstrated within the subplots of our storyline the same type of secret combinations that the early founders and establishers of the United States Constitution had used. We warned the early Americans:

> Wherefore, O ye Gentiles, it is wisdom in God that these things should be shown unto you, that thereby ye may repent of your sins, and suffer not that these murderous combinations shall get above you, which are built up to get power and gain.[21]

These secret combinations of political and business powers, justified by religious belief, are *above the people* now (they are in a position over the masses). Furthermore, they control the people without the people even knowing how they are being controlled. Still, it is the pride of the American people—even the pride of *all* people who are patriotic towards their nation (that they feel God has put above all others)—that is responsible for what is happening in the world and causing the downfall and demise of humanity.

We wrote our new American scripture the way that we did to warn the American people of the inevitability (inescapable conclusion) of the United States of America experiencing the same certain demise. However, we could not disclose the Real Truth™ about these things in plainness and clarity. If we had disclosed it in plainness, as we explained in previous chapters, the people would have never considered or accepted our book as another "word of God."

---

[21] *BOM*, Ether 8:23.

Chapter 4: Exposing Secret Combinations

The pride of the early American people was too great. American pride remains even greater in modern times. Americans do not see their nation as the "most abominable and wicked above all, in the sight of God."[22] Their pride will not let them. They actually believe that God is pleased with their works and what the United States of America has become.

Most disturbing to us is the way that the Church of Jesus Christ of Latter-day Saints uses our book and does not pay attention to its warnings or teachings. The members of this church are some of the most patriotic to the god of this world—to the god of their country.[23] LDS members are among the world's most prideful people. They are deceived by their leaders. They are passive-aggressive in the way that they deal with the rest of the world, and especially how they deal with those who reject their god and religion. They will smile in proclaiming that they have our *Book of Mormon* as evidence of the truthfulness of their religion, but condemn to hell, fire, and damnation any who refuse to accept their church as God's only true and living church upon Earth. (They might not do this outwardly, but this clear doctrine still stands in the LDS Church and in the minds of its believers.)

In the *Prologue* of this book, we gave an extreme example of this pride when one of their prophets, Wilford Woodruff, claimed to have received a spiritual and physical manifestation of all the dead American Founding Fathers.[24] In Woodruff's proclaimed "vision," the Founding Fathers (as well as many others of the "great" men who formed the secret combinations responsible for the success of the American Empire) wanted to join the LDS church through vicarious baptism for the dead. According to this prideful church, ALL of the Founding Fathers, as well as other notable men in

---

[22] *BOM*, Ether 8:18.
[23] *See* "America the Beautiful," "My Country, 'Tis of Thee," "The Star-Spangled Banner," and "God Save the King," *Hymns*, The Church of Jesus Christ of Latter-day Saints, found online at "Hymns," *Music Playlist*, Intellectual Reserve, Inc., churchofjesuschrist.org/music/library/hymns?lang=eng, numbers 338, 339, 340, 341 respectively.
[24] *See* Prologue, xxii.

American history, are now members on the records of the LDS Church (through "baptism for the dead").

As we reveal the citations and actual quotes below, consider the great pride and arrogance of this particular American-based religion:

> Two weeks before I left St. George, the spirits of the dead gathered around me, wanting to know why we did not redeem them. Said they, "You have had the use of the Endowment House for a number of years, and yet nothing has ever been done for us. We laid the foundation of the government you now enjoy, and we never apostatized from it, but we remained true to it and were faithful to God."
>
> Every one of those men that signed the Declaration of Independence, with General Washington, called upon me as an Apostle of the Lord Jesus Christ, in the Temple at St. George, two consecutive nights, and demanded at my hands that I should go forth and attend to the ordinances of the House of God for them.
>
> I straightway went into the baptismal font and called upon Brother McCallister to baptize me for the signers of the Declaration of Independence, and fifty other eminent men, making one hundred in all, including John Wesley, Columbus, and others.
>
> When Brother McAllister had baptized me for the 100 names I baptized him for 21, including General Washington and his forefathers and all the Presidents of the United States, except three. Sister Lucy Bigelow Young went forth into the font and was baptized for Martha Washington and her family and 70 of the eminent women of the world.[25]

---

[25] *See* "Discourse by Elder Wilford Woodruff, delivered in the New Tabernacle, Salt Lake City, Sunday Afternoon, September 16, 1877," *Journal of Discourses*, 26 vols. (London/Liverpool: Latter Day Saints' Book Depot, 1855–86), 19:229.

> I am going to bear my testimony to this assembly, if I never do it again in my life, that those men who laid the foundation of this American government and signed the Declaration of Independence were the best spirits the God of heaven could find on the face of the earth. They were choice spirits, not wicked men. General Washington and all the men that labored for the purpose were inspired of the Lord.
>
> Another thing I am going to say here, because I have a right to say it. Every one of those men that signed the Declaration of Independence, with General Washington, called upon me, as an Apostle of the Lord Jesus Christ, in the Temple at St. George, two consecutive nights, and demanded at my hands that I should go forth and attend to the ordinances of the House of God for them. Men are here, I believe, that know of this, Brother J. D. T. McAllister, David H. Cannon and James S. Bleak. Brother McAllister baptized me for all those men, and then I told these brethren that it was their duty to go into the Temple and labor until they had got endowments for all of them. They did it. Would those spirits have called up on me, as an Elder in Israel to perform that work if they had not been noble spirits before God? They would not.[26]

As we wrote our story, we knew that we had to confront this strong type of pride and diminish it before our message could be heard and accepted. However, when we wrote our new American scripture, we did not "disclose our true identity." This means much more than not disclosing our personal names or whereabouts. It means the same thing as what Joseph Smith often told his followers: "If I told you all that I know about the

---

[26] See Wilford Woodruff, 10 Apr. 1898, Conference Report (Salt Lake City: Deseret News Publishing Co., 1898), 89-90, also found online at archive.org/details/conferencereport1898a/page/88/mode/2up.

mysteries of God, you would rise up and kill me."[27] It means that we did not disclose the Real Truth™.[28] Joseph Smith did not "disclose his true identity" to the people who read our *Book of Mormon* and accepted it as another part of God's word. And we did not disclose ours when we created it.

In the previous chapter, we explained that for someone to write *believable* religious scripture, the person has to know what they're doing. At the very least, they must know what a person who reads scripture (or has scripture read to them) wants to hear. The information must make the person *feel* like it is the word of God—a personal message for the individual. In order to clearly explain what *secret combinations* of political, economic, and religious powers are, we presented appropriate stories, allegories, and symbolism that would affect the mind of a religious reader suitably.

We had Joseph Smith present some of these very important analogies about the power that controls people in a play we created in 1842. To the LDS people, this play is now known as the Temple Endowment—the most sacred ordinance available for their salvation. In this play, we made it very clear that all religion, of every kind, along with all religious writings (scripture "mingled with the philosophies of men") are from the "god of this world"—*Lucifer*. *Lucifer* is the character in our play meant to represent one's natural human pride and ego.[29] The LDS/Mormons do not see this. The members of this church are *blind* and *deaf* when they view our play's presentation.

As we explained in the last chapter, the brain's cognitive functions (thinking processes) are not influenced by any source of energy outside of the brain itself. For example, there is no outside source (i.e., god or angels described by any religion), nor is there any other source of revelation or inspiration that has the power to affect the human mind. Some of the

---

[27] *See* Robert Horne, "Reminiscences of the Church in Nauvoo," *Millennial Star*, vol. 55 no. 36, September 4, 1893, 585; found online at contentdm.lib.byu.edu/digital/collection/MStar/id/19227. (Download the PDF to view all the pages.)

[28] *See JS Bio*, Appendix 3, 676–80.

[29] *See BOM*, Mosiah 3:19.

greatest proof of this is in how we wrote our new American scripture, and, when necessary, changed it to conform to the *feelings* of the reader.

As we have explained, *spiritual* feelings thought to be from God are actually created by a person's own brain. They do not come from an outside source. This is also true for physical *feelings* that people often associate with "evil" or with the devil. To point out that these types of feelings are simple functions of the normal brain, one of our contemporary messengers said of an alleged exorcism (casting an evil spirit out of someone), "Give him some weed [marijuana] and watch how fast the devil leaves." It is an undisputed Real Truth™ that a person who appears to be possessed by the devil can be given a sedative and the evil spirit will "miraculously" depart.

Nevertheless, regardless of the logic, reason, or empirical evidence, one who has experienced a strong *spiritual* event, one who has supposedly seen a spirit, an angel, or a demon, will hardly be convinced that the event was simply made up in one's own head.[30]

There are billions of people throughout the world who would testify of a spiritual experience that convinced them that God is real, or rather, that they felt an overwhelming *real* feeling that could not have come from inside their own head. Although the human brain cannot *feel* without functioning and creating a feeling by itself, billions of people are still convinced that something outside of their own brain can cause their brain to feel.

The *secret combinations* formed by the leaders, to whom the people look for help and guidance, are very skillful at manipulating and using these feelings to accomplish their designs of controlling the people. Over the many milleniums that humans have existed, religious storytellers

---

[30] To watch mentalist Derren Brown cause an atheist to have a strong conversion experience, with a detailed commentary on the methods he is using, *see* Derren Brown, "Do You Believe In GOD? | Faith and Fear | Derren Brown," YouTube, 16 Jan. 2021, youtube.com/watch?v=6-xBFjQjFG4. The most relevant part starts around 7 minutes 30 seconds in.

(scripture writers) and leaders have learned how to make the unsuspecting brain feel these feelings.

So have we. We are masters at doing it.

In order for a person to NOT be manipulated and deceived by these *secret combinations*, the person must understand the power of the feelings that political, religious, and business leaders have been able to create. A person must also be humble enough to acknowledge that they have been deceived and controlled by feelings created by the *secret combinations* in the past.

To help people break the chains of ignorance by which they are bound and controlled by these *secret combinations of power*, we offer the following detailed explanation about the feelings that are responsible for a person who has fallen under their hypnotic and controlling, emotional power:

When people walk into a great and spacious religious church, cathedral, or massive temple, they *feel* small. With their *eyes* they see how small they really are compared to the vastness of the building that they have been told is the "house of God." Their ears can hear the echoes of vastness. Even their own voices succumb to the expanse; and they find themselves whispering in hypnotic reverence for the place. If in one's childhood the practice of lighting a candle to represent God's light was a part of one's upbringing, then in one's adulthood, if a candle is lit in a church, its familiar *sight* and *smell* will remind the adult of whose house was entered.

These feelings are real. These feelings are the result of a person's pride and ego—the basic structural standard of the mortal brain, which we call "*Lucifer.*" How proud is the one who can actually walk into God's house and be accepted there? How proud is the one who feels that the most powerful entity in the universe (God) is aware of just one person's presence and cares for just that one person? How proud are those who feel special because God pays attention to them and hears and answers their prayers and pleas?

Chapter 4: Exposing Secret Combinations

The key to properly understanding where these spiritual feelings come from is available in an honest acceptance of what human pride and ego are, and in understanding how these cognitive influencers manipulate the mind. That which makes each of us *feel* proud is the same as that which makes each of us *feel* human.

To properly understand what creates pride and ego, we need to consider little children. Do little children know who God is? Do they know who the devil is? Do they need a savior?

Our common sense should help us understand that children are not born into this world with any preconditioned or preprogrammed concept about religion, spirituality, or anything else *outside* of their own immediate experience and needs—the things that they make up in their own head.

The *secret combinations* of powers that control the world are masters at using the feelings of spirituality to deceive and control the masses. As the early American Christians began to develop their own nation in the American "promised land," we wanted to warn them not to let these *secret combinations* get the best of them. We intended to end our story with the destruction of the powerful, white-skinned Jaredite Nation as this portent (warning about the future).

Instead of heeding our warnings, the LDS Church has become the wealthiest church on the earth. LDS authorities combine their extensive economic power with their political power in order to have more religious power in the world. This *secret combination* of power allows LDS members throughout the world to openly mock our story, present our book in a fraudulent way, and use our work to entice people to join their church.

Regardless of how much control LDS leaders have over the members, none can deny the spiritual *feeling* they receive when they read our book. Even so, these spiritual feelings deceive them into trusting their leaders. Utilizing the power of LDS *secret combinations*, this religion (and the off-course teachings of its leaders) undermines, transfigures, and replaces our new American scripture with "modern-day revelation" from the *minds* of LDS authorities.

As we proceed to unfold how and why we wrote the *Book of Mormon* the way that we did, it will become very obvious how we did everything that we could to inspire the acceptance of various ideas and doctrines that could help heal humanity. In almost every case, the Americans who read and accepted our book as another "word of God" refused to see and accept what we were presenting. The fault for this lies with their leaders and what happens in secret that the members do not see.

Our goals are to oppose superstition (illogical belief), religious influence over public life, the abuses of state power, and obscurantism (the practice of deliberately preventing the facts or full details of a situation or event from becoming known by the majority). We will do everything within our power to put an end to the machinations (secret plans) of the purveyors of injustice (those who spread lies to create unfairness), to control them without dominating them (without impeding their free will).

Our goals are to expose the *secret combinations* that control the minds and hearts of humanity. We determined that writing a new American scripture was one of the ways that was necessary to "control them without dominating them."

Religious influence, mainly of the Orthodox and Protestant Christian varieties, has held enormous influence over public life. The *secret combinations* of religious and political power and influence exist the same today as they always have in the past. These are responsible for the great success and power of the United States of America. But these *secret combinations*, if not understood and controlled, will cause humanity's demise.

Chapter 5
According to the Portion of His Word

The overall purpose we intended for our new American scripture was to help influence the development of the correct form of government. A proper government would make life upon Earth a fair experience for everyone, according to each human's unique and individual desires of happiness. There was and is no other purpose for our work. Because religion was so strong, influential, and persuasive over the people's hearts and minds, we knew that we would never make any progress with our purpose without also using religion. We had to convince the early American Christians that their god wanted and expected an equal and fair playing field for all of his children (humanity).

We had hoped that this simple idea of a god of equality and fairness would be self-evident and logical. It was not. The natural human ego got in the way. Ego is a person's sense of self-worth and importance. There is nothing wrong with a person having a sense of worth and purpose. However, the ego is responsible for a person's pride, and it is excessive pride that creates ALL of the problems that face humanity.

Pride is the sole perpetrator of the misery and hardships that destroy peace and harmony. *Pride* is responsible for most wars and the destruction of many human civilizations of the past. *Pride* will be the cause of humanity's demise in the future.

Pride is best defined as

a feeling of deep pleasure or satisfaction derived from one's own achievements, the achievements of those with whom one is closely associated, or from qualities or possessions that are widely admired.[1]

---

[1] *See* "PRIDE," *Lexico Dictionaries | English,* Oxford University Press, lexico.com/en/definition/pride.

ALL religions on Earth are established on the foundation of pride ... ALL RELIGIONS. Religion plays on a person's natural ego—one's sense of self-worth and purpose. ALL religions have certain achievements (accomplishments) that the god of each particular religion has prescribed and mandated of its members. A member feels a deep sense of pleasure and satisfaction when the member keeps God's commandments (according to their particular religious beliefs).

A member has "a feeling of deep pleasure or satisfaction derived from [the member's] own achievements" inside the religion, or from the achievements of other members ("those with whom one is closely associated"). A few examples of this in the LDS Church are temple marriages, serving missions, or having a calling, such as being a bishop or stake president. Believing that God is aware of a believer's actions and daily activities, and that while performing these actions and activities the believer is serving God, is vital in feeding the ego and creating self-worth and purpose.

"I exist, not to achieve my own will, but to do God's will," is an easier attitude to have to feel good about oneself. This is because one is not responsible for guiding one's own life and making one's own decisions. Religions make it easier to have self-worth; and religious leaders make sure that members understand what self-worth requires.

Each human starts life upon Earth in the exact same way—doing their own will. Little children do not know anything about any god. Little children's first experience of a god who controls what they do is the parent who leads them, guides them, walks beside them, helps them find the way, teaching them all that they must do in order to continue to live with and please the parent.

Little children are inculcated (taught through repetition) to believe that in order to continue to live with the first god that they are taught to worship and obey—the parent—they must do what their parent asks of them or they will be punished. While growing up and unable to provide for themselves, children are completely dependent on and obligated to do whatever the parent mandates and expects. If not, some kind of physical or psychological punishment is often administered.

Once the child is considered an adult, the child is expected to know the right way to act. The aged child can be kicked out of their parent's house (kicked out of "god's kingdom") for disobedience. This is how an innocent person (a little child) becomes susceptible to strong religious persuasion and control. Because of this, it is easy for one to imagine a Heavenly parent who expects certain things from "a child of God" (from the adult child) in order for the child to "live with him once more."

With great sadness and disappointment, we present below one of the most popular songs that is taught to a little child while the child is exposed to and growing up in the LDS Church. As we have explained, our disappointment is increased by the way this particular church hijacked our new American scripture and transfigured and ignored its message. We have explained how this church uses the spiritual power of our book to get people to join and stay loyal to this church, while referring to itself as God's "only true and living church on Earth."

The following is one of the LDS Church's most popular songs: *I Am a Child of God*. As you read these manipulative lyrics, pay close attention to how much that religion's god mimics and reflects a child's own parent(s) and the experiences a child has while growing up. As a child is taught and sings the verses of this song for the first time, the song's message actually makes a lot of sense to the child's innocent mind because of its close relation to the child's family life experiences:

> I am a child of God,
> And he has sent me here,
> Has given me an earthly home
> With parents kind and dear.

> [Chorus]
> Lead me, guide me, walk beside me,
> Help me find the way.
> Teach me all that I must do
> To live with him someday.
>
> I am a child of God,
> And so my needs are great;
> Help me to understand his words
> Before it grows too late.
>
> I am a child of God.
> Rich blessings are in store;
> If I but learn to do his will,
> I'll live with him once more.
>
> I am a child of God.
> His promises are sure;
> Celestial glory shall be mine
> If I can but endure.[2]

A child growing up in any religion first feels the Holy Spirit, or God's Spirit, because the feeling is associated with the love of a parent. When the child is good, the parent is happy and rewards the child with love and acceptance. With the same influential power that helps the child believe in a "god," the child also first feels the power of the devil. When the child disobeys the parent, the parent's face and countenance change in a way that frightens the child. It does not make sense to a child's mind that a loving God would wield a belt to punish His beloved child. But it makes sense that the devil would.

When threatened by the anger of a parent who was once loving and kind, the child becomes confused and vulnerable. The parent's threatening,

---

[2] "I Am a Child of God." *The Church of Jesus Christ of Latter-Day Saints*, Intellectual Reserve, Inc., churchofjesuschrist.org/music/library/childrens-songbook/i-am-a-child-of-god?lang=eng. Written in 1957 by Naomi W. Randall.

seemingly evil, transformation instills in the child that there actually *does* exist good (God) and evil (the devil). Again, this is how a religious person becomes susceptible to the power and control used by religious leaders who claim to be God's ONLY mouthpieces, and who teach the child what the child must "endure" to be rewarded with "Celestial glory."

Any "good" parent will admit that the best way to keep a child doing what is right (what the *parent* thinks is right for the child) is to keep the child busy doing things so that the child will not act on the child's own free will and do something "wrong" (that the *parent* thinks is wrong). The following quote is attributed to Bible teachings: "Idle hands and minds are the devil's playground."[3] To be a successful religion with a controlled and organized membership, the religion must mandate enough busy work to keep the member's mind associated with and concentrating on religious activities. In this way, the member's personal free will (that which they naturally had as a child) is impeded and controlled.

We have explained how the ancient Hebrew (Jewish) religion began. The Jewish religion (similar to the modern LDS religion) provides a perfect example of religious "busy work" that is so overwhelming for the members that they hardly have any time or energy to think of anything else. The Hebrew religion created what is called the "law of Moses." This religious law contains various "required" rituals and procedures ("busy work"). Similar to the LDS/Mormon religion, Judaism touts itself as the religion of God's chosen people. Jews believe they are the ONLY people on Earth that God has blessed and chosen to whom to deliver His will and commandments for the rest of humanity.

As does Judaism, the LDS Church teaches that it is God's ONLY True and Living Church on Earth. If one were to research the history of these two major

---

[3] "Idle Hands Are the Devil's Workshop," *Wiktionary*, 5 Dec. 2020, en.wiktionary.org/wiki/idle_hands_are_the_devil%27s_workshop.

religions and compare their likenesses, one would be astonished at the obvious similarities. Ironically, even the current membership numbers of both the Jewish faith and the LDS/Mormon faith are eerily equal.[4]

The ancient Mosaic Law mandated many things as "busy work." The Jewish leaders strictly required the members to perform these "ordinances of salvation," or rather, the things that a person must do in order to please God and fulfill God's commandments in order to receive God's richest blessings. This "busy work" included

> a multitude of your sacrifices [volunteer work that supports the church] ... the burnt offerings of rams, and the fat of fed beasts ... the blood of bullocks, or of lambs, or he goats [sacraments] ... vain oblations [any personal offering meant for God] ... incense ... moons and sabbaths, the calling of assemblies [General Conferences and Sunday church meetings] ... the solemn meeting [solemn assemblies held at the dedications of temples and for specially-called meetings to provide instruction to Church leaders] ... and your appointed feasts ... many prayers [Jews and Mormons are taught to pray over everything that they do].[5]

To the ancient Jews, nothing was more important to one's self-worth and purpose (ego) than what they did for their god and church. This pride was demonstrated by the priests who taught the people that God would only speak through the proper channels of priesthood authority. Jewish *pride* is evident not only in their belief system, but in their modern-day political and social expectations and activities.

Nothing is more important to the Jews than the modern State of Israel and its exclusive right to what they consider to be their god's "promised land."

---

[4] *See* "Jewish & LDS (Mormon) Parallels," *Pearl Publishing*, Pearl Publishing, LLC, pearlpublishing.net/tsp/download/JewishLDSParallels.4.4.20.pdf

[5] *Compare* OT, Isaiah 1:11, 13–15.

Chapter 5: According to the Portion of His Word

It is a Jew's "feeling of deep pleasure or satisfaction derived from [Jewish] achievements, the achievements of [the Jewish state], or from qualities or possessions that are widely admired." Not to be outdone, members of one of the wealthiest private institutions upon Earth—the Church of Jesus Christ of Latter-day Saints—also have the same feelings and are widely admired for their qualities and possessions.

We revealed that we were responsible for writing the words of Isaiah. This took place in the fourth (4th) century B.C.E. These words were delivered through our chosen True Messenger at that time. We did this to counter the extreme pride of the ancient Hebrew religion as it was developing under the protection and rule of the Greek and Roman Empires. Christianity, the most powerful religion in this final dispensation of time, is an offshoot of Judaism. The Eastern Roman Empire created it. Christianity's formation ensured this part of the Roman Empire's survival. Had the Eastern Roman Empire not survived, our book of Isaiah would have become obsolete and hardly noticed in the annals (historical records) of religion.

Just as we wrote our New Testament book of Revelation in a poetic (symbolic) way, we also wrote the words of Isaiah so that it was hard for the Jewish priests and scholars to decipher its true meaning. Because they couldn't understand Isaiah's poetic prose, they left his words relatively intact and unchanged. The book of Isaiah was corrupted most when it was translated from its original Greek into other languages. However, it has been largely ignored by modern Judaism. Furthermore, the Islamic religion does not include Isaiah as one of its accepted biblical prophets. Muslims reject Isaiah's writings because Isaiah's prophecies specifically refer to Jews (i.e., the house of Israel) as God's chosen people, implying that all Muslims are following the wrong god.

But why do the Jews overlook and ignore the words of Isaiah? This answer is easy. The book of Isaiah presents the Jewish people as a sinful nation, a people laden with iniquity, a seed of evildoers, children that are corrupters: they have forsaken the Lord, they have provoked the Holy One of Israel ... the whole head is sick, and the whole heart faint. From the sole of the foot [meaning all the membership that supports and carries forth the body of the church] even unto the head [the leaders of the church] there is no soundness in it; but wounds, and bruises, and putrifying sores.[6]

Therefore, obviously, the Jews ignore Isaiah because his prophecies speak of their wickedness. This is the same reason why the LDS/Mormons ignore our words, which speak of the wickedness of the LDS Church. Isaiah's words discount the Jewish church and its law of Moses ... entirely. Isaiah says nothing good about the Jews and their religious laws and ordinances. Isaiah specifically condemns Jewish priesthood authority and leadership while denouncing the pride (specialness) of the Jews (house of Israel).

We began our new American scripture's narrative by introducing characters who were members of the house of Israel. Our first characters lived in Jerusalem right before it was ransacked, as Isaiah's prophecies described it would be:

> Your country is desolate, your cities are burned with fire: your land, strangers devour it in your presence, and it is desolate, as overthrown by strangers. And the daughter of Zion is left as a cottage in a vineyard, as a lodge in a garden of cucumbers, as a besieged city.[7]

Because the major world's religions were generally ignoring Isaiah, it was easy for us to use it and incorporate it into our new American scripture. We used Isaiah's prophecy about "a very small remnant" that had escaped the destruction of Jerusalem. (A remnant is a small remaining number.) This

---

[6] OT, Isaiah 1:4–6.
[7] OT, Isaiah 1:7–8.

Chapter 5: According to the Portion of His Word

"remnant" in Isaiah was the basis and explanation of our new American scripture's first families ("remnants of the house of Israel"). We did this to establish the importance and value of our story's first characters: "Except the Lord of hosts had left unto us a very small remnant, we should have been as Sodom, and we should have been like unto Gomorrah."[8]

Our story's first patriarchs were two Jewish High Priests who ruled in ancient Jerusalem: Lehi and Ishmael. Along with their wives and children, these two families established the "very small remnant" that was saved from Babylonian destruction and captivity. We created this story to match the Old Testament's narrative and the prophecies given in its prophets' warnings. We utilized the Bible's Isaiah, Ezekiel, and Jeremiah as the foundation of biblical proof to explain our "small remnant" that had escaped destruction and was led to a new "promised land" in the Western Hemisphere.

There was nothing however in the Bible's Isaiah, Ezekiel, or Jeremiah that properly presented what we wanted Lehi and Ishmael to hear from God's holy prophets. (Note: the word used in the 1830 publication of the *Book of Mormon* as "Ezias"[9] should have been spelled "Ezekiel."[10] This was an error made by the original printer that was not corrected when the book was first published.)

We needed to make a strong connection to the future Jesus of Nazareth of the New Testament in our new American scripture. We needed to properly and clearly condemn ALL organized religion. To do this, we invented two other prophets who were sent by God to Jerusalem to preach repentance before its destruction: Zenos and Zenock. We introduced them before we presented any of the other accepted biblical prophets in our book's narrative. In our story, these two prophets are the ones that the Jews

---

[8] OT, Isaiah 1:9.
[9] "Ezias" is found on page 430 in the 1830 edition. *See* "Book of Mormon, 1830, Page 430." *The Joseph Smith Papers, Book of Mormon, 1830*, Intellectual Reserve, Inc., josephsmithpapers.org/paper-summary/book-of-mormon-1830/436.
[10] *BOM*, Helaman 8:20.

A New American Scripture

> bound … and carried forth unto the High Priests to see what should be done with them. For the people of Jerusalem mocked the prophets and ridiculed their authority to preach the word of God. For behold, the Jews were not familiar with these prophets, as they had not been acknowledged by the proper authority of the priesthood of Aaron, which the people believed resided only in the High Priests who were called to serve in the church at Jerusalem by lineage of the priesthood, and also by the laying on of hands by those who were in authority.
>
> For the people had been taught that there were none, save he who had been chosen and set apart by a sacred anointing, who could administer the word of God unto the people. And the prophets [Zenos and Zenock] who were sent by the Lord to Jerusalem were not members of this priesthood that was accepted by the people of the church at Jerusalem, nor were they recognized as one having authority to preach the word of God to the people.[11]

A modern *Book of Mormon* scholar would not recognize the above quotation, as it is from our *Book of Lehi*. However, our new American scripture's prophets, Zenos and Zenock, are mentioned in the 1830 publication of our book (the *Book of Mormon*). In the 1830 *Book of Mormon* there is no information about when or from where these two non-biblical prophets came on the scene.

The reader might be interested to know where we came up with the new names for our story's two new ancient Hebrew prophets. We borrowed from Greek mythology, incorporating derivatives (offshoots) of the often-applied surnames of the greatest gods of Greek mythology, Zeus and Hera: Zeus Zygius (Zugia), our Zenos, and Hera Zygia (Zugios), our Zenock. Zenos and Zenock were the two prophets that are mentioned in our original

---

[11] *TSP*, Lehi 1:15–16.

storyline. As mentioned, LDS/Mormon people would recognize our original storyline as the lost 116-page manuscript, or the lost *Book of Lehi*.

Our original storyline was never actually lost. We never would have allowed it to be lost. Here's what actually happened:

We instructed our chosen messenger, the young Joseph Smith, Jr., to form a peer review group with which he would share portions of our story as it was being written. It was our intent to write the storyline in a way that was palatable to early American Christians. Therefore, we instructed Joseph to share the developing manuscript with a certain number of his friends and family.

A peer review group is important for the success of any written document meant to be understood in a certain way by a specific audience. Upon writing our book's storyline, we asked Joseph to share its progress, at different stages, with his family and friends in order to receive their feedback. (As a reminder, the story was written from the gold plates that we prepared. We did this to keep Joseph's attention properly concentrated on exactly what we wanted him to write. We will explain more about this procedure later.)

After the selected peer review group read in our original storyline about the account of "the life and ministry of Lehi, the son of Jeshron, who lived and preached in Jerusalem,"[12] we were astonished at the feedback we received from Joseph. These early American Christians had a hard time, even becoming very angry with Joseph, because of the way that we presented organized religion—its ordinances, its priesthoods, and everything else about the world's religions—as evil and as abominations before God.

In our original storyline, we incorporated the first chapter of the biblical book of Isaiah (some of which is quoted above) that condemns ALL organized religion. In order to make our storyline palatable to early American

---

[12] *See* header of The Book of Lehi. Read for free at realilluminati.org/the-book-of-lehi.

Christians, we dovetailed (linked) its narrative in with what Isaiah wrote ... after condemning ALL religious practices:

> Wash you, make you clean; put away the evil of your doings from before mine eyes; cease to do evil; Learn to do well; seek judgment, relieve the oppressed, judge the fatherless, plead for the widow.[13]

Above we explained that the overall purpose we intended for our new American scripture was to help influence the development of the correct form of government. A proper government would make life upon Earth a fair experience for everyone, according to each human's unique and individual desire of happiness. We also explained how religion stands in the way of this happening. We explained how our natural ego creates *pride*. We explained how this pride is accentuated and supported by organized religion and the "busy work" that religion requires of people.

Those in Joseph Smith's peer review group were greatly offended to think that nothing about their religious organizations, authorities, and purposes was any good ... nothing. How could all church work, all church ordinances, all that organized religion does, be an abomination? These early American Christians were very *prideful* of their Christian heritage. Their pride was great because they saw themselves as God's chosen people. They saw themselves as blessed *Americans* living in the great nation of the United States of America. The pride that they had in their Christian faith and country was too strong for our original narrative.

We realized that there was no way that we could open their minds to the message intended for our new American scripture unless we allowed for the *ego* and *pride* that supported their self-worth and purpose. Owing to what we have explained about the importance of making the reader *feel* the *Holy Spirit of God*, we were forced to change the original storyline of our book in order to ensure that we could create the proper "spiritual" feeling.

---

[13] OT, Isaiah 1:16–17.

Chapter 5: According to the Portion of His Word

We withdrew our original storyline. We counseled Joseph to let the manuscript be taken by some of his enemies. We knew who his enemies were. After the manuscript was *allowed* to be stolen, we stole it back. The original 116 pages of the manuscript are in our possession today. We will bring it forth, if we find it beneficial to do so. We will find it a benefit to bring forth, if we can get the people of the world to listen to us. If they will listen to us, we can then present the actual evidence that what we say to them is the Real Truth™.

As explained, our new American scripture's message has been ignored, transfigured, and distorted by the Christians who read it. They have been deceived into becoming members of organized religion. As the world is today, we know that presenting these documents would not only put the life our chosen contemporary True Messenger in more danger, but the records would be hunted and destroyed. This would be done by the power of politics (which includes judges and lawyers) and the power of business interests that bring great wealth to the powerful, *combined in secret* with the religious power of the church that uses our book to deceive the world.

For these reasons, we chose not to allow our True Messenger (who helped us publish the "sealed portion" of our story in 2004) to provide the empirical evidence of the original 116 pages of manuscript in our possession. Instead, we had him "retranslate" the first part of our "plates [with] the appearance of gold," to logically prove to the world that indeed, the same source was used to write *The Sealed Portion* that was used to write the unsealed *Book of Mormon* (which came from the same gold "plates," as we will explain in another chapter).

An honest researcher reading the original *Book of Lehi* (published in 2004) along with our *sealed portion*, would acknowledge that <u>it could indeed be</u> the lost 116-page manuscript. This can easily be verified by honestly analyzing the word content and comparing it to the known handwriting of Joseph Smith's main scribes, especially to that of Martin Harris. One could study Harris' handwriting, the spacing of his words, and the approximate number of words that would fit on the familiar manuscript of that time period. They could then calculate the approximate number of words in his writing that would have been on 116 pages. An honest scholar would conclude (convincingly) that the 2004 published *Book of Lehi*, could verifiably be the "lost 116-page manuscript."

We have explained how we made a solid connection between the "word of God"—accepted by most early Americans as the King James Bible—and our new American scripture. We explained how our new American scripture fulfills Ezekiel's prophecy about the *stick of Judah* (the Bible) and the *stick of Joseph, which is in the hand of Ephraim* (the *Book of Mormon*) becoming <u>one</u> in the Lord's hand. Our story fulfills many other prophecies given in the Old Testament too.

However, it wasn't that our story actually *fulfilled* these ancient prophecies. Essentially, we *created* a story of skillfully and wisely invented events that fulfilled each specific prophecy. Anything written as a "prophecy," which indicates something that will come to pass in the future, can be fulfilled by someone in the future taking the necessary steps to make it come to pass ... "and it came to pass."

Ironically, we (the Real Illuminati®) did not invent this strategy of deceiving the people into believing that ancient prophecy was being fulfilled—the authors of the Jesus stories did. An obvious example of this in their storyline is when Jesus of Nazareth told his disciples to get an ass and her foal and bring them to him so that he could ride into Jerusalem. This was according to a prophecy given by the ancient prophet, Zechariah. Zechariah had prophesied to the Jews,

> Rejoice greatly, O daughter of Zion; shout, O daughter of Jerusalem: behold, thy King cometh unto thee: he is just, and having salvation; lowly, and riding upon an ass, and upon a colt the foal of an ass.[14]

---

[14] OT, Zechariah 9:9.

The authors who created "Jesus" made sure that any prophecy about his being the promised Messiah was fulfilled. "Jesus" explained the reason for having his disciples get a colt and her foal so that he could ride into Jerusalem:

> All this was done, that it might be fulfilled which was spoken by the prophet, saying, Tell ye the daughter of Sion, Behold, thy King cometh unto thee, meek, and sitting upon an ass, and a colt the foal of an ass.[15]

Before the stories of Jesus were officially compiled and canonized, the pre-Catholic scholars and leaders interpreted many scriptures as *they* wanted to. Here is another of <u>many</u> examples. The book of Jeremiah mentions that:

> A voice was heard in Ramah, lamentation, and bitter weeping; Rahel [*sic*] weeping for her children refused to be comforted … because they were not.[16]

The religious leaders interpreted this as the story about King Herod trying to find and kill baby Jesus, and then killing all the young males in Bethlehem when he couldn't find Jesus. This was one of many ways that early pre-Catholic religious leaders manipulated the Hebrew scriptures to their advantage. They stretched their imaginations to incredibly deceptive lengths in order to get people to believe their interpretation of scripture stories.

There is not one accepted recorded historical event of that time period—not Roman, not Hebrew, nor any other—that relates to the murder of many innocent children for which King Herod was supposedly responsible. It simply never happened. Had it *actually* happened, someone would have reported something, anything, about this terrible event.

In the book of Exodus in the Old Testament, there is a Hebrew story about Moses. Moses was the Jews' prophesied messiah. When Moses was born, the

---

[15] NT, Matthew 21:4–5.
[16] OT, Jeremiah 31:15; *compare* NT, Matthew 2:18.

Pharaoh's "wise men" told him about the Jewish belief that a savior had been born among them. The priests informed Pharaoh that the Jews believed this deliverer would save them and release them from bondage. To prevent this from happening, the Pharaoh ordered the killing of all babies. Moses was "miraculously" saved and protected, thus allowing him to continue his mission.

This entire Old Testament story was copied and plagiarized when the story of Jesus of Nazareth was created. In Jesus' case, there were "wise men" who followed a star (think "star of David") in search of the baby Jesus. They wanted to worship the child and asked King Herod, "Where is he that is born King of the Jews?" As a result, according to the story, King Herod ordered the massacre of all the young males of Bethlehem. Jesus' father was warned by an angel in a dream; therefore, he was able to protect Jesus from the slaughter. This example is just one of many that shows how New Testament stories were plagiarized from Old Testament stories.

In each and every case where the stories of Jesus refer to something being fulfilled of ancient Hebrew prophecy, Rabbinical (Jewish) scholars smile and shake their heads in mockery at the ignorant and deceived Christians. They see the duplicity of the stories and the way that early Christian authors deceived the people with ancient Hebrew prophecies that had nothing to do with Jesus, the Christ.

An honest student of the Bible can confirm the Real Truth™ about these things simply by researching how the Jewish church's scholars and priests interpret *their own scriptures.* Engaging in this honest pursuit, a person will quickly realize how deceptive the early Catholic leaders were in how they used, abused, transfigured, and completely changed the Hebrew scripture. It will become apparent how the authors of the Jesus stories came up with their ideas to make their stories more believable.

We have delivered empirical evidence that this deception continues, even in modern times. In the *Prologue* of this book, we provided indisputable evidence that the General Authorities of the LDS Church use this same deceptive technique when they read *their own scriptures* to their followers. We have provided the evidence of how these deceptive leaders use, abuse, transfigure, and completely change the meaning of our new American scripture to deceive the members of their church.

Religious believers are easily deceived and manipulated by their leaders, especially if the believers do not study *their own scriptures*. Even if the members *do* read and study with real intent and sincerity, they can still be deceived. If *their* individual interpretation of the scripture does not agree with their leaders, they can be convinced that *their* interpretation only applies to themselves, or is wrong. This is because the member is convinced by his or her faith in the god who chose those leaders as His (God's) own mouthpiece. Religious leaders will always hide behind their own "revelation from God." For instance:

> The Lord will never permit me or any other man who stands as President of this Church to lead you astray. It is not in the programme [*sic*]. It is not in the mind of God. If I were to attempt that, the Lord would remove me out of my place, and so He will any other man who attempts to lead the children of men astray from the oracles of God and from their duty. ... It matters not who lives or who dies, or who is called to lead this Church, they have got to lead it by the inspiration of Almighty God. If they do not do it that way, they cannot do it at all.[17]

Joseph Smith never taught this to his followers. It wasn't until Brigham Young created his own spin on Mormonism that this deceptive doctrine was introduced.

This edict (proclamation) from God—that God will never allow His leaders to deceive the people—is what ALL religious leaders, of ALL

---

[17] Wilford Woodruff, as quoted in "Official Declaration 1," *Doctrine and Covenants* (Salt Lake City: The Church of Jesus Christ of Latter-day Saints, 1981), 292.

religions, in ALL time periods, have used in order to control the minds and hearts of the people.

Yet, how wonderful it must be to be a member who does not need to think for him or herself, but can depend on God's chosen mouthpieces to lead them, guide them, walk beside them, help them find the way, teach them all that the members must do to live with God someday. Most members of ALL religions are ignorant, naïve, and very susceptible to being deceived by their accepted religious and spiritual leaders.

As we explained above, most religious followers and members are too busy with the daily drudgery (boring and unpleasant work) of their own mortal lives to worry about spiritual matters. They must procure the basic necessities of life, and therefore, they don't have the time or the mental energy to worry about what God wants them to do. Further, because the members are kept busy with "church work" (assignments and callings), they don't have the time to question doctrine. The members are taught to trust their leaders and depend on them for anything and everything that God would have them do.

The modern LDS Church has corrupted the pure message and intent of our new American scripture. Leaders of that Church have told the members that they don't need to think about doctrine and the plan of salvation, that

> When our leaders speak, the thinking has been done. When they propose a plan—it is God's plan. When they point the way, there is no other which is safe. When they give direction, it should mark the end of controversy. God works in no other way. To think otherwise, without immediate repentance, may cost one his faith, may destroy his testimony, and leave him a stranger to the kingdom of God.[18]

---

[18] *See* Ward Teachers' Message for June, 1945, "Sustaining the General Authorities of the Church," *Improvement Era*, June 1945, 354; also found online at archive.org/details/improvementera4806unse/page/n35/mode/2up.

An "apologist" is someone who defends or justifies their beliefs by presenting information that supports their position. Many LDS/Mormon apologists try to explain that the members *are* taught to think for themselves and depend on personal revelation, as well as have a personal relationship with Jesus Christ. Nevertheless, they can't deny that when an LDS/Mormon leader speaks on behalf of the Church, the leader is not to be questioned or challenged.

As one continues to read this book and discovers the Real Truth™ about the *Book of Mormon*, one will come to understand how easily spiritually-minded people can be deceived and manipulated. In writing our new American scripture, it was not our intent to demean anyone for what they believed. If we had, then we would have lost the opportunity for the people—whose pride would have been hurt—to consider some of the things that we wanted to teach them.

Our chosen Author and Proprietor, Joseph Smith, Jr., said this about the way that *he* tried to teach people:

> If I esteem mankind to be in error, shall I bear them down? No. I will lift them up, and in their own way too, if I cannot persuade them my way is better; and I will not seek to compel any man to believe as I do, only by the force of reasoning, for truth will cut its own way.[19]

"And in their own way too" is *how* and *why* we wrote our new American scripture. We knew that we had to reason with the readers "in their own way," the way that the readers would allow us to. We knew that in order to open their deceived minds we had to do it in the same way and through the same means that their minds were deceived in the first place.

---

[19] Joseph Smith discourse, July 9, 1843, in Nauvoo, Illinois as reported by Willard Richards, found in Andrew H. Hedges, Alex D. Smith, and Brent M. Rogers, eds., *The Joseph Smith Papers, Journals, Volume 3: 1843–1844* (Salt Lake City: Church Historians Press, 2015), 56; also in B.H. Roberts, *History of the Church*, 5:498–9.

Religious people can be very *diligent* in *heeding* the religious teachings that they receive when they listen to the leaders of what they accept as "God's only true church." The leaders ostensibly (supposedly) do not teach the members any doctrine that cannot be backed up by scripture, where "scripture" is God's infallible word. Early American Christians were taught to give attentiveness (heed) to the Bible and to be *diligent* in doing what the Bible tells them to do.

We could not teach Bible-believers anything that might contradict the Bible that the people already had and in which they believed. To explain this, we referred to the Bible as "the portion of his word which [God] doth grant unto the children of men." We explained that our hands were tied in how much Real Truth™ we could teach the people, "according to the *heed* and *diligence*" which they gave unto God and God's word written in the Bible. We gave the following important clue in our new American scripture about how we were limited in our ability to teach the people "the mysteries of God" (i.e., the Real Truth™):

> It is given unto many to know the mysteries of God; nevertheless they are laid under a strict command that they shall not impart only according to the portion of his word which he doth grant unto the children of men, according to the *heed* and *diligence* which they give unto him.[20]

We knew that if a person believed in the Bible and actually *did* what it says to do (giving *heed* and *diligence*), this person's mind would only be open to things that conformed with and supported what the Bible says. We knew we could present information that would get through the filters established in the person's mind by the Bible. If, however, a person did not believe in the Bible, or rather had "hardened his heart" against it, then we could not use the Bible's stories and teachings to penetrate the person's closed mind. We continued the clue, writing:

---

[20] *BOM*, Alma 12:9.

> And therefore, he that will harden his heart, the same receiveth the lesser portion of the word; and he that will not harden his heart, to him is given the greater portion of the word, until it is given unto him to know the mysteries of God until he know them in full.[21]

Those who didn't believe in the Bible and did not give heed and diligence to it didn't receive *any* of God's word. But our new American scripture was not meant for these. In fact, the early Americans who did not believe in the Bible were not as susceptible to being deceived as those who did. Most of the politicians and business leaders of the early United States believed in the Bible, or at least pretended to. As we have explained, they *combined in secret* to use the Bible to get gain and popularity, but mostly, to control the minds and hearts of the early Americans.

Before we presented this clue in our new American scripture about how we teach Bible believers, we had already presented the reader with the concept that the King James Bible was corrupt and lacked the plain and precious things that Jesus taught. We presented our record (the stick of Joseph, by the hand of Ephraim) containing the "lesser portion of the word," that would correct the King James Bible by restoring these plain and precious things. We also introduced the "sealed" or "greater portion of the word" as the *sealed portion* of the plates (from which our *Book of Mormon* was also taken). This portion of the plates (sealed with bands), would not be given to the Americans ("Gentiles") until they "repented of their evil ways."[22]

Our clues were very specific and clear that unless the Americans received the "sealed portion" ("the greater portion of the word"), they would not know anything of Real Truth™ and would then be "taken captive by the devil, and led by his will down to destruction."[23] We finally gave the world the opportunity to read the *sealed portion* of our story in 2004. Amazingly, the members of the LDS/Mormon church rejected this "greater portion of

---

[21] *BOM*, Alma 12:10.
[22] *See BOM*, Mormon 5:22–4; *and BOM*, Ether 4:4–7.
[23] *BOM*, Alma 12:11.

A New American Scripture

the word." LDS apologists justified this rejection because the "lesser portion" (the *Book of Mormon*) specifically says that:

> [The greater portion] shall not go forth unto the Gentiles until the day that they shall repent of their iniquity, and become clean before the Lord.[24]

Astonishingly, "blinded" and "deafened" by the deceptive words of their leaders, the LDS people have been convinced that their church has no need of repentance, that they are doing the right thing "before the Lord," and that they have the restored gospel and priesthood authority to do the right thing. Yet, their excuse that *The Sealed Portion* would not be allowed to come forth among them, is BECAUSE OF THEIR WICKEDNESS.

The LDS/Mormon people who claim belief in our new American scripture do NOT give heed and diligence to the *Book of Mormon*. Therefore, it is impossible for their blind eyes and deaf ears to consider "the greater portion of the word." Members of that church are taught not to delve into or worry about the "mysteries of God." They are counseled not to discuss mysteries; and they certainly do NOT know the "mysteries of God in full." Neither do their *leaders* know these mysteries. Because of the deception and ignorance of their leaders, these "Gentiles" "are taken captive by the devil (their pride), and led by his will down to destruction."[25] We explained that we would do

> a great and marvelous work among the children of men; a work which shall be everlasting, either on the one hand or on the other—either to the convincing of them unto peace and life eternal, or unto the deliverance of them to the hardness of their hearts and the blindness of their minds unto their being brought

---

[24] *BOM*, Ether 4:6.
[25] *BOM*, Alma 12:11.

down into captivity, and also into destruction, both temporally and spiritually, according to the captivity of the devil.[26]

The LDS/Mormon people are "temporally and spiritually" held in the chains of ignorance and hypocrisy, which causes this particular group of people to consume more antidepressants than any other group of people, per capita, in the world.[27]

The American people did not accept the "lesser portion of the word" that was delivered to them as the *Book of Mormon.* They did not *heed* our warnings and were not *diligent* in keeping the commandments of their Lord and Savior Jesus Christ—the "fulness of the everlasting Gospel … as delivered by the Savior to the ancient inhabitants" of the new world.[28] If they HAD done this, they would have received the "sealed portion" with eager hearts and open minds. Instead, they have become one of the wealthiest institutions in the world, completely ignoring ALL the counsel and teachings in the "unsealed part of the plates." Their blatant disregard for our new American scripture and the way that they were and are using it to deceive people into joining their church, forced us to give them, in their prideful, unprepared state, the *sealed portion* of our record.

Every person who has read our sealed portion "with a sincere heart, with real intent," asking God to tell them if it is true or not, has had the truth of it manifested unto them. Most of those who have read and accepted our sealed portion have been led, line upon line, precept on precept "until it is given unto [them] to know the mysteries of God until [they] know them in full."

---

[26] *BOM*, 1 Nephi 14:7.
[27] *See* Julie Cart, "Study Finds Utah Leads Nation in Antidepressant Use," 20 Feb. 2002, *LosAngeles Times*, latimes.com/archives/la-xpm-2002-feb-20-mn-28924-story.html.
See also Insider's chart of global antidepressant users per 1,000 people *found at* Gould Skye and Lauran F. Friedman, "Something startling is going on with antidepressant use around the world, 4 Feb. 2016, Business Insider, Insider Inc., businessinsider.com/countries-largest-antidepressant-drug-users-2016-2?r=US&IR=T.
[28] JSH 1:34.

Our new American scripture (the *Book of Mormon*) confounds the Bible (contradicts it) in a way that a Bible-believer can accept. *The Sealed Portion* confounds the "lesser portion of the word" in a way that a *Book of Mormon*-believer can accept. By the time a person sincerely and with real intent reads *The Sealed Portion* and begins to give *heed* and *diligence* to what it teaches, the scales (filters) of ignorance begin to fall away from the person's mind. The person's eyes are cured of "blindness"; their ears are cured of "deafness"; and the "lame" way in which they have walked is healed.

However, we could have never healed sincere seekers of the truth of their infirmities (weaknesses and failings caused by their ignorance) unless we first convinced them of the error of their ways. To do this we had to "lift them up, and in their own way" persuade them that our way was better (see Joseph's quote above). We did this by the force of reasoning, knowing that the power of the Real Truth™ would become unto them like a "sharp two-edged sword." Our words were delivered unto them from our chosen True Messenger—the "one like unto the Son of man." Thus, we fulfilled another of the Bible's great prophecies by having the Real Truth™ come out of the mouth of "the one like unto the Son of man."[29] We even instructed our contemporary True Messenger to do everything in his power to appear similar to how the Christians perceive Jesus would look.

In the next chapter, we will begin to explain how we revealed unto the children of men the "word of God," "according to the heed and diligence which they give unto him." We will begin with the original storyline of our new American scripture. In order to understand how we did this, so that it makes sense to the reader (and if necessary so that the Bible can be used to prove our story), we need to explain how the "plates of gold" were constructed, compiled, and used.

---

[29] *See* NT, Revelation 14:14–16.

Chapter 6
The Plates of Gold

We have explained how we made solid connections with the Bible's stories and teachings to make our new American scripture as logical, reasonable, and as acceptable as possible for a Bible-believing reader.

What is not taught in accepted and recorded LDS/Mormon history, is that we gave Joseph Smith the narrative of our new American scripture piece by piece ... line upon line, precept upon precept. After each part, we waited for Joseph to return and report to us on how his chosen peer review group (which consisted mainly of his family and friends) responded to each new part of the story they reviewed. Each member of this group had his or her own personal views and Christian beliefs. With a variety of opinions and responses about our writings, we felt that we could offer a new scripture that would fit in with most orthodox (normal) Christian beliefs.

Before we start to explain what we wanted to present and teach the reader as each part of our story progressed, it is important to reiterate that we had to make sure that what we wrote was palatable to our targeted audience: early European American Christians—those responsible for laying the foundation of the United States of America. We had to consider what the Christian mind could absorb, understand, and accept. We had to make sure that the lesson that we wanted the reader to learn, or the information that we wanted them to consider, was clear and easily understood.

Each part of our narrative had its own purpose. Each part was written to present an idea, usually a new idea, that the reader didn't know or consider before reading our story. Each part was expected to accomplish its intent without the reader suspecting that our information was replacing the old information that the reader thought was the infallible truth (the "word of God") of the Bible.

In other words, it was our intent to "*brain wash*" the reader (or better, to *wash* the reader's brain of the religious "old wine") by introducing new, acceptable information ("new wine"). We hoped this "new" information would penetrate the reader's already-established cognitive filters. We have explained that these cognitive filters are a person's thoughts and beliefs that influence one's ability to accept or reject new ideas. If information is allowed to pass through these filters, the reader of our new American scripture will *feel* the same spiritual manifestations that a Christian is accustomed to feeling while reading the "word of God" or thinking about Jesus.

We needed to be able to do this consistently. We also needed to be able to change, if necessary, the way the story flowed in a person's mind so that the change wouldn't confuse the reader and cause the reader to lose their concentration (spiritual *feeling*). Therefore, we came up with the idea of our story coming from lots of different plates that were made and engraved by God's *ancient prophets*, just like the Bible contained the written words of its prophets. Having the ancient record engraved upon different sets of plates allowed us to incorporate a different subplot that taught a specific lesson as needed. Having more than one author gave us the flexibility to make these changes consistent and believable.

As we explained early in this book, we needed to account for the way religious leaders would respond to our "new" information. We explained that the *sealed portion* of our story was the *failsafe* in case the people and leaders who claimed belief in our new American scripture corrupted its meaning and purpose. As we have pointed out, the LDS Church teaches its members that nothing that is written in scripture takes precedence over what its modern, *living* leaders say. This was not the case when we wrote our new American scripture.

Early Americans believed that the Bible, written by *dead* prophets, was the infallible and "complete" word of God. Any preacher who taught otherwise was not successful at retaining a congregation and profiting from his position as a pretended messenger of God's *holy word.* LDS/Mormons

Chapter 6: The Plates of Gold

believe they have priesthood authority (the power to act in God's name). They also believe in the ability of an individual to receive direct communication from God (the Father) or from Jesus (God's mediator). These beliefs negate any importance, authority, and application that new scripture might have. For these reasons, the modern LDS Church ignores the lessons of our *Book of Mormon* no matter how clearly these lessons are presented.

It is relevant here to introduce a great hypocrisy of this powerful and wealthy modern church. The LDS Church teaches that the greatest priesthood ordinance that one can receive is the LDS Temple Endowment. This ordinance is a spinoff from a play that we helped Joseph Smith write in 1842.

As we have reported, Joseph Smith did *not* tell his followers the Real Truth™. He was counseled by us to be very careful about revealing too much of what he actually knew. If he had revealed too much, Joseph's life would have been taken long before it was. If he had been killed earlier than anticipated, any chance our new American scripture had of being accepted and read would have been thwarted. The play we wrote with Joseph in 1842, which eventually became the modern LDS Temple Endowment, was a symbolic presentation of most of the Real Truth™s that Joseph was not allowed to tell his followers.

If the LDS/Mormons were honest about what they see when they sit in their temples and watch the revised 1842 play—transfigured over the years since Brigham Young set up a new church—they would be forced to admit the following:

While the characters *Adam* and *Eve* are going through mortality (life upon Earth), neither God (*Elohim*) nor Jesus (*Jehovah*) has anything to do with mortals. ALL prayers, of ANY kind, of ANY sincerity, are ALWAYS answered by the character *Lucifer*. The play clearly shows that God and Jesus do *not* hear or answer any mortal prayers. It also portrays these gods as having no idea of what is going on upon the earth during the time that

Adam and Eve and their posterity live in what we called "the lone and dreary world," which represents life upon the earth.

This fact about the LDS Temple Endowment's presentation is undeniable. However, this is also why the members are not allowed to speak about what goes on inside of their temples. They are not allowed to ask questions about what the play they see actually means. What we presented here is just one part of the many Real Truth™s that we presented through our 1842 play, ALL of which the LDS/Mormon people reject and ignore.

To help open their closed minds and confront the hypocrisy of their leaders not being able to explain what the LDS Temple Endowment actually means, we gave the LDS people an explanation that would make sense. We helped our contemporary True Messenger write the book, *Sacred Not Secret—The [Authorized and] Official Guide In Understanding the LDS Temple Endowment* (pub. 2007).[1] Our explanations given in that book are indisputable and clear. We did not write it to condemn the LDS people. We wrote it to help them open their eyes to the deceptions that their leaders were perpetuating because their leaders did not understand the purpose of our 1842 play.

LDS/Mormon leaders have a simple explanation as to why our True Messenger can explain all things, and they cannot: Lucifer knows ALL Real Truth™, but will use just one lie to deceive you.

We would counter: the LDS leaders might know one Real Truth™, but the rest of what they teach are lies. There is no getting around the fact of what the LDS Temple Endowment offers in its presentation. The way the LDS leaders have dealt with it is by simply changing it any way they see fit in order to mitigate (lessen) any possibility that their followers might actually pay attention to the Real Truth™s that our play is trying to teach.

---

[1] This book is available to read for free at realilluminati.org/sacred-not-secret.

In the same manner, LDS Church leaders, historians, and scholars know very little to nothing about the *real* source of the *Book of Mormon*. To counter this ignorance, we offer the following easy-to-understand explanation of why we chose "gold plates" as the source of our new American scripture:

It is logical and reasonable according to the time period (600 B.C.E.–400 C.E.) that we chose for our new American scripture story, for it to have been written on papyri. However, papyrus is rolled up on a stick to preserve it. The remnants of papyri that *were* available in the early part of the nineteenth (19th) century were mostly corroded because of time and weather. This would have made it impossible for us to change the flow of the storyline, if needed.

If we had presented the source as ancient papyri, it also would have made it difficult for us to show the actual papyri to three witnesses as our new American scripture prophesied:

> And behold, ye may be privileged that ye may show the plates unto those who shall assist to bring forth this work; And unto three shall they be shown by the power of God; wherefore they shall know of a surety that these things are true. And in the mouth of three witnesses shall these things be established.[2]

Metal plates, especially those made of soft metals that include gold, are virtually indestructible. It made sense that we used soft metals because they are malleable enough to engrave. These soft metals are not affected by the environment like papyri are. Further, archeologists of this time period (early 1800s/nineteenth [19th] century) had found plates of metal upon which other ancient cultures had kept their records; therefore, metal plates weren't so far-fetched (improbable) as being an actual record of an ancient people's history.

---

[2] *BOM*, Ether 5:2–4.

We have revealed that we created the plates that we gave to Joseph Smith in order to help him stay focused.[3] Our plates were made of a gold alloy and were used as a prop, not only to help the young teenager stay motivated and absorbed in the presentation of the story, but also so that we could provide the tangible witness to others of the source from which Joseph had obtained and "translated" the information.

We explained in the first book of our Trilogy, *The True History of Religion*, how we had tried to recruit others, before Joseph Smith Jr., to help us. We had approached Thomas Jefferson and asked him to help us to persuade the early Americans to accept the native Americans as more than just naked, indigenous "heathens" who were "cursed" by the Christian god. We presented ourselves to Jefferson as travelers from Europe. We convinced him that we were part of the Freemasons, but that we disagreed with Freemasonry and the pride and control that this secretive group had in government authority. Freemasonry started in Europe, and Jefferson was not a fan of anything that seemed esoteric (secretive) and deceptive coming out of Europe. Playing on his disdain for Masonic pride, arrogance, and secret meetings meant to control the people, we were able to gain an audience with Thomas Jefferson.

Over the course of about three days, including one day in the presence of Thomas Paine (whom we had already met in Europe), we were able to intrigue Jefferson and convince him that something had to be done. We spoke with Jefferson at some length about Christianity and the way that this particular religion was being used incorrectly to demonize the native Americans and cause the European Americans to justify the North and South American natives' slaughter and marginalization.

We explained how a new American scripture, separate from the Bible, could be introduced to tell the story of how God loves any indigenous native people just as much as God loves His chosen people, the migrating Jews. Jefferson was not agreeable to making up a lie to counter

---

[3] *See Pentateuch Illuminated, 131. See also JS Bio, 297.*

a lie. He did not believe fully in Christianity, but *was* still a fan of the Jesus stories and what Jesus taught.

To make a long story short, we could not convince Jefferson to help us introduce a new American scripture, comparable to the Bible, that would convince the Bible-believers that the native American people were descendants of the house of Israel and loved by God in spite of the color of their skin. A few years after meeting with us, and affected by our meetings, Jefferson wrote his own new American scripture. It would become known as the *Jefferson Bible*.[4] Jefferson's *inspired scripture* was rejected by the American Christians. It was not a secret that Jefferson had personal issues with orthodox Christianity. Jefferson's views on the hypocrisy of most Christian religions did not sit well with contemporary Christian leaders.

Jefferson and Paine, along with a few others, argued with many of the other Founding Fathers to make a complete and strong separation between church (religion) and state (government). Christians had a problem with Jefferson's desire to diminish their pride and belief in the idea of eminent domain (the right of government to take property). As we explained in the *Introduction* of this book, Christians believed that God gave them this right according to what would become a widely accepted Christian doctrine known as *Manifest Destiny*. Again, *Manifest Destiny* is the idea that the United States was chosen and blessed by God to expand its dominion, which included spreading Christianity, along with democracy and Capitalism, across the entire North American continent, and from there, throughout the entire world.[5]

Many early American Christians wanted the United States to be a Christian nation. They forced their will through a democratic republic where the people elected their representatives who made the laws and wielded the power. Most elected officials who made the laws were Christian. These

---

[4] *See* "Jefferson Bible," *Wikipedia*, Wikimedia Foundation, 8 May 2021, en.wikipedia.org/wiki/Jefferson_Bible.

[5] *See* "Manifest Destiny." *Wikipedia*, Wikimedia Foundation, 12 May 2021, en.wikipedia.org/wiki/Manifest_destiny.

members of the U.S. Congress based many of their laws largely on Christian doctrine as it was interpreted from the Bible. However, NONE of the laws incorporated and enacted by the U.S. Congress, ever since its inception to modern times, were based on the simple and straightforward words of Jesus' *Sermon on the Mount.*

Having been rejected by one of the most popular men of that time period (Thomas Jefferson), we decided to approach a lesser-known but equally influential man in the Christian community, Ethan Smith[6] (no relation to Joseph Smith, Jr.). Ethan Smith was an author and a preacher. We spent well over two weeks in his presence discussing our plans for a new American scripture.

At first, Ethan Smith seemed reasonably agreeable to what we were proposing. He was intrigued by our knowledge of not only history, but of the world's religions. He listened intently to us and learned many things that he had never known. As we did with Jefferson, we presented ourselves to Smith as disillusioned Freemasons whose only desire was to make life easier on the native Americans by helping the American Christians see the natives as their equals in the eyes of God. We also spent a great deal of time with Ethan Smith explaining the correct form of government that *should* have been the basis for the foundation of the United States.

We explained things to Ethan Smith that most Americans did not know about their politicians. We discussed the secret combinations that gave government, religion, and business their power and influence over the people. Ethan Smith would not consider writing anything that might counter the Bible, so he outrightly rejected our plans for a new American scripture, even threatening to expose us and our plans to other Christian leaders. We quickly made our departure and had nothing further to do with Ethan Smith. To our

---

[6] *See* "Ethan Smith (clergyman)," *Wikipedia*, 3 Apr. 2020, en.wikipedia.org/wiki/Ethan_Smith_(clergyman).

great dismay, Ethan Smith took a lot of the things that we had discussed with him and wrote his own book called *View of the Hebrews* (1823).[7]

When we found out what Ethan Smith was doing, it became very apparent to us that we needed to move quickly to recruit a messenger whom we could immediately convince to help us. We found a young teenager named Joseph Smith, Jr.

We first became aware of the young Joseph from listening to people mock him and argue with him as he tried to explain what we knew was the Real Truth™. It was while listening to this mere boy, and using other means at our disposal to find such an individual, that we became aware that the young American teenager had received the "transfiguration" of his brain that would be needed to help us properly.

We had known of Joseph's family for many years prior to 1823, the year when we first introduced ourselves to Joseph. The details of the events involving the rest of Joseph's family (more particularly involving his grandfather, Asael Smith; his father, Joseph Smith, Sr.; his mother, Lucy Mack Smith; and his eldest sibling, Alvin Smith) are not necessary in explaining how and why we wrote our new American scripture. However, it *is* important to note that the same year that Ethan Smith published his above-mentioned book (1823), we were forced to make ourselves known to Joseph Smith and recruit him as our new messenger. We had hoped to allow Joseph to mature a few more years, but Ethan Smith's move to publish a book containing information that we gave him forced us to introduce ourselves and attempt to recruit Joseph at a very young age (not quite 18 years old).

During our discussions with Ethan Smith, we realized that we had to provide some kind of tangible evidence of what we wanted to incorporate

---

[7] *See* Ethan Smith, *View of the Hebrews: Exhibiting the Destruction of Jerusalem; the Certain Restoration of Judah and Israel; the Present State of Judah and Israel; and an Address of the Prophet Isaiah Relative to Their Restoration* (Poultney, VT: Smith & Shute, 1823); also found online at archive.org/details/viewhebrewsexhi00smitgoog/page/n4/mode/2up.

into our new American scripture (hence, the construction of the "plates" at that time). Both Jefferson and Ethan Smith had a hard time accepting something that didn't have any evidence to back up its existence. If we claimed to know the true history of the native American people, then we needed some sort of "proof" (empirical evidence) that the history was true. It was our intent to invent the history as we wrote our story about it, according to what we wanted to teach the people. We created the plates upon which this history was supposedly recorded in ancient times. We did this as a way to offer visible and tangible proof of our invented story.

Before we introduced ourselves to Joseph in September of 1823, we constructed the plates the way that we wanted them to look and be presented. Two-thirds (2/3) of the plates were sealed with bands of brass. We made engravings on the unsealed plates that would be easily recognizable as similar to Egyptian hieroglyphics. At the time we presented the plates to Joseph, we had not yet engraved the plates that were *sealed* with the brass bands. We sealed them and Joseph was commanded not to break the seals. Had he broken the seals, Joseph would have seen that there were no other engravings on the *sealed part*.

We needed the "sealed part" in order to be able to "engrave" the story that *we wanted* to reveal to the world later. The "sealed part" of our story would be dependent on what would transpire after the world had our "unsealed part," events that we did not yet know. We have explained how the "unsealed part" (the *Book of Mormon*) came first, so that we could

> try their faith, and if it shall so be that they shall believe these things then shall the greater things be made manifest unto them. And if it so be that they will not believe these things, then shall the greater things be withheld from them, unto their condemnation.[8]

---

[8] *BOM*, 3 Nephi 26:9–10.

Chapter 6: The Plates of Gold

Not knowing how the world was going to react to our *Book of Mormon*, we needed to wait and see. As we explained, once we realized how the religion that embraces and shares our new American scripture with the rest of the world used it to become one of the wealthiest institutions on Earth, and how this church had corrupted most of our new scripture's intended lessons, we had to confront this wickedness. We were forced to break the seals and write the "greater portion of the word."

Had the people who call themselves "Latter-day Saints" accepted the lessons of our *Book of Mormon* and incorporated these lessons into their lives, we would have given them *The Sealed Portion* as a positive reinforcer of their actions. Instead, *The Sealed Portion* condemns them for what they have done. The *sealed part*—the greater portion of our new word of God—could have united the people of the world and praised them for establishing a society of humans with one heart and one mind, so that there was no poor among them (i.e., "Zion"). Instead, we were forced to use the most precious "greater portion" of our story to convince the reader to leave this sinful church.

The true facts will show that most LDS people who read *The Sealed Portion* as if it were the actual remaining two-thirds of our gold plates, leave that church without looking back. We intended to redeem those whose minds had been closed and hearts had been hardened by the leaders of a corrupt church that misinterpreted, abused, transfigured, and destroyed the original message of our new American scripture.

Because it was widely known and accepted that a single hieroglyphic character told a story instead of representing a single word or letter, each of our engraved characters told its own story—a story that only we knew. Although we could have used characters that we knew were part of the Sumerian and Egyptian ancient dynasties, we made up our own characters. In this way, our new American scripture could be a continually evolving and changing story according to the feedback that we received from Joseph's peer review group.

Joseph was a very young and uneducated man under the age of twenty when we showed him our plates. We did not tell Joseph at this first meeting that the meaning of the characters engraved on the plates was whatever we wanted them to mean. It was important for Joseph to concentrate on the task at hand. We wanted his focus to remain on relaying the words that we wanted him to write and to not worry about any changes that we were making along the way.

Joseph was not only convinced by the actual presence of engraved gold plates, but he was fully convinced because of a tool that we presented to him, through which we gave him the words to write. Without going into a complete and full explanation of what this tool was, and in order to protect it from being hunted by our enemies, we have a few words to say about the "two rocks" that we provided to Joseph, upon which words "magically" appeared (according to how it seemed at that time period).

What the world does not know and accept is that human societies existed on Earth in the past that were far more developed and technologically advanced than the current time period. We will only reveal here, that what we gave the young Joseph was a primitive-looking cell phone through which we *texted* the words that he would write for our new American scripture.

It was much easier for our next True Messenger (whom we recruited to write *The Sealed Portion*) to accept the ancient, advanced technology hidden in these "two rocks," and from which he received our text messages for our "sealed portion of the plates." Cell phone technology was on the verge of discovery in 1991, when we first introduced ourselves to him, and widespread and abundant in 2004 when *The Sealed Portion* was published.

However, we had a harder time convincing this more contemporary and older man to focus and concentrate his efforts on *transcribing* what he already knew were engraved characters that could be anything we wanted them to be. However, we still required the same devotion and focus from

Chapter 6: The Plates of Gold

this "Bearer of Christ" (i.e., *Christopher*) that we did from the young Joseph. (Christopher's pride was a bit harder to manipulate and control than an uneducated, young American teenager's.)

Our *Urim and Thummim* are simply a couple of rocks "of curious workmanship." As we presented in our new American scripture's narrative, "the rocks" are a tool used by God's chosen messenger—a small means to bring about great things. The user can

> look upon [the rocks] and behold the things which are written. ... And there was also written upon them a new writing, which was plain to be read, which did give us understanding concerning the ways of the Lord; and it was written and changed from time to time. ... And thus we see that by small means the Lord can bring about great things.[9]

In our new American scripture, we introduced the idea that God can provide His chosen servant with an actual tool that can be held and used. This was because of a discussion that ensued and escalated into an argument, as our story progressed and Joseph's peers reviewed what we wrote. The dispute was about *how it was possible* that Joseph was "translating" the plates with a couple of rocks. We were forced to provide a logical and reasonable explanation that would put their minds at ease. To make such a tool feasible and logical, in our story we introduced the possibility (and reality) of God providing actual technology for a purpose. We would later name this advanced technology the *Liahona* and state, "behold, there cannot any man work after the manner of so curious a workmanship."[10]

The peer review group was able to accept the idea of a prophet of God using advanced technology to do what God wanted done. It made sense to this group because of the way that we introduced and presented the information about our *Liahona*. However, at the time we first introduced this technology

---

[9] *BOM*, 1 Nephi 16:26, 29.
[10] See *BOM*, Alma 37:39.

in "God's word" (at about 590 B.C.E. in the story's timeline), we had not yet considered by what name we would call it. The reader will take note that it wasn't for another 500 years in the future of the story's timeline (about 80 B.C.E.) that we were forced to come up with a name for this advanced technology. We were "forced" because of something else that we presented early on in the story with which the peer review group had taken issue.

At a certain point in our story, we wanted to provide a logical segue (bridge) to a new history of a great white civilization that had existed in North America for almost 2000 years. This would be a civilization that existed before Lehi and his family migrated to South America. We called it the Jaredite Nation. As we explained previously, it was our intent to write a story about these people that mirrored the nation of the United States of America, the citizens of which were mostly all white people. We intended to present the factors that destroyed the Jaredite Nation, which would be the same factors that we knew would lead to the demise of the American nation as well.

Earlier in the story's timeline (about 300 B.C.E., in the book of Omni), we introduced "a large stone … with engravings on it" that was brought to God's chosen prophet and king, Mosiah (according to the story), who was able to "interpret the engravings by the gift and power of God."[11] However, King Mosiah did not have any tool to help him interpret what was written on the "large stone." It was our hope that Joseph's peers would pay more attention to what was being written and taught than *how* it was being written. But, as they often did, Joseph's peer review group disappointed us. We were forced to give them what they wanted and how they wanted it.

The first mention of how God's chosen leader could "interpret … engravings by the gift and power of God," caused some to doubt the authenticity of Joseph's singular and special ability to "interpret" the engravings on the gold plates. If Joseph had only to rely on "the gift and power of God," which Bible believers accept as *inspiration* and *revelation*

---

[11] *BOM*, Omni 1:20.

Chapter 6: The Plates of Gold

that comes into a chosen person's head, then other men might have the same gift and could also interpret ancient engravings. We had to make sure that no other man could make such a claim. This is why we eventually tied the "ball of curious workmanship"[12] to an *actual tool* that was used to interpret ancient engravings.

We initially meant to give a short history of the fallen Jaredite Nation, which we presented as being engraved on the "large stone" that we introduced earlier in our story. We intended to only relate a few of the

> mysteries and the works of darkness, and their secret works, or the secret works of those people who [had] been destroyed, [that these works] may be made manifest unto [the rest of the world].[13]

However, as our storyline progressed, we experienced the stubbornness and resistance of Joseph's peer review group. They did not like the idea that ALL organized religion, rituals, priesthood authority, and everything else introduced in the Old Testament (that was set up through the stories of Moses), was useless and meaningless to a person's salvation. We knew that we had to drive this point home with a clear explanation that the American Christians could not dispute after reading our story.

We had to enhance the history of the Jaredites. We originally intended there to be just a

> few words concerning [the Jaredite ancestors who] came out from the tower, at the time the Lord confounded the language of the people.[14]

We were forced to change it to an entire story with a lot of words. We had to emphasize that God does NOT require any type of church, religion, ordinance, or any type of "church busy work" in order for a person to be saved.

---

[12] *BOM*, 1 Nephi 16:10.
[13] *BOM*, Alma 37:21.
[14] *BOM*, Omni 1:22.

Because our story only presented a "large stone" that gave only a "few words" about such a great nation of millions of people, we had to invent another source, with a lot of words, about the rise and fall of the Great Jaredite Nation. This is when we came up with the idea of introducing twenty-four gold plates[15] that were found in North America and brought to God's chosen messenger to interpret the engravings thereon. (At this point in the narrative, the Nephite prophet lived in the southern regions of South America.) The introduction of twenty-four gold plates instead of just a "large stone" provided us with plenty of leeway to invent whatever story we thought was necessary.

In our story, we connected these twenty-four gold plates with an *actual tool* that a servant of God would use to interpret the engravings. Again, by introducing an actual tool, we hoped that we could convince other men to not make a claim to this particular "gift and power of God." Sadly, making this connection didn't stop other men in Joseph's day from also claiming to have their own "tool."

Shortly after our book was published in 1830, a few men close to Joseph claimed that they too had possession of a tool (a stone) by which they received revelation from God. One example was Hiram Page, who had been one of the Eight Witnesses to the authenticity and existence of our gold plates. (These men were never actually shown the plates.[16]) Page claimed to have possession of a stone that gave him revelations from God. As he was often forced to do, Joseph made up ("received") another one of "the Lord's" revelations to stop any man from claiming to have the same tool that Joseph had. Joseph said, on behalf of "the Lord":

> But, behold, verily, verily, I say unto thee, no one shall be appointed to receive commandments and revelations in this church excepting my servant Joseph Smith, Jun., for he receiveth them even as Moses.[17]

---

[15] *BOM*, Mosiah 8:9.
[16] *See JS Bio*, 312–13.
[17] *D&C*, 28:2.

Chapter 6: The Plates of Gold

In a later chapter, we will get to the part of our story where we introduced the means by which the twenty-four gold plates containing the Jaredite history were interpreted. It was accomplished by means of an actual tool, "a stone, which shall shine forth in darkness unto light."[18] In that chapter, we will give more details about the transition that we made from "a few words" to a lot of words about the Jaredite history.

At the particular part of our story when we introduced a "large stone" that contained the history of an earlier people living in the Western Hemisphere, we introduced a name by which the Lord God referred to his servant, one who had possession of this actual tool. That servant's name was *Gazelem*. We did this with a good purpose in mind. It was done so that at any time in the future, if and when needed, Joseph could reiterate his sole authority as the only one appointed to receive commandments and revelations. God's word (the *Book of Mormon*) had already provided a second witness of God's will concerning "my servant Gazelem," (a pseudonym for Joseph Smith, Jr.), who would be the ONLY ONE provided with the *actual tool* to interpret the plates.

In early editions of what the LDS/Mormons call their *Doctrine and Covenants*, the Lord referred to Joseph Smith as "Gazelam" [*sic*]. Of course, Joseph was the author of these revelations, many times having received instructions and counsel from us on what to have "the Lord" say to his followers. In later LDS editions of their *Doctrine and Covenants*, the name and any reference to our story's "Gazelem" were removed and changed to Joseph's own name. We did NOT command this change. We meant for "the Lord" to say "Gazelem" when the Lord God referred to his servant, Joseph, in modern revelation, just as we meant it in our new American scripture.

Above we have explained how we subtly introduced to the mind of a Christian that an actual physical tool (advanced technology) could be provided by God to one of God's servants to help the servant do God's will.

---

[18] *BOM*, Alma 37:23.

In presenting our story as an actual account of ancient peoples, we had to present a believable explanation of *how* the historical records of these people were preserved. We chose metal plates. We gave the following explanation of why metal plates had to be used:

> we know that the things which we write upon plates must remain; But whatsoever things we write upon anything save it be upon plates must perish and vanish away; but we can write a few words upon plates, which will give our children, and also our beloved brethren, a small degree of knowledge concerning us, or concerning their fathers.[19]

The 1830 first publication of the *Book of Mormon* included a Title Page that prominently showed that our book was written "BY JOSEPH SMITH, JUNIOR, AUTHOR AND PROPRIETOR."[20] There has been a lot of confusion about whether Joseph actually *wrote* the book instead of translating it. Joseph did not initially say that he "translated" the book. A few months after the book was published, we had to quiet a tide of persecution that Joseph's enemies and critics had crashed upon him because of saying he was the "author." Joseph therefore received a "revelation from the Lord" confirming that he was called "to *write* the Book of Mormon" not to translate it.[21]

In the beginning, Joseph was always consistent when he explained where the words came from that he wrote: "they appeared on the Urim and Thummim."[22] Joseph told his peers that he *transcribed*, meaning he copied (or rather read to his scribes), what he saw. The Title Page of the modern

---

[19] *BOM*, Jacob 4:1–2.
[20] *See* "Book of Mormon, 1830," The Joseph Smith Papers – Church Historian's Press, josephsmithpapers.org/paper-summary/book-of-mormon-1830/7.
[21] *D&C*, 24:1.
[22] For a later explanation, *see* Joseph Smith, *Elders' Journal*, July 1838, 42–3; also found online at josephsmithpapers.org/paper-summary/elders-journal-july-1838/10.

Book of Mormon does not say that Joseph was the book's "AUTHOR AND PROPRIETOR." It states, "TRANSLATED BY JOSEPH SMITH, JUN."[23]

Joseph's followers took issue with the Lord's revelation that Joseph had "written" (authored) the book instead of "translated" it.[24] As Joseph did many times, whenever there was controversy about which his followers demanded clarification, he received another "revelation from the Lord."

We told Joseph to always give the people what they wanted … regardless of whether it was right or not. So, a few years after the first edition of our book was published, Joseph made revisions to some grammatical and other minor mistakes in its *second edition*, appeasing the desires of his followers. Then, ten years after the first publication, Joseph would provide a *third edition* in 1840. In this edition, he placed a descriptive page before the *original* Title Page. This new page named him as the "Translator" instead of the "Author and Proprietor." This third edition stated on the descriptive page, that it was "CAREFULLY REVISED BY THE TRANSLATOR.[25]

During each revision, Joseph would counsel with us and ask our permission for any changes that the people wanted to make to our *Book of Mormon*. We had long since realized that the people had rejected the intent for which our book was written; they had "looked beyond the mark" that we intended to set for our new American scripture. In other words, they did not hit the intended "mark" that we describe below. This "mark" represents what we intended for the reader to get from our book—those things that were most noteworthy and important.

In our *Book of Mormon*'s original storyline, this "mark" was simple, even so much that we wrote of it as an answer to the question,

---

[23] See "Title Page of the Book of Mormon," The Church of Jesus Christ of Latter-day Saints, churchofjesuschrist.org/study/scriptures/bofm/bofm-title?lang=eng.

[24] See D&C, 24:1.

[25] For a side-by-side comparison of the 1830, 1837 and 1840 editions of the *Book of Mormon*, see The Parallel Book Of Mormon: The 1830, 1837, and 1840 Editions, Introduction by Curt A. Bench (Salt Lake City: Smith-Pettit Foundation, 2008).

And do ye know the reason for the corruption of our people? ... The answer is simple. Oh, that ye would open your hearts to the simplicity of the answer. Oh, that ye would not look beyond the mark, which mark hath been set since the beginning of time to teach the children of God all things that they need to know in order to have peace and happiness forever.[26]

This "mark" was the most important thing in our book. The "mark" upon which we based the entirety of our original story was nothing more or less than what Jesus told his disciples was the greatest of all commandments. These are the words of our King Mosiah, given to his people before his death according to our *original* story that was presented as being abridged by Mormon in our *Book of Lehi*:

Love your neighbor as yourself. And do unto others as you would have them do unto you—this is the mark, my brothers and sisters; this is the standard by which ye shall be judged and by which ye shall live in the eternities.[27]

The simple teachings of Jesus (Matthew 5, 6, and 7) were "the mark" we aimed to present in our new American scripture. We wanted to get the early European Americans to start seeing the native Americans as their equal neighbors and loving them as they did themselves. We wanted to explain the unimportance of organized religion, of ordinances, of church work, or of *anything* other than simply loving others and doing good to them: "And these are the commandments of God, yea, even the only way unto salvation."[28]

Our intent was to call upon the logic and reason of a person's cognitive paradigms (thinking patterns). We wanted to persuade Christians, in their own way, to actually accept the simple words (teachings) of their Lord and Savior, Jesus Christ, when he explained, <u>according to the Bible</u>, what the two

---

[26] *TSP*, Lehi, 9:40, 45.
[27] *TSP*, Lehi 9:51.
[28] *TSP*, Lehi 9:50.

greatest commandments were. Jesus did not say to go to church. Jesus did not say to pay your tithing. Jesus did not say to get baptized, perform rituals, get priesthood blessings, or do church service. Neither did Jesus require anything of a person in order to have "eternal salvation" other than to simply love your neighbor as yourselves. This was the "mark" set by Jesus.

To hit this "mark," we had no choice but to attempt to shoot a sharp arrow of truth through the thick layers of religious prejudice, ignorance, and hypocrisy. To penetrate these filters, we had to start with the stories of the Old Testament. American Christians were convinced that these stories were true, so we started there.

We started with the law of Moses. We presented these ancient laws as being written on "plates of brass." We chose *brass* as the metal that the plates were made of upon which the law of Moses was engraved. We chose this particular metal because it was the most popular metal used by the artificers (skilled craftsman and inventors) who were responsible for the contemporary arts and crafts of the time period that we began our story.

We chose to begin our story's timeline at 600 B.C.E. We chose this particular time because it could be somewhat accurately verified as the time when the Babylonians destroyed Jerusalem. As we have already explained, we used the prophecies of the Old Testament given by the Hebrew prophets. We especially used Ezekiel's and Isaiah's prophecies about a small remnant (group) of people being saved and led to a "land of promise," and about the "sticks" of Judah and Joseph being made into one.

Now consider *how* we invented our story as we briefly explain below all of the "plates" mentioned in our narrative. We will give more details of these specific events and *why* we invented and presented these events the way that we did in later chapters. For now, we will explain below *how* the history of our story unfolded as it relates to being recorded on numerous metal plates.

Before we do this, we want to explain, so that it is clear, *why* we wrote the following and included it in the modified storyline that replaced our original one.

In an earlier chapter, we disclosed that our original storyline (the 116-page "lost" manuscript) was rejected by Joseph's peer review group. In our new storyline, we included the *reason* for which we revised it. It was because these people were seeking for things that they could not understand, and because they desired these things, we did it so that they would stumble.[29]

The beginning of our original story (the *Book of Lehi*) was written in plainness. Its prophecies were given to the understanding of early American Christians, according to the "Spirit" by which they *could* accept these things (except they did *not*). We gave them what we wanted to teach them about religion; wherefore, we gave them things as they really are, and wrote of things as they really will be, according to their understanding about what would save their souls.[30]

Joseph later related the story of his *First Vision* as an answer to his sincere prayer about "which of all the sects was right." We had him make up the story about what "Jesus Christ" told him during this vision. We tried to make the Real Truth™ plain and clear about ALL organized religion. Jesus answered Joseph clearly that the sects (churches) were "ALL wrong … that ALL their creeds were an abomination in his sight; that those" who believed in religion, ANY AND ALL religions, "were all corrupt."[31]

Joseph reported that Jesus told him "many other things … which [he could not] write at [that] time."[32] But in NOTHING that Jesus said to Joseph, as he reported it, did Jesus EVER condone the restoration of a church or the organization of any new religion. We eventually provided the world with the

---

[29] *See BOM*, Jacob 4:14.
[30] *Compare BOM*, Jacob 4:13.
[31] *See* JSH 1:18–19, emphasis added.
[32] JSH 1:20.

Chapter 6: The Plates of Gold

exact words that Joseph "[could not] write at [that] time." We have added these "many other things" as Appendix 3 to *The Sealed Portion—The Final Testament of Jesus Christ* (2004). Jesus said to Joseph, among many other things:

> And thou shalt desire to establish a church among men according to the commandments and the words that thou shalt receive concerning these things as they shall be given unto thee. But this thing is not that which shall bring happiness unto you; for this reason, I forbid this thing. But unto you it shall be given according to the desires of the Gentiles.[33]

Because Joseph's peer review group missed the "mark," they were given many things that made them stumble. They were given the Church of Jesus Christ of Latter-day Saints.

Our original story included the first chapter of Isaiah, in which Isaiah condemns the Jewish church and discounts all rituals, authority, and "church busy work" that the Jews believed were necessary for their salvation.

We intended to present a story that explained that the "mark" set by Jesus (according to the New Testament stories about him) was the <u>only</u> thing that needed to be observed and "hit" in order for a person to be "saved." Joseph's peer review group could not accept this simplicity. So, instead, we gave them what they wanted. We gave them a revision of our storyline. We were able to do this easily by simply having Mormon, the ancient main engraver, search

> among the records [the plates] which had been delivered into his hands, and he found these plates the Small Plates of Nephi. ... Wherefore, he chose these things, to finish his record upon them [or rather, Mormon put the plates that he found, underneath the other plates that he had originally started engraving].

---

[33] *TSP*, The First Vision 1:25.

> ... And Mormon did this for a wise purpose; ... And now he did not know all things; but the Lord knoweth all things which are to come [those things that were going to happen while Joseph was translating the plates]; wherefore, he worketh in Mormon to do according to his will.[34]

We were essentially the "Lord" in the story; therefore, if you were to replace the word "Lord" with the "Real Illuminati®," you will have more clarity with the following: The "Lord" DID know "all things ... to come." The "Lord" knew that Joseph's peers would have a problem with the simplicity of gaining "salvation" without an organized church. (They had already rejected our original storyline when we wrote this part.) Of course, we controlled what "the Lord" knew in the "past" and what "the Lord" knew as we wrote our new American scripture.

Before we explain in detail what we intended when we wrote each part of our new American scripture, here is a brief description of all of the plates and records in Mormon's possession when he sat down to abridge the history of the native Americans' ancestors, published in 1830 as the *Book of Mormon*. (As a reminder, this is all according to the STORY that we invented.)

The Plates of Brass (Old Testament of the Bible)

According to our story, there were just two ancient Hebrew families that escaped being carried off as slaves and becoming captives of the Babylonians during the Siege of Jerusalem. *Lehi* was the patriarch of one family and *Ishmael* was the patriarch of the other. Both of these men were wealthy High Priests living in Jerusalem and serving as General Authorities of the Jewish Church. They both had access to the *brass plates* upon which the Old Testament, including the law of Moses, was written.

---

[34] *Compare BOM*, Words of Mormon 1:3, 5, 7.

Chapter 6: The Plates of Gold

After Lehi was warned that Jerusalem was going to be destroyed, Lehi had his sons steal the *brass plates* from the church archives so that they would have access to God's commandments, as given through Moses, as they traveled to a new promised land. God led these two families from the Middle East of the Eastern Hemisphere to South America of the Western Hemisphere.

The Plates of Lehi and Nephi

When they got to South America, Lehi copied the format of the *brass plates* and made other plates upon which Lehi started to record his own family's history. Lehi wrote a lot. One of his sons, Nephi, wrote about his father's writings:

> for he hath written many things which he saw in visions and in dreams; and he also hath written many things which he prophesied and spake unto his children, of which I shall not make a full account. But I [Nephi] shall ... make an abridgment of the record of my father [Lehi], upon plates which I have made with mine own hands; wherefore, after I have abridged the record of my father then will I make an account of my own life.[35]

The Large and Small Plates of Nephi

Lehi's son, Nephi, made two separate collections of plates. The first set of plates was called the "Large Plates of Nephi," and the other set was called the "Small Plates of Nephi." To explain these two sets of plates, we had Nephi state:

> And now, as I have spoken concerning these plates [the Small Plates of Nephi], behold they are not the plates upon which I make a full account of the history of my people; for the plates upon which I make a full account of my people I have given the name of

---

[35] *BOM*, 1Nephi 1:16–17.

Nephi [Large Plates of Nephi]; wherefore, they are called the [Large] plates of Nephi, after mine own name; and these plates also are called the [Small] plates of Nephi.

Nevertheless, I have received a commandment of the Lord that I should make these [Small] plates, for the special purpose that there should be an account engraven of the ministry of my people.

Upon the other [Large] plates should be engraven an account of the reign of the kings, and the wars and the contentions of my people; wherefore these [Small] plates are for the more part of the ministry; and the other [Large] plates are for the more part of the reign of the kings and the wars and contentions of my people.

Wherefore, the Lord hath commanded me to make these [Small] plates for a wise purpose in him, which purpose I know not.

But the Lord knoweth all things from the beginning; wherefore, he prepareth a way to accomplish all his works among the children of men; for behold, he hath all power unto the fulfilling of all his words. And thus it is. Amen.[36]

The Gold Plates of Mormon

Our story is called the *Book of <u>Mormon</u>* because of *Mormon*, a character in our story who lived about 1000 years <u>after</u> Lehi and Nephi lived. (We had Mormon live at about 400 C.E. in North America.)

As our story goes, for 1000 years, the descendants of Lehi kept their history engraved upon various metal "plates." Mormon was given ALL OF THESE PLATES and was told to go through them and make an abridgment of the history of the people. You can imagine how many plates were in front of

---

[36] *BOM*, 1 Nephi 9:2–6.

Mormon as he went through all of them. He condensed them into an abridged history that he engraved on the *gold plates*. These same plates were to be given to Joseph Smith, Jr. to "translate" … again, only according to the narrative that we invented for our new American scripture.

The Many Nephite Plates

Let's discuss more about these 1000 years' worth of plates that were in Mormon's possession. Imagine Mormon going through all of these plates. He had to choose which ones he was going to review and use in his own abridged record, written by his own hand on plates made of gold. According to the story we made up, Mormon had the actual template that had been passed down through the centuries, which was the same template that had created the brass plates containing the Old Testament of the Bible.

All of the engravers had used this template to melt ore for the plates and make the plates upon which they engraved the words of their particular time period and history. Therefore, all of the plates that contained Lehi's and Ishmael's history were the exact same size. Being of the exact same dimensions, Mormon could have easily added a set of the ancient plates to his new plates and no one would have been able to tell the difference, as long as the plates were made of the same metals.

Some LDS/Mormon people believe that there is a cave somewhere in the United States that contains numerous plates—the entire 1000 years of engraved history of the native American ancestors, beginning with two families: Lehi's and Ishmael's. That's a lot of plates. Their worth would be astronomical, IF they actually existed. Some opportunistic Mormons have claimed that the Lord showed them in a vision all of the Nephite plates together in one cave.[37] They have called this place *The Dream Mine*.

---

[37] "There are numerous second-, third-, and fourth-hand accounts of there being a cave inside the hill Cumorah containing numerous plates and Nephite/Lamanite relics. All of these

These charlatans have convinced many, many devout Mormons to invest money in this *dream mine*. And many, many did. The deceived investors were convinced that if they bought shares in the yet-to-be-discovered cave, that when it was finally discovered, they would be rich.[38] No cave was ever discovered; and no cave ever will be, because it does not exist. (We are now explaining how we made up the story of all the different "plates.") Sadly, many opportunistic Mormons have used our story and our book any way they could to make money.

Now back to our storyline:

The Large Stone and the Twenty-Four Plates of Gold Containing the History of the Jaredite Nation in North America from about 2200 B.C.E. to 150 B.C.E.

Not all the records in Mormon's possession were made of metal. All of the *plates* were made of metal, but Mormon found a small recorded history of a people written on a "large stone." This contained a small history of what we called the Jaredite Nation.

As we previously mentioned, as our story progressed, or rather, as we wrote it to conform to the palatability of Joseph's peers, we were forced to produce a much more detailed history of the downfall of this Great Jaredite Nation. To do this, we introduced twenty-four gold plates that contained a fuller account of what happened to this great nation of white people who had immigrated to the Western Hemisphere from the Eastern Hemisphere about 1,500 years before Lehi did.

---

accounts can be found together, with LDS commentary, in Cameron J. Parker, "Cumorah's Cave," *Journal of Book of Mormon Studies* vol. 13 no. 1 (2004), 50–7, 170–1, found online at scholarsarchive.byu.edu/jbms/vol13/iss1/6/.

[38] *See* "Dream Mine," *Wikipedia*, 20 Dec. 2020, en.m.wikipedia.org/wiki/Dream_Mine.

Chapter 6: The Plates of Gold

To explain where the twenty-four gold plates came from, we wrote about the explorers who found the ruins of this Great Jaredite Nation:

And they [a few white explorers, who were descendants of Nephi, the son of Lehi] were lost in the wilderness for the space of many days, yet they were diligent, and found not the land of Zarahemla but returned to this land, having traveled in a land among many waters, having discovered a land which was covered with bones of men, and of beasts, and was also covered with ruins of buildings of every kind, having discovered a land which had been peopled with a people who were as numerous as the hosts of Israel. And for a testimony that the things that they had said are true they have brought twenty-four plates which are filled with engravings, and they are of pure gold.[39]

Again, the details of *why* we added the "twenty-four gold plates" to the Jaredite history that was already written on the "large stone" have already been touched upon and will be explained further in another chapter. In this chapter, we wanted to present ALL of the sources that Mormon used to create his abridgment of history, which is what became the *Book of Mormon*.

In front of our character Mormon were a lot of plates, most of which were uniform in size because they were produced from the same template. However, the twenty-four gold plates couldn't have been the same size because they were made by a different people, at a different time period.

When Mormon was ten years old, he first received instructions about all of the plates. He was told that when he reached twenty-four years old, he was to go to where the plates were hidden and ONLY

---

[39] *BOM*, Mosiah 8:8–9.

take the plates of Nephi unto yourself, and the remainder shall ye leave in the place where they are; and ye shall engrave on the plates of Nephi all the things that ye have observed concerning this people.[40]

In our story, our main author "Mormon" would eventually hide ALL of the records "in the hill Cumorah," except for the plates that he made. He gave these plates to his son, Moroni, so that Moroni could add to these plates and make the "sealed portion" of the plates.

At this point, the reader still might be confused about *how* our new American scripture was put together. If this is the case, we hope that the following chapters, in which we will give the exact details about *why* we wrote the story, will clear up any lingering confusion.

---

[40] *BOM*, Mormon 1:4.

Chapter 7
Looking Beyond the Mark

Before we can properly explain more about *how* we put together our new American scripture, it is important that we explain more about *why* we wrote it.

The main goal of our new American scripture—the mark we meant to hit (i.e., achieve our aim)—was to make the world a better place by teaching people how to treat each other with respect and love. No religion on Earth—none that existed at the time we wrote our new American scripture (early nineteenth [19th] century), none that has existed any time in the past, and none today ... NO RELIGION AT ANY TIME—has been able to hit the mark for which we were aiming in order to help create peace and harmony on Earth.

Many religious teachings appear outwardly to be good. Most are centered on what the world recognizes as the *Golden Rule*: do unto others as you would want done unto you. Most religions teach some form of the *Golden Rule*. Religious *teachings* are not the problem. Organized religions that put their leaders above the members and incorporate rituals, ceremonies, rites, passages, baptisms, pilgrimages, and the likes, as well as demand financial contributions of any kind, <u>are</u> the problem.

Sometimes referred to as saving rituals (ordinances), these requirements have nothing to do with the *Golden Rule*. In fact, no religious ritual teaches the participant anything about the way a person should treat another person. Rituals and ordinances are prescribed and overseen by the leaders of organized churches. In most cases, the members are required to pay a tithe or other donation before they can properly perform the ritual or ordinance. Regardless of how kind, compassionate, or good a person might be, religions teach that anyone who does not perform the prescribed rituals will be damned. It is not "doing unto another what one would want done unto you," if one condemns another to hell and damnation in thought or by voice when another does not perform prescribed and mandated religious rituals and ordinances.

As we have explained, we were responsible for helping Joseph Smith invent the final account of how he was "called by God" to perform the work that he did. This account is known by the LDS Church as the *First Vision*. Although very different from the first few accounts[1] that Joseph told his followers, his final account reports the response to his inquiry about "which of all the sects was right":

> I was answered that I must join none of them, for they were all wrong; and the Personage who addressed me [Jesus Christ] said that all their creeds were an abomination in his sight; that those professors were all corrupt; that: "they draw near to me with their lips, but their hearts are far from me, they teach for doctrines the commandments of men, having a form of godliness, but they deny the power thereof." He again forbade me to join with any of them; and many other things did he say unto me, which I cannot write at this time.[2]

We mentioned that when we published *The Sealed Portion* of our new American scripture, we included as Appendix 3 the "many other things" that we had intended for Jesus Christ to say to Joseph Smith. The final version of Joseph's many accounts—known as the *First Vision*—was written and published almost 20 years after the event occurred in the Spring of 1820. Part of the "many other things did he say unto me, which I cannot write at this time," was this:

> And it is the will of the Father that all the children of men come unto the Father through me that they might have this eternal life

---

[1] The various accounts can all be found, along with historical introduction, at "Accounts of Joseph Smith's First Vision," Church Historian's Press – The Church of Jesus Christ of Latter-day Saints, josephsmithpapers.org/site/accounts-of-the-first-vision.

[2] JSH 1:19–20.

of which I have spoken. Behold, there is no other way except by me that this salvation shall come unto them.

And I came unto the Jews that I might teach them that they did not need to follow the leaders of their churches to destruction, but that if they seek the Holy Ghost and keep my commandments, then they would find peace and rest in me, having the fullness of my gospel revealed unto them.

But the Jews rejected me because of the things that I taught unto them, desiring rather to follow the course of their churches and their leaders, which they looked to for the words of salvation.

Behold, the religions and churches of men have always been an abomination before God, for He despiseth them, because they put one man above his neighbor in the things which they believe.

And these churches lead the children of God away from the Father because of the leaders who put themselves above the members of these churches, teaching for commandments the doctrines and precepts of men.

And the people are led to believe that their church is greater than that of another, thus causing a division among them, who should have all things in common before the Father.

Behold, in time it shall be given unto thee—the mysteries of God and the path that He desireth that His children should follow to eternal life; and not only eternal life, but for the establishment of peace and happiness upon the earth.

And thou shalt desire to establish a church among men according to the commandments and the words that thou shalt receive concerning these things as they shall be given unto thee. But this thing is not that which shall bring happiness unto you; for this reason, I forbid this thing. But unto you it shall be given according to the desires of the Gentiles.

And thou shalt desire to do this to prove the Gentiles herewith, and show unto them that they are not above the Jews, and that the Jew is not above the Gentile, that all might know that God is no respecter of persons, and would that all of His children seek not the arm of flesh, but Him and His righteousness.

And thou shalt be called as a prophet among them, being the first who shall prepare the way for the last, that the children of men might have the opportunity to know the Father and receive eternal life as I have explained it unto thee. And the Gentiles shall reject that which shall be given them through you; and they shall cast you out from among them and listen not to your precepts and counsel.

And thou shalt lead those that listen to thy words like my servant Moses led those of the house of Israel, and give unto them my words as thou receivest through me, like unto Moses and Aaron. But the Gentiles shall reject thee, as did the Israelites the law that Moses brought down unto them, that they might have known me and the Father who sent me unto them.

And thou shalt be commanded to give unto them a lower law of ordinances and sacrifice like unto those which Moses gave unto the rebellious house of Israel, who would not hear my words from my own mouth, but wanted that they be given unto them through Moses.

And when they rejected me and trusted more in the arm of the flesh than they did in me, I took the plainness of my gospel from among them and allowed them to be led according to their own desires, which were unrighteous before God. And they did stumble exceedingly because of their wickedness.

And the fullness of my gospel was among them, but they did not understand it, trusting more in their fleshly ordinances and the sacrifices that pointed them towards this gospel.

And when I came down among them, they could not give up the traditions and doctrines of men that had crept in among them and deceived their souls, causing them to trust in their church and its leaders for their salvation.

And behold, as I was led, so shalt thou be led like a lamb to the slaughter, being innocent of the sins of this generation, having given unto them the opportunity to receive the fullness [of] my gospel and establish the kingdom of God upon the earth for the last time.

And the Gentiles shall be led like unto the Jews of old, and they shall do all things in the likeness of the Jews, that the first may be last and the last may be first, showing that the weaknesses of men are the same yesterday as they are today.[3]

How did religion become the way that it is—based on busy work and things that have nothing to do with how to love yourself and your neighbor as yourself?

How did loving your neighbor as yourself turn into: "If I were my neighbor, I would want my neighbor to do everything and anything possible to convince me to join my neighbor's religion and receive the saving ordinances"?

How did priesthood authority originate?

---

[3] *TSP*, The First Vision, 1:18–34.

A New American Scripture

It all started with the Bible.

Christians believe in the Bible. They believe the Bible to be the infallible truth. Therefore, as we have explained, we wrote stories for our new American scripture that complemented and followed the stories of the Bible. By using stories that could be cross-referenced to the Bible, we were able to sow a seed of doubt on the religions that are based on the Bible.

We started our original narrative with what eventually became the "lost" 116-page manuscript—not to be confused with what we published as the *Book of Mormon* in 1830. We started it by explaining that the ancient church at Jerusalem was violating the "lower law" that the Jews were given by Moses. This "lower law" was given to the Jews because they refused to accept the "higher law." The Bible story is clear that God was angry with the people because they rejected His "higher laws."

According to the story, the ancient Hebrews wanted God to tell them what they should do and how to become the best society possible. Their chosen prophet, Moses, told the people that ALL OF THEM could go up to the mountain and talk to God themselves. Moses told the Hebrews that they didn't need him to talk to God on their behalf. But the people refused to accept this and wanted Moses to speak to God on their behalf. After the Jews refused to speak with God personally, they sent Moses up into the mountain to get God's information for them. Reluctantly, Moses went up into the mountain. While he was gone, the Israelites basically ignored everything that Moses had told them previously. The Israelites made a "golden idol" that they could see and worship.

Moses had tried to explain the "higher laws" that would help the Israelites form the perfect, peaceful, humane society. But when they couldn't understand the concepts of this "higher law" well enough, that's when Moses told them to get prepared to hear the higher law from the actual voice of God himself. And again, they were afraid and refused.

Chapter 7: Looking Beyond the Mark

When Moses came down from the mountain with God's "lower law," it was filled with all kinds of "busy work" that the people needed to do in order to keep them doing something, anything, that pointed their minds towards God. God gave the Israelites this "lower law" because he was angry with them that they couldn't understand how to create the perfect society.

As indicated, while Moses was talking to an angry God and receiving commandments for the people, his right-hand man, Aaron, was being threatened by the people. The people wanted something to lead them, guide them, walk beside them, help them find the way, and teach them all that they must do to live with God someday. So, Aaron made an idolatrous god for the people.

According to the Bible story, God knew what was going on with the people while Moses was up on the mountain talking to Him. God told Moses that the people were way too wicked and that He was going to destroy them all. He told Moses that He (God) would make a great nation from just Moses' and Joshua's families. (Joshua was Moses' loyal servant and friend, who was down the mountain a short way waiting for Moses.)

This part of the Old Testament story influenced *our* story of creating a great nation out of just a few families that weren't destroyed by God. As the Bible story goes, God finally allowed ALL of his people to be destroyed by the Babylonians, except for a "small remnant," as prophesied and told by Isaiah.

Moses convinced God that it probably wouldn't be too good of an idea to destroy all of his people, because then the Egyptians would mock Him for telling them that the house of Israel was God's special people. "And the Lord repented of the evil which he thought to do unto his people."[4]

As time went on, the Israelites didn't have a clue why they were doing the acts and rituals that were required of them according to the "lower" law

---

[4] OT, Exodus 32:14.

given to them by Moses. In our new American scripture, we explained that "the Jews were a stiffnecked people; and they despised the words of plainness." The "words of plainness" were given in the higher law. The Jews wanted to kill God's messengers—they had threatened both Moses and Aaron before. They

> sought for things that they could not understand. Wherefore, because of their blindness, which blindness came by looking beyond the mark, they must needs fall; for God hath taken away his plainness from them, and delivered unto them many things which they cannot understand, because they desired it. And because they desired it God hath done it, that they may stumble.[5]

Because the people didn't understand what they were commanded to do, and they depended on Moses to tell them what to do, Moses sat all day long in counsel with the people. This wore him out. His father-in-law, Jethro, saw the great burden placed on Moses because of the people. Jethro suggested to Moses that he appoint others to help him counsel the people. This is how the priesthood started. It wasn't something that God wanted. It was something that Jethro wanted in order to help Moses explain to the people things that they couldn't understand, and to keep Moses from being physically worn out.

God had already commanded Moses to deliver unto the people things that they couldn't understand, because they desired it. Because of this, ALL the information that the APPOINTED HIGH PRIESTS delivered unto the people were things that made the people stumble. There is no part of any established Holy Priesthood that is from God. All priesthoods are the inventions of men, starting with the idea that Jethro proposed.

It is obvious, even from reading Bible stories, that the people were wicked when they wanted religion, rituals, ordinances, and lots of "busy

---

[5] *BOM*, Jacob 4:14.

Chapter 7: Looking Beyond the Mark

work" administered and overseen by priesthood authority. The people could mistreat each other and be as mean and as selfish as they wanted. They could rely on the rituals of their religion to make them feel good about themselves and their relationship with God. As indicated by what we had Joseph Smith report in his final account of the LDS *First Vision*, we knew that ALL Christian religions, of every kind, as well as ALL other religions on Earth were (and are) "drunken with iniquity and all manner of abominations." We reiterated this throughout our new American scripture:

> But, behold, in the last days, or in the days of the Gentiles—yea, behold all the nations of the Gentiles and also the Jews, both those who shall come upon this land [the Americas] and those who shall be upon other lands, yea, even upon all the lands of the earth, behold, they will be drunken with iniquity and all manner of abominations.[6]

We knew that nothing about any religion would help create a society of peace and goodwill towards all men. But we also knew that the *code of humanity* created by the great thinkers who invented Christianity—as we previously explained thoroughly in our book *The True History of Religion*—would put people on the right track.

As explained, to begin our original storyline, we intended to sow seeds of doubt into the reader's mind about religion, and also a seed of hope through Jesus Christ and what he taught the people according to the Bible's stories. Again, as we began the narrative of our new American scripture, we had to make sure that our story was consistent and strongly connected to the Old Testament that the Christians believed was the factual word of God. If they believed it was the factual word of God, then they also believed the history in the Bible was true.

We explained in previous chapters that this solid connection with the Old Testament had to be made according to the timeline that we chose for our

---

[6] *BOM*, 2 Nephi 27:1.

new American scripture. Our chosen timeline began about 600 B.C.E. (before the accepted birth of Jesus Christ). The New Testament containing the stories of Jesus did not exist 600 years before he was born. Furthermore, an honest researcher would admit that the stories about Jesus were not written down for a few hundred years until *after* Jesus supposedly lived upon the earth.

Following what the Hebrews did with their oral traditions and stories, the idea of a Christ, the son of God sent to save the world, was almost entirely spread through oral stories told among the poor and disenfranchised Roman citizens. As Hercules provided a hope of salvation (born as the son of Zeus and a mortal virgin) for the ancient Greeks, an anointed one ("Christ") would become the savior of hope for the poor and marginalized living throughout the Great Roman Empire.

We were creating a story about the importance of Jesus Christ long before he was purportedly alive. To convince a Christian that our story was true, it had to be based on Old Testament "facts," or at least on what early American Christians believed was true. Our narrative had to be focused and centered on the importance of Jesus Christ. Again, our utmost desire was to convince the early American Christians that they should be treating all people, especially the native Americans, as their brothers and sisters, and as their equals in all things, as the Jesus of Nazareth taught.

We wanted to convince early Americans of what the "God of all the earth and of all the inhabitants thereupon" intended the United States of America to become. It was supposed to be a melting pot for all of God's children who were suffering throughout the world. Just as the Statue of Liberty proclaims, it was supposed to be created for

> your tired, your poor, your huddled masses yearning to breathe free, the wretched refuse of [other nations'] teeming shore[s].[7]

---

[7] *See* Poem by Emma Lazarus on Statue of Liberty plaque, transcript and picture found at "Statue of Liberty, The New Colossus," National Park Service, U.S. Department of the Interior, nps.gov/stli/learn/historyculture/colossus.htm.

Chapter 7: Looking Beyond the Mark

We hoped that the Western Hemisphere would become a "promised land" where people could live free of control and persecution by unrighteous governments. We hoped that it would be a place where each person could pursue his or her own desires for happiness, regardless of what these desires were, as long as one's desires didn't impede the desires of another's life, liberty, or the pursuit of another's happiness.

The early United States of America was established by a combination of the Christian faith, ancient Roman politics, and Capitalism. The men who created the government and the Constitution that provided this government's blueprint and power established them in secret and obscurantism (the practice of deliberately preventing the facts or full details of something from becoming known). Again, the following explanation of what we (the Real Illuminati®) do, properly defines our desires and more about *why* we thought it was necessary to create a new American scripture:

> Our society's goals (our goals) are to oppose superstition (false beliefs), obscurantism (hiding the truth), religious influence over public life, and the abuses of state power. Our intent is to put an end to the machinations (secret plans) of the purveyors of injustice (those who spread lies to create unfairness), to control them without dominating them.[8]

Christian belief controlled the early United States' Government. Christianity's influence over public life is undeniable and has led to the abuses of state power, especially abuses against those who are of dark-skinned races, or those who reject Christianity.

Christianity is full of superstition and considerable error about what really happened in the past. Even in modern times, there is no way that Jews, Christians, or Muslims can be convinced that they are wrong. This is true no matter how much common sense, reason, and logic are used, and no matter

---

[8] *Compare* "About Us: The Real Illuminati®," The Real Illuminati®, realilluminati.org/about-us.

how much other information has been discovered through science. Even if the followers of these three major religions are taught things as things really are and as things really were, they do not overcome their pride and accept new information with an honest and objective heart and mind.

The bulk of this superstition and error comes from the Bible. Christians believe that God created the earth and all of its inhabitants—which *should* include the native American people, as well as all other dark-skinned races. But we could not convince Christians of these errors *unless* we used the authority of their own Bible—which they believed was the factual word of God—to convince them.

As we have explained, we wanted to present the native Americans as direct descendants of Abraham through the lineage of his grandson, Jacob (whose name was changed to "Israel," according to the Bible). This was important so we could firmly connect our story to the "house of Israel," which the Bible connects to Abraham, and on and on, back to Adam—God's first creation, according to the Bible.

Many other peoples were on Earth at the time when Abraham supposedly existed and received his *specialness*. But Jewish, Christian, and Muslim pride and superstition do not allow them to accept that they are no more special in the sight of God than those who trace their lineage to any of these other peoples. The prejudice against all other peoples on Earth is soundly presented in the Bible's narrative.

Astonishingly … shockingly … not one Bible-believer can be persuaded to consider that in about 2000 B.C.E., when Abraham supposedly lived, there were at least a million other people on Earth. In their eyes, not one of these other million "houses" (people) was chosen by God to be of any worth to humanity. If these religious groups *could* be convinced, they would be giving up their pride that supports their egos (self-worth and value).

Chapter 7: Looking Beyond the Mark

Among all modern people, no single group is as prideful of their Bible heritage as the American people. And what is most disturbing and sad to us is that among the American people, no single group is as prideful of their Bible heritage as the LDS/Mormon people (members of the Church of Jesus Christ of Latter-day Saints); this church is the only major religious group of people on Earth that *ostensibly* accepts our new American scripture as "Another Testament of Jesus Christ."

Notwithstanding, had our storyline been presented as we had *originally* written it, the LDS/Mormon people would have known of their great unrighteousness. We first wrote our storyline in a way so as to prevent a new church—which would not be fully based on the equality of all people—from being created. This was a doctrine that is clearly taught by the words of Jesus as presented in the Bible. Our original storyline clearly condemned ALL organized churches and ALL works and ordinances ("busy work") of ANY religion. We also condemned ALL of the commandments that these churches required of the people in order to be saved, which are not based on equality, or rather, on "doing unto others as THEY would have you do unto them."

As we have explained, ALL of the great societies that developed in our world in the past failed because of inequality. None of the constitutions of these great societies provided a correct blueprint or established proper laws that supported and protected life, liberty, and the pursuit of happiness of <u>all people equally</u>.

The Church of Jesus Christ of Latter-day Saints (LDS/Mormon Church) is the perfect example of what happens when people are taught that "busy work" is more important than treating others with equality. In order to be recognized as a "member in good standing" in this particular church, one must pay a full tithe, honor and sustain the church's General Authorities and its First Presidency, attend church regularly, and fulfill all church callings and assignments. The worthy member must be honest in business dealings, obey the law of the land, and comply with church rules that control the flesh (sex, drugs, alcohol, and coffee).

In this church, in order to be in good standing "before the Lord" (or rather, before the LDS priesthood leaders), one only has to follow this church's rules, regardless of what the scriptures teach about what Jesus required of a person. There are no requirements about *calling a person a fool, having road rage, lusting after a person in thought, or judging another person as a sinner.* It doesn't matter if a person *goes into debt to buy things* ("let your communication be, Yea, yea; [or] Nay, nay:" any other type of promise leads to evil), or *sues others in a court of law* to gain financially or to protect one's possessions. You don't have to *agree with your adversary quickly, turn the other cheek, only seek riches to do good* (to care for the poor and needy), *love your enemies, do good to those who persecute you and despitefully use you*, or follow any other commandment that is based on loving your neighbor as yourself.[9]

NOTHING that this particular religion requires of its members makes a society of better people because of the way that they treat others. In fact, those who disagree with the LDS ideology, especially those who were once Mormon and left that Church, are condemned to eternal damnation. This is done in a passive-aggressive way: "We love you. But you're not going to be saved in God's Celestial Kingdom unless you obey the Church's leaders and commandments."

Throughout our new American scripture, we warned about these types of religions and described them as

> churches which are built up to get gain [the LDS/Mormon church is the wealthiest church in the world], ... built up to get power over the flesh [sex, drugs, alcohol, coffee], ... built up to become popular in the eyes of the world [nothing is more important to the LDS/Mormon people than how the world perceives their church, thus they promote their church widely and loudly through their missionary and alleged humanitarian efforts], ...

---

[9] See the *Sermon on the Mount*, in NT, Matthew, chapters 5, 6, and 7; and *BOM*, 3 Nephi, chapters 12, 13, and 14.

those who seek the lusts of the flesh and the things of the world [education, material things, success in business and finances].

… They [have their General Authorities] become popular; and [wrongly suppose] they ought not to labor with their hands, but that they ought to be supported by the people.[10]

Of all groups of people on Earth, none has been more successful at Multi-Level Marketing than the LDS/Mormon people.[11] A "MLM" (Multi-Level Marketing) system is a business strategy where one strives to have others under them work hard so that the top person doesn't have to work. It is a pyramid scheme. There is no business plan more evil and abusive. MLM schemes allow for the success of only the very few at the top. The work of the majority benefits the few. This became *America's Way* of doing business. From this business model, one of America's most successful MLM schemes took its name: *Amway* (**Am**erica's **way**).

The American stock market (New York Stock Exchange), has influenced other stock markets of the world. It is another example of how a person desires to become wealthy without actually doing any work. One of our close friends, Mahatma Gandhi, called "Wealth Without Work" one of the world's Seven Social Sins.[12] Our new American scripture specifically and clearly condemns any reason for acquiring wealth that does not have to do with

the intent to do good—to clothe the naked, and to feed the hungry, and to liberate the captive, and administer relief to the sick and the afflicted.[13]

---

[10] *See BOM*, 1 Nephi 22:23; Alma 1:3.
[11] *See* Daryl Lindsey, "Follow the profit: How Mormon culture made Utah a hotbed for multi-level marketers," 8 Sept. 2016, KUTV News, kutv.com/news/local/follow-the-profit-how-mormon-culture-made-utah-a-hotbed-for-multi-level-marketers.
[12] *See* "Seven Social Sins," *Wikipedia*, 10 Jan 2021 en.wikipedia.org/wiki/Seven_Social_Sins.
[13] *Refer to BOM*, Jacob 2:1–21, *especially v.* 19.

When Joseph Smith allowed the first 116 pages of written manuscript of our original storyline to be reviewed, the people reviewing it had a problem. They could not accept that we denounced the accumulation of wealth as something that was NOT a blessing from God, but a result of misapplied religious views and teachings. The early Americans were greatly influenced and inspired to search for and accumulate wealth. At that time, one of the only ways a male was allowed to vote was if he owned land. This provided a great motivation to pursue wealth. Their religious leaders preached that if they accumulated wealth, it was a blessing from God for doing His will (performing rituals and ordinances and following what the leaders said God wanted them to do). To be popular and someone to whom others would pay attention and give respect, an American needed material things.

The Constitution of the United States became an instrument of businesses and corporations. A corporation was eventually given the same rights under the law that citizens were given. No law was established that guaranteed life, liberty, and pursuit of happiness, unless that one used one's life and liberty to pursue one's wealth. This was *America's Way*.

Our original storyline condemned the American dream of pursuing wealth.[14] We made it clear that the pursuit of success and wealth was a great sin that caused human societies to fail. In our original story, we explained this in a religious context by using the Bible's stories about Moses and the "golden idol" that the people wanted more than the counsel of God.[15] After the peer review group was offended by what we wrote of their American lust for material goods and success, we re-wrote it so that it would not be misunderstood or rejected.

Our original story failed to get Joseph's peers to set aside the pride they had as Christian Americans. The peer review group was very uncomfortable

---

[14] *See TSP*, Lehi 5:21–2; 8:7–17.
[15] *See TSP*, Lehi 3:14–21.

Chapter 7: Looking Beyond the Mark

to read and hear that the native Americans were "as precious in [God's] sight"[16] as they were. They were troubled when presented with the storyline implying ALL Christian churches that existed in America at that time were evil. They could not accept our initial explanation that the native American skin color had nothing to do with the Bible curse.[17]

Joseph met with his peers and tried to quiet their doubts and help them accept what had been written. He had already explained to them that what he was "translating" was the "stick of Joseph [by] the hand of Ephraim"[18] in fulfillment of the Bible's prophecy. Our original storyline gave an exact genealogy of the ancestry of the native American people all the way back to *Ephraim*, the half black and half white Egyptian son of Joseph (who was sold into Egypt). Joseph's peers had a hard time accepting that anyone with the "cursed blood" was equal to a white-skinned Christian.

Joseph Smith explained that the plates of brass were actually written in the Egyptian language because the Hebrews did not have their own written language when they were slaves living in Egypt. For this reason, we explained through Joseph Smith that our plates had Egyptian engravings on them instead of Hebrew words. Although we neither explained this in our original storyline, nor did we expect we would have to, we did explain it as our story progressed. We explained that in order to satisfy an honest researcher about the writings that were attributed to Moses, as well as all of the other ancient engravings upon plates that were had among the Jews, our new American scripture's original letters must be engraved in the same way that the Egyptians kept their own history.

No matter how hard he tried (partly because of his young age), Joseph had a hard time convincing his peers of anything. However, we covered every speculation or doubt that might arise about the engravings on our plates of gold. The Hebrew written language could not have existed during the time

---

[16] *BOM*, Jacob 2:21.
[17] *TSP*, Lehi 7:15–17.
[18] OT, Ezekiel 37:19.

that the religious world believes that Moses lived. But Egyptian hieroglyphics did. We used this verifiable fact to present our "reformed Egyptian." In the revision of our story, we made sure that the flow of the story remained consistent. We ensured that we mentioned the fact that the brass plates were written in Egyptian when we continued our revised storyline.

Joseph tried to explain that the native American skin color was actually passed down to them through this Egyptian lineage, but could have genetically evolved to become even darker because of the amount of sun to which the native Americans' ancestors were exposed through their nakedness. The Americans had already accepted that the native Americans, when first discovered, didn't wear much clothing.

But Christians couldn't accept this simple genetic explanation, partly because, at that time, DNA and genetics were not widely studied by science. They had a hard time not being able to apply the "curse of Cain" to people whom they felt deserved to be punished—thus, justifying the way they viewed and treated the natives and stole their land. The Christians' great pride blinded them. It was difficult for them to believe that these "naked heathens" were part of a chosen house of Israel when they believed so strongly that they were *not*.

Christians were "Gentiles." According to their belief, unless they could trace their lineage and identify themselves as Jews, their ancestors were "not chosen." This is demonstrated by the way that they express their pretended Christ-centered attitudes:

> We are Christians! Those of the house of Israel killed our Lord and Savior! Our Christian churches cannot be evil! Our missionary efforts in converting the native Americans to Christianity couldn't possibly be evil! These heathens need Christ! They need to be baptized and receive the Holy Ghost by the laying on of hands, by the ones who have the authority to do it. No man has this authority unless he is called of God! Jesus laid his hands on his disciples and

gave them this authority to baptize and give the Holy Ghost. Jesus gave the authority to Peter, from whom our Christian leaders received their authority ... not Jewish authority ... but Christian authority, directly from Christ himself!

In their minds, there was no way that all of this could be evil. There was no way that all a person had to do was treat others well in order to be saved, and that this simplicity was the fullness of Jesus' everlasting Gospel. There was no way. Without religion, without churches, without priesthood authority, there was no way that the native Americans (or anyone else for that matter) could be saved, so they believed.

From the very beginning of our new American scripture's story, we wanted to show that religious ritual was useless in forming a society of good people. We wanted to influence the early American Christians to recognize that the native Americans were not bad people just because they weren't Christian. Honest American history accounts for thousands of native Americans being murdered because they would not bow down to a different god and perform the ordinances that the Christian god demanded of them.

We knew that many of the native American societies were already more *Christ-like* than all European-American Christian societies were. One of our contemporary (recent) good friends, Howard Zinn, wrote of Christopher Columbus' interaction with the first natives that he encountered:

Arawak men and women, naked, tawny, and full of wonder, emerged from their villages onto the island's beaches and swam out to get a closer look at the strange big boat. When Columbus and his sailors came ashore, carrying swords, speaking oddly, the Arawaks ran to greet them, brought them food, water, gifts. He later wrote of this in his log:

"They ... brought us parrots and balls of cotton and spears and many other things, which they exchanged for the glass beads

and hawks' bells. They willingly traded everything they owned … . They were well-built, with good bodies and handsome features … . They do not bear arms, and do not know them, for I showed them a sword, they took it by the edge and cut themselves out of ignorance. They have no iron. Their spears are made of cane … . They would make fine servants … . With fifty men we could subjugate them all and make them do whatever we want."

These Arawaks of the Bahama Islands were much like Indians on the mainland, who were remarkable (European observers were to say again and again) for their hospitality, their belief in sharing. These traits did not stand out in the Europe of the Renaissance, dominated as it was by the religion of popes, the government of kings, the frenzy for money that marked Western civilization and its first messenger to the Americas, Christopher Columbus.[19]

Again, Christian rituals are based on the Bible. Before there were rituals that were *supposedly* taught in the New Testament, there were rituals of the Old Testament. The law of Moses was the "lower law" given to the Israelites as "busy work" to keep their minds pointed towards God and God's commandments. These ancient rituals were not what saved the people. These rituals *were meant* to keep people always in remembrance of how God told them to treat each other.

Our story confronts organized church, its leaders, and the rituals that do much more harm than good in promoting peace and goodwill. We started with the law of Moses. After Joseph's peers reviewed our original storyline, they could not be convinced that rituals were *not* necessary for a person's salvation. Their pride wouldn't let them.

---

[19] Howard Zinn, *The People's History of the United States of America* (New York: Harper Perennial Modern Classics, 2005), p. 1, emphasis added.

Chapter 7: Looking Beyond the Mark

In the next chapter, we will begin to explain *how* we rewrote the beginning of our story. We re-did it in a way that protected the Christians' pride in performing their rituals. Because our desire was to get Christians to place more importance and value on the *Golden Rule* taught by Jesus, our rewrite emphasized being "baptized, yea, even by water."

We made sure it was clear that this baptism, in order for it to be effective and save a person, was entirely conditioned on following Jesus and doing the things "which ye have seen [Jesus] do. ... Wherefore, my beloved brethren, can we follow Jesus save we shall be willing to keep the commandments of the Father?"[20] We also made sure that the "commandments of the Father" were all about the *Golden Rule* that Jesus taught.

When we wrote each section of our new American scripture, we wanted to present information that accomplished two main objectives: 1) to get people to read it and believe it; and 2) to teach them correct principles by which they could create a peaceful society.

As we have explained, and it is worth reiterating again and again, we needed to create an emotional (*spiritual*) connection with the story, as well as a personal one, for the reader. To accomplish this, we had to write the material so that it was consistent with the reader's already-established beliefs. We needed to include information to which the reader could relate personally. For the *spiritual* connection we used Christianity as the basis; to make the *personal* connection we used a relatable family dynamic (father, mother, brother, sister, etc.) and the struggles associated with the family (child rebellion, sibling rivalry, spousal disagreements, etc.).

We needed to present information that reinforced the moral of the story, or rather, the lesson that we wanted to teach the reader. In order to get the reader to learn something new, or even consider something other than what the reader already believed to be true, we had to open the reader's

---

[20] *BOM*, 2 Nephi 31:12, 10.

mind and heart to the possibility that our new information wasn't going to replace the reader's old cognitive paradigm (ways of thinking).

We hoped to help form a more perfect union of human beings that would treat all people equally and equitably. We knew that this could only be accomplished by inspiring humanity to form and uphold righteous forms of governmental authority that were completely separated from ALL religious belief and authority.

Thomas Jefferson was one of the most successful statesmen and politicians of modern times.[21] He knew what would make a government successful and what would not. Jefferson knew that "the care of human life and happiness, and not their destruction, is the only legitimate object of [a righteous] government."[22] It was reported correctly that Jefferson said, "Peace and friendship with all mankind [should be a government's first and] wisest policy; and I wish [to God that] we may be permitted to pursue them."[23]

Jefferson also penned the most famous sentence recorded in all of American history:

> We hold these truths to be self-evident, that all men are created equal, that they are endowed by their Creator with certain unalienable Rights, that among these are Life, Liberty and the pursuit of Happiness.[24]

Although a hypocrite as a slave owner, Jefferson was one of the few American Founding Fathers who believed that the native American people

---

[21] *See* "Thomas Jefferson," *Wikipedia*, Wikimedia Foundation, 8 June 2021, en.wikipedia.org/wiki/Thomas_Jefferson.

[22] *See* "Thomas Jefferson to the Republicans of Washington County, Maryland," March 31, 1809, paragraph 2, National Archives, founders.archives.gov/documents/Jefferson/03-01-02-0088.

[23] *See* "Thomas Jefferson to C. W. F. Dumas," May 6, 1786, National Archives, founders.archives.gov/documents/Jefferson/01-09-02-0389.

[24] *See* Declaration of Independence, July 4, 1776, paragraph 2, transcript, National Archives, archives.gov/founding-docs/declaration-transcript.

Chapter 7: Looking Beyond the Mark

were "equal men." He believed that they were created by God, just like white men, and endowed with the same unalienable rights. The larger part of the *secret combination* of popular and wealthy political, religious, and business leaders did not. Most of them held strongly to the prejudices taught in the Bible, especially about God choosing a specific race of people as His "chosen people."

These men used democracy (the vote of the majority) to establish laws that upheld their religious beliefs. They claimed to follow the teachings of Jesus Christ as presented in the New Testament stories. But Jefferson knew the stories of Jesus and had studied the Bible. He knew that Jesus never taught anything close to what the early American Christians believed.

Thomas Jefferson was often soft-spoken and hardly raised his voice to engage in argument. His wisdom and power came from his writings. We were aware of Jefferson's disdain for the hypocrisy of the wealthy Christian majority. He attended many of the meetings in which the wealthy combined in secret to figure out ways to use their powers of politics, religion, and business to establish a government for the masses, to control the people. Jefferson was well aware of these *secret combinations*.

For this reason, we met with Jefferson and asked for his help in writing something that might penetrate the prevailing Christian prejudice and belief. Jefferson was an honest man, more so than most other politicians. But Jefferson knew his limits and was wise to what he could say and what he couldn't say while meeting with these men in their secret combinations. Ultimately though, his popularity and standing in the community meant more to him than helping us figure out a way to change the hardened hearts and stiff necks (pride) of the Christian leadership.

We knew that our meetings with Jefferson had greatly affected him. We had discussed a lot about religion, especially about Christianity. We read from the Bible and showed Jefferson the actual teachings that were credited to Jesus in the New Testament Gospels. We explained many details that we knew about the Bible's *true* history and how it became the King James Version.

With care and some gentle guile, we explained that our group had been around a long time and that members of our group had actually written the book of Revelation. We could tell that Jefferson was more than impressed. Nevertheless, he would not sacrifice what he had become. He knew that if he ever spoke of the things that we discussed with him, especially that we were secretly trying to find a way to introduce another Christian-based scripture, he would lose all the prestige and popularity that he had gained.

Our influence on Jefferson is noted in how he originally titled a manuscript that he wrote:

> The Philosophy of Jesus of Nazareth, Extracted from the Account of His Life and Doctrines as Given by Matthew, Mark, Luke and John; Being an Abridgement of the New Testament for the Use of the Indians, Unembarrased [sic] with Matters of Fact or Faith beyond the Level of their Comprehensions.[25]

While writing his manuscript, Jefferson sent a letter to one of his closest political friends, John Adams. In the letter, Jefferson expressed his concern about the Christian religion and the way that its various leaders treated what Jesus taught. Jefferson wrote:

> In extracting the pure principles which [Jesus] taught, we should have to strip off the artificial vestments in which [the teachings of Jesus] have been muffled by priests, who have travestied [(severely distorted) the teachings of Jesus] into various forms, as instruments of riches and power to them.[26]

---

[25] *See* "The Philosophy of Jesus of Nazareth," *Thomas Jefferson Encyclopedia*, Monticello and the University of Virginia in Charlottesville, monticello.org/site/research-and-collections/philosophy-jesus-nazareth.

[26] *See* "Thomas Jefferson to John Adams," October 12, 1813, paragraph 2, National Archives, founders.archives.gov/documents/Adams/99-02-02-6182.

Chapter 7: Looking Beyond the Mark

Jefferson knew that no Christian sect in America was teaching the pure and simple teachings of Jesus as these teachings were presented in the Bible. He knew that religious leaders had completely ignored "The Philosophy of Jesus of Nazareth" and replaced it with errant (corrupt) church doctrines that had nothing to do with the "fulness of the gospel of the Lord, of whom the twelve apostles bear record; and they bear record according to the truth which is in the Lamb of God."[27]

In writing what would become known as the *Jefferson Bible*,[28] Jefferson hoped that his popularity among the people would convince the Christians that the "Matters of Fact or Faith" of Jesus' gospel had been "embarrassed" (i.e., complicated, as he used the word). He believed that if the Christians truly read Jesus' words and abided by them, the Christians would see that the native Americans were equal with all people and deserved a government that would protect *their* unalienable rights too. (Nevertheless, as mentioned, Jefferson did own slaves himself.)

Jefferson failed to convince but a few. He never officially published his book because he was afraid that it would be seen as blasphemous. He knew that Christians would think that he was implying that God's word was incorrect and needed correction.

The original American government, along with its Constitution, were a far cry from being an authority of law that saw all men as equals and supported and protected the rights of ALL people. The United States government, along with its Constitution, were founded on the desires and needs of the secret combinations of the wealthy and powerful men who formed it. These were the exact same desires and needs of the leaders of the ancient Assyrian, Hittite, Babylonian, Egyptian, Greek,

---

[27] *BOM*, 1 Nephi 13:24.
[28] For Jefferson's later work (commonly referred to as the *Jefferson Bible*), see "The Life and Morals of Jesus of Nazareth," in the *Thomas Jefferson Encyclopedia*, Monticello and the University of Virginia in Charlottesville, monticello.org/site/research-and-collections/life-and-morals-jesus-nazareth.

Roman, and Byzantine empires, plus every other great and powerful nation of the past. All of these failed. We know that if the United States of America will not change its ways, it will once again repeat history and follow the same course of failure.

Thomas Jefferson once said, "History in general only informs us of what bad government is."[29] He said this because there had never been a government that had lasted. The information recorded in history about government is primarily "what bad governments did."

There was a significant time in the past when the government of the Great Roman Empire was being threatened from within because of its bad policies and laws. At that time, there were many great thinkers who had studied "bad government" enough to recognize the mistakes that had been made. These thinkers knew that the greatest mistake these failed governments had made was not treating all of their citizens equally—providing, supporting, and protecting the unalienable rights of life, liberty, and the pursuit of happiness of ALL people equally.

Each time that the masses (population of a nation) grew and were not treated properly, the people rebelled against their government. These rebellions and protests were directly responsible for the failure of these great nations ... each and every time.

When the masses of the Great Roman Empire began to complain and resist corrupt government, Emperor Constantine organized his own secret combination of the greatest thinkers, along with some of the most powerful political, religious, and business leaders of that time. They had to come up with a way to quiet and control the people. These great thinkers, which included highly educated philosophers and secular scholars, knew that the people needed something in which they could hope for a better future. And

---

[29] *See* "Thomas Jefferson to John Norvell," June 11, 1807, paragraph 2, National Archives, founders.archives.gov/documents/Jefferson/99-01-02-5737.

Chapter 7: Looking Beyond the Mark

nothing created more hope than the faith that the people had in their gods and their religions.

In the first book of our Trilogy, *The True History of Religion*, we explained well enough how Christianity began. It is important here to reiterate that the new religion of Christianity gave the poor Roman citizens hope.

When Constantine organized this "think tank," he was successful at inviting the most educated minds of that time period. This council of men (loosely based on what history reports as the *Council of Nicaea*[30]) had studied all the bad governments of the past. This council knew what the people believed in and what the people would accept from their leaders. Not all of these men, however, were religious and believed in a god. A few had studied enough philosophy to understand how human nature worked.

While meeting to standardize this new belief system that would provide hope to the people, the few non-believers (of which some of our group influenced) were able to introduce a *code of humanity*. This code was a set of simple rules of how a person should act in order for peace and goodwill to be present in society. To make a long story short, the New Testament account of Jesus' *Sermon on the Mount* (as found in Matthew 5, 6, and 7) was based on this code for humanity, upon which these great thinkers agreed would quiet the masses and bring peace and control.

The most important part of the new Messiah's teachings was based on one thing: EQUALITY—the idea that all people are created to be equal, and *should* be treated as if they are equal, because they ARE. All previous governments lacked this trait, which led to their demise. It is <u>this important code and law</u> upon which all other codes and laws that govern humans should be based.

---

[30] *See* "First Council of Nicaea," *Wikipedia*, 19 May 2021, en.wikipedia.org/wiki/First_Council_of_Nicaea.

These great thinkers wrote this part of Jesus' teachings in clear language that could not be misunderstood. From its original Greek, it was written:

The greatest commandment is to love yourself with all your heart, might, mind, and strength; and then to love your neighbor in the same way that you love yourself. Upon these commandments shall all law be established among the children of men.

Eventually, corrupt Christian leaders changed this great commandment and masked its original meaning (or clothed it in an "artificial vestment [that] muffled" it). The leaders of the Christian churches that evolved from the Catholic Church—which was responsible for saving the eastern part of the Great Roman Empire—could not allow their followers to have more love for themselves and their neighbors than they did for God.

If a person loved their self, at least as much as the person loved God, and the person thought that they were equal with God (one with God, as Jesus taught the people that they should be), why would the people need leaders? Why would the people need an organized religion? A later Christian translation of the original Greek changed the first part of the greatest commandment from "Love *yourself* with all your heart, might, mind, and strength" to "Love God." Christian religious leaders taught the people that God would not talk to the people, but would only talk to His chosen leaders. This is how inequality was introduced and changed "the fulness of the gospel of Jesus Christ."

One of the important purposes of our new American scripture was to provide a story about bad government and bad religion. In our narrative, unlike in all other recorded history, we wanted to present information about *good* government and *good* religion. It was our intent to give the reader hope that it IS possible to have peace on Earth and goodwill towards all equally. Our new American scripture was intended to convince the people of this hope. But we could not convince them simply by telling them the Real Truth™ about all things in the past and in the present that led to humanity's demise, which are the things that humanity must change in order to not make the same mistakes in the future. As we explained in a previous chapter, we could only teach the people "according to the heed and diligence which they gave unto [God]."[31]

We knew that all religion was in error and that none of it was good. We offer here another statement attributed to Thomas Jefferson:

> Ignorance is preferable to error; and he is less remote from the truth who believes nothing [ignorant], than he who believes what is wrong [deceived].[32]

The early Americans were completely ignorant about how their new government was formed and being operated. They were ignorant and deceived (uninformed and misled) then, just as they still are today. Their leaders counted (and still count) on this ignorance to control them. The people's tendency to have faith in their leaders allowed their leaders to teach them the errors that the people accepted about the teachings of Jesus. The people had hope in a better world. This hope gave them faith and caused them to be susceptible to the secret combinations of power that held them in captivity. But it was impossible for us to tell the people that they were ignorant and didn't know anything about Real Truth™—how things really are, and how things really were in the past.

Americans are a very prideful people.

Joseph's peers rejected our original storyline because of this pride. They saw themselves as *Christian Americans*. They felt that they had been blessed because they believed in Jesus Christ and had accepted him as their Lord and Savior. They felt that God had given them the land of North America as a reward for being faithful Christians.

---

[31] *BOM*, Alma 12:9; *see also BOM*, Mosiah 1:16.
[32] *See* Thomas Jefferson, *Notes on the State of Virginia* (Boston: Lilly and Wait, 1832), Query VI, p. 30, also found at Library of Congress, loc.gov/item/03004902/.

Most Christian sects taught that people could only be saved through grace alone. Early American Christians believed that whatever they did, or did not do, outside of believing in and accepting Jesus as their Lord and Savior, didn't matter. Jesus had died for their sins upon the cross. Jesus had taken upon himself all of their sins. They would not have to suffer for their sins because of Jesus' sacrifice.

The path to eternal salvation was through the atonement of Jesus Christ. They had faith in this. It was simple, easy to understand, and easy to follow. Anyone who refused to accept this atoning sacrifice could not be saved, and would not be saved. To Christians, Jesus was the prophesied Messiah, foretold by Old Testament prophets. Along with all unbelievers, the Jews would be punished for not accepting Jesus as the ONLY Messiah, of whom their own ancient prophets prophesied.

Jesus was a Jew. Jesus Christ was white (so they believed).

This Christian belief created great pride for the white-skinned races that overran the Western Hemisphere. This belief gave value to the early American Christians. They believed the native American people had already been punished by the god of the Old Testament in the same way that this god had punished Adam and Eve's son, Cain, for killing his brother, Abel. Certainly, the ancestors of the native American people had done something wrong that caused God to curse them with a dark skin. There was no other way that having dark-colored skin could be explained, according to the Bible.

If the Bible stories were true, then Adam and Eve were God's first creations, created in the image of God. And because it was believed that Adam and Eve were white, God was also white and expected all of His children to be white.

In our original storyline, we attempted to counter this racial prejudice. This attempt was one of the things that made Joseph's chosen peer review group uncomfortable. It affected the faith that they had in our story as "God's

Chapter 7: Looking Beyond the Mark

word." We had threatened the value of their white skin. We had threatened the value of all of their orthodox Christian beliefs. We had threatened the value and worth of the law of Moses written in the Old Testament. We had threatened the value of their Bible.

Christians were taught by their leaders that the law of Moses, along with all of its rituals, ordinances, and busy work, pointed them to Jesus Christ and was necessary for salvation *before* Jesus died on the cross for the sins of the world. They were taught that an organized religion was necessary—that with the proper priesthood authority, God would expect the people to perform outward, physical requirements in order to secure their eternal salvation.

None of these false, early American Christian doctrines or beliefs associated with organized religion were part of the "fulness of the gospel" of Jesus Christ as it is given in the Gospels of the New Testament. Jesus did not teach any of these things. The FULL mission that Jesus Christ was sent to Earth by his Father to do, according to the Gospels of the New Testament, did not include ANY of the above early American Christian beliefs or duties.

In Jesus' last prayer to his Father, he made this perfectly clear: "I have glorified thee on the earth: I have finished the work which thou gavest me to do."[33] When Jesus gave this prayer, he had not yet been crucified. Being murdered by the members and leaders of God's only true church at the time was not something that God "gave [Jesus] to do." Organizing a religion was not something that his Father told him to do. Requiring a person to perform ordinances, rituals, temple work, genealogy work, or any other "church busy work" was not a part of "glorifying God on Earth." Jesus' Father did not tell him to command the people to pay tithes and offerings, to not drink, to not smoke, to not take drugs, to not have premarital sex, to not masturbate, nor to not love and have sex with someone of the same gender. The sins that

---

[33] NT, John 17:4.

Jesus outlined in his teachings were nothing that the early American Christians considered to be "sins."

We wanted to help the American Christians see that Jesus DID glorify his Father in Heaven by teaching the people what they needed to do in order to have peace and eternal life. He taught them with words that came out of his mouth. He taught them EVERYTHING that was required of a person ... EVERYTHING. And when he was asked about the greatest thing that anyone could do ... about the greatest commandment that one should obey, the original Greek translation of Jesus' answer set the "mark" that had to be reached in order to be saved—the ONLY mark:

> The greatest commandment is to love yourself with all your heart, might, mind, and strength; and then to love your neighbor in the same way that you love yourself. Upon those commandments shall all law be established among the children of men.

Again, these two great commandments (love yourself and love your neighbor as yourself) are the basis for creating equality for all of humanity. ALL of Jesus' teachings were based on creating equality, not only among each mortal person, but between each mortal and God. Nothing else is required of humanity in order to be saved except keeping these two commandments.

Our original storyline couldn't have been any clearer about what we have presented above.

In our new American scripture, we intended to present another story about Jesus that made more sense and was more logical than anything that the early American Christians had considered. Everything that we presented was based on the teachings of Jesus Christ ... on the things that came out of his mouth when he was on Earth teaching the people.

The grand finale of our story, our story's most important part, the *magnum opus* of our "great and marvelous work," is the event when the

Chapter 7: Looking Beyond the Mark

resurrected Jesus Christ delivered "the fulness of the everlasting Gospel ... to the ancient inhabitants" of the Western Hemisphere exactly like he had delivered it to the Jews of the Eastern Hemisphere.[34]

As previously mentioned, there was a *code of humanity* that was agreed upon by the greatest thinkers of the past. A government based on this *code of humanity* would create laws and policies that treated all people as equals. It would guarantee **all** people life, liberty, and the pursuit of happiness. We knew that if we could succeed at convincing the early American Christians to establish their government based upon this *code of humanity*, that our "marvelous work and a wonder" would help create the greatest and most righteous nation the world has ever known. This was our intent for creating a new American scripture. We used Christian belief and faith in our efforts to accomplish what we intended.

Our revised storyline was written to explain this intent in a way that the "Spirit of Christ" would fill the heart of the reader and convince the reader that our words were just as true as the Bible. We wanted to give hope to the native American people that life would get better for them because the European-American Christians (the "Gentiles") were going to do the right thing (or so we hoped).

After we had Joseph Smith let his chosen peer review group read and study the first 116 pages of handwritten manuscript, astonishingly, they did not accept the "mark" we meant to hit with our original storyline. A few of the more educated ones actually tried to counsel Joseph about how the story should have been written. In doing this, they were "counsel[ing] the Lord" (see scripture below).

Again, we repeat and reiterate these same things because of their importance in understanding *why* we did what we did. The early American Christians had a hard time with the way that we discounted the law of Moses

---

[34] *See BOM*, 3 Nephi, chapters 12, 13 and 14.

and organized religion. As you read what we wrote to address these concerns, and as you consider every part of our story's presentation, keep in mind that we wrote everything according to the feedback that we received from these early American Christians. We made sure that our new American scripture not only agreed with the Bible's stories, but created a strong *spiritual feeling* in the Christian reader's mind (although some might incorrectly associate this *feeling* with their heart).

Here is how we addressed some of the concerns that the peer review group had about our original storyline:

> For, for this intent have we written these things, that they [the native American people] may know that we [the ancestors of the native Americans] knew of Christ, and we had a hope of his glory many hundred years before his coming; and not only we ourselves had a hope of his glory, but also all the holy prophets [of the Old Testament, an account of which Lehi brought to the Americas as the "brass plates"] which were before us.
>
> Behold, they [the ancient prophets] believed in Christ and worshiped the Father in his name, and also we worship the Father in his name. And for this intent we keep the law of Moses, it pointing our souls to him; and for this cause it is sanctified unto us for righteousness, even as it was accounted unto Abraham in the wilderness to be obedient unto the commands of God in offering up his son Isaac, which is a similitude of God and his Only Begotten Son.
>
> Wherefore, we search the prophets, and we have many revelations and the spirit of prophecy; and having all these witnesses we obtain a hope, and our faith becometh unshaken, insomuch that we truly can command in the name of Jesus and the very trees obey us, or the mountains, or the waves of the sea.

Nevertheless, the Lord God showeth us our weakness that we may know that it is by his grace, and his great condescensions unto the children of men, that we have power to do these things.

Behold, great and marvelous are the works of the Lord. How unsearchable are the depths of the mysteries of him; and it is impossible that man should find out all his ways. And no man knoweth of his ways save it be revealed unto him; wherefore, brethren, despise not the revelations of God.

For behold, by the power of his word man came upon the face of the earth, which earth was created by the power of his word. Wherefore, if God being able to speak and the world was, and to speak and man was created, O then, why not able to command the earth, or the workmanship of his hands upon the face of it, according to his will and pleasure?

Wherefore, brethren, seek not to counsel the Lord, but to take counsel from his hand. For behold, ye yourselves know that he counseleth in wisdom, and in justice, and in great mercy, over all his works.

Wherefore, beloved brethren, be reconciled unto him through the atonement of Christ, his Only Begotten Son, and ye may obtain a resurrection, according to the power of the resurrection which is in Christ, and be presented as the first-fruits of Christ unto God, having faith, and obtained a good hope of glory in him before he manifesteth himself in the flesh.

And now, beloved, marvel not that I tell you these things; for why not speak of the atonement of Christ, and attain to a perfect knowledge of him, as to attain to the knowledge of a resurrection and the world to come?

> Behold, my brethren, he that prophesieth, let him prophesy to the understanding of men; for the Spirit speaketh the truth and lieth not. Wherefore, it speaketh of things as they really are, and of things as they really will be; wherefore, these things are manifested unto us plainly, for the salvation of our souls. But behold, we are not witnesses alone in these things; for God also spake them unto prophets of old.
>
> But behold, the Jews were a stiffnecked [proud] people; and they despised the words of plainness, and killed the prophets, and sought for things that they could not understand. Wherefore, because of their blindness, which blindness came by looking beyond the mark, they must needs fall; for God hath taken away his plainness from them, and delivered unto them many things which they cannot understand, because they desired it. And because they desired it God hath done it, that they may stumble.[35]

There is no way that we could have directly told the peer review group that they had "looked beyond the mark," and that because they had, we were going to rewrite our story how they desired us to write it. *It was supposed to be "God's word," unchangeable and everlasting.*

Once we realized how prideful ("stiffnecked") and blind Joseph's peers were, and once we considered their concerns about the parts of our writing with which they were uncomfortable, we were able to create and reshape our storyline accordingly. We were dismayed, but not surprised, by the early American Christians' complete rejection of the fullness of the Gospel of Jesus Christ as it was given in the New Testament.

We will present the next chapters according to how the subplots and stories are currently laid out in the modern edition of what the world knows as the *Book of Mormon*. We will show the reader how we "took away" the

---

[35] *BOM*, Jacob 4:4–14.

Chapter 7: Looking Beyond the Mark

plainness of the narrative that we had intended and "delivered unto them many things which they [could not] understand, because they desired it."

The people looked beyond our intended mark and unfortunately desired the narrative to be presented according to their errant (incorrect) beliefs. Because of this, we had few options as to how we could tell the story in order to fulfill the desired goal for which we wrote our new American scripture. Again and again, our goal was to help influence the creation of the greatest nation the world had ever known: the United States of America.

Throughout our entire storyline we lead the reader to the Second Coming of the resurrected Christ when he appears to the ancestors of the native Americans. At that point in our story, we give the most important information (lesson, moral of the story). We have Jesus Christ tell the reader, specifically and clearly, that unless the reader has a broken heart and contrite spirit and becomes like a little child, the reader will NOT accept anything that Jesus was about to tell them.

"Alpha and Omega" (in Greek, "the greatest god of all gods") tells the people that the law of Moses, all religious ordinances, all rituals, and all church "busy work" are no longer acceptable. Jesus tells the people that the only thing that he wants from them is a "broken heart and a contrite spirit." A "broken heart" means a person realizes and accepts that nothing they believe is true and nothing they have done in their life was important or valuable. In other words, everything the person believes and has done is useless and of no worth to the rest of humanity.

> I am the light and the life of the world. I am Alpha and Omega, the beginning and the end.
>
> And ye shall offer up unto me no more the shedding of blood; yea, your sacrifices and your burnt offerings [the lower law of Moses] shall be done away, for I will accept none of your sacrifices and your burnt offerings.

And ye shall offer for a sacrifice unto me a **broken heart** and a **contrite spirit**. And whoso cometh unto me with a broken heart and a contrite spirit, him will I baptize with fire and **with the Holy Ghost**, even as the Lamanites, because of their faith in me at the time of their conversion, were **baptized with fire** and with the Holy Ghost, and they knew it not.

Behold, I have come unto the world to bring redemption unto the world, to save the world from sin.

Therefore, whoso repenteth and cometh unto me as a little child, him will I receive, for of such is the kingdom of God. Behold, for such I have laid down my life, and have taken it up again; therefore repent, and come unto me ye ends of the earth, and be saved.[36]

During the telling of the stories in our new American scripture that led up to the appearance of the resurrected Jesus, we presented a dark-skinned people (the Lamanites) who had to let go of everything that they believed was true and throw it all out the window (in other words, they had to get a *broken heart*). These Lamanites felt bad for what they had done because of their false beliefs (this is having a *contrite spirit*).

Our resurrected Savior was only going to save the people who could throw out all of their old beliefs, all of their religious ideas, all of the rituals, ordinances, and all of the "busy work" that their religions required them to do. The people needed to let go of everything they thought was true in order to allow Jesus to teach them the things that made perfect sense ("to baptize them in his name"). "Baptized by fire" meant they learned new information; "with the Holy Ghost" meant that the information would make perfect sense.

Little children don't know anything and trust and believe that their parent knows everything. If the people did not approach "Alpha and Omega"

---

[36] *BOM*, 3 Nephi 9:18–22, emphasis added.

as a little child would approach their parent to learn, Jesus could not save them. He would not save them.

Incredibly, modern Mormon missionaries actually use the above part of our story to prove to a person that unless the person is baptized in their church by their pretended priesthood authority, the person cannot be saved. Most Christians believe that they must submit to some sort of physical baptism. Therefore, it's easy for LDS/Mormon missionaries to miss the true meaning of our scripture and transfigure it, easily deceiving the investigator into believing that he or she *must* be baptized into the LDS church. Nothing could be further from truth. This becomes obvious when one reads the scripture as we wrote it in context. The Lamanite people were "baptized" properly "and they knew it not."

We mention this part of our story here because our original storyline was meant to begin the process of opening the Christian reader's mind. We wanted them to start to see that nothing about religion—including any of religion's rituals, ordinances, offerings, or any other "busy work"—is needed or required for salvation, or rather, required to help create a peaceful and loving human society.

Up to this point we have explained a lot of *why* we wrote the new American scripture: to get the American people to do the right thing and establish a *righteous* society on Earth. We explained how the great thinkers that invented the Jesus stories came up with a *code for humanity* that they knew, from experience and study, would help create a successful human society. This *code* has nothing to do with personal rituals that people do to fulfill their ego and make them believe that they will be saved after death. This *code for humanity* has ALL to do with how the people need to treat each other in order to have peace on Earth.

One need only consider (with a *broken heart* and a *contrite spirit*) each and every religious ritual, ordinance, offering, or any other type of "busy work" required of church members for salvation. What do ANY of these have to do with making society a better place for **all** humans? The answer is clear: ABSOLUTELY NOTHING.

Nothing that any church or religion, of any kind, requires of its believers actually helps society. This is easily recognized when a person considers this fact honestly and with real intent. This requires realizing that everything you think and believe *might not be true*. After truthfully accepting this fact, a person can also come to understand that ALL religious requirements only help to support a person's ego. These religions do nothing to help establish a peaceful human society where no one's free will is controlled or impeded by another. Their "busy work" only spreads discontent, guilt, persecution, strife, envyings, and priestcrafts (where leaders receive a stipend for their church service).

The institutions of power that currently control life upon Earth are greatly influenced by religion. Each religion claims that a person cannot be saved unless the person does what the religion's god demands, which always includes specific "busy work" that has no positive effect on society. EVERYTHING that religion *does* negatively affects society in one way or another. Human nature is the culprit (cause). A person's ego is supported by the person's pride in their religious beliefs: "I fulfill all of the commandments of God; therefore, I am right before God."

We (the Real Illuminati®) know that nothing that religion requires of a person makes the whole of society better. It only serves human nature, a nature that is the "enemy" of a peaceful and humane society. It was our intent to subtly open up the reader's mind to this new information. In writing the beginning of our storyline, it was our intent to get people to question religion, its authorities over them, and the useless "busy work" required of them that does not positively affect the whole of society.

Regardless of how careful and precise we were in aiming the American people towards the mark of creating an equal and equitable society, the American people *missed the mark by a long shot.*

Chapter 8
The 116-page Lost Manuscript

Now that we have explained and reiterated, sometimes superfluously (excessively) and repetitively in order to let it sink in—that NO organized religion has ever led to anything good for humanity—we can begin to explain *how* we presented the narrative of our new American scripture to the hard hearts and closed minds of the early European-American Christians.

Here, it is again important to remind the reader why influencing early American Christians was such an important thing to do. This particular group of people was establishing the foundation and future for the most powerful nation that has ever existed during the current dispensation of human time upon the earth. The United States of America was meant to be

> an ensign to the nations from far, and will hiss unto them from the end of the earth; and behold, [immigrants seeking refuge] shall come with speed swiftly; none shall be weary nor stumble among them.[1]

We took this from the prophecies of Isaiah contained in the King James Bible. We've explained that our group influenced the writings of Isaiah, and that because we wrote the prophecy, we knew that we could help fulfill it as prophesied.

The United States of America was meant to be the best form of human government yet established. It was our intent to do everything within our power to help this nascent (growing and budding) nation

> with righteousness ... judge the poor, and reprove with equity for the meek of the earth ... And righteousness shall be the girdle

---

[1] *See BOM*, 2 Nephi 15:26; OT, Isaiah 5:26.

> of [this great nation's] loins, and faithfulness the girdle of [its] reins [power and control to guide people].²

We had a hope that the United States would be a place where one could live as a

> wolf also shall dwell with the lamb, and the leopard shall lie down with the kid, and the calf and the young lion and fatling together; and a little child shall lead them, [even a nation that] shall stand for an ensign of the people; to it shall the Gentiles seek; and his rest shall be glorious.³

We had hoped to do what we could to fulfill the biblical prophecies that the Christians had ascribed to Jesus Christ's Second Coming, especially those that were written in the book of Isaiah that the Jews and Muslims believe were about their own Messiah. Again, we wrote these prophecies in a way so that we could try to make them come true in the future. It was our hope that the Americans would take the Second Coming of Christ seriously enough to prepare for it, as if Jesus were to come tomorrow.

We used the words of Isaiah to explain how important it was that the Americans ("Gentiles") become the saviors and helpers of the native American peoples, even all the poor, meek, disenfranchised, and persecuted people of Earth. We wrote:

---

² OT, Isaiah 11:4–5.

³ *See BOM*, 2 Nephi, chapter 21 (vs. 6 and 10 quoted above); and OT, Isaiah chapter 11. Ravenous predatory beasts, such as a leopard and wolf were used also in the book of Revelation to describe bad governments that destroy instead of help humanity. (*See* NT, Revelation 13:2.)

See also 666 America, 296: "The '*beast*' has great power over the people of the earth. Its strength is powerful and exercised in darkness ('*leopards*' are dark and hunt at night). It moves with force, crushing under its '*feet*' anything that rises against it (there is no animal as strong in its feet/paws as the '*bear*'). The sound of its voice is both intimidating and fierce ('*the mouth of a lion*') to all who dare challenge it." Read for free at realilluminati.org/666-mark-of-america.

Thus saith the Lord God: Behold, I will lift up mine hand to the Gentiles, and set up my standard to the people; and [the Americans] shall bring [the descendants of the *Book of Mormon* people—the ancestors of the native Americans, according to our story] in their arms, and thy daughters shall be carried upon [the Americans'] shoulders.[4]

We introduced our Marvelous Work and a Wonder® in a way that we hoped could not be misunderstood. Our intended message was about the Americans caring for the *temporal needs* (the basic necessities of life)[5] of the native Americans:

After they shall be nursed by the Gentiles, and the Lord has lifted up his hand upon the Gentiles and set them up for a standard, and [the native American peoples, both of North and South America] have been carried in their arms and … upon the shoulders [of the Americans], behold these things of which are spoken are *temporal*.

… And after our seed is scattered, the Lord God will proceed to do a marvelous work among the Gentiles, which shall be of great worth unto [the native American peoples]; wherefore, it is likened unto their being nourished by the Gentiles and being carried in their arms and upon their shoulders.[6]

In addition, we made it clear that there was no way that the rest of the world would be "blessed"—in other words, know how to set up the best government possible for humanity—<u>unless</u> "he shall make bare his arm in the eyes of the nations. Wherefore, the Lord God will proceed to make bare

---

[4] *BOM*, 2 Nephi 6:6.
[5] *See* "5 Basic Necessities of Life," The Humanity Party®, humanityparty.com/5-basic-necessities-of-life.
[6] *BOM*, 1 Nephi 22:6–8, emphasis added.

his arm in the eyes of all nations."[7] "Making bare his arm," means to show forth the power to do what needs to be done—the arm signifying the strength by which deeds are accomplished.

The world needed to see the rise of the United States and its greatness and importance to all of humanity. For this reason, we helped make sure that the United States was the first nation on the earth to acquire nuclear capabilities. With this "power of God," the United States controlled the world after World War II. With this immense power, the United States could easily, not only set the ultimate standard and become an ensign to the world, but also utilize Capitalism properly to care for the basic needs of all of Earth's population.

Part of the "marvelous work" that we have done among the Americans is to set up a new political party, The Humanity Party®. The political foundation that we present through this party sets this high standard for governments and shows the world how to establish the right form of government. Our plan to eliminate worldwide poverty is viable (possible) and can be put into effect immediately without changing American government or policy. Not only that, but our plan has never been properly challenged or shown to be ineffective (that it wouldn't work).

As we give the details behind *how* and *why* we wrote our new American scripture in the following chapters, always keep in mind that our intent for writing new scripture was to help the United States of America become the prophesied ensign and standard to the world. Yet the LDS/Mormon people—the American Christians who claimed belief in our new American scripture—completely ignored the needs of the native American people. Instead, they chose to become the wealthiest church on planet Earth.

As we share these details, visualize the young Joseph Smith allowing his scribe, Martin Harris, to present 116 pages of handwritten manuscript to a

---

[7] *See BOM*, 1 Nephi 22:10–11.

group of people and then ask for their opinions about it. No matter how hard Joseph tried to explain things to his peers, he could not get past their pride. They were very uncomfortable with the 116 pages of new American scripture that Joseph let them review. The only thing that Joseph could do at that time was convince his peer review group that there was a lot more coming, and what was coming would answer all of their questions and concerns.

Joseph returned and reported to us what had happened in his communications with the peer review group. He knew that we could deal with their questions and concerns. We did. We made our original storyline become "lost" and rewrote the first part of the story. In our rewrite, we knew we had to deal with the pride of the early American Christians and all of their corrupt religious beliefs. If we did not cater to their pride, they would not accept our new American scripture, and we would have not been able to introduce the specific prophecies that we have touched on above.

Joseph was able to convince his peers that he had only translated the beginning, a small part of the entire set of plates. They were satisfied with this explanation and waited for the rest of the story. However, his first scribe, Martin Harris, had a very hard time with Joseph allowing 116 pages of his handwritten manuscript to become "lost." Harris refused to accept the arguments and concerns of the peer review group. Harris fully agreed with the lessons from our original narrative.

History has properly reported that Harris did not support Joseph when Joseph *suffered* his peers to start a new church. Harris refused to attend the formation of an official religion because he knew that the peer group had *missed the mark*. Harris knew that the members of this group had looked beyond the simplicity of the philosophy and teachings of Jesus of Nazareth and wanted explanations of the things that they didn't understand. And, more than anything else, those who reviewed Harris' handwritten manuscript wanted a new church.

Joseph was able to quiet his peers and keep them excited about what was coming next. This was because they fully accepted that our invented history of the native Americans could fulfill the two Bible prophecies upon which we based our new scripture: 1) that a remnant of the house of Israel would be saved and become a great nation; and 2) that the "stick of Joseph, which is in the hand of Ephraim," would become a companion to the "stick of Judah" (the Bible).

In order to fulfill these two prophecies, the native American people would have to become a great and prosperous nation. For the native Americans to become this kind of nation, a record of their ancestors had to come forth and prove that they were descendants of the house of Israel, through Joseph's dark-skinned sons, Ephraim and Manasseh. Because the native American nation had been decimated by European Christians (the "Gentiles"), the only way that it would be possible to fulfill the prophecy about the native Americans becoming a great nation, would be with the help of the Americans (European Christians) *after* the Americans became a great nation. With the help of the "Gentiles," this prophecy could be fulfilled, but *only* if they were willing to help fulfill it.

We wanted to inspire the European Americans to help the native American people become a great nation. (This included all the darker-skinned peoples of both North and South America). The only way to do this was to incorporate a mandate from God. Therefore, our new American scripture was written to manipulate the Americans to use the power and means of their new government to help the native Americans become part of the United States, a nation on its way to becoming the greatest nation upon Earth.

We had Jesus Christ order the "Gentiles" (Americans) to establish a "new Jerusalem"[8] and "Zion" for the native Americans. We described *Zion* as a people "of one heart and one mind, [who] dwelt in righteousness; and there was no poor among them."[9] Unfortunately though, no matter how clearly we presented the mandates from Jesus Christ himself, the *unsealed*

---

[8] *See BOM*, 3 Nephi 20:22; 21:23–4; *and* Ether, chapter 13.
[9] *PGP*, Moses 7:18.

part of our story (the *Book of Mormon*) failed miserably. Thankfully, *The Sealed Portion was* able to convince many staunch LDS/Mormons of the gravity of their error. This caused them to leave that religion and no longer support this church's corrupt policies. Particularly damaging are those policies that support securing the United States' southern border[10] and keeping the descendants of the *Book of Mormon* people from benefiting from our prophecies.

Today (about 2020), the native Americans living in the United States are some of its most impoverished and marginalized citizens. Even more devastating, the native Americans living in the countries that make up South America live in much worse conditions. Crushing to us, the members of the religion that formed by using our book as the foundation of its creed (the Church of Jesus Christ of Latter-day Saints), supports American immigration law and policy that make it very difficult for South Americans to cross the imaginary line (the U.S. southern border).[11] These actions[12] directly impact the descendants of early native Americans and keep them from prospering. Instead, this church ignores the prophecies of our book, uses them to deceive people into joining their church, and has become one of the richest institutions in the modern world.

We anticipated that the early Americans would do this (set up a new religion instead of helping the native Americans become just as prosperous as they were). Therefore, the original narrative of our new American scripture, known as the *Book of Lehi* (and to the LDS people, as the *lost 116-page manuscript*), explained the wickedness of an organized church and

---

[10] *See* "Immigration," *Church News*, Intellectual Reserve, Inc., https://newsroom.churchofjesuschrist.org/official-statement/immigration.

[11] *See* "Most Republican States 2021," World Population Review, worldpopulationreview.com/state-rankings/most-republican-states.

[12] *See* "Immigration: Church Issues New Statement," June 10, 2011, The Church of Jesus Christ of Latter-day Saints, newsroom.churchofjesuschrist.org/article/immigration-church-issues-new-statement, which says, in part, "Most Americans agree that the federal government of the United States should secure its borders and sharply reduce or eliminate the flow of undocumented immigrants."

priesthood, as well as the uselessness of religious rituals and ordinances that have nothing to do with how a person treats another.

We wanted to reiterate that it was evil to organize a religion *instead* of uniting people and helping the poor. We used the book of Isaiah to provide the connection to what the Bible says that condemns organized religion and the priesthood authority thereof. In our original storyline, we included the first chapter of Isaiah in our intended narrative. We did not include verses 1 through 10, but wrote in a way to inspire the reader to study ALL of Isaiah, in context. We wrote an address given by our two chosen prophets (Zenos and Zenock) to the leaders of the church at Jerusalem:

> Behold, ye know not the words of God, but speak vanity and foolishness unto this people. Ye have taught this people that they should worship the church and the ordinances and the traditions thereof, and yet they deny the Spirit of God that will only dwell with the children of men in righteousness.
>
> Do ye not remember the words of the prophet, Isaiah? Ye have them before you, yet ye understand them not. Ye hear them, but ye do not hear their true meaning. Ye read them, but ye do not understand that which ye have read, but ye have changed the doctrine of God to conform to your own selfish interests and desires.
>
> Behold, did not Isaiah say unto this church: Thus saith the Lord, To what purpose is the multitude of your sacrifices unto me? Saith the Lord: I am full of the burnt offerings of rams, and the fat of fed beasts; and I delight not in the blood of bullocks, or of lambs, or of he-goats.
>
> When ye come to appear before me, who hath required this at your hand, to tread my courts? Bring no more vain oblations; incense is an abomination unto me; the new moons and

sabbaths, the calling of assemblies, I cannot abide them; away with them; it is iniquity, even the solemn meeting.

Your new moons and your appointed feasts my soul hateth; they are a trouble unto me; I am weary to bear them. And when ye spread forth your hands, I will hide mine eyes from you: yea, when ye make many prayers, I will not hear: your hands are full of blood.

Wash you, make you clean; put away the evil of your doings from before mine eyes; cease to do evil; Learn to do well; seek judgment, relieve the oppressed, judge the fatherless, plead for the widow.[13]

The first chapter of Isaiah explains how corrupt the church leaders and members were, even though they thought of themselves as righteous leaders and members of the only true church of God on the earth. Instead, Isaiah compared the church to "Sodom and Gomorrah."[14]

In our original storyline, our two prophets, Zenos and Zenock, directly condemned the leaders of the church established in Jerusalem as God's only *true and living church* upon Earth. These prophets came to Jerusalem and condemned this church for caring more about "busy work" than about the poor and the needy, similarly to how Isaiah presented it. Isaiah warned this church (leaders and members), that if it didn't repent, then the same thing that happened to the cities of Sodom and Gomorrah was going to happen to Jerusalem. Isaiah warned the Jews that

your country is desolate, your cities are burned with fire: your land, strangers devour it in your presence, and it is desolate, as overthrown by strangers.[15]

---

[13] *TSP*, Lehi 1:27–35.
[14] *See* OT, Isaiah 1:9–10.
[15] OT, Isaiah 1:7.

In the case of our story's timeline, the Babylonians were the "strangers" that fulfilled Isaiah's prophecy shortly after our Lehi left Jerusalem in 600 B.C.E.

As we have explained, Isaiah's prophecy mentioned "a very small remnant" that would be saved of the house of Israel. According to Jewish history, the entire house of Israel was carried away captive by the Babylonians in about 586 B.C.E. The Jews never accounted for or worried about fulfilling Isaiah's prophecy concerning this "small remnant" of people that was saved, escaping Babylonian captivity. Because the Jewish leaders didn't address this, we were able to fulfill Isaiah's prophecy ourselves. As we have explained, the families of Lehi and Ishmael (characters of our new American scripture) were this "small remnant" from the tribe of Joseph that was saved.

We didn't mention any actual timeline in our original story (the 116 pages of manuscript). This created some confusion among Joseph Smith's peers. Therefore, in our revised storyline, we made the exact year perfectly clear, as well as the events surrounding the time these two prophets came to Jerusalem:

> And now I, Nephi, proceed to give an account upon these plates [the plates that were replacing the 'lost' 116 pages that contained our original story] of my proceedings, and my reign and ministry; wherefore, to proceed with mine account, I must speak somewhat of the things of my father, and also of my brethren [to address the concerns of Joseph's peers].
>
> ... Yea, even six hundred years from the time that my father left Jerusalem, a prophet [Jesus Christ] would the Lord God raise up among the Jews—even a Messiah, or, in other words, a Savior of the world.

> ... And behold he cometh, according to the words of the angel, in six hundred years from the time my father left Jerusalem.[16]

Lehi left Jerusalem in 600 B.C.E. Fourteen years later (586 B.C.E.), according to accepted Jewish/Christian history, Jerusalem was destroyed by the Babylonians, just as our prophets Zenos and Zenock had prophesied.

The following is a brief summary of what was written in our original storyline that we had Joseph allow to be "lost," and which we "found" and took back from his enemies. We have published a full transcript of our original storyline as the *Book of Lehi*.[17]

According to our story, the native Americans are the descendants of two Jewish families that lived in Jerusalem 600 years before Jesus Christ was born. As we have mentioned, **Lehi** and **Ishmael** were the names of these two families' patriarchs. Both men were High Priests in the Jewish church (hereinafter referred to as "the Church").

Laban was the president, prophet, seer, and revelator of the Church. Laban was the highest authority of the Church, according to the Aaronic Priesthood established among the Jewish Church, as prescribed by the "lower" law of Moses presented in the Old Testament of the Bible.

The Old Testament record was written and preserved by the Hebrew Church upon plates of brass. There were more than one set of brass plates upon which the Old Testament was engraved. If there were duplicate sets, it was not a farfetched idea for Lehi to send his sons back to the Church to get one of the sets of brass plates. These sets of brass plates were in possession of the Church. High Priests were the only ones who were authorized to check out a set of the brass plates when needed in order to teach the people from the Mosaic Law that was engraved upon them.

---

[16] *BOM*, 1 Nephi 10:1, 4; 19:8.
[17] *See TSP*, Appendix 2: *The Book of Lehi*, p. 591. Download for free at realilluminati.org/the-book-of-lehi.

We will cover Lehi sending his sons to request the brass plates below. Had there not been more than one set, there was no sensible way that Lehi's sons could have asked Laban for the ONLY set of brass plates that had the law of Moses written upon it. There is no possible way that Laban would have allowed Lehi's sons to take the plates, or buy a set, unless there were multiple sets. (Although this is not explained in our story, we thought it important here to explain our reasoning for having Lehi's sons ask for a set of the brass plates.)

Two prophets were sent by God to call the Church and the people to repent of their evil ways. The Church did not think it was doing anything wrong. The members adored their leaders. The members believed that God would not let their leaders direct them to do evil. The leaders taught the members that God wouldn't allow it. (Likewise, a modern LDS Church prophet told the members that "the Lord will never permit me or any other man who stands as President of this Church to lead you astray.")[18]

Zenos and **Zenock** were the names of the *first* two prophets in our story. There were many more prophets throughout our story who tried to preach repentance to the people, all of whom were killed for speaking against the Church. When Zenos and Zenock were preaching against the Church and calling it evil, the people bound them and took them in front of the High Priests to be condemned for what they were saying.

Laban told his guards to kill them. Lehi was affected by what these two prophets were saying and stood between the guards and the prophets in an effort to protect them. Laban wanted to kill Lehi. However, Laban knew that Lehi was beloved by the people, so he didn't do anything to Lehi except kick Lehi out of the High Priest Group and out of the Church.

Lehi knew that the Church was corrupt. He tried to tell the people that the two prophets were right. The people rejected Lehi and cast him out

---

[18] *See D&C*, Official Declaration 1, "Excerpts From Three Addresses By President Wilford Woodruff Regarding The Manifesto."

as an apostate. Lehi believed everything that Zenos and Zenock had said. Lehi felt guilty for all of his sins, as well as for the sins of the Church. While Lehi was praying for forgiveness, he had a vision in which he saw Jerusalem being destroyed.

In Lehi's vision, he saw the house of Israel eventually return to Jerusalem and rebuild the city. He also saw Jesus Christ and his twelve apostles among the Jews, teaching the correct "fulness of the everlasting Gospel." This was the way that we introduced the future Christ and made the connection between Jesus Christ and the Messiah prophesied in the Old Testament.

We wanted our story to be all about Jesus and what he taught the people. We wanted Jesus Christ to be the main focus of our story. *If* we could not convince the Americans to abandon ALL organized religion, we wanted his words—exactly as they were recorded in the New Testament Gospels—to become the most important part of any future Christian religion, and a standard and ensign of a righteous nation.

Lehi was warned to get out of Jerusalem. God told Lehi that He would lead him to a new promised land. This is how we explained how "a small remnant" of the house of Israel came to the Western Hemisphere.

In our original story, we made it clear that an organized religion was not necessary, and that all church "busy work" was part of the "lower law" that was given. This was because they rejected the simplicity of the "higher law," as we have explained in detail in a previous chapter.

Lehi needed to teach his descendants to continue to observe the "lower law" until Jesus Christ delivered the "higher law." We made it very clear that the only law that would save the people was the "higher law" given in the words of Jesus.[19]

---

[19] See *BOM*, 2 Nephi 11:4; 25:24, 30.

At the time Lehi left Jerusalem, Lehi's family consisted of his wife, **Sariah**, his sons, **Laman**, **Lemuel**, **Sam**, and **Nephi**, and two daughters. In our original story, we only mentioned the name of one of Lehi's daughters, **Sira**, who was

> greatly blessed by the Spirit of the Lord and understood many things which she kept secret and unto herself because of her respect for her father and his authority in the priesthood.[20]

We knew that we could not focus a lot of attention on the women in our story because of the traditions of the Jews, as presented in the Bible's Old Testament, which were honored by early American Christians and demonstrated by the original U.S. Constitution. The reason why early American women could not vote is based entirely on erroneous Bible doctrine that had nothing to do with the words of Jesus:

> Let your women keep silence in the churches: for it is not permitted unto them to speak; but they are commanded to be under obedience, as also saith the law. And if they will learn any thing, let them ask their husbands at home: for it is a shame for women to speak in the church.[21]

It was our intent to show in our new American scripture how corrupt the Bible really was, outside of the actual words attributed to Jesus and the other books that we wrote to confront the way that religious leaders were interpreting the Bible. People cannot pick and choose what is "God's word" and what is not. It used to be a widely held belief in the LDS religion that a woman's role was quite a bit lower than that of a man. But in order to become popular in the eyes of the world, and luckily for women, this LDS/Mormon view has changed over time.

---

[20] *TSP*, Lehi 4:39.
[21] NT, 1 Corinthians 14:34–5.

Chapter 8: The 116-page Lost Manuscript

Our new American scripture was meant to counter all of the evil things that the Bible taught as the infallible "word of God," especially when it came to organized religion. Throughout our narrative, the actual words that came from Jesus' own lips were the only words that mattered, and they did *not* include the subordination of women in any way.

Lehi and Ishmael's families made their way to the new world: to the Western Hemisphere. After Lehi and Ishmael died, Lehi's oldest sons, Laman and Lemuel, rebelled against their younger brother Nephi, who was put in charge over them. Lehi's original family (which included the family of Ishmael), became separated into two main groups: the **Nephites** and the **Lamanites**.

At first, all the descendants of Lehi were a "white and delightsome people" that obeyed Nephi and the law of Moses. But the Lamanites were taught by their patriarchs, Laman and Lemuel, to hate the Nephites, the descendants of Nephi, Sam, and those of Lehi's posterity who chose to follow Nephi. The Lamanites ran around naked. They were lazy and stole from the Nephites instead of being "industrious."[22]

The first area that was established in the new world was called the "Land of Nephi." The Lamanites lived outside of its borders and stole from and murdered the Nephites whenever they had the chance. The Nephites made copies of a sword that Nephi had stolen from Laban to protect themselves.

There are many details of the story that we are not presenting here. One need only review the *Book of Mormon* and compare its narrative to what was "lost" in the *Book of Lehi* in order to understand that many of the important details were *not* changed when we revised the story. We have given a short summary of our original narrative above so that we can then present to the reader the things that we *needed* to change about our story in order to get Joseph's peers to accept it as "God's word."

---

[22] *BOM*, 2 Nephi 5:21, 17.

Chapter 9
The Forced Revision

Before we continue to explain more about how we replaced 116 pages of "lost" manuscript with our revision, imagine (according to how we wrote our story) our character **Mormon** sitting in a cave surrounded by 1000 years of metal plates containing the history of his people. Mormon's job is to make a complete abridgment—a condensed history of the most important events.

Mormon begins this arduous (extremely difficult) task by making new metal plates upon which he will engrave his abridgment. The new plates are created from the same template from which most of the other metal plates were made. Because he doesn't know how long his abridgment is going to be, Mormon has the appropriate metals available in the cave to cast as many plates as he might need. So he begins.

The many plates are not all bound together with rings. In front of Mormon are six separate groups of items. These six items are:

1) the largest group of plates that are *not* bound together, called the "large plates of Nephi";

2) a smaller set of plates that *are* bound together, called the "small plates of Nephi";

3) a "large stone" that contains a very short abridgment of the history of a people called "the Jaredites," whose ancestors first arrived in North America about 2000 years before Mormon was born;

4) the "twenty and four plates of pure gold" that contain more of the history of the Jaredites. The majority of these 24 gold plates contain the writings of the father of the Jaredites—a man simply called "the brother of Jared";

Chapter 9: The Forced Revision

5) a set of two stones, called "*interpreters*";

6) "a ball of curious workmanship," called the "*Liahona.*"

Honest and scrupulous LDS/Mormon historians are perplexed. They are unable to explain how Mormon and his son, Moroni, put together their separate abridgments that became the final set of "gold plates" that were delivered to Joseph Smith to be translated. Part of the confusion comes from their inability to explain how the "large stone" was translated. The engravings on the "large stone" were not written in the same language as those on the "large amount" of plates named after Nephi, which were called the "large plates of Nephi" (see item 1 above). Mormon's ancestors had used "reformed Egyptian" to record that lengthy 1000-year history.

(Keep in mind, that in every way possible, we were careful to ensure that the way we were presenting our new American scripture to the world was both plausible and probable. EVERYTHING had to make sense.)

According to the storyline, the "large" and "small" sets of plates (items 1 and 2 above), both called "the plates of Nephi," were written in Mormon's and Moroni's own language—"reformed Egyptian." This was not a spoken language, but only used for engraving their history on metal plates. Mormon and Moroni didn't need interpreters to read and then abridge their own history. However, the "people of Zarahemla," who had discovered the "large stone"—engraved in an unfamiliar language as presented in our storyline—did not find any interpreters with the stone.

The people of Zarahemla were another group that had escaped Jerusalem while it was being ransacked by the Babylonians. Zarahemla was the name of the leader of this group of people found by Nephite explorers. Like Lehi and Ishmael, the people of Zarahemla "journeyed in the wilderness, and were brought by the hand of the Lord across the great waters"[1] into North America a short time after Lehi and Ishmael had landed their families in South America. When the ancestors of Zarahemla first arrived in North America, they encountered the last surviving person of the Great Jaredite Nation, King Coriantumr.[2]

Because LDS/Mormon historians and scholars do not know *how* and *why* the *Book of Mormon* narrative was created, they cannot explain why it was important to include a subplot about the people of Zarahemla; nor can they explain how Zarahemla's story fit in with the overall narrative. Historians and scholars do not know that Joseph Smith had a peer review group that was reviewing each part of our story. They do not understand that when this group of peers was confused, uncertain, or argumentative about something we wrote, we would try our best to solve the conflict in the next part of our story.

As an example, the peer review group had a very hard time accepting that God would command someone to kill a defenseless Jewish High Priest (Laban), and then rob the Church at Jerusalem of the plates of brass (which, as we have explained, contained the Old Testament of the Bible).

The peer group had reviewed our original storyline when the prophets Zenos and Zenock confronted the Church for its wickedness. (The evil of the Church came from following the letter of the law contained in the *lower* Law of Moses, and denying the spirit thereof). When we presented the plot in which Lehi was commanded by God to take a copy of the brass plates (Old Testament) with him when he fled Jerusalem, Joseph's peers were unsettled. They didn't understand the need to murder someone and steal a record of laws[3] that God could have easily given to Lehi. Joseph's peer review group reasoned that God could have even given Lehi His complete "higher law" without having one of his sons commit murder and steal in violation of

---

[1] *BOM* Omni 1:16.
[2] *BOM*, Omni 1:21.
[3] *See TSP*, Lehi 4:9–30.

the Ten Commandments. God could have given Lehi His will the same way that He gave it to Moses, face to face upon a mountain.

After we "lost" our original narrative and rewrote the story,[4] we explained that Lehi's son, Nephi, was commanded by God to murder the High Priest who had possession of the brass plates. This was so that Lehi's posterity would have the law of Moses because "they could not keep the commandments of the Lord according to the law of Moses, save they should have the law."[5] We did this to adjust what we wrote, because our first try (given in our original narrative) at explaining why stealing the brass plates through murder and deceit was important, hadn't thoroughly convinced Joseph's peers.

Another problem the peer group had was with the part of Nephi's story in our narrative when the Lord tells Nephi:

> After ye have arrived in the promised land, ye shall know that I, the Lord, am God; and that I, the Lord, did deliver you from destruction; yea, that I did bring you out of the land of Jerusalem.[6]

Joseph's peers also wanted to know *how* "ye shall know" that the people of Jerusalem were destroyed, when Lehi and his group were long gone and across the ocean living in South America.

Because of these issues the peer group had, we invented another subplot that we hoped would solve their concerns. The ancestors of the people of Zarahemla were firsthand witnesses of the destruction of Jerusalem. After these people saw Jerusalem being destroyed, we had them travel to North America where they were discovered by the Nephites. The Nephites discovered that the people of Zarahemla were

---

[4] *See BOM*, 1 Nephi 4:6–27.
[5] *BOM*, 1 Nephi 4:15.
[6] *BOM*, 1 Nephi 17:14.

exceedingly numerous. Nevertheless, they had had many wars and serious contentions ... and their language had become corrupted; and they had brought no records with them; and they denied the being of their Creator; and [the Nephites] could [not] understand them.[7]

Once the Nephites taught the people of Zarahemla how to speak Hebrew again, their leader, **Zarahemla**, was able to recount what he knew of their history. This history included the way that the Lord showed the Nephites ("ye shall know") that the people living in Jerusalem had been destroyed, as Zenos and Zenock had prophesied. The people of Zarahemla were the proof that the Nephites needed to know that Jerusalem had been destroyed as prophesied.

Further, without having the brass plates, the Nephites might have done what the people of Zarahemla did and also corrupted their own language and not believed in God. This was another justification of the importance of having Nephi steal the brass plates. The Zarahemla subplot also provided us with an opportunity to first introduce the Great Jaredite Nation that existed in North America. The Zarahemla story satisfied the concerns of Joseph's peers, at least concerning the issues explained above.

The Zarahemla subplot told of a "large stone brought unto [King Mosiah, a Nephite king] with engravings on it; and he did interpret the engravings by the gift and power of God."[8] The problem with the narrative, at least for some of Joseph's peers, was in how King Mosiah interpreted the engravings on the "large stone ... by the gift and power of God," when there was no record of what this "gift and power" was. If King Mosiah's ability to interpret ancient writings, if his "gift and power of God," did not include some kind of physical interpreters, then *how* did he actually interpret the engravings on the "large stone"?

Joseph's peers were confused and began to argue amongst themselves. A few suggested that God could inspire the mind of any man

---

[7] *BOM*, Omni 1:17.
[8] *BOM*, Omni 1:20.

so appointed to know the interpretation of anything. We knew that if we allowed this speculation to continue, then any man could claim the "gift and power of God" and come up with any interpretation that he wanted.

Joseph was quick to explain how King Mosiah interpreted the "large stone." Joseph reminded the group about the *Liahona* (the "ball of curious workmanship"[9]) that Lehi had been given—an actual tool that had been passed down through the generations to whomever kept the records. When we later introduced the "twenty-four plates which were filled with engravings and were of pure gold,"[10] we included a clear explanation of a device that provided "the gift and power of God." We did this to ensure that a deceptive man would not simply claim to be a prophet of God and have "God's inspiration" in interpreting ancient records without possessing an actual, physical apparatus by which to interpret them.

In our story, the plates were brought to a Nephite king who asked, "Knowest thou of anyone that can translate?" To ensure we eliminated the possibility of any person claiming authority over others by having "the gift and power of God," we clearly wrote that to translate one must also have the:

> wherewith that he can look, and translate all records that are of ancient date; and it is a gift from God. And the things are called interpreters, and no man can look in them except he be commanded, lest he should look for that he ought not and he should perish. And whosoever is commanded to look in them, the same is called seer.
>
> ... A seer is a revelator and a prophet also; and a gift which is greater can no man have, except he should possess the power of God, which no man can; yet a man may have great power given him from God.

---

[9] *BOM*, 1 Nephi 16:10.
[10] *Compare BOM*, Mosiah 8:9.

> ... Thus God has provided a means that man, through faith, might work mighty miracles; therefore he becometh a great benefit to his fellow beings.[11]

Imagine Mormon sitting in a cave with the six items that we described in the beginning of this chapter. Now imagine *how* his son Moroni (who wrote about the Jaredites) could have used the *Liahona* to translate the engravings on the "large stone" (like King Mosiah had). However, Moroni also had the two stones called "interpreters." These are what he used to translate the engravings that were on the "twenty and four plates." He also could have used the "interpreters" (two stones) to translate the engravings on the "large stone."

The engravings on the "plates of Nephi" (both large and small) were in a different language ("reformed Egyptian") than the engravings on the "large stone" and those upon the twenty-four gold plates—which told the story of the Great Jaredite Nation. More importantly, according to the story, the engravings on the twenty-four gold plates provided all the information for the *sealed portion* of the final set of plates that were delivered to Joseph Smith, which would later be "translated" by our more contemporary True Messenger, Christopher.

The *sealed portion* of the gold plates that we delivered to Joseph Smith (2/3) was twice as big as the *unsealed part* (1/3). Mormon and Moroni had access to many, many metal plates that had been engraved over 1000 years, from which to make their abridgments. But, from just twenty-four gold plates, a record twice as large as the *unsealed* part was abridged. The twenty-four plates contained a history of the entire world, from its beginning to its end, as told by *the brother of Jared*. Moroni was shown all things by the Lord—even

---

[11] See *BOM*, Mosiah 8:13–18.

the very things which the brother of Jared saw; and there never were greater things made manifest than those which were made manifest unto the brother of Jared.[12]

The story of the ancestors of the native Americans spanned 1000 years of history (600 B.C.E. to 400 C.E.). This required *many* metal plates. The twenty-four gold plates included a history of magnitude that spanned from the beginning of Earth to its end. They also included the entire history of the Great Jaredite Nation that lasted for about 2000 years. How could all of this be recorded on just twenty-four plates?

The answer is simple. All of the engravings on the twenty-four gold Jaredite plates were hieroglyphics. Each hieroglyphic character tells its own story. Whereas the 1000-year history of the Nephite people was written in "reformed Egyptian" and abridged in 1/3 of the final set of "gold plates" delivered to Joseph Smith, the engravings on the twenty-four gold plates were written in "Jaredite hieroglyphics," which were very different from "reformed Egyptian."

Because the Jaredite people came *before* the Egyptians, they had a completely different way of writing and telling their stories. Before writing, people told stories. The storytellers would make marks and symbols about their various stories that would remind the storyteller about the narrative when they retold the same story over and over again. These marks and symbols became *hieroglyphics*. The pre-Egyptian Jaredites came from the time of the Tower of Babel story related in the Bible. Therefore, it is easy to understand how they could have had a much different set and pattern of hieroglyphics than the later Egyptians or other later civilizations. Each of the Jaredite *hieroglyphic* characters told a lot more story than "reformed Egyptian" did. That's why it is understandable that so many words could come from just twenty-four gold Jaredite plates.

---

[12] *See BOM*, Ether 4:4.

A New American Scripture

According to our narrative, the two stones ("interpreters") that were used to translate Jaredite engravings were made by the first Jaredite, the brother of Jared. Joseph Smith used the same two stones to translate (transcribe) the *unsealed* part of the plates he received. According to the official account Joseph revealed to the world, he was instructed properly by **Moroni**, who was resurrected and appeared to Joseph as an *angel sent from God.* We instructed Joseph Smith on what to write. We wanted his experience to match our story's narrative. We had Joseph describe an experience of being visited by the resurrected Moroni and receiving the instructions to translate Mormon's plates of gold (except for the *sealed portion* of the plates).

(As explained, according to the story we made up, Moroni was Mormon's son.) **Mormon** engraved the majority of the *unsealed portion* of the gold plates delivered to Joseph Smith to be translated into what became the *Book of Mormon*. Mormon's son, **Moroni**, wrote the last portion of the *unsealed* part of the plates, as well as all of the *sealed portion* of the plates. The *sealed portion* of the plates, according to our story's narrative, was translated and abridged from the twenty-four gold plates by Moroni. (To clarify, the "complete" gold plates engraved by Mormon and Moroni were comprised of both the *sealed* and *unsealed* portions.)

Ten years passed between the time that Joseph told people that he received his first instructions about the gold plates (1827) and the time that he made a public and official account of his experiences (1837). Over the course of these ten years, Joseph had never been specific about how he got the plates, or about the experiences surrounding their existence. LDS/Mormon critics and honest historians do well to point out that Joseph had given various *incomplete* accounts about what happened. This was true until we instructed him to make a more complete and official account in 1837.

It was our hope that the message and intended lessons of our new American scripture would be accepted and understood without questioning the authenticity and verifiable history of *where* the scripture came from. We based this hope on the fact that although the validity and truthfulness of the Bible had been questioned for many hundreds of years, none of these secular scholars or Bible skeptics could convince Bible believers that the Bible was not authentic and what it claimed to be: God's infallible words. Bible critics had the same problem with the Bible's authenticity and verifiable history that the people in Joseph Smith's time had with what they often referred to as "Joes' Golden Bible." We figured that because the Bible-believers in Joseph Smith's day didn't pay attention to the critics, nor did they question the Bible's history or truthfulness, why would they question our new American scripture's genuineness and legitimacy?

To set our new American scripture at a level of integrity even greater than the Bible, we had to finally give the people a history that they could easily understand and believe. We instructed Joseph to write this:

> He called me by name, and said unto me that he was a messenger sent from the presence of God to me, and that his name was Moroni; that God had a work for me to do; and that my name should be had for good and evil among all nations, kindreds, and tongues, or that it should be both good and evil spoken of among all people.
>
> He said there was a book deposited, written upon gold plates, giving an account of the former inhabitants of this continent, and the source from whence they sprang. He also said that the fulness of the everlasting Gospel was contained in it, as delivered by the Savior to the ancient inhabitants;
>
> Also, that there were two stones in silver bows—and these stones, fastened to a breastplate, constituted what is called the Urim and Thummim—deposited with the plates; and the possession and use of these stones were what constituted

"seers" in ancient or former times; and that God had prepared them for the purpose of translating the book.[13]

Dishonest and unscrupulous (biased and subjective) accounts have been published about Joseph peering into a hat in which he had placed a "seer stone,"[14] from which he allegedly translated the gold plates. Not at any time did Joseph Smith ever explain that he translated the plates in this way.[15] With great care, we instructed both Joseph Smith and Christopher to follow our instructions precisely as the former produced the *Book of Mormon* (1830), and the latter *The Sealed Portion* (2004).

We have revealed, and will continue to reveal throughout the book you are reading, *how* and *why* we created the *Book of Mormon*. Everything that we quote from our book was made up, by us, for a specific purpose. Everything that we did, we hoped would become "a great benefit to [our] fellow beings."[16]

Before we proceed to further explain how we made the transition from the "lost" (original) first part of our narrative, to the finalized story that

---

[13] JSH 1:33–5.
[14] *See* "Mormonism," *Kansas City Daily Journal*, 5 June 1881, 1, whitmercollege.com/interviews/kansas-city-journal-1881/; *and*
"Testimony of David Whitmer," *Saints' Herald*, 15 Nov. 1879, 341; view at rsc.byu.edu/coming-forth-book-mormon/firsthand-witness-accounts-translation-process; *and*
Emma Smith Bidamon, Nauvoo, IL, to Emma Pilgrim, 27 Mar. 1870, in John Clark, "Translation of Nephite Records," *The Return*, 15 July 1895, 2; view at josephsmithpapers.org/intro/introduction-to-revelations-and-translations-volume-3; *and*
"Seer stone," Church Historians Press – The Church of Jesus Christ of Latter-day Saints, josephsmithpapers.org/topic/seer-stone; *and*
Michael Hubbard MacKay and Gerrit J. Dirkmaat, "Firsthand Witness Accounts of the Translation Process," in *The Coming Forth of the Book of Mormon: A Marvelous Work and a Wonder*, edited by Dennis L. Largey, Andrew H. Hedges, John Hilton III, and Kerry Hull (Provo, UT: Religious Studies Center; Salt Lake City: Deseret Book, 2015), 61–79, also found online at rsc.byu.edu/coming-forth-book-mormon/firsthand-witness-accounts-translation-process.
[15] *See* JS Bio, 296–7.
[16] *BOM*, Mosiah 8:18.

Chapter 9: The Forced Revision

was published as the *Book of Mormon* in 1830, we want to make a proclamation here. There have ONLY been two men with whom we have revealed ourselves and asked to help us perform our work: Joseph Smith, Jr. and Christopher (last name withheld for his protection). Any other person claiming access to us, at any time, in any way, is a liar and deceiver who should be avoided at all costs.

Joseph and Christopher are the "seers" of whom we have written. **Only** these two men could have and can produce the actual device, the "wherewith that he can look, and translate all records that are of ancient date."[17] Joseph showed the *Urim and Thummim* to a few people in his day. Joseph had those to whom he showed the device take a vow of secrecy about the presentation. Christopher however, was given our permission to allow many to see and hold what we call the *Urim and Thummim*.

Christopher's life is now in more danger because we are revealing the Real Truth™ about *how* and *why* we created our new American scripture. For this reason, we have forbidden him from showing the device to anyone else. We have taken repossession of the device and will bring it forth in our own due time in order to prove to the world the claims we are making about the work that we have done—a work that we properly call, a Marvelous Work and a Wonder®.

Now, back to our story with **Mormon** sitting in a cave with the six items we described above:

To make his abridgment, Mormon began to review the *larger amount* of the plates of Nephi (the "large plates of Nephi"). In the revision of our narrative, after the 116-page manuscript was "lost," we had Nephi clearly explain the difference between the two sets of plates. Nephi wrote:

---

[17] *BOM*, Mosiah 8:13.

[There was a large set] upon which I make a full account of the history of my people; for the plates upon which I make a full account of my people I have given the name of Nephi; wherefore, they are called the plates of Nephi, after mine own name; and these plates [referring now to the "smaller amount of plates of Nephi"] also are called the plates of Nephi.

Nevertheless, I have received a commandment of the Lord that I should make these ["smaller amount of the plates of Nephi"], for the special purpose that there should be an account engraven of the ministry of my people.

Upon the other plates [the "larger amount of plates of Nephi"] should be engraven an account of the reign of the kings, and the wars and contentions of my people; wherefore these plates [the "small plates of Nephi"] are for the more part of the ministry; and the ["large plates of Nephi"] are for the more part of the reign of the kings and the wars and contentions of my people.

Wherefore, the Lord hath commanded me to make these ["small plates of Nephi"] for a wise purpose in him, which purpose I know not. [We (the Real Illuminati®) know the purpose. We are the "Lord" that commanded Nephi to make two sets of plates.]

But the Lord knoweth all things from the beginning; wherefore, he prepareth a way to accomplish all his works among the children of men; for behold, he hath all power unto the fulfilling of all his words. And thus it is. Amen.[18]

In our revised narrative (which became the *Book of Mormon*), we had Mormon explain why he included the "small plates of Nephi" in his abridgment. Keep in mind that our main character and author, **Mormon**,

---

[18] *BOM*, 1 Nephi 9:2–6.

had already made a few plates and engraved an abridgment of what Lehi had written. (Again, this was according to the story that we made up in response to Joseph's peers' inquiries, questions, and complaints.) Lehi was the first person to make plates of ore based on the brass plates that they stole from the Church at Jerusalem. Once Lehi had made a few plates, he began to engrave the account of his life. Mormon reviewed and abridged Lehi's account (which is part of what the "lost" 116 pages of manuscript contained). Then Mormon explains,

> And now, I speak somewhat concerning that which I have written; for after I had made an abridgment from the [large] plates of Nephi [which included Lehi's account], down to the reign of this king Benjamin, of whom Amaleki spake, I searched among the records which had been delivered into my hands, and I found these plates [the smaller collection, the "small plates of Nephi" that were bound together], which contained this small account of the prophets, from Jacob down to the reign of king Benjamin, and also many of the words of Nephi.
>
> ... Wherefore, I chose these things, to finish my record upon them, which remainder of my record I shall take from the [larger collection, the "large"] plates of Nephi; and I cannot write the hundredth part of the things of my people.
>
> ... And I [include the small plates of Nephi with my abridgment of the large plates of Nephi] for a wise purpose; for thus it whispereth me, according to the workings of the Spirit of the Lord which is in me. And now, I do not know all things; but the Lord knoweth all things which are to come; wherefore, he worketh in me to do according to his will.[19]

---

[19] *BOM*, Words of Mormon 1:3–7.

A New American Scripture

Because all the Nephite plates were the exact same dimension (as they had been constructed from the same template), Mormon simply placed his abridgment of the account of Lehi to the reign of king Benjamin on top of the "small plates of Nephi." This constituted the first part of his abridgment, viewing the plates as they would be bound by rings as the finished product. After putting the small plates of Nephi in with his abridgment, Mormon made more plates and continued his narrative.

The easiest way for a person to understand the changes that we made to our original storyline (116-page "lost" manuscript) is for one to take out the "small plates of Nephi" that Mormon included and read our story as it would have read, had we not changed its beginning.

To grasp the great significance of the changes, one needs to read the *Book of Lehi* as we published it with *The Sealed Portion* (2004). After this, one can skip over 1st and 2nd Nephi, Jacob, Enos, Jarom, Omni, and the Words of Mormon, in the contemporary *Book of Mormon*, and continue to read, as if Mormon had not made the inclusion of the *Small Plates of Nephi*. After the last verse in the *Book of Lehi*, start with Mosiah, chapter 1.

Here's how it would read following the instructions above:

And it came to pass that king Mosiah called the people together to speak with them one last time before his death. And when the people had gathered to hear their leader, Mosiah set his son Benjamin before them and consecrated and anointed him to reign in his stead.

And king Mosiah stood forth and spoke unto his people, saying: My beloved brothers and sisters; Behold, ye are all truly my brothers and sisters, for in God our Father, we have our affiliation.

[What follows for a number of verses are some incredible words given by king Mosiah that we did not include in our revised narrative. As these verses are too numerous to include herein, we would admonish the reader to review these words in context as we wrote them for the 116-page manuscript.]

… And there arose much contention throughout the land of Zarahemla. Yea, everyone blamed another for the wars with the Lamanites. Yea, every man accused his neighbor of sinning against God and bringing the wrath of God upon them, thus denying his own wickedness.

And it came to pass that king Benjamin pleaded with the people to repent of their sins and remember the things that his father had spoken unto them.

… And now there was no more contention in all the land of Zarahemla, among all the people who belonged to king Benjamin, so that king Benjamin had continual peace all the remainder of his days.[20]

The story flows seamlessly, as we presented it, had we not been forced to address the concerns and doubts of Joseph's peers and caused the original narrative to become "lost."

Below we present a few of the reasons why we made our revision (1st and 2nd Nephi, Jacob, Enos, Jarom, Omni, and the Words of Mormon). We are not going to give a lot of quotes from the 1830 *Book of Mormon*. If the reader is truly interested in finding the Real Truth™ about *how* and *why* we wrote the revision, the reader will take the time to review our revision while taking into account what we explain below.

Whereas it was our intent to show the Christians how valuable the native Americans were, Christian pride made it all about themselves. Therefore, in our rewrite, **we made it all about the European-American Christians.**

---
[20] *See TSP*, Lehi 9:32–63; then go seamlessly to *BOM*, Mosiah 1:1.

A New American Scripture

In our revised storyline, we played on the pride of being a Christian, as well as (and probably more important to Joseph's peers) the pride of being an American. We had to show the importance of being both. We had to connect the lessons of our new American scripture to the already established Christian pride and belief so that we could accomplish one of our main desires for our new scripture: to influence the development of the United States of America.

Using a connection to the Old Testament through the law of Moses and the prophets (as we had presented it with the introduction of the "brass plates") wasn't enough. We had to interlock our new American scripture with the *New* Testament as well, which we had not done in our original storyline.

To drive the point home, we introduced the relevance of the New Testament book of Revelation. This was very important, because our group (the Real Illuminati®) was responsible for writing Revelation for the early Roman Catholics. We had done this as another testimony of the pure teachings of Jesus Christ and how these teachings could help humanity. We wrote Revelation to disclose and counter the way that the early Christian leaders had corrupted Jesus' original message as it was recorded in the Gospels.

In a previous chapter, we explained that two-thirds (2/3) of our gold plates were sealed. We revealed that we didn't actually have anything engraved on this sealed portion at that time. This was intended to give us leeway in presenting information that we correctly assumed would be needed to teach prideful Christians.

In this book we have also presented this "sealed part" as a *failsafe*. We needed to be able to put a plan into operation in the event of something going wrong, or to prevent such an occurrence from happening. We presented the "sealed part" of our book as the most important part, as the "greater things" that must be received and accepted by the people in order for them to not be condemned. We warned the Christians (the "Gentiles") that they would not receive the "sealed portion" if they were wicked. We made it perfectly clear that if "the greater portion of the word" was withheld, "then [the Christians would be] taken captive by the devil, and led by his will down to destruction."[21]

It was our hope that such warnings would motivate Christians to not be wicked, "remain[ing in their] awful state of wickedness, and hardness of heart, and blindness of mind."[22] Unbelievably, the modern LDS people seem to be fine with not having the "greater portion." As we prophesied about them, these members are pacified and lulled

> away into carnal security, that they will say: All is well in Zion; yea, Zion prospereth [our church is one of the world's wealthiest], all is well—and thus the devil cheateth their souls, and leadeth them away carefully down to hell.[23]

Members of this church see themselves as righteous, and certainly do not think that they are being led by the devil. Our book could not have been any clearer about the importance of its "sealed portion." However, our book has failed to convince Christians of their great *un*righteousness. Our *failsafe* was put into our storyline to prevent the "Gentiles" from becoming corrupt, by warning them that if they didn't have the *sealed portion*, then they had nothing.[24]

Our *Book of Mormon* failed in its intended purpose. Therefore, as we have explained, in 2004 we put our *failsafe* into operation. Any honest and sincere *Book of Mormon* believer, upon reading our book, *The Sealed Portion*, has no choice but to see the LDS Church for what it really is. Just as powerful as this failsafe is, our *Book of Lehi* (the "lost" 116-page

---

[21] See *BOM*, Alma 12:10–11.
[22] See *BOM*, Ether 4:15.
[23] *BOM*, 2 Nephi 28:21.
[24] See *BOM*, Alma 12:9–11.

manuscript), when read in context with a sincere heart and real intent, can also convince a person of the great evil of organized religion, especially the one that evolved from the misuse of our new American scripture.

Again, it was this convincing power—that condemned the way that churches use rituals and completely ignore the *Royal Law*—that offended many of Joseph's peers. In our revision, we needed to give more prophecies about the wickedness of religion and the churches that had developed among the "Gentiles" living in America. We needed to subtly introduce the foundational operations of the secret combinations of politics, religion, and business that began in Europe. These were responsible for the corruption of the "plain and precious things" about Jesus' teachings. As our friend Howard Zinn wrote:

> These [native Americans] were remarkable (European observers were to say again and again) for their hospitality, their belief in sharing. These traits did not stand out in the Europe of the Renaissance [in the nations of the "Gentiles"], dominated as it was by the religion of popes, the government of kings, the frenzy for money [i.e., the "great and abominable church"] that marked Western civilization.[25]

Our original story didn't get through to the reader by using the example of the law of Moses and what happened to the Jews. We had to convince them with prophecies that came directly from God, through angels, and were aimed specifically at the American "Gentiles."

As we explained previously, it was also very important to us to present the idea that the United States and its inhabitants (early European-American Christians) were responsible for the wellbeing and care of the native Americans. The "Gentiles" were supposed to help establish a "New Jerusalem"

---

[25] Howard Zinn, *The People's History of the United States of America* (New York: Harper Perennial Modern Classics, 2005), 1.

Chapter 9: The Forced Revision

on the American continent, where members of the house of Israel would gather and establish what "Zion" was supposed to represent.

Just a few months after Joseph officially published the "unsealed part" of the gold plates as the *Book of Mormon*, we counseled him to finally give an explanation to his followers of the true meaning of "Zion." In order to teach certain lessons, we had Joseph rewrite the history of the Jews in a particular way. We also had to counter obvious errors in the Bible's narrative. We called this biblical rewrite, the *Book of Moses*. In it, Joseph wrote:

> And the Lord called his people Zion, because they were of one heart and one mind, and dwelt in righteousness; and there was no poor among them.[26]

In previous chapters, we went to great lengths to explain how the LDS people missed the mark about establishing Zion for the native Americans. While their church became the wealthiest in the world, the native American people living in the United States became some of the poorest people. The early American Christians who read our book made it all about them, and *little to nothing* about the native American people who were the intended ancestors of our story's characters.

Another main concern that Joseph's peers had with our new American scripture was the *atonement*. The *atonement* they believed in was a ritual (the actual act of Jesus suffering in the Garden of Gethsemane and being killed on the cross to pay for their sins). This ritual was based on past rituals given in the law of Moses (sacrificing an innocent animal by shedding its blood). But in our new American scripture, we clearly presented the law of Moses as the "lower law." Using logic and reason, we presented this symbolic ritual—the *atonement*—as being <u>fulfilled</u> by Jesus Christ, and therefore *no longer necessary* after Jesus taught everything that a person needed to do in order to be saved: just be nice to others, as his *Sermon on the Mount* expressed.

---

[26] *PGP*, Moses 7:18.

Joseph cleverly *tried* to explain the Real Truth™ about the *atonement* to his peers. He told them that the actual act of Jesus dying on the cross had nothing to do with a person's salvation. This was a big concern to Christians. The act of Jesus dying on the cross was the most important part of Christian belief. In our story, each time we mentioned what the Christians viewed as the *atonement* (when Jesus died on the cross), we connected it to obeying "the law which the Holy One hath given" (i.e., to following Jesus' commandments to be nice to others).

It was our intent to show that Jesus dying on the cross didn't matter, if one didn't do what Jesus instructed them to do. We made Christ the center of our story, and "feasting upon the words of Christ" the main requirement in order to "have eternal life":

> Wherefore, I said unto you, feast upon the words of Christ; for behold, the words of Christ will tell you all things what ye should do. ... and they teach all men that they should do good.[27]

Because the Christians were fixated on the murder of Jesus as all that needed to be done to save them from sin, complying with the *Royal Law* was not important to them. This was because when they sinned (by not treating their neighbor as themselves), they believed the sin was automatically forgiven because Jesus had died on the cross.

<u>There is no way that a good society can exist when people justify treating each other badly</u>, no matter from where the justification comes. A successful community cannot be accomplished when people relieve themselves of any guilt associated with their actions because "Jesus died" to take away their sins. The plain and precious words of Jesus never said *anything* about a person being saved just because he was murdered. But if we tried to even imply that the *atonement* was not real, a Christian would automatically shut their mind to anything else that we said.

---

[27] *BOM*, 2 Nephi 32:3; 33:10.

Chapter 9: The Forced Revision

As explained above, if read carefully and in context, one will see that when we wrote our revisions, we always connected Jesus' *atonement* with "keeping the commandments of God." None of these commandments, not one, required any ritual to be performed, except being "baptized in the name of Christ" as a covenant to always do what Christ says to do.

We made sure there was a solid connection between Jesus and the promised Messiah mentioned in the Bible's prophecies. Then, once we had the reader's mind open using Old Testament prophecies, we invented some of our own in order to give Joseph Smith and our new American scripture more validity and importance. We were then able to introduce Joseph as a person just as important as Moses. Again, the most important first step was writing things that would open the Bible-believer's mind just enough for us to introduce concepts that most Christians would have otherwise rejected outright.

We had to make Joseph Smith part of the prophecy, so we connected him directly to the "Joseph who was carried captive into Egypt."[28] By first mentioning something that we knew Christians already accepted as truth, the familiarity opened their minds to believe whatever followed, as long as it made sense. But with each new concept we presented, we used subtle mind manipulation to reinforce to the reader that the most important focus was to "keep the commandments of the Holy One of Israel."[29]

Giving subliminal messages works. This is evident as one reads our revised story, focusing on how we presented new ideas within the boundaries of belief that Christians had created in their minds. We used subliminal messages throughout our revised storyline. We presented new ideas that the reader did not consciously notice because of the way that we mixed these new ideas in with orthodox Christian belief—even when we knew that the established belief was completely wrong. There was no other way we could

---

[28] *See BOM*, 2 Nephi 3:4–24.
[29] *BOM*, 2 Nephi 3:2.

get our points across without alarming the reader and discounting what they already believed was true.

Consider how we were able to introduce the idea that the King James Bible is corrupt in the *unsealed portion* of our new American scripture (the *Book of Mormon*). First, we introduced the reader to the idea that the "Spirit of God" was upon the early American settlers. The reader was most likely an American, so reinforcing that the reader was "wrought upon by the Spirit of God"[30] complied with the boundaries established by the American reader's pride.

We reinforced this pride by subtly telling the American Christians that "they were white, and exceedingly fair and beautiful." We continued to stroke their egos by writing that they "did humble themselves before the Lord; and the power of the Lord was with them."[31] Nothing boosts a Christian's pride more than feeling the Spirit and the power of God as they read.

We were then able to introduce the Bible and compare it to "the plates of brass" that we had already presented. We then planted a seed of how important the Bible is to the reader: "they are of great worth unto the Gentiles." We reiterated that the Bible was first written "in purity unto the Gentiles, according to the truth which is in God." Of course, the Christian reader already believes this. Then we hit the reader with the Bible being corrupted by the "great and abominable church." Before we wrote that the Bible containing the "word of God" was *not* infallible ("many plain and precious parts were taken away"), we presented this "great and abominable church" as something that was created in Europe.[32]

An American believes "that their mother Gentiles [Great Britain] were gathered together to battle against them" (implying the Revolutionary War that gave America its independence). Because we already told the reader

---

[30] *BOM*, 3 Nephi 7:22.
[31] *BOM*, 1 Nephi 13:15–16.
[32] *See BOM*, 1 Nephi 13:23–9 for all references in this paragraph.

Chapter 9: The Forced Revision

that Europeans were to blame for "the formation of a church which is most abominable above all other churches," the reader's mind was ready to accept that the King James Bible that "was carried forth among [the Europeans]," could be corrupt because of the British royal family. The Americans didn't corrupt it. The Europeans who fought against the Americans did. At least this is the idea that we introduced through our subliminal messages throughout the part in our *Book of Mormon* known as 1 Nephi, chapter 13.

We used the pride of American Christians to make them comfortable so we could then present many, many prophecies of how corrupt the *American* Christian churches actually were. Once we had their minds open by stroking their ego, it wasn't hard for the reader to see that,

> in the last days, or in the days of the Gentiles—yea, behold all the nations of the Gentiles and also the Jews, both those who shall come upon this land and those who shall be upon other lands, yea, even upon all the lands of the earth, behold, they will be drunken with iniquity and all manner of abominations.[33]

The corrupted doctrine that a Christian is saved by grace through the atonement of Jesus, because Jesus was murdered for what he taught, started in Europe and continued in all American churches "drunken with iniquity and all manner of abominations." In our revision, we were able to control what the mind of the reader felt as we introduced many of the iniquities by which ALL Christian churches were drunken in the latter days.

Unfortunately, though hard to believe, the reader always thought we were writing about someone else. We were in fact addressing ALL Christians and the way that they were treating each other. We were especially pointing to the way the "Gentiles" (Americans) were treating the native Americans and justifying their own "iniquity and all manner of abominations," because they believed that Jesus had died for their sins.

---

[33] *See BOM*, 2 Nephi 27:1.

A New American Scripture

Another way we presented counsel in our revision, hoping that the reader's mind wouldn't automatically dismiss their "iniquity and abominations," was with what has been called a "praise sandwich." We said something that the reader's ego wanted to hear, something that praised the reader, and then we pointed out unacceptable behaviors or things that needed to be improved. We then followed it up with a further boost to the ego.

For example, we explained that the "Gentiles" were supposed to be the "nursing mothers and fathers"[34] of the native Americans. We explained through prophecy that God would help the Americans so that they would always have liberty and God's protection, but ONLY IF ... and the "ONLY IFs" are what the American Christian reader's ego often overlooks ...

> [only] IF the Gentiles shall hearken unto the Lamb of God ... and harden not their hearts against the Lamb of God ... they shall be a blessed people upon the promised land forever; they shall be no more brought down into captivity; ... that IF the Gentiles repent it shall be well with them; ... Therefore, wo be unto the Gentiles IF it so be that they harden their hearts against the Lamb of God.[35]

Plainly, the IFs were surrounded with praise and ego boosts. As explained—but is very important to reiterate again—besides subliminal messages and "praise sandwiches," we incorporated prophecies about things that only we could control in the future. We only presented prophecies of events that had already taken place or those events that we could cause ourselves, in order to present further evidence to the Bible believer of the importance of our new American scripture. We presented our book of Revelation as containing

---

[34] *BOM*, 1 Nephi 21:23.
[35] *BOM*, 1 Nephi 14:1–6, emphasis added.

many things which have been [and also] concerning the end of the world. ... And also others who have been, to them hath [the Lord] shown all things, and they have written them; and they are sealed up to come forth in their purity, according to the truth which is in the Lamb.[36]

This is how we introduced our New Testament book of Revelation in our story's revision and connected it to our "sealed portion." We knew that we were the only ones who could properly unfold the mystery of the book of Revelation. We intended to reserve the time of Revelation's unfolding for the same time that we published our *failsafe* to the world. (*The Sealed Portion* was published in 2004; the *unfolding of Revelation* was published in 2006). We made this connection in our revised storyline[37] and finalized its profundity (wisdom and importance) later.[38]

We presented details that we felt would make the reader excited to consider our new American scripture. We attempted to make it appear to be an intriguing book to entice readers. Nevertheless, we continually pointed out how corrupt ALL religion is, and that the actual words that came out of Jesus' mouth were the ONLY way to peace and eternal life.

We could write an entire book about the details of *how* and *why* we rewrote our original storyline. What we have explained in this chapter is sufficient, for now.

---

[36] *BOM*, 1 Nephi 14:21–6.
[37] *See BOM*, 1 Nephi 14:18–28.
[38] *See BOM*, Ether 4:13–17.

Chapter 10
The Atonement—A Christian Delusion

Since the publication of the unsealed portion of our new American scripture, our greatest frustration has been how it has been ignored, misinterpreted, transfigured, and set aside by those who accept it and believe it to be another set of God's holy word.

In 1982, the LDS Church that claims our new American scripture as the "keystone" of its faith, added a subtitle to our *Book of Mormon*'s original title: "Another Testament of Jesus Christ."

> Since 1983 all editions of the Book of Mormon have appeared with [that subtitle]. At that time Church leaders felt a need to further emphasize the purpose of the book as stated on the title page: "… And also to the convincing of the Jew and Gentile that JESUS is the CHRIST, the ETERNAL GOD, manifesting himself unto all nations …" "With the subtitle added to the Book of Mormon, the purpose of the book, 'to the convincing of the Jew and Gentile that JESUS is the CHRIST,' will become immediately apparent to all who hereafter receive the Book of Mormon," said President Ezra Taft Benson, then president of the Council of the Twelve.

> Additionally, according to Elder Boyd K. Packer of the Council of the Twelve, the subtitle clarifies the Book of Mormon's place among the scriptures. He said in an interview at that time: "The Book of Mormon has been misunderstood. With the subtitle, it takes its place where it should be—beside the Old Testament and the New Testament."[1]

---

[1] "Since 1982, Subtitle Has Defined Book as 'Another Testament of Jesus Christ'." *Church News*, Intellectual Reserve, Inc., 2 Jan. 1988, thechurchnews.com/archives/1988-01-02/since-1982-subtitle-has-defined-book-as-another-testament-of-jesus-christ-154250.

Chapter 10: The Atonement—A Christian Delusion

We have pointed out succinctly (clearly and simply) that the *Book of Mormon* "has been misunderstood" by the world, *exclusively **because of*** the LDS Church and its leaders. How can the rest of the world ignore, misinterpret, transfigure, and set aside something that it does not accept or in which it does not believe? The blame rests solely with the LDS Church and the *Book of Mormon* believers.

"LDS/Mormons" and their leaders include those of several various Mormon-based sects that began after the murder of Joseph Smith. This collective group has not only deceived themselves and their followers, but also the entire world. They have completely transfigured the true meaning and intent of our new American scripture—the *Book of Mormon* and its greater part, *The Sealed Portion*. We have provided empirical, sound, and strong evidence of how these leaders deceive their followers in the *Prologue*, when a member of the LDS Church's Quorum of the Twelve Apostles transfigured our book's meaning and message, saying:

> You [addressing the worldwide LDS Church membership] have the benefit of holding in your hands the complete Book of Mormon. Interestingly, one of the Book of Mormon prophets, Moroni, saw our day—YOUR day. He even saw YOU, in vision, many hundreds of years ago![2]

We pointed out that the context in which "one of the *Book of Mormon* prophets, Moroni," saw them and their day, was when Moroni was describing the great wickedness of the people who would receive our book. Our book presents Moroni saying,

> O ye wicked and perverse and stiffnecked people, why have ye built up churches unto yourselves to get gain?[3]

---

[2] *See Prologue*, page x.
[3] *BOM*, Mormon 8:33.

A New American Scripture

The LDS Church is the wealthiest church in the modern history of the world. When considered objectively and transparently, it is easy to understand how the LDS Church has "built up" a church "unto" itself.

To our amazement, when our True Messenger pointed out that LDS apostle's blatant hypocrisy and lie, LDS apologists fired back that Moroni was "not talking about our church, but about other churches that existed at the time when the *Book of Mormon* came forth." However, it was not our True Messenger who specifically addressed the worldwide membership of the LDS Church during one of its semi-annual General Conferences, and was recognized as one of the Twelve Apostles of Jesus Christ. Elder Stevenson himself looked directly into the camera and made his comments all about the LDS/Mormon people, even at one point choking on his emotions when implying how special the LDS people are because "Jesus Christ hath shown YOU unto [Moroni], and I know your doing."

All one needs to do is to view the LDS conference address recorded on video to know without any doubt or question that this LDS apostle was referring to the members of his church ... there is no question about it.[4]

Our great frustration comes from how the LDS/Mormons have turned something that was meant to be good for all of humanity, into something bad, that only caters to their pride and ego.

Twelve-year-old LDS/Mormon boys receive the Priesthood,[5] which they are taught to believe is "the Authority to Act in God's Name."[6] Besides

---

[4] *See* Elder Gary E. Stevenson, "Look to the Book, Look to the Lord," October 2016 General Conference, The Church of Jesus Christ of Latter-day Saints, churchofjesuschrist.org/study/general-conference/2016/10/look-to-the-book-look-to-the-lord?lang=eng.

[5] "3. Priesthood Principles." *General Handbook: Serving in The Church of Jesus Christ of Latter-Day Saints*, Church of Jesus Christ of Latter-Day Saints, 2021, abn.churchofjesuschrist.org/study/manual/general-handbook/3-priesthood-principles?lang=eng#p1.

[6] "Priesthood Is the Authority to Act in God's Name." *Ensign*, June 2011, churchofjesuschrist.org/study/ensign/2011/06/priesthood-is-the-authority-to-act-in-gods-name?lang=eng.

this male privilege, from a young age Mormons are taught that God is always aware of what they are doing and will "lead them, guide them, walk beside them, help them find the way." They are taught that they can pray to God for assistance at any time, for anything, and that God will hear and answer their prayers, BUT ONLY IF the member is doing what church leaders teach them is God's will. To accentuate this pride, the LDS Church claims to be God's ONLY true and living church. This pride is instilled within these children and remains a strong part of the attitudes and prejudices that affect them for the rest of their lives.

The irony of the above is emphasized in what the LDS/Mormons believe are the

> sacred ordinances necessary for salvation, such as baptism, confirmation, administration of sacrament, and temple [ordinances that can only be administered by] those who hold the priesthood [and] are authorized to act in God's name in leading His Church.[7]

This paradox (turning something that was meant to be good for all of humanity into something bad) is established in what the LDS people believe is the most sacred ordinance of all: receiving their Temple Endowment.

We have mentioned and explained a few bits of information about a play that we helped Joseph Smith to write in 1842, just two years before he was murdered.[8] The presentation of this play is what the LDS Church refers to as the Holy Temple Endowment. "Receiving your endowment," simply means that a faithful member watches a play and participates by performing certain acts that the member is taught are necessary for their eternal salvation. The play's acts symbolically represent certain aspects of human existence, or rather, three

---

[7] "Priesthood Is the Authority to Act in God's Name." *Ensign*, June 2011, churchofjesuschrist.org/study/ensign/2011/06/priesthood-is-the-authority-to-act-in-gods-name?lang=eng.

[8] *See* Chapter 6, pages 131–2.

significant stages: 1) before the "fall of mankind" in the Garden of Eden; 2) during mortal life upon the earth in what is described as the "lone and dreary world"; and finally, 3) what happens after death.

The play presents human existence on Earth (after "the fall") and what transpires during this mortal period of time. The audience is well aware that the characters that represent each of them (**Adam** for the men and **Eve** for the women) were kicked out of the Garden of Eden. When they left the Garden, Adam and Eve (the play's characters that represent all mortals) were banned from the presence of God and Jesus. God the Father is presented in the play as *Elohim*. His son, Jesus Christ is presented in the play as *Jehovah*. Being expelled from the Garden of Eden meant that Adam and Eve could no longer communicate with God or His son.

Throughout the play's presentation, during the stage representing mortality on Earth, it is clearly and plainly presented that neither *Elohim* nor *Jehovah* have anything to do with mortals living <u>on</u> the earth. It is obvious that when Adam and Eve pray to God, the ONLY entity that hears and answers their prayers is *Lucifer*, presented in the play as "the god of this world." It is clearly presented that *Elohim* and *Jehovah* do not know what is happening on the earth during this stage of human existence.

Speaking as if they are in heaven, *Elohim* commands *Jehovah* to ask messengers to visit Adam and Eve in the "lone and dreary world," and then "return and report" what is happening. Not at ANY time during the presentation when the characters *Adam and Eve* are in the "lone and dreary world," does God or His son interact in ANY way with mortals, <u>except through chosen True Messengers</u>. Adam is unable to learn anything from God, from the Holy Spirit, or from any other source (besides True Messengers) EXCEPT from *Lucifer*, the god of the mortal world.

There can be no logical and honest argument made about what we have revealed above concerning what is seen during the presentation of the LDS Temple Endowment. LDS apologists (defenders) would agree that the

Chapter 10: The Atonement—A Christian Delusion

play's presentation as given above is correct. However, they would claim that the True Messengers that receive direction and guidance from *Elohim* and *Jehovah* represent *their* Church leaders. We would concede to this if it wasn't for the fact that ALL members of that Church believe that THEY, PERSONALLY, can communicate with God or Jesus, and that their prayers are *not* answered by *Lucifer*, but through the Holy Ghost from God. This belief is NOT consistent with the play's presentation. Furthermore, whenever the LDS leaders start doing something in their church that is *not consistent* with the play's presentation, they simply change the original play to reflect their new beliefs. This is done despite the fact they teach that the play is a holy ordinance of salvation.

Likewise, when the LDS leaders are uncomfortable with what is written about them in our *Book of Mormon*, it is easy for them to explain the inconsistency with the idea that God changes His mind, depending on the situation that is happening on the earth. This is why the Mormons are taught that their *living* leaders receive current direction from God or Jesus Christ, and that the members should not pay attention to what "dead prophets" wrote in scripture. Our new American scripture has become obsolete to that Church's presentations of its current "gospel."

If you consider the totality of that Church's doctrine, precepts, covenants, and teachings, you will see that NONE OF THEM WERE TAUGHT BY JESUS CHRIST. Likewise, NONE OF THEM ARE FOUND IN OUR *BOOK OF MORMON*... ABSOLUTELY NONE. LDS genealogies and ALL of the busy work that are required of the members in order to enter one of their temples to receive the Temple Endowment, including paying a FULL tithing of their income, HAVE NOTHING TO DO WITH BEING A TRUE CHRISTIAN AND FOLLOWING THE TEACHINGS OF JESUS CHRIST.

The LDS/Mormons are not the only people, however, who believe that God and Jesus are aware of them and can inspire and help them on a daily basis. From athletes to movie stars, from politicians to successful business people, those who claim to be Christian give thanks to God or Jesus for their successes, and ask for God's or Jesus' help with their failures.

As we explained in Chapter 3, *The Greatest Human Deception*, the belief that a person can receive personal direction and help from God has caused an enormous amount of suffering for most of humanity. The Christians believe their god is right and inspires and guides them. The Jews believe the same. Considering the other major religions based on the Bible, the Muslims take the idea of God inspiring them to a different level. In each of these three major religions, the believers are waiting upon their god to come to, or return to, Earth to save humanity.

The members of all of these religions are taught by their leaders that, "Surely the Lord God will do nothing, [unless] he revealeth his secret unto his servants the prophets."[9] This particular scripture is widely used by the leaders of these religions. More particularly, it is used by the tens of thousands of LDS missionaries who go throughout the world teaching that *their church*, and their church alone, is the only church that has the prophets to whom God reveals "His secret" and His will for humanity.

We know that believers in God depend on this personal revelation and guidance throughout their daily lives. We also know how this dependence has caused so many of humanity's problems, especially the wars and rumors of wars that create misery and unrest. We wrote that this great "iniquity,"—the idea that God talks to everyone, and that the different gods tell different people many different things—leads to "the hardness of their hearts, and the stiffness of their necks."[10] In other words, this belief that God talks to them specifically, and to no one outside of their group, leads to the great pride that afflicts all of humanity.

For this very reason, we included the part in our 1842 play that directly counters the idea that mortals have ANY connection with God, of

---

[9] OT, Amos 3:7.
[10] *BOM*, 2 Nephi 25:12.

Chapter 10: The Atonement—A Christian Delusion

ANY kind or means. We made it very clear in the original presentation of our 1842 play that when mortals think they are receiving inspiration or an answer to their prayers, they are actually being answered by *Lucifer—the god of this world*. *Lucifer* is the character we included in our play to represent the pride and ego of a human being.

In our new American scripture, we wrote about the Jews and their belief in a Messiah, along with their belief that their particular religion was God's *only truth*. We introduced this "iniquity" as that which created the

> wars, and rumors of wars; and when the day cometh that the Only Begotten of the Father, yea, even the Father of heaven and of earth, shall manifest himself unto them in the flesh, behold they will reject him, because of their iniquities, and the hardness of their hearts, and the stiffness of their necks. Behold, they will crucify him.[11]

The Christians consider the crucifixion of Jesus Christ as the greatest act that God has done for the world. American Christians believe that the blood that *their* Christ shed upon the cross *atoned* for their sins. They believe that all mortals are living in sin, and without Jesus' crucifixion, none will be saved in Heaven. Many Christians believe that it doesn't matter how sinful a person is, so long as the person believes in Jesus and professes that Jesus Christ is their Lord and Savior. Having faith in Christ, most Christians believe that they will be saved, because Jesus died for them and their sins. Others believe that this *faith* in Jesus must be followed with proper *works* or the person will not be saved. However, ALL Christians believe that the blood of Christ means something, and without it no one can be saved.

In previous chapters, we have explained some of the major issues that Joseph Smith's peer group had with the first 116 pages of handwritten manuscript (mostly written by Martin Harris). The *atonement* of Jesus

---
[11] *BOM*, 2 Nephi 25:12–13.

Christ was probably the idea that concerned this group the most. Christians cannot accept that Jesus' death by crucifixion was nothing more than straightforward murder. It hurts their pride and ego to consider that Jesus' death had nothing to do with salvation, or with the mission that Jesus was sent to Earth to perform.

Many Christians, especially Catholics and LDS/Mormons, believe that the sacrament (symbolically eating the flesh and drinking the blood of Jesus Christ) is an essential part of their salvation. These religions believe that before the sacrament can be properly administered, the bread and wine (or water) must be blessed by a man who has been given the priesthood of God to do so. Therefore, organized religion—with proper priesthood authority to administer the sacrament and other saving rituals and ordinances—is not only important, but <u>essential</u> to a person's eternal salvation.

Our original narrative (116-page "lost" manuscript) condemned organized religion, priesthood authority, and all rituals and ordinances. Again, and again, and again, it was our intent to help the early American Christians, who were establishing a new and unique, powerful government in the United States of America. We knew the teachings of Jesus could help them to do this. We wanted to help them base their Christian beliefs on what Jesus Christ taught *before* he was murdered.

We also wanted to teach them that Jesus was murdered *because* of what he taught. Our original intent was to help the Christians see that Jesus did not die *for* the sins of the world, but *because of* the sins of the world. In our revision, we presented a vision of the future that our first character, Lehi, had of the life and times of Jesus Christ. When the New Testament was translated into other languages, and finally into the English language, the translators should have written "because of" the sins of the world, instead of "for" the sins of the world (language conjunctions that can be interchangeable) when translating the reason why Jesus was murdered.

> [Jesus Christ] is the propitiation for our sins: and not for ours only, but also for the sins of the whole world.[12]

Concerning Jesus being crucified, we said this in our new American scripture:

> Wherefore, as I said unto you, it must needs be expedient that Christ ... should come among the Jews, among those who are the more wicked part of the world; and they shall crucify him—for thus it behooveth our God, and there is none other nation on earth that would crucify their God. ... But because of priestcrafts and iniquities, they at Jerusalem will stiffen their necks against him, that he be crucified.[13]

It was *"because of priestcrafts and iniquities"* that the Jews killed Jesus. We defined what "priestcrafts" mean:

> priestcrafts are that men preach and set themselves up for a light unto the world, that they may get gain and praise of the world; but they seek not the welfare of Zion.[14]

Jesus taught the people that they didn't need priesthood leaders, that they didn't need to pay donations, and that they didn't need organized religion. Jesus taught the people that the "kingdom of God is within," and that any person can be one with God and receive God's inspiration for their personal lives without the need of any priesthood leader. (This is not the same thing as inspiration from Lucifer—*the god of this world.*)

Jesus did **not** set up a church and establish church commandments that if violated by the members would cause them to be disfellowshipped or excommunicated. Jesus did **not** base a person's salvation on whether or not the person paid tithing and offerings. The intent of **all** of Jesus' teachings was to

---

[12] *See* NT, 1 John 2:2.
[13] *BOM*, 2 Nephi 10:3–5.
[14] *BOM*, 2 Nephi 26:29.

help a person love their self, and their fellow beings (neighbors) as their self. There was no other intent for anything that Jesus taught.

The Jews thought they were a righteous people because they believed that they were God's chosen people. In our revised story, we had two of Lehi's rebellious sons, Laman and Lemuel, mock their father and their brother, Nephi, for misjudging the Jews and leading them away from Jerusalem into the wilderness:

> Behold, these many years we have suffered in the wilderness, which time we might have enjoyed our possessions and the land of our inheritance; yea, and we might have been happy.
>
> And we know that the people who were in the land of Jerusalem were a righteous people; for they kept the statutes and judgments of the Lord, and all his commandments, according to the law of Moses; wherefore, we know that they are a righteous people; and our father hath judged them.[15]

In our scripture above, we presented the Jews as "among those who are the more wicked part of the world ... and there is none other nation on earth that would crucify their God." We proclaim the same thing about the members and leaders of the LDS Church, that in so many ways they are very similar to the Jews. For our contemporary work, and as a way to prove the similarities between the LDS/Mormon people and the Jews, we chose as our True Messenger a man named after Christ: *Christ*opher, whose name means "Bearer of Christ." What we had Christopher teach the LDS people is nothing more or less than what Jesus Christ taught the Jews. And as Jesus did, Christopher also condemned the LDS Church for its priestcrafts. And if the LDS/Mormon people had their way, they would also choose to get rid of Christopher in the same way that the Jews got rid of Jesus Christ.

---

[15] *BOM*, 1 Nephi 17:21–2.

Chapter 10: The Atonement—A Christian Delusion

Our *bearer of Christ's* words confronted the LDS Church and its doctrine, calling this religion, its leaders and members, "among those who are the more wicked part of the world." Our judgment of them is based on what this organized religion has done with our *Book of Mormon*, as we have revealed throughout this book about our new American scripture. Through Christopher, we brought forth the most important part of our new American scripture, the *sealed portion* of our narrative. Amazingly, most LDS/Mormon people refuse to even read *The Sealed Portion*. Most of those who do, recognize how wicked their church really is and end up leaving it.

Christopher is hated vehemently, in most cases, by the members of this church and its leaders. They "stiffen their necks against him." If it were possible, and if the LDS Church ran the government of the United States, Christopher would be jailed, silenced, and most likely murdered like his predecessor, Joseph Smith, was.

Many faithful members of this church have left it after reading *The Sealed Portion*. The families of those who have left this church become devastated, but still refuse to read our book. These faithful LDS families blame our book and True Messenger for their loved ones' abandonment of the saving ordinances that they believe are only available and properly administered in the LDS Church. IF it were possible that these angered members and families could have a choice between having Christopher crucified or releasing a felon, the LDS people would assuredly vote to end Christopher's life.

It was our intent to have Christopher confront the LDS Church at Salt Lake City in the same manner as Jesus confronted the Jewish Church at Jerusalem. He has done nothing but teach people the same things that Jesus taught the people of his day. In one instance, while teaching, Christopher interchanged some of his own words with what we had written in our new American scripture. (This is quoted below, from a recording that we took of him.)

We must warn the reader that Christopher has often used profanity in his delivery. Although we have often discouraged him from using profanity, we also recognize the reason behind it. Christopher does not want people to put him up on a pedestal like they do with their religious leaders. Anything that Christopher could do to mitigate a person worshipping him as a prophet, or as people usually worship and adore their spiritual leaders, he has done.

Christopher said (in June of 2012):

> The Mormons are some of the most prideful ... people on Earth. They stumble all over themselves trying to figure out how they can prove to the rest of the world how great they are. Think about all those temples they are building throughout the world. They're trying to tell people that unless someone has been baptized and received the ritual of the temple endowment ordinance they can't be saved. What a load of ... ! They think they are so ... smart.
>
> They don't consider anything that anyone outside of the Church says. They think the *Book of Mormon* talks about them [those outside of the LDS Church] preaching up to themselves their own wisdom and their own learning. And look what they've done with all that wisdom and learning. They've become the richest church in the entire world, and they did it on the backs of the poor, grinding their faces as the good books says they would. The idiots demand tithing from even the poorest of the poor of the members, and don't let members who don't pay a ... full tithe enter their temples to be saved. Can you believe this ... ?!
>
> The leaders of the Church work in darkness, behind the scenes, combining the power that they have over politics, because of all their ... money, to get what they want. Can you ... imagine if Mitt Romney wins the election? The ... Mormons would obviously

think that God wanted him in there [in as the U.S. President], then they could continue their works of darkness with their secret combination of religious, business, and political power. What a ... mess that would be!

This church thinks it's so good and righteous, yet it causes more strife and malice than any other group that touts its humanitarian efforts in helping out the poor. These idiots don't have a clue how their so-called humanitarian efforts destroy local economies and leave the people wanting more, more that ain't gonna come. Their own pride ... which you now know is how we present the devil ..., leads them around by the neck.

Their own book talks about the Lord only doing things for the benefit of humanity, not for the benefit of a ... Brigham Young-made church. Jesus told people that they didn't have to pay ... to be saved ... Come unto me all you and buy honey and milk without money 'cause there isn't a price attached to salvation.' Jesus told the people that salvation was completely free, and that you didn't need to worship in a ... synagogue or temple in order to be saved. Salvation is free to everyone equally ... that's what he said in their own ... *Book of Mormon*. Geez Louise, you gotta wonder if the idiot Mormons even read their own ... scriptures. If they actually did and paid attention, they might learn a few things about their own salvation.

It's all about charity, the pure love of Christ, the way that Jesus loved people, the things that Jesus did ... that's what salvation is, it's nothing else. But those ... General Authorities who put themselves up as a light unto the world and preach over their grand pulpits to get praise from the members, and from the world; everything these idiots do is about pleasing the world. And don't be fooled by these ... hypocrites who say they don't receive a good income from being who they are. Oh, yeah, they receive both gain and praise from their pretended positions of priesthood authority. They ... do not labor for Zion, they labor to make the Church look good and become richer. They forgot what the definition of "Zion" is ... to help the people become one heart and one mind so that there is no poor among them. But the idiots ... Who was it? I think, Dallin "Hitler" Oaks, who said that the poor will always be among us, implying that there wasn't much we could do about it. What a ... idiot!

Mormons think that if they just obey the commandments given by their leaders, not a ... one that was actually given by Christ, and most which the *Book of Mormon* condemns as great wickedness ... they think that if they just obey their ... leaders they'll be saved. To hell with being a nice person to others ... condemn the ... non-believers to hell, no matter how good of a person a non-Mormon might be. Yeah, what happened to charity, the pure love of Christ? Oh, that means giving to the poor for a day, destroy their local economic structure and don't keep helping them, because Ol' Oaks was inspired by God ... we'll always have the poor among us. What a ... idiot!

There ain't no commandment given that a person has to be baptized and receive any ordinances in order to be saved. The book says that everyone is invited to partake of goodness and salvation, don't matter if you have a tan that's darker than mine, if you're bond or free, male or female ... and what does he say, even the heathen ... which would include me ... even the ... heathen are saved because they are all alike unto God.[16]

From the few of Christopher's words that we have shared above, it is no wonder why the LDS/Mormon people are angered with him and denounce that God would choose someone of his character to do God's work.

---

[16] All profanity has been omitted. *Compare* these excerpts of Christopher's sermon *to BOM*, 2 Nephi 26:20–3.

Chapter 10: The Atonement—A Christian Delusion

We can assure this world that we chose the right person to help us do our work. We have no doubt about it.

The revision of our story cleared up many of the issues that Joseph's peers had with our original presentation. It was also our intent to present a story that would once and for all prove that baptism, sacraments, and any ritual or ordinance prescribed by and administered by priesthood authority were *not* necessary for a person's eternal salvation. We wanted to present the *atonement of Jesus Christ* with an entirely different meaning than what was believed in orthodox Christianity. We did this through the presentation of the story of King Benjamin. King Benjamin was the Nephite king who had received

> the plates of brass; and also the [large, meaning larger amount] plates of Nephi; and also, the sword of Laban, and the ball or director [later named the *Liahona*].[17]

We again addressed the problems that Joseph's group had with how Nephi was commanded by God to murder Laban and steal the brass plates. We reiterated the importance of the plates:

> were it not for these plates, which contain these records and these commandments, we must have suffered in ignorance, even at this present time, not knowing the mysteries of God. … except it were for the help of these plates; for [Lehi] having been taught in the language of the Egyptians therefore he could read these engravings.[18]

Just before King Benjamin died, he conferred the kingdom and authority on his son, Mosiah. King Benjamin commanded all the people to gather to hear his final words to them. King Benjamin's final words explained how we wanted to present the *true atonement of Christ*. Also, we wanted to present a correct

---

[17] See *BOM*, Mosiah 1:16.
[18] See *BOM*, Mosiah 1:3–4.

idea of how a righteous government and church leader should act. The way we presented both the atonement and how a leader *should* act was simple, clear, and straightforward. King Benjamin begins:

> My brethren, all ye that have assembled yourselves together, you that can hear my words which I shall speak unto you this day; for I have not commanded you to come up hither to trifle with the words which I shall speak, but that you should hearken unto me, and open your ears that ye may hear, and your hearts that ye may understand, and your minds that the mysteries of God may be unfolded to your view.[19]

(For the rest of our explanation about what we had King Benjamin teach the people, we will not include specific footnotes with the verses. All of the following quotes not referenced are taken from Mosiah, chapters 1 through 6.)

King Benjamin was one of the most beloved kings in our story. The people loved and respected him. What he was about to tell the people, they had never heard before ("the mysteries of God may be unfolded to your view"). He reiterated that he was nobody special, that

> I have not commanded that ye should fear me, or that ye should think that I of myself am more than a mortal man. But I am like as yourselves.

King Benjamin then outlined the proper way that all government and religious leaders should act, not as leaders of the people, but as *servants* of the people. He explained that he did not tax the people, nor require any donations from them to support himself and his family:

---

[19] *BOM*, Mosiah 2:9.

Chapter 10: The Atonement—A Christian Delusion

> And even I, myself, have labored with mine own hands that I might serve you, and that ye should not be laden with taxes, and that there should nothing come upon you which was grievous to be borne.

After he died, his son, Mosiah,

> did cause his people that they should till the earth. And he also, himself, did till the earth, that thereby he might not become burdensome to his people.

One thing that all failed governments and societies had in common was that the leaders were paid by the people through forced taxation. The leaders of these failed institutions always manipulated the system to benefit themselves, corrupting the idea that a person should be *serving the people* instead of leading them. Also, we had King Benjamin reiterate the evils of Capitalism, which we presented earlier on in our narrative as "the great and abominable church."

Before presenting this subplot about King Benjamin, we presented as blatant "priestcraft" the idea that a person must perform a "saving ordinance" in order to "partake of [Christ's] salvation," or pay tithes and offerings to the church as part of being saved. We wrote,

> Hath he commanded any that they should not partake of his salvation? Behold I say unto you, Nay; but he hath given it **free** for **all** men; and he hath commanded his people that they should persuade all men to repentance.

> Behold, hath the Lord commanded any that they should not partake of his goodness? Behold I say unto you, Nay; but **all** men are privileged the one like unto the other, and none are forbidden.

He commandeth that there shall be no priestcrafts; for behold, priestcrafts are that men preach and set themselves up for a light unto the world, that they may get gain and praise of the world; but they seek not the welfare of Zion.[20]

Around the time that Capitalism, the stock market, bonds, securities, and most other economic structures developed, the idea of the "atonement" also developed in the Christian churches in Europe. These fiscal (financial) ideas were started so that a person with money could invest and increase their "wealth without work."

These economic structures were responsible for slaying the saints of God, torturing them, binding them down, yoking them with iron, and bringing them down into captivity.[21] These economic forces altered the pureness and plainness of Christianity and changed its meaning by transfiguring what was written in the Bible as the pure and simple teachings of Jesus Christ. In so doing, "an exceedingly great many do stumble, yea, insomuch that Satan hath great power over them."[22] This means that their pride and ego—*Lucifer*—had great power over them.

We addressed all of this in the revised storyline of our new American scripture:

And it came to pass that the angel spake unto me, saying: Look! And I looked and beheld many nations and kingdoms. And the angel said unto me: What beholdest thou? And I said: I behold many nations and kingdoms. And he said unto me: These are the nations and kingdoms of the Gentiles.

And it came to pass that I saw among the nations of the Gentiles the formation of a great church. And the angel said unto me:

---

[20] *BOM*, 2 Nephi 26:27–9, emphasis added.
[21] *Compare BOM*, 1 Nephi 13:5.
[22] *BOM*, 1 Nephi 13:29.

> Behold the formation of a church which is most abominable above all other churches, which slayeth the saints of God, yea, and tortureth them and bindeth them down, and yoketh them with a yoke of iron, and bringeth them down into captivity.
>
> And it came to pass that I beheld this great and abominable church; and I saw the devil that he was the founder of it. And I also saw gold, and silver, and silks, and scarlets, and fine-twined linen, and all manner of precious clothing; and I saw many harlots.
>
> And the angel spake unto me, saying: Behold the gold, and the silver, and the silks, and the scarlets, and the fine-twined linen, and the precious clothing, and the harlots, are the desires of this great and abominable church. And also for the praise of the world do they destroy the saints of God, and bring them down into captivity.[23]

We had King Benjamin reiterate the evils of priestcrafts and Capitalism, where a person is forced to become a slave to another person, or to an institution: "Neither have I suffered that ye should be confined in dungeons, nor that ye should make slaves one of another."

King Benjamin goes on and tells the people that they are indebted to God for their lives, and

> that if ye should serve him who has created you from the beginning, and is preserving you from day to day, by lending you breath, that ye may live and move and do according to your own will, and even supporting you from one moment to another—I say, if ye should serve him with all your whole souls yet ye would be unprofitable servants.

---

[23] *BOM*, 1 Nephi 13:1–9.

A New American Scripture

As we've pointed out in two examples of extreme self-righteousness, the Jews and the LDS people believe that theirs is the only true church of God upon the earth, and that if their particular ordinances and practices are not administered and performed, a person cannot be saved after death.

The people in King Benjamin's kingdom had the" lower law of Moses." They were fulfilling it as they had been taught. As they gathered to hear their king speak, "they also took of the firstlings of their flocks, that they might offer sacrifice and burnt offerings according to the law of Moses."

In saying what he did above, King Benjamin was getting the minds of his people prepared to receive a new "name, that thereby they may be distinguished above all the people which the Lord God hath brought out of the land of Jerusalem." In other words, the people were no longer to be referred to as members of the house of Israel, or Jews, or the chosen people, but would be given "a name that never shall be blotted out, except it be through transgression." Transgression of what laws? The people were already serving God with their "whole souls" and complying with the law of Moses, but they were still "unprofitable servants" according to what King Benjamin was telling them.

The *new name* by which the people would be distinguished was *Christians—followers of Christ's words*. As we have explained, Christ's words are all about what is required for a people to prosper and have a successful society.

> If this highly favored people of the Lord should fall into transgression [i.e., not follow the things that Christ told them to do], and become a wicked and an adulterous people ... the Lord ... will no more preserve them by his matchless and marvelous power.

What we had King Benjamin say at this point was the same warning that we gave earlier in the narrative of our new American scripture about the people (the "Gentiles") who would establish the United States of America.

Chapter 10: The Atonement—A Christian Delusion

King Benjamin told the people that if they wanted to have a successful society that prospered, the ONLY thing that was required of them was to keep the commandments of God:

> I would desire that ye should consider on the blessed and happy state of those that keep the commandments of God. For behold, they are blessed in all things, both temporal and spiritual; and if they hold out faithful to the end they are received into heaven, that thereby they may dwell with God in a state of never-ending happiness.

King Benjamin then talked about Jesus Christ and how Jesus was going to

> come down from heaven among the children of men, and shall dwell in a tabernacle of clay. ... And he shall be called Jesus Christ, the Son of God, the Father of heaven and earth, the Creator of all things from the beginning; and his mother shall be called Mary.

The way in which we had King Benjamin introduce Jesus Christ was sufficient to get the Christian reader spiritually (emotionally) hooked on what was about to happen. King Benjamin explained that Christ's

> blood atoneth for the sins of those who have fallen by the transgression of Adam, who have died not knowing the will of God concerning them, or who have ignorantly sinned. But wo, wo, unto him who knoweth that he rebelleth against God! For salvation cometh to none such except it be through repentance and faith on the Lord Jesus Christ.

This was all perfectly in line with orthodox Christian belief. We then had King Benjamin clearly tell the people that the law of Moses was "appointed unto them a law [because they] were a stiffnecked people ... that the law of Moses availeth nothing [doesn't accomplish anything] except it were through the atonement of his blood."

A New American Scripture

Again, this was all perfectly in line with orthodox Christian belief. The Christian reader of our new American scripture would be completely agreeable with what we had written and presented so far as the atonement of Jesus Christ in our King Benjamin subplot. Once the reader felt the spirit of Christ in our words, we subtly introduced the way that we wanted to present the atonement.

Christians are taught that the act (the *atonement*) of Jesus Christ being killed on the cross and having his blood spilt in this manner relieves them of their sins. Yet, many, many years BEFORE Jesus came in the flesh, because of what their king taught them of the "mysteries of God," King Benjamin's people:

> cried aloud with one voice, saying: O have mercy, and apply the atoning blood of Christ that we may receive forgiveness of our sins, and our hearts may be purified;

> ... And it came to pass that after they had spoken these words the Spirit of the Lord came upon them, and they were filled with joy, having received a remission of their sins, and having peace of conscience.

Many more than one hundred years BEFORE Christ came to the earth (at the time that the people lived in our story's timeline), the "atoning blood of Christ" atoned for the people's sins and purified them. They did not perform any ritual, nor did Jesus Christ do anything—because he wasn't alive then to do anything—that caused the people to receive "a remission of their sins, and have a peace of conscience." King Benjamin's people had

> offered for a sacrifice unto [the Lord] a broken heart and a contrite spirit ... and were baptized with fire and with the Holy Ghost ... because of their faith in [Jesus Christ, who was yet to

Chapter 10: The Atonement—A Christian Delusion

come] at the time of their conversion, and they were baptized with fire and with the Holy Ghost, and they knew it not.[24]

This is what we would later write in our storyline about the Lamanites, who did exactly the same thing and went through the same procedure and experience as King Benjamin's people did in being converted and taking upon them the new name of Christ.

The Lamanites and the people of King Benjamin did it right. They were baptized the proper way *without knowing it*, or rather, without performing any church-mandated ordinance; and the "atoning blood of Christ" did the rest. We were introducing a completely different concept about the "atoning blood of Christ" than the *atonement* in which the American Christians believed.

As we continued the story about King Benjamin, we wanted to cause the reader to *feel* a broken heart and a contrite spirit. This is prerequisite (something that must happen first) to doing the right thing so that the "atoning blood of Christ" can work properly for the reader. Then,

> all that he requires of you is to keep his commandments; and he has promised you that if ye would keep his commandments ye should prosper in the land; and he never doth vary from that which he hath said; therefore, if ye do keep his commandments he doth bless you and prosper you.
>
> And now, in the first place, he hath created you, and granted unto you your lives, for which ye are indebted unto him. And secondly, he doth require that ye should do as he hath commanded you; for which if ye do, he doth immediately bless you; and therefore he hath paid you. And ye are still indebted unto him, and are, and will be, forever and ever; therefore, of what have ye to boast? And now I ask, can ye say aught of

---

[24] *Compare BOM*, 3 Nephi 9:20.

yourselves?" ["Can ye say aught of yourselves," means to have a broken heart and be humble.]

... Therefore, as I said unto you that I had served you, walking with a clear conscience before God, even so I at this time have caused that ye should assemble yourselves together, that I might be found blameless, and that your **blood should not come upon me**, when I shall stand to be judged of God of the things whereof he hath commanded me concerning you.[25]

How was it possible that King Benjamin could keep his people's "blood" from coming upon him? The answer is presented in the story of Jesus, which we also reflected in our own story: "blood" is the life of the "flesh." In other words, "blood" means the "spirit" in which a person performs an act of the flesh. The spirit in which we do something in the flesh (while we are mortal, here on Earth) gives us life. King Benjamin wanted to teach the people the right way to do the right things, for the right intent. He did not want the people's intent for doing something to be improper. This righteous king teaching the people to treat each other well is how "their blood" (their intent) would "not come upon" him.

If a person does not understand *why* they are doing something, then the *mal-intent* (intent for the wrong reason) becomes the responsibility of the teacher. We could say that because we did not want the blood of the American Christians to be upon us, we wanted to make sure that they understood *why* they should be doing the things that we wanted them to do. Again, the "life of the flesh is in the blood." The true intent and reasons behind what a person does is indicative of the goodness or evil of the individual. A person can do what appears outwardly to be something good, but if what is done causes others harm, the "blood" of the act is on the person's hands or clothes.

---

[25] *BOM*, Mosiah 2:22–7.

Chapter 10: The Atonement—A Christian Delusion

To understand this more clearly, one needs to understand why Christ is presented in Revelation as coming to save the world in red clothing ("vesture dipped in blood"). Jesus was responsible for teaching the people, not only what they had to do, but *why* they had to do it. Jesus' own blood symbolizes the *intent* for why he did what he did. Like King Benjamin, everything that Jesus did, he did it with the *intent* to be in the service of his God, which was always in the service of his fellow beings.

In our book of Revelation, we dressed the Son of man coming in his glory in the color red. We did this to symbolize that the people's *intent* in worshipping him (the people's *blood*) was upon him; or rather, that he was responsible for what the people did, IF the people listened to him and kept his commandments.

Jesus *did* teach the people properly. King Benjamin wanted to make sure that he taught his people properly. And in presenting both Jesus and King Benjamin in our story, we (the Real Illuminati®) wanted to teach properly as well. Therefore, we did it according to what we knew the people's real and pure intent *should be*.

One must also understand what Jesus actually meant when he said what a person needed to do in order for a person to be saved: a person must

> eat the flesh of the Son of man, and drink his blood, [or] ye have no life in you. Whoso eateth my flesh, and drinketh my blood, hath eternal life; ... He that eateth my flesh, and drinketh my blood, *dwelleth* in me, and I in him.[26]

What does it mean to "dwell in Jesus," so that Jesus will "dwell in you"? A better word in the English language would be "live" instead of "dwell"—to "live in Jesus," so that Jesus "can live in you"; or rather, to have Jesus' own "blood in you, as the life of your flesh." For this reason, it has been taught to

---

[26] NT, John 6:53–6, emphasis added.

Christians to *drink the blood of Christ*. In other words, a true Christian should act for the same reason and with the same intent as Jesus would act. (One can know how Jesus would act by reading the words that he taught.)

Again, drinking the blood of Christ simply means that whatever you do, you do it "in the same spirit" in which Jesus would do it. In other words, you have the same intent. When you do something, you should do it for the same reasons that Jesus would do it.

We gave a clear example of this in the revised storyline that replaced our original story. Jacob, the brother of Nephi, spoke to the people about *their thoughts*, or the reason and intent behind what the people were doing at the time:

> I can tell you concerning **your thoughts**, how that ye are beginning to labor in sin, which sin appeareth very abominable unto me, yea, and abominable unto God.[27]

Whatever it was that the people were doing (their actions), wasn't the problem that was "abominable unto God." It was *why* they were doing what they were doing; it was the *intent* behind their actions; it was the true *reason why* they were doing what they were doing that was an abomination before God.

In this part of our story, we wanted the reader to understand *what* the people were doing that Jacob was condemning. Again, *what* the people were doing wasn't an abomination before God, it was **their thoughts** (their intent) in doing what they were doing that caused the people "to labor in sin, which sin appeareth very abominable unto me, yea, and abominable unto God."

Jacob referred to the "wickedness of [their] hearts,"[28] not of their actions. Jacob wanted to make sure that he spoke plainly and clearly about

---

[27] *See BOM*, Jacob 2:5.
[28] *BOM*, Jacob 2:6.

Chapter 10: The Atonement—A Christian Delusion

what was causing the people to sin: "Wherefore, I must tell you the truth according to the plainness of the word of God."[29] Here's what the people were doing that was an "abomination," which is directly related to Capitalism:

> Many of you have begun to search for gold, and for silver, and for all manner of precious ores, in the which this land, which is a land of promise unto you and to your seed, doth abound most plentifully. And the hand of providence [in other words, the hand of God] hath smiled upon you most pleasingly, that you have obtained many riches.[30]

The people had been obeying God's commandments. As a result, they had been successful. Acquiring assets that a "promised land" provided, after God had given the land to the people, wasn't the problem. It certainly wasn't a sin for the people to take advantage of the bounteous blessings that they enjoyed while living in a "land of promise." Acquiring lots of worldly goods that made the people happy *wasn't* what was "abominable [before] God." He was the one who had guided them to a land where these things "doth abound most plentifully." If it *were* a sin, why would God "smile" upon the people and bless them with these things?

The great and abominable sin actually came from the **thoughts** (*the intent*) behind acquiring the wealth. One might ask, "Why does a person acquire wealth? In 'what spirit,' or better, in what state of mind, does a person begin to search for worldly success?" Does the person do it in the "same spirit" in which Jesus would do it (i.e., to feed the hungry and help the poor)? Does the person "drink the blood of Christ" and "eat his flesh"? Again, the blood represents the "spirit" in which a person does something. The "flesh" represents what is being done in the flesh (or with a mortal body).

In order for a person to receive "eternal life," the person must do what Jesus would do, in the same spirit—which means for the same reason—that

---

[29] *BOM*, Jacob 2:10.
[30] See *BOM*, Jacob 2:11–13.

Jesus would do it. Better said, one's actions should be *sanctified in the blood of Christ.* What this means is that your *actions* must be sanctified in the blood of Christ by your *intentions* being pure, and by having the same intentions that Jesus would have in doing the act himself.

Keep in mind that the *American Dream*[31] is all about performing works of the flesh (through hard work and opportunity) that are NOT *sanctified in the blood of Christ.* The *American Dream* is to become rich and successful by the works of your flesh for the benefit of yourself and your family only. American Christians honor Christ with their lips (they *believe* they are *doing* good works) but their hearts (the reason *why* they do what they do) are far from him.

Of all their creeds, of all the doctrines and commandments of men in which the American Christian believed, none was more abominable to the meaning of a *true Christ* than the idea of an *atonement* being made to take away a person's sins without the person having to do anything.

Our Jacob told the people that they were wicked because they were becoming wealthy for the wrong reasons. He told the people that they should be more worried about seeking for the "kingdom of God" than "seek[ing] for riches." He told them that if they truly had a "hope in Christ," then they would ONLY seek for riches "for the intent" … according to the spirit and blood of Christ …

> to do good—to clothe the naked, and to feed the hungry, and to liberate the captive, and administer relief to the sick and the afflicted.[32]

The Jesus of the New Testament told the people "the truth according to the plainness of the word of God"[33] about what would save them in the

---

[31] See *666 America*, 310, 360, 380–1. Read for free at realilluminati.org/666-mark-of-america.
[32] See *BOM*, Jacob 2:18–19.
[33] *BOM*, Jacob 2:11.

eternities, and what would not. His words, as given in Matthew chapter 25, are very clear. Nothing is plainer than what separates a person who does things according to the "spirit of Christ" from one who does it for their own benefit and purpose. Jesus couldn't have spoken more clearly about what the people needed to do in order to avoid "everlasting punishment," or to receive "life eternal."

We intended for our prophet Jacob to utilize Jesus' words given in Matthew chapter 25 about what Jesus was going to do when he came "in his glory, and all the holy angels with him ... to sit upon the throne of his glory."[34] Jacob was very clear about the *intent to do good* that Jesus expected of the people—"to clothe the naked, and to feed the hungry, and to liberate the captive, and administer relief to the sick and the afflicted."

In our story, we presented the people of Nephi as those who were doing the right things (living righteously). By doing the right things, they prospered in the land. Doing the "right thing" is using the earth's resources for the benefit of all people equitably (fairly and equally). King Benjamin was also clear that living correctly included NOT making "slaves one of another," and,

> for the sake of these things which I have spoken unto you—that is, for the sake of retaining a remission of your sins from day to day, that ye may walk guiltless before God—I would that ye should impart of your substance to the poor, every man according to that which he hath, such as feeding the hungry, clothing the naked, visiting the sick and administering to their relief, both spiritually and temporally, according to their wants.

The only way that anyone can fulfill the *American Dream* today (circa 2020) is to "make slaves one of another." Successful business pursuits are all

---

[34] NT, Matthew 25:31.

about having employees who work hard for the company and receive a wage that creates a profit for the owner. No American business is set up to enrich the employees. Businesses are set up to fulfill the *American Dream*. If everyone was able to live the *American Dream*, there wouldn't be any employees (slaves) to do all the work needed to make the businesses successful.

Christians do not see it as a sin to make millions of dollars in pursuit of the *American Dream* when they are using all of that money to benefit their self and their family. If they are doing that, then they are only honoring Christ with their lips, but their hearts are far from him. They are not using their success and money the way that Jesus would.

In order to be recognized as a millionaire that is financially independent, the person must have saved enough money to warrant the status. If a business is making millions, and the business saves millions, then in saving the money, the money just sits there and doesn't benefit anyone else.

Investment is one of the only ways that the *American Dream* can be reached by most. A person works hard and earns money. They invest their money into things that create more money without them having to do any more hard work. The more money you invest, the more money you make off your investments without having to work for it. But somebody ALWAYS has to do the hard work so that your investments are successful.

You invest in the stock market with *the hope* that the "slaves" that create the profit for the business in which you have invested continue to work hard and make the company more profitable. You place a "hope" in your investments with the intent to live the *American Dream* so that you don't have to work as hard. Christians believe that the hard work that you do in order to invest is *not* "abominable to God."

But if the "name of Christ" is on your lips, then you would have a "hope in Christ," instead of in your investments. "And after ye have obtained a hope in Christ" (which is not the same hope that you have for your investments),

Chapter 10: The Atonement—A Christian Delusion

"ye shall obtain riches, if ye seek them; BUT YE WILL SEEK THEM FOR THE INTENT TO DO GOOD"—and not good for only yourself or your family—people who already have enough food to eat, clothes to wear, and are not sick and afflicted with poverty.

The hope that you have placed in your investments creates poverty and inequality. What you do is an unrighteous act. You are partaking of the flesh of Jesus unworthily. (In other words, you are not taking care of the poor and the needy.) We wrote about this later in our story (when Jesus was among the Nephites), making another connection between the New Testament and our new American scripture. We reiterated the importance of not eating the flesh of Jesus and drinking his blood unworthily.

A Bible story tells of the last supper that Jesus had with his disciples, during which he introduced the sacrament. This sacrament (that the Christian world later incorporated into their rituals) symbolically represented eating the flesh of Christ and drinking his blood:

> Wherefore whosoever shall eat this bread, and drink this cup of the Lord, unworthily, shall be guilty of the body and blood of the Lord. ... For he that eateth and drinketh unworthily, eateth and drinketh damnation to himself, not discerning the Lord's body.[35]

In other words, if a person does not understand the symbolism of the sacrament, and doesn't take it for the purpose for which it was instituted and intended, the person is condemned, rather than blessed. We knew that there weren't <u>any</u> American Christians who were "partaking of Jesus' blood and flesh" worthily. ALL were an abomination before God, because they honored him with their lips (took the sacrament), but their hearts were far from him. This was because the American Christians were being taught "for doctrines the commandments of men, having a form of godliness, but they [were] deny[ing] the power thereof."[36] The power of what Jesus did was centered

---

[35] NT, 1 Corinthians 11:27–9; *see also* BOM, 3 Nephi 18:28–9.
[36] JSH 1:19.

on making the world a better place in which to live. Jesus was all about saving the people by teaching them how they should treat each other, which would save humanity, if they followed his words.

Our friend, Mahatma Gandhi, not only said that "Wealth Without Work" was one of the world's worst social sins, but also said, "A nation's greatness is measured by how it treats its weakest members." This is how Jesus reportedly said it:

> Inasmuch as ye have done it unto one of the least of these my brethren, ye have done it unto me. ... Inasmuch as ye did it not to one of the least of these, ye did it not to me.[37]

The overall intent of our new American scripture was to somehow penetrate the pride of the American people, who claimed to be Christian, but who did NOTHING that Jesus would do. Through the way that they perceived the atonement of Jesus Christ, American Christians learned from their leaders that it didn't matter if they were all sinners doing the wrong thing. They were taught that as long as they believed in Christ and were baptized in his name, they would be forgiven for all of their sins; they just had to do what God's servants on Earth told them to do. The people put their trust and salvation in the hands of their corrupt religious leaders, none of whom taught Jesus' pure and simple teachings.

Currently (around 2020), many Americans are protesting in the street about racial injustice and demanding change, chanting, "No justice. No peace." Often these protests become violent, and all of these protests disobey law and order by shutting down streets and threatening civil unrest. At the front of many of these protests are Christian preachers who call upon the name of Jesus while supporting protests and disruptions of law and authority. NONE of these preachers uses the words of Jesus Christ to create peace and goodwill in society. Jesus' teachings were very specific and clear about how to deal with

---

[37] *See* NT, Matthew 25:40, 45.

Chapter 10: The Atonement—A Christian Delusion

people who persecute a group of people and "despitefully use them." Jesus taught to love your enemies and do good to them. Jesus taught compassion and forgiveness. Jesus taught people NOT to sue in court and use the justice system for revenge. Again, the American Christian leaders are contributing to the problems that are creating division and misery. They honor Jesus with their lips, but their hearts are FAR from him.

Society cannot and will not improve unless its members act to improve it. If no action is taken, no improvements will be made. Nothing stands in the way of motivating people to make the necessary improvements to society more than their religious beliefs. *Religious people take no action unless God commands them to act.* Therefore, the religious leaders, who control the members and who speak for God, can influence what the people do.

If the commands of God, given through religious leaders, improve a society to the point where the society no longer needs improvement, then what use do religious leaders have, except to remind the people to keep doing the things that made a good society? And if the people realize that *their actions* make a good society, then for what else do the people need God?

ALL religious ritual is invented by religious leaders so they can keep control of and be needed by the people. If people are taught that they must perform certain acts in order to be saved, then whoever has the proper authority to administer the acts becomes a savior to the people. The leader is the most popular and respected person in the community and usually gains monetarily (in money) from the administration of the saving ordinance (act). (For one example, people pay tithing to the LDS/Mormon church in order to be allowed to go to the temple to be "sealed for eternity" as a family.)

A "saving ordinance" is a specific act that a church requires of a member in order to be saved in Heaven. There is no saving ordinance that benefits society as a whole. The act only benefits the person doing the ordinance. Conveniently, no church allows a person to administer a saving ordinance to their self. You need a religious (priesthood) leader to administer the ordinance for you.[38]

All of the world's greatest societies have failed in the past and are failing today. This is because the people believe that performing saving ordinances of the churches is more important than following the teachings that tell them how to treat their neighbor. Societies flourish when their citizens treat each other correctly. No society has EVER become successful because of the existence of churches in which leaders administer saving ordinances to the people. The only societies that have worked are those whose citizens have learned the proper way to treat each other.

With great sadness, we are forced to report that those who honor our new American scripture with their lips have hearts that are far from it. The people who call themselves after our book, "the Mormons," are members of the "great and abominable church of the devil," as we have presented it in our storyline.

The investments of the Church of Jesus Christ of Latter-day Saints have made that church one of the worldliest, most successful institutions in all of the world. The LDS/Mormons do not use their wealth and power to do good. Instead, they use it to remain part of the "great and abominable church" that keeps the descendants of the Nephites and the Lamanites from entering the borders of their land. They do not use their great wealth and the combination of power that they have in secret with governments and businesses to make the world a better place. They use their great wealth to build temples and churches, malls, and structures from which they receive the praise of the world.

And when they take the sacrament, when they take upon themselves the "flesh and blood of Christ," there is not a group of Christian people on Earth that does so as unworthily as the members of the LDS Church. If we

---

[38] Contrast this with *BOM*, Mosiah 18:12–15, where Alma baptizes himself.

could, we would prohibit that religion from mocking us and misusing one of the only books ever written that can make a person ONE with God.

Truly, this is what AT-ONE-MENT should mean: making a person Christ-like (at one with Christ) by doing the things that Jesus would do, but most importantly, for the same reasons and intents that he would do them.

Becoming "one with God" is defined by religious leaders as doing what they claim God tells a person to do by listening to them. The teachings of Jesus in the Bible teach no such doctrine. "The Kingdom of God is within" was taught in the Jesus stories, which means "God is within" each and every person equally.

No religion on Earth properly teaches a person to believe in their own self, and to listen to no other source, but their own self. And just as important, the true self-god is not a god meant for any other person except for the ruler who sits on the throne in the "kingdom of God within"—the individual.

Until the people of Earth start to believe in themselves above all the false gods created by religious leaders—gods that were created in order to control and subject the people to these false messengers—the Atonement can only be a Christian delusion.

Chapter 11
Transfiguring the Holy Word of God

In the Prologue of this book, we introduced indisputable evidence of how modern LDS Church leaders change the meaning of our new American scripture to fit their intentions. They mislead and misguide the members of this church against the counsel and lessons we intended for our scripture. This church Apostle's actions forced us to come forward and confront his blatant fraud against what we intended to help the American Christians become better people—our *Book of Mormon*. Publishing this book (*A New American Scripture—How and Why the Real Illuminati® Created the Book of Mormon*) was necessary to challenge this unrighteous church and hopefully stop its fraud against our work.

In American law, there are four essential elements of the crime of wire fraud (similar to those of mail fraud): 1) electronic communication was used in the furtherance of the scheme; 2) the voluntary act of intentionally devising or participating in a scheme to defraud another out of money; 3) the act was done with the intent to defraud; and 4) it was reasonably foreseeable that the act would require the use of electronic communication.

"Defraud" means to "illegally obtain money from someone by deception."[1]

On October 2, 2016, during the 186th Semiannual General Conference of the Church of Jesus Christ of Latter-day Saints (LDS Church), being broadcast via television (electronic communication), one of this church's members of the Quorum of the Twelve Apostles, Elder Gary E. Stevenson,

---

[1] *See* "defraud," Lexico – Oxford University Press, lexico.com/en/definition/defraud.

committed the crime of wire fraud in his conference address, titled "Look to the Book, Look to the Lord."[2]

Here are the details of our complaint:

LDS/Mormon members are required to listen to and accept the words of their Twelve Apostles, as if God were speaking to them. LDS/Mormon leaders mandate the payment of tithing (money) in order for a person to be saved. These leaders emphatically state that the LDS Church is God's ONLY true and living church upon Earth, and that paying religious donations to this church is the ONLY way to true salvation. ("True and living" is intended to mean that there are *living* prophets, seers, and revelators who speak to God and receive God's *true* will for the rest of humanity.)

Stevenson's crime was not the result of his belief and teaching others that their church is the only true church of God on the earth.[3] This is protected as the free practice of religion. However, this pretended Apostle of Jesus Christ committed fraud when he used our new American scripture in a deceitful way to reiterate the importance of being a member of the LDS Church. Many of the members of this church have joined and remained faithful to it because of our *Book of Mormon*. Trusting their Apostle, a reasonable member would assume that the way Stevenson was interpreting the verses he used was correct. His powerful words, along with his expressions of emotion, made the listener believe that the LDS/Mormon people are special because an ancient prophet of God "saw YOU [the modern LDS/Mormon people], in vision, many hundreds of years ago!"

Stevenson also lied when he emphatically stated that the members of the LDS church have "the complete book," implying that the *Book of*

---

[2] *See* Elder Gary E. Stevenson, "Look to the Book, Look to the Lord," October 2016 General Conference, The Church of Jesus Christ of Latter-day Saints, churchofjesuschrist.org/study/general-conference/2016/10/look-to-the-book-look-to-the-lord?lang=eng.

[3] *See* "Latter Day Saint movement," in "One true church," *Wikipedia*, 24 May 2021, en.wikipedia.org/wiki/One_true_church#Latter_Day_Saint_movement.

A New American Scripture

Mormon had no other part to it, and that the LDS/Mormon people were a righteous and blessed people because they have the *Book of Mormon*.

We have already given these details of Stevenson's deception. We have explained that the ancient prophet to whom Stevenson was referring DID see the modern LDS/Mormon people in vision, but this prophet, Moroni, said *nothing good* about the LDS/Mormon people. Moroni's vision clearly condemns the modern LDS Church, all of its members, and all of its leaders.[4]

Stevenson presented the members of the LDS Church as righteous and blessed. Had he not, had Stevenson read Moroni's vision in context as we had written it, his words would have implied that the LDS Church and its members are, as we wrote in our new American scripture, "the more wicked part of the world."[5] We wrote specifically in this part of our story of the importance of "the plates" upon which was engraved our intended history of the native American ancestors. These plates contained both an *unsealed* (1/3) and a *sealed* part (2/3). Besides our *Book of Mormon* and *The Sealed Portion*, we gave the reader a clue that there were many more

> greater things than these [and that] whoso receiveth this record,
> and shall not condemn it because of the imperfections which are
> in it, the same shall know of greater things than these.[6]

Throughout the narrative of our new American scripture, we wrote of "greater things" that would be revealed. These would be provided only *if* those who received the *unsealed* portion (the *Book of Mormon*) repented and worked righteousness—which meant to become better people by following the simple teachings attributed to Jesus Christ of the New Testament. We made it very clear to the Americans that they had to comply with the lessons and instructions given in our new scripture or they would always be under condemnation. There is no part of our story, if presented

---

[4] *See BOM*, Mormon, chapter 8.
[5] *BOM*, 2 Nephi 10:3.
[6] *See BOM*, Mormon 8:12.

Chapter 11: Transfiguring the Holy Word of God

correctly and honestly, that justifies the actions of the LDS Church and its leaders. In fact, "this record" clearly condemns them.

To keep members believing in their prophets, seers, and revelators, and faithfully paying their tithing—which meets one of the necessary criminal elements of fraud—the LDS/Mormon leaders have no choice but to deceptively *transfigure* and misinterpret (and in Stevenson's case, blatantly lie about) what our *Book of Mormon* teaches.

To be fair, Joseph Smith was also accused of defrauding the people of his day. This was not because he misread or transfigured the words contained in the *Book of Mormon*, but because he claimed to have received gold plates and translated these plates through "the gift and power of God"[7] (in order to produce the *Book of Mormon*).

There is nothing that can be done in defense of the fraud that Stevenson committed. The evidence is too overwhelming. However, we did something to ensure that any charge of fraud made against Joseph (or later Christopher) would not stand. We allowed Joseph to show the actual metal plates that we had constructed to three men. We created a prophecy in our revised storyline that would allow for this:

> Wherefore, at that day when the book shall be delivered unto the man of whom I have spoken, the book shall be hid from the eyes of the world, that the eyes of none shall behold it save it be that three witnesses shall behold it, by the power of God, besides him to whom the book shall be delivered; and they shall testify to the truth of the book and the things therein.[8]

Two of these Three Witnesses were Joseph's original scribes, Martin Harris and Oliver Cowdery. The third was David Whitmer, a friend of

---

[7] *See* the Preface of the 1830 edition of the *Book of Mormon*, found online at realilluminati.org/the-book-of-mormon. *See also BOM*, Omni 1:20

[8] *See BOM*, 2 Nephi 27:12.

Cowdery's. These men were also part of the peer review group that Joseph put together to review our book as we wrote it. Others in the peer review group included members of Joseph's own family; Martin Harris' family (including his wife, who was a staunch Christian and very critical of what Joseph was doing); most of the adult members of David Whitmer's family (including his father, Peter Whitmer Sr.; his mother, Mary; and his other siblings); and also Hiram Page, Whitmer's brother-in-law.

Joseph allowed the peer review group to be open to anyone who wanted to review his claims of translating an ancient record. There were a few other curious family friends and neighbors who sat in on a few peer review discussions, but these people didn't last long. Most were offended by the claims about where the material originated.

Joseph received some financial help while he was translating the plates. A generous donation came from Martin Harris ($50 USD), which added to Harris' wife's dismay and reluctance. Once money was exchanged because of Joseph's claims, an element of fraud could be claimed: *the voluntary act of intentionally devising or participating in a scheme to defraud another out of money.*

We needed to ensure others would give their testimonies that Joseph was not devising or participating in a scheme. This is also one of the reasons why we created actual plates when we could have just told our True Messengers what to write, as is the case with the authors of the Bible. The Bible has no physical evidence of where it came from. It has no evidence to show that it came from anywhere but the minds of the authors who wrote its stories. We wanted to provide physical proof of our claims of authenticity and origin.

As we have explained, we made the plates and engravings on them in hieroglyphics of a language of our own construct: both "reformed Egyptian" and pre-Egyptian Jaredite hieroglyphics. With this physical evidence, neither Joseph nor Christopher could be charged with fraud or deception. Both men claimed, honestly and correctly, that they took their writings directly from the plates we provided them. Neither man was educated enough to read the engravings. They testified that they were able to read our homemade engravings with an apparatus of "curious workmanship" that we provided to them.

Neither Joseph nor Christopher intentionally devised or participated in a fraudulent scheme to produce the *Book of Mormon* or *The Sealed Portion*, respectively. We were the ones who intentionally devised and participated in creating something that was not real or true—yes, in order to deceive the people, but we did this for a wise and good purpose because of the previous deceptions of the Bible. We never intended, however, for Joseph to receive any money for what he did, and we strictly forbade Christopher from accepting any donations that were for his personal use or directly associated with someone purchasing *The Sealed Portion*. All of our works can be downloaded free of charge on the Internet.

Harris, Cowdery, and Whitmer actually saw the gold plates. Joseph set up the experience. He had the men follow him into the trees nearby his home at an early morning hour when the sun was shining at a particular spot that we had previously arranged. One of us (the Real Illuminati®) dressed in the appropriate attire (to appear like an *angel*) and stood in the sunlight's rays that showed through the trees. The sun's light infused the otherwise shadowed location with spectacular brilliance. Joseph had instructed the men not to speak with "the angel" who would show the plates to them.

Cowdery and Whitmer approached together. Harris had a hard time gaining the courage, but was eventually shown the plates by "an angel of God"—as Harris perceived the appearance. It was a short meeting and no words were spoken. The prophecy had been fulfilled.

When Christopher published *The Sealed Portion*, many critics wanted proof. They asked about his witnesses. Christopher's response was to the point, and given in typical Christopher fashion:

Read your damn book [meaning the *Book of Mormon*]! The prophesy states that the eyes of NONE shall see the plates EXCEPT THREE. The prophecy was fulfilled. If I had shown the plates to anyone else, you shits would have accused me of wrong because MORE THAN THREE saw the plates! You idiots!

LDS/Mormon history reports that there were eight other men who were also shown the plates, not by us ("by an angel of God"), but by the hand of Joseph. We approved an "official and authorized" biography that was written about Joseph's life (under our direction). In it, we explained these events and the Real Truth™ behind the sworn affidavits of these eight additional witnesses who claimed they too saw the plates.[9]

These other witnesses never actually saw our gold plates. Joseph did not show the plates to them. To protect Joseph and the other Three Witnesses from being convicted of fraud, these eight men were convinced to sign a false affidavit. This was necessary because our book was being sold, and many people had given money to support its publication and dissemination. By signing the affidavit, these men protected Joseph and the Three Witnesses. Upon certifying their testimonies under the law, these eight knew that they could never reveal the falsity of their testimonies or they would be convicted of fraud themselves.

David Whitmer's mother later told other church members that an angel had shown her the plates.[10] This was not true and was a selfish attempt to gain more value for herself. Except for the three men named above, and a few others "according to the will of God, to bear testimony of his word unto the children of men,"[11] no other mortal has seen these plates. However, we can now reveal that there have been two women who have actually held the

---

[9] *See JS Bio*, 312–13.
[10] Royal Skousen, "Another Account of Mary Whitmer's Viewing of the Golden Plates: The Interpreter Foundation," *The Interpreter Foundation | Increasing Understanding of Scripture One Article at a Time*, 25 Apr. 2014, journal.interpreterfoundation.org/another-account-of-mary-whitmers-viewing-of-the-golden-plates/.
[11] *BOM*, 2 Nephi 27:13.

gold plates and could give their testimony of the experience: the ex-wife of our last True Messenger (who was married to him at the time *The Sealed Portion* was published in 2004), and Ida Smith, who was mentioned in the *Prologue* of this book. (Ida passed away in 2015.)

ALL of the "official" witnesses, except for Joseph's intimate family members, later left him and called him a "fallen prophet." The *eight other witnesses* who turned on Joseph, but who knew they had signed a fraudulent affidavit, began to call Joseph a fraud and a charlatan. These eight men turning against Joseph makes logical sense. However, one would assume a person who *actually saw* the plates of gold, especially if shown by an "angel of God," as one perceives, could never fall away from Joseph and denounce (speak out against) him.

Although they vehemently turned against him, none of the Three Witnesses ever referred to Joseph as a "fraud" or "charlatan." As mentioned, the few men who did were among those *eight* who committed fraud themselves when they gave their signed, *fraudulent* oath that Joseph had shown them the gold plates. Again, we act as we must in order to protect our True Messengers the best way we can.

Accepted LDS/Mormon history does not report the Real Truth™ about *why* the three main witnesses turned on and abandoned Joseph. These men loved our new American scripture, and until the day that each died, none ever recanted his love for it. In fact, it was their love for our book that caused them to scorn and condemn Joseph.

The Three Witnesses were very upset when Joseph began to allow the early LDS/Mormon Church authorities to *transfigure*, ignore, and misinterpret the prophecies and teachings of the *Book of Mormon*. After Joseph's death, Brigham Young's continuation of church leadership and authority, as well as the leadership of those who did not follow Young and "reorganized" the church in Illinois, continued to relentlessly damage our book's meaning and message.

"Transfigure" usually means to give new meaning to something and transform it into something better than what it was. In this case, however, nothing that Joseph *suffered* (allowed) the early LDS leaders and members to do to our new American scripture was good, especially nothing that was done to our story *after* Joseph was gone. It was all bad. Nothing that the LDS/Mormon-based religions have done has made the world a better place and helped humanity. Although the Mormon people might argue this, if one sincerely and with real intent considers the evidence that we provide in this book (*A New American Scripture*), the LDS/Mormon argument fails to prevail.

We knew that it was highly possible that the believers in our *Book of Mormon* would do what the modern Apostle Stevenson did in transfiguring the meaning of our words. This became very apparent to us after we were forced to *transfigure* the beginning of our own storyline. However, we did not change its intended lessons. (In contrast, Brigham Young and others later *did* change its meaning and ignored its lessons in the way they read our scripture out of context and interpreted it in *their own way*). We only added more details in our revision in order to help the Christian reader accept it and to more clearly understand our book's intent and purpose.

Everything that the LDS/Mormon sects did to our book after it was published in 1830 was abhorrent and repulsive to us. Many times, their changes directly contradicted what was written in our new American scripture. These ignorant, unscrupulous, and deceptive men misread our book to the members, spinning the meaning of its lessons and passages into a web of lies and deceit.

This brought the whole church under great condemnation. Through Joseph Smith, "the Lord" (words given to Joseph by us) condemned the LDS Church for how the leaders and members of that faith were treating our book:

> And the whole world lieth in sin, and groaneth under darkness and under the bondage of sin. And by this you may know they are under the bondage of sin, because they [meaning the early

Latter-day Saints] come *not* unto me. For whoso cometh not unto me is under bondage of sin. And whosoever receiveth not my voice [as given in the *Book of Mormon*] is not acquainted with my voice, and is not of me.

And by this you may know the righteous from the wicked [<u>those who accept the words of the Lord in the *Book of Mormon* and those who don't</u>], and that the whole world groaneth under sin and darkness even now.

And your minds in times past have been darkened because of unbelief [in the *Book of Mormon*], and because you have treated lightly the things you have received—which vanity and unbelief have brought the **whole church** under condemnation.

And this condemnation resteth upon the children of Zion, **even all**. And they shall remain under this condemnation until they repent and remember the new covenant, even the Book of Mormon and the former commandments which I have given them, not only to say, but to do according to that which I have written [in the *Book of Mormon*].[12]

We could provide pages upon pages of information about what the LDS/Mormon Church did and does to our book's meaning. We can show how "the whole church ... even all" say that they believe in the *Book of Mormon* but do not do anything that is taught therein. However, we want to focus on a few issues that caused the Three Witnesses to turn against Joseph. These issues are very important. They are of such importance that these few issues caused the Three Witnesses to testify that Joseph had become a fallen prophet, although they continued their belief in our *Book of Mormon* until their deaths.

---

[12] *See D&C*, 84:49–57, emphasis added.

Joseph allowed a church to form, but not according to the "word of God," as he might have received it through direct revelation. Joseph was mandated (by us) to allow an organized religion to form into an official new American church according to the protocol of democracy—the vote of the majority. Nothing official in the Church was done unless it was done "by the uplifting of hands." This means that the members themselves voted on most of this church's policies and procedures by raising their hands in the affirmative or in opposition to whatever they were voting on. It was initially reported correctly in LDS/Mormon history:

> On April 6, 1830, Joseph Smith and several newly baptized Saints gathered in a small log farm home belonging to Peter Whitmer Sr. in Fayette, Seneca County, New York.
>
> Joseph stood and asked those participating if they "desired the organization of The Church of Jesus Christ of Latter-day Saints."
>
> Exercising the principle of common consent, the newly baptized members raised their hands in a unanimous vote. Next they consented to accept Joseph Smith and the other elders of the Church as their "spiritual teachers."
>
> "In one sense, sustaining the leaders was a major reason for having the first meeting of the Church on April 6, 1830," said Steven C. Harper, a historian in the Church History Department.[13]

Although the LDS/Mormons tout that their religion is the *restored* church that Jesus Christ had organized anciently, nowhere can it be found where Jesus asked people to vote on his decisions. Nevertheless, we instructed Joseph to not do *anything* or perform *any* function as an

---

[13] "Raising Our Hands to Sustain Is Also a Promise to 'Do Our Part.'" Edited by Sarah Jane Weaver, 31 Mar. 2018, *Church News*, Intellectual Reserve, Inc., churchofjesuschrist.org/church/news/raising-our-hands-to-sustain-is-also-a-promise-to-do-our-part?lang=eng.

organized church without taking a vote to see if the members agreed. At first, only by a majority vote of ALL members would official church business be carried out. This was in line with our new American scripture's warning that the people would be getting what they wanted, which would cause them to stumble, *IF* they rejected the lessons of our book. The LDS/Mormons "looked beyond the mark and they must needs fall."[14]

While Joseph was alive, he tried to allow the people to govern themselves *after* he had already attempted to teach them correct principles. Although Martin Harris strongly opposed organizing a new church, the other two witnesses didn't see a problem with a church that was established, but *only if* the majority voice of the people was considered.

After the Church was officially organized, Cowdery and Whitmer were able to convince Harris that the Church could be good while the people had their vote in how it was governed. During the time that "the uplifting of hands" governed the Church that had been organized, the Three Witnesses stayed loyal to the Church. They were agreeable to the Church when the majority of the members had a say in Church policies and procedures.

We explained that when the Church was first formed, Martin Harris wanted nothing to do with its formation because of the information he knew was in the "lost" 116 pages of manuscript that he had transcribed. The other two Witnesses were part of the original six official members of the "Church of Jesus Christ," as it was called when it was officially organized on April 6, 1830.

Everything felt right for the members, and for the Three Witnesses, until the members wanted a *governing body of priesthood authority.* Cowdery, Harris, and Whitmer were strongly opposed to any governing body of priesthood authority. They were outnumbered by the majority of people that voted for Twelve Apostles like they supposed that Jesus had.

---

[14] *Compare BOM*, Jacob 4:14.

They wanted to *restore* Jesus' original church, which they believed consisted of twelve apostles. Arguments ensued until Joseph intervened.

There is a good reason why NONE of the Three Witnesses was chosen for the original first Quorum of the Twelve Apostles. And it doesn't make sense that the governing body of men didn't include at least *one* of these important men in LDS/Mormon history. We have explained why above. None of them wanted a governing body. Again, the Three Witnesses felt that having the members vote on church procedure was the right way to run a church. They felt that as long as the majority of the members had a say in church policies and procedures, they could accept their new church.

Because there was so much contention over the issue, Joseph needed "the Lord" (us) to intervene. "The Lord" gave Joseph a revelation that the Three Witnesses should be the ones who chose the twelve men to perform the apostolic role. Contention solved. The Three Witnesses were full of pride that the Lord singled them out specifically to elect the first LDS Church Quorum of the Twelve Apostles.[15] With their egos satisfied, the Three Witnesses conformed to and accepted the outcome of the vote when the members were asked by uplifted hands if their church should have a Quorum of the Twelve Apostles.

Besides Cowdery, Harris, and Whitmer, there were only six members of the Church who refused to vote for the organization of this new priesthood quorum: Joseph and Emma Smith, Hyrum and Jerusha Smith, and Lucy Mack and Joseph Smith, Sr. (It's well to note that, in most Church votes, Joseph's family always looked to him first to see how he was voting.)

After the vote had passed, Joseph said nothing. These words from our new American scripture were ringing in his ears:

---

[15] *See D&C* 18:37–8.

Chapter 11: Transfiguring the Holy Word of God

> Because of their blindness, which blindness came by looking beyond the mark, they must needs fall; for God hath taken way his plainness from them, and [given them their Quorum of the Twelve Apostles], because they desired it. And because they desired it God hath done it, that they may stumble.[16]

After the establishment of the Quorum of the Twelve Apostles in 1835, these twelve men started making all of the final decisions for this church, regardless of what the majority of people wanted. The Quorum could override any vote.

The people wanted Twelve Apostles because they believed that this is what Jesus would do and would have done. They believed this even though—for all the years after our book was available—Joseph never once suggested having a Quorum of Twelve Apostles. The ringing of the words of our new American scripture in his ears was too loud. We had warned Joseph against establishing apostles for a church. Being warned by us, Joseph had nothing to do with choosing the first twelve men who became this church's selected Quorum of the Twelve Apostles.

Knowing the terrible results that would come from this action, and (as we explained) trying to appease the concerns of the Three Witnesses, Harris, Cowdery, and Whitmer were elected to choose the twelve men themselves. The prophet, seer, and revelator whom God had chosen—Joseph Smith Jr.—had NOTHING to do with choosing these twelve apostles.[17]

None of the Three Witnesses liked it when this new priesthood authority of their church began to make all the decisions and override the majority. When the group of twelve men, whom the Three Witnesses had selected, started

---

[16] *Compare BOM*, Jacob 4:14.

[17] *See* "Record of the Twelve, 14 February–28 August 1835," February 14, 1835, p. 1, The Joseph Smith Papers – The Church of Jesus Christ of Latter-day Saints, josephsmithpapers.org/paper-summary/record-of-the-twelve-14-february-28-august-1835/7, for the official historical account of the calling of the Twelve Apostles. Joseph Smith's name is not mentioned as being involved.

exercising "unrighteous dominion" over the rest of the Church, these Witnesses could sense that their church would soon become corrupt.

It was only a few years after THEY chose these twelve men, that all of the Three Witnesses left this church. They were very upset that Joseph didn't do something about the men of the Quorum of the Twelve to rein in their apostolic authority (related to being an apostle). Joseph's response to the Three Witnesses' complaints was epic: "You chose them. The blood of this church is on your hands."

The Three Witnesses now had no choice but to see Joseph as a fallen prophet. How could the blood of the people be on *their* hands? Didn't the Lord ask them to choose the twelve men? The Three Witnesses were very confused.

While this church was developing in Kirtland, Ohio, the members voted on creating their own currency.[18] There were a lot of negative votes, but the majority won out. The Three Witnesses voted against creating a new currency; but the ringing in Joseph's ears grew even louder,

> because of their blindness, which blindness came by looking beyond the mark, they must needs fall; ... And because they desired it God hath done it, that they may stumble.

Many times, "the Lord" condemned the early church for how its members were treating the *Book of Mormon*.

---

[18] Known as the Kirtland Safety Society. For more details, *see JS Bio*, p. 392, 401, 447–8, and 454; *and*

Scott H. Partridge, "The Failure of the Kirtland Safety Society," *BYU Studies* vol.12 no. 4 (Summer 1972), 437–54, found online at byustudies.byu.edu/wp-content/uploads/2020/02/12.4PartridgeFailure-1518c5ab-4202-41eb-84b4-0cc8fce9fc5e.pdf.

Chapter 11: Transfiguring the Holy Word of God

The LDS/Mormon people claim that the *Book of Mormon* contains, as the "angel Moroni" told Joseph, "the fulness of the everlasting Gospel ... as delivered by the Savior to the ancient inhabitants" of this continent.[19] (This means ALL of the Western Hemisphere of Earth). LDS/Mormons say, but do not do, what has been written in our new American scripture. They say, but do not do, the things that the resurrected Jesus told the ancestors of the native Americans (the ancient inhabitants) to do.[20] They say that the *Book of Mormon* contains the fullness of Christ's Gospel, but they do not do ANY of Jesus' simple commandments, nor do they teach of the things that Jesus teaches in our new American scripture.

This behavior was also prevalent at the time this church was organized in Joseph's day. This church, now being led and directed by the Quorum of the Twelve Apostles, was ignoring the *Book of Mormon.* This was a huge issue for the three men who could not deny the existence of the gold plates. Martin Harris, particularly, had a very hard time with where their church was headed.

We have explained that Joseph's peers and family had a hard time accepting that an organized church—including all of its ordinances, priesthoods, and "busy work"—did not contribute to the success of a righteous nation (human society). We made it clear that the *code of humanity* invented for the story of Jesus—his *Sermon on the Mount*—contains the basic rules on which a society **must** be built in order to establish peace and goodwill. We stated that this was the "mark," set by Jesus, towards which a person's heart and mind should be aimed.

We have illustrated that the way Christians view the *atonement* is not only in error respecting what Jesus actually taught, but has nothing to do with actual salvation. We have explained that "salvation" means the success, preservation, and continuation of a good human society, where peace and equity exist for the benefit of all Earth's inhabitants. What churches demand

---

[19] JSH 1:34.
[20] *See BOM*, 3 Nephi, chapters 12, 13 and 14.

of their members as "busy work" has nothing to do with helping society flourish. Instead, religion causes society's greatest problems, largely because each religion thinks that it is the correct one, and that the rest are from the devil.

We have explained that Martin Harris was Joseph's main scribe when the 116-page original manuscript was finished. The manuscript was given to Joseph's peers to be reviewed and discussed. It made perfect sense to Harris that an organized religion and a church were not needed for salvation. He knew it would only lead to what had happened to God's church in Jerusalem, as presented in the narrative we wrote for the *Book of Lehi*.

After we (the Real Illuminati®) made sure the 116-page manuscript was "lost," Joseph resumed "translating" with Martin Harris. At that time, Harris had a huge problem with some of the things that Joseph translated from the "small plates of Nephi." Harris wrote down the "Words of Mormon" first. These words introduced the "Small (less-numerous) Plates of Nephi." They explained how these small plates got put in with the other gold plates that Mormon was engraving, as an abridgment of the "Large (more numerous) Plates of Nephi."

Joseph said a little bit too much to Harris about how blind and hardhearted Joseph's peers were in "looking beyond the mark" of what Jesus taught. Joseph expounded to Harris on what was about to be rewritten as the "Book of Jacob." He also said that the American Christians were no different than the Jews of old. Joseph told Harris that he had received a commandment to take away the

> plainness from them, and [deliver] unto them many things which they cannot understand, because they desired it. And because they desired it God hath [commanded Joseph to do what the people wanted], that they may stumble.

Joseph related to Harris that it was not his intention to allow a church to form, but that the people needed a church in order to keep them busy and *aimed at the mark* set by the "fulness of the everlasting Gospel ... delivered by the Savior to the ancient inhabitants." The actions of the early American LDS/Mormons were exactly like the ancient Hebrews who wanted the lower Law of Moses instead of the "higher law" they could have received had the Hebrews not "looked beyond the mark."

Joseph was going to lie to the people, and Martin Harris knew it. As he did throughout his life, Joseph often told his followers that if they knew everything that he knew about the beginnings and foundations of this church, and the mysteries of God, they would rise up and kill him.[21] Harris knew why Joseph said this. Few others did.

Harris, however, was incensed at having to lie to the people. He refused to continue as Joseph's scribe. Joseph understood and made up an excuse that released Harris from his sacred duties without affecting Harris' and Joseph's integrity with their mutual peers. This made-up excuse began the rumors of what had happened to the 116 pages of "lost" manuscript that is the accepted history of the LDS/Mormon people today.[22]

Harris knew that allowing a church to be organized would not be good. He knew this would eventually have the same results as all churches that started and failed to implement the *code of humanity* given by Jesus Christ in the *Sermon on the Mount*, as presented in the New Testament.

LDS/Mormons have never been able to explain why Martin Harris did not attend the official and legal organization of their religion on April 6, 1830.[23]

---

[21] *See* Robert Horne, "Reminiscences of the Church in Nauvoo," *Millennial Star*, vol. 55 no. 36, 4 Sept. 1893, 585; also found online at contentdm.lib.byu.edu/digital/collection/MStar/id/19227. (Download the PDF to view all the pages.)

[22] *See* "Lost 116 pages," *Wikipedia*, 10 May 2121 en.wikipedia.org/wiki/Lost_116_pages.

[23] For details on who the original six members of the Church of Jesus Christ were, *see* "The Organization of The Church of Jesus Christ of Latter-day Saints," American Prophet – Timeline, PBS, pbs.org/americanprophet/18300406.html.

A New American Scripture

The world now knows the Real Truth™. Harris refused to be involved in something that he knew would cause the people to stumble. The ringing in Harris' ears about the people getting what they wanted, so that they would stumble, was insurmountable.

The other major issue that the Three Witnesses had with Joseph was how the American Christians who joined the new church ignored the native American people. Reading our new American scripture with an honest mind, one will come to understand that our book is about the native American people being a "remnant of the house of Israel." In our story, this remnant (a small surviving group) was led to a new "promised land" in order to set up "Zion" with the help of the "Gentiles."[24]

This was the "covenant which [God] made with" the ancient ancestors of the native Americans. As we presented above, according to revelation given to Joseph "from the Lord," the *Book of Mormon* **is** "the new [and everlasting] covenant."[25] The modern LDS/Mormon Church has changed this simple definition of God's "new and everlasting covenant" (the *Book of Mormon*) into something that benefits the priesthood leadership of this erroneous church.

According to modern LDS/Mormon doctrine, "the new and everlasting covenant" is

> a contractual arrangement in which God and man agree to abide by certain terms and conditions in return for certain benefits. Man agrees to keep all of God's commandments and observe every ordinance of salvation.[26]

---

[24] *See BOM*, 3 Nephi, chapter 20.
[25] *See D&C*, 84:57.
[26] *See Doctrine and Covenants Instructor's Guide* (Salt Lake City: The Church of Jesus Christ of Latter-day Saints, 1981), Lesson 25, found online at churchofjesuschrist.org/study/manual/doctrine-and-covenants-instructors-guide-religion-324-325/the-everlasting-covenant-the-fulness-of-the-gospel-lesson-25-sections-66-68?lang=eng.

Chapter 11: Transfiguring the Holy Word of God

Completely excluding the *Book of Mormon*, but including the way that the modern LDS/Mormon Church has *transfigured* the "word of God," allows this church's leadership to make up "certain terms and conditions" and "all of God's commandments," NONE of which is found in the ***true*** "new covenant, even the *Book of Mormon*"[27]:

> They draw near to me with their lips, but their hearts are far from me, they teach for doctrines the commandments of men, having a form of godliness, but they deny the power thereof.[28]

It was with the introduction of this important covenant (promise) that we intended to end the history of the ancient inhabitants of the Western Hemisphere, regarding "a remnant of the house of Israel." This "remnant" (Lehi and his family) had been led away from Jerusalem and saved in a new "promised land." We intended for Mormon's son, Moroni, to end the story about the Nephites and Lamanites with this narrative (at the end of the Book of Ether) and finish our book with the story about the Great Jaredite Nation. This story was written as a warning to the white race of people living in the United States of America.

Joseph's peers wanted more things that they could not understand (which we knew would cause them to stumble).[29] They wanted a church. They wanted directions given them in "the new covenant—even the Book of Mormon" about how to organize a church. They even wanted to know what God would want them to call their church.

To appease them and give them more that would make them stumble, we therefore had to continue the story about the Nephites and Lamanites <u>after</u> we had already given "an account of those inhabitants who were

---

[27] *D&C*, 84:57.
[28] *See* JSH 1:19.
[29] *See BOM*, Jacob 4:14.

destroyed by the hand of the Lord upon the face of this north country [North America]."³⁰ We were forced to

> write a few more things, contrary to that which [we] had supposed; for [we] had supposed not to have written any more.³¹

The early Americans wanted a new religion for themselves, a religion that was not centered ONLY on "the fulness of the everlasting Gospel," but one that catered to their pride. Along with many other messages, which we will explain in later chapters, we had to warn the Americans to

> take heed, my beloved brethren, that ye do not judge that which is evil to be of God, or that which is good and of God to be of the devil.³²

We knew that the American Christians and all of their churches and creeds, "yea, even every one,"³³

> were all wrong … that those professors were all corrupt because they draw near to Jesus' everlasting Gospel with their lips, but their hearts are far from it.³⁴

This <u>included</u> the church that the professors (supposed supporters) of our book wanted to form.

The Three Witnesses of our *Book of Mormon* could see how the LDS Church began to "teach for doctrines the commandments of men, having a form of godliness, but they deny the power thereof." It was very apparent to these three men, who never lost their love for our new American scripture, that the early "Saints" were not "saints" at all. They had changed something

---

³⁰ *BOM*, Ether 1:1
³¹ *BOM*, Moroni 1:4.
³² *BOM*, Moroni 7:14.
³³ *BOM*, Mormon 8:36.
³⁴ *Compare* JSH 1:19.

Chapter 11: Transfiguring the Holy Word of God

"good and of God" *(that one doesn't need a church to be saved)* into something "evil and of the devil" *(that one **does** need a church, priesthood, and ordinances in order to be saved)*. The early Latter-day "Saints" had turned something "evil and of the devil" (Priesthood) into something "good and of God." The evidence of this is overwhelming.

A few years before most of the witnesses to the plates (eleven men) left Joseph, Oliver Cowdery was asked by Joseph to write some *Articles of Faith* for the Church. Under Joseph's direction, and with our consent, Cowdery wrote the following explanations of church doctrine as *Eight Articles of Faith*:[35]

1. We believe in God, and his Son Jesus Christ.

2. We believe that God, from the beginning, revealed himself to man; and that whenever he has had a people on earth, he always has revealed himself to them by the Holy Ghost, the ministering of angels, or his own voice. We do not believe that he ever had a church on earth without revealing himself to that church; consequently, there were apostles, prophets, evangelists, pastors, and teachers, in the same.

3. We believe that God is the same in all ages; and that it requires the same holiness, purity, and religion, to save a man now, as it did anciently; and that, as He is no respecter of persons, [He] always has, and always will reveal himself to men when they call upon him.

4. We believe that God has revealed himself to men in this age, and commenced to raise up a church preparatory to his second advent, when he will come in the clouds of heaven with power and great glory.

---

[35] *See* Oliver Cowdery, "Address," *Latter Day Saints' Messenger and Advocate* vol. 1 no. 1 (October 1834), 2; also found online at contentdm.lib.byu.edu/digital/collection/NCMP1820-1846/id/7002.

5. We believe that the popular religious theories of the day are incorrect; that they are without parallel in the revelations of God, as sanctioned by him; and that however faithfully they may be adhered to, or however zealously and warmly they may be defended, they will never stand the strict scrutiny of the word of life.

6. We believe that all men are born free and equal; that no man, combination of men, or government of men, have power or authority to compel or force others to embrace any system of religion, or religious creed, or to use force or violence to prevent others from enjoying their own opinions, or practicing the same, so long as they do not molest or disturb others in theirs, in a manner to deprive them of their privileges as free citizens—or of worshipping God as they choose, and that any attempt to the contrary is an assumption unwarrantable in the revelations of heaven, and strikes at the root of civil liberty, and is a subversion of all equitable principles between man and man.

7. We believe that God has set his hand the second time to recover the remnant of his people, Israel; and that the time is near when he will bring them from the four winds, with songs of everlasting joy, and reinstate them upon their own lands which he gave their fathers by covenant.

8. And further: We believe in embracing good wherever it may be found; of proving all things, and holding fast that which is righteous.

A few revisions to these original eight articles were made before Joseph was killed, and a lot of revisions after. Most of the later modifications to LDS Church doctrine were not accepted by the Three Witnesses. There were specifically two changes to the above "principles" that caused a great amount of concern to these three men and stood out to them as the most "evil."

Chapter 11: Transfiguring the Holy Word of God

Here is how Cowdery's article number 2 was revised:

> We believe that a man must be called of God, by prophecy, and by the laying on of hands by those who are in authority, to preach the Gospel and administer in the ordinances thereof.[36]

Furthermore, the LDS/Mormon Church teaches that no one can receive "the gift of the Holy Ghost"[37] unless the person receives it in the manner listed above, in the corrupted version of Cowdery's original number 2 article. Clearly, this revision is completely contrary to what Cowdery wrote about how God reveals himself to his people.

Here's the revision they made to Cowdery's article number 7:

> We believe in the literal gathering of Israel and in the restoration of the Ten Tribes; that Zion (the New Jerusalem) will be built upon the American continent; that Christ will reign personally upon the earth; and, that the earth will be renewed and receive its paradisiacal glory.[38]

We wrote a prophecy about the "Gentiles" who would bring "my gospel, saith the Lamb, and my rock and my salvation"[39] to the descendants of the ancient native Americans, upon whose history our story was based:

> And blessed are they who shall seek to bring forth my Zion at that day, for they shall have the gift and the power of the Holy Ghost; ... they shall be lifted up at the last day, and shall be saved in the everlasting kingdom of the Lamb; and whoso shall publish peace, yea, tidings of great joy, how beautiful upon the mountains shall they be.[40]

---

[36] *PGP*, Article of Faith 5.
[37] *PGP*, Article of Faith 4.
[38] *PGP*, Article of Faith 10.
[39] *BOM*, 1 Nephi 13:36.
[40] *BOM*, 1 Nephi 13:37.

A New American Scripture

The "Gentiles" were supposed to create Zion for the latter-day native Americans by giving them the Bible with the plain and precious parts put back, which our *Book of Mormon* did. Through the teachings of these two books, the "fulness of the everlasting Gospel" was confirmed, as delivered by the mouth of Jesus to both the Jews and to the ancient inhabitants of the Western Hemisphere.[41]

As written above, our prophecy *specifically* states that those "who shall seek to bring forth my Zion at that day ... shall [be blessed and] have the gift and the power of the Holy Ghost." The prophecy presents a person who "seek[s] to bring forth my Zion" as one who "shall publish peace, yea, tidings of great joy, how beautiful upon the mountains shall they be."

Our prophecy *did not* say that one must be given "the gift and the power of the Holy Ghost" by the "laying on of hands by those who are in authority, to preach the Gospel and administer in the ordinances thereof." Nowhere is this corrupted doctrine taught in our new American scripture. In fact, we *discounted* "the laying on of hands by those who are in authority" as the proper way for the people to receive "the gift and power of the Holy Ghost."

In a previous chapter, we explained how King Benjamin's people had

> offered for a sacrifice unto the Lord a broken heart and a contrite spirit, and were baptized with fire and with the Holy Ghost because of their faith in Jesus Christ, who was yet to come at the time of their conversion, and they were baptized with fire and with the Holy Ghost, and they knew it not.[42]

The Lamanites (to whom we referred in the passage above) and the people of King Benjamin did it right. They were baptized the *proper way*, without knowing it, or rather, without performing any church-mandated

---

[41] The fullness of Jesus' Gospel is found in the *New Testament*, Matthew, chapters 5, 6, and 7, and in the *Book of Mormon*, 3 Nephi, chapters 12, 13, and 14.
[42] *See* Chapter 10, pages 262–4. *Also compare BOM*, 3 Nephi 9:20.

ordinance, allowing the *true* "atoning blood of Christ"—who had not lived or died—to do the rest of the redeeming of the soul.

We explained the "blood of Christ" represents that a person does things (of the flesh) with the same intent (in the same spirit) that Jesus would do things. When a person does the things that Jesus taught them to do, with the intent that Jesus had in mind for the act, they will automatically receive "the power and gift of the Holy Ghost."

No one "in authority" laid their hands on the heads of the people of King Benjamin. Neither did anyone "lay their hands" on the heads of the Lamanites, who were converted, received "the gift and power of the Holy Ghost," and were baptized "and they knew it not."

As we listened to Joseph's reports about what his peers had said concerning what he was writing, we knew that this idea of "laying on of hands" to receive God's authority was going to be an issue. This manner of priesthood authority had started in the early Roman Catholic Church. It ensured that the Pope could remain in charge. People were taught that Jesus laid his hands on Peter and gave Peter the authority to administer in God's church. We knew that we had to address this issue.

We addressed it before we ended our story about the history of the Nephite and Lamanite (ancient American) peoples. Keep in mind what we explained above about continuing our storyline being "contrary to that which [we] had supposed." We had to confront this accepted Christian policy of the "laying on of hands" and have it make sense to our intended Christian audience.

There was another, more subtle way, that we *discounted* the idea that the laying on of hands was necessary for Jesus' disciples in order for them to teach other people after he left. In our story, we introduced the twelve disciples whom Jesus had chosen. Nine of the disciples wanted that after we have lived unto the age of man, that our ministry, wherein thou hast called us, may have an end, that we may speedily come unto thee in thy kingdom.[43]

According to the story, the other three disciples wanted to remain alive and continue to teach Jesus' gospel until Jesus came again in his glory. They "desired the thing which John, my beloved, who was with me in my ministry, before that I was lifted up by the Jews, desired of me."[44]

This was the point in our narrative when we introduced the idea behind our group, the Real Illuminati®: "And it came to pass that when Jesus had spoken these words," he *did not* lay his hands on these disciples to give them any authority. After Jesus had taught the people his everlasting Gospel, he did *not* command them to form a church. In fact, Jesus was greatly disturbed because the people didn't understand what he had just taught them, which were the only thoughts and behaviors they had to do to be saved.

> Jesus groaned within himself, and said: Father, I am troubled because of the wickedness of the people of the house of Israel.[45]

To appease Joseph's peers, we had the people in our story desire to be part of a church. They wanted what they were used to and were comfortable with when they thought they were receiving the "saving ordinances" (as they supposed) according to the law of Moses.

Before he left his disciples, Jesus "touched every one of them with his finger save it were the three who were to tarry." At this point, it was not our intent to give any credence to the "laying on of hands by those in authority." Our story would have remained very clear on this subject had Joseph's peers not "desired things that they could not understand" because they were "looking beyond the mark" that Jesus wanted his disciples to aim the people towards.

---

[43] *BOM*, 3 Nephi 28:2.
[44] *BOM*, 3 Nephi 28:6.
[45] *BOM*, 3 Nephi 17:14.

In fact, the irony that we used in this part of our new American scripture's narrative was that Jesus did NOT touch the three disciples who would remain on Earth to teach the everlasting Gospel. And as well as teaching the Gospel, these *three Nephites* would also help the people to

> come unto [Jesus] as a little child ... with a broken heart and a contrite spirit ... [and to be] baptize[d] with fire and with the Holy Ghost, even as the Lamanites, because of their faith in [Jesus] at the time of their conversion, were baptized with fire and with the Holy Ghost, and they knew it not.[46]

The LDS/Mormons believe that no one on Earth can or will be saved, unless the person receives baptism and the gift of the Holy Ghost, administered properly "by the laying on of hands by those who are in authority" in *their* church. The Three Witnesses knew that the *Book of Mormon* taught something completely different. This is why Oliver Cowdery wrote the part of his *Eight Articles of Faith* the way that he did.

Dishonest LDS/Mormon leaders *transfigured* the word of God and turned something that was "good and of God" into something that was "evil and of the devil." They did this in order to control the people, and to make their followers, and everyone else in the world, value them and their priesthood authority. It is "good" that salvation is free to all people. It is "evil" when the people have to depend on men—priesthood authority and the laying on of hands—and pay tithing to their leaders in order to be saved.

The Three Witnesses began to condemn Joseph Smith for allowing these evil doctrines to creep into their church, contrary to the teachings of the *Book of Mormon*. However, this was not the only reason why they left this church. They also recalled the actual "covenant" God made to the native American people, that they would be "reinstate[d] upon their own lands which [God] gave their fathers by covenant." (Refer to Cowdery's article number 7.)

---

[46] *BOM*, 3 Nephi 9:22, 20.

It is this "new covenant" given in the *Book of Mormon* that the LDS/Mormons do not accept, and for which they are under condemnation. Because of their vanity and unbelief in their own *Book of Mormon* prophecies, "the whole church [is] under condemnation ... even all."[47] They are vain because they believe that "Zion" is theirs to own and build for themselves. In actuality, "Zion" is supposed to be built upon both of the main continents of the Western Hemisphere (all of North and South America), not just in the United States. The LDS/Mormons give no attention or heed to what Oliver Cowdery explained was *supposed to be* the doctrine of this church:

> We believe that God has set his hand the second time to recover the remnant of his people, Israel; and that the time is near when he will bring them from the four winds, with songs of everlasting joy, and reinstate them upon their own lands [all of the Western Hemisphere] which he gave their fathers by covenant.

The Three Witnesses approached Joseph shortly after the *Book of Mormon* (our book) was officially released and published in 1830. They asked him to please explain what the Lord meant by "Zion." They also asked Joseph to expound upon what the resurrected Christ said about a "New Jerusalem" being "establish[ed] in this land, unto the fulfilling of the covenant which I made with your father Jacob; and it shall be a New Jerusalem. And the powers of heaven shall be in the midst of this people; yea, even I will be in the midst of you."[48]

Harris, Cowdery, and Whitmer loved what the resurrected Jesus said concerning the future church and religion of the "Gentiles" and what it was supposed to do for the native Americans. However, they needed Joseph to explain this better to the other members. This was especially the case when Jesus was speaking about the "Latter-day Saints" (those who believe in the *Book of Mormon*), from whom the native Americans were *supposed* to be receiving Christ's everlasting Gospel:

---

[47] *D&C*, 84:55–6.
[48] *See BOM*, 3 Nephi 20:22.

> But if they [the American Christians/Mormons] will repent and hearken unto my words, and harden not their hearts, I will establish my church among them [the American Christians/Mormons], and they [the American Christians/Mormons] shall come in unto the covenant and be numbered among this the remnant of Jacob, unto whom I have given this land for their [the remnant of Jacob's/the native American's] inheritance;
>
> And they [the American Christians/Mormons] shall assist my people, the remnant of Jacob, and also as many of the house of Israel as shall come, that they [my people, the remnant of Jacob, and also as many of the house of Israel as shall come], may build a city, which shall be called the New Jerusalem.
>
> And then shall they [the American Christians/ Mormons] assist my people that they [my people, the remnant of Jacob, and also as many of the house of Israel as shall come] may be gathered in, who are scattered upon all the face of the land, in unto the New Jerusalem.[49]

Christ was NOT referring to the European-Christian Americans as those "unto whom I have given this land for their inheritance." The entire Western Hemisphere was the covenanted "promised land" for the native American people, and for millions of other immigrants for whom the land was saved from being taken and controlled by the "Gentiles" (non-Jewish people) like the Eastern Hemisphere had been.

There was and is NOTHING being done in the Church of Jesus Christ of Latter-day Saints that is **assisting** the native Americans to establish "Zion"—not in the church that was established in Joseph's day; not in the church that continued after Joseph's murder under the control of Brigham Young; and not in the present-day church.

---

[49] *See BOM*, 3 Nephi 21:22–4.

A New American Scripture

Joseph explained "Zion" to be this: "And the Lord called his people **Zion**, because they were of one heart and one mind, and dwelt in righteousness; and there was no poor among them."[50]

The LDS/Mormon people had rejected the simple words of Jesus that would save their society and help create "Zion" and a "New Jerusalem." These new "cities from heaven" were not supposed to be built ***for** them*, but ***by** them*. These prophecies were about the native American people. We wrote these prophecies in hopes that the "Gentiles" (Americans) would remember these prophecies and assist the native American people, and many other immigrants, to establish themselves as the Lord's people, called **Zion**.

The LDS Church does <u>not</u> help humanity become of one heart and one mind; and this religion certainly does not work towards ensuring that there are no poor among them. Because this church is like this, while pretending to believe in our new American scripture, we can honestly say that this church is among the most unrighteous and corrupt in the world.

As we have explained—and it bears such importance to continue repeating it throughout this book—the modern-day native American people are some of the poorest, most marginalized, and ignored citizens of the United States of America. The LDS/Mormon people support political policies that keep the "remnant of the house of Israel" out of *their* country (as they suppose). They believe that God gave them this country. They support strong anti-immigration laws and strong borders.

Little do they know that the people who are struggling throughout this world to immigrate to the "promised land" are those people of whom we refer in our new American scripture as the "lost Ten Tribes of Israel." We had hoped to impress upon the minds of the early American people the importance of keeping their borders open and inviting into this "promised land" ANY and ALL of the children of God that needed God's

---

[50] *PGP*, Moses 7:18.

help—help with which the "Gentiles" were blessed by God to provide to those less fortunate throughout the entire world.

We were connected to the man who gifted the Statue of Liberty to the United States government. Our discussions with this man, and with others, also inspired the writing that this symbol of God's nation promised to ALL of God's children, equally:

Give me your tired, your poor,
Your huddled masses yearning to breathe free,
The wretched refuse of your teeming shore.
Send these, the homeless, tempest-tost to me,
I lift my lamp beside the golden door![51]

NOTHING that the LDS/Mormons do, NOTHING that most other Christians do, glorifies Jesus. The American Christians do not hold up a candle (a lamp) to invite God's needy children into the United States of America. Instead, they do the exact opposite. The vanity and pride of the American Christians, along with their policies and procedures (established by law according to the U.S. Constitution), are based on keeping people OUT of the United States of America.

The Americans believe that their Constitution was inspired by God. In this way, they have turned that which is evil and of the devil into something they think is good and of God.

We warned them.

---

[51] *See* Poem by Emma Lazarus on Statue of Liberty plaque, transcript and picture found at "Statue of Liberty, The New Colossus," National Park Service, U.S. Department of the Interior, nps.gov/stli/learn/historyculture/colossus.htm.
See also "The New Colossus," *Wikipedia*, 26 May 2021, en.wikipedia.org/wiki/The_New_Colossus.

We tried to work with their pride and vanity. We wrote our story to imply that God would help them become the greatest nation on Earth; BUT ONLY, BUT ONLY, **if** they would

> assist my people, the remnant of Jacob, and also as many of the house of Israel as shall come, [to] build a city, which shall be called the New Jerusalem. And ... assist my people that they may be gathered in, who are scattered upon all the face of the land, in unto the New Jerusalem.[52]

The Three Witnesses could not believe how proud and unrighteous the LDS/Mormon people had become in such a short time. They were justified in leaving their church, which to them, had become sinful. But they were NOT justified in leaving Joseph alone to have to deal with those unholy people.

Joseph's followers never understood that we were influencing Joseph's actions behind the scenes. We told Joseph to give them things "that they could not understand, so that they may stumble." We wrote the prophecy and made sure it was fulfilled. Joseph could not speak openly about our existence. At that time, the technology that we could use to stay in touch with him and guide him did not exist. But we provided him with a compass of "curious workmanship" that he used for us to guide him under our direction.

One of us (the Real Illuminati®) met the Three Witnesses, when we posed as an "angel of God." We wrote a prophesy about our existence in our new American scripture, that we "are as the angels of God, and if [we] shall pray unto the Father in the name of Jesus [we] can show [ourselves] unto whatsoever man it seemeth [us] good."[53]

The leaders and members of the LDS Church do not acknowledge our existence and what we do. Regardless, there was a time when it

---

[52] *BOM*, 3 Nephi 21:23–4.
[53] *See BOM*, 3 Nephi 28:30.

Chapter 11: Transfiguring the Holy Word of God

"seemed good" to us to introduce ourselves to one of the modern General Authorities of this church.

We wanted this man to know that we were aware of him. We introduced him to our last True Messenger. We did this to give this General Authority comfort and support, because this man was the only General Authority who was a descendent of the "remnant of the house of Israel." He was a direct descendent of Jacob, as we presented the lineage in our new American scripture. He was the only native American, modern-day LDS General Authority. Like the earlier Three Witnesses, he recognized the great unrighteousness and hypocrisy of this church. This man was aware his church was a religious institution that was (and is) under condemnation for *transfiguring the holy word of God*.

This man's name was George P. Lee. The LDS Church to which he belonged has done to Lee's name what it has done to our last True Messenger's name, and also to Joseph's name, because of the way that this church misrepresents what Joseph was asked to do. This church has maligned (defamed) their names (George's, Christopher's, and Joseph's) and presented fabrications of all sorts against them.[54]

Our work brought great joy to George P. Lee. For many years, he saw the great hypocrisy of the LDS/Mormon Church, but he never gave up *wanting* to believe in our *Book of Mormon*. Lee witnessed for so many years how the LDS Church got away with misusing our book and *transfiguring* its message.[55] He suffered greatly at the hands of that "great and abominable church." Lee began to doubt his testimony and faith in the prophecies that we wrote in our new

---

[54] For a brief biography of George P. Lee, *see* "George P. Lee," *Wikipedia*, 24 Sept 2020, en.wikipedia.org/wiki/George_P._Lee.

[55] Lee wrote two letters to Church leaders describing the hypocrisy he saw. Both letters can be found in "The Lee Letters," *Sunstone* vol. 13 no. 4 (August 1989), 50–5; also found online at sunstonemagazine.com/wp-content/uploads/sbi/issues/072.pdf;
see also "Press Coverage of Lee's Excommunication Ambivalent," *Sunstone* vol. 13 no. 4 (August 1989), 47–9; also found online at sunstonemagazine.com/wp-content/uploads/sbi/issues/072.pdf.

A New American Scripture

American scripture, which were meant to bless *his* people and ancestors. But finally, he became the FOURTH WITNESS that we exist and are doing everything in our power to do what we prophesied we would do for his people:

> Great and marvelous works shall be wrought by them, before the great and coming day when all people must surely stand before the judgment-seat of Christ;
>
> Yea, even among the Gentiles shall there be a great and marvelous work wrought by them, before that judgment day.[56]

The LDS Church has greatly transfigured and corrupted our "word of God." We wrote the prophecies in our new American scripture that told them they were going to do this. Regardless of how sincerely and clearly we tried to tell them, they have completely ignored the new and everlasting covenant, even our new American scripture. This church, along with all other religious organizations on Earth, "hath brought forth much fruit, and there is <u>NONE</u> of it which is good."[57]

In one of our most prolific (highly creative and beneficial) prophecies written for our new American scripture (quoted from above), "the master of the vineyard" asks his servant, "Who is it that has corrupted my vineyard?" To which the servant replies, "Is it not the loftiness of thy vineyard?"[58]

PRIDE and VANITY ("loftiness") are responsible for the way that the LDS/Mormon people, and the rest of the world, treat our new American scripture, denying the great blessings of peace and prosperity to those for whom it was written.

We will now further explain this "loftiness" that has corrupted the whole Earth.

---

[56] *BOM*, 3 Nephi 28:31–2.
[57] *BOM*, Jacob 5:32, emphasis added.
[58] *BOM*, Jacob 5:47–8.

Chapter 12
Pride and Vanity—Destroyers of Civilization

No human attributes are more devastating to peace and harmony than *pride* and *vanity*. Throughout our new American scripture we present scenarios (subplots) about the rise and fall of different groups of people. Our stories explain how the people establish a good society—where there is peace, equality, and goodwill towards all—and then show how these societies become corrupt and are destroyed. In each and every case, the culprits (causes) are always *pride* and *vanity* ... ALWAYS.

There are two general definitions for the term "pride" that we need to explain in order for one to fully comprehend *why* we wrote our new American scripture the way that we did. There is a positive connotation and a negative one.

<u>The negative definition and connotation of **pride**</u> *is a feeling of deep pleasure or satisfaction derived from one's own achievements, the achievements of those with whom one is closely associated, or from qualities or possessions that are widely admired by others.* <u>The positive side of pride</u> is *the consciousness of one's own dignity.* The negative undertone greatly affects the positive feeling that a person experiences when one is conscious of one's own dignity.

Our current world *only* promotes the *consciousness of one's own dignity.* Success in our world, and thereby the perception of what brings joy to a person, depends on a person striving for the pleasure and satisfaction that their achievements, qualities, and possessions are greater than those of others. This *standard of joy* is set by the world and is responsible for how a person defines their *own dignity.*

Competition to become *the best* at something is viewed as a positive thing. Being *rich* and able to buy anything you want is viewed as a positive thing. Being a *leader* to whom others look up to for counsel and governance is viewed as a positive thing. Being *popular and known* is viewed as a positive thing.

There are many more ways that the people of the world derive *a feeling of deep pleasure or satisfaction from their own achievements, the achievements of those with whom they are closely associated, or from qualities or possessions that are widely admired by others.*

All the things listed above can also **negatively** affect the way that the majority of Earth's inhabitants view themselves and *their own dignity.* If you are not striving to be the best in what you do, you are not praised, nor do you have anything of which to be proud. If you are not striving to be popular and successful in the world, you do not have anything of which to be proud. If you need and depend on others to lead you, guide you, walk beside you and help you find your way, your need and dependency on these others *reflects your own lack of self-esteem*—another term that means the lack of *consciousness of your own dignity.* If you care about what others think of you, you are *not conscious of your own dignity*, and you are seeking and waiting to be dignified by others.

One of the main goals in writing our new American scripture was to confront the negative connotation of *pride* and promote its *positive* side. Excessive *negative pride* is the definition of "vanity." It is our experience that whenever any group of people, of any number (the masses or the few), shows the negative *pride* in an excessive way (i.e., *vanity*), it always leads to the destruction of that society.

However, just as destructive, the *lack* of positive pride can do the same. When people lack a sense of their own dignity, they cannot become positive members of society; nor can they do anything beneficial for society. People then are susceptible to the control of those whom they believe are more dignified than they are.

In our narrative, whenever the people were prideful (in a negative way) and vain, for whatever reason, society failed and was destroyed. When they humbled themselves and got rid of their pride and vanity, the people succeeded and prospered. Our entire story centers around what makes people stumble in pride and what makes them happy.

In our new American scripture, it was very important to give a lot of examples of how pride can destroy humanity and cause problems that keep people from forming a good society. We made it as clear as possible that the cause of the downfall of human society is how humans react once they feel successful and "blessed" by God.

All of humanity's problems can be traced to economic, religious, or political inequality—all justified by individual pride. When a group of people (nation) prospers, and another nation does not, the group that is prospering wants to ensure that their prosperity increases and continues. The nation that is not prospering is seen as a threat. Instead of thinking that another group of people can become equally successful and prosperous in the same way, by doing the same things that the wealthy nation did, the people of the more successful nation are deceived by their leaders. In their pride, they put themselves above the people of the less successful nations.

To bring value to themselves and their positions of authority, and to make sure they continue to have power and prestige (which usually includes wealth without labor), the government leaders take the credit for a nation's success. They deceive their citizens by convincing them that unless another nation has *them* as its leaders, it cannot become successful.

When people of the less successful nation have a different idea of how to live "according to their own will and pleasure" than that of the people of a successful nation, their ideas of how they live become a threat to the successful nation. In order to confront the perceived "threat" to their "righteous" society, the leaders of the more successful nation will try to convince *their* citizens that the way the less successful people are living is wrong. When a society places expectations on its members to conform to *its* ideas and concepts of happiness, those who do not conform become a threat.

For example, think of a group of people who gain happiness from being in a family unit, and these family units are the result of a man and a woman having children through sexual intercourse. If another person gains happiness from having sex with a person of the same gender, which does not result in having children, the homosexual act seems to threaten the supposed sacredness of the family unit. The conventional family-oriented group of people (husband/wife/children) believe that if they condone the homosexual act, and if a lot of other group members start gaining happiness from homosexuality, then this might lead to the end of their happiness—a happiness that is based on pride and vanity as we have explained above.

In this way, the wants of the group (the majority) outweigh and seem more important than the wants of the minority. In the above example, to fight the threat and protect their way of life, the group teaches their children that homosexuality is wrong and is not the way to happiness. They will use any means possible to protect *their* idea of happiness, according to *their* will and pleasure.

Somehow, having a family unit gives the people of the majority group a feeling of deep pleasure or satisfaction. This is what *pride* is. This is the negative aspect of "pride" that we are focusing on in this chapter and have used throughout our new American scripture. The other definition of pride, which is a positive force, focuses on a person being properly conscious and aware of their own dignity. Dignity is derived from a person acting or being acted upon in a way that makes the person happy. Humans are that they might have joy in doing what makes them happy.

Humans are the only life form found anywhere in the universe that has a consciousness of individual dignity and self-worth. Only humans take pride in their singular, personal, and individual existence. This is the most endearing and dignified part of being human, which separates us from all other life forms.

The questions should be asked: "Why are we like this? What makes us different from all other life forms? What makes us feel pride?"

Again, the negative aspect of pride is in believing that "I'm right and you're wrong." For example, we feel a deep pleasure or satisfaction in doing what makes each of us happy. Thinking that what we each do individually to achieve our own happiness is the *only* way to feel pleasure or satisfaction negates what others feel and experience. With that reasoning, we then *must* believe that if another person is not achieving happiness the same way that we are then the other person is wrong or a threat. This is the negative aspect of pride.

These negative feelings are instilled in us by religion, patriotism, and economic success: "If you would just believe in God the way *I* do, God would bless you with happiness. If you would just obey the laws of the land that *I* do, you would not go to jail. If you would only work as hard as *I* do, you would have money."

How is it that when a person does not believe in the same God as you do, does not obey the same laws you do, and does not want to work as hard as you do, that person does not deserve the same happiness as you do? This attitude is the *negative* aspect of pride. This attitude creates division, and when considered honestly is the overall and overwhelming antithesis (opposite) of peace, equality, and harmony.

Yet pride, when enhanced by its positive aspects, makes us uniquely human. The consciousness of our individual dignity makes us happy. Human nature makes us human. We are that we might have *positive* pride. It is very hard for a mortal to be convinced that each one of us is the most important person (life form) in existence. But this is the Real Truth™ behind *why* we are full of pride.

In considering what we have already explained about *why* we wrote a new American scripture the way that we did, consider the idea and concept of a "Christ." Consider that the word "Christ" signifies one chosen or anointed to be the best of the best—a person who has all of the best qualities of being a human being.

Humans are the only life form that hopes, loves its own kind, and loves other life forms (species) as well. Humans can unite in strength and purpose in times of joy, or in times of conflict. If a group of people is standing near a lake, and a person is drowning, humans have the unique ability to forget their personal prejudices and opinions for as long as it takes to save the one drowning. Even if another species is drowning, humans have a unique and natural propensity to unite to save the other species.

In other words, the *spirit of humanity* is what makes us different and unique from all other life forms. It is a *spirit of hope*. It is a *spirit of kindness* and *of compassion*. And it is the same *spirit* that makes humans hope for a better future when things are not going too well upon Earth. It is this *uniquely human spirit* that embodies the idea of a "Christ." It is this hope that humans have in their own humanity that causes them to look for someone greater than themselves—for someone who embodies all that is good about them—to save them. This is the *spirit of a messiah*—someone who makes us feel human and have hope for a better world. It is this *spirit* that gives Christians the belief that someday all things will be better when their *Messiah* comes to Earth.

This *spirit* manifests and incorporates the particulars as to *why* we wrote our new American scripture the way that we did. To better understand how and *why* we wrote the *Book of Mormon* the way that we did, we need to explain and demonstrate *how* we dealt with the *pride* and *vanity* of the people. In chronological order, according to our storyline as

Chapter 12: Pride and Vanity—Destroyers of Civilization

presented below, consider all the ways that we dealt with pride and vanity. Pay close attention to the efforts we made to confront pride regarding nationality, race, religion, and personal ego. In each of our story's subplots, focus on how inequality, hopelessness, and unhappiness affected the people and *how* pride and vanity were responsible.

In the "lost" 116-page manuscript, the *Book of Lehi* (the *original storyline*), we presented some words from the prophet Zenos about pride and vanity. Zenos' profound words were retold in more detail in our revised story as the *Allegory of the Tame and Wild Olive Trees*, found in Jacob, chapter 5.

In our narrative, we depicted the groups of people (societies) growing throughout the world as *trees of the vineyard*. We presented that ALL of the fruit of ALL the trees was corrupt; that there was no good fruit being produced by any of the trees of the vineyard. The "Lord of the vineyard" asked his servants why there was no good fruit being produced by any group of people on the earth (in the *vineyard*). The servant answered,

> Is it not the loftiness of thy vineyard—have not the branches thereof overcome the roots which are good? And because the branches have overcome the roots thereof, behold they grew faster than the strength of the roots, taking strength unto themselves.[1]

We explained this "loftiness" in our *Pentateuch Illuminated* book. It has to do with the members of a group of people hardening their hearts against their own humanity (the root of the tree) because of the way that they view themselves in comparison to everyone else on Earth.[2]

Little children are FULL of a *consciousness of their own dignity* and have no natural inclination, nor disposition, to experience *a feeling of deep pleasure or satisfaction from their own achievements, the achievements of*

---

[1] *BOM*, Jacob 5:48.
[2] *See Pentateuch Illuminated*, 274–7. Read for free at realilluminati.org/pentateuch-illuminated.

those with whom they are closely associated, or from qualities or possessions that are widely admired by others. Little children do not care, in the least, what other people think of them. Little children do not start caring until they are punished and rewarded, not based on their innate *consciousness of their own dignity*, but on how they act and give pleasure and deep satisfaction to their parents and peers—to the world. Children seek to be rewarded, not punished.

If we think of each person on Earth as a "*tree of the vineyard,*" then the "*roots of their own tree*" can be viewed as their foundational humanity, the innate knowledge and self-esteem that each had as a little child. In this sense, we wrote in response to why no *tree* on Earth is producing any good fruit (it merits repeating again):

> Is it not the loftiness of thy vineyard—have not the branches thereof overcome the roots which are good? And because the branches have overcome the roots thereof, behold they grew faster than the strength of the roots, taking strength unto themselves.

In other words, competition (trying to beat others), attempting to become wealthy, trying to become popular and successful, and the rest of the negative connotations of *pride* are the *branches* that one's personal *tree* has grown to bear fruit. The *fruit* is what people produce throughout their life. As the branches of competition, popularity, and success begin to grow during a person's early life, this constant desire to be recognized and accounted as an important and successful person becomes one's only purpose and desire.

As one proceeds to desire and accumulate these negative parts of pride, the desire gets stronger, and the need to succeed propels a person to work harder and faster; the person begins to lose sight of what was important to them as a child.

Chapter 12: Pride and Vanity—Destroyers of Civilization

The person doubts their own dignity and is constantly striving to obtain *a feeling of deep pleasure or satisfaction from their own achievements, or from qualities or possessions that are widely admired by others*. Thus, "the *branches* grow faster than the strength of the roots, taking strength unto themselves." People lose their innocence and the comfortable way they once experienced life as little children. Instead, they choose to pursue success, popularity, and to be known as someone special and important (*the branches overcome the roots, which are good*).

The more that people become successful, and the faster that they do, the more they forget to be good to each other. People claim success because of their own strengths and accomplishments. They forget to treat each other equally and humanely, like they did as little children. Nevertheless, deep down, all humans recognize the goodness of little children (*the roots which are good*) and long to return to their childhood experiences.

In our original storyline, we expounded more upon what we meant by our *allegory of the olive trees*. The two prophets, Zenos and Zenock, who confronted the Hebrew Church at Jerusalem, condemned the Jews for believing that they were chosen by God and that their church was the only true church of God on Earth.

When people believe that their religion is the correct religion, and that no other is, *pride* is the culprit. Again, the members of a church who believe this have *a feeling of deep pleasure or satisfaction* (*first, from their own achievements, and second, from the achievements of those with whom they are closely associated*). They believe that they and the other faithful members of their church are doing God's will and that no one else is. They feel they are wealthy and successful and *widely admired* for their work ethic, honesty, and morals (*qualities or possessions that are widely admired by others*) because they are righteous and blessed by God.

In the case of early America, Christians had tremendous pride in being *American*. They felt they were a righteous people, blessed with the land of

North America, *because* they were Christian and blessed by God. This *pride* and *vanity* led to the decimation of all of the indigenous native American groups of people. It was the way we confronted this excessive pride in our original storyline that upset many of Joseph Smith's peers. One of our story's prophets confronted this church, saying:

> And it came to pass that Zenos expounded [on] the meaning of the parable [the allegory of the olive trees] unto the High Priests, saying: Behold, in the latter days the church of God shall be like unto this church at Jerusalem. For the Lord will give unto them the pureness of his everlasting gospel and provide for them a way whereby they might be saved in the kingdom of God at the last day.
>
> Nevertheless, because of the branches, or in other words, because of the church of God and its supposed greatness, the roots of the tree, which is the pure gospel of God, shall be overcome. The leaders and members of the church of God shall become lofty and prideful, and their desires shall be towards the church and not set upon the gospel, which is the root of the tree, thus the branches overcoming the roots that are good.
>
> And they shall be like unto you, and also like unto those who will be at Jerusalem when God sendeth His Son among them. For behold, they shall not understand the gospel that the Son of God, shall preach unto them. And because of the examples of the leaders of the church of God the people shall harden their hearts towards the gospel and turn their hearts towards the church for their salvation, thus denying the power of the Holy Spirit and its righteousness.
>
> And their hearts and their minds shall be set upon the things of this world and the honors and glories of men.[3]

---

[3] *See TSP*, Lehi 2:21–4.

Chapter 12: Pride and Vanity—Destroyers of Civilization

In our story, our character Lehi, one of the High Priests of the Hebrew Church, and a very wealthy and popular man among the people, stood up and tried to defend Zenos and Zenock. What we wrote as Lehi's condemnation of the Jewish Church is eerily appropriate to what we would say to the leaders of the LDS Church.

In the last chapter, we introduced George P. Lee, the first native American to be called as an LDS General Authority. When our True Messenger met with Lee in private, Christopher reported that Lee teared up when recounting what we had Lehi say in our "lost" original narrative. Lee was moved by what he read because he had confronted the LDS/Mormon leadership with many of the exact same comments and complaints, which eventually led to his excommunication and expulsion:

And Lehi pleaded with the other High Priests that no harm should come to these two prophets of God. And he pleaded unto them, saying: What cause have we against these two men? Do they not speak the truth concerning us? Do they not speak unto us of our iniquities and corruption? Know we not that they have been sent by God to preach repentance unto us that we might not experience the pain and anguish of the wrath of God because of our sins?

Behold, my soul hath been burdened much because of the ways of this church and those things which we teach unto the people. And have we not set ourselves up above the people, even so much that when we walk by them on the street or in the synagogue that they do worship us and bow down before us? How can we not see that these things are an abomination before God and that we are misleading this people to trust more in the church and its leaders than in the gospel that we are supposed to be teaching unto them?

And have we not taken the money that hath been given to the church, because of the commandment of the Lord regarding the tithing of his people, and have we not used this money to build great synagogues and great temples, yet we suffer that there remain the poor and needy among us? Doth this not bear testimony that we do love our money and our substance, and our fine apparel, and the adorning of our churches, more than we love the poor and the needy, the sick and the afflicted?

And in our solemn assemblies do we not justify our actions and doings because of the praise of the world? Do we not make concessions to the word of God because we believe that we will be mocked and ridiculed by the pride and ignorance of the world? In fine, do we not change the precepts and doctrines of God, and even the pure ordinances that were given unto us by the prophet, Moses; do we not change them to suit our whims and satisfy the desires of the world that we may be accepted by it?

Behold, my soul is racked with anguish because I know that these things are true, and I also know that these two men are prophets of God who have been sent unto this church to bring us unto repentance so that we might not be destroyed.

… And it came to pass that the people of Jerusalem rejected the words of Lehi and cast him out from among them and mocked him. For behold, the people at Jerusalem were hardened by their pride, and also by the pride that they had in the church of God to which they belonged. [In other words, "We know that we belong to the ONLY true and living church of God, so no matter what this guy says about us, it can't be true!"]

And they mocked Lehi, saying: How can thee, being one man alone, claim that the church of God is corrupt? Dost thou not believe that the Lord hath prospered this church and sanctified it because of its righteousness? Do we not attend regularly to the ordinances and traditions that Moses handed down to us? And

Chapter 12: Pride and Vanity—Destroyers of Civilization

we know that Moses was a prophet of God and that he showed us all things that we must do in order to be saved in the kingdom of God at the last day. And do we not do all the things that he hath commanded us?[4]

In our original narrative, we presented what happened to the people once they traveled to the Western Hemisphere to the new "land of promise" and started to establish new communities:

> And it came to pass that the people began to spend their days in pursuit of gold and silver, and other precious ores that gave no sustenance to their lives, except to their pride and to their arrogance.
>
> For behold, the people began to believe that their gold and their silver, and their precious things were gifts from God because of their righteousness. And the church of God was becoming like unto the church that was at Jerusalem when Lehi was commanded to leave.
>
> And it came to pass that the people began to separate themselves into groups according to the amount of gold and silver and precious things that they had accumulated.
>
> Now this would not have been such a gross sin in the eyes of the Lord had it been an accumulation that was made through their own industry and hard work. But their accumulation of wealth was from the sweat and work of others who were the less fortunate and had not the ability to accumulate wealth due to the scarcity of the gold, and the silver, and the precious ores; and also because they were the more ignorant part of the people. Nevertheless, these more ignorant ones were more righteous in

---

[4] See *TSP*, Lehi 2:48–52; 3:13–14.

keeping the commandments of God—their ignorance coming in worldly affairs only.

And it came to pass that a small group of Nephites had accumulated most of the wealth among them, and the other Nephites were forced to labor continuously for this minority who owned the machinery and the tools and the businesses and the crafts on which they were all dependent for their survival.

And thus did the Nephites divide themselves into a rich class and a poor class, thus denying the commandments of God in which they were commanded to be equal in all things.

And the rich class refused to do manual labor, but hired out all manner of work that required sweat to those who were poor and in need of that which the rich provided for them.

And the rich controlled the guards that kept watch at the borders of the city. And the leaders of the people began to become rich, leading the people to believe that because they were leaders, they deserved more sustenance than others.

And it came to pass that the guards began to exercise authority over the Nephites under the direction of the rich. And any Nephite who complained against the rich was arrested by the guards and brought forth to be judged according to the Nephite system of justice, which was set up and controlled by the rich.

Nevertheless, the guards had no authority over the church, nor did they have any authority over the High Priests, who had also set themselves up as leaders of the people and convinced the people that they deserved more sustenance than the average Nephite, like unto the rich class. And in this way did the leaders of the church of God begin to separate themselves from the people.

Chapter 12: Pride and Vanity—Destroyers of Civilization

And in this way did pride and envying enter into the hearts of the Nephites. And this pride began to threaten and destroy the very foundation of truth and righteousness, which foundation was set up in the beginning by Nephi and his brothers Jacob and Joseph, and which was based upon the commandments of God.

For behold, because the church was not accountable to the laws of justice established by the Nephites and enforced by the guards, the leaders of the church began to become the most wicked of all the leaders of the people. Yea, because these leaders were not accountable to the people, they were left to do whatever their hearts desired. And the church became more wicked than the church at Jerusalem at the time of Lehi and his ministry unto the Jews.

… And Mosiah listened to the voice of the prophets and recognized the wickedness of the pride and envying of his people because of their exceeding possessions, and their gold, and their silver and the classes in to which they had divided themselves.[5]

After we revised the beginning of our story, we introduced a vision in which Lehi partakes of the "tree of life" (in contrast to eating other "trees of the vineyard"). We presented a tree that represented a group of people who found the Real Truth™ (the fruit) growing upon a tree, "whose fruit was desirable to make one happy." As people began to eat the fruit of this tree, many fell away because of what was happening in

> a great and spacious building; and it stood as were in the air, high above the earth. And it was filled with people, both old and young, both male and female; and their manner of dress was

---

[5] *TSP*, Lehi 8:7–18, 26.

exceedingly fine; and they were in the attitude of mocking and pointing their fingers towards those who had come at and were partaking of the fruit.[6]

We explained that this building represents "the world and the wisdom thereof; ... the pride of the world ... vain imaginations and the pride of the children of men."[7]

We have explained that "vanity" is the excess of pride. Again, pride does not have to be a bad thing, if one does not have an excess of it. Pride is not bad when ALL people feel a personal dignity of self-worth and value to society. When a people become successful, rich, and "prospered" by what they believe are "blessings from God," their imagination convinces them that those who are not worldly, successful, rich, and do not live prosperously must be doing something wrong or they would be blessed by God too. In this way, they justify the existence of poverty. And because they believe that poverty is a punishment from God, they do nothing to solve it, although they *could*. Before they act to help eliminate what they believe to be a punishment from God, these self-righteous wait upon God to remove his punishment first.

The people who live in poverty do not see themselves as "less than" the rich and prosperous people. And when the poor people are told that they have to do what God tells them to do (or rather, what religious leaders tell them that God wants them to do), the god of the rich then becomes the devil of the poor (see explanation below). This is how divisions and wars start. The poor imagine their own god and believe that it is the devil that is making the rich people prosper; and therefore, they must fight the devil at all costs.

---

[6] *BOM*, 1 Nephi 8:26–7.
[7] *BOM*, 1 Nephi 11: 35–6; 12:18.

Chapter 12: Pride and Vanity—Destroyers of Civilization

Today, the State of Israel, for just one of many examples, prospers exceedingly with the help of the United States of America.[8] Its neighbors residing in the Gaza Strip and the West Bank (as these areas are known and recognized by the rest of the world) live in abject poverty.[9] The god of the poor people in these areas is Allah. Their devil is the god of the house of Israel and Christianity.

As other Muslim countries observe the obvious differences between the economic state of Israel compared to the economic state of the "occupied areas," they see both Israel and the United States as enemies of Allah. Muslim *prideful* chants of "death to Israel" and "death to America" fill the minds and hearts of many other Arab nations.

The Arab nations that do not hate the United States are those nations that are *as prosperous as the United States*. These prosperous Arab nations are considered enemies of the poorer Arab nations, because these prosperous Muslim nations are not following Allah (according to the poor nations' religious convictions [consider *Sunni* and *Shia*]). The poorer Muslim nations believe that the prosperous Muslim nations, aligned with the United States and Israel, are being deceived and led by Islam's devil.

With great faith, believing that they would be rewarded by Allah for destroying Satan, a group of young Muslim men diverted four planes on September 11, 2001. Their intent was to destroy the means of the devil that were creating such economic inequality among "Allah's people," according to their perception and belief—entirely based on *pride*. They believed that the center of the economic world, the World Trade Center,

---

[8] *See* Stephen Zunes, Tom Malthaner, Richard H. Curtiss, "U.S. Financial Aid To Israel: Figures, Facts, and Impact," Washington Report on Middle Eastern Affairs – American Education Trust, wrmea.org/congress-u.s.-aid-to-israel/u.s.-aid-to-israel-1948-present.html.

[9] *See* "Report: Poverty Rate in Gaza Strip Highest Worldwide," 21 Oct. 2019, Asharq Al-Awsat - H H Saudi Research and Marketing LTD, english.aawsat.com/home/article/1954881/report-poverty-rate-gaza-strip-highest-worldwide.

was Satan's base for creating economic inequality. They also attacked the U.S. Military Headquarters—the Pentagon, which was the center that gave power to Satan's followers (Americans and Israelis) to fight Allah.[10]

In their minds and hearts, these *proud* Muslim men were doing God a great service. They were fighting Allah's Satan, and sacrificed their lives in service of their fellow men, which is only in the service of their God. In this way, Muslims took something "good and of God" (service to one's fellow men) and turned it into something "evil and of the devil."

But could God blame them? Would Allah blame them? If most of Allah's children are suffering from the economic policies of non-Muslim nations, or from those of other Muslim nations that are in bed with Allah's enemies, wouldn't Allah want something done about it?

Every argument and contention that exist on Earth today (circa 2020) can be traced to the economic insecurity and deprivations (the lack of basic necessities) of one side that fights the other. In the example we used above, it's not Allah's fault that his people are suffering. It's the devil's fault. On the other hand, the God of the Jews and Christians is not going to allow the devil to destroy "His chosen people" either.

The traditions of the world's major religions, spawned from the Bible, are one of the main underlying causes of human *pride* and *vanity*. The idea that God chose Abraham's younger son (Isaac) over Abraham's eldest son (Ishmael—the son of Sara's dark-skinned handmaiden) is one of the legends that causes the Muslims to hate the Jews. And later, according to Bible stories, when Rebecca deceived her husband (Isaac) and guided his hands to bless Jacob, her younger son, instead of Esau, who rightfully deserved the birthright blessing, how should the descendants of Esau feel about this deception?[11]

---

[10] *See* "September 11 attacks," *Wikipedia*, Wikimedia Foundation, 28 May 2021, en.m.wikipedia.org/wiki/September_11_attacks.

[11] For a visual of the genealogy, *see* "Abraham's family tree," *Wikipedia*, 13 May 2021, en.wikipedia.org/wiki/Abraham%27s_family_tree#Family_tree.

Chapter 12: Pride and Vanity—Destroyers of Civilization

Who are the descendants of Esau? Who are the descendants of Ishmael? Who are the descendants of Cain? According to the Bible's foolish traditions, Ishmael is Cain's descendent, who received his dark skin as a "curse from God." However, as we have explained, Joseph's ("Israel's") two sons Ephraim and Manasseh are also descendants of Cain.[12] It was our desire to show that Cain's descendants were just as important to God as Abel's descendants.

Throughout our new American scripture, we showed how pride in the traditions of the people's fathers can cause hate and war. The Lamanites hated the Nephites in our story for some of the same reasons that the Palestinians hate the Jews—

> Believing that they were driven out of the land of Jerusalem because of the iniquities of their fathers [Lehi and Nephi], and that they were wronged in the wilderness by their brethren, and they were also wronged while crossing the sea. And again, that they were wronged while in the land of their first inheritance [in the promised land of the Western Hemisphere].[13]

A lot of our new American scripture's narrative addressed the great pride of those who would have access to our *Book of Mormon*. We hoped to teach the reader all we could about *pride* and *vanity*. We gave many examples of what pride can do, and would do, to the American people. About ALL the religions on the earth during the latter days, we wrote:

> Yea, they have <u>ALL</u> gone out of the way; they have become corrupted. Because of pride, and because of false teachers, and false doctrine, their churches have become corrupted, and their churches are lifted up; because of pride they are puffed up.

---

[12] *See* Introduction, pages 10–12.
[13] *BOM*, Mosiah 10:12–13.

> They rob the poor because of their fine sanctuaries; they rob the poor because of their fine clothing; and they persecute the meek and the poor in heart, because in their pride they are puffed up.
>
> They wear stiff necks and high heads; yea, and because of pride, and wickedness, and abominations, and whoredoms, they have all gone astray save it be a few, who are the humble followers of Christ; nevertheless, they [the humble followers of Christ who have not strayed from his teachings] are led, that in many instances they do err because they are taught by the precepts of men.
>
> O the wise, and the learned, and the rich, that are puffed up in the pride of their hearts, and all those who preach false doctrines, and all those who commit whoredoms, and pervert the right way of the Lord, wo, wo, wo be unto them, saith the Lord God Almighty, for they shall be thrust down to hell!
>
> Wo unto them that turn aside the just for a thing of naught and revile against that which is good, and say that it is of no worth![14]

Incredulously (unbelievably), no matter what we wrote about the religions of a future time period within the United States of America (about the "Gentiles" of the latter days), no religion sees itself as what we have described above. The "wise and the learned" (college educated) and the well-off people certainly do not think they have done anything wrong. Their pride will not let them. They get a feeling of deep satisfaction from their own (and their particular church's) achievements—also, from the achievements of their peers and other members, along with their qualities of being spiritual. Their possessions also provide them with a feeling of satisfaction. (The reader can refer back to the definition of *pride* at the beginning of this chapter).

---

[14] *BOM*, 2 Nephi 28:11–16, emphasis added.

If logically considered, the *only* people to whom we were referring and addressing were those who were *supposed* to be reading our *Book of Mormon*. The LDS/Mormon people's actions, because of their *pride* and *vanity*, fit the description we gave and quoted above … perfectly.

Truly, there is no religion on Earth as hypocritical as the Church of Jesus Christ of Latter-day Saints. This church has taken something "good and of God" (our book) and made it "evil and of the devil" in the eyes of the rest of the Christian world. Apart from a few small off-shoots, no other religion has access to our words and to the things that we tried to teach the world through our True Messengers. And because of how the LDS/Mormons treat our new American scripture, the rest of the world has little to no interest in it.

We have explained that the core of our new American scripture was to inspire the Americans to make the world a better place, starting with helping the marginalized indigenous native American people (of both North and South America). The LDS/Mormon people should be doing everything and anything in their power to help the native American peoples of the Western Hemisphere establish a "New Jerusalem," a city of "Zion," in the promised land. Instead, that prideful Church secretly combines its spiritual power over its members with the power of its riches and with the power of its political connections. The direct result of this church's actions

> cause that widows should mourn before the Lord, and also orphans to mourn before the Lord, and also the blood of their fathers and their husbands to cry unto the Lord from the ground, for vengeance upon [their] heads.[15]

---

[15] *BOM*, Mormon 8:40.

At the present time (circa 2020), thousands of Latino-American people struggle to enter the United States of America.[16] Children are separated from their mothers and fathers and have become orphans. Many of their fathers have been killed because the only jobs available to them are in the business of illegal drugs, which jobs their fathers have no choice but to accept or their children will starve. Their mothers' cries are being heard by the true god of humanity whose wrath is soon to be felt in its fullness. But this prideful, wealthy church does nothing to succor (help) the children of our story's "remnant of the house of Israel."

The vanity of the LDS/Mormon people convinces them that they are fulfilling the prophecies concerning their involvement in possessing our *Book of Mormon*. LDS/Mormons believe that their "feet are beautiful upon the mountains," not because of what they do for the poor, needy, and afflicted of this world, but because of the shoes that they purchase from their City Creek Mall. Many members believe they are doing good for those who are suffering. In this they greatly err.[17]

Here is what we wrote in our new American scripture about how "blessed are they who shall seek to bring forth my Zion at that day"—that which the LDS/Mormon people believe of themselves:

> And it came to pass that the angel of the Lord spake unto me, saying: Behold, saith the Lamb of God, after I have visited the remnant of the house of Israel [the native American people]—and this remnant of whom I speak is the seed of thy father—wherefore, after I have visited them in judgment, and smitten them by the hand of the Gentiles, and after the Gentiles do

---

[16] *See* Marta Tienda and Susana M. Sanchez, "Latin American Immigration to the United States," *Daedalus: Journal of the American Academy of Arts & Sciences*, vol. 142 no. 3 (Summer 2013), 48–64, found online at amacad.org/sites/default/files/daedalus/downloads/Su2013_Immigration-and-the-Future-of-America.pdf.

[17] *See JS bio*, 694 n.13–696. Read for free at realilluminati.org/without-disclosing-my-true-identity.

stumble exceedingly, because of the most plain and precious parts of the gospel of the Lamb which have been kept back by that abominable church, which is the mother of harlots, saith the Lamb—I will be merciful unto the Gentiles in that day, insomuch that I will bring forth unto them, in mine own power, much of my gospel, which shall be plain and precious, saith the Lamb.

For, behold, saith the Lamb: I will manifest myself unto thy seed, that they shall write many things which I shall minister unto them [in the *Book of Mormon*], which shall be plain and precious; and after thy seed shall be destroyed, and dwindle in unbelief, and also the seed of thy brethren, behold, these things shall be hid up, to come forth unto the Gentiles, by the gift and power of the Lamb.

And in them shall be written my gospel, saith the Lamb, and my rock and my salvation. [The *Book of Mormon* explains this "rock" and "salvation," but the LDS/Mormon Church does nothing that is taught in the *Book of Mormon*.]

And blessed are they who shall seek to bring forth my Zion at that day, for they shall have the gift and the power of the Holy Ghost; and if they endure unto the end they shall be lifted up at the last day, and shall be saved in the everlasting kingdom of the Lamb; and whoso shall publish peace, yea, tidings of great joy, how beautiful upon the mountains shall they be.[18]

It is the LDS/Mormon "loftiness" that has corrupted them. The same thing that happened to the characters in our story's narrative, happened to the LDS/Mormons. After they had developed righteous, very prosperous societies, these societies fell into great wickedness because of their own

---

[18] *BOM*, 1 Nephi 13:34–7.

success. Now consider what caused the downfall of our new American scripture's peoples:

> And when [the people stop doing the things that Jesus told them to do] a speedy destruction cometh unto my people; for, notwithstanding the pains of my soul, I have seen it; wherefore, I know that it shall come to pass; and they sell themselves for naught; for, for the reward of their pride and their foolishness they shall reap destruction; for ... they yield unto the devil and choose works of darkness rather than light.
>
> ... And the Gentiles are lifted up in the pride of their eyes, and have stumbled, because of the greatness of their stumbling block, that they have built up many churches; nevertheless, they put down the power and miracles of God, and preach up unto themselves their own wisdom and their own learning, that they may get gain and grind upon the face of the poor.[19]

The modern LDS/Mormon Church became one of the wealthiest institutions on Earth[20] because of their financial investments.[21] We have explained clearly that investing in financial markets and securities to get gain without working "grind[s] upon the face of the poor." LDS/Mormon leaders "preach up unto themselves their own wisdom and their own learning" in how to make money and have their money make more money. This economic strategy is taught in their universities. It is their proud, vain, and foolish imagination to think that God would have one part of His people

---

[19] *See BOM*, 2 Nephi 26:10, 20.
[20] *See* "Religious Organizations," in "List of wealthiest organizations." *Wikipedia*, 24 May 2021, en.wikipedia.org/wiki/List_of_wealthiest_organizations.
[21] *See* Jon Swaine, Douglas MacMillan and Michelle Boorstein, "Investigations: Mormon Church has misled members on $100 billion tax-exempt investment fund, whistleblower alleges," 17 Dec. 2019, *The Washington Post*, washingtonpost.com/investigations/mormon-church-has-misled-members-on-100-billion-tax-exempt-investment-fund-whistleblower-alleges/2019/12/16/e3619bd2-2004-11ea-86f3-3b5019d451db_story.html.

suffer while the other part prospers. But the LDS/Mormon God will only choose General Authorities who are financially and worldly successful men.[22] It is worth repeating:

> Because of pride, and because of false teachers, and false doctrine, their churches have become corrupted, and their churches are lifted up; because of pride they are puffed up.
>
> They rob the poor because of their fine sanctuaries; they rob the poor because of their fine clothing; and they persecute the meek and the poor in heart, because in their pride they are puffed up.
>
> ... O the wise, and the learned, and the rich, that are puffed up in the pride of their hearts, and all those who preach false doctrines, and all those who commit whoredoms, and pervert the right way of the Lord, wo, wo, wo, be unto them, saith the Lord God Almighty, for they shall be thrust down to hell!
>
> Wo unto them that turn aside the just for a thing of naught and revile against that which is good, and say that it is of no worth![23]

In 2016 we had our contemporary True Messenger present a plan to eliminate poverty throughout the world (The Humanity Party®).[24] We had him introduce a plan that would end forced prostitution, where a young person is forced into prostitution because of poverty.[25] We had our True

---

[22] *See* "Current Apostles Previous Profession," LDSminds, ldsminds.com/current-apostles-previous-profession/.
[23] *BOM*, 2 Nephi 28:12–16.
[24] *See* The Humanity Party®, (THumP®), 2020, humanityparty.com; *and* "The Humanity Party® introduces their Economic Plan To End Worldwide Poverty – Official Release," YouTube, 14 Dec. 2020, youtu.be/xruLy1LG-f0.
[25] *See* "The Humanity Party® Challenges the United States to End Worldwide Underage Prostitution in One Week!" 8 Oct. 2020, YouTube, youtu.be/vg6-AX8hhJ0.

Messenger introduce a plan that would help create peace and prosperity in the Middle East among the Israelis and the Muslims.[26]

These plans are unchallengeable. There is no "learned" person in the world who can logically explain why these plans would not work. The wisdom of the world did not come up with these plans. We did. The world responded to these plans and called them "a thing of naught." They "revile against [these plans] which are good," and say that these plans are "of no worth!" It is the pride and vain imaginations of the children of men that fight against that which is good.

Religious people reject these plans, just as they do the rest of our "marvelous work and a wonder," because these plans and our work were not given to them from *their god*—the god that answers their prayers and leads them through their god's chosen leaders.

As we have explained, in the play that we helped Joseph Smith write in 1842, it is clearly presented *whom* the "god" is that the people *actually* follow: "*Lucifer, the god of this world.*" This is the character we used in the play to symbolically represent the *pride* and *vanity* of the world.

It is with considerable irony that we can now reveal that on September 11, 2001, the day that the Muslims fought for Allah, our chosen modern-day True Messenger was in jail. He had been put there by an LDS/Mormon U.S. District Court Judge. That fateful day never would have happened had economic equality existed throughout the Muslim world. And our True Messenger would not have been incarcerated if the judge were not LDS/Mormon.

That judge, Denise P. Lindberg, found out about our True Messenger's claim that he had been chosen to publish *The Sealed Portion* of our new American scripture. This claim incensed Judge Lindberg (made her very angry). She ordered him to be incarcerated because of her prejudice and

---

[26] *See* "The Humanity Party® Solves the Israeli - Palestinian Conflict - www.HUMANITYPARTY.com," YouTube, 25 Sept. 2017, youtu.be/502SfQ6Mues.

Chapter 12: Pride and Vanity—Destroyers of Civilization

hate for him. She even said in open court, as our True Messenger stood before her: "It is no secret that I do not like you."

The very man who would introduce a plan that could help mitigate future attacks by poor nations on wealthy nations, was held bound by a deceived judge who believed that she was righteous. This same situation occurred to all True Messengers as we presented it in the narrative of our new American scripture.

In a previous chapter, we explained that the only reason why anyone, who is a professor of Christ,[27] and who has a "hope in Christ," should have pride and seek for riches, is for the

> intent to do good—to clothe the naked, and to feed the hungry, and to liberate the captive, and administer relief to the sick and the afflicted.
>
> And now, my brethren, I have spoken unto you concerning pride; and those of you which have afflicted your neighbor, and persecuted him because ye were proud in your hearts, of the things which God hath given you, what say ye of it?
>
> Do ye not suppose that such things are abominable unto him who created all flesh? And the one being is as precious in his sight as the other.[28]

No matter how we wrote it, we failed to get the reader of our new American scripture to see the excess of pride (i.e., vanity) as an "abomination of God." Our greatest effort was when we presented the resurrected Christ and the effect his presence and teachings had on the people.

---

[27] A person who believes in Jesus and professes that Jesus Christ is their Lord and Savior.
[28] *BOM*, Jacob 2:19–21.

A New American Scripture

In our new American scripture, we presented the resurrected Christ teaching the ancient inhabitants of the Western Hemisphere the same doctrine that he taught the Jews in Jerusalem before he ascended to his father. After he had taught them these things, Jesus told the people to remember "these sayings of mine, and doeth them,"[29] so that the people would be "raise[d] up at the last day"[30] (i.e., be saved).

It was the tradition of their fathers (those things "concerning the law of Moses") that made Jesus "groan within himself" and say, "Father, I am troubled because of the wickedness of the people of the house of Israel."[31] Jesus had just taught them everything that they needed to do so that "the hearts of thousands and tens of thousands shall greatly rejoice," and his "fame [would] spread to foreign lands."[32] But the "wicked one came and took away light and truth from the children of men because of the tradition of their fathers."[33]

In the next chapter, we will give more details about how Jesus dealt with the pride and vanity of the people, according to the stories written about him. Before we do, we think it is important to point out how we presented Christ dealing with the world's pride and vanity in our book of Revelation.

When we unfolded the true meaning of the book of Revelation, along with the *sealed portion* of our new American scripture, we explained what we meant by repeating the words of Jesus, when he said, "Behold, I come as a thief."

We wrote (in our book unfolding Revelation):

> **16:15** *If any man have an ear, let him hear what the spirit sayeth:* Behold, I come as a thief. Blessed is he that watcheth, and keepeth his garments **upon him**, lest he walk naked and see his **own** shame.

---

[29] NT, Matthew 7:24.
[30] NT, John 6:54.
[31] *BOM*, 3 Nephi 17:14.
[32] *D&C*, 110:9–10.
[33] *Compare D&C*, 93:39.

Though John mentions Christ as a *"thief"* in Revelation 3:3, he has led us into a proper understanding of what Christ meant when he said:

"But know this, that if the goodman of the house had known in what watch **the thief would come**, *he would have watched, and would not have suffered his house to be broken up. Therefore be ye also ready: for in such an hour as ye think not* **the Son of man cometh**.*" (Matthew 24:43–44)*

Christ's gospel robs us of our pride, our materialism, and our disrespect for others and their beliefs. He robs us of our family units, communities, nations and borders, and makes us equal to others in all things. He robs us of our heroes, our leaders, even all those to whom we look as the quintessential example of a successful human being. He robs us of our ignorance, our degrees, our doctorates, and our worldly intelligence that creates our classes, our castes, and our divisions. He robs us of our businesses, corporations, and all other means by which the "*miracles*" of this life have divided us and caused us misery.

He is truly a ***thief***.[34]

Our new American scripture teaches that <u>any type of society humans create on Earth—that promotes pride and vanity in its members—will always fail</u>. The greatest mistake made by all great societies of the past, which have fallen, is that they have allowed *pride* and *vanity* to create and place a value on one person that is not the same value placed on all others equally.

All great nations (groups of humans) have failed for this reason and will fail for the same reason in the future.

---

[34] *See 666 America*, 367. Read for free at realilluminati.org/666-mark-of-america.

Before we move on with other subjects revealing *how* and *why* we created the *Book of Mormon*, and because of how important it is to understand how *pride* and *vanity* can destroy humanity, we need to consider even more details and explanations about this devastating human trait.

Chapter 13
The Family of Pride

At the time we are writing this book (*A New American Scripture*)—which we are doing in order to reveal the true meaning and purpose of our new American scripture (the *Book of Mormon* and *The Sealed Portion*)—the United States of America is on the verge of collapse. We do not speak of a physical collapse, but of a mental collapse[1] that will create a literal hell for the American people—a hell that will affect all of humanity on Earth unlike anything the world has ever seen in recorded history.

We wrote of this "hell which hath no end" in one of the prophecies we included about the people of the United States of America (the "Gentiles"). We described what would happen to them if they rejected the counsel and lessons of our new American scripture:

> Therefore, wo be unto the Gentiles if it so be that [the Americans for whom our new American scripture was written] harden their hearts against the Lamb of God [i.e., against the words spoken by Jesus Christ as we presented them in our scripture].[2]

We warned them of a "great pit" that was dug by Capitalism and the secret combinations of political, religious, and economic power. We warned them that the

> great pit, which hath been digged for [the Americans] by that *great and abominable church* [which we meant to represent *Capitalism* that began in Europe before the United States was

---

[1] *See* William Wan, "The coronavirus pandemic is pushing America into a mental health crisis," 4 May 2020, *The Washington Post*, washingtonpost.com/health/2020/05/04/mental-health-coronavirus/.

[2] *Compare BOM*, 1 Nephi 14:6.

established], which was founded by the devil and his children, that he might lead away the souls of men down to hell—yea, that great pit which hath been digged for the destruction of men shall be filled by those who digged it, unto their utter destruction, saith the Lamb of God; not the destruction of the soul, save it be the casting of it into that hell which hath no end.[3]

This hell of which we wrote is not a physical death. Nevertheless, this mental state will result in a tremendous rise of suicides throughout the world.[4] It is a mental and emotional state out of which a person finds it hard to climb ... thus, a "great pit." About this, we prophesied (wrote what we knew we could one day in the future make come to pass) that we would perform

> a great and a marvelous work among the children of men; a work which shall be everlasting, either on the one hand or on the other.[5]

Our work, a Marvelous Work and a Wonder®, was meant to convince humanity

> unto peace and life eternal, or [deliver the people of Earth] to the hardness of their hearts and the blindness of their minds unto their being brought down unto captivity, and also into destruction, both temporally and spiritually, according to the captivity of the devil, of which [we wrote].

Describing this "captivity of the devil" created by European Capitalism, we wrote:

> And it came to pass that the angel spake unto me, saying: Look! And I looked and beheld many nations and kingdoms. And the

---

[3] *BOM*, 1 Nephi 14:3.
[4] *See* "Suicide Rate by Country 2021," World Population Review, worldpopulationreview.com/country-rankings/suicide-rate-by-country.
[5] *BOM*, 1 Nephi 14:7.

angel said unto me: What beholdest thou? And I said: I behold many nations and kingdoms. And he said unto me: These are the [European] nations and kingdoms of the Gentiles.

And it came to pass that I saw among the nations of the Gentiles the formation of a great church. And the angel said unto me: Behold the formation of a church which is most abominable above all other churches, which slayeth the saints of God, yea, and tortureth them and bindeth them down, and yoketh them with a yoke of iron, and bringeth them down into captivity.

And it came to pass that I beheld this great and abominable church; and I saw the devil that he was the founder of it. And I also saw gold, and silver, and silks, and scarlets, and fine-twined linen, and all manner of precious clothing; and I saw many harlots.

And the angel spake unto me, saying: Behold the gold, and the silver, and the silks, and the scarlets, and the fine-twined linen, and the precious clothing, and the harlots, are the desires of this great and abominable church. And also for the praise of the world do they destroy the saints of God, and bring them down into captivity.[6]

We explained in our *Pentateuch Illuminated* book[7] that we called this "great and abominable church" a great "beast" in our book of Revelation.[8] Both terms refer to an economic and political system in which property, businesses, and industry are owned and controlled by private owners for profit, rather than by a central government.[9] Private owners do what they

---

[6] *BOM*, 1 Nephi 13:1–9.
[7] *See Pentateuch Illuminated*, 123–6.
[8] *See 666 America*, 9–16, 51, 295–6, and 303–6. Read for free at realilluminati.org/666-mark-of-america.
[9] *See* "capitalism," Macmillan dictionary, Macmillan Education Limited, macmillandictionary.com/dictionary/american/capitalism#capitalism_3; *and* "Capitalism – definition and meaning," Market Business News, marketbusinessnews.com/financial-glossary/capitalism-definition.

do for the benefit of themselves and their families, regardless of the consequences to others.

In the same religious, allegorical prose in which we wrote all of our new American scripture, we presented that there are basically only two types of people in the world: 1) those who seek the welfare and benefit of all of humanity equally and equitably; and 2) those whose actions and dedication are specifically for their own benefit and that of their own loved ones. We wrote that

> there are save two churches only; the one is the church of the Lamb of God, and the other is the church of the devil; wherefore, whoso belongeth not to the church of the Lamb of God belongeth to that great church, which is the mother of abominations; and she is the whore of all the earth.[10]

We explained that there are very few people living on the earth who dedicate their lives to the whole of humanity, outside of their own family unit. We wrote the reason why there are so few people who are not completely centered on their own family units. It is because of the wickedness of the "great whore." We then pointed the reader to the importance of reading our book of Revelation for a continuation of our prophecy about Capitalism. If Revelation is read honestly, and with direction from what we unfolded in our book, *666, The Mark of America—Seat of the Beast: The Apostle John's New Testament Revelation Unfolded*, one will find that Revelation is *not* about the end of the world, but the end of Capitalism.

It's not that the good parts of Capitalism are no longer used, but that this "great beast" upon whose back humanity is riding, is finally *bridled* and ridden properly. Revelation portends (foretells) of the end of the power of "kings and merchants" (religious, political, and business leaders) and of their secret combinations of power that are set up for the

---

[10] *BOM*, 1 Nephi 14:10.

benefit of one's self and one's family. Revelation speaks of a righteous government that is set up that "renews" humanity and ushers in a time of "peace and eternal life" upon Earth.

We have done a lot to convince the world to change its ways before it is too late. We have explained that what we have done and are doing is a "great and marvelous work." This work will either convince people of what needs to be done to bring "peace and life eternal" to Earth, or we will deliver them to the hardness of their hearts and blindness of their minds, to their emotional destruction. We have explained how our *Book of Mormon* has been greatly misused by the LDS/Mormon people. It is no surprise that, per capita, this group of people consumes more antidepressant drugs than any other single group of people on Earth.[11] The LDS/Mormon people have been "delivered to the hardness of their hearts and blindness of their minds."

It is our duty to explain in full detail and transparency what has caused, is causing, and will continue to cause the downfall of humanity. If not addressed, this world will be destroyed. We can no longer depend on the clues we have written through our new American scripture. We will no longer expect that we can convince the people of Earth of what needs to be done through subtle religious persuasion. (We tried to use religious persuasion so as not to impede the free will of a person that allows one to believe according to the dictates of one's own mind.) In the last chapter, we explained that *excessive pride* is the cause of all of humanity's problems. We wrote that humanity (i.e., "the saints of God") is under bondage and captivity to Capitalism "for the praise of the world." Except for the very few, most people do what they do *to be praised* by others.

---

[11] *See* Julie Cart, "Study Finds Utah Leads Nation in Antidepressant Use," 20 Feb. 2002, *Los Angeles Times*, latimes.com/archives/la-xpm-2002-feb-20-mn-28924-story.html.

See Insider's chart of global antidepressant users per 1,000 people *found at* Gould Skye and Lauran F. Friedman, "Something startling is going on with antidepressant use around the world, 4 Feb. 2016, Business Insider, Insider Inc., businessinsider.com/countries-largest-antidepressant-drug-users-2016-2?r=US&IR=T.

A New American Scripture

In the last chapter, we gave a lot of information about pride and vanity. In this chapter, we are going to make sure that we very clearly explain the negative causes and effects of *pride* to the reader. We will be very plain and obvious about what is actually causing humanity to fail. Unfortunately, what we are going to explain will challenge all of humanity, especially all the things about which the people of Earth are proud, and which most people believe are "good and of God," when these things are actually "evil and of the devil" (*their pride and ego*).

Before we give a clear, simple, and detailed explanation of the "evil fruit" that ALL of the "trees of the vineyard" are producing, we desire to briefly point out the important clues about this evil fruit that we added to our new American scripture's narrative. Keep in mind that our new American scripture also includes what we wrote as the *sealed portion* (the "greater part") of our book.

As we have explained, we wrote a subplot about an all-white nation of people called the Jaredites. According to our story, these people were the most ancient inhabitants of North America—the exact location of the United States of America. This subplot explains how this people became a very populous and great nation of people *without* organized religion of *any* kind. The only thing the people of this nation were taught was that God did exist and spoke to their first leader, *the brother of Jared*.

While speaking to the brother of Jared around the time of the Tower of Babel (according to the Bible's narrative), God told the brother of Jared that He would lead him, his brother Jared, and a few of their friends to the Western Hemisphere. There, God would bless them and make them a great people, regardless of what was going to happen in the Eastern Hemisphere as a result of the people rebelling against God (during the Tower of Babel time period of the Bible's narrative). After God was done speaking with the brother of Jared, He commanded the brother of Jared to go down out of the mount from the presence of the Lord, and write the things which he had seen. [We wrote] upon these plates the very things which the brother of Jared saw; and there never were greater things made manifest than those which were made manifest unto the brother of Jared.[12]

... [God] showed unto the brother of Jared all the inhabitants of the earth which had been, and also all that would be; and he withheld them not from his sight, even unto the ends of the earth.[13]

This means that the brother of Jared saw Adam and Eve, and all of their posterity. The brother of Jared wrote everything down, making his own record. God commanded him to write what he saw "in a language that ... cannot be read."[14] To comply with this commandment, the brother of Jared wrote the record in a language that only could be interpreted through the means by which God had prepared—two stones called *Interpreters*.

The Jaredites prospered in the land and became a great people. Our narrative does not say *how* or *why* they became such a righteous and prosperous people. It's implied however, that the brother of Jared taught his followers what God told him on the mount, which he wrote down in the record that he "brought across the great deep."[15] The record that the brother of Jared made was the ONLY set of scriptures that the people had to guide them in what they were supposed to be doing, a record that was *not* the Bible. And nothing that the Jaredites did had anything to do with the law of Moses, priesthood, churches, ordinances, rituals ... ABSOLUTELY NOTHING.

Jared and his special, God-chosen brother, got old and were about to die. Before they died, they had to give the record and the means to translate

---

[12] *BOM*, Ether 4:1–4.
[13] *BOM*, Ether 3:25.
[14] *BOM*, Ether 3:22.
[15] *BOM*, Ether 8:9.

the record to someone else. Jared and his brother asked the people what they could do for them before they died. The people wanted Jared and his brother to anoint one of their sons to be their king.

The request of the Jaredite people "was grievous unto them. And the brother of Jared said unto them: Surely this thing [appointing a king] leadeth into captivity."[16] A king would mean that a person was placed in a position of authority over all the other people. This was unacceptable. But unacceptable according to what? It was unacceptable according to the information written upon the record that contained the will of God pertaining to all of Earth's inhabitants, since the beginning of time "even unto the ends of the earth."[17]

We made it obvious that the brother of Jared taught the people according to the "record which [they] brought across the great deep." The details written on the record taught them what happened to the descendants of Adam and Eve and how the children of Adam and Eve ended up the way that they were at the time of the Tower of Babel. It was all written in the record. Jared and his brother gave the people the king that they wanted … exactly *why* and *how* Joseph Smith gave his followers what they wanted … so that they would stumble.

The brother of Jared's record contained a history of humanity from its beginning "even unto the ends of the earth." This record also included a history of what went wrong. The record gave an accounting of the terrible ways that humans behaved, causing their own demise. Jared and his brother warned their descendants of these evils, as was written in the record. After Jared and his brother died, the people still had access to everything written on the record through the person who kept it—usually the Jaredite king. The king was meant to use it to teach the people how they were supposed to live and deal with each other.

---

[16] *BOM*, Ether 6:23.
[17] *BOM*, Ether 3:25.

Chapter 13: The Family of Pride

The Jaredite story goes on. With a king appointed, the people set up a government made up of those who were not their *servants*, but their *leaders*. These leaders did not serve the people, but instead forced the people to do what *these leaders* wanted. Because of this, many wars and contentions began that brought the people into captivity, as the brother of Jared had warned them. It came to a point when the king (who also happened to be named Jared), who had possession of the record and the means to read it, was captured. This king Jared

> became exceedingly sorrowful because of the loss of the kingdom, for he had set his heart upon the kingdom and upon the glory of the world. ... Now the daughter of Jared was exceedingly fair. And it came to pass that she did talk with her father, and said unto him: Whereby hath my father so much sorrow? Hath he not read the record which our fathers brought across the great deep? Behold, is there not an account concerning them of old, that they by their secret plans did obtain kingdoms and great glory? [18]

And it came to pass ... that eventually the Great Jaredite Nation, of millions and millions of exceedingly beautiful people, was completely destroyed because of the "secret plans" that were explained in the brother of Jared's record.

As the author of the *unsealed* part of our new American scripture (*Mormon*) wrote his abridged history of the native American people, he would not discuss or reveal what he knew of these "secret plans" that led to the demise of an entire, once-populous, and prosperous nation. *The Sealed Portion* of our new American scripture was abridged by Mormon's son, Moroni, from the *twenty-four plates of gold* that contained the Jaredite history. This included the record that the brother of Jared "brought across the great deep."

---

[18] *BOM*, Ether 8:7–9.

Ether was a Jaredite prophet who was eventually given the Jaredite record many, many years after the Jaredites first arrived in North America (shortly before they were destroyed). Ether added to the record written on plates of gold, being commanded to write the end of the Jaredite history.

According to the record of the brother of Jared, something happened after Adam and Eve were cast out of the Garden of Eden. Some believe that if Cain and Abel were Adam and Eve's first children, they would've had to have had sex with their sisters, and maybe Adam with his daughters, in order to perpetuate the human race. This is the only thing that makes sense; but in making sense, it gives license to incest. Because of this narrative, many Bible-believing men foolishly (yet reasonably) justified lusting after their own daughters. To counter this (along with other things that the Bible's narrative had caused), Joseph Smith, under our direction, rewrote the Adam and Eve story. He produced the *Book of Moses*.[19]

In Joseph's new narrative, Adam and Eve had many sons and daughters *before* Cain and Abel were born. This revised story explained that their sons and daughters

> loved Satan more than God. And men began from that time forth to be carnal, sensual, and devilish. ... And Adam and Eve, his wife, ceased not to call upon God. And Adam knew his wife, and she conceived and bare Cain, and [Eve] said: I have gotten a man from the Lord; wherefore he may not reject his words [like all of the rest of our sons and daughters had].[20]

(For reference to the excerpts that we mention above, see Joseph Smith's rewrite of the Adam and Eve story in Moses, chapter 5.)

In *The Sealed Portion*, we presented the story of Adam and Eve as it was shown to the brother of Jared. We are not going to include it here. If our

---

[19] See *PGP*, Moses.
[20] See *PGP*, Moses 5:12–18 for the full details.

words and explanations mean anything to the reader of this book (*A New American Scripture*), this person will read the complete story. But because of the great importance of this part of *The Sealed Portion*, in understanding how pride first caused the downfall of humanity, we have included it in the back as Appendix 1 of this book.

The Sealed Portion of our new American scripture explains what the brother of Jared saw, including what caused the start of humanity's failure, which always leads to its complete annihilation (destruction). What we present in Appendix 1 are the very things that we intended to show the world that cause all of humanity's problems. The causes that we are going to describe below can be verified in *The Sealed Portion*'s narrative in Appendix 1.

The family unit is the single greatest cause of humanity's failure. Possessions, money, people being placed in positions of power and control *above* other people (i.e., leadership), patriotism, race, gender, sexuality, and anything else that causes anger, contention, and division, are also part of humanity's failure.

And the primary cause of everything we listed above can honestly be traced to one's excessive *pride*. This includes *pride* in one's family, *pride* in one's possessions and success, *pride* in one's position of power, *pride* in one's nation, *pride* in one's race, *pride* in one's gender, and *pride* in one's sexuality. We mentioned above that

> we will be very plain and obvious about what is actually causing humanity to fail. Unfortunately, what we are going to explain will challenge all of humanity, especially all the things about which the people of Earth *are proud*.

The reader's initial reaction may be: "There's *no way* these things lead to the demise of the human race." However, if one genuinely reads the *sealed portion* of our book[21] with a sincere heart and real intent, that one will be convinced that the things we listed above, in very deed, are what has, is, and will continue to corrupt human life upon Earth.

In *The Sealed Portion*, Moroni explains these ideas perfectly. He outlines three main problems. First, he explains how Adam and Eve's children began to separate themselves into these family units. He then describes how they started using money. Finally, he addresses how they began to see their individual family unit as something better and more important than ALL of Adam and Eve's family as a whole. The way these concepts are presented is very logical, reasonable, and convincing. If people believe that Adam and Eve were all of humanity's first parents, how can anyone place their individual family above any other family unit on Earth? A sincere person would consider reading our explanations in *The Sealed Portion*.

We asked the Americans, regarding the things that we had written in our new American scripture (both the *unsealed* and *sealed* portions), to "exercise faith" in the words that we ascribed to Jesus Christ,

> that they may become sanctified in me, then I will manifest unto them the things which the brother of Jared saw, even to the unfolding unto them all my revelations, saith Jesus Christ, the Son of God, the Father of the heavens and of the earth, and all things that in them are. [We warned them that] he that will contend against the word of the Lord, let him be accursed; and he that shall deny these things, let him be accursed; for unto them will I show no greater things, saith Jesus Christ; for I am he who speaketh.[22]

Everything that we listed above, and which the current world sees as something "good and of God," is actually "evil and of the devil." We call these things "evil" because they have caused, are causing, and will continue to

---

[21] Read *TSP* for free at realilluminati.org/the-sealed-portion.
[22] *BOM*, Ether 4:7–8.

Chapter 13: The Family of Pride

cause the demise of the human race. We challenge the world to study our words because they are good, because they

> persuadeth men to do good. And whatsoever thing persuadeth men to do good is of me; for good cometh of none save it be of me. I am the same that leadeth men to all good; he that will not believe my words will not believe me—that I am; and he that will not believe me will not believe the Father who sent me. For behold, I am the Father, I am the light, and the life, and the truth of the world.[23]

In our new American scripture, we call this the "Spirit of Christ ... given to every man, that he may know good from evil."[24] We counsel people to be careful that they do not judge that which is good to be evil, and that which is evil to be good. A belief in Jesus Christ is a very powerful motivator. The mere belief can change a person's mind and cause that one to become a better person. Many people find Jesus while incarcerated. Many find him when they are at their lowest point emotionally. Many find Jesus by thinking about everything that causes one to

> becometh as a child, submissive, meek, humble, patient, full of love, willing to submit to all things which the Lord seeth fit to inflict upon [the person].[25]

People don't actually *find Jesus*. He was never lost—he never existed. But the feelings and *spirit* surrounding the idea of Christ have given hope to billions of mortals living in a world where they feel lost and lonely. They long for their younger experiences when they did not feel this way. In finding Jesus, they find their childlike innocence again. As explained, the "Spirit of Christ" is the *spirit of love*, *compassion*, *forgiveness*, *kindness*, and *humility*—all of the

---

[23] *BOM*, Ether 4:11–12.
[24] *See BOM*, all of Moroni, chapter 7.
[25] *BOM*, Mosiah 3:19.

characteristics that we think of as being "good and from God" and all of which are possessed by little children.

Considering that the "Spirit of Christ" can tell us what is good and what is not, how does Jesus view the family unit? Is one family unit more important to Jesus than all the rest? How does Jesus view the accumulation of money and possessions? How does Jesus view anger, contention, protests, and confrontations? How does the "Spirit of Christ" respond to people who hate their enemies? How do people feel when they stand up against those who abuse them, persecute them, and despitefully use them? What does Jesus think about people suing another person in court for money, perhaps to cause the person to lose everything and have nothing?

Isn't what we wrote here applicable to the human race?

For human nature is an enemy to all that is good, and has been from the fall of human nature, and will be, forever and ever, unless we yield to the enticing of our mutual humanity, and put off our human nature and become a better person, like we used to be as a child.[26]

Consider the state of the world. There is much more hate and contention than love, compassion, forgiveness, and acceptance. "I'm right and you're wrong! Your opinion doesn't matter when it affects mine! I want what I deserve! You should be punished for what you've done to me! I'm going to sue you!"

Consider what the world views and recalls as the Arab Spring:

> The Arab Spring was a series of anti-government protests, uprisings, and armed rebellions that spread across much of the Arab world in the early 2010s. It began in response to oppressive regimes and a low standard of living, starting with

---

[26] *Compare BOM*, Mosiah 3:19.

protests in Tunisia. From Tunisia, the protests then spread to five other countries: Libya, Egypt, Yemen, Syria, and Bahrain, where either the ruler was deposed (Zine El Abidine Ben Ali, Muammar Gaddafi, Hosni Mubarak, and Ali Abdullah Saleh) or major uprisings and social violence occurred including riots, civil wars, or insurgencies. Sustained street demonstrations took place in Morocco, Iraq, Algeria, Iranian Khuzestan, Lebanon, Jordan, Kuwait, Oman, and Sudan. Minor protests took place in Djibouti, Mauritania, Palestine, Saudi Arabia, and the Moroccan-occupied Western Sahara. A major slogan of the demonstrators in the Arab world is *ash-sha'b yurīd isqāṭ an-niẓām!* ["the people want to bring down the regime"].[27]

Nothing good has come from these uprisings. In fact, the countries listed above have become worse. The peoples' standard of living has suffered. Wars have decimated these nations. These uprisings were seen as good, but they have led to nothing but "evil." None of these protestors were kind, considerate, humble, or forgiving. Can an honest Christian really believe that Jesus Christ would have supported any of these events?

What good has come from constant protests fueled by anger and frustration—all of which are motivated by *excessive pride*? Whether it's pride in one's race, one's gender, one's sexuality, or justification of one's economic situation, what *good* justifies the illegal act of blocking a road, or yelling at people who are simply going about their day attempting to get to their destination unmolested?

If you were God, and you saw all of your people as equal children, what would you do to try to get your children to see each other as *one family unit*? What could you do when all of your children have very different opinions of what each views as their freedom to act and be acted upon? What would you

---

[27]*See* "Arab Spring," *Wikipedia*, 11 May 2021, en.wikipedia.org/wiki/Arab_Spring.

A New American Scripture

do about all the different religions that claim to be the only true religion? What could you do?

What would you do to help your impoverished children? What would you do to end war and strife? What would you do to show your children that YOU ARE REAL AND AWARE OF THEM?

If you were "the Father, the light, and the life, and the truth of the world,"[28] what would you do to solve the problems of humanity? What could you do? Would you send a prophet to the people and call them "unto repentance lest they should be destroyed"? What if this prophet said to the people,

> by faith all things are fulfilled—Wherefore, whoso believeth in God might with surety hope for a better world, yea, even a place at the right hand of God, which hope cometh of faith, maketh an anchor to the souls of men, which would make them sure and steadfast, always abounding in good works, being led to glorify God?[29]

Would the people believe the "great and marvelous thing" that this prophet said to them?

No matter how careful and clever we were about helping the Americans see where their pride was going to lead them, and lead the world, they have rejected our new American scripture. As explained, in our new American scripture we gave stories about the rise and fall of the people. Our stories explained how the people established a good society—where there was peace, equality, and goodwill towards all—and then how these societies became corrupt and were destroyed. In each and every case, the culprits (causes) were always *pride* and *vanity*.

---

[28] *Compare BOM*, 3 Nephi 11:10–11; *and* NT, John 14:6.
[29] *See BOM*, Ether 12:3–5.

Chapter 13: The Family of Pride

Our stories revolved around a couple families (of Lehi and Ishmael) who were Jews—a "remnant of the house of Israel." Therefore, we needed to address the *pride* and *vanity* of the Jews, or rather, what made the Jews have an excessive feeling of deep pleasure or satisfaction derived from their achievements.

The Jews believe that they are God's chosen people. They believe that their Messiah is yet to come. They believe that when their Messiah comes to the earth, he will save the Jewish people from all of their enemies and rule and reign over the world.

The Jews perform many ordinances, including those described in the Bible's law of Moses. However, Jews do not make a connection between any of their ordinances and a savior or redeemer who is going to appear and usher in the kingdom of God on Earth. The Jews believe that their Messiah will restore Israel to its proper glory and order. They believe that the Jewish state (Israel) will become the greatest nation on Earth—the only nation that will survive the wrath of his coming.

Faith in the future coming of the Messiah is a fundamental requirement for all Jews. They believe he will be coming for the first time; they do not believe in a Second Coming. Their religion teaches that if someone does not believe in this Messiah and is not faithfully waiting for his arrival, then this person is denying the whole of Judaism. This includes denying the Torah (first five books of Moses), Moses himself, and the rest of the biblical prophets.

Jews do not believe that the true Messiah "of heaven and earth" was meant to be killed, or *could* be killed by mere mortals. They believe that *their* Messiah will come to restore the Jews to their proper place among all of humanity as "God's chosen people," and such a Messiah cannot and will never be killed by mere mortals. To the Jews, the claims of Christianity are blasphemous. They believe there is no way that Jesus could be the prophesied *Christ* (the anointed one). Not only was Jesus easily killed, but

A New American Scripture

he did nothing to restore the Jews to what they believe was their original glory. Jesus condemned the Jews because of their religious beliefs.

Jews believe their Messiah is God—the only true "God, yea, the very Eternal Father of heaven and earth."[30] They believe that after the Messiah comes in the flesh (for the first time), he will resurrect the dead to be judged, along with the living. The good people that died will be awakened to everlasting life and the bad people to everlasting shame and contempt.

In the Jesus stories, the role of John the Baptist was to "prepare the way of the Lord Jesus and make his paths straight."[31] The Jews were following a path that was "crooked" and evil. As Jesus mocked the Jews' pride and vanity, the prophet sent to prepare the people to hear him (John the Baptist), also mocked Jewish pride.

According to the Bible story, the Jews sought out John to be baptized by him. John didn't want to baptize them. He called them a "generation of vipers" and referred to them (the Jews) as being of no more worth to God than stones. John told the people that if they wanted to truly repent and become clean before God, they must "bring forth therefore fruits worthy of repentance. ... And the people asked [John], saying, What shall we do then?"[32] What John told the people to do in order to "prepare ... the way of the Lord, and make his paths straight"[33] was profound:

> John answered and said unto them, He that hath two coats, let him impart to him that hath none; and he that hath meat, let him do likewise.[34]

John and Jesus discounted everything the Jews believed made them special above all other people. None of the ordinances that the Jews were

---
[30] *See BOM*, Mosiah 15:4; and *BOM*, Alma 11:38–9.
[31] *Compare* NT, Mark 1:3.
[32] NT, Luke 3:7–10
[33] NT, Luke 3:4.
[34] *Compare* NT, Luke 3:11.

performing for their church were of any good to anyone but to the Jews themselves. Isaiah also clearly said this, as we have explained. John, Isaiah, and Jesus all taught the same thing.

Jesus told an important parable about what he was going to do when he came "in his glory [with] all the holy angels." He was going to take care of the poor and needy. According to the simple-to-understand parable found in Matthew, chapter 25, the ONLY way that people could be saved—the only way that they would avoid eternal damnation—was to take care of the poor and the needy. In other words, they needed to do things that would benefit ALL of humanity, not just boost Jewish or Christian pride and vanity (as was the case with their ordinances and rituals).

There is no mistake about the evil of *pride* and *vanity* in the teachings of Jesus, IF a person honestly and sincerely studies *the philosophy of Jesus of Nazareth*, as Thomas Jefferson called it. Jesus taught, by his own example, that no one was above any other. He never placed himself above any other. Jesus taught that he was God, and that he was no better than any other man. In everything that Jesus taught, he stripped away the pride and vanity of the "natural man."

Pride and vanity are the downfall of all nations when the laws and powers that control that nation (government, religion, and businesses) allow people to put the value of their own life above another's. When people see their own existence and purpose in life as more valuable than another's, their pride and vanity cause them to protect their status and value at all costs.

In politics—kings, prime ministers, presidents, senators, members of Congress, and the likes—are the most popular and are usually chosen from the most successful. None of these serve the whole of humanity. These serve their own interests, or the interests of their constituents (those who elect them). When one group of people votes for a leader, that group's pride in their platform and issues are represented by the leader of their political party.

Democracy allows the demands that one group of people has (the majority) to be placed above, and become more valuable than, the losing group's demands (the minority). The winning party does not care about the values and desires of the losing party. Democracy breeds strife, persecution, and great inequality.

The best politician is one who is *not a leader* (a king), but who *serves* ALL people equally by implementing laws that are fair and equitable for all people. There should be no powers given to government other than those that *serve* ALL of the people equally. This is what Jesus taught. He taught that "he that is greatest among you shall be your servant."[35]

The life of Jesus, as it was invented by those who were wise to what constitutes a "righteous" and successful government, gave the ideal example of the perfect political leader. Jesus did not place one group of people's interests over those of another. His teachings did not place the majority's interests above the minority's. In confronting the pride of the people, Jesus was murdered.

The Church of Jesus Christ of Latter-day Saints (LDS/Mormon Church) has become exceedingly rich.[36] Many of its members are lifted up in **pride**, such as in the wearing of costly apparel, and all manner of fine pearls, and of the fine things of the world—which they purchase from this church's own mall (City Creek Mall, located adjacent to their main temple in Salt Lake City, Utah).[37] The LDS/Mormons do not have their goods and their substance in common among them. They are divided into classes. They build up their church to get gain. This church has now become the wealthiest church in the modern history of the world.[38]

---

[35] NT, Matthew 23:11.
[36] *See* "Religious Organizations," in "List of wealthiest organizations." *Wikipedia*, 23 May 2021, en.wikipedia.org/wiki/List_of_wealthiest_organizations.
[37] *See* "City Creek Center," *Wikipedia*, 26 May 2021, en.wikipedia.org/wiki/City_Creek_Center.
[38] *See* Paul Glader, "Mormon Church Stockpiled $100 Billion Intended for Charities and Misled LDS Members, Whistleblower Says," 17 Dec. 2019, *Newsweek*, newsweek.com/mormon-church-stockpiled-100-billion-intended-charities-misled-lds-members-whistleblower-says-1477809.

LDS/Mormons profess Christ, yet they deny the more parts of his gospel—the words that Jesus taught in both the Bible and in the *Book of Mormon*. They practice all manner of wickedness, in that they focus their time and efforts on worldly success, education, and popularity. Nothing that is required of a good and faithful member to enter their temples and receive their priesthood-sanctioned "saving ordinances," is based on the words of Jesus—"the fulness of the everlasting Gospel … as delivered by the Savior to the ancient inhabitants" of the Western Hemisphere.[39]

The LDS Church administers "that which was sacred unto him to whom it had been forbidden because of unworthiness."[40] This is explained by what we wrote in a previous chapter:

> And when they take the sacrament, when they take upon themselves the "flesh and blood of Christ," there is not a group of Christian people on Earth that does so as unworthily as the members of the LDS Church. If we could, we would prohibit that religion from mocking us and misusing one of the only books ever written that can make a person ONE with God [the *Book of Mormon*].[41]

The LDS/Mormon Church sends tens of thousands of deceived young people to the rest of the world as missionaries. These young people think they are doing something righteous, but they couldn't be more wrong. They carry our book to the world and are trained to lie and deceive *others* who read OUR book. These *others* are convinced of our book's power and truthfulness because of the way we wrote it. This church is full of priestcraft. Its leaders "set themselves up for a light unto the world that they may get gain and praise of the world; but they seek not the welfare of Zion," where "Zion" is a society of people who are "of one heart and one mind [with] no poor among them."

---

[39] JSH 1:34.
[40] *See BOM*, 4 Nephi 1:27.
[41] *See* Chapter 10, pages 274–5.

We knew that throughout our new American scripture we had to confront this *pride* and *vanity*. We continued to make the attempt as we presented the storyline:

> And there was a strict command throughout all the churches that there should be no persecutions among them, that there should be an equality among all men; That they should let no pride nor haughtiness disturb their peace; that every man should esteem his neighbor as himself, laboring with their own hands for their support.[42]

Investing in someone else's labor creates inequality in a society. If one invests in the stock market, for example, one is depending on the labor of those who work for the company in which one has invested. The investors hope (certainly not having a "hope in Christ") that the employees work hard to create a profit for the company so that the investors' dividends will increase without their having to "labor with their own hands for their support." And it is because of their investments that,

> the people of the church began to wax proud, because of their exceeding riches, and their fine silks, and their fine-twined linen [*even everything that was sold at City Creek Mall*], and because of their many flocks and herds, and their gold and their silver, and all manner of precious things, which they had obtained by their industry; and in all these things were they lifted up in the pride of their eyes, for they began to wear very costly apparel. ... the people of the church began to be lifted up in the pride of their eyes, and to set their hearts upon riches and upon the vain things of the world, that they began to be scornful, one towards another, and they began to persecute those that did not believe according to their own will and pleasure.[43]

---

[42] *BOM*, Mosiah 27:3–4.
[43] *Compare BOM*, Alma 4:6, 8.

The LDS/Mormons persecute others who do not believe in their church and who live according to their own will and pleasure. They condemn people who smoke, drink, and do certain things on a Sunday, according to their own will and pleasure. They persecute those who have sex outside of marriage, masturbate, or have sex with those of the same sex, according to their own will and pleasure. They criticize those who do many other things, according to their own will and pleasure—things with which LDS/Mormons do not agree. The LDS/Mormons condemn other people to hell for doing many things "according to their own will and pleasure."

> There began to be great contentions among the people of the church; yea, there were envyings, and strife, and malice, and persecutions, and pride, even to exceed the pride of those who did not belong to the church of God. ... and the wickedness of the church was a great stumbling-block to those who did not belong to the church.[44]

We briefly mentioned that the successful, Tony Award-winning musical, *The Book of Mormon*,[45] is a mockery of our new American scripture because of the way that the LDS/Mormon Church uses our book. Thus, our book has become a stumbling block to those who have never read or studied it. Therefore, one can see that,

> the wickedness of the church, and ... the example of the church began to lead those who were unbelievers on from one piece of iniquity to another, thus bringing on the destruction of the people.

> Yea, he saw great inequality among the people, some lifting themselves up with their pride, despising others, turning their backs upon the needy and the naked and those who were hungry, and those who were athirst, and those who were sick and afflicted.

---

[44] *See BOM*, Alma 4:9–10.
[45] *See* "The Book of Mormon (musical)," *Wikipedia*, 28 May 2021, en.wikipedia.org/wiki/The_Book_of_Mormon_(musical).

Now this was a great cause for lamentations among the people, while others were abasing themselves, succoring those who stood in need of their succor, such as imparting their substance to the poor and the needy, feeding the hungry, and suffering all manner of afflictions, for Christ's sake.[46]

In our book, we asked those who profess a belief in Christ, especially members of the LDS/Mormon Church,

> if ye have experienced a change of heart, and if ye have felt to sing the song of redeeming love, I would ask, can ye feel so now? Have ye walked, keeping yourselves blameless before God? Could ye say, if ye were called to die at this time, within yourselves, that ye have been sufficiently humble? ... Behold, are ye stripped of PRIDE? I say unto you, if ye are not ye are not prepared to meet God. ... Behold, I say, is there one among you who is not stripped of envy? ... And again I say unto you, is there one among you that doth make a mock of his brother, or that heapeth upon him persecutions?[47]

In your pride, do you believe that your church is the only true church of God on Earth? Do you envy worldly success, a nice car, a nice house, and other nice things that you do not possess? Isn't this envy? Don't you mock your neighbor because they do not believe like you do? Don't you tell them that they can't be with their loved ones forever, unless they join your church and pay tithing so that they can enter into your "fine sanctuaries" to receive the saving ordinances that *only* your priesthood leaders can give them? Doesn't this create strife and contention?

Don't you heap persecutions on those young women who are not ready to be a mother, who seek for an abortion of a fetus that is certainly not a "child of

---

[46] *BOM*, Alma 4:11–13.
[47] *BOM*, Alma 5:26–30, emphasis added.

God" any more than an egg or a sperm is a child of God? How many other persecutions do you heap on those who do not believe as you do?

> [We] say unto you, can ye withstand these sayings; yea, can ye lay aside these things, and trample the Holy One under your feet; yea, can ye be puffed up in the pride of your hearts; yea, will ye still persist in the wearing of costly apparel and setting your hearts upon the vain things of the world, upon your riches [*for example, by investing in the stock market and shopping at your City Creek Mall*]? Yea, will ye persist in supposing that ye are better one than another?[48]

Yea, do you actually read our new American scripture?

We presented one of our characters (who represents a True Messenger) observing some of the financially successful Nephites meeting each Sunday at church. Their leaders (such as bishops and counselors) sat above the people behind a pulpit. In our story, we called this place, "Rameumptom, which, being interpreted, is the holy stand."[49] Likewise, each Sunday, the LDS/Mormons

> offer up, every man, the selfsame prayer unto God, thanking their God that they were chosen of him. ... Now, after the people had all offered up thanks after this manner, they returned to their homes, never speaking of their God again until they had assembled themselves together again to the holy stand, to offer up thanks after their manner.[50]

---

[48] *BOM*, Alma 5:53–4.
[49] *BOM*, Alma 31:21.
[50] *BOM*, Alma 31:22–3.

A New American Scripture

Just one day a week, Mormons act the part of "professors of Christ." The rest of the week, although they might be giving lip service to God and participating in the "busy work" of their church, "their hearts [are] set upon gold, and upon silver, and upon all manner of fine goods. ... Their hearts [are] lifted up unto great boasting, in their pride."[51]

As we have explained, LDS/Mormons are the consummate (supreme) Multi-level Marketing capitalists. They rejoice in becoming rich. They present the sales plans associated with these insidious (deceitful and crafty) pyramid schemes, which make the few at the top wealthy by having the majority at the bottom do all the labor. They pitch increasing their "downline" in order to increase their wealth, justifying this great unrighteousness by proclaiming that they are God's people. They believe that they will receive God's blessings of salvation as long as they pay their tithing and do what their leaders tell them God wants them to do, nothing of which is taught in our new American scripture.

Knowing that this would happen, we wrote the following, crying through the words of Alma (the character in our story who represents a True Messenger):

> And he lifted up his voice to heaven, and cried, saying: O, how long, O Lord, wilt thou suffer that thy servants shall dwell here below in the flesh, to behold such gross wickedness among the children of men?
>
> Behold, O God, they cry unto thee, and yet their hearts are swallowed up in their pride. Behold, O God, they cry unto thee with their mouths, while they are puffed up, even to greatness, with the vain things of the world.

---

[51] *BOM*, Alma 31:24–5.

Chapter 13: The Family of Pride

> Behold, O my God, their costly apparel, and their ringlets, and their bracelets, and their ornaments of gold, and all their precious things which they are ornamented with; and behold, their hearts are set upon them, and yet they cry unto thee and say—We thank thee, O God, for we are a chosen people unto thee, while others shall perish.[52]

The unrighteous people of our day (circa 2020) will claim that because they believe in Christ, this part of our story does not apply to them. The people to whom Alma was referring didn't believe in the "foolishness" of a future Christ coming to save and bless the people. They didn't need to—they were already being blessed with riches and great prosperity. But we apply Alma's words properly to the LDS/Mormon people, because they act the same way as the example of the church that we gave in our storyline.

We presented in our story that we (the Real Illuminati®) do not suffer "save it be for the sins of the world." The excessive pride of, not only the LDS/Mormon people, but of all Christians in the world, as well as of the Jews, of the Muslims, and of all other religions that claim to be God's true religion, causes us to relate to the words we wrote for our book's character, Alma:

> O Lord God, how long wilt thou suffer that such wickedness and infidelity shall be among this people? O Lord, wilt thou give us strength, that we may bear with our infirmities. For we are infirm, and such wickedness among this people doth pain our souls.

> O Lord, our hearts are exceedingly sorrowful; wilt thou comfort our souls in Christ. O Lord, wilt thou grant unto us that we may have strength, that we may suffer with patience these afflictions which shall come upon us, because of the iniquity of this people.[53]

---

[52] *BOM*, Alma 31:26–8.
[53] *Compare BOM*, Alma 31:30–1.

We also explained in our story that it *is* possible for righteous people to prosper and become rich. A prosperous society can succeed as long as they are not excessively prideful. They must also always remember how they became that way—by following the words of the prophets who taught them the good principles that make a great society of people. We wrote:

> And the people of Nephi began to prosper again in the land, and began to multiply and to wax exceedingly strong again in the land. And they began to grow exceedingly rich. But notwithstanding their riches, or their strength, or their prosperity, they were not lifted up in the pride of their eyes; neither were they slow to remember the Lord their God; but they did humble themselves exceedingly before him.[54]

Our new American scripture's narrative seems to be a roller-coaster ride of the successes and failures of the people. These people

> did fast and pray oft, and did wax stronger and stronger in their humility, and firmer and firmer in the faith of Christ, unto the filling their souls with joy and consolation, yea, even to the purifying and the sanctification of their hearts, which sanctification cometh because of their yielding their hearts unto God.

Yet, once again, not that many years later,

> exceedingly great pride [got] into the hearts of the people; and it was because of their exceedingly great riches and their prosperity in the land; and [their pride] did grow upon them from day to day.[55]

Throughout our story, we called out and explained in detail what excessive pride does to a society. We explained that the downfall of a society

---

[54] *BOM*, Alma 62:48–9.
[55] *BOM*, Helaman 3:35–6.

Chapter 13: The Family of Pride

would not have happened had it not been for their wickedness and their abomination which was among them; yea, and it was among those also who professed to belong to the church of God.

And it was because of the pride of their hearts, because of their exceeding riches, yea, it was because of their oppression to the poor, withholding their food from the hungry, withholding their clothing from the naked, and smiting their humble brethren upon the cheek.

... O how foolish, and how vain, and how evil, and devilish, and how quick to do iniquity, and how slow to do good, are the children of men; yea, how quick to hearken unto the words of the evil one, and to set their hearts upon the vain things of the world!

Yea, how quick to be lifted up in pride; yea, how quick to boast, and do all manner of that which is iniquity; and how slow are they to remember the Lord their God, and to give ear unto his counsels, yea, how slow to walk in wisdom's paths![56]

Throughout our story, we presented many other factors that cause a society's downfall. We explained that

the foundation of the destruction of this people is beginning to be laid by the unrighteousness of your lawyers and your judges.[57]

The United States' judicial system touts itself as being the most just and reliable of all the world. When considered honestly however, the U.S. court system does not serve the needs of the people. It serves the wants and desires of judges and lawyers seeking gain and power over the people. The rules of the court make it extremely difficult, if not impossible, for a person to present a

---

[56] *BOM*, Helaman 4:11–12; 12:4–5.
[57] *BOM*, Alma 10:27.

case that is not properly presented by a lawyer. We wrote of what we knew was already happening in the American justice system:

> Now the object of these lawyers was to get gain; and they got gain according to their employ. ... Now, it was for the sole purpose to get gain, because they received their wages according to their employ [most attorneys make $250–$350 per hour], therefore, they did stir up the people to riotings, and all manner of disturbances and wickedness, that they might have more employ, that they might get money according to the suits which were brought before them.[58]

People who are poor usually lose in a United States court. The person who has enough money to employ a lawyer has a significantly better chance of winning. These wicked and unsympathetic courts have established rules that prohibit a person from coming before a court who does not know their rules. The judges used to be lawyers attempting to get gain, so the sympathy of a judge, which should be towards fairness and justice, is overshadowed by the rules of court procedure that deny justice to anyone who does not follow this procedure. This is a great cause of the downfall of the American society, which *could have been great* and led the world by example in how to create a good human society.

There are other factors we have not covered in this chapter that can cause a society to become corrupt because of *excessive pride*. It is our hope, by providing the examples and explanations that we have in the last two chapters, that a sincere person will be inspired to read all that we have written on the subject.

It is very important to understand that excessive pride creates a mental and emotional hell. This hell leads to the most devastating physical result of this pride—war. We will discuss this next.

---

[58] *BOM*, Alma 10:32; 11:20.

Chapter 14
Wars and Rumors of Wars

Our new American scripture is filled with stories of wars. What a reader often wonders is, "*Why* so much emphasis on war?"

The *why* should be obvious if one takes an honest and hard look at how the human world operates. Unlike *any* other species, humans kill each other for reasons that have nothing to do with protecting the species and helping it to survive. Most human-made wars are about emotional battles, almost always about *pride*. Again, the negative aspect of pride is

> *a feeling of deep pleasure or satisfaction derived from one's own achievements, the achievements of those with whom one is closely associated, or from qualities or possessions that are widely admired by others.*

The positive side of *pride* is *the consciousness of one's own dignity*.

Every war and rumor of war that has ever started was caused by a person or group of people protecting what they have achieved (as an individual or as a group), which includes their possessions. What individuals and groups accomplish, and what they possess, gives them their dignity (*makes them conscious of their own self-worth*). To protect their accomplishments and defend their self-worth, humans will sacrifice their existence at all costs. It is very important for people to be *conscious of their own dignity*—that's a positive thing that is part of *good* human nature. However, this becomes a negative thing when consciousness of one's self-worth is derived from the politics one supports, from the religion that one follows, or from the worldly success (money and possessions) for which one strives. Again, these things lead to *pride* and *vanity*. This *pride* and *vanity* are the cause of all human conflicts that result in ending human life.

Groups of people achieve a degree of prominence by believing and proclaiming that they belong to the greatest and most significant nation on Earth. Being a loyal patriotic citizen of this nation gives the members of this group personal dignity. To protect this personal dignity, the members will fight for and defend their nation against any other group of people that believes and proclaims that their nation is more special than another.

Groups of people achieve a degree of prominence by believing and proclaiming that they belong to God's only true religion on Earth. Being a faithful member of this religion gives them personal dignity. To protect this personal dignity, they will fight for and defend against any other group of people that might believe and proclaim that theirs is the true religion.

Groups of people achieve a degree of prominence by having a higher standard of living than other groups of people, owning more land, possessing more *things*, having access to more opportunity to possess whatever *thing* they desire. These groups of people will fight and defend against any other group of people that threatens its members' economic status.

However, it is not always a *group* of people that seeks to defend its prominence and dignity (self-worth). More often than not, it is a few individuals trying to protect their own power, popularity, and economic security. Political, religious, and business leaders realize that their power and possessions can be overthrown and threatened by the masses. Therefore, the plight of the masses is not as important to political leaders as their own dilemma of protecting the *consciousness of their own dignity*. These leaders in society will do anything in their power to defend the source of their self-worth and possessions. And because they are the few against the majority, they do anything and everything they can to keep the majority under their control—whatever it takes and whatever war they must start, or about whatever war they must start a rumor.

Consider what would have happened in the ancient Hebrew culture if the people had figured out that the rituals and ordinances of the law of Moses

Chapter 14: Wars and Rumors of Wars

were not actually mandated by God. What if people had understood that it was just a way for the priests to get the first fruits of the fields and the best cuts of meat? (The law of Moses even made sure the Hebrew priests got their liquor.) God told the people to not revile (criticize) God's chosen priesthood holder,

> nor curse the ruler of thy people. Thou shalt not delay to offer the first of thy ripe fruits, and of thy liquors: the firstborn of thy sons shalt thou give unto me. Likewise shalt thou do with thine oxen, and with thy sheep: seven days it shall be with his dam; on the eighth day thou shalt give it me.[1]

The people of ancient Israel were convinced that: 1) their group of people (the nation of Israel) was the *only* group of people that God wanted anything to do with; 2) their religion and priesthood laws of sacrifice were what God expected of his people; and 3) if they supported numbers 1 and 2, God would give them everything that they wanted. The Israelites (ancient Hebrews/Jews) were very conscious of their own dignity because of how they viewed themselves (children of Abraham) compared to everyone else in the world (who were *not* children of Abraham).

We have mentioned a play that we helped Joseph Smith write for his followers a few years before he was murdered (by some of his disgruntled ex-followers and others who hated him). The play was written with symbolic undertones that represented what we know is the Real Truth™ about human existence. The modern LDS/Mormon people view this play as the most sacred priesthood ritual (ordinance) they can perform while being a mortal on Earth. However, as we previously explained, Joseph did not present this play as such. Brigham Young was the one responsible for changing its significance and original presentation. Young never understood the true symbolism of the play. Young used it to keep power and authority over his followers (just like the LDS/Mormon Church leadership does today).

---

[1] OT, Exodus 22:28–30.

In this play, we demonstrated the two sides of *pride*. Here, we would like to give more details about these two sides as each is demonstrated symbolically in the play's presentation. The following is what the character *Elohim* says to the character *Lucifer*, after He (God) finds out that the devil *Lucifer* has deceived Adam and Eve and caused them to partake of the forbidden fruit (according to our play's original presentation):

> ELOHIM: Lucifer, because thou hast done this, thou shalt be cursed above all the beasts of the field. Upon thy belly thou shalt go, and dust shalt thou eat all the days of thy life.
>
> LUCIFER: If thou cursest me for doing the same thing which has been done in other worlds, I will take the spirits that follow me, and they shall possess the bodies thou createst for Adam and Eve!
>
> ELOHIM: I will place *enmity* between thee and the seed of the woman. Thou mayest have power to bruise his heel, but he shall have power to crush thy head.
>
> LUCIFER: Then with that enmity I will take the treasures of the earth, and with gold and silver I will buy up armies and navies, popes and priests, and reign with blood and horror on the earth![2]

Before one can understand what the above conversation between God and the devil represents, we need to briefly explain who the characters *Elohim* and *Lucifer* were meant to represent. Although we have touched upon the true meaning of *Lucifer* and how we used it in our new American scripture, it is good that we review what we have explained. Herein, we hope to provide a clearer explanation of what the devil, or *Lucifer*, actually means.

We know that the "devil," "Satan," or whatever other name is used to define the bad things that humans do, is nothing more or less than "the natural man," who "is an enemy to God, and has been from the fall of

---
[2] SNS, 57–60. Read for free at realilluminati.org/sacred-not-secret.

Adam." The "natural man" (or rather, *natural*, intrinsic human nature) is full of *pride*. Humans act continually to protect their *pride* and ego, as we have explained above, and as we presented the idea within the flow of information that we wanted to present in our new American scripture:

> For the **natural man is an enemy to God**, and has been from the fall of Adam, and will be, forever and ever, unless he yields to the enticings of the Holy Spirit, and **putteth off the natural man** and becometh a saint through the atonement of Christ the Lord, and becometh as a child, submissive, meek, humble, patient, full of love, willing to submit to all things which the Lord seeth fit to inflict upon him, even as a child doth submit to his father.[3]

Our contemporary True Messenger explained in the Foreword of this book that a supernatural god, of any kind, does <u>not</u> exist, and that each person has a *higher True Self*.[4] In other writings, we explain that our mortal experience is occurring as a dream sequence of events in the physical brain of our *True Self*, similar to how our mortal brain creates its dreams.[5] To make this easier to understand, we can say that when a mortal dies, the person will immediately become *conscious of their own dignity* (the positive aspect of *pride*) as the advanced human that the person was *before* connecting to an infant mortal body.[6]

In our play, we present the Holy Trinity (Godhead) of the Father, the Son, and the Holy Ghost as the characters *Elohim*, *Jehovah*, and *Michael*, respectively. *Michael* is put to sleep by *Elohim* and *Jehovah* and dreams that he is having experiences involving the characters *Adam*, *Eve*, and *Lucifer*. Whereas a person's *True Self* is this *Godhead*, we meant to allegorically explain how a *part of this Godhead* is participating in the Earth experience

---

[3] *BOM*, Mosiah 3:19, emphasis added.
[4] *See THOR*, 15, 22–3, 241–4 for more information about one's True Self.
[5] *See THOR*, 15–23, 101, 241–4, 316.
[6] *See THOR*, 22–4. Download free at realilluminati.org/the-true-history-of-religion.

asleep. However, all three members of this Godhead are just ONE GOD, just ONE person, one's *True Self.*

When a person is born into mortality, the infant, not yet affected by any experience of mortality, is a near perfect example of the person's *True Self*—the *Michael part* of one's *Godhead.* A little child is

> submissive, meek, humble, patient, full of love, willing to submit to all things which the Lord seeth fit to inflict upon [the child], even as a child submits to his father.

No little child is born "an enemy of God." No human starts out being prejudiced, lofty, or with any other negative emotional traits associated with excessive pride. This doesn't happen to a little child until the child is affected and *tempted* by the *pride of this world*. Keep in mind, there are three main sources of the pride of this world that begin to affect a young mind—nationality, religion, and economic status. Although innocent and unaffected at birth, the child gives in to temptation and *falls* prey to *excessive pride*, which turns the child into a "natural man—an enemy of [the child's *True Nature*]."

Regardless of what children are exposed to during the mortal experience, they possess a deep personal feeling that they are *the* most important human in their own existence. This emotional *feeling* is actually caused by the person's continual connection to the other parts of what we symbolically presented in our play as a person's personal *Godhead: Elohim* and *Jehovah*, the non-sleeping parts of their *True Self.*

When we presented that *Elohim* placed "enmity" between *Lucifer* and "the seed of the woman,"[7] we meant that mortals are in a constant battle (a war). This war comes from having a *consciousness of their own dignity* (which is a natural feeling from the mortal connection to one's *True Self*) and

---

[7] *SNS*, 58–9.

what the world expects of people in order to be valued and have what the world defines as "dignity."

As people experience life upon Earth, it is very *natural* for them to pursue and want to *feel* self-worth and have a *consciousness of their own dignity*. This feeling never leaves a human being, regardless of what is done to the person. This struggle to maintain a sense of self-worth is the "*enmity*" that our play's character *Elohim* places between *Lucifer* and "the seed of the woman" (i.e., everyone born into mortality). *Enmity* means a feeling of distaste, or a feeling of constant dislike.[8] As portrayed symbolically in our play, this is the conflict that one experiences when the person does not feel of worth to the world.[9]

In a religious sense, people do not like *Lucifer*, or anything that they perceive as "evil." As we explained above, anything that threatens a person's self-worth is hated and fought against. If people are taught by a religion that something that they desire or do is "evil," then when they feel the desire to do it, the feeling *bruises* their ego.

For example, if a homosexual person desires to have sex with someone of the same gender, and a religion forbids it as something evil, the person will not have a *consciousness of their own dignity* and will feel a sense of extreme guilt. Gay groups of men and women fight for their right to exercise their free will. When they are free to do what they feel is best for them in order to become *conscious of their own dignity*, they are acting consistent with the desires and needs of their *True Self*. If the feeling were not consistent, then the act would not bring them joy. The *pride* (Lucifer) of religious groups wages a war of "blood and horror on the earth" against homosexuals.

In our play, we made it as clear as possible that whenever a mortal person prays to God for an answer, the person (no matter how sincere or

---

[8] *See also* "enmity," Lexico – Oxford University Press, lexico.com/en/definition/enmity.
[9] *SNS*, 45–6.

righteous), is ALWAYS answered by *Lucifer*.[10] In other words, when a person prays, the answer that one receives does not come from anywhere but that person's own *pride* and ego. Unfortunately, more often than not, this is a consequence of the prejudices they have been *taught*. In the example we used above, what little child would care in the least whether or not the child's parents were gay?

Usually, the answer that a person receives from prayer supports and upholds whatever it is that gives the person *consciousness of their own dignity*. Therefore, when Muslims pray to Allah, for example, they will ALWAYS receive a feeling consistent with the self-worth that they have derived from following Islam. Likewise, when LDS/Mormons pray to Heavenly Father, they will ALWAYS receive a feeling consistent with the self-worth that they have derived from following Mormonism.

We have a good example of this in an actual experience that our contemporary True Messenger had. In 2009, his nephew was killed in what is known as the *Fort Hood Massacre*.[11] His nephew was killed by a Muslim fanatic who was trying to keep American soldiers from going to war against his Muslim brothers and killing them because of their beliefs.

Our True Messenger shared a story about his nephew. This nephew had been forced by his father (our True Messenger's brother) to make a decision—either go on an LDS/Mormon mission, or join the military. Our contemporary True Messenger's nephew chose the military and was attending Fort Hood (an American Army base). He was preparing to go to war against the Taliban (an Islamic faction) in Afghanistan. During this time the Muslim man mentioned above shot our True Messenger's nephew and as many newly recruited soldiers as he could kill.

---

[10] *SNS*, 85–8.
[11] *See* "2009 Fort Hood shooting," *Wikipedia*, Wikimedia Foundation, 16 May 2021, en.wikipedia.org/wiki/2009_Fort_Hood_shooting.

After the incident, our True Messenger explained the Real Truth™. The Muslim man who had killed our True Messenger's nephew was just as justified in his actions of killing a Christian American solider as a Christian American soldier was in preparing to kill Taliban soldiers.[12] As is often the case when our True Messenger tells the Real Truth™, he was greatly persecuted and ostracized for pointing out the comparison between the reasoning of the Muslim man to kill and his nephew preparing to kill.

As the Muslim man said his daily prayers, asking Allah for strength and courage to carry out Allah's will to protect Muslims, the man's *Lucifer* answered his prayers. In support and protection of the Muslim man's *consciousness of his own dignity*, *Lucifer* told him to kill as many American soldiers as he could before they killed Allah's people.

Our 1842 play is very clear that during a person's mortal life, in what we call "the lone and dreary world," *Elohim* and *Jehovah* have NOTHING to do with, nor do they communicate with, nor do they know what is happening with, any mortal going through the mortal earth experience.[13] Regardless of how clearly we tried to explain this symbolism, the LDS/Mormon people believe they are in constant contact with, and under constant direction from, their Heavenly Father and Jesus, through the Holy Ghost/Spirit.

As we pointed out, this group of people consumes more antidepressants, per capita, than any other group of people on Earth. This consumption is a direct result of the *enmity* that their hearts feel in trying to be faithful members of that burdensome religion and not becoming a "natural enemy" to their *True Self*. The drugs help them avoid their real feelings and justify their reliance on "the god of this world" (*Lucifer*), from whom they have been conditioned to receive answers to their prayers.[14]

---

[12] *See* "Human Reality - A Message to the Youth of the World," Marvelous Work and a Wonder, 21 Oct. 2015, YouTube, youtu.be/z0U3aeUNtck.
[13] *See SNS*, 85–6.
[14] *See SNS*, 87.

In the presentation of our play, the *enmity* that is provided by *Elohim* is a very good thing. *Elohim* tells *Lucifer* that with this *enmity* mortals will be able to "crush" their pride and ego, although their *consciousness of their own dignity* will be "bruised" throughout their mortal experience.[15] It is later revealed that in order for mortals to be able to "crush the head" of Lucifer, they will need help doing it.[16]

Earlier in the play, *Elohim* explains that "Lucifer [is] our common enemy, whom we shall also place upon the earth and whom we have thrust out [of our advanced existence]."[17] This earlier part symbolizes our existence as advanced humans before and after participating in the *mortal dream of life*. There is no *excessive pride* that exists in a world full of advanced humans. In our *real world*, ALL of us are VERY conscious of our own dignity and nothing exists in that world that threatens or affects our eternal self-worth. Thus, we wrote into our play that *Lucifer* (pride) was a "common enemy" of the Godhead, and someone that they, the *Godhead—Elohim, Jehovah, and Michael*—thrust out.

Mortals have a desire to protect and support their self-worth. This desire is *natural* and perfectly normal, as well as a *good* human desire to have. However, because of this desire, our *excessive pride* has taken

> the treasures of the earth, and with gold and silver has bought up armies and navies, popes and priests, and reigned with blood and horror on the earth![18]

Above we explained the three main reasons that mortals will go to war and kill others. They desire to protect their: 1) nation, which does everything possible to have the strongest "armies and navies"; 2) religion ("popes and priests"); and finally, 3) economic stability ("gold and

---

[15] *See SNS*, 58.
[16] *See SNS*, 116, 119–23.
[17] *SNS*, 31.
[18] *SNS*, 59.

silver"). We have pointed out how these three divisions have caused all the "blood and horror on the earth" (a result of war), which also *causes* rumors of war.

Likewise, we give many examples of *emotional* battles in our new American scripture. We do this to demonstrate that what starts out as an emotional-based argument because of pride usually ends up in the actual physical destruction of countless people. Each and every battle in our new American scripture, if taken in context, teaches something about "fallen" human nature and how the devil (*Lucifer,* i.e., *excessive pride*) causes people to do his bidding. The wars in our story start with the sibling rivalry experienced in the first family we created for our narrative (Laman and Lemuel versus Nephi). Our narrative's wars end with the complete destruction of millions and millions of people living in a great nation we invented to represent the United States of America (the Jaredite Nation).

There was a specific reason *why* we included each and every battle mentioned in our book. Each battle has its own particular purpose and object. Each has a unique lesson we intended to teach about human nature and what causes humans to fight with each other. And the battle that *ended the Great Jaredite Nation* was meant to warn the American people and the world that the United States influences and controls— that **unless the people of the world change their emotional attitudes towards each other, there will be wars in which millions "of mighty men, and also their wives and their children will be destroyed."**[19]

This book, *A New American Scripture*, is the second of a Trilogy that we present to the world in order to attempt to save humanity. We know what humanity's fate will be, IF the people of this world do not set aside their emotional differences and contentions and see each other as equal members of the same family unit—the HUMAN FAMILY.

---

[19] *See BOM,* Ether 15:2, emphasis added.

We have presented as Appendix 1 of this book a <u>very important explanation</u> about how pride crept into the human family, at least according to the Bible's narrative. If one reads *The Sealed Portion* of our new American scripture, one will be convinced by reason and logic just how many "evil" beliefs "fallen humans" think are good and of God, when actually these beliefs are evil and of the devil.

The *sealed portion* of our new American scripture presents Adam (the father of all living) discussing with his children how *evil* they became because of *family units*, money, and the secret combination of politics, religion, and economics, all of which crept in and started deceiving the human race (the family of Adam and Eve).[20]

The Sealed Portion explains the full details in clarity (although it was written in religious prose that was meant to match the *unsealed Book of Mormon)* the many ways that wars were started throughout the history of the world. After reading *The Sealed Portion* with a sincere heart and real intent, most are convinced that their personal pride in their nation, their religion, and their economic standing is the main cause of all the problems facing humanity. Readers are convinced to change their lives so that their own personal acts no longer contribute to the downfall of humanity. As we have explained, most LDS/Mormons who read *The Sealed Portion* finally realize how unrighteous the religion is that gave them their *consciousness of their own dignity* and in so doing also destroyed their humanity.

As explained, the story of the Great Jaredite Nation in the *unsealed portion* of our new American scripture was meant as an allegorical similitude of the United States of America. (It was a symbolic representation of the events and people of the United States.) This great nation (the U.S.) was humanity's last hope to save itself. For this reason, we backed its establishment and have done everything in our power to give it its strength

---

[20] *See* Appendix 1, page 946.

(through advanced nuclear technology and power) and help protect it from other nations that hate it and want to destroy it.

We (the Real Illuminati®) have done things for humanity that we cannot divulge at this time. But in everything that we have done, our intent was to open people's eyes and soften their hearts, and to help them set aside their personal emotional battles and join hands to combat the true enemy of peace and life eternal: **excessive pride in one's own nation, religion, or economic position**, *i.e., Lucifer.*

In the last battle described in our new American scripture, we present how the leader of one side began to see the evil and futility of the cause for which the two sides were fighting. We wrote, and herein present an analogy to the United States:

[The leader of the United States of America] began to repent of the evil which he had done; he began to remember the words which had been spoken by the mouth of all the prophets, and he saw them that they were fulfilled thus far, every whit; and his soul mourned and refused to be comforted.

And it came to pass that he wrote an epistle unto [the other side's leader, a leader of the people who hated America], desiring him that he would spare the people, and he would give up the kingdom for the sake of the lives of the people.

And it came to pass that when [the other side's leader, a leader of the people who hated America] had received his epistle, he wrote an epistle unto [the leader of the American people], that if he would give *himself* up, that he might slay him with his own sword, that he would spare the lives of the people.

And it came to pass that the [American] people repented not of their iniquity; and the people of [America] were stirred up to anger against the people [who hated America]; and the people [who hated America] were stirred up to anger against the people of [America]; wherefore, the people [who hated America] did give battle unto the people of [America].[21]

The above was meant as a warning. However, we can no longer choose sides in the great conflicts of wars and rumors of wars that are devastating humanity. The United States of America has not done what was expected of it.

We have explained our involvement in the 2019 pandemic that was meant to unite the world in a mutual war against an unseen enemy—an enemy more powerful than any possible nuclear weapon. Despite this worldwide pandemic that affects all people equally, the American people and those around the world who embrace their own particular nation, religion, or economic status, who embrace their pride's image, and accept the mark it has made on humanity, "repented not of their iniquity."

Because the people of the world, properly warned, did not repent of their iniquity, we can no longer intervene. The nations that hate the beast (that disagree with the American economic system), as we reported in our book of Revelation, are nations that

> receive power as kings [from] the beast [for the last] hour. These all have one mind, and shall give their power and strength unto the beast. These shall [cause the] peoples, and multitudes, and nations, and tongues [to] hate the whore [the United States of America's economic system], and [they] shall make her desolate and naked, and shall eat her flesh, and [they shall] burn her with fire.[22]

---

[21] *Compare BOM*, Ether 15:3–6.
[22] *Compare* NT, Revelation 17:12–16. See *666 America*, 376, 383–7, and 395 to learn the meaning. Read free at realilluminati.org/666-mark-of-america.

We have warned the Americans that other countries that hate America's power and control over the world's economy finally have the potential of possessing powerful nuclear weapons. When we were involved, we did everything in our power to stop these nations from acquiring and developing nuclear technology.[23]

In our new American scripture, we had a man (Nephi) who was shown a vision of the future development of the United States of America. Nephi viewed what would happen up until the time that the United States prospered and expanded Capitalism (the "great and abominable church ... of the devil") throughout the world. The

> wrath of God was [then] poured out upon that great and abominable church, insomuch that there were wars and rumors of wars among all the nations and kindreds of the earth.[24]

This "wrath of God" simply means the non-intervention by those (of us) who know how to establish peace and life eternal upon the earth. We know how to heal the world from any pandemic. We know how to give the world advanced technology and understanding that will end all disease, all death, and all inequality, which literally

> either ... convinc[es humanity] unto peace and life eternal, or unto the deliverance of them to the hardness of their hearts and the blindness of their minds unto their being brought down into captivity, and also into destruction, both temporally and spiritually.[25]

At this point in our scripture's narrative (during Nephi's vision of the future), we direct the reader towards our New Testament book of Revelation. Our character Nephi writes:

---

[23] *See THOR*, 49–55, 311–12.
[24] *BOM*, 1 Nephi 14:15.
[25] *BOM*, 1 Nephi 14:7.

I am forbidden that I should write the remainder of the things which I saw and heard; wherefore the things which I have written sufficeth me; and I have written but a small part of the things which I saw.[26]

Joseph allowed his scribes to show and discuss the manuscripts with the peer review group. To our great surprise, they failed to see the powerful significance of the book of Revelation and its importance to humanity's salvation. Because of this ignorance and oversight, we made it perfectly clear later in our story that the "unfolding" of the book of Revelation would herald (announce) the beginning of "the work of the Father [that] has commenced upon all the face of the land. Therefore, repent all ye ends of the earth."[27]

In the first book of our Trilogy, *The True History of Religion*, we explained that we will no longer intervene in the affairs of humanity. This is what we mean when we write about the "wrath of God."[28] Because of our non-intervention, humanity will first experience great pandemics that all have in common, physically.[29] These events will occur as an attempt to open the eyes of humanity to see that all people on Earth are of the same creation and must unite together to fight an unseen enemy that can destroy *all* of humanity.

It was our hope that fighting the COVID-19 pandemic would stop the wars and rumors of wars. For a time it did, at least among all nations upon the earth. However, in the hearts and minds of the people, who depend on their patriotism, religion, and economic standard of living, the pandemic proved devastating to the *consciousness of their own dignity*. People were not allowed to attend sporting events, rallies, and other activities associated with *national pride*. They were forbidden to go to church and congregate together, not able to partake of the sacraments and rituals that

---

[26] *BOM*, 1 Nephi 14:28.
[27] *BOM*, Ether 4:17–18.
[28] See *THOR*, 314–21.
[29] See *Pentateuch Illuminated*, bottom of page 115–22. Read for free at realilluminati.org/pentateuch-illuminated.

many religions teach are necessary for one's salvation. Most devastating, many people lost their jobs and were unable to support and maintain their expected lifestyle.

All of these things (attending patriotic and religious events, and sustaining a certain standard of living) were a "great pit" that was dug by the people. And as we prophesied,

> that great pit which hath been digged for the destruction of men shall be filled by those who digged it, unto their utter destruction, saith the Lamb of God; not the destruction of the soul, save it be the casting of it into that hell which hath no end.[30]

Except for the people who can no longer handle the "casting of [their soul] into that hell which hath no end," and end their life through suicide, most continue to live, but in a state of "hell" which seems to have no end. Thus, drugs help them assuage the hell and deal with life.

COVID-19 was one of our attempts to stop the people of Earth from continuing their wars and rumors of wars based on their emotional divisions (political, religious, and economic). If our attempts fail, as we have explained, all sides of the battle will eventually have nuclear weapons. With these weapons, as we have prophesied in our book of Revelation to the world (and "the time is at hand that they shall be made manifest in very deed"[31]), they shall "burn her with fire." This means that nuclear wars will begin to destroy pockets of humanity until the entire world is destroyed, UNLESS humanity sees its great iniquity and changes its course.

We could write many pages to describe the numerous wars and contentions we placed in our new American scripture to warn humanity. We could explain how the sibling rivalry between brothers led to the eventual destruction of an entire civilization, a society of people that should have

---

[30] *BOM*, 1 Nephi 14:3.
[31] *BOM*, Ether 4:16.

been united as one family. Each of the wars in our story—from this sibling rivalry to the end of the Great Jaredite Nation that we have described above—has its own significance. The reader need only consider each war in context, both what transpired to begin the war and how the war ended, to understand *why* we used so much war in our story. Again, each subplot teaches a very important lesson about human failures and weaknesses, but also the strengths of our humanity.

For one example, the great patriotic military leader, Captain Moroni, united a people because of a nation's military strength and patriotism. *But this never led to peace.* It only led to more war. It wasn't until the people of Ammon (a dark-skinned people who once hated their white-skinned neighbors) decided that they would bury their weapons of war and never kill another person that both sides began to see the awfulness and misery that war causes humanity. The gentle people of Ammon gave up pride, patriotism, and all the things that cause war. They were the supreme example of what it takes to unite the people of the world under one heart and one mind so that there are no poor among them.

In regards to the gentle people of Ammon, to present the obvious point that a righteous people will give up any and all titles that separate them from anyone else upon Earth, we

> called their names Anti-Nephi-Lehies; and they were called by this name and were no more called Lamanites. And they began to be a very industrious people; yea, and they were friendly with the Nephites; therefore, they did open a correspondence with them, and the curse of God did no more follow them.[32]

It is hard to imagine that the Canadians, Americans, and South American people could come together and stop using the national names that separate them. *Anti-American-Canadian-Latino.* Why is it so hard to

---

[32] *BOM*, Alma 23:17–18.

imagine this type of unity? But this unity will remain impossible because of all of the people's pride and because they gain their self-worth through their nation, religions, and economic status.

The people of Ammon, in our story, would not take up weapons to hurt another person, even if it meant sacrificing their own lives and the lives of their loved ones:

> And this they did, it being in their view a testimony to God, and also to men, that they never would use weapons again for the shedding of man's blood; and this they did, vouching and covenanting with God, that rather than shed the blood of their brethren they would give up their own lives; and rather than take away from a brother they would give unto him; and rather than spend their days in idleness they would labor abundantly with their hands.
>
> And thus we see that, when these Lamanites were brought to believe and know the truth, they were firm, and would suffer even unto death rather than commit sin; and thus we see that they buried their weapons of peace, or they buried their weapons of war, for peace.[33]

This group of people was the most righteous example of humanity that we could possibly present to the reader of our new American scripture. We continued the subplot by explaining how their example changed the hearts of other people, and these others, who were once their sworn enemies, "did also bury their weapons of war, according as their brethren had, and they began to be a righteous people."[34] Truly, good humans would

---

[33] *BOM*, Alma 24:18–19.
[34] *BOM*, Alma 25:14.

rather sacrifice their lives than even to take the life of their enemy; and they have buried their weapons of war deep in the earth, **because of their love towards their brethren**.[35]

With great dismay, we report that within days of the United States government declaring a state of emergency because of the COVID-19 pandemic,[36] people lined the streets to buy and stockpile guns and ammunition. This happened in the city in which the most concentrated population of LDS/Mormons exist.[37] These hypocritical people should know better because they are the ones who claim to believe in our new American scripture.

There is no other group of people more angered and militant about their government restricting what they believe is their God-given "right to bear arms" (guns and ammunition) than the conservative-voting LDS/Mormon people.[38] The majority of the "latter-day Saints" will only opt for politicians who support their right to bear arms. There is no other group of people upon Earth, when their per capita number is taken into consideration, that owns more weapons meant to kill their neighbor in times of anticipated turmoil than the hypocritical LDS people.[39] This causes us to "suffer because of the sins of

---

[35] *BOM,* Alma 26:32, emphasis added.

[36] See Lesley Kennedy, et al., *President Trump Declares State of Emergency for COVID-19,* National Conference of State Legislatures, 25 Mar. 2020, ncsl.org/ncsl-in-dc/publications-and-resources/president-trump-declares-state-of-emergency-for-covid-19.aspx.

[37] *See* Thomas Burr, "Utah gun sales spike amid coronavirus scare," *The Salt Lake Tribune,* 24 Mar. 2020 sltrib.com/news/politics/2020/03/24/utah-gun-sales-spike-amid/.

[38] *See* Jana Riess, "Mormons and guns: It's time to set limits," 24 July 2018, Religion News Service, religionnews.com/2018/07/24/mormons-and-guns-its-time-to-set-limits; *and*

"Gun laws in Utah," *Wikipedia,* Wikimedia Foundation, 17 May 2021, en.wikipedia.org/wiki/Gun_laws_in_Utah; *and*

Brittany Tait, "Hundreds Of People Line Up Outside Gun Store In Orem," 9 Jan. 2021, KSL TV – Bonneville International, ksltv.com/452788/hundreds-of-people-line-up-outside-gun-store-in-orem.

[39] *See* Robert A. Rees and Clifton H. Jolley, "Commentary: Utahns and Mormons need to recalibrate our love of guns," 5 Mar. 2018, *The Salt Lake Tribune,* sltrib.com/opinion/commentary/2018/03/05/commentary-guns-utahns-and-mormons/; *and*

this world."[40] More so, because their leaders say NOTHING about this great evil, nor do these unrighteous leaders use our *Book of Mormon* for what it was intended to do: teach the people to love others.

Above we mentioned a very patriotic character in our story named **Captain Moroni** (not to be confused with Mormon's son, Moroni, who wrote *The Sealed Portion* of our narrative). LDS/Mormons do not speak much of the Anti-Nephi-Lehi people, but with great excitement and pride, they love the stories about *Captain* Moroni[41] and the 2,000 stripling warriors (the Army of Helaman).[42]

Truly, taking all things into consideration, there are no people upon Earth as hypocritical as the LDS/Mormons. This is especially true due to the fact that this group of people gains a lot of their self-worth from our *Book of Mormon*. As we have explained, our book was written to support the native American people. Yet the LDS/Mormons support keeping them out of their country, due to their conservative political beliefs.[43]

Ashley Imlay, "Bill to allow Utahns to carry concealed guns without any permit ignites debate," 22 Jan. 2021, *Deseret News*, deseret.com/utah/2021/1/22/22244734/concealed-carry-bill-gun-rights-legislature-concealed-weapons-ignites-debate-mental-health-crisis; *and*

McKay Coppins, "Bloomberg Report Takes Aim At Mormon Church For Online Gun Sales," 6 Feb. 2012, *Buzz Feed News*, Buzz Feed, buzzfeednews.com/article/mckaycoppins/bloomberg-report-takes-aim-at-mormon-church-for-on; *and*

Mya Jaradat, "Understanding America: Is there a connection between faith and firearms?" 3 Dec. 2020, *Deseret News*, deseret.com/indepth/2020/12/3/21455886/america-faith-firearms-gun-control-gun-rights-gun-violence-evangelical-christian-gun-policy; *and*

"Gun History Connected To Church History," *LDS Gunsite*, Reddpublishing, ldsgunsite.blogspot.com/p/john-browning.html.

[40] *See BOM*, 3 Nephi 28:38; *see also BOM*, 4 Nephi 1:44.

[41] *See* "Captain Moroni and the Title of Liberty," YouTube, 26 Dec. 2014, youtu.be/V106VTMRAN4?t=58.

[42] *See* "How can we become like the 2,000 stripling warriors and Captain Moroni?" *Gospel Lessons for LDS Members Attending Basic Training*, The Church of Jesus Christ of Latter-day Saints, abn.churchofjesuschrist.org/study/manual/gospel-lessons-for-lds-members-attending-basic-training/how-can-we-become-like-the-2000-stripling-warriors-and-captain-moroni?lang=eng.

[43] *See* "Most Republican States 2021," World Population Review, worldpopulationreview.com/state-rankings/most-republican-states.

A New American Scripture

We could fill many pages detailing *why* we included all the rest of the wars we presented in our narrative, each with its own purpose and intent. If readers are *really* interested, they will read our *Book of Mormon* and *The Sealed Portion*, incorporating the details and commentary provided in this book (*A New American Scripture*). The information we have provided here will allow the reader to make the connection to each war and its analogy to human nature.

We took each of the war scenarios from recorded history. If studied, a well-read historian will recognize the strategy and specific details of the wars we created for our story. We took most of them from what are recorded as the wars of the Great Roman Empire, as well as many of the wars that lasted throughout the centuries of medieval times.

As we further explain *why* we wrote our narrative the way that we did, we draw your attention to something else of great importance. Being forced to cater to the pride of the early American people, as well as the pride of the modern American people, we unfolded our story in a specific way. We purposefully presented situations in a way that *should* cause a reader to rethink who the heroes and the villains are in our story. It should be hard for the reader to justify the actions of some of our main characters, especially in light of our story being centered on Jesus Christ and what he taught the people.

Jesus would NEVER take up arms to hurt people, not even in defense of himself or others. Jesus would NEVER hurt another human being. Jesus would NEVER condemn a person for their religious beliefs, as long as their beliefs did not harm another.

We intended to show that the actions of people who did not center their lives on the *teachings* of Jesus Christ would ALWAYS lead to war and turmoil. Our story started out with a family that lived according to the law of Moses because they didn't have the "fulness of the everlasting Gospel of Jesus Christ" yet. We subtly introduced the idea that obeying the law of Moses ALWAYS led to war and turmoil.

Chapter 14: Wars and Rumors of Wars

Consider the beginning of our story when Lehi's son, Nephi, confronted his brothers and told them they were wicked. We gave no indication of what Nephi's brothers had done to cause them to be wicked, except for becoming upset that they were being called wicked by their father and younger brother. Nephi's brothers, Laman and Lemuel, were very upset that their father and younger brother started condemning them for what they believed. Laman and Lemuel believed and lived what their own father had taught them throughout their childhood and early adult lives.

These eldest sons did not want to leave their comfortable and secure homes in Jerusalem to go into the wilderness. They felt that they were doing everything that the Church of God wanted them to do. Thus, they argued with Nephi:

> Yea, he hath led us out of the land of Jerusalem, and we have wandered in the wilderness for these many years; and our women have toiled, being big with child; and they have borne children in the wilderness and suffered all things, save it were death; and it would have been better that they had died before they came out of Jerusalem than to have suffered these afflictions.
>
> Behold, these many years we have suffered in the wilderness, which time we might have enjoyed our possessions and the land of our inheritance; yea, and we might have been happy.
>
> And we know that the people who were in the land of Jerusalem were a righteous people; for they kept the statutes and judgments of the Lord, and all his commandments, according to the law of Moses; wherefore, we know that they are a righteous people; and our father hath judged them, and hath led us away because we would harken unto his words; yea, and our brother is like unto him.[44]

---

[44] *BOM*, 1 Nephi 17:20–2.

What if Lehi and Nephi had followed the words of Jesus Christ? Would they have condemned their sons and brothers? Why didn't Lehi have compassion and love for his eldest sons and allow them to remain in Jerusalem? Why would Lehi condemn his sons for being faithful and true to all that he had taught them from the law of Moses?

Because of the way that Laman and Lemuel were treated by their father and brother, their children rebelled against the Nephites and were responsible for most of the wars that took place between the Nephites and the Lamanites. If Laman and Lemuel and the sons of Ishmael (Lehi's friend) had been treated with respect and kindness and allowed to stay in the "land of their inheritance," would there have been any conflict or wars among the descendants of Lehi?

The brass plates (the Old Testament) contained the law of Moses that caused people to stumble. Why would it be that important to God that he would command someone to kill, deceive, and steal to obtain it? We needed to include these things in our narrative to show the world what religious fanaticism and adherence to corrupt religious beliefs (the law of Moses) would do to a people. If our story is read properly and according to what we would later present as the "fulness of the Gospel of Jesus Christ," NOTHING that Lehi and Nephi did helped the people to become of one heart and mind, where there was no poor among them. What Lehi and Nephi did actually caused the wars and contentions that would eventually lead to the annihilation (total destruction) of most of their descendants.

It was our desire to present a narrative that would not affect the free will of our targeted audience—the early European-Christian-American people. We knew how important the Bible was to the American people. The Bible (the brass plates of Laban that Nephi stole and murdered for) was the main cause of the problems between the Nephites and the Lamanites.

Chapter 14: Wars and Rumors of Wars

In more recent times, we had members of our peer review group contribute their opinions and comments on our *Book of Mormon*. One man in particular was able to finally see through what we were trying to do in our narrative. This man had studied the *Book of Mormon* for many years. He does not know how many times he read it and tried desperately to understand its great lessons. Finally, after we explained a few Real Truth™s to him about *why* and *how* we wrote the *Book of Mormon*, his blindness was removed. This man wrote:

> The arrogance and pride with which Nephi describes himself, performs his role through the next few dozen chapters and exercises power and authority over his brothers is sickening. It is not surprising why his older brothers murmured, rebelled, and became angry. Nephi's pride within himself, thinking he was favored and blessed by God to accomplish certain things, laid the foundation for the future wars between the Nephites and Lamanites.
>
> Both sides, Nephi on one hand and Laman and Lemuel on the other, were wrong. Over the course of centuries through the *Book of Mormon* stories, according to the precedent and example of Nephi, the Nephites quickly became self-righteous and holier-than-thou, while at the same time, the Lamanites, according to the precedent and examples of Laman and Lemuel, became vengeful, vindictive, and angry. These contrasting attitudes permeate the storyline of the wars in the *Book of Mormon* ... . For the most part, though, the Nephites' self-righteousness and the Lamanites' vengefulness, both of which are due to pride in themselves, are the cause of most of the wars throughout the *Book of Mormon*.[45]

This honest and sincere student of our new American scripture pointed out that, with a few exceptions, most of the wars between the

---
[45] Bret Powelson, written December 15, 2020.

A New American Scripture

Nephites and Lamanites were caused as a result of the backlash towards the white-skinned Nephites' self-righteousness. The other exceptions were greed, caused by the economic disparity of the people, and the political alliances made in secret that combined the political, religious, and economic powers that existed at that time.

In a previous chapter, we explained more about these *secret combinations*. We told the story of the Great Jaredite Nation and how these *secret combinations* caused the downfall of a once powerful and prosperous nation. We did not give a lot of detail in the *unsealed part* of our story about what these secret combinations were and how they started. We wanted to allow the Americans to establish these combinations of *excessive pride* and then experience the consequences of the way that Americans support and defend the things that give them their self-worth—the things that make them *conscious of their own dignity*.

By writing our new American scripture the way we did, allowing contrasting ideas to exist to represent that the "loftiness of the vineyard" caused no "tree in the vineyard" to produce good fruit, we wanted the American people to stumble, hoping they would learn from their mistakes.

We had hoped that the Americans would accept our new scripture and incorporate its lessons into their lives. We did not intend for the Americans to ignore how pride started and how these *secret combinations of pride* entered the hearts and minds of once little children, who grew to become "natural men, an enemy of God."

In Appendix 1 of this book, *The Sealed Portion* explains in detail how these issues began. Briefly, Adam and Eve's first son was not Cain. Their first son's name was *Beneli* (meaning "son of God" in Hebrew). Beneli's birth was the result of what actually took place in the Garden of Eden that caused Adam and Eve to fall. We presented a story that made sense, according to science. It did not follow that a serpent deceived Eve and told her to eat some forbidden fruit.

Eventually, starting with Beneli, all of Adam's children started dividing themselves into family units and hoarding their possessions. Beneli taught the people that it was a righteous thing to separate themselves into family units and stockpile material goods for the sake of their own family (i.e., food storage meant to sustain *only* their immediate family in time of need). Beneli is the mortal who first introduced the concept of money based on gold.

Eve prayed for a righteous child and had Cain; later, she had Abel. Abel confronted Beneli about what he was doing. Abel tried to explain how wrong it was to break up the human family into separate units and hoard things for the benefit of just these individual units (one's family). Beneli was very angry at being called out by Abel. Beneli conspired with Cain to kill Abel, convincing Cain that Abel was trying to destroy their happiness and limit the ability of Beneli's followers from being secure in their homes and possessions.

In the course of convincing Cain to kill Abel, the *secret combinations* of power and authority in politics, religion, and economics began. To gain a better understanding, we recommend that the reader review Appendix 1 of this book, as well as the preceding chapters of this book (*A New American Scripture*), which put the explanation of these secret doings in context.

Everything about the fall of humanity, and that which continues to cause all war and rumors of war, is in fulfillment of what we symbolically had *Lucifer* threaten in our 1842 play. However, our play gave clarity to *why* we included so many stories and subplots about war and misery in our new American scripture:

> Then with [the desire of a person to protect and support their self-worth and dignity, they] will take the treasures of the earth, and with gold and silver [they] will buy up armies and navies, popes and priests, and reign with blood and horror on the earth![46]

---

[46] *SNS*, 59.

Chapter 15
True Messengers

We, now known as the Real Illuminati®, are the only people on Earth who have the answers to humanity's problems. We are the only group that has advised and counseled public True Messengers. We work behind the scenes to inspire good things to happen on Earth. If humanity would consider our counsel and review what we reveal, we know that this information can lead the world to peace and salvation.

We wrote our new American scripture with the intent to inspire the early American people to establish a nation on the earth that would do right for ALL of humanity, not just for the citizens of the United States of America. We helped the United States establish itself as the most powerful nation on Earth. Without disclosing our true identities, we have been involved behind the scenes in motivating, inspiring, and subtly manipulating anyone whom we believed was engaged in accomplishing something that could benefit all of humanity.

Here is an example of how we work behind the scenes:

In many situations we befriend low-level employees who work for some of the world's most successful research organizations. Without the employee knowing of our purposes, we discuss with them what is happening at their work. We listen to the employee explain what their employers are working on, as well as some of the difficulties the company or organization might be experiencing in reaching a successful result on a certain project. If we know that the project would benefit all of humanity, we give information to the low-level employee that can solve a particular problem and help the project to succeed.

Chapter 15: True Messengers

As is the case with most great discoveries that have to do with technologies, only a few get the credit for what many others have done. Low-level employees, lab assistants, research students and others spend countless hours helping to develop these technologies; but only a few of their bosses take the credit. However, some of the most successful companies always listen to what their employees have to contribute (offer). This open communication can lead to the company's success.

As we have revealed, we were also successful at meeting with a few of the American Founding Fathers as they finalized the groundwork for the new government of the United States. We kept our identities secret, not wanting to draw attention to ourselves. We did everything we could to inspire as many of the American Founding Fathers as possible. We often found that these leaders were reluctant to listen to something new that they had never considered before because of their personal pride in their nation, religion, or economic status. We covered this pride and vanity in previous chapters. Religious belief was the main obstacle that we encountered with these men. We worked our best to ensure that *secularism* was firmly, legally, and powerfully inserted into government protocol and procedure. *Secularism* means separation of all government authority and power from religious influence, or at least arriving at an agreeable and fair consensus with those of religious persuasion.

We attempted to influence the American Founding Fathers who leaned more towards secularism—leaders like Thomas Jefferson, James Madison, Ethan Allen, and Thomas Paine, among others. Our goal was specifically to ensure that the new American government would not allow any religious views, practices, beliefs, or ideologies to overwhelmingly influence American government. However, in spite of our efforts behind the scenes, most of the men who were known as America's "Founding Fathers" were deeply religious Christians.[1] Furthermore, almost every government meeting was called to order by a Christian prayer invoking the Christian idea of God.[2] And as we have explained, in every instance, *Lucifer, the god of this world—excessive pride*—heard and answered each prayer.[3] The United States of America is a result of the excessive pride of its original founders.

The first draft of the new U.S. Constitution had no part that protected secularism.[4] If the U.S. Congress had wanted to pass a law that established Christianity as the new nation's only religion, Congress could have done so at that time. There was no constitutional law forbidding it. Congress could have enacted laws that were based on Bible references alone, if the majority voted for these laws. After the first Constitution was incorporated, it quickly became obvious to us that the religious views of the members of a Christian Congress were behind almost all of the proposed bills aimed at becoming laws. We saw what was taking place and worked at every angle within our power to stop this from happening.

The Bill of Rights[5] was finally accepted and became the rule of law. The incorporation of these important human rights as the First Amendment somewhat mitigated (lessened) the problem of religion taking over government. The original U.S. Constitution was amended so that Congress

---

[1] *See* David L. Holmes, "The Founding Fathers, Deism, and Christianity," *Encyclopedia Britannica*, found online at britannica.com/topic/The-Founding-Fathers-Deism-and-Christianity-1272214.

[2] *See* Chad West, "Legislative Prayer: Historical Tradition and Contemporary Issues," *Utah Law Review* vol. 2019 no. 3, 709–34; found online at dc.law.utah.edu/cgi/viewcontent.cgi?article=1214&context=ulr.

[3] *SNS*, 87.

[4] *See* "The First Draft," in "Constitution of the United States—A History," National Archives, archives.gov/founding-docs/more-perfect-union.

[5] *See* "United States Bill of Rights," *Wikipedia*, Wikimedia Foundation, 28 May 2021, en.wikipedia.org/wiki/United_States_Bill_of_Rights.

would be forbidden by law to "make [any] law respecting the establishment of religion, or prohibiting the free exercise thereof."[6]

Jefferson, Madison, Allen, and Paine, among just a few others, wanted the law to be more constricting on religious influence over government. They argued that when a person was elected to represent the people, that person should not exercise their personal religious beliefs in any manner. These men argued for their version of the first amendment to the U.S. Constitution. Madison proposed the amendment to express that NO Representative in Congress, NOR President elected to the Executive Branch, NOR a person of the Judicial Branch, shall exercise a personal religious belief or idea in the exercising of the power given to each Branch.[7]

This constitutional amendment should have ended all prayers offered to open up government meetings. However, these more secular-leaning leaders failed to convince the majority that its religious views and beliefs were not important when it came to governing people with fairness and equity. Although the compromise agreed to is in the current U.S. Constitution as its First Amendment, this amendment proved very weak in establishing a strong separation of government authority and religious persuasion.

As a consequence of its weakness, all sessions of Congress and of the Supreme Court still begin by invoking God through a prayer or a statement about God.[8] United States politicians make the frail argument that showing

---

[6] *See* "Amendment I," in "The Bill of Rights: A Transcription," National Archives, archives.gov/founding-docs/bill-of-rights-transcript.

[7] *See* James H. Read, "James Madison," in *The First Amendment Encyclopedia: Presented by the John Seigenthaler Chair of Excellence in First Amendment Studies*, 2009, Middle Tennessee State University, mtsu.edu/first-amendment/article/1220/james-madison.

[8] Offering this opening prayer is part of the duties of the Chaplain of the United States Senate, and the Chaplain of the United States House of Representatives. *See* "Chaplain of the United States Senate," *Wikipedia*, Wikimedia Foundation, 13 Feb. 2021, en.wikipedia.org/wiki/Chaplain_of_the_United_States_Senate; *and*

faith in and asking for the help of "God as Sovereign Lord of our Nation," does not violate the law. They argue that separation of *Church* and State is not the same as separation of *God* and State.⁹

On June 1, 2020, sitting U.S. President Donald J. Trump walked from the White House to the nearby St. John's Episcopal Church and held up a Bible for the cameras covering the event for all the world to see.¹⁰ Many have speculated as to why Trump did this. We need not add to speculation and unsubstantiated opinion. We need only point out that the laws for the United States of America have been established according to the U.S. Constitution for over 200 years. It was even amended to separate church and state. Yet after all of this, religion still persists and is very significant and important in the minds and hearts of the American people today (circa 2020).

We would not have had to write our new American scripture if the United States government had actually been established with a strict, legal, and powerful separation of government and religion. We hoped that the government would have granted and protected by law the right and ability of the individual to believe whatever the individual wanted, without having religion in any way related to government authority. The American people rejected the notion of absolute secularism (a political system that rejects all forms of religious faith and worship). Therefore, we were forced to write the storyline of our new American scripture to include examples of a government that was not separated from religion and one that was.

There is no way that our work could have proceeded without a *known* public representative. We need one who is chosen, not to hide as we do, but to deliver our message to the world and confront the world for its hypocrisy

---

"Chaplain of the United States House of Representatives," *Wikipedia*, Wikimedia Foundation, 5 May 2021, en.wikipedia.org/wiki/Chaplain_of_the_United_States_House_of_Representatives.

⁹ *See* AFA attorneys on freedom of religious expression Q & A, in "The state of Church and State," *AFA Journal* (July 2001), afajournal.org/past-issues/2001/july/the-state-of-church-and-state.

¹⁰ *See* "Donald Trump photo op at St. John's Church," *Wikipedia*, Wikimedia Foundation, 20 Dec. 2020, en.wikipedia.org/wiki/Donald_Trump_photo_op_at_St._John%27s_Church.

Chapter 15: True Messengers

and corruption. We designate these public representatives as our "True Messengers." So that there is no confusion or conflict in delivering our message and helping us in our work, we have never chosen and recruited more than one True Messenger at a time. Throughout the entire history of humanity, throughout all dispensations of time, there has only been ONE chosen True Messenger at any given time who sacrifices his life for our cause. Again, let us reiterate *our cause* as found on our website:

> One of the world's definitions presents an agreeable undertone to the purpose of our secretive group:
>
> *"The society's goals are to oppose superstition, obscurantism, religious influence over public life, and the abuses of state power. Our intent is to put an end to the machinations of the purveyors of injustice, to control them without dominating them."*[11]

We do not make ourselves known to the world. We work behind the scenes as we have explained. The reason for this is that every one of our chosen public True Messengers has been killed by the people to whom he was sent to deliver our message, without exception. We do not plan to be killed ourselves. If all the members of our group were killed, there would no longer be a group of people fighting for *our cause*.

To protect our current chosen True Messenger, we instructed him to "flee into the wilderness" away from society. Only if a True Messenger isolates himself from the rest of the world can his life be protected. We protect him in instances when we see the need for a public representative. Otherwise, when we see that the people of the world have no intention, desire, or interest in doing the right thing, we allow our True Messenger to be killed. His death is a witness to the corruptness of the world. Our True Messengers teach nothing

---

[11] *See* "About Us - The Real Illuminati®," The Real Illuminati®, realilluminati.org/about-us. For the definition, *see* Richard van Dülmen, *The Society of Enlightenment: the rise of the middle class and Enlightenment culture in Germany* (Polity Press: 1992) p. 110.

but things that are meant to help humanity. None of them has ever taught anything that would not benefit all people living upon the earth, if heeded. But because what we teach confronts the powers that control humanity, condemning these powers because of the personal gain taken by these leaders, the secret combinations of political, religious, and business entities are the main instigators in the deaths of our True Messengers.

In the early nineteenth (19th) century, the American people were not ready for our message. They rejected our new American scripture. We allowed them to murder our True Messenger, Joseph Smith, Jr. However, Joseph was not allowed to "disclose his true identity," or rather, tell the people the Real Truth™.[12] Had he tried, the people (even his own followers), would have risen up and killed him sooner than they did.[13] Because nothing that we were trying to accomplish for the early Americans had any success, we withdrew from our True Messenger and allowed him to be killed as a testimony of the wickedness of the American people—the "Gentiles" whom we condemned throughout our new American scripture.[14]

Two hundred (200) years after the U.S. Constitution was first ratified, we became aware that there was another man being prepared to help us. On June 16, 1987,[15] our contemporary (modern) True Messenger—whom we have now isolated away from society to protect him—went through the *two phases* of becoming a True Messenger. To explain the phases that a person must go through in order to become a True Messenger involved with our case, we incorporated these two phases into our new American scripture's narrative.

We introduced our story's characters as the descendants of two family units: Lehi's family and Ishmael's family. In our revised narrative, Lehi was the first True Messenger we introduced. Lehi held a prominent position in the

---

[12] See *SNS*, 95–8; and *JS Bio*, 22–3.
[13] See *JS Bio*, 207.
[14] See *JS Bio*, 443–4.
[15] See *TSP*, 584–6.

city of Jerusalem. He was a High Priest. The Jews had no separation of church and state. Every aspect of law and authority was based on the law of Moses. The High Priests were the law administrators (the General Authorities) and also held absolute authority in government. As most modern-day LDS/Mormon Church General Authorities, the High Priests in our story were wealthy men who had many possessions. Lehi had "gold, silver, precious things and property that was exceedingly great."[16]

In our original storyline (the 116-page "lost" manuscript), Lehi listened to the words of two True Messengers (or in religious terms: *true prophets of God*), Zenos and Zenock. Zenos was the ONE True Messenger appointed. Zenock was called as Zenos' companion. This unique relationship between an appointed True Messenger—called one at a time—and a companion was reiterated in the later story of Alma and Amulek.[17] These two prophets convinced Lehi that the church (religion) and state (government) of the Jews were both corrupt and evil. Another member of the High Priesthood, Ishmael, was also convinced by Zenos and Zenock, but did not act on what he knew was the truth about the church and state that were established in ancient Jerusalem.

Lehi acted upon his feelings. He attempted to save the lives of the prophets who were sent to Jerusalem to tell the people about their wickedness and their abominations. When he failed to protect them, Lehi left his position in the established priesthood body and went home in anguish and turmoil.

Being in anguish and turmoil is the first step—the *first phase*—in becoming a True Messenger. This is a sorrow that takes place in the heart. It is what we refer to as a *broken heart and a contrite spirit*. People must open their heart to the possibility that everything that they are doing, everything that they have done, and everything that they believe is true and good, is not. This psychological realization causes people to completely open their minds,

---

[16] *See BOM*, 1 Nephi 3:24–5.
[17] *See BOM*, Alma 8:18–22.

so that whatever happens next, whatever enters into their thoughts, can pass through the filters of prejudice and belief that had closed their mind, blinded their eyes, and hardened their heart.

Joseph Smith, Jr. and our contemporary True Messenger both experienced this anguish and turmoil ("sorrowed in their hearts") before they were able to open up their minds sufficiently enough to allow the *next phase* of becoming a True Messenger to take place. The *second phase* is having an "illuminating" experience that is not allowed to happen to any mortal unless the person has been specifically chosen, but ONLY to help all of humanity in some way.

We described this *second phase* in our new American scripture as an experience that happened to three of our story's characters, who were identified in the narrative as the *Three Nephites*. These Three (representative of three of us—the Real Illuminati®) went through the *first phase* required to become a True Messenger: "And they sorrowed in their hearts"; and then the *second phase:*

> And behold, the heavens were opened, and they were caught up into heaven, and saw and heard unspeakable things. And it was forbidden them that they should utter; neither was it given unto them power that they could utter the things which they saw and heard; And whether they were in the body or out of the body, they could not tell; for it did seem unto them like a transfiguration of them, that they were changed from this body of flesh into an immortal state, that they could behold the things of God.[18]

What happens during this *second phase* is that the person's mind immediately begins to perceive the Real Truth™—things as they *really* are, as they *really* were, and as they *really* will be. Next in our story's subplot, we introduced how True Messengers are selected. At this point, we explain what it

---

[18] *BOM*, 3 Nephi 28:5, 13–15.

Chapter 15: True Messengers

means when a True Messenger does not disclose his true identity. There are strict mandates that are given to True Messengers about what they know and what they can teach to the rest of the world. About the *Three Nephites*, we wrote:

> But it came to pass that they did again minister upon the face of the earth; nevertheless they did not minister of the things which they had heard and seen, because of the commandment which was given them in heaven.[19]

We have continually mentioned a play that we helped Joseph write in 1842. This play symbolically presents, through acts and actors, many of the "mysteries of God" (i.e., Real Truth™) that Joseph was not allowed to tell the world. In this play, we presented True Messengers as a group of *three*,[20] hoping those who read our book would make the connection between these characters in the play and the *Three* Nephites in the storyline of our new American scripture. The religion that hijacked our book and is using it to deceive people into joining their church completely ignores what our story presents about what we are doing. They thus negate any connection at all with the *Three Nephites*, or with *John the Beloved*, who is also mentioned in our new American scripture in conjunction with the *Three Nephites*.

We made it clear, according to the story, that we couldn't be killed, and would continue on Earth doing

> great and marvelous works … Yea even among the Gentiles shall there be a great and marvelous work wrought by us; that we will be among the Gentiles, and the Gentiles shall know us not. We will also be among the Jews, and the Jews shall know us not; that the powers of the earth cannot hold us.[21]

---

[19] *BOM*, 3 Nephi 28:16.
[20] Represented in the play as "Peter, James, and John."
[21] *Compare BOM*, 3 Nephi, chapter 28, esp. verses 27–39.

These powers are the secret combinations of politicians, religious leaders, and business owners, whose power and control over the world are threatened by our Marvelous Work and a Wonder®.

When it comes to what we do and what we ask of our public True Messengers, there are no miracles or supernatural interventions that take place. Everything that we do is done according to the laws of nature that control any act performed by <u>any</u> person living upon this earth. What we have that no others have, is a proper intelligence of all things: a knowledge of things as they are, as they were, and as they are to come.

In the first book of our Trilogy, *The True History of Religion*, we mentioned *Inpendius*.[22] He was our first (1st) century B.C.E. True Messenger living in the area of Palestine in the Roman Empire. We wrote that he performed "miracles" that the people of that time perceived as supernatural power. For example, one of his friends had a simple heart attack and stopped breathing. Inpendius performed CPR (cardiopulmonary resuscitation) and brought his friend back to life. This is a very simple procedure that has saved many lives since it was first discovered and widely used about 60 years before the writing of this book (in 1960). It is no longer perceived as a miracle when one gives the "breath of life" to another and brings the dead back to life.

Many people are convinced that there exists a force (a god) that can perform acts beyond scientific understanding or the laws of nature (things that common sense cannot explain). Therefore, whenever we have had an appointed True Messenger claiming to be a true prophet of a god (a supernatural force or entity), the people demand a miracle according to their perception of what a miracle is.

We addressed this in our 1842 play. The character who portrays a *Preacher* in our *original* play was told by *Lucifer*, the character that represents pride and vanity, that

---

[22] *See THOR*, 124–43.

we should never have any [True Messengers], but if any should come professing to be [a True Messenger, you are] to ask them to cut off an arm or some other member of the body and then restore it, so that the people might know that they came with power.[23]

We wrote a detailed explanation for the LDS/Mormon people who watch our play every day, but have no idea what it means. In this book (*Sacred, not Secret—The [Authorized and] Official Guide In Understanding the LDS Temple Endowment*, pub. 2008), we mention the type of "miracles" we actually perform as True Messengers. We gave an explanation according to the beliefs of these LDS/Mormon people:

> The religions of the world perceive a "*great miracle*" as some supernatural intervention in healing, or any supplementary task, the accomplishment of which they cannot understand. Lucifer's instruction is to not believe anyone proclaiming the truth unless they can show forth such a miracle. However, the *miracle of truth* is not in magic, but rather in transformation. Real truth™ is intended to show people all things as they were, are, and are to come, so that they are brought to a state of understanding, thereby eliminating "miracles" as we think of them. No miracle would be considered as such if one understood how it was performed; the miracle therefore remains in the mystery of how it is performed. True messengers who *disclose their true identity* will not speak in parables as Jesus did; they will perform nothing that is not understood ("miracles") in order to capture the attention of potential followers. In fact, they are not looking for followers at all—but rather, speak truth in such manner that those looking for it may find *them*. They will not be wearing an "*apron ... of their priesthood*," say anything that is confusing, or charge people money for the truth. Everything they say will make perfect sense.

---

[23] *SNS*, 116–17. Read for free at realilluminati.org/sacred-not-secret.

The "*miracle*" a *true messenger* of the Father demonstrates is the figurative healing of *the blind who do not see and the deaf who do not hear*. In other words, they remove the stumbling blocks so that people do not stumble in their efforts to understand *real truth*. There is no religious leader on this earth who can do this. It can only be done by *true messengers* whose teachings oppose the **God of This Earth [i.e., Lucifer, ego and pride]**.[24]

In the above excerpts from our explanation of our 1842 play, we mentioned "true messengers who disclose their true identity." At another part in the play, the True Messengers receive specific instructions from *Elohim through Jehovah*—two significant characters that represent the Godhead—but who have NOTHING to do with the "man Adam in the Telestial world" (i.e., Earth). The True Messengers are told that they should deal with mortals "without disclosing their identity" (i.e., without telling the people the Real Truth™).[25]

True Messengers can only deal with the people according to the people's desire to change their actions and seek for understanding of things as they *really* are, and as they *really* have been. If people remain in their stiffneckedness (pride) and blindness and hardness of heart (closed mind), there is nothing that a True Messenger can do to help society.

Sadly, there are very few people who are humble enough to admit that what they believe to be true, is not. The most hard-hearted are religious people who believe that their church is the "only true church on Earth," and that they are righteous because they follow the counsel and instruction of their appointed General Authorities.

---

[24] *SNS*, 112–13. Read for free at realilluminati.org/sacred-not-secret.
[25] *See SNS*, 94–5.

Chapter 15: True Messengers

In our story, after Lehi experienced a "great ... anguish for the sins of the people,"[26] thus completing the *first phase* of becoming a True Messenger, he went home and experienced the *second phase*, where "he was carried away in a vision, even that he saw the heavens open."[27] Lehi then did his best to teach the people about their sins:

> And it came to pass that the Jews did mock him because of the things which he testified of them; for he truly testified of their wickedness and their abominations.[28]

True Messengers tell the world that it is wicked. These messengers are hated, hunted, and killed because of what they say about people who think of themselves as righteous. If a True Messenger didn't make a lot of sense, his message would be ignored. Because what a True Messenger says makes so much sense, the only way that the leaders of a deceived world can act is in anger to kill the True Messenger in order to silence him.

We sent our contemporary True Messenger to the General Authorities of the Church of Jesus Christ of Latter-day Saints. He offered to these leaders our exclusive help in introducing the *sealed part* of our gold plates, as prophesied in our new American scripture. These leaders refused and mocked our messenger.[29] They mocked him "because of the things which he testified of them; for he truly testified of their wickedness and their abominations."

Our True Messenger was a member of the LDS Church and was cast out because he could no longer ascribe to the wickedness that he beheld. It was what he saw and witnessed as a security officer employed by this church, behind the scenes, that led him to becoming a True Messenger. He

---

[26] *TSP*, Lehi 2:59.
[27] *BOM*, 1 Nephi 1:8.
[28] *BOM*, 1 Nephi 1:19.
[29] See Christopher's words in *The Sealed Portion*, 594–7. Read free at realilluminati.org/the-sealed-portion.

attempted to tell other members how far off course this church was. Their response was the same as Lehi's oldest sons, Laman and Lemuel, in our story. These two sons believed

> that the people who were in the land of Jerusalem were a righteous people; for they kept the statutes and judgments of the Lord, and all his commandments, according to the law of Moses; wherefore, we know that they are a righteous people; and our father hath judged them, and hath led us away because we would hearken unto his words; yea, and our brother is like unto him.[30]

This sibling rivalry among the sons of Lehi eventually led to the development of two separate societies of Lehi's descendants: those who followed his son Nephi (Nephites), and those who followed his other son Laman (Lamanites). Laman taught his children that Nephi stole the right of government from him—the one who *should* have been given their father's blessing and birthright, according to tradition.

Similar to how Lehi's rebellious sons thought that their church was righteous and true, the modern LDS/Mormon people do not see themselves as wicked. In fact, they see themselves as God's ONLY chosen people—as "Saturday's Warriors"[31]—as the ONLY elect group of people meant for the latter days as an ensign and example of righteousness to the rest of the world. They believe this about themselves and their church because they keep the "statutes and judgments of the Lord," and all of his commandments—according to what their church leaders teach them—ALL of which is an abomination to God, as we have explained throughout the narrative of our new American scripture.

---

[30] *BOM*, 1 Nephi 17:22.
[31] Referring to the musical Saturday's Warrior, *see* "Saturday's Warrior," *Wikipedia*, Wikimedia Foundation, 16 Apr. 2021, en.wikipedia.org/wiki/Saturday%27s_Warrior.

Chapter 15: True Messengers

All of our True Messengers have a "perfect love" for humanity. It is this love that motivates them to sacrifice their own lives and face persecution and threats in order to help us save humanity. However, the world does not see their "speak[ing] with boldness, having authority from God"[32] as love. The people of the world condemn True Messengers for condemning the world's sins. The world hates them because of the hate that True Messengers have, not for the *people* of the world, but for *what the people of the world do*. The world persecutes them. And if we did not protect them by having them "flee into the wilderness," the world would find a way to kill them in order to silence them.

We have explained throughout this book how deceived the Church of Jesus Christ of Latter-day Saints is when it comes to what it does, compared to what our *Book of Mormon* tells it to do. This is the same church to which our contemporary True Messenger belonged for twenty-five years of his life. Allegorically, the events in this True Messenger's life follow the same as the story of Lehi. In our new American scripture, we tried our best to make it clear what the wickedness and abominations of the Hebrew Church were. Our contemporary True Messenger also tried his best, but like Lehi's eldest sons, our True Messenger's two older brothers, along with the members of the LDS Church, believe that they are righteous, and cannot be convinced to the contrary. (It is well to note that the younger brother of our modern True Messenger supports his older brother very similar to how our story's character, Sam, protected and supported Nephi.)

As our story proceeded with Lehi's descendants making their way over to the Western Hemisphere, we made the distinction between state (government) authority and church (religious) authority. We invented subplots to our narrative that presented both situations—one where the government and religion were one and the same; and one where they were separated.

---

[32] *BOM*, Moroni 8:16.

A New American Scripture

Lehi's son, Nephi, was not a chosen True Messenger like his father. For this reason, we have Nephi "desiring to know the things that his father had seen."[33] If Nephi had been a True Messenger, he would have gained an understanding on his own. It was not Nephi's role to preach repentance to the Church at Jerusalem. Nephi, however, was chosen over his elder brothers to be a governing leader because of his faith in what their father, a True Messenger, had taught them.

Our story explained that Lehi tried to teach his sons about what was going to happen when they reached the Western Hemisphere, "the land of promise," *if* his sons didn't do the right things. After Nephi had an understanding of his father's message, he explained how the native Americans came to be, all of whom were dark-skinned. He explained how the "Gentiles" (the North Americans) would be tasked with helping ALL native Americans living in the Western Hemisphere to prosper in the "land of promise" and establish a "new" Jerusalem where the people could become "Zion" (a people of one heart and one mind, who have no poor among them).

As we have explained, we used the prophecies given in the Bible's book of Isaiah to present to and convince the early Americans (the "Gentiles") of their important role. They were supposed to establish a great nation where the native Americans could be "nourished and carried upon the shoulders" of the "Gentiles." With the example of this great nation, the fullness of the everlasting Gospel of Jesus Christ (the *saving* code of humanity) could then be spread throughout the entire Earth.

Using the words of Isaiah, we hoped to inspire the Americans (the "Gentiles") to help humanity, by first establishing the right form of government that would

> set up my standard to the people; and [the Americans] shall bring [the native Americans] in their arms, and [the native Americans]

---

[33] *Compare BOM*, 1 Nephi 11:1.

shall be carried upon their shoulders. And kings [the government of the United States of America] shall be thy nursing fathers, and their queens thy nursing mothers.[34]

This "standard" should have been established by the U.S. Constitution. It was not. Therefore, in the narrative of our new American scripture, we had Nephi's brothers ask him for an explanation that would clarify what Isaiah's words meant. We invented an interpretation of the words of Isaiah, as they are presented in the Bible, to meet the expectations of our "marvelous work among the Gentiles, which [we hoped would have been] of great worth unto [the native Americans]."[35]

We explained that "these things of which are spoken are temporal"[36] (relating to ordinary practical life rather than religious matters). It was our expectation and hope that the Americans would help the native Americans, not just spiritually, but temporally—helping the native Americans in issues related to worldly matters as opposed to only spiritual affairs. These worldly matters are the *basic necessities of life*.[37] We put in our story what is required of one who has wealth:

> to do good—clothe the naked, and to feed the hungry, and to liberate the captive, and administer relief to the sick and the afflicted.[38]

As we have explained, before we intervened in 2004 and began to point out the great hypocrisy of the very wealthy church that carried our *Book of Mormon* to all of the world, this church had three main missions: 1) proclaim the gospel (and baptize people into the church); 2) perfect

---

[34] *Compare BOM*, 1 Nephi 21:22–3.
[35] *Compare BOM*, 1 Nephi 22:8.
[36] *BOM*, 1 Nephi 22:6.
[37] *See* "5 Basic Necessities of Life," The Humanity Party®, humanityparty.com/5-basic-necessities-of-life.
[38] *BOM*, Jacob 2:19.

the Saints; and 3) redeem the dead (do vicarious temple work).[39] This church's mission statement did not include a provision for taking care of the poor until AFTER some of the leaders were confronted by Ida Smith with our information (2009).[40]

As we showed throughout the storyline of our new American scripture, the people of the established churches focused more on spiritual matters than they did on temporal matters (food, clothing, shelter, etc.). This always led to the church becoming wicked because the people failed to take care of those in need. It is when a church becomes wicked that a True Messenger becomes necessary and is sent to call the members and leaders of the church to repentance.

After his older brothers separated themselves from him, Nephi became the first king and appointed his younger brother, Jacob, as the spiritual leader. There was a complete separation between church and state at that time. The people began to prosper under a strong government; but, in becoming prosperous, they began to do things that were "abominable unto him who created all flesh."[41] The people became prideful because of spiritual matters. They believed that their prosperity came because they were a blessed and chosen people of God, even though they had forgotten about the *temporal* matters—economic equality for <u>all</u> people.

Before his death, Nephi appointed another man to be king. The government continued to be separated from religion. But then we presented a subplot that told of the people having the same person as their king as their religious leader. This led to a part of our story in which we introduced the wicked King Noah, who was also the authority that controlled the Church. The people's religious institution was under the authority of a group of High

---

[39] *See* Spencer W. Kimball, "A Report of My Stewardship," *Ensign* (May 1981), 5, churchofjesuschrist.org/study/ensign/1981/05/a-report-of-my-stewardship?lang=eng.

[40] *See JS Bio*, 694–6, n. 12–13. Read free at realilluminati.org/without-disclosing-my-true-identity. *See also* "Four-fold Mission of the Church," *MormonWiki*, 21 Sept. 2020, mormonwiki.com/Four-fold_Mission_of_the_Church.

[41] *See BOM*, Jacob 2:20–1.

Chapter 15: True Messengers

Priests, with King Noah being the highest religious authority of all. The next True Messenger we wrote a subplot about, Abinadi, was sent to the people under the reign of King Noah.

Because there was no separation between church and state, the Nephites became wicked under King Noah's reign. Understanding the subplot of King Noah is very important in understanding how we set up the stories of our new American scripture to reflect the reality of human nature and to teach the lessons we wanted the American people to learn.

The story of King Noah told of a white race of people who had the law of Moses (from the brass plates—the Bible's Old Testament). By ONLY following that religion, they began to prosper; but then they became very wicked.

To contrast what happened to the people of King Noah, we incorporated a subplot about the people of King Benjamin. King Benjamin introduced Jesus Christ and made Jesus' name (the works he did in the flesh) the uniting order of the religion that the people followed. Although the people of King Benjamin continued to observe the law of Moses, their hearts were fixed on the *higher law of Jesus Christ*. To properly explain more about this contrast and the lessons we intended the American Christians to learn, we need to carefully and simplistically outline how the groups of Nephites (white-skinned) and Lamanites (darker-skinned) became separated and what happened after the separation, according to our new American scripture's intended narrative.

The stories that we created for our new American scripture portrayed what would happen to the Americans who made the *Book of Mormon* (the lesser part) their main "word of God," but paid no attention to the "higher law" given in the "greater portion of the word"— *The Sealed Portion*. As the story about King Noah and his people is told, a direct correlation to Brigham Young and his people can be made—and is uncanny (to the honest reader), to say the least.

However, to us it is no mystery that human nature is, was, and will always be what it is. It is easy to invent stories that follow the course of history and invent prophecies that we know will be fulfilled, because human nature doesn't change and often repeats itself. What happened in Joseph Smith's day and what followed after his murder retold the history that we invented for our new American scripture.

Brigham Young was a modern-day King Noah in almost every way. How Young became the king of the Mormons living in Utah is similar to how Noah became the king of the Nephites living in Shilom. King Noah became king after his people fled persecution into the wilderness. Young became "king" after he fled across the plains from the persecution that the early Mormons were experiencing in Nauvoo.

The events in our story reflected how the early Mormons would flee from one city to another in search of a place where they could live their religion. They wanted to set up a righteous society where their people could dwell in peace, equity, and harmony with the rest of the world. But what the modern LDS/Mormons fail to realize or accept of their history is that the true cause of their (the early Latter-day Saints) many failings was *their own wickedness.*

One part of our story explained how the American Civil War could happen. We gave an example of how a united group of people, of the same family units, of the same race, could start a war in which "father fought against father, and brother against brother."[42] We could rewrite our new American scripture and replace the names, places, and events with those of the early American people. If we did, the narrative would remain the same and result in the same outcome.

Lehi and his family arrived in the Western Hemisphere. We intended for the reader to recognize the south part of South America on its western

---

[42] *BOM*, Mosiah 9:2.

Chapter 15: True Messengers

coast (where the modern nation of Peru exists), as the place that Lehi, Ishmael, and their families first arrived, traveling "eastward [from Jerusalem]." We called this first area and city "the land of Lehi-Nephi."

It is very important to note here that we made Jesus Christ the focus of our story. Because our story was about a people who lived 600 years *before* Jesus lived, we had to use prophecies and visions of the future to present the concept of Jesus as the world's only Savior. Because Christians are made to believe that the words of Isaiah contain prophecies about Jesus, we used Isaiah as the source of our new American scripture's prophesying.

We incorporated the King James Version of Isaiah, chapters 1 through 14, word for word in our new American scripture. We chose chapter 14 of Isaiah to finish our interpolation (inserting it into our new American scripture), solely because of how it ends:

> What shall then answer the messengers of the nations? That the
> Lord hath founded Zion, and the poor of his people shall trust in it.[43]

We've explained how Joseph's peer review group had a problem with the way that we started our original storyline because it condemned organized religion and ALL religious ordinance work. Those people could not understand how organized churches that speak of Christ could be bad for society. In the first part, as we originally wrote it, we began quoting the words of Isaiah (chapter 1) from "the brass plates" (our story's Old Testament). However, as we have already explained and reiterated many times, we then had to rewrite the beginning of our story because of the early Americans' pride in being American Christians.

Nevertheless, if one reads our new American scripture with a sincere heart and a real intent to learn the lessons that we intended to teach, one will clearly recognize our original intent. It will become apparent to the reader

---

[43] *BOM*, 2 Nephi 24:32.

that organized religion, in all of its forms, with all of its priesthoods, powers, rituals, ordinances, assemblies, etc., is one of the main causes of the pride of the people, which then results in the downfall of human society.

We have explained that excessive pride is the main cause of the problems that humanity faces. If one were to use modern technology and word-search the words "pride" and "proud," and read the mention of these words in context of the story in which we used each word (in the *Book of Mormon*), the downfall of humanity would be revealed. Again, any time we mention in our writings the devil, or any other title by which people associate "evilness," these words could be replaced with "pride and vanity," where "vanity" is excessive pride.

In our narrative, we reflected on the Bible story where Moses told the Israelites they didn't need *him* in order to speak to and receive direction from God—they could speak with God themselves. The people refused. God got angry and gave the people the "lower law," which is reflected in the ordinances and rituals that the priests and leaders of all organized religions demand of their members.

These perfunctory (routine) practices cause the people to focus more on performing the acts than on treating other people respectfully, equally, and harmoniously. Like the modern LDS/Mormon people, the ancient Israelites believed that they were the only chosen people of God, and that all others were not—only the Israelites had the saving ordinances according to how these practices were administered to the members by priesthood authority. We made it clear that if the people had been given the "higher law," they would not be doing any ordinances at all—that the basis of the "higher law" is loving oneself and loving one's neighbor as one loves oneself.

In our story, we made a distinct difference between the law of Moses and the teachings of Jesus. Yet, we connected them in a way that would make the reader believe that it was okay to perform church-mandated ordinances, as long as they observed the words of Christ and made his

Chapter 15: True Messengers

words of a more important focus. Again, we had to do this because of how the first readers (peer reviewers) of our story resisted our condemnation of organized religion.

While we used a few more of the words of Isaiah in other parts of our storyline, our main emphasis had been on Isaiah, chapters 1 through 14. We made sure to end this highlight by focusing on Isaiah's words that mentioned the "messengers of the nations." His message centered on the establishment of "Zion," creating a society of people "of one heart and one mind, and … no poor among them." <u>The *true message* of Jesus Christ always focuses on this.</u>

The American people, as well as all Christians, Jews, and Muslims throughout the world, love their scriptures. They have been grossly deceived into believing that their written scripture is the infallible word of God. They believe if others do not ascribe to the God of Abraham, Isaac, and Jacob (Israel) and perform the rituals, acts, and commandments mentioned in their scriptures, that these others are sinners, blasphemers, and infidels. It was our desire to change this mindset. We wanted to prove the law of Moses is a "dead law" that is not important to salvation.

We also wanted to teach that the words of Jesus Christ—the simple things Jesus taught the people to do while he was among them—were the way to life and salvation. Jesus' words were all about how we treat ourselves and each other. Christians, Jews, and Muslims are

> a stiffnecked (prideful) people; wherefore, we write plainly unto you, that ye cannot misunderstand. And the words which we have written shall stand as a testimony against you; for the words of our new American scripture are sufficient to teach any man the right way.[44]

---

[44] *Compare BOM*, 2 Nephi 25:28.

Consider how we presented the law of Moses in contrast to the ideology of Christ without offending any of the Bible believers. Consider how "we labor[ed] diligently" to write our new American scripture:

> For we labor diligently to write, to persuade our children, and also our brethren, to believe in Christ, and to be reconciled to God; for we know that it is by grace that we are saved, after all we can do.
>
> And, notwithstanding we believe in Christ, we keep the law of Moses, and look forward with steadfastness unto Christ, until the law shall be fulfilled.
>
> For, for this end was the law given; wherefore the law hath become dead unto us, and we are made alive in Christ because of our faith; yet we keep the law because of the commandments.
>
> And we talk of Christ, we rejoice in Christ, we preach of Christ, we prophesy of Christ, and we write according to our prophecies, that our children may know to what source they may look for a remission of their sins.
>
> Wherefore, we speak concerning the law that our children may know the deadness of the law; and they, by knowing the deadness of the law, may look forward unto that life which is in Christ, and know for what end the law was given. And after the law is fulfilled in Christ, that they need not harden their hearts against him when the law ought to be done away.
>
> And now behold, my people, ye are a stiffnecked people; wherefore, I have spoken plainly unto you, that ye cannot misunderstand. And the words which I have spoken shall stand as a testimony against you; for they are sufficient to teach any man the right way; for the right way is to believe in Christ and deny him not; for by denying him ye also deny the prophets and the law.

Chapter 15: True Messengers

> And now behold, I say unto you that the right way is to believe in Christ, and deny him not; and Christ is the Holy One of Israel; wherefore ye must bow down before him, and worship him with all your might, mind, and strength, and your whole soul; and if ye do this ye shall in nowise be cast out.
>
> And, inasmuch as it shall be expedient, ye must keep the performances and ordinances of God until the law shall be fulfilled which was given unto Moses.[45]

The law of "performances and ordinances" ended when Jesus came to the people and told them how to treat each other. In the next chapter, we will discuss these things—this way of life and salvation that a society must follow in order to succeed. We will show how, immediately after Jesus had taught the people EVERYTHING that they needed to do—how they needed to treat each other—the people still

> marveled, and wondered what he would concerning the law of Moses; for they understood not the saying that old things had passed away, and that all things had become new.[46]

This caused Jesus to "groan within himself, and say: Father, I am troubled because of the wickedness of the people of the house of Israel."[47]

Before he died, Lehi blessed his posterity and admonished them to follow Nephi. Lehi specifically spoke to his oldest sons, Laman and Lemuel, and told them that if they would "hearken unto the voice of Nephi [they should] not perish." Lehi tried to convince his older sons that Nephi was not trying to seek "for power nor authority over you, but he hath sought the glory of God, and your own eternal welfare."[48]

---

[45] *BOM*, 2 Nephi 25:23–30.
[46] *BOM*, 3 Nephi 15:2.
[47] *Compare BOM*, 3 Nephi 17:14.
[48] *BOM*, 2 Nephi 1:25.

Lehi tried to tell his oldest sons that they would be the ones whom he would leave his "first blessing" with, *if* they listened to him and did what was right. Doing "what was right" entailed living according to the future Christ's commandments, which they had learned through Lehi's visions and revelation. This had NOTHING whatsoever to do with the law of Moses in which Laman and Lemuel focused their attention. Doing what was right was believing in Christ and doing what Christ revealed to their father Lehi and their brother Nephi (through vision and revelation), which was necessary for a successful society. Again, the things that Christ would teach the people were NOT part of the "lower law" given to Moses.

According to Hebrew tradition, this "first blessing" was usually given to the eldest son as a way of confirming this son's prominence and authority to govern the people (the rest of the family). The most important role of the eldest son who received this "birthright" was to be the head of the family and provide for the widows, unmarried sisters, and other members of the family who didn't have any hereditary rights.[49]

When a family was successful at acquiring possessions (such as gold, silver, livestock and grains that the family needed in order to survive), the father made sure all of his children were treated equally and fairly in distribution of these goods, regardless of their spiritual beliefs. The head of the family was to make sure that each member had the basic necessities of life provided without cost or concern. Lehi told Laman and Lemuel,

> if ye will hearken unto the voice of Nephi ye shall not perish. And if ye will hearken unto him I leave unto you a blessing, yea, even my first blessing. But if ye will not hearken unto him I take away my first blessing, yea, even my blessing, and it shall rest upon him.[50]

---

[49] *See* Morris Jastrow, Jr., B. Eerdmans, Marcus Jastrow, Louis Ginzberg, "Birthright," *Jewish Encyclopedia*, jewishencyclopedia.com/articles/3323-birthright.

[50] *BOM*, 2 Nephi 1:28–9.

Chapter 15: True Messengers

Laman and Lemuel could have been the political leaders of the people, holding all the power and authority of government (in the family). But this power and authority had to be based on that which would maintain peace, equality, and harmony among the people. The law of Moses did not teach this peace, equality, and harmony. Lehi taught his children that this is why the people living in Jerusalem had become wicked. The prophets Zenos and Zenock came to Jerusalem and told the people of their great wickedness because the people were *only* obeying the laws of performances and ordinances (of Moses) and were not caring for the poor and needy of their society.

Laman and Lemuel rejected the idea of a future Christ that had not yet come but had given commandments to their *visionary* father and brother. Lehi's oldest sons believed only in the law of Moses and thought that their dad and brother had misjudged the Jews and made up lies in order to control them and take away their (Laman's and Lemuel's) right to lead the people.

Lehi and Nephi knew that their people would never thrive as a successful and righteous society without the words of the future Christ. After Lehi died, Laman and Lemuel, and others who followed them, were angry with Nephi and separated themselves from those who followed their younger brother.

Nephi was greatly saddened that he had to alienate his brothers. Although Nephi was not a True Messenger, he felt the same way as all True Messengers feel when they are forced to use sharp words that cause others to hate them: his "heart wept and his soul lingered in the valley of sorrow."[51]

Because his brothers rebelled and began to persecute the people who followed him, Nephi became the *political* leader of the people and appointed his brother, Jacob, as their *spiritual* leader. Again, this separation of church

---

[51] *Compare BOM*, 2 Nephi 4:26.

and state was very important. If there is not a complete separation, then the people can quickly become wicked.

Nephi's brother, Jacob, was not a politician. Nephi was the head of the state (government) and Jacob was the head of the church. This separation was important because the people were living the "lower law" (the law of Moses). The right form of government, headed by whichever son was given the father's birthright, would assure that all people (all members of the family) had their basic needs met. It would allow people the right to choose *not* to believe as others. They would be allowed to choose *not* to follow the law of Moses or the words of the future Christ. In the proper government, unbelievers would not be persecuted by those who chose to believe, nor would they be permitted to persecute those who chose to believe. This is what a righteous government, one established "for the people, by the people, and of the people,"[52] is supposed to do.

Jacob's job as the *spiritual leader* was to keep the people focused on Christ and the things that were *not* associated with the perfunctory (routine) performances and ordinances of the law of Moses. Nephi's job as the *political leader* was to make sure that ALL people, regardless of their beliefs, were provided for equally as the ancient Hebrew *birthright given to the eldest* required.

As our story relates, the Nephites became very prosperous; however, in their prosperity, their pride took over and they began to hoard riches for themselves and their families and not care about the people going without these things. Jacob confronted the people of the church because of their excessive pride. He called this excessive pride that leads a person to put their own family above others an "abomination." Then Jacob explained that the Nephites (the people of the Church) were starting to do something even

---

[52] Original phrase used by Abraham Lincoln, *see* "The Gettysburg Address," 19 Nov. 1863, multiple accounts found at Abraham Lincoln Online, abrahamlincolnonline.org/lincoln/speeches/gettysburg.htm.

more abominable before God, even "a grosser crime"—the men wanted to live polygamy (plural marriage).

This "grosser crime" started because many of the men had been killed in the wars between the Nephites and the Lamanites. The government took care of the widows and orphans. Some men became prosperous because of their hard labor and industry. These wealthy ones were required by law to help the women and children who had lost their husbands and fathers. The men became lustful and wanted compensation (sex) from the widowed women. This compensation was an "abomination" and a "grosser crime" before God, according to the

> commandments [of Christ that] were given to our father, Lehi; wherefore, ye have known them before; and ye have come unto great condemnation; for ye have done these things which ye ought not to have done.[53]

The history of the Jews and the law of Moses did not condemn a man for having more than one wife. Jewish oral history, which became the Bible's narrative, gave examples of men who lived polygamy.[54] This practice eventually led to the destruction of the house of Israel. This practice would have also destroyed the LDS Church, if it had not been forced to rescind polygamy.[55]

We were specific in our new American scripture explaining that Lehi and Nephi had received the instructions and commandments of a *future* Christ, none of which allowed plural marriage, in any way, shape, or form, or

---

[53] *BOM*, Jacob 2:34.
[54] *See* "Judaism," in "Polygamy," *Wikipedia*, Wikimedia Foundation, 27 May 2021, en.wikipedia.org/wiki/Polygamy#Judaism.
[55] Under pressure from the United States Government, the LDS Church officially ended polygamy in 1890. For more details, *see* "Latter Day Saint polygamy in the late-19th century," *Wikipedia*, 5 Apr. 2021, en.wikipedia.org/wiki/Latter_Day_Saint_polygamy_in_the_late-19th_century.

for any reason. The Jews didn't have the words of Jesus because he had not yet been born. All they had were the words of Moses and the "lower law" of "performances and ordinances." However, the Jews were told not to desire their neighbor's wife.[56]

Even when the people were doing everything that they were told according to the law of Moses, there was *not one time* that they created a society that wasn't eventually destroyed. ONLY the words of Jesus Christ could help the people create a good society that would not be destroyed. Our desire was to make sure that the reader of our new American scripture understood this clearly.

Brigham Young was the one who committed the "abomination" and "grosser crime" of plural marriage. He was the one who presented polygamy to the LDS/Mormon people in the early history of the church. Joseph Smith was against such doctrine and practice. However, when the men of the early Mormon church desired to live polygamy, Joseph was under strict mandate to let them do what they wanted so that they would stumble and experience the consequences of their actions.

In a biography that we authorized and mandated our contemporary True Messenger to write about the life of Joseph Smith, we proved this and made it perfectly clear how polygamy crept into the early LDS/Mormon Church and how Joseph dealt with it.[57]

In our new American story, after Jacob condemned the people for their pride (in creating economic divisions), as well as condemning the lust of the men (wanting to be rewarded with sex for taking care of the women and their children), we wrote of a Nephite named Sherem. This wicked Nephite taught

---

[56] OT, Deuteronomy 5:21.
[57] See *JS Bio*, Appendix 2, "Mormon Polygamy—The Truth Revealed" 638–75. Read for free at realilluminati.org/without-disclosing-my-true-identity.

the people "that there should be no Christ. And he [Sherem] preached … that he might overthrow the doctrine of Christ."[58] The "doctrine of Christ" condemned the men for lusting after more than one wife and the wealthy people for not helping the poor and the needy.

Sherem (a Nephite) taught the people the prejudices and pride associated with the law of Moses that Laman and Lemuel (Lamanites) had taught their children. He taught that Lehi, Nephi, and Jacob had

> led away much of this people that they pervert the right way of God, and keep not the law of Moses which is the right way; and convert the law of Moses into the worship of a being which ye say shall come many hundred years hence.[59]

We invented this subplot in our story to warn a person who thinks the "law of performances and ordinances" is more important than the law of treating your neighbor as you treat yourself. We had Jacob "smite" Sherem as a sign of his wickedness.[60] Later on in our story, we introduced another character, Korihor, who did the same thing with the law. We had our True Messenger, Alma, "smite" Korihor so that he could not speak.[61] We included these references to show how a True Messenger can confront and "smite" (have a sudden serious effect on) a leader who misleads the people. We did this in order to warn the modern-day people that our contemporary True Messenger could do the same thing.

We mentioned one of the modern LDS/Mormon Twelve Apostles in the *Prologue* of this book. His name is Elder Gary E. Stevenson. Stevenson lied to the members of his church and grossly misled them about our *Book of Mormon*. When the world receives the publication of this book, the proof that we are who we say we are, that we created the *Book of Mormon* for the

---

[58] *BOM*, Jacob 7:2.
[59] *BOM*, Jacob 2:7.
[60] *BOM*, Jacob 7:14.
[61] *BOM*, Alma 30:47.

purposes for which we did, and that the world has a True Messenger, can be certified in the following manner:

If Elder Gary E. Stevenson, who claims to be one of the Twelve Apostles of the Lord Jesus Christ, would meet in a public meeting with our contemporary True Messenger, our True Messenger would confound him, silence him, and "smite him" that he could not speak. In fact, if the entire leadership of the Church of Jesus Christ of Latter-day Saints (General Authorities) were to meet with our True Messenger in public, our True Messenger would confound them and cause them incredible uneasiness. These leaders would fear and tremble in the presence of our True Messenger because his words would truly condemn them and cause them to become exceedingly angry, comparable to how we presented the subplot of another True Messenger in our storyline—Abinadi.

Our True Messenger would convince the world that the LDS/Mormons follow the law of "performances and ordinances" that has nothing to do with the "fulness of the everlasting Gospel [of Jesus Christ] as delivered by the Savior to the ancient inhabitants" of the Western Hemisphere.[62] Every doctrine, every principle, everything taught to the members of the LDS Church is an abomination to the true God of humanity.

In addition, in attempting to prove their righteousness to others, the LDS/Mormons tout their humanitarian efforts throughout the world. These efforts have devastated local economic infrastructures and destroyed the ability of the local people to end the misery of poverty and inequality that American policy and forces have caused.[63]

These latter-day religious High Priests are comparable to King Noah's High Priests in our story. These LDS/Mormon High Priests have authority in

---

[62] JSH 1:34.
[63] *See* "Memorandum," The Humanity Party® Board of Directors in collaboration with The Marvelous Work and a Wonder®, May 25, 2018, humanityparty.com/memorandum; *see also* "The Humanity Party®, in collaboration with a Marvelous Work and a Wonder®, Publishes Memorandum … ," The Humanity Party®, May 25, 2018, humanityparty.com/post/the-humanity-party-in-collaboration-with-a-marvelous-work-and-a-wonder-publishes-memorandum.

the church and religion that Brigham Young created, which, as we will show, mirrors the Nephite Church that was established under the leadership of King Noah in an uncanny (peculiar) way.

In our story, through his spiritual counsel, Jacob was able to restore "peace and the love of God ... again among the people." The Nephites tried hard to convince the Lamanites to come to the table and have peace. The Nephites wanted the Lamanites to understand that they were not trying to take away the traditional authority of the patriarch of their side of the family, Laman. Their attempts to reason with the Lamanites were

> vain in restoring them to the true faith. And they [the Lamanites] swore in their wrath that, if it were possible, they would destroy our records [the plates of Nephi and the brass plates] and us, and also all the traditions of our fathers.[64]

We explained that the Nephite people, because of their prosperity and the many wins they had in battles with the Lamanites, became

> a stiffnecked people, hard to understand. And there was nothing save it was exceeding harshness, preaching and prophesying of wars, and contentions, and destructions, and continually reminding them of death, and the duration of eternity, and the judgments and the power of God, and all these things—stirring them up continually to keep them in the fear of the Lord. I say there was nothing short of these things, and exceedingly great plainness of speech, would keep them from going down speedily to destruction. And after this manner do [we] write concerning them.[65]

Our new American scripture is full of "exceeding harshness, preaching and prophesying of wars, and contentions, and destructions, and continually

---

[64] *BOM*, Enos 1:14.
[65] *BOM*, Enos 1:22–3.

A New American Scripture

reminding [the American Christians/Gentiles] of death." There was no other way to warn the American Christians that they had better focus on the simple words of Jesus Christ.

We presented a time when the Nephite government was *not* separated from religion—from the teachings of Christ ("the ways of the Lord"). We wrote of how "our kings and our leaders were mighty men in the faith of the Lord; and they taught the people the ways of the Lord." This non-separation helped the Nephites to "multiply exceedingly ... and become exceedingly rich."[66] This is **because it united the people under the words of Christ**, which were the words that would ensure a society's success—something that the *lower* law of Moses could not do.

Throughout our story, we reiterated that a righteous government *could* unite the people and care for all citizens equally and equitably, as Jesus taught. We explained that it wasn't wickedness to become "exceedingly rich," **as long as the teachings of equality, fairness, free will, and a people of one heart and one mind, existed** so that there were no poor among them. Again, we ended our insertions of Isaiah's words with:

> What shall then answer the messengers of the nations? That the Lord hath founded Zion, and the poor of his people shall trust in it.[67]

This final insertion of our quotes from Isaiah was to emphasize the importance of creating a government in which "the poor" can trust. This trust can only be maintained by righteous principles and consistency in caring for all people, as Jesus taught. To underscore the importance of this, we wrote the following:

> Wherefore, the prophets, and the priests, and the teachers, did labor diligently, exhorting with all long-suffering the people to

---

[66] *Compare BOM*, Jarom 1:7–8.
[67] *BOM*, 2 Nephi 24:32; *compare also* OT, Isaiah 14:32.

diligence; teaching the law of Moses, and the intent for which it was given; persuading them to look forward unto the Messiah, and believe in him to come as though he already was. And after this manner did they teach them.

And it came to pass that by so doing they kept them from being destroyed upon the face of the land; for they did prick their hearts with the word, continually stirring them up unto repentance.[68]

Regardless of how hard the prophets tried, the Nephites became wicked again because of their pride. Our story presents different situations where a small group of people is saved from the larger group's destruction. This was done by our theme of "flee[ing] into the wilderness." We repeated this pattern when we introduced a character named Mosiah. (We'll call him *Mosiah I*.) Mosiah I was

> warned of the Lord that he should flee out of the land of Nephi [also known as the land of Lehi-Nephi—the first great city in the Western Hemisphere], and as many as would hearken unto the voice of the Lord should also depart out of the land with him, into the wilderness.[69]

Mosiah I took the plates of brass with him, traveling northward from the modern area of Peru towards the area that would eventually become the United States. After fleeing, Mosiah I and his people discovered the "land of Zarahemla." In this land, they discovered a new people from the house of Israel (the Mulekites). These people were a different group of people who had fled from Jerusalem just before it was destroyed by the Babylonians (around 600 B.C.E.).

---

[68] *BOM*, Jarom 1:11–12.
[69] *BOM*, Omni 1:12.

We introduced these people so that we would be able to write "other books" in the future. We would then be able to use these books to "convince the Gentiles and also the Jews who were scattered upon all the face of the earth that the words of Jesus are true.[70] In another chapter, we will give details about what we had intended for these "other books, which came forth by the power of the Lamb." We never had the chance to write these "other books" because we realized that it would have made no difference. The Latter-day Saints ignore and overlook the many lessons of our *Book of Mormon*, so we felt that introducing any "other book" would be futile.

Had the LDS/Mormons accepted the lessons of the *Book of Mormon* and worked towards implementing its teachings into their lives, we would have written these "other books unto the convincing of them that the records of the prophets and of the twelve apostles of the Lamb were and are true."[71]

The people of Mosiah I (the Nephites) and the people they found in the land of Zarahemla (the Mulekites) united as one people. They were taught about the future Christ by King Mosiah I and his son, **Benjamin**. It was in the story of King Benjamin that we first introduced how the people were "redeemed from the fall" and received salvation long before Jesus died on the cross, and without performing any *saving* "performances [or] ordinances."[72] King Benjamin established peace in the land of Zarahemla. His son, Mosiah (we'll call him **Mosiah II**), was appointed to be king after Benjamin died. King Mosiah II followed the words of the future Jesus Christ, besides the law of Moses, and was a righteous king, who

> himself, did till the earth, that thereby he might not become burdensome to his people, that he might do according to that which his father had done in all things.[73]

---

[70] *Compare BOM*, 1 Nephi 13:39.
[71] Again, c*ompare BOM*, 1 Nephi 13:39.
[72] *BOM*, Mosiah 13:30.
[73] *BOM*, Mosiah 6:7.

Chapter 15: True Messengers

Throughout our story, we wanted it well documented that a righteous leader (whether of religion or of state) would not demand taxes or tithes to compensate the leader for his service. From the experience of history, we know that these things (taxes and tithing) lead to great wickedness and result in the formation of the secret combinations of politics, religion, and business, which can and do destroy society.

Previous to King Benjamin's reign, a "considerable number" of people had wanted to return to the land of their inheritance. They left the land of Zarahemla to travel back to dwell in the land of Lehi-Nephi. This group of people hadn't returned to Zarahemla, so years later, Mosiah II's people became curious about what had happened to this group of "a considerable number" who had left.[74] Therefore, King Mosiah II chose sixteen "strong men" to go find out.

The men were led by a man named **Ammon**. Leaving from Zarahemla (in the north country), Ammon and his men traveled to the land of Lehi-Nephi (located near Peru). There they found a group of Nephites who were prospering, except that these Nephites were under the power and control of a larger group of Lamanites. These Nephites were the descendants of the "considerable number" of people who had left during King Mosiah I's reign.

When these Nephites (who had desired to go back to the land of Lehi-Nephi) first left the land of Zarahemla they had had an army. This army had sent men to spy on the Lamanites. The men found that the Lamanites could easily be killed because the Lamanites didn't have the good weapons that the Nephites had. One of the spies, Zeniff, "saw that which was good among [the Lamanites, and he] was desirous that they should not be destroyed."[75] This is when a civil war broke out. One side saw the goodness in the Lamanites and wanted to make a treaty with them. The other side did not and wanted to destroy them.

---

[74] *BOM*, Mosiah 7:1.
[75] *BOM*, Mosiah 9:1.

We put this part in our story to represent the arguments that the early Americans had about what to do with the native Americans who lived in the "new promised land." There were Americans who wanted to help the people because they saw that which was good among them, and there were Americans who didn't view the native Americans as anything but a "lazy" people.[76]

During the later American Civil War, there were some arguments about how people should be treated. Our story referenced this issue. One side of the dispute during the Civil War supported the view that some humans existed that could be subjected to others (slavery) according to Bible teachings in the Old Testament. Believing that one group of people is of less value than an all-white race because of the different color of their skin and their chosen way of life is an issue that has plagued humankind since the darker-skinned race of humans was first created.

We are not going to reveal the details here about how the different races of humans came to be; but when appropriate, we will explain what happened in the past—when the dark-skinned human was bioengineered to be recognized as "less than" the lighter-skinned people living in an advanced society that actually manufactured these types of human bodies in order to produce slaves. Racism is a problem that cannot exist in a successful society. For this reason, our new American scripture is about bringing equality to ALL races upon the Earth.

After this mini civil war broke out in our narrative, the surviving Nephites who wanted to live in the land of their first inheritance returned to the land of Zarahemla. Zeniff then led the "considerable number" of people to the land of Nephi (the land of their first inheritance) to make a treaty with the Lamanites.

---

[76] *See* John Sutton Lutz, *Makuk : a New History of Aboriginal-White Relations* (Vancouver: UBC Press, 2014), Chapter 3 "Making the Lazy Indian," p. 31–47; also found online at web.uvic.ca/stolo/pdf/Lutz%20CHap3%20frm%20Makuk%20(2015_08_30%2007_20_22%20UTC).pdf.

Chapter 15: True Messengers

Previous to Zeniff arriving, the Lamanites had killed most of the Nephites and subjected them to slavery. However, the Lamanites had not been industrious like the Nephites; therefore, the city and the land of Lehi-Nephi had deteriorated. When Zeniff arrived, he met with the king of the Lamanites and asked for his people to be allowed to live among them. The Lamanite king (named appropriately, King Laman), was a very "cunning and crafty" leader. King Laman cleared out all of his people from part of the land of Lehi-Nephi and let the Nephites live there in peace as long as they paid a hefty tax to King Laman and his people.

Zeniff's people were very industrious, fixed up the land of Lehi-Nephi, and grew all kinds of foods that the Lamanites did not. King Laman's plan was to bring the Nephites in, have them fix up the land, plant all kinds of food stuffs, and then eventually destroy them and take it all. When this began to happen, however, Zeniff caused the Nephites to fight back. The Nephites eventually ended up destroying a large part of the Lamanites. In this way, the Nephites regained control over the land of their first inheritance.

Zeniff was a righteous king who cared about his people, but set up a government that did not separate church and state. The king had High Priests whom he controlled. The High Priests controlled the people. Zeniff died and his son, Noah, became king. Noah didn't want to do what his father and the kings Mosiah and Benjamin had done—work with their own hands. Noah started to tax the people. The tax was also a religious offering, a tithe, that the people paid to support the king and his High Priests.

We explained how we had to change our original storyline. By including the story of King Noah and his people in our revised narrative, we let Abinadi, a True Messenger, say the words that were similar to what the prophets Zenos and Zenock had said in our original narrative. The plot was the same: A prophet confronted the High Priests and condemned them for their wickedness.

A New American Scripture

In our revision, we replaced Lehi with a High Priest named **Alma**. We had the same scenario play out, where the High Priests wanted to kill the prophet who called them to repentance. One of them (Lehi/Alma) recognized the wickedness of the people and tried to save the prophets (Zenos and Zenock/Abinadi). One need only read this story and compare it to our *Book of Lehi* (original "lost" 116 pages) to see the similarities.

In every instance when we presented a True Messenger in our storyline delivering a message to an unrighteous people, it centered on Christ. In our revised narrative, Abinadi was later followed by a True Messenger named Samuel the Lamanite. Like Zenos and Zenock, Abinadi and Samuel the Lamanite were each sent to a wicked people who didn't think that they were wicked. In each case, the religious leaders justified their actions because of the law of Moses. In each case, the True Messengers explained that the law of Moses meant nothing compared to the words that the Messiah/Christ would teach the people. We were very careful in how we presented these subplots in our story after Joseph Smith's peer review group had rejected our original narrative.

A True Messenger's role is to teach the people what they need to do to create and support a successful society of human beings. There is no other role that such a messenger performs, or should perform. We have always been very selective about who we recruit as our True Messenger. In each and every case, the same scenario always takes place. The world hates a True Messenger because of what our True Messenger says about the way religious leaders have corrupted society.

Our contemporary True Messenger has often been mocked, ridiculed, and condemned for the way he speaks with boldness about the wickedness of religion, especially the American religion that is misusing our new American scripture (the LDS/Mormon Church). LDS leaders tell their followers that God would not choose a True Messenger who acts like ours. Yet, as we have challenged above, if the Quorum of the Twelve Apostles of Jesus Christ, as they call themselves, were to allow our True Messenger to come before them so that

Chapter 15: True Messengers

they could "question him, that they might cross him, that thereby they might have wherewith to accuse him," our True Messenger would stand boldly against them. He would withstand

> all their questions, yea, to their astonishment; for he [would] withstand them in all their questions, and … confound them in all their words.[77]

Those prideful leaders, who act as if they are humble and contrite towards God condemn our True Messenger for his boldness, and the "sharp two-edged sword" that comes out of his mouth. They would say that a prophet of God would not be so arrogant, bold, and forthcoming. Those dishonest leaders tell the people that a true prophet of God would be one like them, who

> bringeth good tidings; that publisheth peace; that bringeth good tidings of good; that publisheth salvation; that saith unto Zion, Thy God reigneth.[78]

When Abinadi was in front of the High Priests, they mocked him for the way he confronted them and condemned them. The High Priests used the words above to basically say, "God's True Messenger wouldn't be so mean. He would bring good tidings and publish words of peace, blessing the people by telling them that their God is good and in control. But you, Mr. True Messenger, do not publish good tidings of peace."

Dishonest leaders tell the people that God would never allow a leader of God's "only true church" to deceive the people—that if God was going to bless the people with the *sealed portion* of our new American scripture, God would not choose someone down at "Joe's Bar and Grill."[79]

---

[77] *BOM*, Mosiah 12:19.
[78] *BOM*, Mosiah 12:21.
[79] LDS Apostle Jeffrey R. Holland used this phrase referring to the current True Messenger. For details, *see* "Ida Smith and The Man From Joe's Bar and Grill," The Real Illuminati®, realilluminati.org/the-man-from-joe-s-bar-and-grill.

However, the True Messengers in our new American scripture upend and confound this statement. <u>ALL of the prophets sent to the people in our narrative were either non-members, or former members who saw the great wickedness of church leaders. Our True Messengers are sent to confront and confound corrupt church leaders.</u> Our storyline follows the same narratives about a True Messenger throughout its presentation with a few nuances that are important for each subplot and the lesson we intended to teach.

A society of people *will* prosper economically by cooperating and following a *righteous* religion, as long as the religion is a good one based on how people should treat each other. No matter how wealthy a group of people becomes, and no matter how righteous the members of the group *believe* they are, they must beware of pride. When pride enters the hearts of the people—when some start to place their own individual existence (and that of their families) above that of another's—the society starts downwards on a slippery slope towards inequality, division, and wickedness.

Again, we measure the righteousness and wickedness of a group of people (society) by how well that society creates peace, equality, and harmony on the entire Earth, not just for the society itself.

When Brigham Young took over the reins of the LDS Church, he did the exact same things that the wicked King Noah did. He lived in polygamy and tithed the people to support him and his wives, and his High Priests and their wives.[80] Young did not work by the labor of his own hands. He was both Governor and prophet, seer, and revelator. He would not separate church and state.[81] Young built one of the most extravagant temples of his day. Leaders of the vain church that followed him were inspired to do the same, building even more extravagant temples. Inside, the people are taught the

---

[80] *See* "Remarks by President Brigham Young, made in the Tabernacle, Great Salt Lake City, November 6, 1863," *Journal of Discourses* (London/Liverpool: Latter Day Saints' Book Depot, 1855–86) vol. 10, 282–8; also found online at jod.mrm.org/10/282.

[81] *See* "Governor of Utah Territory," in "Brigham Young," *Wikipedia*, 26 May 2021, en.wikipedia.org/wiki/Brigham_Young#Governor_of_Utah_Territory.

Chapter 15: True Messengers

"performances and ordinances" that they must do in order to be saved, NONE of which has anything to do with the words of Christ.

These leaders built a tabernacle (Conference Center) where they sit high above the people and flatter the members of their church with their seemingly kind words and humble expressions. All the while, they are leading the people completely contrary to the words of Jesus Christ as they are given in our new American scripture.

Although these religious leaders would like their followers to see them as *true* messengers sent from God, there is only one True Messenger at any given time upon Earth. And there is only one group that advises and counsels this True Messenger. This group is the same that authored the *Book of Mormon*, a new American scripture. It is us, the Real Illuminati®.

Chapter 16
Humanity's Salvation—The Fullness of the Everlasting Gospel

There is only one way that humanity can be saved: each person living upon the earth must be respected, treated, and valued equally and equitably.

All humans must agree to this.

A centralized, one-world government must be established that exists for no other purpose than to ensure that each living person upon the earth is respected, treated, and valued equally and equitably. There is no other way that humanity will survive.

Human salvation—peace and life eternal—is the hope and premise of a *Messiah*. The Greeks were the first to invent the idea that there are gods that intervene in mortal activity to help humankind. The idea of a god-mortal (the son of the head god and a mortal virgin) was the basis of the birth of Hercules. From the idea of the great and immortal Mount Olympus where the gods live that govern the universe, there has always been a hope that a savior of the world would come to Earth and set up a powerful centralized government that controlled all human action the way that the gods do it in the heavens.

Ironically, the idea of a One-World Government is feared and resisted, especially by American Christians. In writing our new American scripture, we used the Christian god, Jesus Christ, upon which we premised the idea of a righteous and powerful god setting up a One-World Government that could stop all the misery on Earth and save humanity.

What we know, that the rest of the world does not, is that over the nearly 5 billion years that planet Earth has existed, there have been five (5) different times when humanity (groups of humans) evolved and flourished to the point that humans controlled and had dominion over all the earth. Each of these times ended in the destruction of most of humanity. The end of a cooperative humanity leaves the world to the effects of time and natural law and void of human control and intervention. When humans do not cooperate together for the sake of their species' (own) existence, the laws of nature take control and do what these laws have always done to sustain the existence of planet Earth. What we observed 10,000 years ago was the result of nature taking control of its own. What we see today is the result of humans taking back power and dominion over the earth and all of its creations.

We are currently living in what we like to call the *Sixth Dispensation of Humanity*. From what we know about the rise and fall of humanity in the past, we can portend (warn) that the human race has very little time remaining, before humans repeat history and cause their own demise (near extinction) again.

We have explained throughout the pages of this book, that nationalism (politics), religion, and economic disparity are the three main causes that inhibit and impede the respect, treatment, and value that each living person upon the earth deserves and desires. We have explained how humans have divided themselves into isolated groups that protect the pride they have established in their government, religion, and economic stability. We have explained that this *pride*—responsible for how humans separate themselves into nations, churches, and economic classes—has caused, is causing, and will continue to cause the destruction of the human race.

We have explained that the United States of America was one of humanity's last hopes in establishing the right form of government that would guarantee a person's life (respect), liberty (treatment), and pursuit of happiness (value).¹ We have detailed some of the efforts we made in order to help the United States establish itself and develop properly. We helped the U.S. get nuclear weapons before any other nation. We have done everything possible to influence this nation's lawmakers to incorporate better laws for all people.

We did all that we could to try to influence the U.S. government and to ensure a solid separation between church and state. We wanted to ensure this *complete* separation because we knew that the American Christians and all of their creeds wielded the power and control over the early European-Americans. We knew that these creeds were

> an abomination in [Christ's] sight; that those professors [of Christianity] were all corrupt; that: "they draw near to me with their lips, but their hearts are far from me, they teach for doctrines the commandments of men, having a form of godliness, but they deny the power thereof."²

Had these Christians truly been *Christians* and had they implemented what the Jesus of the New Testament would have implemented into his government (if he were a real person and created a government), **what a different nation the United States of America would have become.**

To counter their great hypocrisy, we wrote our new American scripture for the early Americans. In so doing, we tried everything we could to inspire a "government of the people, by the people, for the people" that kept itself separated from corrupt Christianity, without getting rid of Christianity altogether. Had the Christians not been hypocrites, and had ALL American law been built upon the foundation of Jesus' two greatest

---

[1] The phrase "life, liberty and the pursuit of happiness" was used in the Declaration of Independence. For more on this phrase, *see* "Life, Liberty and the pursuit of Happiness," *Wikipedia*, 20 May 2021, en.wikipedia.org/wiki/Life,_Liberty_and_the_pursuit_of_Happiness.
[2] JSH 1:19.

Chapter 16: Humanity's Salvation—The Fullness of the Everlasting Gospel

commandments—love thyself and love thy neighbor as thyself—then the society of America would be as strong as a rock:

> Therefore, whatever nation heareth these sayings of Jesus and doeth them, Jesus likened this nation unto a wise man, who built his nation upon a rock—And the rain descended, and the floods came, and the winds blew, and beat upon that nation; and it fell not, for it was founded upon Jesus' two greatest commandments.[3]

Instead, because American Christians ignored this solid foundation,

> the rain descended, and the floods came, and the winds blew, and beat upon that nation; and it will fall, and great will be the fall of it.

We prophesied of the fall of the United States of America in our new American scripture, a fall that has not yet occurred (circa 2020), but will. We warned the Christian Americans about their pride in rejecting and "fighting" against the simple Gospel of Jesus Christ, as taught in the New Testament by "the twelve apostles of the Lamb":

> And it came to pass that I saw and bear record, that the great and spacious building [*the sandy foundation upon which the United States of America was built*] was the pride of the world; and it fell, and the fall thereof was exceedingly great. And the angel of the Lord spake unto me again, saying: Thus shall be the destruction of all nations, kindreds, tongues, and people, that shall fight against the twelve apostles of the Lamb.[4]

---

[3] *Compare BOM*, 3 Nephi 14:24–5.
[4] *BOM*, 1 Nephi 11:36.

That which causes great nations to fall is not a mystery or a secret. History is full of examples.[5] However, the histories of these great nations are told by liars—biased, nationalistic, often religiously bent, and patriotic historians who write subjectively (based on their own personal feelings and opinions). They do this to please the ears of the people of their particular nation. Hardly has there ever been an honest history written that explains and details the "wickedness and abominations" of the people that led to any great nation's downfall.

We have explained how the greatest minds of the fourth (4th) century C.E. got together to create a *code of laws* upon which a nation must build its foundation in order to succeed. Greek and Roman authors reviewed hundreds of years of experience in order to come up with this code. The Greek Empire had failed, and the Great Roman Empire was failing. This was when Emperor Constantine motivated church, state, and business to unite (*combine*) in secret under a new flag, with a new standard and a new code for humanity. The masses were unaware of this *secret combination* of powers. These powers convened (got together) in an effort to control the masses of people who were beginning to rise up in protest and rebellion against them.

A new god for the masses—Jesus, the Christ—and new teachings—the fullness of Christ's everlasting gospel—were created.

Unlike all the other religions of that time period, this new code, meant to be **of and for** humanity, had nothing to do with perfunctory (routine) performances and ordinances that brought pride to the people's minds and hearts. The fullness of the gospel of Jesus Christ was completely based on how to treat yourself and each other so that a peaceful, equal, and harmonious society could exist. But because religion and spirituality were so important to the masses, this new foundation still gave glory and control to the people's idea of what "God" is. It played on their desire for a Messiah to save them from their

---

[5] *See* R. David Harden, "How nations fail: Lessons for America," 27 Oct. 2019, *The Hill* – Capital Hill Publishing Corp., thehill.com/opinion/national-security/467595-how-nations-fail-lessons-for-america.

miserable circumstance. This *secret combination* of Greco-Roman intelligence and influence created a new god that would continue to control the people, while *they* controlled this new god.

This unprecedented unification of both church and state under the banner of Christianity saved the Eastern Roman Empire. The Western part of the Great Roman Empire fell, and great was the fall thereof. And the main cause of its fall was economic inequality caused by Roman pride and prosperity. Controlling the economy, resulting in poverty, led to the inability of the local governments established in the Western part of the Roman Empire to continue to control the masses.

No matter how hard we tried, no matter how many times we reiterated it, no matter how many different ways and examples we used in our storyline to get the American Christians to focus on the words of Christ, notwithstanding all that we could possibly do, the American Christians denied the *true Christ* and rejected the message intended for our new American scripture.

We were addressing *them* and warning the early Americans, whom we named the "Gentiles," in every way possible, as eloquently as we could without offending their *pride* and belief in organized religion. We warned them of their pride ("stiff necks and high heads"). We warned them of their wickedness, abominations, and whoredoms. We warned them that "they have all gone astray." Consider the way we presented some of our greatest warnings:

> They wear stiff necks and high heads; yea, and because of pride, and wickedness, and abominations, and whoredoms, they have all gone astray save it be a few, who are the humble followers of Christ; nevertheless, they are led, that in many instances they do err because they are taught by the precepts of men.

O the wise, and the learned, and the rich, that are puffed up in the pride of their hearts, and all those who preach false doctrines, and all those who commit whoredoms, and pervert the right way of the Lord, wo, wo, wo be unto them, saith the Lord God Almighty, for they shall be thrust down to hell!

Wo unto them that turn aside the just for a thing of naught and revile against that which is good, and say that it is of no worth! For the day shall come that the Lord God will speedily visit the inhabitants of the earth; and in that day that they are fully ripe in iniquity they shall perish.

But behold, if the inhabitants of the earth shall repent of their wickedness and abominations they shall not be destroyed, saith the Lord of Hosts.

But behold, that great and abominable church, the whore of all the earth, must tumble to the earth, and great must be the fall thereof.

For the kingdom of the devil must shake, and they which belong to it must needs be stirred up unto repentance, or the devil will grasp them with his everlasting chains, and they be stirred up to anger, and perish;

For behold, at that day shall he rage in the hearts of the children of men, and stir them up to anger against that which is good.

And others will he pacify, and lull them away into carnal security, that they will say: All is well in [*America*]; yea, [*America*] prospereth, all is well—and thus the devil cheateth their souls, and leadeth them away carefully down to hell.

And behold, others he flattereth away, and telleth them there is no hell; and he saith unto them: I am no devil, for there is none—and thus he whispereth in their ears, until he grasps them with his awful chains, from whence there is no deliverance.

Yea, they are grasped with death, and hell; and death, and hell, and the devil, and all that have been seized therewith must stand before the throne of God, and be judged according to their works, from whence they must go into the place prepared for them, even a lake of fire and brimstone, which is endless torment.
Therefore, wo be unto him that is at ease in [*America*]! Wo be unto him that crieth: All is well!

Yea, wo be unto him that hearkeneth unto the precepts of men, and denieth the power of God, and the gift of the Holy Ghost!

Yea, wo be unto him that saith: We have received [*the word of God in the Bible*], and we need no more [*new American scripture*]!

And in fine, wo unto all those who tremble, and are angry because of the truth of God! For behold, he that is built upon the rock receiveth it with gladness; and he that is built upon a sandy foundation trembleth lest he shall fall.

Wo be unto him that shall say: We have received the word of God, and we need no more of the word of God, for we have enough!

For behold, thus saith the Lord God: I will give unto the children of men line upon line, precept upon precept, here a little and there a little; and blessed are those who hearken unto my precepts, and lend an ear unto my counsel, for they shall learn wisdom; for unto him that receiveth I will give more; and from them that shall say, We have enough, from them shall be taken away even that which they have.

Cursed is he that putteth his trust in man, or maketh flesh his arm, or shall hearken unto the precepts of men, save their precepts shall be given by the power of the Holy Ghost.

Wo be unto the [*Americans*], saith the Lord God of Hosts! For notwithstanding I shall lengthen out mine arm unto them from day to day, they will deny me; nevertheless, I will be merciful unto them, saith the Lord God, if they will repent and come unto me; for mine arm is lengthened out all the day long, saith the Lord God of Hosts.[6]

The church that uses our new American scripture to promote itself and get people to join it was the very first authentic *American Christian* religion. It *should have been* the best church. It would have been, *if* it had been based on our *Book of Mormon*. Instead, this church is one of the most duplicitous and dishonest of all American Christian religions. The LDS Church's great prosperity has caused its members to believe that "all is well in Zion; yea, Zion prospereth, all is well."[7] It is this church that claims that its members are the chosen people of God,[8] that they are the ones who have established Zion on the American continent, and that THEY have the only true church of Christ upon Earth.

It is the LDS Church that "teaches for doctrines the commandments of [its leaders]." This church is not honest about its history. Its members are deceived into believing that the early Latter-day Saints were righteous, unjustly persecuted and driven out of their homes and away from their

---

[6] *BOM*, 2 Nephi 28:14–32.
[7] *BOM*, 2 Nephi 28:21. Incredulously, the LDS/Mormons often sing a song from their Hymn Book that uses this phrase numerous times. *See* William Clayton, "Come, Come, Ye Saints," in Hymns of The Church of Jesus Christ of Latter-day Saints (Salt Lake City: The Church of Jesus Christ of Latter-day Saints, 1985), #326; also found online at churchofjesuschrist.org/music/library/hymns/come-come-ye-saints?lang=eng.
[8] *See* "Mormonism," in "Chosen people," *Wikipedia*, Wikimedia Foundation, 23 May 2021, en.wikipedia.org/wiki/Chosen_people#Mormonism.

Chapter 16: Humanity's Salvation—The Fullness of the Everlasting Gospel

possessions. Nothing could be further from the Real Truth™ about this church's history.

The early Latter-day Saints (Mormons) rejected the "fulness of the everlasting Gospel ... as delivered by the Savior to the ancient inhabitants" of the Western Hemisphere. *Their* church replaced Jesus' simple teachings with performances and ordinances that corrupted the members. This is exactly how we explained that the law of Moses (a law of performances and ordinances) corrupted the church of the Nephites in our new American scripture's narrative.

It was not the righteousness of the LDS/Mormon people that caused their persecutions; it was their wickedness and abominations. For one of many examples of this, the early Mormons created their own money system[9] in Kirtland, Ohio, and stole countless goods and services from non-members who had been deceived into accepting the *Mormon Money*. The bogus scripts were actually worth nothing. The people who trusted the Mormons (their neighbors) lost much, and some lost most of their savings and livelihood.

The LDS/Mormons gave scathing prophecies about non-members, especially those living in the state of Missouri. They used our new American scripture to prophesy that THEY—not the native American people, but THEY—would eventually inherit all of North America, beginning in Far West, Missouri and in Jackson County. This is where the LDS/Mormons believe that Christ will return one day[10] and wipe out

---

[9] *See* "Kirtland Safety Society," The Joseph Smith Papers – Church Historian's Press, josephsmithpapers.org/topic/kirtland-safety-society; *and* "Kirtland Safety Society," *Wikipedia*, Wikimedia Foundation, 22 Apr. 2021, en.wikipedia.org/wiki/Kirtland_Safety_Society.

[10] *See* Tim Townsend, "Missouri remains land of religious promise for Mormons," *The Washington Post*, 20 Sept. 2021, washingtonpost.com/national/on-faith/missouri-remains-land-of-religious-promise-for-mormons/2012/09/20/d40cbbd4-0348-11e2-9132-f2750cd65f97_story.html.

everyone who is not a member of their church. This pride caused wars and mayhem because of what the Mormons said to the non-members.[11] The people were afraid of the Mormons.

The Mormon men wanted a priesthood that gave a few leaders control over the entire church. Church democracy (the "vote and voice" of the people) was replaced with the vain and foolish decisions of priesthood leadership. LDS/Mormon men lusted after women who were not their wives. They would associate with non-member women and flirt with them (even if the woman was married), touting their priesthood authority that non-member men did not have. When non-member women would leave their own husbands to join a Mormon man (after being promised goods, security, and eternal salvation), the non-member men were furious. (Can you blame them?)

As we have explained, and reiterated time and time again, Joseph Smith was under strict mandate to allow the Mormons to do whatever they wanted.[12] Joseph was mandated to stand back and watch them stumble as they corrupted the everlasting Gospel of Jesus Christ. And as we have explained, Joseph lost not just a few of his close friends because of the way that he allowed the people to do what they wanted. The people had lost faith in Joseph. In the city of Nauvoo, the LDS/Mormon prophet, seer, and revelator ran for Mayor, and lost to a man who would become one of his most bitter enemies—John C. Bennett.[13] One might ask, "How could the man who was chosen to bring forth what the people believed was another 'word of God,' that even trumped the Bible, lose an election where *all the voters were Mormon*?"

---

[11] *See* "The Missouri Mormon War," Missouri Office of the Secretary of State - Missouri State Library - Missouri State Archives, sos.mo.gov/archives/resources/mormon.asp.

[12] *See BOM*, Jacob 4:14.

[13] For a brief history of the Mayoral election of February 1, 1841 in Nauvoo, IL, which Bennett won, *see* Arnold K. Garr, "Joseph Smith: Mayor of Nauvoo," *Mormon Historical Studies* vol 3 no. 1 (Spring 2002), 30–2; also found online at ensignpeakfoundation.org/wp-content/uploads/2013/05/MHS3.1Spring2002Garr.pdf

Chapter 16: Humanity's Salvation—The Fullness of the Everlasting Gospel

What if the Mormons had actually read and believed our new American scripture? What if they had viewed polygamy as a "gross crime" and an abomination before God? What if the men would have helped the widows without lusting after them? What if the Mormons had loved their enemies and done good to those who persecuted them and abused them? What if the Mormons never sued in a court of law, but supported a reaction to evil with kindness, compassion, forgiveness, and being like a little child? Again, what if the Mormons would have complied with the prophecies of our *Book of Mormon* and did everything in their power to create a "New Jerusalem"—a Zion on the American Continent—that blessed the native Americans?

Speaking modernly of the LDS Church, imagine how non-members feel when they realize that LDS/Mormons do genealogical research and perform ordinance work in their temples for these non-members' dead relatives—*without* their permission? After their vicarious ordinance work is done, the Latter-day Saints put the names of these dead people on the roles of their church membership, whether the person's non-member family agrees or not—because the LDS Church does not tell them what they are doing. This practice of baptizing dead non-members is in direct violation of the counsel given in our new American scripture, concerning "they that die who are without the law."[14]

What would have happened modernly, if the LDS/Mormons, in their prosperity, had sought for riches with "a hope in Christ ... for the intent to do good?" What if they desired riches "to clothe the naked, and to feed the hungry, and to liberate the captive, and administer relief to the sick and the afflicted" of their neighbors who were *NOT* members of their church?[15] What would have happened if,

> because of the steadiness of the church they began to be exceedingly rich, having abundance of all things whatsoever they stood in need—an abundance of flocks and herds, and

---

[14] *See BOM*, Moroni 8:22–6.
[15] *See BOM*, Jacob 2:19.

fatlings of every kind, and also abundance of grain, and of gold, and of silver, and of precious things, and abundance of silk and fine-twined linen, and all manner of good homely cloth [even 100 billion dollars of investments[16]].

And thus, in their prosperous circumstances, they did not send away any who were naked, or that were hungry, or that were athirst, or that were sick, or that had not been nourished; and they did not set their hearts upon riches; therefore they were liberal to all, both old and young, both bond and free, both male and female, **whether out of the church or in the church**, having no respect to persons as to those who stood in need. And thus they did prosper and become far more wealthy than those who did not belong to their church.[17]

The LDS/Mormons are NOT liberal to all when it comes to their riches. If they were, they wouldn't have so many riches. But having riches, as our story explains, is good for a society, as long as "whether out of the church or in the church" the people receive the same care equally and equitably. This is NOT the case with the modern LDS Church. A person who seeks help from this church must do what its leaders command. A person who is kind, compassionate, patient, longsuffering, and is simply a great person, but who refuses to conform with the requirements set by this church, is not helped.

As we have explained, the LDS Church touts its worldwide humanitarian efforts. But we have proven that these efforts do much more damage than good to the people whom this church pretends to help and serve.[18] Furthermore,

---

[16] *See* Paul Glader, "Mormon Church Stockpiled $100 Billion Intended for Charities and Misled LDS Members, Whistleblower Says," 17 Dec. 2019, *Newsweek*, newsweek.com/mormon-church-stockpiled-100-billion-intended-charities-misled-lds-members-whistleblower-says-1477809.

[17] *BOM*, Alma 1:29–31, emphasis added.

[18] See "Memorandum," The Humanity Party® Board of Directors in collaboration with The Marvelous Work and a Wonder®, 25 May 2018, humanityparty.com/memorandum.

Chapter 16: Humanity's Salvation—The Fullness of the Everlasting Gospel

LDS/Mormon popularity and worldly status, demonstrated by their extravagant temples throughout the world, as well as this church's great financial success, is much more important to this church than eliminating poverty—something their own Jesus warned would be his final judgement of them.[19]

What would have happened had the early Mormons made the words of the resurrected Jesus Christ the ONLY foundation upon which they had built their religion? What would have happened had they invited all to join with them in worshipping Christ, freely, without obligation of paying tithing or performing saving ordinances that could only be administered by priesthood leadership, and *only* after paying a full tithe?

We could fill pages with descriptions of the pride, arrogance, and many things the early Latter-day Saints did that warranted a negative response from outside communities (and this behavior continues in the LDS Church today). Wherever they went, the early LDS/Mormons created anger and fear in the hearts of the people. Again, they misinterpreted our new American scripture claiming that their "Golden Bible" prophesied that they (the Mormons) would one day take over the United States of America. This is how they incorrectly presented it to non-members.

Had the Mormons learned the lessons that we clearly presented in our new American scripture, they would have become one of the kindest, most compassionate, fairest, most honest, and successful societies upon the earth. One can just imagine what would have happened had the Mormons made helping the native American people the focus of their religion, which was the main focus of our *Book of Mormon*. (The hundreds of billions of dollars that the LDS Church has now amassed could be used to fulfill the prophecies of our *Book of Mormon* with regards to the native American people who are ignored at the southern borders of the United States.)

---

[19] *See* NT, Matthew 25:31–46.

And had the readers of our new American scripture accepted it and had faith in it, we would have created other books that would have told of the other "lost ten tribes of Israel" and other of Earth's inhabitants. We would have told a story about how the resurrected Jesus Christ visited these people and taught them *the code of humanity* that can save ALL people on Earth.

We have explained how and why we presented stories in our new American scripture demonstrating what happened when there was no separation between government and religious authority. In our narrative, we showed how easily society becomes corrupt when a religion is corrupt, thus the need for a separation. But we also included subplots showing what happened when there was no separation and the people still flourished and were successful. This prosperity came ONLY when the words of Christ were the basis of both church and state. Any deviation from the simple words contained in the fullness of Christ's everlasting gospel caused society to fail.

We wrote the prophecies in our new American scripture according to Christian belief. We told of a redeemer—a savior, who comes to Earth to bring salvation to ALL of humanity. Our story complemented and reflected the eschatological (related to death, judgment and the final destiny of humanity) beliefs held similarly by Christians, Jews, and Muslims. It is Christ, Jehovah, or Allah, respectively as the Messiah of each of these religions, who will eventually get rid of all separate governments and establish one government and religion.

We call this establishment "Zion." It is when government and religion are one and the same, where all people are "of one heart and one mind," and there is "no poor among them" ... no poverty upon Earth.[20]

---

[20] *PGP*, Moses 7:18.

Chapter 16: Humanity's Salvation—The Fullness of the Everlasting Gospel

As we have clearly pointed out and proven throughout this book, the message of Jesus Christ culminates in judging the nations on how well the poor and the needy are cared for—on nothing more and nothing less.[21] Our book of Revelation is not a prophecy about the end of the world, but a prophecy about a "renewing" that takes place. Revelation explains that the only people who will suffer in the end, are those of

> all nations [that] have drunk of the wine of the wrath of her fornication, and the kings of the earth [who] have committed fornication with her, and the merchants of the earth [who have] waxed rich through the abundance of her delicacies.[22]

The "woman" mentioned above, as described in Revelation, represents humanity. "The beast" upon which she rides, as it applies to modern society, represents Capitalism. *She* represents the "abundance of delicacies" that this economic system provides for the few, while millions of others suffer because of "her."

Before a society can start treating the poor with economic equality, it must first establish itself as a society that treats everyone with equal respect and value. There can be no *leaders* that are put above the people whom the leaders are supposed to *serve*. Kings, presidents, magistrates, prime ministers, and the likes are positions of authority and power that must be replaced with constitutional laws that establish equal fairness and justice. A written constitution MUST establish the basis of all laws. In order to write this type of constitution, its authors must be influenced by a philosophy and ideology that is fair to ALL people. It must promote

> that which is good among the children of men ... denying none ... black and white, bond and free, male and female, and even the heathen who does not believe in God.[23]

---

[21] *See* NT, Matthew 25:31–46.
[22] *See* NT, Revelation 18:3.
[23] *Compare BOM*, 2 Nephi 26:33.

We presented this philosophy and ideology in our new American scripture as the "everlasting Gospel" of Jesus Christ. Following the words that Jesus taught is not the whole of what a society must do to be successful. The simple and straightforward teachings of Jesus are that upon which a society must <u>build its foundation</u>. Nevertheless, successful governing requires much more than just telling people how to treat each other with respect, which is the overall message that Jesus delivered in the stories told about him.

Again, Jesus' teachings are only a foundation upon which to build. Once the people respect each other as equals, and nothing separates or divides them emotionally, a foundation for the laws that will support humanity *temporally* must be built. This *temporal foundation* must equitably provide the five basic necessities of life for all people living upon Earth.[24]

The words of Jesus that we call the "fulness of the everlasting Gospel" are found in the Bible, in Matthew, chapters 5, 6, and 7, and copied in our new American scripture as 3 Nephi, chapters 12, 13, and 14. These words are all about how people should treat each other. Again, these words are *only the foundation upon which a great nation is built.* This gospel says very little about how to solve poverty. There is only one thing that is said about poverty, "Give to him that asketh thee, and from him that would borrow of thee turn not thou away."[25]

From not calling a person a fool, to loving and treating your enemy with compassion, forgiveness, and kindness, this simple counsel speaks of equality and respect, the very foundation of a successful society. <u>All people on Earth must be respected as equals.</u> If not, there is no way that peace, equality, and harmony can be established, and war and misery will always be the result. This universal respect is simply that you should not put yourself above another, and you should not allow another to put their self above you.

---

[24] How to provide **all** with these five basic necessities, **for free**, is detailed here: "What are the Five Basic Necessities of Life (FBNL®)," The Humanity Party®, <u>humanityparty.com/5-basic-necessities-of-life</u>.

[25] NT, Matthew 5:42; and *BOM*, 3 Nephi 12:42.

When religious ideologies exist, the group of people that believes it is *right* and that everyone else is *wrong*, puts itself up above the other group that does not believe as this prideful group does. A strong government of law and order must be established, protecting the unbeliever from the believer, as well as protecting the believer from the unbeliever. Based on our experience and what we know about the rise and fall of the past five different *Dispensations of Humanity*, we will write and publish (free of charge) another entire book about how to form the perfect human government.

The third book of our Trilogy will be called *One People, One World, One Government*. In this book, we will provide humanity with the proper blueprint for the perfect human government. However, if we cannot convince the people to treat and value each other with emotional equality and respect, a perfect and equitable government will be impossible. Therefore, the first two books of our Trilogy attempt to break down the emotional barriers that have kept humanity from having successful societies.

In the first book of our Trilogy, *The True History of Religion—How Religion Destroys the Human Race and What the Real Illuminati® Has Attempted to do Through Religion to Save the Human Race*, we explained how we attempted to influence religion throughout history. In the second book of our Trilogy (that you are reading now), we have given specific details and provided empirical evidence of what we did through religion to try to help establish a nation built upon the right *kind* of religion—a faith-based system that would establish mutual respect as its foundation. We call this system's foundation "the everlasting Gospel."

Joseph Smith was very vague for many years about how he received the commission to write our new American scripture. He never revealed the Real Truth™ about how he was recruited as our True Messenger. For many years, no one really knew anything about what had happened to Joseph when he was a teenager and experienced his "transfiguration." His followers and supporters didn't know about when the heavens were opened, and he was caught up into heaven, and saw and heard unspeakable things. And it was forbidden him that he should utter; neither was it given him power that he could utter the things which he saw and heard; And whether he was in the body or out of the body, he could not tell; for it did seem unto him like a transfiguration of him, that he was changed from this body of flesh into an immortal state, that he could behold the things of God.[26]

Various accounts of what the LDS/Mormons call the *First Vision* still confuse many people.[27] As we have explained throughout this book, *ad nauseam*, the American Christians would not accept the simplicity of the words of Jesus as the *only* thing necessary for salvation. Because of this, Joseph gave various accounts of what happened to him. These different versions gave his followers "many things that they could not understand, because they desired it ... so that they would stumble."

Just before we left Joseph alone so that we wouldn't intervene and keep him from being murdered, we instructed him how to write a simple explanation about what happened to him. What he wrote became the accepted history of the LDS/Mormon people. Included in this final and official account, we had Joseph Smith clearly explain what our new American scripture was about:

> [A messenger sent from God] said there was a book deposited, written upon gold plates, giving an account of the former inhabitants of this continent, and the source from whence

---

[26] *Compare BOM*, 3 Nephi 28:13–15.
[27] *See* "Recorded accounts of the vision" in "First Vision," for a summary of each account: en.wikipedia.org/wiki/First_Vision#1830s_reference_to_early_Christian_regeneration.
See also See Joel B. Groat, "Joseph Smith's Changing First Vision Accounts," 15 July 2011, Mormons In Transition - Institute for Religious Research, mit.irr.org/joseph-smiths-changing-first-vision-accounts.

they sprang. He also said that **the fulness of the everlasting Gospel was contained in it, as delivered by the Savior to the ancient inhabitants.**[28]

How could we have been any clearer that the "fulness of the everlasting Gospel" were the words that the resurrected Jesus Christ spoke to the people, from his own mouth, as presented in our story? This "fulness" is "everlasting," which means it is the same yesterday, today, and forever. It means that whatever Jesus said yesterday to the Jews, was the same thing that he would say when he visited the ancient native Americans, according to our story. And if he visited any other people tomorrow, what he would tell them to do would be the exact same.

Here's how we presented this concept to the American Christians who doubted our new American scripture and claimed that the Bible was the ultimate word of God, and that "there cannot be any more Bible":

And because my [Jesus'] words shall hiss forth—many of the Gentiles shall say: A Bible! A Bible! We have got a Bible, and there cannot be any more Bible.

But thus saith the Lord God: O fools, they shall have a Bible; and it shall proceed forth from the Jews, mine ancient covenant people. And what thank they the Jews for the Bible which they receive from them? Yea, what do the Gentiles mean? Do they remember the travails, and the labors, and the pains of the Jews, and their diligence unto me, in bringing forth salvation unto the Gentiles?

O ye Gentiles, have ye remembered the Jews, mine ancient covenant people? Nay; but ye have cursed them, and have hated them, and have not sought to recover them. But behold, I will

---

[28] JSH 1:34, emphasis added.

return all these things upon your own heads; for I the Lord have not forgotten my people.

Thou fool, that shall say: A Bible, we have got a Bible, and we need no more Bible. Have ye obtained a Bible save it were by the Jews?

Know ye not that there are more nations than one? Know ye not that I, the Lord your God, have created all men, and that I remember those who are upon the isles of the sea; and that I rule in the heavens above and in the earth beneath; and I bring forth my word unto the children of men, yea, even upon all the nations of the earth?

Wherefore murmur ye, because that ye shall receive more of my word? Know ye not that the testimony of two nations is a witness unto you that I am God, that I remember one nation like unto another? Wherefore, I speak the same words unto one nation like unto another. And when the two nations shall run together the testimony of the two nations shall run together also.

And I do this that I may prove unto many that I am the same yesterday, today, and forever; and that I speak forth my words according to mine own pleasure. And because that I have spoken one word ye need not suppose that I cannot speak another; for my work is not yet finished; neither shall it be until the end of man, neither from that time henceforth and forever.

Wherefore, because that ye have a Bible ye need not suppose that it contains all my words; neither need ye suppose that I have not caused more to be written.

For I command all men, both in the east and in the west, and in the north, and in the south, and in the islands of the sea, that they shall write the words which I speak unto them; for out of the books

Chapter 16: Humanity's Salvation—The Fullness of the Everlasting Gospel

which shall be written I will judge the world, every man according to their works, according to that which is written.

For behold, I shall speak unto the Jews and they shall write it; and I shall also speak unto the Nephites and they shall write it; and I shall also speak unto the other tribes of the house of Israel, which I have led away, and they shall write it; and I shall also speak unto all nations of the earth and they shall write it.[29]

We invented a narrative that was consistent with how the Christians believed that the resurrected Christ would come to Earth. We set up the story to teach certain key points that we wanted to reiterate and emphasize to the reader. We wrote how the Nephites and Lamanites were sometimes good and sometimes bad. We explained that when they were good, and when they incorporated the words of the future Christ into their society, or rather when they built their society on *a foundation* of Christ's "everlasting gospel," they prospered. Our narrative explained how when the church of God prospered too much, its members got prideful and stopped following the words of Christ.

We provided scenarios of how the people would doubt Christ and call the belief in Christ a

> wicked tradition, which has been handed down unto us by our fathers, to cause us that we should believe in some great and marvelous thing which should come to pass, but not among us, but in a land which is far distant [Jesus was born in the Eastern Hemisphere], a land which we know not; therefore they can keep us in ignorance, for we cannot witness with our own eyes that [it is] true.[30]

---

[29] *BOM*, 2 Nephi 29:3–12.
[30] *BOM*, Helaman 16:20.

A New American Scripture

We have not detailed the entire storyline in this book. But we have given enough examples of what we wrote to help the reader understand *why* we wrote it and *how* we did. After reading this book (*A New American Scripture—How and Why the Real Illuminati® Created the Book of Mormon*), one who reads our *Book of Mormon* (1830) and *The Sealed Portion* (2004) will enjoy the story even more. After knowing *why* and *how* we wrote what we did, one will be able to understand more clearly *why* we told a certain story and presented a particular subplot the way that we did.

Every part of our narrative funneled the reader's attention towards the story of the coming of Jesus Christ to the Western Hemisphere (after he was killed by the Jews in the Eastern Hemisphere).

The day before Jesus was born, we had him speak to our designated prophet in the Western Hemisphere, another character named <u>*Nephi*</u>. This Nephi and others were being persecuted for their belief in Christ. A few years previous, a True Messenger, Samuel the Lamanite, was sent to the wicked members of the Nephite church. Samuel told these people, who thought that they were righteous and doing what God wanted them to do, to repent of their wickedness. In his preaching and condemnation of the Church of God (similar to the LDS Church of modern times), Samuel told the people the exact year when the future Christ would be born.

In this part of our story, we wanted to reiterate the importance of listening to a True Messenger. We made Samuel's prophecy come true. The year came that Samuel prophesied Jesus would be born. But when the prophesied sign of his coming—"one day and a night and a day, as if it were one day and there were no night"[31]—didn't happen as expected, the doubters threatened to kill Nephi and the other believers.

---

[31] *BOM*, Helaman 14:4.

The night before he was born, the adult Jesus Christ, whose mortal infant body was still developing inside Mary (who was living in the Eastern Hemisphere), spoke to Nephi (in the Western Hemisphere). Jesus told Nephi to "be of good cheer; for behold ... on the morrow come I into the world."[32] We knew this would leave Christians wondering about when the human spirit actually enters the physical body of a mortal person. This part of our story should help understand this important "mystery."[33]

We also wanted to reiterate that the Father and the Son were the same entity, as we had presented earlier in our story:

> God himself shall come down among the children of men, and shall redeem his people. And because he dwelleth in flesh he shall be called the Son of God, and having subjected the flesh to the will of the Father, being the Father and the Son—The Father, because he was conceived by the power of God; and the Son, because of the flesh; thus becoming the Father and the Son—And they are one God, yea, the very Eternal Father of heaven and earth. ... to do the will, both of the Father and of the Son—of the Father because of me, and of the Son because of my flesh.[34]

It was important for us to give another clue about a Real Truth™ (i.e., "mystery of God") that few mortals understand. It is that all of us are our own God the Father, our own Christ, and our own Holy Ghost—three cognitive parts of the same eternal being that we have always been, and always will be. Our mortal flesh is an avatar that exists in our advanced mind, similarly to how we exist in our mortal dreams and have dream experiences. In our dreams, we have experiences on a *dream earth* while existing as our *dream self*. Likewise, when our mortal flesh dies, our advanced brain will disconnect from our mortal brain and we will no longer *dream* the mortal life experience.

---

[32] *BOM*, 3 Nephi 1:13.
[33] *See* Anonymous, *Human Reality—Who We Are and Why We Exist!* (Melba, ID: Worldwide United Publishing, 2009), 47–9. Read free at realilluminati.org/human-reality.
[34] *BOM*, Mosiah 15:1–4; *BOM*, 3 Nephi 1:14.

We will return to being completely conscious of our *true nature as an eternal advanced human*.

This concept is hard for a person to grasp, especially a religious person who believes in a god that is higher and more important than a mere mortal. However, the following <u>false</u> ideas are even harder to understand:

> We are spiritual children of God ("Heavenly Father"), and we existed as spirits before we were born on Earth. We came to Earth to physical bodies that were created by mortal parents.[35]

Why would God (a loving parent) want to cause a great deal of inequality among us (some are handsome, some are not; some are too tall, some are too short)? What are we going to look like in Heaven after we die? Are the ugly ones still going to be ugly? Are the short ones still going to be short? Are we going to look like we did *before* our spirit came to Earth? Or, will we look forever, in Heaven, like we do now upon Earth, except in a perfect form of ugliness (for some)? Christian belief on this matter is quite perplexing. For this reason, we wanted to provide those two clues about Jesus Christ that presented a close reflection to a Real Truth™ about our existence as humans—the greatest compendium of matter possible.

Because the Christians mocked our book, and those who didn't mock it ignored its message, we warned them about not reading our book carefully enough. We had Joseph give his followers another thing which "they could not understand." This other thing we gave them was the *First Vision*, where Joseph reported that he saw *both* the Father and the Son as *separate*, glorified beings. Joseph did not tell the people about these two separate

---

[35] *Compare to True to the Faith: A Gospel Reference* (Salt Lake City: The Church of Jesus Christ of Latter-day Saints, 2004), 164, found at churchofjesuschrist.org/study/manual/true-to-the-faith/spirit?lang=eng.

beings until many years after[36] the people had already rejected our new American scripture and wanted another corrupt Christian religion.

No LDS/Mormon scholar can properly explain and justify the contradiction—of Jesus being both the Father and the Son—between what our *Book of Mormon* teaches about this and Joseph's later account of the *First Vision*. What critics point out is that Joseph gave other accounts of the *First Vision* that are vastly different from the *official* version[37] in which the LDS/Mormons believe. Indeed, these things cause the LDS/Mormon people to stumble.

Needless to say, we are very upset at the way the LDS/Mormon people have treated our new American scripture. Their pride and blindness have made a mockery of our masterpiece, which was meant to do good. The world mocks our *Book of Mormon*, not because our book is corrupt, but because of the unrighteousness of those who present it as "another word of God."[38] Because of their pride, we have done things to cause them to stumble, but also tried to teach them important lessons in our new American scripture. One of these important lessons is that a person does not need a spiritual guide or religious leader to actually *hear* the *voice of God* in their own mind. Here is how we presented this Real Truth™:

After Jesus was killed by the Jews, there were three days of darkness in the Western Hemisphere. These three days of darkness fulfilled the prophecies that the native American prophets had told them about the death of Jesus. During these three days of darkness, many of the great Nephite and

---

[36] This was the 1838 account, written 18 years later. *See* Joseph Smith—History in the *Pearl of Great Price*.

[37] *See* Joseph Smith-History in *Pearl of Great Price*. For the manuscript version, *see* "History, 1838–1856, volume A-1 [23 December 1805–30 August 1834]," Church History Library in Salt Lake City, UT; also found online at josephsmithpapers.org/paper-summary/history-1838-1856-volume-a-1-23-december-1805-30-august-1834/1.

[38] *See* "Title Page of the Book of Mormon," The Church of Jesus Christ of Latter-day Saints, churchofjesuschrist.org/study/scriptures/bofm/bofm-title?lang=eng.

Lamanite cities were destroyed by earthquakes, fires, tornados, and other natural causes. Millions of people were killed.

We included this violent description in order to present a believable event that the Christians accept will herald Christ's "Second Coming" to Earth. It was our intent to give Christians an example of what it was going to be like when Jesus came again (as they believe). Christians do not realize that we presented a story in which Jesus *did come again*, to the ancient inhabitants of the Western Hemisphere. In our new American scripture, we presented an example of what the *Second Coming* of Jesus Christ would be like (if it were to occur). While in the darkness, the voice of Christ spoke to the people from Heaven. He did not tell them that those who were spared from destruction were righteous. He said,

> O all ye that are spared because ye were more righteous than they, will ye not now return unto me, and repent of your sins, and be converted, that I may heal you?[39]

Right after the darkness lifted, Christ's voice then told the people what they needed to do to be converted and healed. And what Christ told them to do in the darkness had nothing to do with performing any ordinance or being involved with any organized religion. We had Christ tell the people that he wanted them to become like a little child, with a broken heart and a contrite spirit, so that he could heal and "baptize [them] with fire and with the Holy Ghost," just like what had happened before in our story when the Lamanites were baptized and they

> knew it not. Behold, I have come unto the world to bring redemption unto the world, to save the world from sin. Therefore, whoso repenteth and cometh unto me as a little child, him will I receive, for of such is the kingdom of God. Behold, for such I have

---

[39] *BOM*, 3 Nephi 9:13.

Chapter 16: Humanity's Salvation—The Fullness of the Everlasting Gospel

laid down my life, and have taken it up again; therefore repent, and come unto me ye ends of the earth, and be saved.[40]

The salvation that Christ offers comes from a person <u>changing the way that they see their self and how they see others</u>—as a little child views themselves and others with the proper respect and value that causes them to treat each other properly. Unlike adults, a little child's mind is always open for instruction. This is what is required for "salvation."

After the darkness went away, we presented how the people

> heard a voice as if it came out of heaven; and they cast their eyes round about, for they understood not the voice which they heard; and it was not a harsh voice, neither was it a loud voice; nevertheless, and notwithstanding it being a small voice it did pierce them that did hear to the center, insomuch that there was no part of their frame that it did not cause to quake; yea, it did pierce them to the very soul, and did cause their hearts to burn.[41]

The people heard the voice of God in Heaven a couple of times, but did not understand it. Because they couldn't understand what they were hearing in their heads, an actual person had to appear to teach them. This is the part in the story when we had the physical resurrected *Christ* appear.

This part of our story is how we explained that mortals have the ability to hear from their advanced True Self, from *the Father*. But because of their fallen mortal flesh, they will not understand what they hear, unless they hear actual words from *the Son*—from someone with a physical mortal body, who shares the same kind of flesh that they have (i.e., from a True Messenger). We presented this scenario so that Christians might be convinced that,

---

[40] *BOM*, 3 Nephi 9:20–2.
[41] *BOM*, 3 Nephi 11:3.

although they feel like they are receiving communication from heaven (from God), mortals **do not** have the capacity to understand what "God" is trying to tell them.[42] Thus, they need a True Messenger. This is important.

Unfortunately, there have been many mortals who hear voices in their heads[43] and *feel* a physical sensation associated with what they assume is "God's voice." These people are deceived by what they *think* they hear. This is how people create religions and tell other people that God spoke to them, when in reality they are hearing voices that they do not understand,[44] all of which are caused by their personal pride and vanity (i.e., *Lucifer*).

In this part of the story, we wanted to teach the Christians that they shouldn't be listening to anyone but Christ himself; and that they shouldn't believe any voice in their head, because they would not be able to properly understand what the voice was telling them. We meant for this to be a rule that applies to everyone equally. We wanted to teach the people that there is ONLY one person whom "the Father" has designated to give "his will" to the people—Jesus Christ. If a person says that God has told them something, and what is told is NOT consistent with the words that Jesus spoke, the revelation or inspiration that came from the "still small voice" inside the person's head should be ignored.

In our story, the resurrected Jesus "descend[ed] out of heaven; and he was clothed in a white robe; and he came down and stood in the midst of them." The people verified it was Jesus Christ because of the marks in his hands and feet, as per the prophecies about his crucifixion.

Jesus called Nephi out of the crowd and gave him power to baptize the people after he had taught the people and left. There was no laying on of hands to confer this power to baptize at this time, nor did we have any

---

[42] *See BOM*, 3 Nephi 11:3–7.
[43] Anonymous, *Human Reality—Who We Are and Why We Exist!* (Melba, ID: Worldwide United Publishing. 2009), 64–5. Read for free at realilluminati.org/human-reality.
[44] *See Human Reality*, 467.

Chapter 16: Humanity's Salvation—The Fullness of the Everlasting Gospel

intention of including it in our narrative. It will be explained that we had to include the "laying on of hands" later on in our narrative in order to make our new American scripture more palatable to the Christians, especially to the men. Men value their priesthood authority and power more than anything else. If only men can hold the priesthood authority and power to properly baptize, then the male's value in the community increases. In early America, men ruled without question.

Baptism was important to Christians. We had presented in our storyline that actual physical baptism wasn't necessary, as previously explained. Nevertheless, we knew that this one "performance and ordinance" was important enough to the American Christians that it could not be completely excluded. Therefore, we included it in relation to having people do the following: 1) hear the words of Jesus; 2) repent of their sins with a broken heart and contrite spirit (which means that they were sorry for all the things that they were doing that went against what Jesus taught); and 3) desire to demonstrate their faith in Jesus through baptism. This was all presented after we

> had supposed not to have written any more ... Wherefore, we wrote a few more things, contrary to that which we had supposed; for we had supposed not to have written any more.[45]

Joseph's peers had been baptized in various churches that had been established throughout the United States. There were a lot of disputations among them about the right way to baptize and what baptism actually meant. In our new American scripture, we associated baptism with "becoming one with the Father, one with the Son, and one with the Holy Ghost," which is actually just one God. But first, people had to do the things that Jesus taught them. The entire presentation of baptism in our new American scripture, as well as all of the words and terms we used in the presentation of the "Second Coming of Jesus Christ," were meant to prepare the Christian readers' minds to

---

[45] *Compare BOM*, Moroni 1:4.

do the things that Jesus would tell them to do—things that would "save them," or in other words, create a successful society.

Jesus set up the proper protocol (order). His chosen apostles would give the people his teachings, and HIS TEACHINGS ONLY, and then baptize the people in water. Jesus told the people that after this, he would "baptize [them] with fire and with the Holy Ghost." At this point in our story, no apostle, no one but Jesus, could "baptize ... with fire and with the Holy Ghost." Jesus told his chosen apostles that after the people had been baptized, "they shall be visited with fire and with the Holy Ghost, and shall receive a remission of their sins." This protocol was how we hoped to end the disputations (arguments) about baptism and receiving the Holy Ghost. We wanted Christians to learn that no mortal man had the power to give the "baptism of fire and the Holy Ghost."

Sadly, after Joseph's peer group reviewed this part of our story, they were still confused. They argued about how people were supposed to know if they had actually received the "Holy Ghost." They admitted that people would know that they were baptized, because they would be immersed in water. But how would people be assured that they were going to be "visited with fire and with the Holy Ghost"?

Joseph's peers were beyond incorrigible (unable to change). They couldn't let go of what they had read in the Bible—how the Bible patriarchs and priests laid their hands on the heads of others to confer the priesthood and administer the "lower law." They looked beyond the mark and needed performances and ordinances that would *prove* to them they were special. To address this, we had our Jesus respond to this same wickedness by "groan[ing] within."[46] We were forced to respond by continuing our storyline (after we had already ended it with Jesus delivering the fullness of his everlasting Gospel). We had to add additional writings that would allow the people to receive the gift of the Holy Ghost by the laying on of hands from "men."

---

[46] *BOM*, 3 Nephi 17:14.

Chapter 16: Humanity's Salvation—The Fullness of the Everlasting Gospel

Our original intent was to end the book with the story of the Jaredites, after the subplot that had Jesus Christ deliver the fullness of his Gospel. After Joseph's peers reviewed our Jaredite story, they were astonished and dismayed that there was no mention of any priesthood, churches, or anything like what the Bible had presented as associated with the law of Moses. In the account of the Jaredites, we made it clear that no ordinance, no performance, *nothing* needed to be done to be "redeemed from the fall" <u>except to know the Real Truth™ about all things.</u>[47]

It's important here to reiterate how offended the men of Joseph's peer review group became when our story diminished the need for a male-dominated and -controlled religion. Jesus' *Sermon on the Mount* (the fullness of his everlasting Gospel) said nothing positive about the male role in a religion. His words didn't say anything about any religious organization being necessary or needed, and did not emphasize any difference between men and women, in any way. Therefore, we did what we had to do in order to get people, especially the men, to read and accept our new American scripture as another "word of God" comparable to the Bible. We were forced to give them what they desired; thus, we had to "write a few more things" pertaining to organized religion and priesthood performances and ordinances.

We knew that if the people depended on the priesthood authority of men to be saved, this dependence would lead to great inequality and wickedness. The men would use this authority to gain power over others, especially over the women who were not allowed to hold the priesthood. Women would need men in order to be saved and redeemed of their sins. This was of great concern to us. But there was nothing we could do about it at that time, except warn the reader that there was a lot more that Jesus taught the people that wasn't included in the unsealed part of Mormon's gold plates. There was a lot that wasn't included *because of the wickedness of those who first reviewed our new American scripture.*

---

[47] *See BOM*, Ether 3:13.

A New American Scripture

As our character *Mormon* was finishing up his account of the visit of the resurrected Christ to the people, we had him write:

And now there cannot be written in this book [the *Book of Mormon*] even a hundredth part of the things which Jesus did truly teach unto the people;

But behold the plates of Nephi do contain the more part of the things which he taught the people. And these things have I written, which are a lesser part of the things which he taught the people; and I have written them to the intent that they may be brought again unto this people [the native Americans], from the Gentiles [the American Christians], according to the words which Jesus hath spoken [the fullness of Jesus' everlasting Gospel].

And when they shall have received this [the *Book of Mormon*], which is expedient that they should have first, to try their faith, and if it shall so be that they shall believe these things then shall the greater things be made manifest unto them.

And if it so be that they will not believe these things [that are written in the *Book of Mormon*], then shall the greater things be withheld from them, unto their condemnation.

Behold, I was about to write them [the things that Jesus truly taught the people], all which were engraven upon the plates of Nephi, but the Lord forbade it, saying: I will try the faith of my people.[48]

The American Christians who *claim* to embrace and accept our new American scripture do NOT believe in it. They honor it with their lips, but their hearts are far from it. They ignore all of its prophecies and all of its

---
[48] *BOM*, 3 Nephi 26:6–11.

teachings, and completely transfigure its message to fit their own incorrect paradigm of religion and spirituality. Their faith in our book was tried. They failed to accept what they were given. The greater things, even that which Jesus did TRULY TEACH THE PEOPLE, were withheld, because of their unrighteousness. The LDS/Mormon people today are condemned for their lack of faith and lack of belief in our new American scripture.

As we explained above, the "everlasting Gospel" of Christ is only a *foundation* upon which to build a righteous society. Our new American scripture's narrative presents this *foundation* upon which to build such a society as the simple and clear words that Jesus taught the people. However, our story withholds many other things that "Jesus truly taught" the people. We had Mormon explain this as quoted above. If the American people refused the proper *foundation* <u>upon which to build a successful human society, they didn't need to know the "many other things" that Jesus taught, which Mormon withheld from his abridgment, because they wouldn't have done any of these other things anyway.</u>

As we have pointed out poignantly throughout this book, NOTHING—no lesson that our story teaches—is incorporated into the religious practices and beliefs of the LDS Church and its members. As we mentioned, they made all of the prophecies ABOUT THEM. Instead of helping the native Americans establish "Zion" (so that "Christ" could reign personally on the earth, in the Western Hemisphere with the native Americans), the LDS/Mormons teach that *their religion* will fill the earth after all the non-believers (non-Mormons) are destroyed.

NONE of the LDS/Mormon people or their leaders understands the "mysteries of God ... in full." And we were very specific about what happens when people do not understand Real Truth™ (i.e., "the mysteries of God in full"). As mentioned above, in reference to the "Gentiles" who do not want a new Bible or any more revelation or understanding of the "mysteries of God," we warned:

for unto him that receiveth [and believeth the *Book of Mormon*] I will give more; and from them that shall say, We have enough [we don't want to read the *Sealed Portion* of the record], from them shall be taken away even that which they have.[49]

The "fulness of the everlasting Gospel" of Jesus Christ has been taken from LDS/Mormons because of their unrighteousness. As we wrote and warned,

> he that will harden his heart, the same receiveth the lesser portion of the word; and he that will not harden his heart, to him is given the greater portion of the word, until it is given unto him to know the mysteries of God until he know them in full.

> And they that will harden their hearts, to them is given the lesser portion of the word [i.e., the *Book of Mormon*, not even a hundredth part of the things which Jesus did truly teach the people] until they know nothing concerning his mysteries; and then they are taken captive by the devil, and led by his will down to destruction. Now this is what is meant by the chains of hell.[50]

The litmus test of whether or not the people are righteous and are being led properly by the right people is HOW WELL THE PEOPLE KNOW THE MYSTERIES OF GOD. If the people know nothing of the mysteries of God, then the lesser portion of the word that they were given is taken away, until they know nothing. If one were to ask any LDS/Mormon person to explain the "mysteries of God in full," their response, if honest and forthright, would be, "We are counseled by our leaders to avoid discussing the mysteries."

There are people who accept and believe in our *Book of Mormon* and look forward to the fulfillment of the prophecy that spoke of the greater portion—the sealed part of the gold plates. When we fulfilled this prophecy

---

[49] *BOM*, 2 Nephi 28:30.
[50] See *BOM*, Alma 12:9–11.

in 2004, some of these people read *The Sealed Portion—The Final Testament of Jesus Christ* and were given some of the greater part, the greater things. In every case, reading *The Sealed Portion* has helped them understand the mysteries of God ("line upon line, precept upon precept") until it is given unto them to know the mysteries of God until they know them in full. The LDS/Mormons who have read and studied our *Book of Mormon* (pub. 1830) and our *Sealed Portion* (pub. 2004) have been released from the "chains of hell" by which they were bound by their ignorance.

We explained earlier in our storyline (before the account of Christ's Second Coming) that our book does not contain:

> a hundredth part of the proceedings of this people, yea, the account of the Lamanites and of the Nephites, and their wars, and contentions, and dissensions, and their preaching, and their prophecies, and their shipping and their building of ships, and their building of temples, and of synagogues and their sanctuaries, and their righteousness, and their wickedness, and their murders,*[51] and their robbings, and their plundering, and all manner of abominations and whoredoms, cannot be contained in this work.

> ... And there had many things transpired which, in the eyes of some, would be great and marvelous; nevertheless, they cannot all be written in this book; yea, this book cannot contain even a hundredth part.[52]

In writing our record the way we did, admitting that a great deal was left out of the story, we opened up the possibility for us to add to our story in the future. We will explain how we did this in another chapter about the "other books."

---

[51] Keep reading.
[52] *BOM*, Helaman 3:14; *BOM*, 3 Nephi 5:8.

A New American Scripture

We presented the Second Coming of the resurrected Christ to the people (in our story). We had Christ provide instructions to his chosen disciples about *how* to give his words to his people. After transcribing this part of our new American scripture, Joseph instructed his scribe, Oliver Cowdery, to use the King James Version of the New Testament and copy word for word from Matthew, chapters 5, 6, and 7.

These words became the same words that the *resurrected* Jesus Christ gave to the people in our story. These words established his *everlasting Gospel*, as we explained above. Joseph told Oliver Cowdery to give the story and words of Jesus from the Bible to the peer review group so that it could be reported to us how it was accepted by Joseph's peers. To us, this was the most important part of our new American scripture.

When Joseph reported back to us, we "groaned within ... because of the wickedness of the people." We were forced to continue the storyline based on Joseph's peers' reaction to the words that were supposed to be the ONLY way to salvation. What we wrote in our narrative, after presenting the words of Christ, reflects the great wickedness and pride of the early American people. However, we could not offend them and tell them plainly of their wickedness—they wouldn't have accepted our story as God's word.

We wrote the rest of the story in a way that presented those ancient people, who had received the words of Jesus, as an example of how the American Christians received the same words and "looked beyond the mark." We continued the story after Jesus delivered the fullness of his Gospel:

> And now it came to pass that when Jesus had ended these sayings he cast his eyes round about on the multitude, and said unto them: Behold, ye have heard the things which I taught before I ascended to my Father; therefore, whoso

Chapter 16: Humanity's Salvation—The Fullness of the Everlasting Gospel

remembereth these sayings of mine and doeth them, him will I raise up at the last day.[53]

We made this part of the story PERFECTLY CLEAR—that the ONLY THINGS required of the people in order to be "raised up at the last day" was to remember, and more importantly, DO, "these sayings of Jesus." We were clear that this was "the fulness of the everlasting Gospel ... as delivered by the Savior to the ancient inhabitants."

At this point in the story, had the people not questioned Jesus, if they had instead believed his words, Jesus would have left them straightway in order to fulfill the commandments that he had received of the Father:

that I shall go unto [the rest of the world, to other sheep], and that they shall hear my voice, and shall be numbered among my sheep, that there may be one fold and one shepherd.[54]

Instead of accepting the clear words of the resurrected Christ as the "fulness" of his everlasting Gospel, the incorrigible (unable to reform) American Christians questioned and wondered about organized religion. Thus, we wrote:

And it came to pass that when Jesus had said these words he perceived that there were some among them who marveled, and wondered what he would concerning the law of Moses [organized religion of performances and ordinances]; for they understood not the saying that old things had passed away, and that all things had become new.[55]

This part reflects the problems Joseph's peer review group had—that the simple words of Jesus were all that was needed to begin to create peace

---

[53] *BOM*, 3 Nephi 15:1.
[54] *BOM*, 3 Nephi 16:3.
[55] *BOM*, 3 Nephi 15:2.

on Earth and gain eternal salvation. They "marveled, and wondered" about religion, church, organization, priesthood—all the Christian traditions that meant so much to them.

We had our Jesus explain and reiterate to the people of our new American scripture's narrative, as we had to explain and reiterate to the American Christians, that:

> I am the law, and the light. Look unto me, and endure to the end, and ye shall live; for unto him that endureth to the end will I give eternal life. Behold, I have given unto you the commandments; therefore keep my commandments. And this is the law and the prophets, for they truly testified of me.[56]

Because of the reaction of Joseph's peers, we knew that the American Christians had already rejected the fullness of Christ's gospel. Therefore, we had Jesus himself prophecy about what was going to happen to the "Gentiles" (the Americans) after they received our book containing the "fulness of the everlasting Gospel ... as delivered by the Savior to the ancient inhabitants," and after they completely "looked beyond its mark."[57]

Jesus prophesied:

> And thus commandeth the Father that I should say unto you: At that day when the Gentiles [Americans] shall sin against my gospel, and shall reject the fulness of my gospel, and shall be lifted up in the pride of their hearts above all nations, and above all the people of the whole earth, and shall be filled with all manner of lyings, and of deceits, and of mischiefs, and all manner of

---

[56] *BOM*, 3 Nephi 15:9–10.
[57] *BOM*, Jacob 4:14.

Chapter 16: Humanity's Salvation—The Fullness of the Everlasting Gospel

hypocrisy, and murders,*⁵⁸ and priestcrafts, and whoredoms, and of secret abominations; and if they shall do all those things, and shall reject the fulness of my gospel, behold, saith the Father, **I will bring the fulness of my gospel from among them.**⁵⁹

The LDS/Mormons no longer teach, preach, or present the simple words of Christ as the "Gospel." Their religion teaches a completely different idea about the Gospel of Jesus Christ. We have given evidence of how they lie, are deceitful, and mischievous when we gave empirical evidence of what one of their Twelve Apostles said about our new American scripture. (See *Prologue*.) These people are hypocrites and engage in priestcrafts. Their top leaders are paid handsomely for what they do.⁶⁰ Their church combines its power in secret with the political and business powers of the world.⁶¹

The LDS/Mormons would outwardly deny that they murder people (*see above scripture quotes).⁶² But we have given an explanation in our new American scripture of how they DO commit murder, as we referred to it in Jesus' words above. In our story, we present a character named "Alma," who was rebellious against the commands of the Lord. Through his bad example and the way he lived, he was "destroying the people" by leading them away unto eternal destruction, not of the body, but of the soul. Alma says of this, "I had *murdered* many of his children, or rather led them away unto destruction."⁶³

The early Mormon Church that Joseph *suffered* to be, as well as the even more corrupt church under the leadership of Brigham Young, "murdered* many of his children, or rather led them away unto [their spiritual]

---

⁵⁸ Explained later.
⁵⁹ *See BOM*, 3 Nephi 16:10, emphasis added.
⁶⁰ *See* Peggy Fletcher Stack, "How much do top Mormon leaders make? Leaked pay stubs may surprise you.," The Salt Lake Tribune, 26 Jan. 2017. archive.sltrib.com/article.php?id=4800350&itype=cmsid.
⁶¹ For a list of prominent LDS/Mormons in various fields and industries, *see* "List of Latter Day Saints," *Wikipedia*, 8 May 2021, en.wikipedia.org/wiki/List_of_Latter_Day_Saints.
⁶² *BOM*, Helaman 3:14; *BOM*, 3 Nephi 16:10; how we defined *murder*.
⁶³ *See BOM*, Alma 36:14.

destruction." We had our Jesus prophesy that the "Gentiles," by rejecting the fullness of his Gospel, were committing *spiritual murder*.

And as to Jesus' mention of the "whoredoms" that the "Gentiles" would commit because they rejected his gospel, our story was VERY clear. One of these "whoredoms" was polygamy. We also used the word "whoredom" throughout our new American scripture to indicate "worldliness." In our book of Revelation, we refer to "whoredom" as "fornication" with

> the great whore that sitteth upon many waters: With whom the kings of the earth have committed fornication, and the inhabitants of the earth have been made drunk with the wine of her fornication.[64]

The ancient Hebrews used the word "Babylon" to describe excessive worldliness and the lust for things of the world. The woman that we mention in Revelation represents:

MYSTERY, BABYLON THE GREAT, THE MOTHER OF HARLOTS AND ABOMINATIONS OF THE EARTH.[65]

We wrote how when the Nephites and the Lamanites became excessively worldly and focused on their possessions, we called these things "whoredoms." Few modern-day religions are more focused on worldly success, materialism, possessions, education, and popularity than the LDS Church.[66] Truly, the "Gentiles" commit "murders" and

---

[64] NT, Revelation 17:1–2.

[65] *See* NT, Revelation 17:3–5.

[66] *See* "Why So Many Good Business Leaders Are Mormons," The Economist, Business Insider, May 4, 2012, businessinsider.com/why-the-mormon-faith-produces-so-many-good-business-leaders-2012-5; *see also*

Aimee Groth, "The REAL REASON So Many Mormons Become Executives And Political Leaders," *Business Insider*, 22 June 2011, businessinsider.com/mormon-business-leaders-2011-7.

Chapter 16: Humanity's Salvation—The Fullness of the Everlasting Gospel

"whoredoms," as our Jesus explains, because they have rejected the *true* fullness of his everlasting Gospel.

Our story continued with Jesus not only "groan[ing] within ... because of the wickedness of the people of the house of Israel," but with Jesus giving strict warnings to the "Gentiles" who would be reading our *Book of Mormon*.

In our story, the people at Jesus' Second Coming questioned his mission to teach them the things that his Father had commanded. If the people had not wanted religion, and had Jesus done what he said he was going to do before he "groaned within," there would have been no sacrament, no laying on of hands, and no organization of any type of church. Jesus would have left the people in the hands of his chosen apostles, who would have continued to teach ONLY the fullness of the Gospel—"those same words which Jesus had spoken—NOTHING VARYING FROM THE WORDS WHICH JESUS HAD SPOKEN."[67]

Instead of the fullness of the everlasting Gospel—the foundation upon which a successful nation must establish itself—the American Christians

> sought for things that they could not understand. Wherefore, because of their blindness, which blindness came by looking beyond the mark [set by Christ's Gospel], they must needs fall; for God hath taken away his plainness from them, and delivered unto them many things which they cannot understand, because they desired it. And because they desired it God hath done it, that they may stumble.[68]

We, the Real Illuminati®, invented the God of the *Book of Mormon*. We invented the Messiah of the ancient inhabitants of the Western Hemisphere. We presented the idea of "the Father," "the Son," and "the Holy Ghost" being just one entity that exists in each and every person.

---

[67] *See BOM*, 3 Nephi 19:8.
[68] *BOM*, Jacob 4:14.

A New American Scripture

We invented the *Three Nephites* and *John the beloved* to introduce ourselves. We have written our new American scripture to present the "way, the truth, and the life" that the world must follow in order to establish a successful world filled with peace, equity, and harmony.

Our work is called a Marvelous Work and a Wonder®. What we have done in presenting the stories upon the gold plates of Mormon is truly

> a great and a marvelous work among the children of men; a work which shall be everlasting, either on the one hand or on the other—either to the convincing of the American Christians and ALL religious people throughout the world unto peace and life eternal, or unto the deliverance of them to the hardness of their hearts and the blindness of their minds unto their being brought down into captivity, and also into destruction, both temporally and spiritually.[69]

The Americans, the Christians, and the rest of the world have made their choice concerning the "great and marvelous work" that we are doing. The people chose their religions over peace and life eternal. Because of their choice, we have made our choice, and have delivered them to their own destruction, both temporally and spiritually.

What more could we say about the salvation of humanity—the fullness of the everlasting Gospel?

---

[69] *Compare BOM*, 1 Nephi 14:7.

Chapter 17
The Great White Nation of the United States

We have explained how the first early European-American Christians who had accepted our new American scripture and called themselves Latter-day Saints, rejected its clear and profound lessons. We have explained that we warned them "in every way possible, as eloquently as we could without offending their *pride* and belief in organized religion." And throughout this book (*A New American Scripture—How and Why the Real Illuminati® Created the Book of Mormon*) we have quoted the following verse of our new American scripture more than any other:

> But behold, the Jews [Joseph's peer review group] were a stiffnecked people; and they despised the words of plainness, and killed the prophets, and sought for things that they could not understand. Wherefore, because of their blindness, which blindness came by looking beyond the mark [the fullness of the everlasting Gospel of Jesus Christ], they must needs fall; for God hath taken away his plainness from them, and delivered unto them many things which they cannot understand, because they desired it. And because they desired it God hath done it, that they may stumble.[1]

We have explained how we wrote the above verse *after* we were forced to rewrite the original storyline (presented as the *Lost 116-page Manuscript—*the *Book of Lehi*) and replace it with the *Small Plates of Nephi,* which include *1 and 2 Nephi, Jacob, Enos, Jarom,* and *Omni.* We wrote the part called *The Words of Mormon* to make a believable transition from what we wanted "lost" to the rest of our intended narrative. "And [we did] this for a wise purpose."[2]

---

[1] *BOM*, Jacob 4:14.
[2] *BOM*, Words of Mormon 1:7.

There was little doubt in our minds that the American Christians who read our new scripture would not let go of their ideas about organized religion. We have explained how important the outward performances and ordinances (religious rituals) were to them. These people felt that these rituals would save them in Heaven. We have explained how the early LDS/Mormon people made our new American scripture ALL about them and their *spiritual salvation.* We've explained how they ignored the prophecies we created to inspire them to help the native Americans living in the Western Hemisphere attain *temporal salvation.*

We have condemned this people throughout this book, *A New American Scripture—How and Why the Real Illuminati® Created the Book of Mormon.* Our justified attacks against the LDS/Mormon people and their organized churches, no matter how large or small, are needed, not only to convince these people of the error of their ways, but to convince the world that our *Book of Mormon* and *The Sealed Portion* were meant for the "intent to do good." We have fairly and honestly explained that the LDS/Mormon people, their ideologies and their churches, are far from good, neither do they follow ANY part of our new American scripture.

We have explained that the United States of America is currently on a slippery slope towards its own demise,

> not the destruction of the soul, save it be the casting of it into that hell which hath no end ... unto the deliverance of [the Americans and the rest of the world] to the hardness of their hearts and the blindness of their minds unto their being brought down into captivity, and also into destruction, both temporally and spiritually.[3]

We did not write this prophecy until *after* the early LDS/Mormons had rejected our original narrative's beginning and "looked beyond the mark and

---

[3] *BOM*, 1 Nephi 14:3, 7.

sought for things that they could not understand." We then made one last attempt to convince these early American Christians (notwithstanding the fact that they had rejected the idea) that they didn't need any religion of any type, of any means, or any outward performances and ordinances. This was one of the main reasons for creating a story to represent the American people (the "Gentiles")—a nation of millions and millions of "white, and exceedingly fair and beautiful … people before they were slain."[4]

We created the Great Jaredite Nation.

The subplot we inserted into our new American scripture's narrative about this Great Jaredite Nation is known as the *Book of Ether*. This was our last attempt in the *unsealed portion* of our record (book) to convince the Americans to take the right steps in establishing and developing the greatest modern nation of all the nations on Earth.

Our main prophet of God mentioned in this subplot was named Ether. We made certain that Ether would leave a clear prophecy about what was *supposed* to happen in North America—the area of the Western Hemisphere where the Great Jaredite Nation began and ended. This is the same area where the United States of America began, and will end, IF the American people do not heed our warnings and learn the lessons that we have presented *about them* in our new American scripture.

We tried one last time to convince the Americans "that [North America] was the place of the New Jerusalem, which *should* come down out of heaven, and the holy sanctuary of the Lord."[5] We did *not* write that the New Jerusalem "will" come down out of heaven. We wrote that it "*should*."

> A New Jerusalem *should* be built upon this land, **unto the remnant of the seed of Joseph … wherefore, the Lord brought a remnant of the seed of Joseph out of the land of Jerusalem, that he might be**

---

[4] *BOM*, 1 Nephi 13:15.
[5] *BOM*, Ether 13:3.

> merciful unto the seed of Joseph that they should perish not. ... Wherefore, the remnant of the house of Joseph shall be built upon this land; and it shall be a land of their inheritance; and they shall build up a holy city unto the Lord ... and they shall no more be confounded, until the end come when the earth shall pass away. And there shall be a new heaven and a new earth; and they shall be like unto the old save the old have passed away, and all things have become new.[6]

We have explained and given a plethora of ample and honest evidence that the LDS/Mormon people (who in modern times tout our *Book of Mormon* as the "keystone of their religion") do NOTHING to help the native American peoples living in both North and South America. THESE NATIVE PEOPLES ARE the "remnant of the house of Joseph," according to our narrative. The American "Gentiles" are NOT. The United States of America *should be* a "land of inheritance" for the native American peoples "that [these people] should perish not." Great promises are given to the white-skinned "Gentiles" in our scripture's prophecies, **IF** they help the native American peoples to prosper in the land.

Outside of the *Book of Ether* (which presents the story of the Jaredite Nation), we gave many other prophecies, including actual words Jesus Christ spoke to the people (according to our story) that explained what *should* have happened in the United States of America:

> The kings of the Gentiles [the American politicians] shall be the nursing fathers unto [the native American peoples], and their queens shall become nursing mothers; wherefore, the promises of the Lord are great unto the [Americans], for he hath spoken it, and who can dispute? But behold, this land, said God, shall be a land of [the native American people's] inheritance, and the Gentiles shall be blessed upon the land.[7]

---

[6] *BOM*, Ether 13:6–9, emphasis added.
[7] Compare *BOM*, 2 Nephi 10:9–10.

Chapter 17: The Great White Nation of the United States

Who can dispute how great and powerful the United States of America is? After World War II, the United States had the power to control and cause all nations to bow down to its power. This power came from the nuclear weapons that *we* (the Real Illuminati®) helped America obtain, as we have explained in our writings. We helped the Americans in order to give them the power they would need to fulfill the prophecies that we wrote for our new American scripture. It was our hope that they *should* do what was expected of a righteous nation of human beings. The United States of America *should have* become a melting pot of all marginalized and persecuted people throughout the world, starting with those of native American ancestry whose lands the Americans stole and controlled without proper compensation.

"The promises of the Lord are great unto the [people of the United States of America]." (See quote above.) We made it clear that these promises had restrictions and requirements. One was that

> this land shall be a land of liberty unto the Gentiles, and there shall be no kings upon the land, who shall raise up unto the Gentiles. And I will fortify this land against all other nations. And he that fighteth against Zion shall perish, saith God.[8]

Although the Americans (the LDS/Mormon people) ignored the lessons and prophecies of our *Book of Mormon*, and although Joseph Smith was under strict mandate to give them things that would make them stumble (because they *missed the mark* of our lessons and prophecies and desired these things that they could not understand), we still allowed Joseph to try all that he could to persuade his followers to do the right thing. For this reason, we mentioned that we helped Joseph write what is known in the LDS faith as the *Book of Moses*.[9]

---

[8] *BOM*, 2 Nephi 10:11–13.
[9] See *PGP*, "Selections From The Book of Moses."

The *Book of Moses* is basically a rewrite of the Old Testament up until the story of Noah, when "God said unto Noah: The end of all flesh is come before me, for the earth is filled with violence, and behold I will destroy all flesh from off the earth."[10] It was in the *Book of Moses* that we had Joseph Smith attempt to give his followers a different view of the Bible stories. Why would God want to destroy all humankind? Why is "the earth filled with violence"? What can save humanity?

It was in this new account of the Bible stories that we had Joseph expound upon what happened to Enoch, when the Bible account states: "And Enoch walked with God: and he was not; for God took him."[11] Where the Bible left a hole regarding *how* "Enoch walked with God," and *how* "God took him," we found an opportunity to create another story that would teach the lessons we intended for our new American scripture.

We intended for the story of Enoch in the *Book of Moses* to be supportive evidence of what happened to the brother of Jared in our subplot about the Jaredite Nation. Enoch came before the brother of Jared. Both Enoch and the Brother of Jared shared the same experiences. Both went upon a great mountain to converse with God. Both "saw the Lord; and he stood before my face, and he talked with me, even as a man talketh one with another, face to face." Both were shown "the world for the space of many generations."[12]

We have explained that Joseph's peer review group's members were all staunch Bible-believers. Even after the *unsealed portion* of our record was published as the *Book of Mormon* in 1830, those who had accepted it as another "word of God" still had a lot of questions, concerns, and doubts. A few wondered why God wouldn't have tried to set up a righteous people in the Eastern Hemisphere *before* contacting the brother of Jared and sending him, his brother (Jared), and a few of their friends over to the Western Hemisphere.

---

[10] *PGP*, Moses 8:30.
[11] OT, Genesis 5:24.
[12] *See PGP*, Moses 7:2–4 and *BOM*, Ether 3:1–26.

Chapter 17: The Great White Nation of the United States

This is when we took advantage of the hole in the Bible's account about what happened to Enoch. The *Book of Moses* was written just a few months after the *Book of Mormon* was published. We had to make the story about Enoch consistent with what the *Book of Mormon* story states about the brother of Jared being the first person on Earth who saw God with his own physical eyes. Our new American scripture states, in regards to the brother of Jared: "never have I [God] showed myself unto man whom I have created, for never has man believed in me as thou hast."[13]

Of course, Joseph's peers questioned the authenticity of the story of Enoch, because of what the *Book of Mormon* states about the brother of Jared (who came after Enoch) being the first mortal to see God "face to face." These questions were what we intended by presenting the *Book of Moses* the way we did, especially including the story about Enoch. Enoch "was not; for God took him." In other words, because Enoch saw God, he couldn't remain on the earth as a mortal any longer. Therefore, it made sense that the brother of Jared was the first *living* mortal who saw God and lived to tell about it.

Their doubts and questions opened up the opportunity for us to write another story that we hoped would have inspired the people to create a righteous society. We created the idea that Enoch was given certain instructions to create what the LDS/Mormon people believe to be the perfect city upon the earth—the *City of Enoch*. This gave us a way to present more details about what the people needed to do to create such a society. If Enoch was able to create such a city, then it is possible for other people to do so as well, *IF* the people will start with the correct foundation. Enoch taught his people this "correct foundation."

The account of Enoch in the *Book of Moses* was preceded by something that the American Christians, as well as members of all other religions, could not comprehend very well or accept. It is this concept that MUST BE THE

---

[13] *BOM*, Ether 3:15.

FOUNDATION UPON WHICH ALL HUMAN ACTION IS BASED: ALL humans can be EQUAL TO GOD, IF THEY FOLLOW THE WORDS OF CHRIST.

The story of Enoch starts by God calling Enoch to

> prophesy unto this people, and say unto them—Repent, for thus saith the Lord: I am angry with this people ... for their hearts have waxed hard, and their ears are dull of hearing, and their eyes cannot see afar off.[14]

Enoch's preaching culminates in presenting the time when Adam was first told about Jesus Christ, the

> Only Begotten Son, who is full of grace and truth, [and] the only name which shall be given under heaven, whereby salvation shall come unto the children of men.[15]

Enoch continues his teachings about the importance of listening to and doing what Jesus Christ tells the people to do. He is very clear that it doesn't matter that Jesus would be murdered to die for sin—if a person does not do what Jesus says, they will not be saved.

> This is the plan of salvation unto all men, through the blood of mine Only Begotten, who shall come in the meridian of time.[16]

We told Enoch's story in a way that we knew would capture the hearts and minds of the Christian people. In this story, we were able to confront the Christian belief that Jesus died to "atone for the original guilt." We presented this as a misunderstanding that the children of Adam had about what Adam taught them regarding Jesus Christ. We wrote,

---

[14] *PGP*, Moses 6:27.
[15] *PGP*, Moses 6:52.
[16] *PGP*, Moses 6:62.

Chapter 17: The Great White Nation of the United States

> Hence came the saying abroad among the people, that the Son of God hath atoned for original guilt, wherein the sins of the parents cannot be answered upon the heads of the children, for they are whole from the foundation of the world.[17]

In Enoch's story, we confronted the idea that a person needed someone else of priesthood authority to baptize them. In the story, Adam baptizes himself,

> and the Spirit of God descended upon him, and thus he was born of the Sprit, and became quickened in the inner man. And he heard a voice out of heaven, saying: Thou art baptized with fire, and with the Holy Ghost. This is the record of the Father, and the Son, from henceforth and forever.[18]

This was exactly what we wrote in our new American scripture about how the Lamanites were converted and baptized and "they knew it not."[19]

Rewriting the Bible would not have been necessary, if the American Christians would have read our new American scripture and learned the lessons that it was meant to teach. The Christians wanted their religions, they wanted their churches, and they wanted their own "promised land" that God set aside just for them and their white skin. Catering to this extreme pride, we were forced to give them more lessons about what it was going to take to create a society of people that would not end up destroying itself. For this reason, we created the story about the righteous *City of Enoch* in contrast to how the white Great Jaredite Nation was destroyed from within.

This righteous *City of Enoch* was based on the idea that all people are equal to God as long as they do what God would do if God were among them living as a mortal. And because our *Book of Mormon* prophesied that the

---

[17] *PGP*, Moses 6:54.
[18] *See PGP*, Moses 6:64–6.
[19] *BOM*, 3 Nephi 9:20.

"Gentiles" (Americans) *should* establish *Zion* in North America, we gave them a direct and clear explanation of what God meant for "Zion":

> And the Lord called his people Zion, because they were of one heart and one mind, and dwelt in righteousness; and there was no poor among them.[20]

We had hoped that there would have been no question about what foundation of law and order would create a successful society. For this reason, all of our writings pointed the reader towards the simple teachings that the mortal god Jesus the Christ, taught the Jews, for which he was murdered. These were the EXACT SAME WORDS that the resurrected Jesus, the Christ, taught when he came in his power and glory.[21] If the United States of America based ALL of its law and order on the *Sermon on the Mount*, this nation would rise to be another *City of Enoch*.

We wrote prophecies that explained how great the United States would *or could* become because of God's help (or rather because of *our* help, because *we* wrote the prophecy), and that "he that fighteth against Zion shall perish." Joseph's followers had no idea what "Zion" actually meant until we incorporated a clear definition in our *Book of Moses*. We meant to explain that anyone—any government, group, or faction of people—that fights against <u>*becoming of one heart and one mind and dwelling in righteousness,* and as a result of living this way, has *no poor among them*</u>, will cause the demise of humanity.

We wrote that

> [God] must needs destroy the secret works of darkness, and of murders, and of abominations. Wherefore, he that fighteth against

---

[20] *PGP*, Moses 7:18.
[21] *See BOM*, 3 Nephi, chapters 12, 13, and 14; and Matthew, chapters 5, 6, and 7.

Zion, both Jew [believer] and Gentile [non-believer], both bond and free, both male and female, shall perish; for they are they who are the whore of all the earth; for they who are not for me are against me, saith our God [Jesus Christ].[22]

Consider a few examples of what is happening in the United States today (circa 2020). Those who consider themselves *African American*—whose ancestors were those in "bondage"—are rising up in anger and protest against those whose ancestors were considered "free." The *excessive pride* of these descendants of early American slaves causes them to *fight against becoming of one heart and one mind* with the lighter-skinned Americans, even though most of the white-skinned Americans disagree with slavery in every shape and form.

The Real Truth™ modern African-Americans refuse to see is that the laws that emancipated their ancestors from slavery, as well as the laws that would eventually desegregate America and allow more freedom and equality for a dark-skinned person, were NOT introduced or voted upon by ANY African-American United States member of Congress. ALL were white.[23] If a majority of white-skinned Americans did not support and vote for emancipation and desegregation, the unjust position of an African-American would have remained as it was many years ago.

---

[22] *Compare BOM*, 2 Nephi 10:15–16.

[23] The 13th, 14th, and 15th Amendments were ratified on 6 Dec. 1865, 9 July 1868, and 3 Feb. 1870, respectively. For a brief summary of these Amendments, *see* "Landmark Legislation: Thirteenth, Fourteenth, & Fifteenth Amendments," United States Senate, senate.gov/artandhistory/history/common/generic/CivilWarAmendments.htm.

The first African-American Senator took office Feb 25, 1870. The first African-American United States Representative took office 12 Dec, 1870. *See* "List of African-American United States senators," *Wikipedia*, Wikimedia Foundation, 22 May 2021, en.wikipedia.org/wiki/List_of_African-American_United_States_senators; *and*

"List of African-American United States representatives, *Wikipedia*, Wikimedia Foundation, 22 May 2021, /en.wikipedia.org/wiki/List_of_African-American_United_States_representatives.

A New American Scripture

Countering the way that the African-American leaders cause fear, anger, protests, uprisings and conflict, the Real Truth™ maintains that there is no overall *systemic racism* in the United States of America. The "system" of law and order established by the U.S. Constitution was entirely responsible for the changes and laws that brought equality of the races to America. A majority of the white-skinned, non-racist U.S. Congress was solely responsible for these changes.

The leaders of the African-American movements are creating great strife, anger, hatred, and division. These leaders call Jesus their god, yet not one of them promote the words of Jesus to their followers. The *Black Lives Matter* movement and protests[24] are causing this unprecedented division, anger, and sometimes fear and violence. These angry, unforgiving, and prideful groups block roads, yell at people passing by their protests, and instill a threat: "No Justice. No Peace."[25] These groups, most of whom identify as Christians, do NOTHING that Jesus would do.

We have explained in some of our writings how we influenced early American slave traders to help the African people come to America. We knew that slavery was happening and that the early Americans were transporting slaves from other countries, besides Africa. *We knew of the* **potential** *of the United States.* Therefore, it is both prudent and wise for modern people, who insist on identifying themselves as *African American*, to consider the sufferings and struggles their ancestors endured, which ensured that they (the modern people) now have access to the innovations and opportunities afforded to American citizens.

An African man (born, bred, and still living in Africa today) found our Marvelous Work and a Wonder®. He commented on what is happening in the world with those who identify themselves divisively as of African descent:

---

[24] *See* "At least 6,070 Black Lives Matter protests and other demonstrations have been held in the past 2,504 days," Elephrame, elephrame.com/textbook/BLM.
[25] *See* "No justice, no peace," *Wikipedia*, Wikimedia Foundation, 26 Apr. 2021, en.wikipedia.org/wiki/No_justice,_no_peace.

Chapter 17: The Great White Nation of the United States

The pride of African Americans doesn't only end there in America but transcends down to their African counterpart. As an African, I have always found my environment troubling. There is an unending segregation, discrimination, tribalism, hate, envy, and pride among Africans themselves. I'm not trying to be the good sheep here, but truth be told, we Africans kill ourselves [more] than any [other] race killing Africans.

We don't seem to be solving problems but rather destroying and creating more problems. We claim ... things that we have no empirical evidence of. There is a lot of misleading information among Africans about how the white race invaded Africa, stole their natural resources, rape[d] their women, kill[ed] their brave men that stood against them and took them as slaves. [Instead,] empirical evidence, coupled with common sense points to us as Africans that we had no idea nor enough knowledge about the uses of these natural resources that we have in abundance. [Until] today, Africa remains the poorest continent in the world with [this] so-called abundance of natural resources that Africans make noise off.

The lifestyle of almost [all] African leader[s] will certainly make you sick and throw [up]. The abuse of women, sex, and power is common. The lifestyle of almost [all] African Americans in America doesn't surprise me when compared to the lifestyle of almost [all] Africans in Africa. Most Africans are not law-abiding people. We seem to have [a] problem with law and order. We seem to prefer [a] chaotic environment [rather] than [a] peaceful one. George Floyd's disobedience to the law and law enforcers is no way different from his counterparts in Africa. Instead of aligning ourselves to other race[s] to promote peace and unity among humanity, we [would] rather promote disunity and segregation by forming pan African and African emancipation groups that create [a] more chaotic world.

The Real Truth™ is the only thing that calms me down, knowing I have no atom of intelligence and knowledge within me to solve humanity's problems. My only hope is placed in those who know [that] they know.[26]

We would wisely, cautiously, and with great love and compassion for all "bond" people, ask those so insistent on protesting and *fighting* "free" people to consider what it would be like if they returned to the modern African nations where a *part* of their DNA originated.

What would your life be like in Africa compared to what it is like in the United States? Some of the most revered actors, athletes, and statesmen have a dark-skinned complexion. These demand great respect and accolade from all people, of all races; and they receive it. Further, there are many lighter-skinned people who suffer the same injustices of which you march and protest, all suffering of which can be traced to poverty and inequality among ALL skin colors. We must warn you that you are digging a deep pit that will be "filled by those who digged it."[27]

Our warning to the American people was to ALL the American people: "[God] must needs destroy the secret works of darkness, and of murders, and of abominations," not only of fair-skinned people, but of "both bond and free, both black and white, both male and female … **for they are they who are the whore of all the earth.**"[28]

NONE OF THESE GROUPS follow the gentle words of Jesus Christ to love their enemies and do good to those who persecute them and despitefully use them. "For they who are not for me are against me, saith our God [Jesus Christ]."[29]

---

[26] John A. Davies, written April 22, 2021.
[27] *See BOM*, 1 Nephi 14:3.
[28] *BOM*, 2 Nephi 10:16.
[29] *BOM*, 2 Nephi 10:16.

We humbly, and again, with compassion for all people, ask the *Black Lives Matter* leaders to consider what would have happened, in most cases, if the darker-skinned Americans had been humble, meek, and kind when law enforcement was trying to take the person into custody. Had they (whose fighting, anger, and pride led to their death at the hands of law enforcement) complied with the teachings of Jesus Christ and submitted to the law (that forces a person to submit to ALL the commands of law enforcement), would they have been killed?

We realize how confrontational the above statements are to those who *fight against Zion*, as we have explained it above. Regardless of the ramifications of our statements, honest and reasonable people, setting aside their pride, would agree. We call upon the youth of the world to stop their anger, hate, strife, and persecution, and submit to a love and compassion for ALL of humanity, loving your enemies and doing good to those who persecute you and despitefully use you. And those of you who believe in Jesus, what do you think Jesus would have you do? We condemn the leaders of these movements, many of whom claim to be ministers and preachers of Christ's words. YOU are NOT.

We also reiterate this: EVERY person, regardless of race, gender, nationality, or belief, who is insistent on giving in to their

> natural man [or woman] is an enemy to God, and has been from the fall of Adam, and will be, forever and ever, unless he [she] yields to the enticings of the Holy Spirit, and putteth off the natural man [woman] and becometh a saint through the atonement of Christ the Lord, and becometh as a child, submissive, meek, humble, patient, full of love, willing to submit to all things which the Lord seeth fit to inflict upon him, even as a child doth submit to his father.[30]

---

[30] *BOM*, Mosiah 3:19.

People who are excessively prideful or angry, or who fight back, complain, protest, seek vengeance, and who do not submit to the law (regardless of the unrighteousness of the law), are causing and will cause the demise of humanity. At no time in the history of the world has taking up the sword ended well for humanity. We wrote of this in our book of Revelation:

> If any man have an ear, let him hear. He that leadeth into captivity shall go into captivity: he that killeth with the sword must be killed with the sword. Here is the patience and the faith of the saints.[31]

Our new American scripture is full of subplots about this. We wrote of how people who were slaves humbled themselves and submitted to slavery, law, and law enforcement of corrupt governments. These people did not protest or overthrow the government, but many times were delivered from their bondage because they were humble, meek, and a righteous people.

We explained early in this book about the Anti-Nephi-Lehi people who refused to fight, protest, or rise up against those who persecuted and despitefully used them (even killed them for no apparent reason). **It will take this type of people to bring peace and salvation to humanity.** These are the core of the lessons we presented in our new American scripture.

In our Jaredite story, the prophet Ether did everything in his power to point the people towards actions that would not make them a "natural man, an enemy to God." Ether

> cried from the morning, even until the going down of the sun, exhorting the people to believe in God unto repentance lest they should be destroyed, saying unto them that by faith all things are fulfilled—Wherefore, whoso believeth in God might with surety hope for a better world, yea, even a place at the right hand

---

[31] NT, Revelation 13:9–10.

of God, which hope cometh of faith, maketh an anchor to the souls of men, which would make them sure and steadfast, always abounding in good works, being led to glorify God.[32]

Regardless of how patient and full of long-suffering Ether was in trying to teach the people

a more excellent way ... in which man might have a more excellent hope; ... they did reject all the words of the prophets, because of their secret society and wicked abominations.[33]

"And it came to pass that Ether did behold **all the doings** of the people [the Jaredites]"[34] that led to their complete destruction. We included a subplot in our new American scripture in which the prophet Moroni also saw **the doings** of the people that developed the United States of America. **These doings** were the things that are currently causing the American society to fail, a failure that can be traced to poverty.

Moroni saw "the great pollutions upon the face of the earth." He saw how "polluted" the churches were that claimed to be the "holy church of God." Moroni saw the great pride of the American people. He saw their "love of money, and their substance, and their fine apparel, and the adorning of their churches," that this love was more than the love they have for the native American people at their southern borders who are "the poor and the needy, the sick and the afflicted." Moroni saw the "secret abominations to get gain" and that the "stiffnecked people" caused that "widows should mourn before the Lord, and also orphans to mourn before the Lord, and also the blood of their fathers and their husbands to cry unto the Lord."[35]

---

[32] *BOM*, Ether 12:3–4.
[33] *BOM*, Ether 12:11, 32; 11:22.
[34] *BOM*, Ether 15:13, emphasis added.
[35] *Compare BOM*, Mormon 8:27–41.

A New American Scripture

To our great sadness, we have presented empirical and indisputable evidence of how a leader of the LDS Church (that touts our *Book of Mormon* as the keystone of its religion) "transfigured the holy word of God."[36] This church has "built [itself] up to get gain." It has not accumulated this great gain righteously, as Jesus would, as the exemplary people presented in our *Book of Mormon* did, by their own industry.[37] The LDS Church did not become successful in the same way that the early, *righteous* Jaredites did. We wrote that the Jaredites "were exceedingly industrious, and they did buy and sell and traffic one with another, that they might get gain."[38]

This unrighteous and hypocritical church did NOT gain its massive wealth from its own industry. The LDS Church acquired the majority of its wealth from investments in the stock market and other investments through the industry of others—especially of the poor who work for the corporations that do not pay dividends to investors unless they make a profit. The companies and corporations that make enough profit to pay out dividends to investors—investors who perform NO work or labor for the dividends that they receive—"beat my people to pieces, and grind the faces of the poor" to make a profit.[39]

The LDS/Mormon people are a good example of the "Gentiles," or rather, of the American people for whom we wrote our new American scripture:

And the Gentiles are lifted up in the pride of their eyes, and have stumbled, because of the greatness of their stumbling block [i.e., the church that Joseph allowed them to create, because they looked beyond the mark, causing them to stumble], that they have built up many churches; nevertheless, they put down the power and miracles of God, and preach up unto themselves their own

---

[36] *BOM*, Mormon 8:33.
[37] *Contrast BOM*, Alma 4:6 with *BOM*, Mosiah 27:3–5.
[38] *See BOM*, Ether 10:22.
[39] *BOM*, 2 Nephi 13:15; OT, Isaiah 3:15.

Chapter 17: The Great White Nation of the United States

wisdom and their own learning, that they may get gain and grind upon the face of the poor.[40]

We have shown how an LDS leader "put down the power and miracle" of Moroni's vision of "their doings," and "preach[ed to the members of this church his] own wisdom and [his] own learning." These dishonest leaders must do everything in their power to justify the great wealth that their church has amassed. Nevertheless, they cannot hide from the Real Truth™ that their investments would not have yielded such an amount, UNLESS others were performing labor that they didn't.

In all of these warnings and prophecies about the United States of America, there is one underlying and familiar theme about the cause of this wickedness and abominations—"secret combinations, even as in times of old, according to the combinations of the devil."[41]

In our Jaredite story, we explained *why* the people "rejected all the words of the prophets." They rejected their words, even the words and fullness of the everlasting Gospel of Jesus Christ, "because of their secret society and wicked abominations."[42]

> And it came to pass that [the Jaredites] formed a secret combination, even as they of old; which combination is most abominable and wicked above all, in the sight of God; For the Lord worketh not in secret combinations, neither doth he will that man should shed blood, but in all things hath forbidden it, from the beginning of man.[43]

We dedicated an entire previous chapter to explain these *secret combinations*. In the story of the Jaredites, we reiterated how devastating

---

[40] *BOM*, 2 Nephi 26:20.
[41] *BOM*, 2 Nephi 26:22.
[42] *BOM*, Ether 11:22.
[43] *BOM*, Ether 8:18–19.

these things were and how they contribute to the demise of humanity. We warned the American people that these things

> have caused the destruction of this people of whom I am now speaking [the Jaredites], and also the destruction of the people of Nephi.
>
> And whatsoever nation shall uphold such secret combinations, to get power and gain, until they shall spread over the nation, behold, they shall be destroyed; for the Lord will not suffer that the blood of his saints, which shall be shed by them, shall always cry unto him from the ground for vengeance upon them and yet he avenge them not.
>
> Wherefore, O ye Gentiles, it is wisdom in God that these things should be shown unto you, that thereby ye may repent of your sins, and suffer not that these murderous combinations shall get above you, which are built up to get power and gain—and the work, yea, even the work of destruction come upon you, yea, even the sword of the justice of the Eternal God shall fall upon you, to your overthrow and destruction if ye shall suffer these things to be.
>
> Wherefore, the Lord commandeth you, when ye shall see these things come among you that ye shall awake to a sense of your awful situation, because of this secret combination which shall be among you; or wo be unto it, because of the blood of them who have been slain; for they cry from the dust for vengeance upon it, and also upon those who built it up.[44]

---

[44] *BOM*, Ether 8:21–4.

Chapter 17: The Great White Nation of the United States

We did not include a complete explanation of these things in the chapter about these *secret combinations*. We explained how the Jaredites had the record that the brother of Jared wrote, which he "brought across the great deep."[45] We explained that "there never were greater things made manifest than those which were made manifest unto the brother of Jared."[46] We gave a brief summary of the things that cause ALL wars and rumors of wars that have led to the downfall of humanity. *The Sealed Portion* of our new American scripture gives greater details.

The Sealed Portion of our new American scripture describes how the family unit and money can destroy humanity. There are many other parts of the story of the Jaredites that we will not discuss here. One so disposed may read the entire story and gain an appreciation for how we tried to help the American Christians set aside the pride in their individual family units, and unite as a people of ZION as we have defined it, as a people of "one heart and one mind, [with] no poor among them."

We have shown how, because of these family units, the system of money began. This money system enables one to support just one's own family and ignore the plight of the rest of humanity—Adam's family, according to how American Christians believe. Humanity cannot establish *Zion* where "there are no poor among them," unless the economic powers are controlled properly. Again, there is only one thing that can save humanity—establishing *Zion* as we have explained it above.

In our *Book of Moses*, Enoch tells how Adam explained what humanity needed to do to create a nation like his *City of Enoch*. The evils of the current system of money that has caused most of humanity's problems cannot exist in such a city. When the world's economic and political systems (humanity's trade and industry) are controlled by private owners for profit, rather than by a righteous government, human nature (the natural man, an enemy to God) takes over. This is CAPITALISM.

---

[45] *BOM*, Ether 8:9.
[46] *BOM*, Ether 4:4.

We have discussed the Real Truth™ throughout this book. Humanity cannot be saved, unless people know the Real Truth™ about the secret acts performed and supported by the powers that control humanity. People cannot be saved in ignorance. On the other hand, if the people know the Real Truth™, they shall be "redeemed from the fall."[47]

Unlike the story about the Nephites and the Lamanites (the remnant of the house of Joseph), the Jaredite story was written to present a narrative that was *not* filled with any superstition, tradition, or religion of any kind. However, these two stories *do* have something in common that led both nations to their eventual demise—*obscurantism* (the work of secret combinations). In all of history, when the powers of religion, politics, and business combine (without the majority of people knowing what is happening behind the scenes), they cause society to fail.

By including the subplot of the white Great Jaredite Nation, it was our desire to introduce "a more EXCELLENT way," by giving the people "a more EXCELLENT hope."[48] It <u>is</u> possible for a society of humans to exist where peace, equality, and harmony exist. The Nephites, Lamanites, and Jaredites could never establish this society. This more excellent way will *never* happen when the leaders of the people meet behind closed doors (in secret) and do things of which the people are not aware. This can only happen when ALL things are known and out in the open.

In our Jaredite story, we used the word "excellent," as it is presented, in reference to what Jesus Christ did, as related in the New Testament stories. The commandments given to the brother of Jared on the mount, were "a more EXCELLENT way" than those given to Moses on the mount. This "more EXCELLENT way" was explained in our Jaredite story as that which "redeemed the people from the fall." This "way" had nothing to do with what the people did (performances and ordinances), but this "more EXCELLENT WAY" to be redeemed had all to do with what the people KNEW.

---

[47] *BOM*, 2 Nephi 2:26.
[48] *BOM*, Ether 12:11, 32.

Chapter 17: The Great White Nation of the United States

Knowing the Real Truth™ about God, about human existence, and about life upon Earth, is the ONLY way that humans can be "redeemed from the fall." We made this clear, and presented this "MORE EXCELLENT WAY" to being redeemed, in what "Jesus Christ"—both "the Father and the Son"—revealed to the brother of Jared.

Before the brother of Jared, no other man upon Earth—not Adam or any other man UNTIL the brother of Jared—was "redeemed from the fall of Adam." (The only exception was Enoch and his righteous city, which was taken from the earth.) When our Jaredite Moses (the brother of Jared) spoke to God, he saw God for who He *really* was: a human being who looked like every other human being. This was something that was never known before we introduced it in the story of the Jaredites. Because of this knowledge, a knowledge of this "mystery of God"—that all humans are gods—the brother of Jared and those who listened to him were "redeemed."

People must recognize that they alone hold the power of their own salvation. When people are taught that God is more powerful than they are, and that they can do nothing without God, NOTHING GETS DONE. We wrote:

> Because thou [singular, meaning the brother of Jared] knowest these things, ye [plural, meaning all those who listen to the brother of Jared] are redeemed from the fall; therefore ye [plural] are brought back into my presence.[49]

We did not write, "Because thou knowest these things, *thou art* redeemed from the fall." We meant for it to read that *anyone* who knows (or accepts and believes) what was revealed to the brother of Jared is redeemed from the fall. Only True Messengers know what God revealed to the brother of Jared.

---

[49] *BOM*, Ether 3:13.

We are True Messengers. In the 1842 play that we helped Joseph Smith pen (write) for his followers, in order to give them the first symbolic representation of the Real Truth™ about human existence, the character Adam's last words were (referring to us):

> These are true messengers sent down from the Father. I exhort you to give strict heed to their counsel and teachings, and they will lead you in the way of life and salvation.[50]

No matter how hard we tried to convince the American Christians of a "more EXCELLENT way," they did NOT heed the counsel and teachings of our new American scripture.

---

[50] *SNS*, 123. Read free at realilluminati.org/sacred-not-secret.

Chapter 18
Other Books, Other Peoples

In Appendices 1 and 2, we provide some examples of how we wrote the *sealed part* of our new American scripture. Appendix 1, taken from *The Sealed Portion*, explains (in scripture prose according to the Bible's narrative) how the family unit and money started in the *Family of Adam* (the human race). Appendix 2 deals with specific instructions that Adam gave to his children after they became corrupt and separated into family units and economic classes. Adam's instructions are the *Everlasting Gospel of Jesus Christ*, according to our intended narrative. **Following these instructions is the *only way* humanity will ever be saved.**

We highly recommend that the reader take the time to review these parts of *The Sealed Portion* in order to gain a greater appreciation for our ability to write scripture.

Throughout our writings, we have explained how the written word actually began, and how men began to use it to invent scripture to make themselves more valuable to the community. We gave a more detailed and thorough explanation of this in the first book of our Trilogy, *The True History of Religion*.[1] By providing empirical evidence of our ability to write scripture that can cause a person to *feel the Spirit of God* and believe that the writing is from a supernatural source, we hoped to convince the reader of ALL scripture's *true* mortal source—the mind and will of a mortal human being.

Our 1842 play was meant to symbolically reveal the Real Truth™ about human existence upon Earth. It is currently known as the LDS Temple Endowment, although it has been changed from our original presentation. In that play, we made it very clear that ALL religion and ALL scriptures were from

---
[1] *See THOR*, 82–99. Free to read or listen at realilluminati.org/the-true-history-of-religion.

the *pride of "the natural man, an enemy of God."* They were ALL made up in the head of mortals who had a certain and specific reason for writing the scripture—usually to aggrandize their self and gain some value from others.

Consider the full verse from which we took the quote above in our new American scripture:

> For the natural man is an enemy to God, and has been from the fall of Adam, and will be, forever and ever, unless he yields to the enticings of the Holy Spirit, and putteth off the natural man and becometh a saint through the atonement of Christ the Lord, and becometh as a child, submissive, meek, humble, patient, full of love, willing to submit to all things which the Lord seeth fit to inflict upon him, even as a child doth submit to his father. [2]

This was the first time that we replaced the terms "the devil, Satan, and Lucifer" in our scripture writing with what we know is the *true source* of all human evil—a person's natural susceptibility to excessive pride and vanity, as we have explained it in previous chapters.

To understand the power and profundity (profound nature) of this single verse of scripture, consider what our world would be like if EVERYONE became again like they were as a little child—more submissive, meek, humble, patient, and full of love. Again, it is important for a sincere person seeking to understand Real Truth™ to take the time to read the Appendices (1 & 2) of this book (*A New American Scripture*). Upon reading them—now with better eyes that understand who wrote it and why this scripture was written—we ask each person to sincerely contemplate what we were trying to present as the way humanity got messed up because of this pride. Also consider the *only way* that humanity can be saved through the lessons taught by our story's character, Adam.

---

[2] *BOM*, Mosiah 3:19.

Chapter 18: Other Books, Other Peoples

What we presented throughout our scripture is a *code of salvation* that we call: *The Everlasting Gospel of Jesus Christ*. We only call it this because of the great power that Christianity holds over the hearts and minds of the people living in our current world. Especially consider those leaders who use this power to control humanity. We believe that we have sufficiently explained *how* and *why* we wrote a new American scripture and based it on Christianity.

In one of the scenes of our 1842 play's presentation, we have the characters **Adam** and **Eve**, who represent the people living upon Earth during mortality, sincerely pray to God for answers and guidance. We have the character **Lucifer** answer Adam's prayer. We clearly show that each person (Adam) is actually a *dreaming god*. We introduce Adam's *True* Self—the god Michael—during the first scene of the play. The god **Michael** is an equal god with the other two members of the godhead, **Elohim** and **Jehovah**. In portraying each mortal as the characters Adam and Eve in our play, we felt we couldn't have made it any clearer that a person's life experience upon the earth is a result of the person's own godhead (Elohim, Jehovah, and Michael)—one's *True Self*—"and they are one God, yea, the very Eternal Father of heaven and of earth."[3]

In our play, we made it clear and unmistakable that a person's *Elohim* and *Jehovah* part has NOTHING to do with the *Michael part* of a person, while the person is participating in the experience of life upon Earth, in what we present as "the lone and dreary world." Our play is clear that the characters *Eve* and *Lucifer*, which were meant to represent **another** part of *Adam*, do not exist *until* the god *Michael* is put to sleep and starts dreaming of life upon Earth, a planet that the godhead created exclusively for the mortal experience.

No matter how reluctant and evasive the LDS/Mormon leaders and people are about what they believe is the most sacred ordinance that they

---
[3] *BOM*, Mosiah 15:4.

can receive, what we have explained about the presentation of this ordinance throughout this book is undeniable. We made it very clear that *Lucifer* was responsible for ALL religion. We present *religion* in our play as the "philosophies of men mingled with scripture." In other words, the fallen human natures of mortal kind, mostly of men, caused the excessive pride and vanity that led to ALL religious beliefs and writings (scriptures) of ALL types. Outside of our scripture and other religious-based writings, we have produced other books (including the one you are reading now) and have explained how this pride and vanity led to first, writing and language, and then to how men used writing and language to deceive and control the masses who could not read or write.

Our play explains clearly that religion is responsible for all the mayhem and "blood and horror on the earth." There is no honest and reasonable person who can dispute this. We have explained that humanity is failing fast. Religious people are waiting upon their particular god to save humanity. They sit on their hands and do nothing, having faith in their religious leaders who teach them there is nothing they can do until their god comes to Earth, or returns to Earth (as the Christians believe) to save humanity. And the main source of these religious leaders' deceptions is the way they interpret the written word of God (scripture). We have pointed out, particularly, how the LDS Church leaders openly and unabashedly (blatantly) deceive the members of this church by transfiguring, misquoting, and ignoring the *unsealed portion* of our new American scripture, the *Book of Mormon*.

We have explained that the only way humanity will be saved is if humans start uniting together and solving the problems that they created themselves. Humans are completely responsible for all of the problems that exist. Being thus responsible, humans can solve all of these problems. All that stands in humanity's way is the *pride and vanity* that individuals and groups of individuals depend upon for their self-worth and value. We have explained how this excessive pride and vanity (i.e., *Lucifer*) "takes the treasures of the

Chapter 18: Other Books, Other Peoples

earth, and with gold and silver buys up armies and navies, religions and governments, and reigns with blood and horror on the earth!"[4]

The Trilogy of books that we are publishing at this time (of which this book is the second) is meant to do all that we can to open the hard hearts and closed minds of the human race. In our first book, we confront and explain *the true history of religion* and how we tried everything we could within religion to counter it and help religious people overcome their pride and become a united people "of one heart and one mind, and dwell in righteousness so that there is no poor among them."[5]

This book, the second of our Trilogy, was meant to provide empirical and indisputable evidence that we have the ability to write convincing and powerful scripture. Our scripture can affect the pride and vanity of those so inclined to choose religion as the basis of their self-worth and value. We hope to convince the world that ALL scripture is made up by humans. To do this, we were forced to write scripture, as we have explained.

Chapter 1 of this book presents what we offered as our *Opening Statement*. We stated that the evidence will show that our *Book of Mormon* was able to convince some Bible believers to accept it as another "word of God," comparable to the Bible. The evidence will also show that *The Sealed Portion* was able to convince some *Book of Mormon* believers that *The Sealed Portion* is, without a doubt, the prophesied *greater part* of our new American scripture. There is NO WAY that we could have done any of this without writing the books that we have written.

Owing to how much religious people rely on God's "written word" for guidance, in the prophecies that we wrote for our new American scripture, we purposefully left ourselves plenty of leeway and freedom to introduce more stories about other peoples and nations. In these *other* stories, we

---

[4] *Compare SNS*, 59; *see also TSP*, 20:50.
[5] *Compare PGP*, Moses 7:18.

A New American Scripture

intended to teach whatever lesson, in whatever way necessary, to further our purpose and intent.

We wrote a vision that our character *Nephi* had about the United States of America:

> And after [the *Book of Mormon*] had come forth unto [the native Americans living in the Western Hemisphere] I beheld **other books**, which came forth by the power of the Lamb, from the Gentiles unto them, unto the convincing of the Gentiles and the remnant of the seed of my brethren, and also the Jews who were scattered upon all the face of the earth, that the records of the prophets and of the twelve apostles of the Lamb are true.[6]

We prophesied that

> out of the books which shall be written [God] will judge the world, every man according to their works, according to that which is written.[7]

At this point in our narrative, we were making reference not only to the Bible, but also to our *Book of Mormon*, to *The Sealed Portion*, and to these "other books."

> For [God commands] all men, both in the east and in the west, and in the north, and in the south, and in the islands of the sea, that they shall write the words which I speak unto them.

We wrote these prophecies in a very specific way so that leaders of a corrupt religion would not be able to write "other books" and claim that *their personal* writings fulfill our specific prophecies. Regardless of our clear prophecies and warnings, the LDS Church claims that other books written by

---

[6] *BOM*, 1 Nephi 13:39, emphasis added.
[7] *BOM*, 2 Nephi 29:11.

Chapter 18: Other Books, Other Peoples

its General Authorities are part of these prophesied "other books." Nevertheless, it is not "God" who is speaking to the members of this church in these published books—it is their leaders. These leaders have made a very handsome profit by writing their own books and selling them to the members. We were very specific to point out that these "other books" would be from people outside of North America (where the United States of America exists).

We specified that these "other books" would be from "other tribes of the house of Israel [and] all nations of the earth," and that they will contain "the words which I [God] speak unto them."[8] Again, dishonest religious leaders make claim that *their words* are what God speaks to them for the people. We were very specific in the way we presented our prophecies. We hoped this would make it very difficult for the reader to believe that these deceitful leaders' books (written with their own words) fulfilled our prophecies about "other books." About the Bible and the *Book of Mormon*, we wrote clearly:

> For behold, I shall speak unto the Jews and they shall write it [the Bible]; and I shall also speak unto the Nephites and they shall write it [the *Book of Mormon*]; and I shall also speak unto the other tribes of the house of Israel, which I have led away, and they shall write it [*The Sealed Portion* taken from the record of the Jaredites, a group that was led away from the Eastern Hemisphere at the time of the Bible's account of the Tower of Babel]; and I shall also speak unto all nations of the earth and they shall write it. And it shall come to pass that the Jews shall have the [*Book of Mormon*], and the Nephites shall have [the Bible]; and the Nephites and the Jews shall have the words of the lost tribes of Israel [the "other books" that we have not yet written]; and the lost tribes of Israel shall have the [*Book of Mormon* and the Bible].[9]

---

[8] *BOM*, 2 Nephi 29:11–12.
[9] Compare *BOM*, 2 Nephi 29:12–13.

A New American Scripture

We had hoped that our new American scripture would have taught the Americans the fullness of the everlasting Gospel, persuading them to establish a great nation in which a New Jerusalem, a city of *Zion*, was built exclusively for the native American people. If our scripture had accomplished this, we would have been able to provide more "plates" upon which was written the history of the other tribes of Israel and other nations, which the Christians are taught are the "lost ten tribes of Israel."

Had our new scripture, written exclusively for the American people, worked, we would have brought forth <u>other</u> of the many plates of Nephi from which Mormon abridged the Nephite history, according to our new American scripture's narrative. On these other Nephite plates, we would have written what "Jesus truly taught the people," as well as many of the things that were mentioned as being left out on purpose in the "lesser portion":

> And now there cannot be written in this book [the unsealed *Book of Mormon*] even a hundredth part of the things which Jesus did truly teach unto the people; But behold the plates of Nephi do contain the more part of the things which he taught the people. And these things have I written, which are a lesser part of the things which he taught the people; and I have written them to the intent that they may be brought again unto this people, from the Gentiles, according to the words which Jesus hath spoken. And when they shall have received this [the *Book of Mormon*], which is expedient that they should have first, to try their faith, and if it shall so be that they shall believe these things then shall the greater things be made manifest unto them. And if it so be that they will not believe these things, then shall the greater things be withheld from them, unto their condemnation.[10]

---

[10] *BOM*, 3 Nephi 26:6–10.

We have explained how the people who accept our *Book of Mormon* and carry it forth into the world, testifying that it is "another word of God," are under great condemnation. These people have rejected the intended message of our new American scripture. They have no interest in fulfilling the prophecies that we wrote for the native Americans, but have made our message all about themselves. This has resulted in that particular church becoming one of the wealthiest institutions on Earth. We have provided sound evidence that, in their great hypocrisy, the LDS/Mormons have transfigured the word of God, as well as performed many other "doings" that we prophesied about them. Again, because of the powerful and strong evidence against the LDS Church, we mention once more what we presented in the *Prologue* of this book. We were shocked and greatly disappointed (but not surprised) that one of the Twelve Apostles of this church made a public record of his deception and hypocrisy.

As we have explained and reiterated throughout this book, it is because of how far the LDS/Mormon religion had gone in warping and distorting our message and using our book to entice people to join their church, that we were forced to bring forth the sealed part of our record before its time. Even so, there have been very few who have read the prophesied *sealed part* of our record, which is part of the "greater things," the "greater portion of the word,"[11] as we have presented it. Most of the world could not care less about our *Book of Mormon*. Most believe that Joseph and Christopher made up the *Book of Mormon* and *The Sealed Portion*, respectively. If this were true, the world should admire these two men as geniuses. Instead, they are mocked, persecuted, and one was killed because of this belief. But of Christopher, we wrote the prophecy in our new American scripture:

> Therefore, when these works [the *complete* record, both the *unsealed* and *sealed* portions of our new American scripture] shall come forth from the Gentiles ... For in that day, for my sake [Jesus

---

[11] *BOM*, Alma 12:10.

is speaking] shall the Father work a work, which shall be a great and a marvelous work among them; and there shall be among them those who will not believe it, although a man shall declare it unto them. But behold, the life of my servant shall be in my hand; therefore they shall not hurt him, although he shall be marred because of them. Yet I will heal him, for I will show unto them that my wisdom is greater than the cunning of the devil.[12]

The LDS/Mormons erroneously believe that "my servant" mentioned in the above passage referred to Joseph Smith, even when Joseph was killed "because of them." To fulfill this prophecy, which we wrote, and the outcome of which we can control, we protect Christopher, our former contemporary True Messenger. One who investigates Christopher will find many salacious and terrible things written about him, all of which are lies created to *mar* his character. Like Joseph's name, Christopher's name is "had for good and evil among all nations, kindreds, and tongues, or that it should be both good and evil spoken of among all people."[13]

With the release of our three-book Trilogy, we expect our books to eventually make an impact on the religious world. If that happens, and if the world continues to believe that Joseph Smith and Christopher made up the *Book of Mormon* and *The Sealed Portion*, respectively, Christopher's name will be *marred* to even a greater degree than Joseph's. Again, we will ensure that our prophecy about "my servant" is fulfilled. His life is in our hands.

Because of the LDS/Mormons' rejection of these "greater things," we were forced to write this book about our new American scripture. We wrote this book to reveal to the world how impure ALL religion is, but more so, how impure the LDS Church is. This particular church provides empirical evidence of how far off people can misinterpret and apply what they believe to be "God's holy word" in order to support their own personal pride and ego.

---

[12] *BOM*, 3 Nephi 21:5, 9–10.
[13] JSH 1:33.

Chapter 18: Other Books, Other Peoples

In so doing (writing this book), we have limited our ability to bring forth any of the "other books" of which our story prophesies. Because we have already explained *why* and *how* we wrote the *Book of Mormon* (consistent with the title of this book), any new written word we bring forth will not do what we intended for these prophesied "other books":

> to convince the Gentiles and the remnant of the seed of my brethren, and also the Jews who were scattered upon all the face of the earth, that the records of the prophets and of the twelve apostles of the Lamb are true.[14]

We cannot convince people of something that we have now revealed is not actually true. In the first book of our Trilogy, as well as in this one, we have revealed that the Bible is *not* true and that the stories of Jesus were invented for a wise purpose during the time when the Great Roman Empire was collapsing. Again, we had hoped that we could have convinced the world that the *Philosophy of Jesus of Nazareth* was all that a good society should be built upon. (We previously revealed that we were initially able to convince one of the American Founding Fathers, Thomas Jefferson of this.) If we had succeeded in our goal, we could have brought forth a lot more of the "mysteries of God" (Real Truth™) through these "other books."

As we mentioned earlier, we could have written a believable history about, not only the lost ten tribes of Israel, but also about the people of Ishmael (Isaac's half-brother and Abraham's "other" son, according to the Bible's narrative). We could have written a history about Esau, Isaacs's "other" son; about Cain, Adam's "other" son; as well as about many "other nations on the earth" that existed at the time that Abraham existed, according to the story of the Bible.

In revealing *how* and *why* we wrote the *Book of Mormon*, we have given strong evidence and proven a strong point about the rest of the scriptures that exist in the religions of the world: ALL scripture is the philosophies of men.

---

[14] *Compare BOM*, 1 Nephi 13:39.

There is no true religion, and there is no true scripture. Again, because of this revelation and the proof that we have provided about how we have the ability to write new scripture, writing any "other book" would now be futile.

Regardless of whether we would have written more *new scripture*, humanity no longer has the time to continue to worry about religion and the gods of religion. Humanity is failing fast. Humanity is faced with a threat of destruction unlike at any other time during this current *Sixth Dispensation of Humanity [Time]*.

Therefore, we cannot waste any more time and energy trying to convince people to believe in God and presenting a God to them that can change the course of history, when only <u>they</u> can change it. We cannot continue using our skill in writing scripture to prolong their belief in imaginary gods—gods that are invented and controlled by ego and pride (*Lucifer—the god of this world*). We are giving the people of Earth the Real Truth™ in its fullness. In the third and final book of our Trilogy, *One People, One World, One Government*, we will present political strategies and plans that can be, and must be, implemented in order to save humanity.

If our Trilogy is ignored and rejected and if we are rejected in this last part of our work, at least we can say that the blood of this generation is not on our hands. We will rest knowing that we have warned the people of Earth sufficiently and have done everything humanly possible to open the closed minds and soften the hard hearts of the people living on Earth.

In *The Sealed Portion* of our new American scripture, we wrote some very relevant things about the prideful American religion that has misused our new American scripture. The following excerpts are among many other words that have helped many LDS/Mormons shake off the chains of ignorance by which they were bound as members of this church. It is our hope that upon reading and *feeling* the power of *how* we wrote scripture, that the reader will understand *why*:

And it shall come to pass that the people of the church that he shall establish shall reject the pure message of the gospel of Jesus Christ and be given lower laws of sacrifice and ordinances like unto the children of Israel when they desired that Moses be their leader.

And because of the wickedness of this church, this prophet [Joseph Smith] shall be taken from among them. And because he is taken from among them, they are left to themselves to establish a church according to the dictates of their own conscience, which dictates are not based upon the words of Christ as I have explained them in this record.

And because the church is named after the name of Jesus Christ and not in his name, or in other words, based upon his gospel, this holy endowment shall be changed and modified according to the desires and precepts of the leaders of this church, who do so because of the praise of the world.

And my soul [Moroni, who wrote *The Sealed Portion*] is burdened exceedingly as I read the words of the brother of Jared who hath seen the coming forth of this church among the Gentiles, yea even the very same church which shall preach the words of the record of my father, and also many of my own words, and carry them forth to many parts of the world.

... And no other people on earth will have these two testimonies which the Lord hath given unto the children of men. And the Lord will use your pride and your arrogance against you. For in your pride and arrogance, ye think ye are better than the rest of your brothers and sisters in the world, and that ye enjoy a happiness that they do not enjoy. And with this pride, ye send out missionaries to take your message of pride throughout the world.

And ye shall carry the record of my father with you, and pretend that ye believe in this record. And ye shall testify unto the world that the fullness of the gospel of Jesus Christ is contained in this record. And in this ye testify correctly, but by so testifying, ye are securing your own damnation. For ye testify of those things that ye do not do. And though the Lord will have exceedingly great mercy for the sinner, he shall condemn and punish the hypocrite.

And these words which I write unto you at this time, even in the sealed part of the plates upon which my father and I have written, and which I have been commanded to complete and hide in the earth to come forth in the own due time of the Lord; even these things shall ye reject because they were not given unto you by the leaders of your church, which leaders are all men of the world, which have received the fine things of the world and the praises and honors of men.

But these things shall condemn you and shall confound your false doctrines and the traditions that ye have allowed to creep into the foundations of the church that is called after the name of Jesus. For in the beginning, the foundation of your church was given in its purity, and the Lord suffered it to be organized according to the power of the Holy Priesthood and under the direction of the Holy Ghost.

... And I have explained many things regarding this church unto you in this record; for this church shall have the record of my father among them, but they shall be like unto the Jews of old, who had the records of all the holy prophets, yet they did not read them, nor did they understand them.

And the Father shall use this church and its greatness and its glory and its money and the deception of its people to allow this record to be given unto all the earth.

Chapter 18: Other Books, Other Peoples

For these people shall believe that they are the only righteous children of God upon the earth, and that a man cannot be saved unless he joineth their church and receiveth the ordinances that its leaders have prescribed for the salvation of the people.

And because of this pride, many people shall carry the record of my people to others upon the earth, who are the elect of God and are searching for the truth of God in all things.

And these shall join this church, but shall come to know that its works are evil, and then they shall depart from it. Nevertheless, they shall take with them the record of my fathers, which Joseph was commanded to bring forth unto them.

And after they have received a testimony of the things that are written in the part of the record which is not sealed, then shall their hearts and minds be ready to receive these things, which are sealed, and have been preserved for them, who are elect, even those who shall have the name of the Lord written in their hearts and in their foreheads.

And they shall know that the things revealed unto them are true, because they testifieth of the wickedness of the world and the great corruption of the children of men as they live by the plan of Lucifer.

But these things which have been sealed up shall come forth and give unto them a better understanding of the plan of the Father that they did not consider.[15]

Again, there was no other purpose in our writing new scripture than to help humanity. Had we written any other books about the "lost ten tribes of

---

[15] *TSP*, 10:14–17; 18:53–6; 82:85–92.

Israel," or any other history of the many peoples that have lived upon the earth, we would have had our new American scripture's Jesus visit these people, as he said he was going to do after visiting the ancestors of the native American peoples. In ALL the narratives of our "other books," our resurrected Jesus would have taught the exact same things to ALL people living on the Earth. And as we have explained and proven, NOTHING that any of the Christian religions now upon the earth teach their congregations includes the simple fullness of the everlasting Gospel of Jesus, the Christ.

We wrote of the condition of ALL of humanity when our new American scripture would come forth:

> But behold, in the last days, or in the days of the Gentiles [during the greatness of the United States of America]—yea, behold all the nations of the Gentiles and also the Jews, both those who shall come upon this land [the Western Hemisphere, especially North America] and those who shall be upon other lands, yea, even upon all the lands of the earth, behold, they will be drunken with iniquity and all manner of abominations—
>
> ... Forasmuch as this people draw near unto me with their mouth, and with their lips do honor me [claiming to be Christians and saved by Jesus Christ], but have removed their hearts far from me, and their fear towards me is taught by the precepts of men—
>
> Therefore, I will proceed to do a marvelous work among this people, yea, a marvelous work and a wonder, for the wisdom of their wise and learned shall perish, and the understanding of their prudent shall be hid.[16]

And now it is appropriate that we clearly explain, without using religious prose, but plainly and without reservation, our Marvelous Work and a Wonder®—a promise of peace and life eternal.

---

[16] *BOM*, 2 Nephi 27:1, 25–6.

Chapter 19
A Marvelous Work and a Wonder®— A Promise of Peace and Life Eternal

We based the official name of our work, a ***Marvelous Work and a Wonder***®, on the inference (idea) found in the Bible's book of Isaiah. We also recopied this part into our new American scripture's prophecies about what we were going to do in the United States of America:

> Therefore, behold, I will proceed to do a marvelous work among this people, even a marvelous work and a wonder: for the wisdom of their wise men shall perish, and the understanding of their prudent men shall be hid.[1]

What is so *marvelous* about our work? Why is what we do a *wonder* that confounds the wisdom and understanding of the world? How is the "wisdom of the wise" going to perish? Who are the "prudent men" whose understanding will be hid?

When one is considered "wise" or "prudent," the person is lifted up "as if it were in the air, high above [everyone else living upon] the earth."[2] University and college degrees and doctorates cause graduates to hold their heads high with a stiff neck, hoping that others see the value of the education and study that gives them self-worth and glory.

Political, religious, and business leaders are trained in the ministry of their occupations. This training allows these people to administer what they have learned. They are generally paid more money for their training than those to whom they administer. And as stated above, these people (doctors, lawyers, and engineers, to name just a few) proudly display their wisdom,

---
[1] *Compare* OT, Isaiah 29:14; and *BOM*, 2 Nephi 27:26.
[2] *Compare BOM*, 1 Nephi 8:26; 11:36.

understanding, and accomplishments as something better, more distinguished, and more valuable than those who lack such training.

What have these wise and prudent ones *really* accomplished? Is the world becoming a better place for ALL of humanity? Is there more peace, security, and freedom today than there was in times past? Is humanity safe and prosperous for one and ALL? Do humans retain a hope in the future? Do they think that things are going to get better?

We know that the answer to all of these questions is a resounding "NO." We know that

> the world and the wisdom thereof, that great and spacious building that stands as it were in the air, high above the earth … filled with people, both old and young, both male and female; and their manner of dress was exceedingly fine, will one day fall and the fall thereof will be exceedingly great.[3]

In recent history, the "wise and prudent" were warned of what could happen to their wisdom, understanding, and personal value. What is known in history as the *Cambodian genocide* should have been a wake-up call to political, religious, and business leaders. The poor, disenfranchised, and marginalized—those who were once meek, humble, patient, and willing to submit to whatever power was forced upon them—rose up against the Cambodian government and any foreign government that supported it. They rose up against business professionals, intellectuals, and Buddhist monks.

Uniting in blood and calling themselves the *Khmer Rouge* (rouge: *French*, meaning "red"), these once humble people were fed up with poverty and inequality. Their new leaders inspired and motivated them to kill their oppressors. They wanted to kill those whom they felt were in that

---

[3] *Compare BOM*, 1 Nephi 8:26–7; 11:35–6.

Chapter 19: A Marvelous Work and a Wonder®—A Promise of Peace and Life Eternal

great and spacious building; and it stood as it were in the air, high above the earth ... filled with [political, religious and business leaders, and those who thought they were "wise and prudent." And the political, religious, and business leaders, and those who thought they were "wise and prudent"] were in the attitude of mocking and pointing their fingers towards ... the poor, humble, meek, patient, and submissive people.[4]

The "wise and prudent" *did* learn something from the *Cambodian genocide*. They learned how to strike first and hard against any uprising. They used their "training" to keep any rebellion in check. They did *not* use their training, their knowledge, and their "wisdom and understanding" like the ancient Roman political, religious, and business leaders did in creating *Christianity*. These contemporary "wise ones" did not create a new religion for the masses. They did *not* create and establish a *new* belief and faith in which the poor, they that mourn, the meek, the merciful, the pure in heart, and the peacemakers could have hope. They didn't need to. They had powerful militaries and nuclear weapons.

The "wise ones" did not consider *why* the once meek and humble people became so violent and vengeful. These leaders had their PRIDE. And with that pride, they utilized their "armies and navies, popes and priests, [to] reign with blood and horror on the earth."

Contemporary leaders also did not consider *why* Islamic terrorists attacked the World Trade Center and the U.S. Pentagon on September 11, 2001. They didn't need to. They used their "armies and navies," inspired and egged on by their "popes and priests," to "reign with blood and horror" on the Muslim people, whose religion, *Islam*, actually means "*PEACE.*"

We have warned these "wise" and "prudent" ones about what is going to happen in the future when these disenfranchised and marginalized groups get

---

[4] Compare *BOM*, 1 Nephi 8:26–7; and *BOM*, Mosiah 3:19.

their own nuclear weapons—and THEY WILL. We warned them through prophecy, written exclusively for the United States of America (the "Gentiles" in our new American scripture), that

> the world and the wisdom thereof... that great and spacious building ... the pride of the world [shall fall] and the fall thereof [will be] exceedingly great. ... Thus shall be the destruction of all nations, kindreds, tongues, and people, that shall fight against ... becom[ing] as a child, submissive, meek, humble, patient, full of love, willing to submit to all things.[5]

Thus, "the wisdom of their wise shall perish, and the understanding of their prudent men shall be hid." It is our marvelous work and a wonder to do all that we can to lead humanity to peace and life eternal. We know how it can be done. We know how it *should* be done. We know a "more EXCELLENT way."

This "*more EXCELLENT way*" cannot be done without the help and support of the masses, the poor, the meek, the humble, those who are persecuted, marginalized, disenfranchised, and scorned because of their poverty and ignorance. The only way that we can gain their trust and their support is to reveal and expose

> them that seek deep to hide their counsel ... and their works are in the dark, and they say, Who seeth us? And who knoweth us?[6]

The secret combinations of power, fueled by personal pride and vanity, have turned things upside down in our world. As clay in the hands of selfish and wicked potters, they have formed and framed governments, religions, and economic systems that are destroying humanity.

---

[5] *BOM*, 1 Nephi 11:35–6; and *BOM*, Mosiah 3:19.
[6] OT, Isaiah 29:15.

> Surely [their] turning of things upside down shall be esteemed as the potter's clay: for shall the work say of him that made it, He made me not? Or shall the thing framed say of him that framed it, He had no understanding?[7]

Our work has the power to teach the people about these works of obscurantism, i.e., their works of darkness—things they do behind the scenes, about which the masses know nothing. Our work can teach the religious

> that erred in spirit [to] come to understanding, and they that murmured shall learn [true] doctrine ... the eyes of the blind shall see out of obscurity, and out of darkness. The meek also shall increase their joy ... and the poor among men shall rejoice.[8]

On our website, www.realilluminati.org, at the "About Us" link, we give one of the world's definitions of our covert group:

> The society's goals are to oppose superstition, obscurantism, religious influence over public life, and the abuses of state power. [Our intent] is to put an end to the machinations of the purveyors of injustice, to control them without dominating them.[9]

Political, religious, and business leaders are "purveyors of injustice" who are master magicians. The masses are their audience, held captive by their great deceptions. Their tricks, their sleight of hand, their illusions, are magical. Notwithstanding "the means of those miracles which [they have] power to do ... saying to them that dwell on the earth:"[10] ... "You must do what we tell you to do" ... there is no such thing as magic. There is no miraculous power seemingly (supposedly) influencing the course of events

---

[7] OT, Isaiah 29:16; *compare also* BOM, 2 Nephi 27:27.
[8] OT, Isaiah 29:14–24.
[9] *See* "About Us - The Real Illuminati®," The Real Illuminati®, realilluminati.org/about-us.
[10] NT, Revelation 13:14.

by using mysterious or supernatural forces. We now reveal the *tricks* that these *master magicians* use to retain control over their audiences.

Every trick that a magician does is accomplished by the magician's degree of knowledge and experience (know-how). The ignorant audience members are the ones left in astonishment and in awe of the trick. Other magicians are not astonished, nor in awe of what their peers do. When a magician invents a new magic trick that fools other magicians, the others praise the magician who was able to deceive them. But at no time does any magician believe that *magic* was involved. Magicians try their best to not only discover how the trick was done, but how to do it better.

Magicians have an unspoken, informal code of secrecy intended to protect their tricks from being exposed to the unknowing public. Magicians perform to make money. To become successful at what they do, they use their knowledge *secretly combined* with the desire of people to be entertained by their tricks. This does the exact same thing for the magician that the *secret combinations* we have discussed throughout this book do for politics, religion, and economics. It provides a means of profit to benefit those thus *combined in secret*, especially for their own families and loved ones. The biggest difference between magicians and political, religious, and business leaders is that a magician's audience makes the choice and has the freedom to choose to attend the performance. In contrast, the world's political, religious, and economic leaders *force* their will upon the masses. They force the masses to be part of their *audience*.

We are the Real Illuminati®. There is no magician on this planet as knowledgeable and adroit as we are at using power to influence the course of events happening in this world. Our *tricks* in the past were done by using mysterious or supernatural forces attributed to God—whatever this god might be to the masses. In the first book of our Trilogy, we revealed what *magical tricks* we used to influence Judaism, Christianity, and Islam—the three major religions spawned from how the masses perceive the stories in the Old Testament (about how God created the heavens and the earth and all things therein).

Chapter 19: A Marvelous Work and a Wonder®—A Promise of Peace and Life Eternal

We revealed how one of our group was involved with the (well-paid) Greek writers who were commissioned to transcribe the oral history of the ancient Hebrew people into a written history, now known as the Old Testament of the Bible.[11] There is a part of the Hebrew myths that was *not* orally passed down for hundreds of years. We invented this part and influenced the Greek writers to incorporate it into the written production of the Hebrew's oral myths. It was a part that compared the power of *magic* to the power of God. We wrote how the Pharaoh asked to see a miracle to prove that Moses had been sent by God. Moses showed the power of God by having

> Aaron cast down his rod before Pharaoh, and before his servants, and [the rod] became a serpent. Then Pharaoh also called the wise men and the sorcerers: now the magicians of Egypt, they also did in like manner with their enchantments. For they cast down every man his rod, and they became serpents: but Aaron's rod swallowed up their rods.[12]

This part was to symbolically show that, no matter how magical anything appears to be, no matter what a True Messenger does that seems God-related, no matter what power we use in our attempts to influence the course of events by using mysterious or supernatural forces, simple *magic* can do the same.

In the example above, Hebrew mythology about Moses taught that Pharaoh hardened his "heart, that he hearkened not unto them."[13] Likewise, regardless of the extent of the apparent "miracles" that a True Messenger can do, the people's hearts remain hardened against the Real Truth™.

We have explained what the Real Truth™ is. The Real Truth™ and magic are opposites. In essence, the Real Truth™ is science—how things

---

[11] *See THOR*, 121–3.
[12] OT, Exodus 7:10–12.
[13] Exodus 7:13.

really are today, and how things *really* were in the past. Scientists publish all of their findings for their peers to see and evaluate. Science is "the intellectual and practical activity encompassing the systematic study of the structure and behavior of the physical and natural world through observation and experiment."[14] In contrast to *secret combinations*, science is an open system. Science only works if people share and verify each other's results. If magicians shared all of their secrets, they could potentially destroy the mystery of magic that makes it unique and entertaining for audiences. Not understanding how a trick is done is what makes it special, entertaining, and profitable.[15]

We are religious "magicians." Our intent in writing this book, the second in our Trilogy, was to share *how* we wrote our new American scripture, known by the world as the *Book of Mormon*. In doing so, it was our intent to give empirical evidence of what other *religious magicians* have done throughout history to create the *magic* of religion and the feelings of awe and wonder that create what humans interpret as *spirituality*. We used our knowledge, skill, and experience to create a masterpiece that would have the same effect on our intended audience as the Bible does. The Bible is nothing more than a *trick* that was and is used to perform an act before an ignorant and unaware audience—an act that provides its performers (religious leaders) with a profit to benefit themselves, their families, and their loved ones.

The more these performers practice and use charisma, charm, and their perceived humility and sincerity to perform—the more believable their trick is to their unsuspecting audience. NONE of these performers would act and use the trick of the Bible, if they did not gain something for their pride and ego. The Pope's robes, the preacher's wardrobe, the cleric's collar, the LDS General Authorities' expensive suits are just a few of many

---

[14] *See* "science," *Lexico Dictionaries | English*, Oxford University Press, lexico.com/en/definition/science.

[15] *See* Christopher Ornelas, "The Magician's Oath: A Conversation with Pat Hammond on Magic, Science, and the Wind," *Disclosure: from the end of the line* (May 2021), 16–29; also found online at drachen.org/wp-content/uploads/2012/06/DiscourseIssue12_0.pdf.

examples of costumes worn. These costumes are nothing more or less than the magician's—a performer's—cape. Ironically, most Christian priests are recognized by their dress of darkness (dark-colored robes). The only part of their wardrobe that is white is their collar. From their throat (the location of their white collar) they speak of righteousness, but their works are covered in darkness.

It was our intent in writing this book, *A New American Scripture*, to thoroughly explain the trick that was played on humanity with the Bible. We showed how the trick was done. We have shown and provided empirical evidence of how religious scripture, that is believed to be from a mysterious or supernatural force (God), is nothing more than *spiritual magic* performed by an experienced *religious magician*. We have explained how religion creates the same physical types of feelings and emotions that an audience senses when it observes a good magic trick or illusion. Both religion and magic seemingly influence the course of events (an act) by using mysterious supernatural forces.

In writing this book, we have tried to explain *WHY* we wrote a new American scripture, but specifically pointed out that our intentions for doing so were not the same as those responsible for most of the Bible. In fact, our intentions for writing a new American scripture were completely opposite to *why* the Bible was written. We have proven in this book that ALL religions, of every kind and of every name, are nothing more than the philosophies of men mingled with scripture, inspired and caused by PRIDE.

We claimed above that we are *religious magicians*. In a larger sense, we are also *master* scientists. As scientists, we have published all of our findings for other honest and sincere people to review and study and for other scientists who "systematically study the structure and behavior [of religion] through observation and experiment." What we have admitted in this book, we have done in an "open system." We have shared our results. We hope that others will study and verify our results. We have shared our secrets, knowing fully well, and expecting to "destroy the magic" that makes religion "unique and entertaining for audiences."

We have not done this to be malicious. We have done this to help humanity. Religion has done nothing good for humanity. Regardless of the claim or belief, there is no religion upon Earth that can show any evidence that it has benefited humanity in any way. The Real Truth™ is that religion has done just the opposite. Religion has tricked humanity into being divided by family units, by nationality, by race (skin color), by tribal affiliation, by language, and by cultural traditions. Most insidious (attractive, yet harmful) of all, because money is the basis of most world power, religion is directly responsible for poverty. The people of planet Earth have sold the sign and token of their humanity for money. Experiment on our words. Refuse to give any money, donation, tithe or offering to religious leaders and watch how fast their religion dissolves.

When it comes to money and wealth, we made it very clear in our new American scripture what we intended from the *trick* that we used. In writing the following scripture the way that we did, we wanted to make our audience feel the *spirit* and *power* of a mysterious and supernatural force. We *tricked* the audience's feelings of a "hope in Christ."

As we have explained before, notwithstanding our previous mention, the following part of our *trick* (the *unsealed part* of our new American scripture) is of such great importance to humanity, that we need to repeat it. We wrote about the worldly success that some people achieve, because

> the hand of providence hath smiled upon you most pleasingly, that you have obtained many riches.

We continued,

> and because some of you have obtained more abundantly than that of your brethren ye are lifted up in the pride of your hearts,

Chapter 19: A Marvelous Work and a Wonder®—A Promise of Peace and Life Eternal

and wear stiff necks and high heads because of the costliness of your apparel, and persecute your brethren because ye suppose that ye are better than they.[16]

We explained how this division of economic success is an "iniquity and abomination ... that such [successes] are abominable unto him who created all flesh." We continued,

> Think of your brethren like unto yourselves, and be familiar with all and free with your substance, that they may be rich like unto you. But before ye seek for riches, seek ye for the kingdom of God. And after ye have obtained a hope in Christ ye shall obtain riches, if ye seek them; and ye will seek them for the intent to do good—to clothe the naked, and to feed the hungry, and to liberate the captive, and administer relief to the sick and the afflicted.[17]

We wrote above that, "in a larger sense, we are also scientists." We are much more knowledgeable than any scientist on Earth—much more. We do not need to "systematically study the structure and behavior [of human society] through observation and experiment." We do not need to study what we already know. We know what we know because of what we have already observed throughout the history of the human race.

And WE KNOW that the first step in saving humanity from its own demise is to eliminate poverty.

We have shown how the Great Roman Empire fell because of the disparity between the rich and the poor, where the former thrived in few numbers, and the latter increased in mass. In other words, the gap between the rich few and the poor majority (economic inequality) widened to such an expanse that the Roman Empire had no choice but to split its power between the *secret combinations* of the Western Empire (where a large part of the

---

[16] *BOM*, Jacob 2:13.
[17] *BOM*, Jacob 2:12–22.

wealthy lived) and those of the Eastern Empire, where the masses fell under the spell of a *magician's act*.

There was only one reason why the Eastern part of the Great Roman Empire succeeded when its Western part failed: *hope was provided for the impoverished masses*. We have explained how the wisest of the wise combined in secret to figure out what to do. These "wise" ones (of the "*wise and learned*")[18] were *magicians*. These Eastern Roman *secret combinations* of political, religious, and business leaders *tricked* the people into supporting them, which kept the masses entertained and feeling *awe* and amazement. This stopped the masses from rising up in rebellion against these deceptive magicians. Their *trick* was complementing the ancient Hebrew myths with new myths—the stories of Jesus that led to Christianity.

It was easy for these *religious magicians* to write words that Jesus said, teachings that gave the masses a hope of eventual economic equality. The *act, the performance*, included a prophecy that Jesus gave of what he was going to do when he came again. He would come

> in his glory, and all the holy angels with him, then shall he sit upon the throne of his glory: And before him shall be gathered all nations: and he shall separate them one from another.[19]

The *act* was this prophesied *separation*. The masses were told to have a hope in Jesus, that when he came again in his glory, he was going to straighten everything out equitably by judging how well the political, religious, and business leaders did in eliminating poverty.[20]

Another part of the *trick* was what they wrote about what Jesus taught the people when he was alive. He taught the people to not be angry, but to love their enemies and to do good to those who persecuted them and

---

[18] *See BOM*, 2 Nephi 9:42.
[19] NT, Matthew 25:31–2.
[20] NT, Matthew 25:31–46.

despitefully used them. The masses were being persecuted and despitefully used by their political, religious, and business leaders. The people were taught that they would not be saved if they sinned against Jesus and rose up and killed the members of the *secret combinations* that controlled them. The Greco-Roman "wise and prudent" knew what brought peace to a society of numerous people. These magicians knew what *illusion* they needed to perform to keep the audience's attention, awe, and wonder.

We have explained how the surviving Eastern Roman Empire transitioned into the powerful Christian nations that would eventually control most of planet Earth. None of these nations would have been as successful as they were without Christianity—without the people being controlled by religious authority through *faith* and *hope* in the Second Coming of Jesus Christ.

These leaders knew that, until Jesus Christ came again, they—these *secret combinations* of power and authority—could use

> the treasures of the earth, and with gold and silver [they could pay for] armies and navies, popes and priests, [to] reign with blood and horror on the earth![21]

These powerful and prideful Christian nations realized that

> now is the great day of [their] power. [They] reign from the rivers to the ends of the earth. There is none who dares to molest, or make afraid.[22]

There was none who dared to molest or make these *secret combinations* afraid, until we—the Real Illuminati®—came along. We have exposed their secret works of darkness. We have given the world all the evidence that is needed to prove what these institutions have done to humanity—none of which is good.

---

[21] *SNS*, 59–60.
[22] *SNS*, 110.

Religious leaders opportunistically keep their followers under control by pointing them towards the coming of God, or God's son, a Savior, to clean up the world's mess. These leaders do nothing to turn things right-side-up. The clay in these potters' hands was not used to create a *melting pot* of ALL of Earth's inhabitants, but to create an

> image whose head was of fine gold, his breast and his arms of silver, his belly and thighs of brass, his legs of iron, his feet part iron and part clay.[23]

As this "secret [was] revealed unto Daniel in a night vision," only we can explain what this image means. Religious leaders cannot properly interpret this Bible passage. Religious leaders use a *sleight of hand trick*, focusing the attention of their audience away from what they are *really* doing so that they can take advantage and profit for themselves and their own families.

We used this Bible story about Daniel and the image that he saw in vision (the same that King Nebuchadnezzar saw) to create our own beast in our *Apocalypse*, the book of Revelation. These two images (Daniel's and the king's) represent what gives power to the people who control humanity—the gold, the silver, and the brass as money, and the iron that forges the chains that hold the masses captive in slavery. Daniel's vision tells of a latter-day

> kingdom set up, which shall never be destroyed, that shall break in pieces and consume all these kingdoms, and it shall stand for ever.[24]

But King Nebuchadnezzar's pride was too great. He could not accept that anyone or anything was greater than he and his kingdom. Therefore, the king made an image that corresponded with his dream. The king commanded all people to bow down and worship the image and caused that all should be killed who did not worship the image he created. Four

---

[23] *Compare* OT, Daniel 2:19, 32–3.
[24] *Compare* OT, Daniel 2:44.

Chapter 19: A Marvelous Work and a Wonder®—A Promise of Peace and Life Eternal

men, Daniel and his three friends, *Shadrach, Meshach, and Abed-nego*, refused to worship the image. And it was on this Bible narrative that we focused the attention of the audience in introducing the members of our group as the *Three Nephites*.

In presenting our group in our new American scripture, we copied the story of what happened to Daniel and his friends. We wrote that

> thrice they were cast into a furnace and received no harm. And twice were they cast into a den of wild beasts; and behold they did play with the beasts as a child with a suckling lamb, and received no harm.[25]

Yet, in performing this *sleight of hand*, we failed to get our audience to focus on our message—on our *act*. Of ourselves, we wrote that

> there are none that do know the true God save it be the disciples of Jesus, who did tarry in the land until the wickedness of the people was so great that the Lord would not suffer them to remain with the people; and whether they be upon the face of the land no man knoweth.[26]

We cannot suffer ourselves, or our True Messenger, to "tarry in the land" any longer. The wickedness of the people living upon the earth is too great. Nevertheless, "for all this [our] anger is not turned away, but [our] hand is stretched out still."[27] We wrote

> Wo unto them that decree unrighteous decrees, and that write grievousness which they have prescribed; to turn away the

---

[25] *BOM*, 3 Nephi 28:21–2.
[26] *BOM*, Mormon 8:10.
[27] *Compare* OT, Isaiah 9:12, 21 and *BOM*, 2 Nephi 19:12, 21.

needy from judgment, and to take away the right from the poor of my people, that widows may be their prey, and that they may rob the fatherless! ... For all this his anger is not turned away, but his hand is stretched out still.[28]

In spite of our "anger" against the secret combinations of powers that are destroying humanity, our hand is stretched out still. Our work, a Marvelous Work and a Wonder®, is this "outstretched hand." We have explained that the only way humanity will be saved is if humans start uniting together and solving the problems that humans created. We have explained that <u>humans are completely responsible for all of the problems that exist. Being thus responsible, humans can solve all of these problems</u>.

All that is standing in humanity's way is the *pride and vanity* that individuals and groups of individuals depend on for their self-worth and value. We have explained how this excessive pride and vanity is the only evil thing that exists. It is *Lucifer, the god of this world.*

An honest look inside the office of one of the most powerful people on the earth reveals the real reason why this person fulfills the role of President of the United States of America. Behind the desk of the U.S. President, pictures of his family adorn his space. If anything threatens any member of the President's immediate family, this powerful human would use all means at his disposal to protect his and his family's interests and well-being. There is no question about this. In most cases, the office of the President of the United States has been held by a Christian man[29] whose belief in Christ and the Bible *trick* him into believing that the United States of America is God's "promised land" for the sake of his family, and for those who believe in the same God.

Because of the belief of this powerful nation (the U.S.), in writing our new American scripture for it we intended to introduce a new identity for

---

[28] *BOM*, 2 Nephi 20:1–4; *compare also* OT, Isaiah 10:1–4.
[29] *See* "Religious affiliations of presidents of the United States," *Wikipedia*, 23 May 2021, en.wikipedia.org/wiki/Religious_affiliations_of_presidents_of_the_United_States.

Jesus Christ and Christianity. We openly admit that we intended to *trick* the Americans into believing our story—but ONLY for the intent to do good.

We wrote plainly about our work, which we called "a great and marvelous work among the children of men." As mentioned, we introduced ourselves in our story's narrative as a few chosen ones who experienced "a transfiguration" of our minds so that we "could behold the things of God." We introduced the idea that we would "be among the Gentiles, and the Gentiles would know us not. We would also be among the Jews, and the Jews would know us not."[30] We explained that we would be doing "a great and marvelous work" in the latter days during the time when the United States of America was at its peak, just before it began to fall.

We explained that our "great and marvelous work among the children of men" would be

> a work which shall be everlasting, either on the one hand or on the other—either to the convincing of [the people of Earth] unto peace and life eternal, or unto the deliverance of them to the hardness of their hearts and the blindness of their minds.[31]

It is with great sadness that we report we have delivered the American people, as well as all the other "Gentile" nations of the earth that embrace the wrong form of Capitalism, to the hardness of their hearts and the blindness of their minds. The emotional hell that many will feel who belong to what we called "a great and abominable church" is unprecedented.[32]

There is nothing more we can do for them, except to continue to explain the Real Truth™ of all things. We can take away their stumbling blocks so that they begin to see how important it is for all of humanity to be "of one heart and one mind, and [to have] no poor among them."

---

[30] *Compare BOM*, 3 Nephi 28:27–8, 31–2.
[31] *BOM*, 1 Nephi 14:7.
[32] *See* "The State of Mental Health in America," 2021, Mental Health America, mhanational.org/issues/state-mental-health-america.

The people of Earth might have had an excuse *before* we publicly presented our plan to eliminate poverty throughout the world. Before we presented this plan, the people did not know what to do. They have no excuse now. Our political platform, The Humanity Party®, has presented the perfect plan that can bridle the great beast of Capitalism and ride it throughout the Earth for the benefit of all of humanity. But the "children of men," especially the Americans, have "turn[ed] aside the just for a thing of naught and revile against that which is good, and say that it is of no worth!"[33]

Part of the *trick* in getting people to pay attention to the *act* (the performance of the trick) is to keep the audience fixated on one part of the stage, while creating the illusion on another part. This is in preparation for when the audience's focus is again back on the main *trick*. We used this *misdirection* to subtly force the audience (the reader of our scripture) to concentrate on their *hope* and *faith* in Jesus Christ, while we introduced important concepts that were vital to our overall message.

Our *illusion* was a Second Coming of Jesus Christ in his power and glory. The narrative of our story kept the reader subtly misdirected by the conflict, war, and human drama, while we got the reader excited about the coming of Jesus Christ (after he was resurrected). For this part of our trick, we filled our new American scripture with wars, misery, mayhem, condemnations, warnings, and negativity to such a degree, that one might wonder if any of it is good. One might wonder why anyone would want to see our *act*—read our new American scripture. Why subject one's mind to such negativity, despair, and emotional depression?

Upon reading *A New American Scripture—How and Why the Real Illuminati® Created the Book of Mormon*, one would be hard pressed to find anything positive about our writings, but ONLY IF we did not take the opportunity to explain *how* and *why* we wrote our new American scripture

---

[33] *BOM*, 2 Nephi 28:16.

Chapter 19: A Marvelous Work and a Wonder®—A Promise of Peace and Life Eternal

the way we did. From what we have revealed so far, it appears that even we have given up on humanity. We mentioned that we do not write

> the things which are pleasing unto the world ... but the things which are pleasing unto God and unto those who are not of the world.[34]

We pleaded with the reader of our new American scripture to

> give ear to our words. ... Do not say that we have spoken hard things against you; for if ye do, ye will revile against the truth; for we have spoken the words of your Maker. We know that the words of truth are hard against all uncleanness; but the righteous fear them not, for they love the truth and are not shaken.[35]

Nothing that we wrote took away from the orthodox idea of Jesus Christ. We presented the *true Christ*. We taught that all that is good about being human—the *spirit of love*, the *spirit of kindness*, the *spirit of compassion*, the *spirit of equality*, the *spirit of joy and happiness*—all these positive human traits—are encompassed in the *Spirit of Christ*. We taught that the *Spirit of Christ* is given to every one of us, so that each of us may know good from evil, and that the way to do this is easy and straightforward and that everything that persuades us to do good is of Christ, and of the Father, and of the Holy Spirit, which is in each of us.[36]

Our story and all of its subplots taught that good acts by good people make a good society. Bad acts by bad people make a bad society. People who are convinced of their power to act, do good things. People who are convinced that they have no power, do not act without being told what to do and how to act. Our new American scripture's narrative postulated (claimed) and proposed that a human society can only be as good as the

---

[34] *BOM*, 1 Nephi 6:5.
[35] *Compare BOM*, 2 Nephi 9:40.
[36] *Compare BOM*, Moroni 7:16–17. *See also* Galatians 5:22.

people who make it good. It was our desire to unite all people under one *Spirit of God*, using the *Spirit of Christ*—that which we hoped Christians would recognize as something good and not evil—as the unification of our hearts and minds.

When we made the audience focus their attention on the resurrected Jesus Christ, we knew that the illusion we would present would grab them and leave them in awe and wonder. While people focused on this illusion, we introduced simple teachings that we knew could help save humanity.

We did not need to reveal the *tricks* and *magic* that we used in writing our new American scripture. We could have entertained the audience without offending the Christians. Of this we wrote:

> It grieves us that we must use so much boldness of speech concerning you, before those of you who are innocent, many of whose feelings are exceedingly tender and chaste and delicate before God, which thing is pleasing unto God; And it supposeth us that they read our words to hear the pleasing word of God, yea, the word which healeth the wounded soul. Wherefore, it burdeneth our souls that we should be constrained, because of the strict commandment which we have received from God, to admonish you according to your crimes, to enlarge the wounds of those who are already wounded, instead of consoling and healing their wounds; and those who have not been wounded, instead of feasting upon the pleasing word of God have daggers placed to pierce their souls and wound their delicate minds. But, notwithstanding the greatness of the task, we must do according to the strict commands of God, and tell you concerning your wickedness and abominations, in the presence of the pure in heart, and the broken heart, and under the glance of the piercing

eye of the Almighty God. Wherefore, we must tell you the truth according to the plainness of the word of God.[37]

We know that the strictness and plainness of our words offend many people. We write with much boldness and have condemned all of the religions of the world. We especially condemn the religion that is known throughout the world because of our new American scripture, but is not known for its righteousness. As we explained earlier in this book, because of how the LDS/Mormon people use our book to get converts, those who have never read our *Book of Mormon* see no value in reading it.

It is easy for the world to see the great hypocrisy of the LDS Church, for not only disregarding all of our book's teachings, not only for changing our book's meaning to fit this church's own cognitive paradigm of the Gospel of Jesus Christ, but also for using our new American scripture to become *the* wealthiest religion in modern times. As we mentioned earlier in this book, the American Broadway, Tony Award-winning play, *The Book of Mormon*, presents a storyline that perfectly and honestly portrays our book, as it is being used by this church.

In the musical play, Mormon missionaries are sent to a poor nation in Africa to convert the people of that nation to their church—which they erroneously claim is the "Zion" mentioned in the *Book of Mormon*. The missionaries promise the people that they can be saved and sealed to their families forever in Heaven. The people who the Mormon missionaries are trying to convert are poor, have very little food, few clothes, terrible houses, no healthcare, and are afflicted with civil war between different warlords. This play is profound in presenting an honest and general view that the people of the world have about our book.

We have explained that we had to do something to stop the way that the LDS Church is deceptively using our book, which caused the negative

---

[37] Compare *BOM*, Jacob 2:7–11.

way that the rest of the world perceives our new American scripture. To mitigate the terrible effects that this church caused our scripture, we published the "sealed portion of the gold plates," as well as many "other books," including this one (as we explained in a previous chapter). We are doing everything in our power to confront this religion and expose "all manner of iniquity" that this church does to "fight against Zion."

Ironically, one of our new American scripture's prophecies condemns the LDS religion and all others, that are

> built up to get gain, ... to get power over the flesh [in the commandments it gives its members about what they can and cannot do in the flesh, and] to become popular in the eyes of the world, and [to] seek the lusts of the flesh and the things of the world.[38]

Although we have offended them, we have pointed out and proven the truth of all the things in which we have condemned them. We wrote above that the LDS/Mormon Church "fights against Zion." Mormons would vehemently (strongly) and angrily argue this point. But it is true. We have proven that the LDS/Mormon Church fights against the idea of a righteous society existing, which righteous society is one where all the people are of one heart and one mind, and they dwell in righteousness; and there is no poor among them.

We have proven that the LDS/Mormon people who live in the United States are generally very patriotic[39] and lean towards conservative values that the U.S. Republican Party embraces.[40] Those in the U.S. support strong borders

---

[38] *Compare BOM*, 1 Nephi 22:23.

[39] See "America the Beautiful," "My Country, 'Tis of Thee," "The Star-Spangled Banner," and "God Save the King," Hymns, The Church of Jesus Christ of Latter-day Saints, found online at "Hymns," Music Playlist, Intellectual Reserve, Inc., churchofjesuschrist.org/music/library/hymns?lang=eng, numbers 338, 339, 340, and 341 respectively.

[40] *See* "Party affiliation among Mormons," Pew Research Center, pewforum.org/religious-landscape-study/religious-tradition/mormon/party-affiliation.

and anti-immigration laws and policies that keep the majority of the native American descendants *out* of the United States. We have proven that the native Americans living in the Western Hemisphere ARE the "remnant of the house of Israel" about whom the *Book of Mormon* was written.

There are countless prophecies concerning what the Americans ("Gentiles") *should* be doing for the native American people. The "city of holiness," the righteous city of Zion, "the New Jerusalem" that is prophesied of and promised in our *Book of Mormon* is <u>not</u> about the "Gentiles." It is about the native American peoples, both of North and South America. We have proven this. We have proven that the Americans' role in ALL the prophecies given in our *Book of Mormon* is <u>only</u> to care for the native Americans, both temporally and spiritually, with the majority emphasis placed on their temporal needs.

We had our main character, Mormon, address the modern-day native American people. In some of his last words he wrote

> to the Gentiles **who have care for the house of Israel**, that realize and know from whence their blessings come.[41]

We specifically wrote "who have care for the house of Israel," because we wanted it to be perfectly clear that the Americans had the responsibility, and the God-mandated obligation, to "care for the house of Israel." This specifically meant they were supposed to take care of the native Americans, both of North and South America, and upon the "isles of the sea." The phrase "isles of the sea" was meant to include all indigenous peoples who do not live on the Eastern and Western Hemispheres' mainland.

Throughout our new American scripture, we explained how the Americans were going to help do this. These explanations should have given much hope to the native American people, as well as to the people who live

---

[41] *BOM*, Mormon 5:10, emphasis added.

A New American Scripture

"upon the isles of the sea," or in other words, in the rest of the world. However, with each prophecy that we wrote to this end, we were forced to ALWAYS include the word "if." All of the prophecies we wrote about the "Gentiles" helping the native Americans were *conditioned* upon the righteousness of the "Gentiles" and how they received and accepted these prophecies.

We already knew how the early Americans were treating the native Americans. We saw how Joseph Smith's peer review group responded in their initial review of our writings. In almost every case, we were forced to condemn the "Gentiles" (who received and read our book) for NOT fulfilling the prophecies.

Among his last words, we had our character Mormon write:

> And then, O ye Gentiles, how can ye stand before the power of God, except ye shall repent and turn from your evil ways? Know ye not that ye are in the hands of God? Know ye not that he hath all power, and at his great command the earth shall be rolled together as a scroll? Therefore, repent ye, and humble yourselves before him, lest he shall come out in justice against you—lest a remnant of the seed of Jacob shall go forth among you as a lion, and tear you in pieces, and there is none to deliver.[42]

In our new American scripture, we demonstrated the improbabilities that threaten each person's *faith* and *hope* by presenting the reality of earth life—with all of its vicissitudes (uncertainties and hardships). By applying all of this negativity in our story (wars, struggles, natural disasters, etc.), we could then introduce a way to fulfill one's hope. We tied the intrinsic (inner) feeling of *hope* to the extrinsic (outward) *faith in Christ*. Once people have the inner feeling of hope, they are motivated to take the extrinsic action of faith and *do* something. Having "faith in Christ" is taking action on the words that he gave us. It is applying his words into our lives. We then taught the correct

---

[42] *BOM*, Mormon 5:22–4.

Chapter 19: A Marvelous Work and a Wonder®—A Promise of Peace and Life Eternal

application of this faith—of the *power of the glory* that we possess as humans over all other lifeforms. We have presented this as "charity," the "pure love of Christ." Having *charity* causes us to apply our knowledge (have *faith*/take action) with a mutual effort, intelligently, in order to form a better society— "a more EXCELLENT way."⁴³

Excessive pride keeps society from becoming a people of one heart and one mind and having no poor among them. People have been convinced and deceived into giving up their power. They have been convinced that they don't have the capability—that they are not in control of what happens upon the earth. The people of Earth are deceived by the *magicians* who want the people to depend upon them for salvation and to depend on *them* to entertain them and keep them in awe—instead of saving humanity.

Because of this codependency with religious authority, society does nothing that is good. Religions have never done anything that is good. Religious disempowerment (reducing one's power, because of religion) keeps this world from uniting as a people with one heart and mind and convinces people that there will always be poor among them.

"Commandments of men" are created to give value to men. They deny the *true* power of God, which we tried to trick the reader into accepting as the "Spirit of Christ" that each person has been given equally. The commandments of men cause people to feel guilt and unworthiness to be themselves—i.e., to be ONE with God. These *religious magicians* cause people to feel that God wants nothing to do with them and that they need a *magic act* in order to communicate with God and receive His guidance—an *act* that only these *magicians* can perform properly.

Religion, or taking away the power of the individual (disempowerment), cannot lead us to peace and life eternal. "Peace" is the word we use to define how we *could* live with each other. "Life eternal" is

---

[43] This "more excellent way" has been presented through The Humanity Party®. See humanityparty.com.

created by living in peace with each other for as long as we desire. We have explained that our work, a Marvelous Work and a Wonder®, can lead humanity to peace and life eternal. Everything that we, the Real Illuminati® do, we do to this end.

Our new American scripture was not meant to be negative. It was meant to give hope to a world that has been deceived. As we have explained, we connected the book of Revelation to our new American scripture in a positive way. Revelation does not tell of the end of the world, but of Earth's *renewal* to peace and equality.

Revelation's story brings Heaven back to Earth in a reunification that ushers in a time of peace and prosperity for all of Earth's inhabitants, where

> God shall wipe away all tears from their eyes; and there shall be no more death, neither sorrow, nor crying, neither shall there be any more pain: for the former things are passed away. ... [There will be] a pure river of water of life, clear as crystal. [There shall be a] tree of life ... and the leaves of the tree [will be] for the healing of the nations. And there shall be no night there; and they need no candle, neither light of the sun; ... and they shall reign for ever and ever.[44]

> Imagine for a moment, that in the future we eventually figure out how to live with each other in peace and harmony. As science and technology advances, we learn to use these advancements for the mutual benefit of the human race, and at that same time, we learn to live in harmony with the natural environment of the earth. We learn to correct both our social and environmental mistakes of the past, and the earth becomes a wonderful place for humans to live. With our increased knowledge and advancements, we learn to engineer the DNA makeup of our bodies and eliminate aging and

---

[44] NT, Revelation 21:4; 22:1–2, 5.

death altogether. We learn to live as vibrant, healthy human beings with equal opportunities to enjoy our individual lives. Imagine that this existence then becomes an eternity.

Imagine that we finally develop and live in a perfect human world. [It is] *improbable* with the current forms of governments and socioeconomic systems [the way people interact with each other that] we allow to control our lives. [But] it is *not impossible* to **imagine** that we can accomplish this goal as a unified human race. It is not impossible to *imagine* a perfect world. In fact, it is what we hope for. "Hope" is the intrinsic measure of our humanity, or better, that which we feel can be *possible* in spite of the *improbabilities* that seem to be part of our present experience.[45]

Our new American scripture is full of hope, but the *secret combinations* of power threaten this hope. To confront these combinations that destroy humanity, we needed to reveal their secret works. If we explained each "wickedness and abomination" committed by the combinations of political, religious, and business powers, we would cause an unnecessary amount of emotional insecurity and hopelessness.

What we *can* explain is some of the *magic* that we have performed in an effort to make a difference. Again, there's no such thing as *magic*. Everything that occurs upon the earth can be explained scientifically. Below we will provide some detail of what we have condoned and supported, behind the scenes, to perform one of our *magic acts*. In this example, *magic* wasn't used. It was nature's laws that rid the world of one of the worst presidents in U.S. history—William Henry Harrison.

We are revealing this to prove that we have yet to reveal many of the secret abominations and whoredoms that have been committed. These especially include those carried out by the American Founding

---

[45] *See* Anonymous, *Human Reality—Who We Are and Why We Exist!* (Melba, ID: Worldwide United Publishing, 2009), 26. Free to read at realilluminati.org/human-reality.

Fathers and also by the founder of the prideful church that has destroyed the faith of the world in our new American scripture. We are going to reveal these events to give empirical evidence of our intelligence, of our work, and to prove that the secret combinations that exist in our world must be confronted.

First, in our new American scripture, we wrote a description of a certain conflict of war—a conflict that was more devastating and more revealing of the potential of evil than anything else we presented in our story. At this part, we had Mormon explain why he (or rather *we*, the Real Illuminati®)

> speak the word of God with sharpness [that makes people] tremble and anger against [us]; and when [we] use no sharpness they harden their hearts against it; wherefore, [we] fear lest the Spirit of the Lord hath ceased striving with them.[46]

We know of many of the great evils occurring behind the scenes that the public knows nothing about. These great evils are hidden in darkness, and unless we bring them to light, they will continue to destroy civilization as we know it. This will also explain why we continue to labor diligently to "conquer the enemy of all righteousness."[47] Below we offer a description of some terrible and treacherous acts that we included in our narrative. We wrote into our story some particularly hideous and very evil things that both George Washington and Brigham Young actually did. Here is how we presented this evil, as we had our author *Mormon* witness it and report it to his son, *Moroni*. This is referring to the acts of soldiers who were mandated by their commanders while fighting for their cause:

> For so exceedingly do they anger that it seemeth me that they have no fear of death; and they have lost their love, one towards another; and they thirst after blood and revenge continually.

---

[46] *BOM*, Moroni 9:4.
[47] *BOM*, Moroni 9:6.

Chapter 19: A Marvelous Work and a Wonder®—A Promise of Peace and Life Eternal

> ... And now I write somewhat concerning the sufferings of this people. For according to the knowledge which I have received from Amoron, behold, the Lamanites have many prisoners, which they took from the tower of Sherrizah; and there were men, women, and children.
>
> And the husbands and fathers of those women and children they have slain; and they feed the women upon the flesh of their husbands, and the children upon the flesh of their fathers; and no water, save a little, do they give unto them.
>
> And notwithstanding this great abomination of the Lamanites, it doth not exceed that of our people in Moriantum. For behold, many of the daughters of the Lamanites have they taken prisoners; and after depriving them of that which was most dear and precious above all things, which is chastity and virtue—
>
> And after they had done this thing, they did murder them in a most cruel manner, torturing their bodies even unto death; and after they have done this, they devour their flesh like unto wild beasts, because of the hardness of their hearts; and they do it for a token of bravery.
>
> O my beloved son, how can a people like this, that are without civilization ... How can we expect that God will stay his hand in judgment against us?
>
> Behold, my heart cries: Wo unto this people. Come out in judgment, O God, and hide their sins, and wickedness, and abominations from before thy face![48]

During the time before we left Joseph Smith to be killed by the American Christians who had rejected our message, we were engaged in certain matters

---

[48] *BOM*, Moroni 9:5, 7–11, 14–15.

involving other powers that we hoped to influence to do good. We were involved in dealing with the native Americans and their discussions with the American leaders. It was our intent to do good and do whatever we could to bring the sides of the conflicts together in peace, without bloodshed.

During our association and dealings with some of the American Founding Fathers, incognito, usually using the servants of these men as intermediaries (as a go-between), we became aware of some native American conflicts in which William Henry Harrison was involved. We became aware that under the leadership of George Washington, as one of Washington's officers, Harrison was involved in treating some native Americans as the native Americans had treated some of the white men, whom they had killed in battle. The native Americans had "[fed] the [white] women upon the flesh of their husbands, and the children upon the flesh of their fathers; and [had given them] no water, save a little."[49]

In response and in vengeance, and under the direction and orders of George Washington, the American army did the same thing to the native Americans. We overheard Harrison boasting about

> depriving [some of the native American women] of that which was most dear and precious above all things, which is chastity and virtue—And after they had done this thing, they did murder them in a most a cruel manner, torturing their bodies even unto death; and after they [had] done this, they devour[ed] their flesh like unto wild beasts, because of the hardness of their hearts; and they [did] it for a token of bravery.

---

[49] *See* Thomas S. Abler, "Scalping, Torture, Cannibalism and Rape: An Ethnohistorical Analysis of Conflicting Cultural Values in War," *Anthropologica* vol. 34 no. 1 (1992), 3–20; also found online at academia.edu/2573207/Scalping_Torture_Cannibalism_and_Rape_An_Ethnohistorical_Analysis_of_Conflicting_CulturalValues_in_WarAuthor_s_Thomas_S_Abler?auto=download) WARNING—ACTS OF HORRENDOUS CRUELTY ARE DESCRIBED.

Chapter 19: A Marvelous Work and a Wonder®—A Promise of Peace and Life Eternal

Of course, these insidious (terrible) acts were wiped clean out of American history, obscured because of the pride that the American people have in their Founding Fathers.

Before we left the United States and shortly before Joseph was murdered, Joseph had been in the presence of William Henry Harrison. Joseph confronted Harrison about the atrocities that Harrison had committed, of which he had boasted, and continued to boast. Smirking, without denying his involvement, Harrison replied to Joseph, "Who are you to condemn me and the memory of President Washington?" At this point, Harrison threatened Joseph's life.

Joseph had been greatly misjudged and misaligned (slandered), and his pleas for justice for his people had been ignored by the politicians in Washington. This was true especially during the Mormon conflicts with the citizens of Missouri after the Haun's Mill Massacre. To protect our then True Messenger, we condoned and supported the removal of Harrison from his reign as President of the United States of America. As we have explained, we support what might ensure that humanity has a chance of increasing its hope of success. Had Harrison remained in office full term, and possibly a second, Joseph Smith would have been killed much sooner than he was.

To our great disappointment and sadness, a few years later in Utah Territory, Brigham Young did to some white settlers traveling through Utah, the same atrocities that George Washington had done to the native Americans. Young ordered the massacre of innocent men, women, and children. Some of the men who carried out Young's orders "deprive[d some of the white travelers] of that which was most dear and precious above all things, which is chastity and virtue."[50]

---

[50] *See* "Killings and aftermath of the Mountain Meadows Massacre," *Wikipedia*. 26 Feb. 2021, en.wikipedia.org/wiki/Killings_and_aftermath_of_the_Mountain_Meadows_Massacre.
For a more detailed treatment, including several firsthand accounts, writings, reminiscences, and letters, *see* Will Bagley, *Blood of the Prophets: Brigham Young and the Massacre at*

We have now reported these events to provide evidence of how far removed from the "true Spirit of Christ" the hearts of the American "Gentiles" were.

How can we expect that God will stay his hand in judgment against these people? Behold, our hearts cry: Wo unto this people. Come out in judgment, O God, and hide their sins, and wickedness, and abominations from before thy face!⁵¹

It is no longer our desire to *trick* the people of Earth and to use an *act of magic* to save them. We have delivered the people of this world to the hardness of their hearts and blindness of minds. We, the Real Illuminati®, are those who have *really* been illuminated with the light and "spirit of Christ," which is nothing more or less than the "spirit of Real Truth™." We can lead humanity to peace and life eternal, *IF* the people of the earth will only listen to us. We can only have faith and hope that one day the world will listen and pay some attention to our Marvelous Work and a Wonder®. With this hope, we wrote:

Wo be unto the Gentiles, saith the Lord God of Hosts! For notwithstanding I shall lengthen out mine arm unto them from day to day, they will deny me; nevertheless, I will be merciful unto them, saith the Lord God, **IF** they will repent and come unto me; for mine arm is lengthened out all the day long, saith the Lord God of Hosts.[52]

Mountain Meadows (Norman, OK: University of Oklahoma Press, 2002); also found online at books.google.gm/books?id=eakce2R_mdkC&lpg=PP1&pg=PP1#v=onepage&q&f=false.
See also David Bigler, Will Bagley, *Innocent Blood: Essential Narratives of the Mountain Meadows Massacre (Kingdom in the West: The Mormons and the American Frontier, vol. 12)* (Norman, OK: The Arthur H. Clark Co., 2008).
[51] *Compare BOM*, Moroni 9:14–15.
[52] *BOM*, 2 Nephi 28:32, emphasis added.

Chapter 20

The Great Apocalypse—A Message to the Youth of Planet Earth
(Our Closing Argument)

With the evidence that we have presented throughout this book, we have proven beyond any reasonable doubt that our group, now known as the Real Illuminati®, was responsible for writing and publishing a new American scripture—the *Book of Mormon* (the *unsealed* part), and *The Sealed Portion* (the *sealed* part).

We have proven that the organized churches that claim the *unsealed part* of our new American scripture as the "keystone of [their] religion" mislead their members and everyone else about the true content, teachings, and intent of our scripture.

We have proven that the overall intent of our new American scripture is to inspire those who call themselves *Christians* to actually read and pay attention to the simple philosophy and teachings of Jesus Christ, as given in the New Testament of the Bible. These philosophies and teachings are uncomplicated, easy and light,[1] the opposite of how they have been corrupted by ALL Christian sects.

We have proven that our new American scripture was meant to inspire the foundation and establishment of the United States of America as the best form of human government possible at this time. We have presented sound conclusions that the United States of America, as a nation, *could* have become the world's standard of excellence in the governance of human beings. This would have happened if it had been established according to

---
[1] NT, Matthew 11:30.

A New American Scripture

simple principals of equity and respect for ALL humans. This respect *must* include all people: "black or white, bond or free, male or female ... or heathen [a non-believer]."² But as we have proven, the Americans—referred to as "Gentiles" in our new American scripture—have failed to become this "ensign to the nations from far."³

We are confident that if one would take the time to review the evidence that we have submitted, one would invariably conclude that we have overwhelmingly proven our case. With this confidence, we challenge anyone to perform an extensive review of the evidence and prove otherwise.

In our opening statement—included as Chapter 1—we introduced ourselves and explained that each chapter of this book was purposefully written to be able to stand alone, providing the reader with enough information to encourage the person to read the rest of the book. In each chapter, we reiterated what we felt were the most important evidences of *why* we wrote our new American scripture—the *Book of Mormon* and *The Sealed Portion*. Also in each chapter, we tried to give the reader some insight into *how* we wrote our new American scripture to accomplish *why* we did.

We understood that for the more adroit (learned) reader, the repetition of certain points (explaining *why* we wrote our new American scripture) might have been somewhat superfluous and unnecessary. However, as we explained in our opening statement, we wrote this book so that the majority of our fellow humans could understand it easily and clearly. To accomplish this desired clarity, the repetition of important points was vital.

We dedicate our closing arguments, given as this final chapter, to the youth of this world.

Youth, we hope YOU will be the jury who will honestly and sincerely weigh the evidence presented. We encourage you to be objective and have

---

² *Compare BOM*, 2 Nephi 26:33.
³ *See* OT, Isaiah 5:26 and *BOM*, 2 Nephi 15:26.

an open mind, thoroughly considering any evidence that the opposing side might present *against* our case.

The youth of our world, living in all nations, upon all continents, are this specific jury. We speak to you. We argue that humanity has no hope of surviving the next 200 years unless the next few generations of humans strive to do everything within their power to save humanity. To do this, you must first reject the *status quo* of how things have been done and are being done; and second, you must join together and save humanity yourselves, which is the *only* way it can be done.

To begin to save your world, you must be taught what to do *now*. You must be open to doing things that haven't been tried in the past—things that can *really* make a difference and change our world. It is our hope that you, the youth of this world, will recognize that the present state of affairs was set up by older generations of other humans, who now control your lives and shape your destinies.

We call upon the youth living on planet Earth to take a good look at the world around you. Consider where humanity is currently (circa 2020) and where it is headed in the future. Are things getting better for humans? Or worse? Are humans becoming kinder, more amiable, compassionate, and considerate of each other? Or are humans becoming more antagonistic, harsh, hateful, disagreeable, discourteous, and more aloof (detached and separated) from each other?

Consider what is happening as your generation rises up and takes to the streets in protests and demonstrations that challenge the *status quo*—i.e., the existing state of affairs, especially regarding social or political issues.[4]

---

[4] Two examples of these protests are the March for Our Lives and School Strike for Climate movements. *See* "March for Our Lives," *Wikipedia*, Wikimedia Foundation, 20 May 2021, en.wikipedia.org/wiki/March_for_Our_Lives; *and*

Have ANY of these protests *really* done any good? The unrest that many of you have caused and experienced includes your protests, your discord, your revolts, and your objections to the secret combinations of political, religious, and economic powers that control your lives. Yet in spite of all of this, has any *real* change resulted from your uprisings and frustration?

The honest answer is a resounding, "NO."

In spite of all that you have done, or what you as the youth of this planet are planning to do, things have gotten a lot worse for humans living upon the earth. We hope, therefore, that you (the youth) can set aside your own pride and admit that the way you are going about seeking and demanding change from the powers that be does not work. We hope that the youth of this world can take an honest and hard look at your doings, and consider that the way you are going about it is actually contributing to the problems that you seek to change.

Youth, do you realize that your parents and these older generations were once young like you? Do you realize that they, too, in their youth, did many of the same things that you are doing? When they were between the ages of 15 and 35 years, the current older generations, then young, stood up for their right to live their lives the way that they wanted to, without the control of older adults. They sought for peace, freedom, and justice for all.[5] Yet still, in spite of past generational protests and uprisings, the world has not gotten any better for the majority of the human race. Maybe it has gotten better for a few, but NOT for the majority. This fact is undeniable. The world

---

"School strike for climate," *Wikipedia*, Wikimedia Foundation, 22 May 2021, en.wikipedia.org/wiki/School_strike_for_climate.

Another example is the Black Lives Matter movement, *see* "Black Lives Matter," *Wikipedia*, Wikimedia Foundation, 28 May 2021, en.wikipedia.org/wiki/Black_Lives_Matter.

[5] *See for instance*, "Civil rights movement," *Wikipedia*, Wikimedia foundation, 27 May 2021, en.wikipedia.org/wiki/Civil_rights_movement; *and*

"List of protests against the Vietnam War," *Wikipedia*, Wikimedia Foundation, 18 May 2021, en.wikipedia.org/wiki/List_of_protests_against_the_Vietnam_War; *and*

"Women's liberation movement," *Wikipedia*, Wikimedia Foundation, 9 May 2021, en.wikipedia.org/wiki/Women%27s_liberation_movement.

Chapter 20: The Great Apocalypse—A Message to the Youth of Planet Earth

has not changed since *their* rebellion against the *status quo*. Things have gotten much worse since the uprisings and protests that they held when they were young like you.

Do you realize that if they were once YOU, and you follow the same course of action that they followed, YOU will one day become just like THEM: complacent, tired of fighting, unsympathetic towards what they now see as an irreversible and unchangeable *status quo*?

The questions that you should be asking of your generation are:

What have WE done to change the world to become better? Is what WE are doing actually doing anything productive? In spite of all the complaining we have done, all the protests, all the anger, frustration, and resentment, what <u>solutions</u> have WE offered?

If the current *status quo* is responsible for the system of life that made your parents into who they are today (and unchanged, will make YOU into your parents)—what part of that status quo do you want to change, and what exactly do you recommend needs to be done ... specifically and exactly? What are YOU going to do so that you do not follow in your parents' footsteps and become complacent (too comfortable), acquiescent (passive), and acceptant? What will prevent you from settling in to a world that is not changing for the better, but is actually getting much worse?

Youth, consider for a moment what happened to YOU. What happened to you, to your friends, and to your peers that changed you from the carefree little children you used to be? At one time, you were submissive, meek, humble, patient, full of love, and willing to submit to all things that your parents, and *their* world (the *status quo*) inflicted upon you. As children, you seemed to be able to handle the world pretty well, for the most part, at least when all of your basic needs were being met. It wasn't that long ago when you were children. Your parents seem to have long forgotten the carefree days of their own childhood that once brought them joy. Your memories are not so distant.

WHAT HAPPENED TO YOU? How did you lose the basic core of your innate humanity—the roots of our species that make us very different from all other life forms?

Is it not true that you are indeed becoming just like your parents? And if you do, then what are you going to say to future generations of youth who rise up and protest against YOU?

For this answer, it might be wise to ask your parents why the world is the way that it is, what they did to make it that way, and what they are going to do to change it, if anything. Their honest answer will depend on their personal belief and attitude.

We suggest that all humans, if honest, fall into one of three general *cognitive paradigms* (attitudes), which is the inner workings of the mind—how people view their personal experiences and interpret them, and how acting upon these experiences affects their own lives and the lives of the rest of humanity.

These three general attitudes are: 1) a *theological paradigm* of religion and spirituality; 2) an *agnostic paradigm*, wherein one admits that one does not know anything that cannot be seen, heard, smelled, tasted, or touched—although wherein one does *not* consider a theological outlook (a belief in god) to be impossible; or 3) an *atheistic paradigm*, in which one bends towards nihilism—the rejection of all belief that cannot be proven empirically through the senses, which includes that humans cease to exist completely upon death.

Using your parents, families, and the culture in which you grew up as our example, of those from whom you received your knowledge and behavioral construct, we offer the following:

Chapter 20: The Great Apocalypse—A Message to the Youth of Planet Earth

If you hold a *theological paradigm* and outlook on life, you might state that only God can clean up the mess—that faith and hope in God doing so is all that humanity can hope for. If you belong to the few families that are prospering and living relatively well and secure in a theologically based nation that caters to carnal security (prospering and living comfortably), your parents might argue: "All is well in *our* lives. God has blessed us for living His commandments; and if the rest of the world would live as we do, God would bless them too."[6]

Perhaps your upbringing leaned towards *agnosticism* and you feel that you are non-religious, but your family is also one of the few that is well and secure in a nation that caters to carnal security. Perhaps you have learned:

"Don't worry about things. IF there is a heaven or a hell (something we don't know), let's eat, drink, and be merry. If tomorrow we die, and *if* there is a God, as long as we are good people, God will justify us in committing a little sin. He might beat us with a few stripes ('slap us on the wrists'), and at last we will all be saved in the kingdom of God. Because, wouldn't a good God want us to be happy? Everyone sins. It's part of human nature to lie a little and take advantage of another because we're more intelligent and have been to school and received a degree and they have not. There is no harm in having a business that is successful and profitable, relying on the sweat and hard work of others so that we don't have to sweat and work, and because of our opportunity we can live comfortably. There's no sin in investing and having our money make more money for us without us having to do anything."[7]

Perhaps your background is *atheistic*, and you generated *no belief* in a conscious life before or after death. Perhaps you have been taught that you have just one life to live and you better make the best of it and do everything that you can to enjoy yourself. That's what humans do. That's why humans have dominion and control over all the rest of the animals that haven't

---

[6] *See BOM*, 2 Nephi 28:21.
[7] *See BOM*, 2 Nephi 28:7–8.

evolved to the same state to which we have evolved. Humans are the end of evolution, the highest degree of intelligence possible since the Big Bang occurred and set the process of life in motion.

In summary, we present these three general attitudes found in all of humanity: 1) God will save us; 2) God will not condemn us for saving ourselves and our families, even if we commit sin, which is part of our human nature; and 3) there is no god and we must save ourselves to the best of our ability, no matter what it takes, starting with our self and those we love—because in the end, nothing matters.

Youth, THIS IS THE EMOTIONAL STATE OF THE CURRENT WORLD IN WHICH YOU LIVE. These are the prevailing cognitive paradigms (attitudes) that exist. Because of these attitudes, our world is not getting better for **all** of humanity. It is getting worse—much worse—and failing faster than at any other time in all of Earth's long history. Because these three attitudes are prevalent, then couldn't it be reasonably calculated and resolved (carefully thought out and decided) that these three attitudes *ARE* the CAUSE of all of our problems? Isn't it reasonable to consider that, unless we change these attitudes, humanity will not and cannot change?

Youth, what do you REALLY know? Is it not true that ALL that you know you learned from someone else? Is it not true that you learned a lot of what you know from what you have read in a book, in a newspaper, or from an Internet online publication or video? How do you know if the words you have read, studied, and listened to are actual Real Truth™? Consider how we have explained Real Truth™ to be things as they are *really* happening behind closed doors, doors which are shut by those who want you to believe according to their benefit? How is it possible that you can believe what is written in history? How did things *really* happen in the past?

Consider a comment attributed to one of the members of our species to whom the world has bestowed a reputable degree of intelligence (a person who is recognized as smart). Albert Einstein is credited with saying:

"Common sense is actually nothing more than a deposit of prejudices laid down in the mind prior to the age of eighteen."[8]

Youth, was Einstein's summation of YOUR knowledge and intelligence, of your *common sense*, correct? We are certain that Einstein's comments confront the pride that you possess in your own intelligence. It is reasonable and worthy that the youth of this world do not see themselves as ignorant and unintelligent. Youth, are you humble and honest enough to admit that Einstein might have been correct?

Each of you has one of the above cognitive attitudes; and it's not your fault that you do. Yes, there will be those of your peers, who in search of more significance and value from you, argue that they have a different cognitive paradigm from the general ones we present above. If people argue in response to their pride being hurt, ask them to explain *their* attitude about life. In spite of this egoism, do any of you *really* have a choice in *not* belonging to one of the general paradigms above? Logically, it seems to be that no one has a choice, because there are no other choices available.

No other person has provided any viable alternative that can sensibly replace any of these attitudes with something that makes more sense. You have not found anyone enlightened enough to offer an alternative. You have found none *illuminated* with the wisdom and experience to offer an alternative—UNTIL NOW.

We call ourselves the Real Illuminati® because we know that we belong to a small group of humans, the members of which *have* been *illuminated—really*. We can indeed provide you with an alternative attitude, one that is not part of the *status quo*. It is one that we know and have gained from our experience and intelligence. What we know can stop humanity's course on a slippery slope towards its own demise. The best part of our claim is that we

---

[8] *See* "Common Sense Is Nothing More Than a Deposit of Prejudices Laid Down in the Mind Before Age Eighteen," 29 Apr. 2014, Quote Investigator, quoteinvestigator.com/2014/04/29/common-sense/.

can provide you with empirical and sound evidence that we are who we claim to be, that we know what we claim to know, and that what we know will do what we claim it will do.

Your parents' value comes from the *status quo*. When you fight what has given your parents their value, they will naturally fight back, usually responding that you and your generation are too young and lack enough life experience to know what to do and how to do it. They will try to convince you that they, too, once had the same attitude and hope for humanity that you do. They will attempt to persuade you, that like they have, you will one day give up your unrealistic hope and rely on their experience to counsel and guide you to become like they are. If you love your parents, you do not want to cause them to be uncomfortable by confronting their wisdom. They are offended to think that their children are smarter than they are.

Youth, you do not have to confront anyone in the older generations. Let us confront them. Let our wisdom and knowledge argue against theirs. As you learn from us, humbly take what you have learned to your parents, and in sincerity and love for them, call upon your parents' wisdom and life experiences to explain how and why our information is not the Real Truth™. Approach them with love, blaming the information on its proper source. Then—in the quiet corners of your own inner mind, where your cognitive paradigms are formed, where cognitive dissonance exists—you will come to know the Real Truth™ that your parents' ego will never allow them to know.

The values that the older generations hang onto and protect were formed and provided by the political, religious, and economic powers that are combined in secret to control human life. Your parents never realized that their minds were being controlled. Do you?

Whenever we have tried to present an alternative paradigm (different set of ideas) for consideration, we have always ended up fighting these secret combinations. These powers have always prevailed (won) against us. In every instance, our True Messengers have been killed. For your

Chapter 20: The Great Apocalypse—A Message to the Youth of Planet Earth

consideration, we would like to give a brief account of what happened to the famed Greek philosopher, Socrates.

In the first book of our Trilogy, *The True History of Religion*, we gave a brief explanation of how our group was involved in recruiting and supporting Socrates as one of our True Messengers.[9] As we review below what happened to Socrates, we humbly ask you to consider what has happened to the last two contemporary True Messengers that we recruited to our current cause. The two men who wrote both parts (*unsealed* and *sealed*) of our new American scripture, Joseph Smith, Jr. (who wrote the *Book of Mormon*) and Christopher (who wrote *The Sealed Portion*), have both suffered ridicule and persecution. Joseph was killed for our cause. The comparison between these two men and Socrates is uncanny.

The only historical source of information about what happened to Socrates comes from two of his students—Plato and Xenophon. Sometimes their views on *what* Socrates taught, *how* he taught, and *why* he taught what he did, are different. However, we have explained that our group (the Real Illuminati®) has access to ancient documents that the world does not have. It is our hope that, if and when we find it safe and productive to reveal our true identities to the world, we can then produce many documents that we have in our possession. These documents will not only prove the authenticity of our group's existence, but of our group's knowledge, which is of great worth to the human race.

We have many of the original documents that were written by Plato. In the treatise currently known as the *Apology of Socrates*, history reports Plato as its source. We know that this particular document was written in collaboration with his fellow student, Xenophon. The *Apology of Socrates* is a document that purports (claims) to be an account of the trial of Socrates, similar to a court reporter's accounting of trial events for the record. We wrote "purports" purposefully, because what the world has is *not* a complete and

---

[9] See *THOR*, 107–11.

correct translation of the Greek treatise collaboration written by Plato and Xenophon. Regardless, if one is willing to study the *Apology of Socrates*, one will generally be apprised of (aware of) the main and significant parts of the actual trial that serve our purpose here.[10]

The secret combinations of political, religious, and business powers that existed in Socrates' time, tried, convicted, and sentenced Socrates to death in order to silence him. Likewise, Joseph Smith and Christopher, each in their relative positions as our recruited True Messengers, have had similar confrontations with secret combinations. We want to prove these stark similarities. We offer the example from the *Apology of Socrates* to confront our critics, who often discount our work because we hide our true identities. (All of the following quotes are from the referenced document.)

The life of Socrates gives ample evidence and testimony of what would happen if we did reveal ourselves to the world. The secret combinations of political, religious, and business leaders (the *status quo*) would do everything in their power to do what they have always done. (The testimony for this is presented below in the account given about Socrates).

Youth, these powers will do everything possible to slander us and convince you that we are evil. The term "illuminati" has often been associated with secret, nefarious (criminal) organizations that seek to take away freedom and control the world. There is no proof of this type of *illuminati*. This imaginary idea has made some movie producers and authors very wealthy; but there has never been one ounce of proof that any such organizations have existed or do exist.

Although titled as such, Socrates is *not* apologizing for what he did. Socrates does not deny, nor does he defend, that what he did was something that should have been considered a criminal offense, especially not an act that

---

[10] *See* "Apology," in G.M.A. Grube, *PLATO – Five Dialogues* (Indianapolis/Cambridge: Hackett Publishing Co., 2002) Second Edition revised by John M. Cooper, 21–44; also found online at sas.upenn.edu/~cavitch/pdf-library/Plato_Apology.pdf. Hereafter, "Apology."

would be prosecuted with a death sentence. As we quote from the *Apology of Socrates* below, we imply the assumption that Plato's and Xenophon's account is true, as far as it is translated correctly from Greek into modern English.

Socrates, talking about all of the witnesses that the prosecution put on the stand to testify against him, told the jury "hardly anything of what they said is true. Of the many lies they told [about me] … practically nothing they said was true."[11] Socrates testified,

> From me you will hear the whole truth, though not, by Zeus, gentlemen, expressed in embroidered and stylized phrases like theirs [indicating the court officers (attorneys) that knew how to speak in court and follow the prescribed rule of law and civil procedure of which attorneys are trained], but things spoken at random and expressed in the first words that come to mind, for I put my trust in the justice of what I say, and let none of you expect anything else.
>
> … One thing I do ask and beg of you, gentlemen [of the jury]: if you hear me making my defense in the same kind of language as I am accustomed to use in the marketplace by the bankers' tables, where many of you have heard me, and elsewhere, do not be surprised or create a disturbance on that account. … I am … simply a stranger to the manner of speaking here [in court. But] concentrate your attention on whether what I say is just or not, for the excellence of a judge lies in this, as that of a speaker lies in telling the truth.
>
> … There have been many who have accused me to you for many years now, and none of their accusations are true.[12]

---

[11] "Apology," 22.
[12] "Apology," 22–3.

A New American Scripture

The above statement by Socrates is what we can present as our own testimony against the accusers of both Joseph Smith and Christopher: "NONE of their accusations are true."

The evidence we have provided in this book proves that when a True Messenger confronts the *status quo* (the way things are) of the secret combinations of power that control human life, what our messenger says, makes sense. The words of our True Messenger threaten the power and value of the *status quo*. When this happens, *slander* is the only means by which these powers are able to turn people against our message and our messenger. If that doesn't work, a death sentence is carried out.

The word "slander" is used in Socrates' defense (the part from which we are quoting) 15 times. In his defense of the lies told about him that accused him of harming another person, in any way, Socrates said,

> I am convinced that I never willingly wrong[ed] anyone, but I am not convincing you of this, for we have talked together but a short time. If it were the law with us, as it is elsewhere, that a trial for life should not last one but many days, you would be convinced, but now it is not easy to dispel great slanders in a short time.[13]

Joseph Smith never wrote his own autobiography. What he did write about his life, he summed up with some important words that were attributed to him:

> You don't know me; you never knew my heart. No man knows my history. I cannot tell it: I shall never undertake it. I don't blame any one for not believing my history. If I had not experienced what I have, I would not have believed it myself. I

---

[13] "Apology," 40.

never did harm any man since I was born in the world. My voice is always for peace.[14]

We did not intend for Joseph Smith, Jr. to tell his true history. He was also quoted as saying, "If I were to tell you all I know of the kingdom of God, I do know that you would rise up and kill me."[15] As we have reiterated and proven throughout the chapters of this book, Joseph Smith was under strict mandate to *not* tell the Real Truth™, but to "deliver unto them many things which they could not understand, because they desired it."[16]

We did not allow Socrates to write an autobiography; nor did we allow him to leave ANY of his personal writings. We knew that if he had, the secret combinations of powers that were threatened by him would have either destroyed his writings or changed them and presented them differently from how Socrates actually wrote them. (We have explained and given evidence of this throughout our writings.)

Socrates did not tell ALL the Real Truth™, but he said enough to cause the Greek youth to question EVERYTHING that their parents, teachers, politicians, religious and business leaders told them. Socrates confronted them all and was very successful at "corrupting the youth" against their parents and the *status quo*, which resulted in one of the main accusations brought against him.

Socrates recognized that if he had held a public office and joined the secret combinations of power, he would not have been of any use. He said,

> Do not be angry with me for speaking the truth; no man will survive who genuinely opposes you or any other crowd and

---

[14] Joseph Smith Jr., found in B. H. Roberts, *History of the Church*, 6:317. Also known as the *King Follett Discourse*, 1844.

[15] *See* Robert Horne, "Reminiscences of the Church in Nauvoo," *Millennial Star*, vol. 55 no. 36, 4 Sept. 1893, 585; also found online at contentdm.lib.byu.edu/digital/collection/MStar/id/19227. (Download the PDF to view all the pages.)

[16] *Compare BOM*, Jacob 4:14.

prevents the occurrence of many unjust and illegal happenings in the city. A man who really fights for justice must lead a private [life], not a public life, if he is to survive for even a short time.

… Do you think I would have survived all these years [Socrates was about 72 years old[17]] if I were engaged in public affairs and, acting as a good man must, came to the help of justice and considered this the most important thing? Far from it, [gentlemen of the jury], nor would any other man. Throughout my life, in any public activity I may have engaged in, I am the same man as I am in private life.[18]

Socrates testified that he never charged a fee for teaching:

If anyone, young or old, desires to listen to me when I am talking and dealing with my own concerns, I have never begrudged this to anyone, but I do not converse when I receive a fee and not when I do not. I am equally ready to question the rich and the poor if anyone is willing to answer my questions and listen to what I say. And I cannot justly be held responsible for the good or bad conduct of these people [referring to his followers], as I never promised to teach them anything and have not done so. If anyone says that he has learned anything from me, or that he heard anything privately that the others did not hear, be assured that he is not telling the truth.

Why then do some people enjoy spending considerable time in my company? You have heard why, [gentlemen of the jury]; I have told you the whole truth. They enjoy hearing those being questioned who think they are wise, but are not.[19]

---

[17] Consider the clue given in the *BOM*, 3 Nephi 28:3: "therefore, after that ye are seventy and two years old ye shall come unto me in my kingdom; and with me ye shall find rest."
[18] "Apology," 36–7.
[19] "Apology," 37.

Chapter 20: The Great Apocalypse—A Message to the Youth of Planet Earth

People wanted to know where Socrates got his information. It was because of his honest answer to this question that the other criminal charge was brought against him. The other main charge against Socrates was introducing new gods, or rather, a new concept of God (a new attitude/*cognitive paradigm*). This new way of thinking was not in line with the ideology (beliefs) that the Greek powers of politics, religion, and business depended upon for their value, authority, and power, which was needed in order to control the people.

Socrates taught very similarly to what the Bible reports Jesus taught about God and the kingdom of God. Both taught that heaven and hell—both the kingdom of God and the kingdom of the devil—were "within."[20] Both taught that humans were the children of gods, and being such, each could be ONE with God and receive God's instructions and guidance personally, WITHOUT the need for a secondary intermediate.

In the story of Jesus, the religious leaders spearheaded the political and legal trial that led to the same sentence for Jesus that Socrates received—death. According to the stories told about them, Socrates and Jesus were both killed, not because they did anything wrong to any other person, but because they "corrupted the youth." Their teachings about God threatened the power and control that the secret combinations of politics, religion, and business held over the people.

In his defense, Socrates mentioned some of those in authority and power whom he had offended. Above, we mentioned Socrates teaching "in the marketplace by the bankers' tables." Likewise, the Roman Emperor Constantine secretly had *powers* convene to create a new hero—a Christ, a new god for the people. This combination of *powers* included philosophers, priests, and business people who had studied Plato's and Xenophon's accounts about Socrates. What Socrates said near "the bankers tables" was

---

[20] *See* NT, Luke 17:21.

very similar to what the Greco-Roman authors of the Jesus stories had Jesus say when he overturned "the tables of the moneychangers."[21] Both Socrates and Jesus confronted the corrupt practice of religious leaders combining with businesses to sell the items that people needed to sacrifice to the gods.

The people in both Socrates' and Jesus' days were convinced that they could not unite and save themselves. The people believed that only the gods could save them; and the gods would not save them unless they made offerings to them, which offerings supported the lifestyles of those who taught the people about these gods. The "bankers" and "moneychangers" were set up outside of the temples of Athens and Jerusalem to sell the people the articles of salvation. Socrates and Jesus were destroying the ability of these businesses to combine with religious ideologies in order to make a profit.

Both men taught that salvation is free, and that no one should be charged for salvation. Consider the modern LDS Church that requires a FULL payment of tithing before a person can enter a temple and receive the "saving ordinances," as this corrupt church supposes. Requiring the payment of money, in any form, is one of the greatest abominations of this church and is of such grievousness that we have addressed it throughout this book.

Our True Messengers do exactly what Socrates was accused of doing. Socrates testified that he had gained

> a reputation for wisdom, for in each case the bystanders thought that I myself possessed the wisdom that I proved that my interlocutor [the person whom he was debating] did not have.[22]

Speaking of the source of his wisdom as "the god," Socrates testified:

> What is probable, gentlemen, is that in fact the god is wise and that his oracular response meant that human wisdom is worth

---

[21] *See* NT, John 2:13–16.
[22] "Apology," 27.

little or nothing, and that when [the god] says this man, Socrates, he is using my name as an example, as if [the god] said: "This man among you, mortals, is wisest who, like Socrates, understands that his wisdom is worthless." So even now I continue this investigation [trying to find a person who is actually wise] as the god bade me—and I go around seeking out anyone, citizen or stranger, whom I think wise. Then if I do not think he is, I come to the assistance of the god and show him that he is not wise.[23]

We have challenged this world to put any of our group (which includes our contemporary True Messenger) into a room with ANY man or woman, young or old, bond or free, rich or poor, of any degree of education. The bystanders in the room will be soundly convinced we possess the wisdom we have proven that our "interlocutors" do not have. It is for this very reason that all True Messengers have been killed. It is for this reason that we have pulled our contemporary True Messenger out of public life to protect him for the time being.

We again reiterate that we are the **Real** *Illuminati*® and that there is no other group outside of ours that knows what we know and that has the power to do what we can do. But there is one thing that we will NOT do. There is one thing that we CANNOT do. We cannot impede nor frustrate free will, nor compel against it in any way. The best we can do is share our knowledge with you, the youth of this world, hoping that in so doing, by your own free will, you will come to know what we know.

The words of "Isaiah," although greatly mistranslated and transfigured, are found in the King James English translation of the Old Testament. We have revealed throughout our writings and given evidence that Socrates was the actual person who wrote the words attributed to the prophet Isaiah. For this

---

[23] "Apology," 27.

reason, we used many of Isaiah's words in our new American scripture. We wrote, coming from the mouth of the resurrected Jesus Christ:

> And now, behold, I say unto you, that ye ought to search these things. Yea, a commandment I give unto you that ye search these things diligently; for great are the words of Isaiah ... And all things that he spake have been and shall be, even according to the words which [Isaiah] spake.[24]

We have revealed in this book and provided substantial (strong) evidence of how we wrote prophecies that we knew we could fulfill. We explained that the non-fulfillment of these prophecies was a result of the "wickedness of the Gentiles." In other words, they did not do the right things upon which any particular one of our prophecies was based and predicated (founded).[25]

We have given ample evidence throughout the work that we do (a Marvelous Work and a Wonder®), that we are the ONLY ones upon Earth, and throughout recorded history, who can properly explain the esoteric symbolism of the books of Revelation and Isaiah, as given in the King James Bible. There is no "interlocutory" who can give any evidence against these claims. One need only read what we have published about Revelation and Isaiah to understand *why* we call our work "a marvelous work among this people, even a marvelous work and a wonder." When our *wisdom* is compared with that of the wisdom of the world, Isaiah's prophecy is fulfilled: "for the wisdom of their wise and learned shall perish, and the understanding of their prudent shall be hid."[26]

Youth, we are making some very strong claims here. In essence, we are saying that the whole world is deceived, and that none of its wisdom (knowledge and understanding) is of any worth to humanity. Notwithstanding

---

[24] *See BOM*, 3 Nephi 23:1, 3.
[25] *See* Chapter 9, pages 238–9.
[26] *Compare* OT, Isaiah 29:14 and *BOM*, 2 Nephi 27:26.

Chapter 20: The Great Apocalypse—A Message to the Youth of Planet Earth

the bravado of our claims, IF you (the youth of this world) give us a chance, we can prove them.

As in the case of Socrates, if you, the youth of the world, were the bystanders in the room where we were confronting the wisdom of the political, religious, and business leaders, we have no doubt that we would *corrupt your minds* with a new understanding of many things, especially by "failing to acknowledge the gods that the city acknowledges."

Youth, we can provide enough evidence to *corrupt your minds* (according to the view of your parents and the *status quo*). According to your parents, leaders, and all those who gain value from you (because you look to them for wisdom and guidance), we "make the worse the stronger argument" (as quoted from the *Apology of Socrates*[27]). In other words, what society now thinks is the best, we can argue with more sense that it is indeed the worst.

May we finalize our quote from the *Apology of Socrates* by plagiarizing his reported words and inserting ours in order to make our point:

> Furthermore, the young ... who follow [us] around of their own free will, those who have most leisure, the sons [and daughters] of the very rich, take pleasure in hearing people questioned; they themselves often imitate [us] and try to question others. [We] think they find an abundance of men who believe they have some knowledge but know little or nothing. The result is that those whom they question are angry, not with themselves but with [us]. They say: "That [the Real Illuminati® are] a pestilential [group which] corrupts the young." If one asks them what [we do] and what [we teach] to corrupt them, they are silent, as they do not know, but, so as not to appear at a loss, they mention those accusations that are available against all philosophers, about "things in the sky and things below the

---

[27] "Apology," 23.

earth," about "not believing in the gods" and "making the worse the stronger argument;" they would not want to tell the truth, [we are] sure, that they have been proved to lay claim to knowledge when they know nothing. These people [these secret combinations] are ambitious, violent, and numerous; they are continually and convincingly talking about [us]; they have been filling your ears for a long time with vehement slanders against [us]. From them [they] attacked [us], and [they attack us] on behalf of the poets, ... on behalf of the craftsmen and the politicians, ... on behalf of the orators, so that, as [we] started out by saying, [we] should be surprised if [we] could rid you of so much slander in so short a time. That, [gentlemen of the jury], is the truth for you. [We] have hidden or disguised nothing [while leaving human free will intact]. [We] know well enough that this very conduct makes [us] unpopular, and this is proof that what [we] say is true, that such is the slander against [us], and that such are its causes. If you look into this either now or later, this is what you will find.[28]

With much humility, but knowing that it is quite possible that we might end up offending the youth to whom we address our last words, albeit far from our natures to say such things as might be considered condescending, we must proclaim: you, the youth of this world, are just as ignorant, just as deceived, and just as prideful as those before you. And unless you, the youth, change your attitudes, you will become like the generations before you, except this time you will cause more damage to humanity than at any other time in Earth's history. This damage will come because you, the youth, now have opportunities, technologies, and scientific advancements that will either aid you in saving humanity or curse you in destroying it.

There is a profound statement that has been made by a few people to whom you give accolades of intelligence and insight. Edgar Allan Poe

---

[28] "Apology," 28.

(an American author) was the first to include this profound statement in one of his stories:

> "You are young yet, my friend," replied my host, "but the time will arrive when you will learn to judge for yourself of what is going on in this world, without trusting gossip of others. Believe nothing you hear [or what you read], and only one half that you see."[29]

Our group has influenced many great thinkers throughout the history of the world. In fact, if you were to ask some of the most recognized and popular, yet humble people about their experiences in gaining knowledge, many would report that much of what they learned was from simple and ordinary people. As we have revealed throughout our writings, posing as *simple and ordinary*, we were able to influence those whom we thought could make a difference for humanity and for our cause without calling attention to ourselves or revealing our true natures.

In everything that we have done, in all that we do, we protect individual free will at all costs. We desire that every human living on Earth know what we know, and to be *enlightened* as we are illuminated.

The masses (the majority of humans) are not protected in their free will. The masses are being forced to do and think what the secret combinations of politics, religion, and business want them to do and think. Humanity is being held in captivity, subservient to these forces. It is our desire to help humanity learn how to break the chains of ignorance that hold the people of Earth in captivity to these corrupt powers.

We have provided you with evidence that whenever we have recruited a person to be our messenger, whom we call our *True Messenger*, the powers that control the course of humanity do everything they can to stop our messenger. And in every case, except the present (for now), these

---

[29] *See* Edgar Allen Poe, "The System of Dr. Tarr and Prof. Fether," found online at *Wikisource*, en.wikisource.org/wiki/The_System_of_Doctor_Tarr_and_Professor_Fether.

powers have succeeded at silencing our message by killing our True Messenger. If our chosen messengers always end up being killed, it doesn't make sense that we would continue to recruit one. For this reason (as mentioned above), throughout most of history we have posed as *simple and ordinary*, quietly attempting to influence society using others without drawing attention to ourselves.

In this book we reported how we tried to inspire Thomas Jefferson to help us. Jefferson would not put his popularity, power, and character on the line to help us. We chose, in the alternative, a young American teenager from among the unthinking (ignorant) masses, who had been enlightened in the same way that we were. This young American teenager, Joseph Smith, Jr., was one of YOU.

In our new American scripture, we introduced ourselves (the Real Illuminati®) as we explained in this book. Relevant to our story's narrative, we wrote about a time when we would reveal ourselves to the world and teach the things that we know. We included, in part of a verse:

> And it shall come to pass, when the Lord seeth fit in his wisdom that [we] shall minister unto all the scattered tribes of Israel, **and unto all nations, kindreds, tongues and people.**[30]

Now that we have revealed that "the Lord" of our new American scripture is "us," we can proclaim that *we see it fit, according to our wisdom, to minister unto all the people on the earth.*

Youth, we can only hope that you will give us a chance to prove to you that we *are* who we claim to be. We know that you will not consider the alternative that we can offer you, as mentioned above, if we cannot convince you of our experience and intelligence and prove to you that those to whom you presently look for knowledge and guidance, have NONE. To convince you, we have provided some of the empirical evidence of our work. Here are just three (3) strong evidences of our claims:

---

[30] *BOM*, 3 Nephi 28:29, emphasis added.

Chapter 20: The Great Apocalypse—A Message to the Youth of Planet Earth

EMPIRICAL EVIDENCE NO. 1:

The Book of Revelation could not be explained properly, except by us.

Do you believe that the number sequence "666" refers to the devil or to evil in any way? If you do, you've been deceived.

Do you believe that the term "Apocalypse" refers to the end of the world? If you do, you've been deceived.

As explained, our group was responsible for the Bible's New Testament book of Revelation. For hundreds of years, no one on Earth was able to decipher the true meaning of the symbolism that we used in writing Revelation. Many have tried. All these *many* have done is create more confusion and misdirection.

When we wrote the *unsealed part* of our new American scripture (the *Book of Mormon)*, we made the Bible's book of Revelation, along with the Bible's book of Isaiah, two of the most relevant parts of our narrative. We did this to introduce how and when we would *unfold* the true meaning of Revelation (a book that has been used by religious authority to deceive you and take advantage of your ignorance).

In its original Greek, the title of the last book of the Bible's New Testament (Revelation) was actually "*Apocalypse,*" not "Revelation." The general definition of "*apocalypse*" (in Greek) is "to make known or public, to expose to view, to open up, to reveal"; thus, it can be called a *revelation*.

We have explained that, because we wrote the Bible's book of Revelation, we could also write a prophecy with integrity that one day we would *unfold* Revelation's true meaning "in the eyes of all the people."[31] We have explained that the "unfolding" of the mystery behind the symbolism

---

[31] *See BOM*, Ether 4:16.

used in Revelation was accomplished with the publication of our book, *666, The Mark of America—Seat of the Beast: The Apostle John's New Testament Revelation Unfolded* (pub. 2006).[32]

There is no "interlocutory," no scholar, priest, nor any "doctor of knowledge" of any degree, who has or can dispute what we have *unfolded* about the symbolism found in Revelation.

We mandated the man whom we recruited as our True Messenger to apply his first name *only* as the book's author: *Christopher*—a name that means, *Christ, Bearer of*. However, as we have explained, we were the authors of Revelation. We were the authors of many of the words of Isaiah and Malachi. Our group was instrumental in providing information to the Greek writers responsible for the original New Testament Gospels (Matthew, Mark, Luke, and John), and for a few other New Testament references (particularly, Timothy, James, Peter, and John).

We influenced much of the ancient Greek philosophy that started with Socrates, as well as the beginnings of Christianity and Islam. (See *The True History of Religion—How Religion Destroys the Human Race and What the Real Illuminati® Has Attempted to do Through Religion to Save the Human Race*, pub. 2019.)[33]

For tens of hundreds of years, there have been many attempts to explain Revelation. Because we wrote it, we knew what all of Revelation's symbolism meant; and we knew that no one would be able to "unfold" it besides us. We did this to provide some strong empirical evidence of our existence and purpose.

It would be easy for one so inclined to prove that we are not who we claim to be, and that we have not done what we claim to have done. One need only present an explanation for the esoteric (hidden) symbolism used in

---

[32] This book is free to read at realilluminati.org/666-mark-of-america.
[33] This book is free to read at realilluminati.org/the-true-history-of-religion.

Revelation that makes more sense than what we have published in our 2006 book. We have no doubt that no one can.

We wrote Revelation for the same reasons, and with the same intent, that we wrote our new American scripture—to confront corrupt religion and the way that religious leaders use scripture to deceive, control, and mislead people. Humanity has been led to believe that there exists a God, and that God speaks with a few chosen ones on behalf of everyone else. Those who accept this false doctrine lose their free will and are susceptible to being misled and controlled by these *falsely* chosen few. Our evidence proves that NONE of these religious leaders know anything about the Real Truth™.

EMPIRICAL EVIDENCE NO. 2:

Our True Messengers, armed with the Real Truth™, can confound any political, religious, business, social, secular, or scientific authority.

We have proven that it is futile to attempt to convince others (the masses) that there is no god outside of one's own consciousness, and that all those who claim to receive revelation from God are making it up in their own heads. In confronting the idea that one needs a religious or spiritual leader to teach them, we have challenged the religious world to place any religious or spiritual leader in the same room as our True Messenger and let each respond to the inquiries and comments of the other. Compare our message with that given by any religious leader, during *any* time, now or throughout all of history.

We have explained that throughout history, when religious leaders have known of a True Messenger and then realized that the True Messenger could actually confound them, these religious leaders convinced their followers that the True Messenger was of the devil and worked with the power of something evil. In the Jesus stories, they called him a messenger of "Beelzebub the prince of the devils."[34]

Religious leaders know that if the people listen to a True Messenger, the people might realize none of the religious leaders know any more than they (their followers) do. Upon listening to the common logic of a True Messenger, IF they would, religious followers would begin to realize that everything their religious leaders teach them about God, or propose as "God's word," comes from their leaders' own heads.

Our message uncovers religious leaders' deceptions, and when it does, they begin to lose their followers. One of the greatest deceptions of all—that which keeps humanity from improving and solving its own problems—is the assumption that if God wanted to solve the problems, God would tell his chosen leaders how to do it. Religious leaders teach that most of humanity's problems are a result of humanity not listening to *them*, who are God's ONLY *true* messengers on the earth. Religious leaders blame humanity's problems on God punishing humanity for not following *their* commands, which they pretend to receive from God. This is a great deception. It causes humanity to continue to suffer from problems that could easily be solved by people uniting and fixing the problems they created themselves.

We have explained that the modern LDS Church will not confront our True Messenger. When members of this church read our words, or listen to our words given through our True Messenger, they recognize in their hearts that what we say makes more sense and is more logical than anything taught by their leaders.

As we pointed out in the *Prologue* of this book, with empirical evidence, this particular church's General Authorities openly deceive the members. Many members of this church have found our work and questioned their authorities

---

[34] NT, Matthew 12:24.

about why our information makes more sense than what they are taught in church. The general response of these deceptive leaders is often:

> Satan knows all truth. Once your mind is focused on what the devil is trying to get you to believe, Lucifer will give you 99% of the truth and then 1% lies to deceive you. The devil's messenger might be able to explain everything, but he will use your attention on him to distract you from what God's leaders are teaching.

We have mentioned a woman named Ida Smith. We explained how she was very connected to the General Authorities of the LDS Church and to certain United States politicians. Ida courageously confronted some of these men with our book that explains the symbolism of the Bible's Revelation, in conjunction with questioning the LDS Church as to why solving poverty was not part of its public mission statement. This is one part of the response she was given:

> Of course, Lucifer knows what the symbolism is behind the meaning of Revelation. But Lucifer wants to convince you not to listen to us. If God wanted misery to end, God would tell us how to end it. But as revealed through the appropriate lines of priesthood authority [and here this man quoted the actual words of one of the LDS Twelve Apostles, Dallin H. Oaks] "we [will] have the poor always with us."[35]

---

[35] *See* Dallin H. Oaks, *The Lord's Way* (Salt Lake City: Deseret Book, 1991) 111. Reference can be seen on LDS Living, Boyd K. Packer, "Thoughts on Lesson Thirty-Eight, by Boyd K. Packer, Ensign August 1975 | Sep. 21, 2005," section titled "Dallin H. Oaks, *The Lord's Way*," 21 Sept 2005, ldsliving.com/Thoughts-on-Lesson-Thirty-Eight/s/5388.

See also Marion G. Romney, "The Role of Bishops in Welfare Services," Oct. 1977 General Conference, The Church of Jesus Christ of Latter-day Saints, churchofjesuschrist.org/study/general-conference/1977/10/the-role-of-bishops-in-welfare-services?lang=eng, wherein Marion G. Romney stated, "The prime duty of help to the poor by the Church is not to bring temporal relief to their needs, but salvation to their souls."

Here we provide another strong piece of evidence of who we are and what we have done, more particularly regarding the church that pretends belief in and reverence to the *unsealed portion* of our new American scripture, the *Book of Mormon*.

Our former contemporary True Messenger confronted the LDS Church's false doctrine about God allowing human suffering so that it would lead people to their "restored Gospel of Jesus Christ."[36] He also challenged them about their belief that because of the fall of Adam and Eve, the world will not and cannot be saved until Jesus Christ comes again to usher in a millennial time. The LDS people are taught that, until that time, there is nothing that they should be doing EXCEPT listening to and obeying the General Authorities and local leaders of their church. There are many questions one could ask an LDS/Mormon member:

Why does God allow so much misery to occur upon the earth?

Why did God create different colors of skin (races) and different languages (confounding human language at the Tower of Babel)?

Why did God create vicious animals that eat humans, bacteria, and viruses that cause humans to suffer, as well as noxious weeds and plants to torment and afflict humankind?

If any of these questions were asked, the LDS/Mormon's response would be:

"God wants us to learn so we can become what He is. We believe that as man is, God once was, and as God is man may become. And to become like God, to gain His knowledge, the way that he did, we must learn to comprehend that everything has its opposite—good and evil, virtue and

---

[36] *See* Elder Dale G Renlund, "Infuriating Unfairness," Apr. 2021 General Conference, The Church of Jesus Christ of Latter-day Saints, abn.churchofjesuschrist.org/study/general-conference/2021/04/25renlund?lang=eng.

vice, light and darkness, health and sickness, pleasure and pain. We believe that experiencing all of the misery and vicissitudes of life is how God, who was once a man, became who He is, an exalted man. We believe that all of human suffering is appropriate and God-mandated so that our eyes will be opened and we will have the same knowledge that God has."

For the above reason, the members of the Church of Jesus Christ of Latter-day Saints do nothing to solve poverty. They do nothing with their money and power to influence their government to open ALL borders so that the poor and suffering people of the world can find peace, security, and a better life in a more prosperous nation. These LDS/Mormon members have been greatly deceived to believe that all of the suffering that happens in the world is God-mandated and God-supported.

Below is our response to this false doctrine and corrupt ideology. (In fact, we tried to teach the LDS/Mormon people about this false concept in the presentation of the Real Truth™ that we helped Joseph Smith present to them in what they call their Temple Endowment.) May we provide testimony of how our True Messenger would respond to such hypocrisy and blatant nonsense, i.e., that God approves of human suffering, and that human suffering is what humans must go through in order to become gods themselves:

> TRUE MESSENGER: *(Addressing an LDS/Mormon believer.)* Where are you taught that all human suffering is the way that the Father gained His knowledge; that we have to comprehend that everything has its opposite—good and evil, virtue and vice, light and darkness, health and sickness, pleasure and pain; and that thus your eyes will be opened and you will have knowledge?
>
> LDS/MORMON: We are taught these things in our temples when we receive the highest saving ordinance—the endowment. We do not talk about or discuss these things outside the walls of the

A New American Scripture

temple. These things are too sacred to be discussed, and others might mock what is most sacred to our religion.

TRUE MESSENGER: Well, if you will not discuss these things, maybe you might consider actually listening to and paying attention to what you are seeing while you watch the temple endowment presentation. Which character in the presentation tells Adam and Eve that they must go through all kinds of misery and human suffering in order to become like God?

LDS/Mormon: Again, we do not discuss these things outside of the temple.

TRUE MESSENGER: Of course, your leaders do not want you considering or discussing things that they cannot explain and answer. But we both know that it is *Lucifer, the god of this world*, who tells Adam and Eve that they have to suffer in order to become gods, and that suffering is a good thing that God wants us to experience. You know this. You should also know that *Lucifer* is known as the "father of lies." EVERYTHING that the character *Lucifer* does in the presentation of the play the *Three Nephites* and *John the Beloved* helped Joseph Smith to write a couple years before he was killed, IS A LIE!

(At this point in the discussion, cognitive dissonance sets in and the LDS/Mormon person becomes very uncomfortable, frustrated, and angry, doing everything possible to leave the conversation.)

TRUE MESSENGER: Before you leave, consider what else you see as you experience the temple endowment. Consider that the characters **Adam** and **Eve** represent you as a mortal. **Elohim** and **Jehovah** represent Heavenly Father and Jesus Christ, respectively. Adam and Eve (you) are living in the "lone and dreary world," which represents life upon Earth.

Chapter 20: The Great Apocalypse—A Message to the Youth of Planet Earth

During this time (mortality), Elohim and Jehovah have ABSOLUTELY NOTHING to do with Adam and Eve. Pay attention and you will find out that the ONLY source of a person's answers to his or her prayers, no matter how contrite and sincere, IS ALWAYS LUCIFER.

We present the above example of a typical conversation that might be held between our True Messenger and an LDS/Mormon person. We hope it demonstrates why it is impossible for a True Messenger to teach anything to one who is deceived by religion and spirituality, taught by those who know nothing. The pride and self-worth of the believer creates impenetrable walls and beliefs that impede the ability of the person to think.

In our new American scripture, we wrote that we can explain "all things [that] shall be revealed unto the children of men which ever have been among the children of men, and which ever will be even unto the end of the earth."[37] The very last prophecy given by one of the main characters of our story, *Nephi*, was:

> Wherefore, the things of all nations shall be made known; yea, all things shall be made known unto the children of men. There is nothing which is secret save it shall be revealed; there is no work of darkness save it shall be made manifest in the light; and there is nothing which is sealed upon the earth save it shall be loosed. Wherefore, all things which have been revealed unto the children of men shall at that day* be revealed; and Satan shall have power over the hearts of the children of men no more.[38]

* **THIS DAY** has come.

---

[37] *BOM*, 2 Nephi 27:11.
[38] *BOM*, 2 Nephi 30:16–18.

EMPIRICAL EVIDENCE NO. 3:

This book. We have given strong evidence that we wrote scripture, like the Bible, that deceives people into believing, like they do the Bible, that God inspires men to write His words and give them to others. We have proven that the *Book of Mormon* and *The Sealed Portion* were written by us.

Throughout this book (*A New American Scripture—How and Why the Real Illuminati® Created the Book of Mormon*), we have used many examples from our new American scripture to help explain *how* and *why* we used Christian beliefs to attempt to open the minds and hearts of the "Gentiles" (Americans). We have explained that our *Book of Mormon* was purposefully written in a way that would cause an emotional (spiritual) response. This response can convince the God-fearing reader that what they are reading truly came from God.

In the stories that we wrote, we revealed many of the "works of darkness" (things done behind the scenes by the secret institutions of power) that led to the destruction of civilizations. It was our hope to persuade the reader to apply these stories to their current life experiences.

LDS/Mormon leaders counter this (that the scripture applies to them and their followers). These deceptive leaders explain that these stories were about *another* people, and that God has a "restored" church now that is doing the right thing. As a result of listening only to their leaders, few LDS/Mormon people read and study our *Book of Mormon* and honestly apply its teachings to their own life. Those who have, have seen through the great hypocrisy of the LDS/Mormon Church and have left it. Our work has helped the blind to see and the deaf to hear.

We have explained how our scripture (the *Book of Mormon* and *The Sealed Portion*) are filled with subliminal (hidden) messages that produce a sensation or a perception. We controlled these sensations and perceptions throughout our books' narratives in the way we wrote the stories, and in how

Chapter 20: The Great Apocalypse—A Message to the Youth of Planet Earth

we presented the intended lessons. Subliminal messages work with the mind below the threshold of consciousness. This is what we wanted. We wrote in a manner that the reader would *feel* that what they were reading was a message coming from their own subconscious, which most believers ascribe to inspiration coming from their god. Through this *feeling*, religious people believe that God (or the "Holy Ghost") is communicating with them.

We used Christianity because of its emotional power in creating sensations that *feel "good and righteous"*—feelings the people associate with Jesus Christ. This is why we used Jesus Christ as the main focus of our storyline.

Below is how we would have presented some of the points of doctrine (truths) that we wanted people to learn, *without* using the subliminal concepts by which religion has seduced a person's mind. We introduced the lesson explained below in our new American scripture, with a hope that we could convince the reader that a person who is a *true* Christian is not only a "peaceable follower of Christ," but also "walks peaceably" with everyone else.

If we could have written it differently, without basing it on Christ, we would have written it as follows:

We would speak unto you who are good people and the peaceable followers of all things that are good and humane. We speak to those of you who have obtained a sufficient hope, because of your goodness, that a society of goodness can exist.

And now my fellow human beings, we judge these things of you because of your peaceable walk with everyone else. For we remember some words that are good, which say, by their works ye shall know the people who are good and those who are bad; for if their works be good, then they are good also.

For behold, a person who is evil cannot do that which is good; for if this person acts like they are doing good, and does things that seem to be good, but the things cause the person to not walk peaceably with everyone else, how can the things that the person believes to be good, actually be good?

A person who is truly good will not do anything that is evil. We judge this person by their peaceable walk with everyone else. We judge every person by how what each person does affects each person's peaceable walk with everyone else. That which is good causes a person to walk peaceably with others. That which is bad causes a person to not walk peaceably with everyone else.

Wherefore, all things which are good come from a person who walks peaceably with everyone else continually; and those people who are bad do things continually that negatively affect the peaceful way they walk with others.

That which makes a person walk peaceably with others is what we know to be good. Therefore, we can say that this peaceable walk is inspired by the good part of our human nature. And that which causes a person to not walk in peace with everyone else is inspired by the bad part of our human nature.
Wherefore, we counsel you to pay attention to what you do. If you do something that causes you to not walk peaceably with everyone else, then you will know of a certainty that it is not good. Be careful not to believe something to be good, when it does not cause you to walk peaceably with everyone else. Be careful not to believe that something is bad, when it causes you to walk peaceably with everyone else.

For behold, my fellow humans, it is given unto us to judge, that we may know good from evil; and the way to judge is as plain, that we may know with a perfect knowledge, as the daylight is from the dark night.

Chapter 20: The Great Apocalypse—A Message to the Youth of Planet Earth

For behold, it is given unto us to know what causes us to walk peaceably with everyone else and what does not. Our unique human conscience guides us to *know*, without having to believe. We know because what we are doing causes us to walk peaceably with everyone else. We also *know* when we are not walking peaceably with everyone else. Therefore, as we said, by our works we know whether or not we are good or evil.

Wherefore, we beseech of you, our fellow humans, that you should search diligently that which you know causes you to walk peaceably with everyone else, and what causes you not to walk peaceably; and if you will lay hold upon every good thing that causes you to walk peacefully, and condemn it not, ye certainly will be a good person.[39]

We could not write in plainness, as we have given in the above example, if we wanted people to believe that the words came from a supernatural being. Religious people need to *feel* that the words of scripture claiming to come from God are *actually* coming from God. People are convinced that they cannot receive these feelings from the message without a messenger (a religious leader chosen by God) to deliver it to them. For this reason, people often feel the "Spirit of God" while they listen to those whom they accept as "God's chosen leaders."

The same feeling that is felt by Christians while listening to their leaders, is also felt by the Jews listening to theirs, by the Muslims listening to theirs, and by the followers of any person who has deceived others into believing that God is talking to them on behalf of the world.

Because we realized this power that religious leaders held over their followers, and because our message was for the American Christians, we chose the leader to whom we knew and hoped they would listen—Jesus

---

[39] *Compare BOM*, Moroni 7:3–19.

A New American Scripture

Christ. Using the above example that we wrote in plainness, consider how we wrote it in our new American scripture to make it all about Christ. We wanted to teach an important lesson that the reader would *feel* was from their Christ.[40]

We wrote about the people who considered themselves "followers of Christ." People who follow Christ do so for a reason. Christians have a hope that, in following Christ, they "can enter into the rest of the Lord, from this time henceforth until [they] shall rest with him in heaven."[41] Our subliminal message was that only people who get along well with others shall "rest with him" as "***peaceable*** followers of Christ."

It was this subtle description that allowed us to affect the reader's emotions and get through their *Christian cognitive filters* in order to present a description of a true Christian: "I judge these things of you because of your ***peaceable*** walk with the children of men."[42]

With this simple description of a true Christian (one who walks peaceably with everyone else), we hoped to have introduced a set of commandments, a code of instructions for those who wanted an organized church. This is why we presented the actual words of the resurrected Jesus Christ in our story. We knew, however, that the leaders of any organized religion could transfigure or completely ignore our words. We chose not to provide an exact code of instructions in our story. We wrote that Jesus *did* deliver this set of commandments to the people he taught (in our story), but that our story's presented author, Mormon, *did not* include "even a hundredth part of the things which Jesus did truly teach unto the people."[43] Because we knew that the people who read our book wanted an organized religion, we reserved "the things which Jesus did truly teach unto the people" for the *sealed part* of our record.

---

[40] *See BOM*, Moroni 7:3–19.
[41] *BOM*, Moroni 7:3.
[42] *BOM*, Moroni 7:4.
[43] *BOM*, 3 Nephi 26:6.

Chapter 20: The Great Apocalypse—A Message to the Youth of Planet Earth

In Appendix 2 of this book, we provide some VERY strong evidence of just how powerful our written words are in this *sealed part* of our new American scripture. Appendix 2 (*TSP*, chapters 18, 19, and 20) tells the story of Adam teaching his children "the fulness of the Gospel of Jesus Christ." Adam's teachings are based on the *Sermon on the Mount*, although expounded upon in greater detail. The simple teachings of Jesus help break down a person's pride in their own family and the way a person views other people, even if the other person is their enemy. *The Sealed Portion*'s account gives a much greater insight to Jesus' *Sermon on the Mount.*

We encourage the youth of this world to consider how profound, clear, and powerful our written scripture is compared to what you might have read in the Bible or in any other source of scripture. Upon reading our scripture and comparing it with the Bible, strong evidence of our ability to write scripture is given. We included Appendix 2 in this book as further proof of our abilities. Most of the people who have read *The Sealed Portion*'s account of the "fulness of the everlasting Gospel," as first given by Adam to all of his children, have been convinced that our claims are true—that they must be true, *if* the *unsealed Book of Mormon* is true.

It was our hope that the Christians who read our new American scripture and were convinced it was from God would judge their own life and what they did[44] on how *peaceably they walk with their fellow humans*.

As further empirical (factual) evidence of how the lessons given in our new American scripture would work, if followed, consider the following. ALL of the persecution experienced by the early LDS/Mormons, and ALL that is currently experienced by the modern Mormons were and are unnecessary. It has and does occur because their church "teaches for doctrines the commandments of men"[45] that do not let them *walk peaceably* with others. LDS/Mormons have commandments that strictly control the flesh, where others find that

---

[44] *See BOM*, 1 Nephi 19:23.
[45] JSH 1:19; NT, Matthew 15:9.

when they "break" these Mormon laws and commandments, it brings them happiness.

For one of **many** examples, when two homosexual men or women are in love and only want to have sex with each other, how much peace do these "children of God" feel when they know that their Mormon neighbors condemn them to hell? One who condemns another to hell for not obeying man-made commandments is *not* walking peaceably with others.

In this book, we have shown how we controlled the way Joseph responded to his peer group. Joseph saw how his peers reviewed the part of our story that presents Jesus Christ teaching the fullness of his everlasting Gospel, or in other words, when Jesus taught people how to walk peaceably with others. If we had not controlled Joseph's response when he confronted the peer review group, he might have reacted towards them very differently. But because Joseph was not allowed to interfere in his followers' free will, he allowed them to organize a religion that they thought was Jesus' "restored church."

Our True Messengers know *how* and *why* we created the *Book of Mormon* the way that we did. If a person reads our story correctly, after Jesus had taught the people, and had the people not wanted a religion, Jesus would have left them without one. There would have been no need for a church to be "restored," because he didn't set one up when he lived among the Jews. According to our narrative, Jesus would have commanded his Nephite Apostles to continue to teach the people the words that he had just spoken, without variation.

It was our intent to end the story at the point right after Jesus told the Nephites that he was going to teach the same things to the rest of the people of the world, who had not yet heard his voice. Jesus was going to go throughout the world and teach everyone how to walk peaceably with everyone else.

Consider what kind of religion and church would exist if the members had all judged their own acts based on whether or not their religious "performances" caused the members to walk peaceably with everyone else. What kind of religion and church, if any, would have developed?

How do present-day "non-members" feel when LDS/Mormon members explain the doctrine of their church? Their church claims that non-members will go to hell unless they believe in the Father, Son, and the Holy Ghost, as entities that will only give direction to the people through *their* appointed priesthood leaders. This church claims that unless all of humanity does what *their* leaders say, humanity will be punished by God and not be redeemed. This religion's foolish doctrine states that non-members will not receive the same blessings as the Mormons (Latter-day Saints).

How much peace exists when one group of people sets itself up above others and claims to be right while everyone else is wrong?

The church that was established in 1830 by the American Christians who read our book and accepted it as "God's Holy Word" did NOT walk peaceably with everyone else. We have given many examples of how this organized church, due to the pride of those who participated in it, caused all kinds of problems for the rest of their neighbors who did not want to join their church.

The wars between the Mormons and everyone else were not about the Mormons' desire to help the native American people establish Zion and be accepted as worthy members of "the house of Israel." These wars were about the arrogance and pride of the Mormon people and how they *didn't* walk peaceably with everyone else. Nothing that this religion and church ever did, or does, shows an example that its members are "peaceable followers of Christ," judging by their "[UN]peaceable walk with the children of men."

We have filled the pages of this book with facts that condemn the Church of Jesus Christ of Latter-day Saints for how it uses our *Book of Mormon* to do everything *but* demonstrate a "peaceable walk with the children of men." We have written this book as plainly as we could have written it to fulfill our prophecy of "reveal[ing] all things unto the children of men."⁴⁶

We have used enough scripture. We have tiptoed around the Real Truth™ because we, the Real Illuminati®, are like unto the Jesus character that we created for our new American scripture. We suffer within. We *groan within*⁴⁷ because of the unrighteousness of the people who read our book and reject it.

And now, out of great respect and love for the YOUTH of this world, in whom we place all of our hope, consider our words of Real Truth™ about all things—things as they are, as they were, and as they are to come:

Humanity will continue to fail as long as you, the youth, are continually held in the same chains of ignorance that have held your parents, teachers, and whomever you look to for understanding and guidance. If these teachers knew what to do to make the world a better place, don't you think they would have already done it?

We have used the word "evil" throughout this book to describe the religious organizations and people that have corrupted, and continue to corrupt, our world. We used this word because we were addressing religious issues. A better and more apropos (appropriate) term to use would be "ignorant." Truly, your parents and the secret combinations of politics, religion, and business they support are not "evil." In fact, to the few, these powers are believed to be good—at least *for* the few.

Chains of ignorance keep humanity in captivity. The links of these chains are directly related to *pride*. Those who have forged the chains by which humanity is held captive gain personal value and worth from the links that create the ignorance.

---

⁴⁶ *Compare BOM*, 2 Nephi 30:16–18.
⁴⁷ *BOM*, 3 Nephi 17:14.

Some believe that their government is the best. Some believe that their religion is the best. Some believe that their business plan is the best. And of course, whatever benefits you is always "the best." But these things that are considered "the best" cause a considerable amount of inequality and misery for the majority of humanity. IF these really were "the best" things, they would benefit every human equally and equitably.

Above we presented three general attitudes that the people of Earth hold. <u>Please consider an alternative to these attitudes.</u> Consider that we are our own saviors and that we are our own gods—the *only* gods that exist and have ever existed.

The more you learn through science, the more you will begin to realize that humans have much more power over the laws of nature than they could have ever imagined. Consider that with this new power, you can use your knowledge to do good for the benefit of all of humanity. But do you? Will you? Will you use your knowledge of nuclear energy, for one of many examples, to do good for humanity or to destroy it?

We mentioned earlier in this book that we know a great deal about human life upon Earth that has not yet been discovered by science. We know how human life first started on the earth, how humans developed into successful societies that lasted for many years, and how these societies were destroyed.

We know, and have documentation to prove that the *First Dispensation of Humanity* on Earth lasted for almost two million years. A "dispensation" is a measure of time that we (the Real Illuminati®) distinguish as a period when all humans upon the earth know of each other and are cooperating together.

During the First Dispensation of human time, all of humanity was cooperating as a people of one heart and one mind, and there were no poor people among them—until they ended up destroying themselves. We have not yet explained clearly *how* these highly advanced civilizations of humans ended up destroying themselves. One day, we intend to explain all things clearly.

For now, we ask you, the youth, to consider what you are learning: humans can control the laws of nature. In the past recorded history of this, the *Sixth Dispensation of Human Time*, people did not know how much control they could have over these laws. In ignorance, our ancestors created gods whom they believed had power and control over nature. Now that you have learned that YOU are the life forms that can control nature, doesn't it make sense that you could also learn to control *God*? And if you learned to control *God*, you could also learn how to control those who speak for God, who act in God's name, and who control your lives in the name of *God*.

Isn't losing control over you the thing that your religious leaders fear the most? For this very reason, religion fights science.

Almost 30 years ago, humans knew how to clone another human. With this knowledge, why haven't we (humanity) cloned the best, the strongest, and the most beautiful human body possible? With the knowledge humans have of DNA and the genetic codes thereof to create the perfect human body, why haven't we done it? What stands in the way of <u>making us the gods</u> that we depend on <u>to save us</u>?

One day we will reveal what happened during the five past *Dispensations of Human Time*. We will explain *how* and *why* every virus, every bacterium, and every species of flora and fauna was created by Earth-bound humans, for human pleasure and purpose. We will explain how human nature—pride and arrogance of one's own existence compared to that of others—caused the downfall and demise of the human race.

We hope to prove to you, the youth of this world, *how* you can become the gods that you are destined to become. We hope to inspire you to reject the false notion that poverty, inequality, and everything that contributes to human suffering and misery is the will and desire of a god who does not live

Chapter 20: The Great Apocalypse—A Message to the Youth of Planet Earth

on planet Earth. As we expose the works of darkness of those who do not want to lose their power and control over your minds and lives, we know that the Real Truth™ will provide you with the proper alternative attitude to the three attitudes (explained above) that are prevalent in the world today.

Here is this alternative attitude:

We are each very equal gods. We should love and respect ourselves with all of our heart, might, mind, and soul. And because all others are equal gods with us, we must love and respect all others like we do ourselves. There is no other doctrine or idea upon which any human should operate their conscious existence.

It is upon this alternative attitude that all laws that govern humans should be established in order to save humanity. Once we respect all others as we do ourselves, we will not allow any of us to live in poverty and inequality.

This is what Socrates knew. It was one of his main teachings by which he was accused of corrupting the youth. Socrates taught that there is no other person, nor any other life form, as important as each *human* person.

We refer to each person as an eternal advanced human, who was never created, nor can be destroyed. With this new attitude, each person can refer to their *higher* self, to the part of them that makes them human and different from all other life forms, as one's "True Self."

If you had all the words of Socrates, unadulterated and unburdened by the prejudices, pride, and fear of the status quo that Plato and Xenophon had, you would find that Socrates taught that our True Selves (our true natures) exist in a dimension of time and space that has no beginning and no end. He taught that we exist with other human beings of the same eternal nature and standing.

Socrates taught that when we die, or once we experience a mortal death, we will immediately be aware that the same type of social interactions we enjoy here on Earth, exist there, only they will be coupled with an eternal glory. An "eternal glory" is the "glory of any god, which is intelligence, or in other words, light and truth"—i.e., the Real Truth™ that all gods know.[48]

Each human being, each one of you, is as intelligent as any other human being. You are gods, each and every one you, equally and separately. There is no god above or below any of you. Each of you made a choice about belonging to a GROUP of humans in which you could have new experiences and through which you could seek joy.

In this book, we (the Real Illuminati®) chose not to explain all there is to know and understand about our *True Selves*. This is the same information that Socrates, we, and all of our True Messengers have known in the past. But it would extend beyond the scope and purpose of this book.

Youth, this world, which includes your family and friends, has been deceived and is being controlled by powers that do not know what they are doing. Some of these powers have set themselves up and convinced your family and friends that God speaks to them.

So, if you embrace this new attitude and see yourself as an individual person equal with God, but your family and friends do not, you will be mocked, scourged, cast out, and disowned by them. Your belief that you are a god will threaten their belief that you are not, and that they are not. How can they accept this? If they do, then their religious leaders are ordinary, just like them. If their religious leaders are just like them, then God can just as easily speak to them as God does to their leaders.

Their pride will not allow them to accept that they have been deceived. Everything that they "know" gives them value and places them

---

[48] *Compare D&C*, 93:36.

above others. They cannot see that everything they have been taught about God is false and, even worse, that these things are actually a "great abomination and wickedness."

Recognizing that you are an equal god with everyone else, you will begin to see the power that you have to act and be acted upon. But they, believing that someone else has power over them, will not act or allow themselves to be acted upon, except when they are commanded by someone else.

The essence of your True God, your true power, comes from your ability to do what you feel is best for you—what makes you happy. There is no other way that a person's brain can properly function towards the end for which the brain exists—to serve the needs of the individual by providing joy. If your brain is being influenced or powered by an *outside* source, you will never reach your potential and personal power over your own life. Your brain must be dependent upon and receive power from itself (from one's "True God") in order for you to reach and maintain the energy level of equilibrium that creates a physical feeling a mortal recognizes as joy. (One day we know that science will also be able to explain this.)

When a person acts according to the power of the person's own brain, peace is felt. And when the person uses their brain to "walk peaceably with the children of men," it means that what the one is doing creates peace for the person themselves, and for the ones with whom the person desires to "walk."

There is no *true* joy when one tells another what to do, especially when one forces another to do something (to act or be acted upon) that one does not want to do.

It is this *joy* that all humans search for, in what they do, in how they act, and in how they allow themselves to be acted upon. In order to have a "peaceable walk" with others, one must be doing what one wants, and one must allow others to do what they want. This is good. But when a person forces another to act, this force takes away another's peace and is not good.

A New American Scripture

To understand the way to "peace and salvation," one need only to observe a little child. A little child is at peace when the child does what the child wants, being the child's own god. If allowed to be a little child, the *flesh* obeys the will of the *spirit* in all things. The little child knows no other god, no other power, than their own.

Human beings should be like little children—always. The difference between the state of peace in which a little child exists and the state in which mortals currently live upon Earth is in the inability of the person to exercise unconditional free will—the inability of the *flesh* to do the will of the *brain*. This creates a *state* of a "hell which hath no end."

Only in exercising unconditional free agency will an individual human find joy. When there is a group of individuals, and just one does not have joy, the others are affected and can lose their joy. Therefore, if it is the choice of individuals to form groups, then by this choice, it becomes the responsibility of each to ensure that whatever is affecting the joy of one is changed so that all can experience joy equally.

It is this peace that people feel when Christians think about Christ. Jesus Christ encompasses all that is good. But Christians do not follow Christ. They follow their pride. Their pride is established in what their religious leaders tell them to do. Their pride condemns those who do not do what *their* leaders say.

ALL of humanity's problems, EVERY ONE, can be traced to how false religions teach people that there exists a power higher than their own, and that this power gives God's will to leaders. When will the people stand up against these false gods and take back their power? When will humanity become like a little child again? In our new American scripture, becoming like a little child is a prerequisite (a necessity) to following the *true Christ* and having the *true Spirit of Christ* and the *true love of Christ* guide one's actions.

Chapter 20: The Great Apocalypse—A Message to the Youth of Planet Earth

What little child, having two cookies, who sees another child crying because that child has none, does not give one of their cookies to the child who doesn't have one? What child playing on the southern border of the United States behind a fence that separates them from other little children, would not cross over the border, without a second thought, to play with an isolated child?

How long will our True Selves put up with how their mortal avatars are treating other mortal avatars? How long will our True Selves allow the earth to continue to exist? Our True Selves know who the problem is. They know that it is a part of their mortal self that is full of pride and that sees its own life as more valuable and of greater worth than the mortal avatar of another equal god.

When you die, how will you see yourself? If you are conscious after this life, it will mean that you were conscious before this life. For now, you may wonder what you were like before your True Self connected to your mortal self.

Nothing keeps this world divided more than false religious teachings that have you thinking you are not the god that you are and that others can tell you who your true god is and what God expects of you.

We fully admit that nothing we have done on Earth has accomplished the goals of why we did it. Nothing we have accomplished through religion has affected the blindness and hardheartedness of the spiritually deceived. In humility, we bow before the only humans who can solve the problems that humanity is experiencing—the YOUTH.

We can do nothing more than pass our wisdom on to you. What more can we do without being accused of corrupting your minds and hearts and facing a sure death sentence from the secret combinations that control your minds? What more can we do to teach humankind that we are all equal gods? Regardless of gender, race, religion, or economic status, nothing can change the fact that we are all equal gods.

Humbled by war, famine, pestilence, poverty, suffering, and misery, may ALL of humanity learn that we are all equal and that none of us is above another. May we unite as ONE HEART AND ONE MIND with a new attitude towards ourselves and each other. We cannot unite and see each other as equals, until we finally realize that we ARE the gods upon whom we depend for salvation.

Youth, it is your work now. We will serve the only true gods that we know exist—YOU. We are your servants, whether you accept us or not. To aid you, we wrote this book, the second book of our Trilogy. In this book we revealed *how* and *why* we, the Real Illuminati®, created a new American scripture—the *Book of Mormon*, and its greater part, *The Sealed Portion*.

We hope that this book has helped you discover your *true god*. We hope that you are now convinced that together, united in equality, we can create peace and joy on Earth by solving humanity's problems, which are our own problems.

The next and final book of our Trilogy will provide you with further evidence of who we are, what we know, and why we exist. We have written much about a righteous government—the *right* form of government that can save humanity. It is a form of government that was instituted and followed in a few dispensations of human time *before* the one in which we now find ourselves. It worked then—until it didn't. And it will work now.

With the instructions and knowledge that we will provide you in the final book of our Trilogy, we can rest and place our eternal hope in your hands—in the power of the YOUTH OF THIS WORLD.

Only YOU can create ONE PEOPLE, ONE WORLD, ONE GOVERNMENT.

Appendix 1
The Sealed Portion—How Money and Secret Combinations Began

CHAPTER 16

Beneli is the first mortal child born to Adam and Eve. He discovers that he is not Adam's son. Beneli discovers his true father and begins to deceive the other children of Adam and Eve. Cain is born

AND it came to pass that the brother of Jared saw many things pertaining to the way in which Adam and Eve began to have dominion over the earth, and also over the beasts of the field, and this because of the intelligence of Adam and Eve, and the things that they had learned of the Father. For the beasts were created on a lower order than the children of men. And these beasts were driven by their instincts, not knowing right or wrong, and therefore, not being able to partake of the joys of which the children of men partake.

2 And when the time arrived for the birth of the child conceived in the garden of Eden, both Adam and Eve rejoiced in his birth. And they called his name Beneli, which being interpreted means, a son of God.

3 And it came to pass that Adam and Eve had many sons and daughters. And these grew and were taught to worship the Lord according to the manner in which Adam and Eve were instructed by the Lord in the garden of Eden, and also by way of the Holy Endowment that hath been explained unto you previously in this record.

4 And the Lord also suffered that Adam should organize a church for the benefit of his children, and also that the Holy Priesthood of God, with its lower and higher appendages, should be established among them for their instruction and their learning.

5 For behold, the children of Adam and Eve were not in the garden of Eden, and they did not know the Lord, nor had they ever seen him with their mortal eyes. And it was required of them to live by faith, even faith in the words that Adam taught unto them.

6 And the ministrations of the Holy Ghost began to fall upon the children of Adam, which ministrations bear record of the Father and of the Son and of the plan that they have established for the children of Adam.

7 And it came to pass that after many years Adam also began to doubt that which he had experienced before in the garden of Eden, even believing that it had been a dream. And thus was the power that Satan had over the hearts of all men, even unto the convincing of the very elect, if it were possible, that they should not believe that which they cannot see with their eyes or listen to that which they do not hear with their ears.

8 And the Father sent an angel from His kingdom unto Adam to help him remember the things that he had forgotten by faith. For behold, in the beginning, Adam did not have faith, for he knew that the Father existed, and that he was begotten of the Father, this having been taught to him by Jehovah immediately after being expelled from the garden of Eden, and also by his own personal experiences with the Father.

9 And it is the condition of mortality that causeth a pure and simple knowledge to become a matter of faith after a long time; and this because of the manner of thought which is permitted by a mortal body. For it was necessary that the Father limit the ability of the children of men to remember their lives before their births, thus ensuring that they do not reach forth and partake of the Tree of Life and live forever in their sins as I have previously explained it unto you.

10 And Adam kept all the commandments that he had received from Jehovah when he was expelled from the garden of Eden. And he taught these commandments to his children according to the manner that was shown unto him.

11 And it came to pass that Beneli grew and became a popular man among the other children of Adam. And he began to notice a difference in his appearance from those who were the other sons and daughters of Adam. For his skin was darker, and his features were different than the rest of his brothers and sisters. And his father Adam did not think anything of the differences that were obvious in the appearance of Beneli, even because he did not understand all of the mysteries of God pertaining to the creation of a mortal body at this time, and therefore accepted that Beneli was conceived of him.

12 And Beneli went unto his mother Eve and questioned her concerning these things. And Eve could not hide the truth from Beneli any longer, and explained unto him that which had occurred in the garden of Eden.

13 And Eve petitioned fervently unto her son and asked that he would promise her that he would not reveal these things unto Adam, who did not know that this thing had happened, and who loved Beneli with all of his heart. And Beneli loved his mother and hearkened unto her, and promised her at this time that he would not tell Adam that which she had revealed unto him.

14 But from that time forth, Beneli began to search out his natural father, even that he began to pray unto Satan and ask for his guidance and his blessing. And Satan came unto Beneli, calling him his son and giving unto him all that he desired.

15 And Beneli began to teach his other brothers and sisters the things which he had learned from Satan, which things were contrary to the commandments that Adam had taught unto them. And because the words of Beneli were enticing unto many of his brothers and sisters, they began to rebel against the words of their father Adam and follow the commandments of Satan that were taught unto them by their eldest brother, Beneli.

16 And in this way did Satan begin to have success in possessing the bodies that the Father had created for Adam and Eve. And from that time forward, men began to be carnal and sensual and devilish in their ways.

17 And the Lord raised up prophets among the children of Adam and gave unto them the Holy Ghost, and commanded them to preach repentance unto their brothers and sisters. And Adam did spend much of his time counseling and directing the church through the priesthood that had been established among them, that he might also bring many of his children unto repentance.

18 And it came to pass that the creatures that had been possessed by Satan and his followers found their way into the land in which lived the children of Adam and Eve. And the sons and daughters of Adam and Eve, who did not hearken to the words of their father, or to the words of their brothers who had been called by the Lord as prophets to preach repentance unto them; yea, even these began to breed with those creatures who were not created by the Father to house the spirits of His children.

19 And from these unions there came to be many different peoples upon the earth. And the bodies that were created by these unions begin to be the vessels in which the Father was required by the eternal laws of heaven to put the spirits of His children. And thus had Satan corrupted the natural bodies that God had created for Adam and Eve.

20 Nevertheless, all this was done according to that which the Father had already known and that which He had expected. For in this same manner did the other worlds in which life was created bring about the mortal bodies for the spirits of the children of God.

21 And all these things were necessary so that the children of God might partake of that which is imperfect, so that they might know that which is perfect. And the bodies that the Father created for Adam and Eve were perfect according to the laws of the nature in which they were formed. And their bodies were also like unto the bodies that He and their Eternal Mothers possess.

22 And how is it that we might know that these bodies are perfect, unless it so be that we experience the effects of a body that is imperfect, and therefore, have some type of comparison that we might know these things?

23 And Satan continued to do that which had been done before in the worlds that were created for the salvation and happiness of the children of God.

24 Therefore, in the beginning, the children of men were given a body like unto that of the Father, and they were also given commandments pertaining to this body that it might not be defiled. But in the space of not many generations, all of the children of men began to possess bodies that were imperfect and unlike the perfect bodies that had been created for Adam and Eve.

25 And it came to pass that the brother of Jared wrote concerning Adam and his efforts to teach his children the commandments of God. For behold, the major part of them had rebelled against these commandments.

26 And because of the agency given unto his children, Adam could not force them to do his will. And he saw the effects of his sons and daughters who were creating children with those that were not chosen vessels of the Father. And Adam saw the effects of his eldest son Beneli as he set himself up as a leader among them, and also as he began to persuade his brothers and sisters to disregard the commandments of God and seek after the things of the earth.

27 And it came to pass that Eve bore another son unto Adam and called his name Cain, believing that he was one that she could raise up righteously before the Lord, and that he would obey the commands of his father.

28 And it was also the desire of Adam that he might preserve in the next generation the similitude of the physical body that he had received from the Father, and therefore Adam was desirous that Cain follow in his footsteps and maintain this purity.

29 And Eve conceived again and bore unto Adam another son and called his name Abel.

30 And it came to pass that as Cain and Abel grew together in the house of their father, that Cain began to become jealous because of the love that he perceived his father Adam had for Abel. And truly Adam loved all of his children the same, but this was not the perception of Cain.

31 And Cain became familiar with the teachings of his eldest brother, Beneli, and went unto him and inquired of the things that he had taught his other brothers and sisters. And Beneli was glad that his younger brother had come unto him, and he blessed him and treated him like his own son.

32 And Cain began to follow the words of Beneli and reject the things that his father had taught unto him.

33 But Abel grew and became righteous and did those things which were expected of him by his father, and also the things that were commanded him of the Lord. And Abel became a High Priest in the church that Adam had established among them. And Able began to preach repentance to his brothers and his sisters.

34 And it came to pass that Abel went unto the house of his eldest brother, Beneli, to inquire of him as to why he had corrupted the teachings of their father, and why he did not worship God as he had been commanded.

35 And Abel said unto him: How is it that thou, being our eldest brother, persuadeth us to disobey father? Knowest thou not that our father hath taught the truth unto us concerning the beginning of our existence in this world, and that he and our mother Eve were commanded by the Lord to teach us the laws that are necessary for our happiness?

36 And Beneli answered him, saying: I have said nothing about our father. For he is a man of many dreams and visions and his imagination doth cause him to believe things that do not exist. And this happiness of which thou hast spoken?—Are we not a happy people? Do we not enjoy our wives and our children and live in peace and happiness? And behold the work of our hands and the accomplishments that we have done with the things of the earth, do they not bring us the joy of which thou speaketh?

37 Did not our father give unto us a commandment that we should multiply and replenish the earth and have dominion over the beasts of the field and the fowls of the air and the fish that are in the water? And do we not have dominion over these things and find joy therein?

38 I say unto thee, that we do find joy in these things, and that we shall continue to find joy in these things all the days of our lives.

39 And Abel rebuked his brother, saying: The joy of which thou speakest is not the everlasting joy of which our father hath taught us existeth in the kingdom of God, and which shall be given unto all those who believe in Him and keep His commandments.

40 The joy of which thou speakest shall only last among thee and those who follow thee for a short time. And the causes of this joy shall require that ye continually pursue that which hath given you this joy for a short season only. But ye do not consider that which shall come to pass by the pursuit of this joy. Yea, neither do ye consider those things that shall also be the cause of much sorrow among you because of this joy that ye seek.

41 For behold, ye do eat the flesh of beasts and of fowl, and of the fishes in the water, which example hath not been given unto you by our father, but hath been given unto you by those beings whom ye have taken as your wives, and unto whom ye give your daughters that they might bring forth children unto you. And these are not those of the children of our father who have the pure blood within them, but ye have corrupted this blood because of your unions with them.

42 And because ye do eat the flesh of the beasts and also the flesh of the fowls and the flesh of the fish in the waters, ye have also corrupted and defiled your own bodies, which bodies were not intended to partake of such things. And even if ye were hungry, and forced by famine to eat the flesh of a creature, ye would not receive the nourishment that your bodies require to live in this joy of which thou speakest. For ye have caused the destructive force of fire to destroy the nutrients that the Father hath placed in the flesh of these animals and also in the plants that these animals eat to gain their nourishment.

43 And because ye have become used to the taste of seared fat and boiled plants and fruits, yea, because ye receive this joy from eating that which hath none of the natural nutrients that the Father hath provided therein to give our bodies health and strength, ye have caused that disease and pestilence should come upon you. And can ye call this an everlasting joy?

44 And thou hast taught thy followers that it is not a sin to take from the earth more than what is necessary to sustain their lives, because thou hast taught them that there is no life after this life in which we find ourselves, and that they should eat and drink and be merry and take unto themselves of all the fine things of the earth that they might have an abundance for themselves.

45 And with these teachings thou hast caused them to become selfish and carnal and share none of the joy of which thou hast spoken with their neighbors, or with their friends, but that they should hoard all that they can for the benefit of their own wives and their own children.

46 And in separating yourselves into these family units in which ye have found this joy of which thou hast spoken, ye have destroyed the sense of fellowship and unity that our father taught us should exist among us. For do we not all share the same father and the same mother? Therefore, to whose family do we pertain, seeing that we are all brothers and sisters?

47 And the ramifications of this joy that you describe are that there shall be contentions among you, in that ye will be more concerned about the welfare of your own family and the things that ye have hoarded from the earth for its welfare, than you will be about sharing that which ye have with those who do not have that which ye have hoarded, because ye have taken it all unto yourselves.

48 And your joy will cause the misery of others. And these—because they, too, want the same joy of which thou hast spoken—will take by force, if necessary, those things that ye have hoarded for the benefit of your own family. And thus will contentions and disputations arise among you. And these things would not arise among you. if ye would do the things that our father hath commanded us.

49 And our father hath given unto us the commandments that he received from the mouth of God when he was banished from the garden of Eden. And ye know that this garden did exist because ye have seen its borders and have experienced the exceedingly verdant nature that existeth therein, which nature is not like any that we can find in other parts of the land in which we live.

50 And even though it is also subjected to the laws of nature, which laws will cause all things therein to decay and to die a natural death, even so, its beauty and exceedingly great natural order doth even now continue to exist. And if this garden of which our father hath spoken doth exist, then why thinkest thou that the God who created this garden doth not exist? And if God doth not exist, then where did our first parents come from? For behold, they are unlike all the other animals that exist upon this land.

51 And even this land, from where thinkest thou that it came? And seest thou not the great order of nature that is all around us? How can this order exist except there be laws given that establish this order and cause it to remain in the state in which it hath been established?

52 And if these laws were given unto nature to keep it in its proper order by Him who created it, then why thinkest thou that this same Being would not give unto us laws that would help us maintain order among ourselves?

53 For we are not of the same order as the order of the nature that is around us. And by these natural laws we do not need to abide. For in this nature it is requisite that only that which is needed to sustain life is taken from it, and under this law are all the creatures that dwell on this world with us subjected.

54 But we are not subjected by this law. And ye have proven this by your actions, even that which ye take from nature; of which ye have no need except to consume it upon the lusts that ye have for this temporary joy that ye pursue.

55 And it is also a law of this nature that those who are subjected to it shall live in a symbiotic state with it, in that they give to its order as it giveth unto them. But what is it that thou supposeth that ye give unto nature from which ye receive many things? Behold, ye give nothing unto nature, but it provideth for you all the things that ye desire.

56 And because thou and thy followers are not subjected by all the laws of nature, by what laws are ye subjected? I say unto thee, that thou and those who follow thee are subjected under your own laws, which are laws of selfishness and carnality, and which shall bring about more sorrow and misery for you than the short time that ye shall experience the joy which ye seek.

57 But there is one law of nature to which ye are all subjected, which law was brought to pass because of the choice of our first parents to provide bodies for us and allow us to enter into mortality with them. And this law is the natural law of death, to which all things in nature are subjected.

58 And thou knowest this law, and hath convinced these people that there is no escaping this law under which we are subjected, thus giving them reason to live their lives as if the only joy that they can experience is that joy that they receive here in mortality.

59 But I have already shown unto thee that we are not subjected to the laws of nature as are the rest of the creations that are found therein. But we are subjected to the laws of the God by whom we were all created.

60 And if it so be that we are subjected to His laws, then there must be a law that He is subjected to that supercedeth the law of nature that we have been subjected to because of the desires of our parents.

61 And because we are not a part of this nature, we are not subjected to its laws, but because we live in this order of nature at this time, and take from it that which bringeth us joy, we are forced into submission to its laws. And for this reason we shall die, thus submitting to the laws of nature.

62 But when we are no longer a part of this nature, then we are no longer subjected to its laws. And after our spirits depart from this mortal body, which was created from this nature, we are no longer a part of it, and are therefore subjected to other laws which govern the environment in which we will find ourselves.

63 And in this spiritual state, or this spirit environment, we shall be subjected to the laws of Him who created our spirits, or to Him from whom we shall receive our joy. And if it so be that we do not abide by His laws, then we cannot receive any joy from Him. And if we do not receive any joy from Him, then we shall be miserable forever in the state in which we shall find ourselves.

64 And there is a law of God that compensateth for the law of nature, or the law of death. And even as it was death that came upon us and cut short the joy that we find in this natural environment, even so shall this law of God be given that we shall once again find life. And this life shall be eternal, for such are all the laws of God.

65 And the law of sacrifice which our father hath given unto us is in similitude of this law that shall give us eternal life and eternal joy.

66 And this law shall be given unto us by the Son of God, who shall come down among us and teach us all the laws of God that shall bring us eternal life, in which we shall experience eternal joy and happiness.

67 And he shall sacrifice his own life for us by presenting himself as a sacrifice for all of us, in that he will teach us the laws of God that we must be subjected to in order to be saved in the kingdom of God, where the laws of happiness and joy are eternal, as well as the laws of life, which are also eternal.

68 And now, I would that thou shouldst know that these are the things which our father hath taught us. And these are the things that we must live by in order to find the happiness and joy that we seek, both in this state of nature, and also in the spiritual state of our God who hath created us.

69 And it came to pass that Abel did confound Beneli in all of his words. And because of the words of Abel, many people left from following Beneli and followed once again after the things that they had been taught by their father.

70 But there were also many others who did not listen to the words of Abel. And many of these were those who had been born into the imperfect bodies as I have explained it unto you. Nevertheless, there were some of those who were born of the imperfect body who did follow the counsel of Abel and sought out Adam to hear his words. And there were also those who had the similitude of the perfect body, in that they were direct descendants of the sons of Adam and the daughters of Eve, and some of these did remain under the power of Beneli.

71 And from that time forth Beneli was wroth with Abel and devised a way in which he could destroy him.

72 And Beneli called Cain unto him and spoke with him, saying: Thou knowest that I love thee as my own son and that I would give my life for thee if it so be that I could save thee. And thou also knowest that I have provided a means whereby these people, even our brothers and our sisters, might find great joy. And this joy is that for which I would give my life.

73 Behold, our brother Abel hath come among us and hath taken away the joy of many of our brothers and sisters and hath caused them to feel guilty for feeling the joy that they have experienced. And he hath caused considerable damage to our families, claiming that our family units are not important, and that they are not part of the laws of this God whom none of us hath seen.

74 And in this way he hath deceived us by taking away our means of this joy that we have experienced. And he doeth this that he might take that which we possess unto himself. For did he not say unto us, that we should impart of our substance unto those who do not have that which we possess? And he doth not have that which we have. And by his cunningness, he desireth to take from us so that he can have part of all that we have.

75 And thou seest that this, our brother, hath lied unto us, for he hath said unto us that we should not take from nature except that we should give back in the same portion of which we have taken. Yet, he offereth up for sacrifice the firstlings of his flocks unto this unknown God, and pretendeth that it hath been commanded of him by God. And he shedeth their blood, but doth not partake of their flesh. And in this way he taketh away from nature without giving back any portion of that which he hath taken.

76 And even thou strugglest all of thy days to grow food from the earth. And thy sweat is the testimony of the hard work that is the lot that hath been given unto thee by our father Adam. And doth not our brother Abel eat of the fruit of thy hands? Doth he not take from thee even that which he doth not return?

77 And is it fair of our father that he requireth of thee to toil in this manner to provide food for thy brother, whose only toil is watching after his flocks and tending to their needs, which needs do not come by his hand, but by the hand of nature that hath given these flocks unto him?

78 And who is he that he thinketh that he shall rule over me, who is his eldest brother, and also over thee who is his elder brother?

79 And it came to pass that by the words of Beneli, the heart of Cain was hardened against his brother Abel.

80 And Beneli entered into a secret pact and covenant with Cain, that if he would kill Abel, he would be protected and watched over by Beneli and those who follow him. And Beneli convinced Cain that the things that he was to do would bring a greater peace and happiness among the people, and that he would be held in respect among them for that which he would do.

81 And they made this pact according to all that Beneli had learned from his father, who was Satan in the beginning. And this pact was held secret among them. And thus began the children of men to form alliances and make covenants one with another in secret that they might get gain and destroy those who prevented them from getting that which they desired.

82 And Cain did that which Beneli desired of him. And he went unto Abel while he was tending to his flocks, and slew him. And this was the first time that a child of Adam was slain by the hand of another. And thus began murder to enter into the hearts of the children of men.

83 And Beneli and those who followed after him came to Cain and gave unto him the title of Master Mahan, which title was given to him of the highest order of this secret society, which society was set up to get gain and maintain power among the people. And Beneli also gave one of his daughters unto Cain as his wife for that which he had done.

84 And those who belonged to this society did not think of themselves as evil men, but they thought of themselves as the most righteous among the people. And they took upon themselves oaths and covenants that would protect them, and also protect their desire for gain and power among the people.

85 And their desire for power, as they had convinced themselves, was to assure the prosperity and freedom of all those who belonged to this secret order. And they took the endowment that they had learned from Adam and changed the signs and the symbols and the penalties to fit the desires of their secret society.

86 And they began to convince themselves that their ways and their teachings were the right ways, and that if there was a God, then that God would want the same things that they desire, which things are joy in their families, and joy in their worldly possessions, and joy in their freedom.

87 And this society began to enforce the desires of their hearts upon the people throughout the land. And if any man or woman refused to live by the laws that they had established according to these desires, then they would call upon those who had taken the secret oaths and covenants to protect their society to kill this man or this woman.

88 And they began to set up a system of law that served this society and its desires, even the desire to get gain and hold on to this gain for the benefit of their families. And in this way did the laws of men begin to supercede [*sic*] the laws of God. And in this way did Lucifer do that which he had promised upon being cast out of the presence of the Father, even that he would take the treasures of the earth, and with gold and silver, he would buy up the means of force, and that he would buy up the means of justice and laws that the children of men would be subjected to through the governments and religions of men, and reign with blood and horror upon the earth.

89 And this society began to use gold and silver and the precious elements of the earth to measure and control the gain that they desired. For behold, among the children of Adam there did not exist a means whereby the value of the things of the earth was measured. For all things were free unto all. And everyone did that which they could, according to their individual abilities, and all received according to their individual needs. And this was done by the sweat of their brow, which was commanded of them by the Father in the beginning.

90 Nevertheless, it had come to pass earlier among the children of Adam, that there lived some who did not want to work by the sweat of their own brow, but who had put themselves up above their brothers and their sisters. And these thought that because of their words, or because of their intelligence, they should not have to work by their own sweat.

91 And it was the eldest son of Adam, even Beneli, who had learned from Satan a way in which he could get gain by not working with his hands. And he had been convinced by Satan that because he was the eldest, and one of the most intelligent among them, that he should not be required to toil like unto the others.

92 And it came to pass that Beneli spent many days wandering throughout the land observing the toil and labor of the rest of his brothers and sisters, and even of his father Adam and his mother Eve, whom he loved.

93 And he was shown by Satan the gold that glittered in its natural state, and that it was beautiful to the eyes and smooth to the touch, even that it was everlasting and that which could not tarnish and age with time. And he also knew that this gold, and also silver which had the same attributes of gold, was sparse and was not found in abundance throughout the land.

94 And Beneli gathered up a large quantity of this gold and this silver and began to shape jewelry in a fashion that was most beautiful to be seen, and most comfortable against the skin of those who would wear it. And he went unto his wife and adorned her with the jewelry which he had made and convinced her to show it unto her friends and her neighbors and let them touch it and see its beauty.

95 And the other women began to covet the things of the wife of Beneli; and they desired of their husbands that they might have jewelry like unto hers. But these men did not know where to get this gold and this silver of which to make these things. And when they searched throughout the land, they could not find any, because of that which Beneli had taken unto himself.

96 And when their wives knew that their husbands could not find that which they desired, they pleaded with them to go unto Beneli and request of him some of his gold and his silver that they might have these things.

97 And the men went unto Beneli and asked of him that he might give unto them some of his gold and his silver, even that which he had gathered up in abundance unto himself.

98 And Beneli answered them, saying: My dear brethren, it is my utmost desire that I should share that which I have with each of you, so that ye might give unto your wives that which I have given unto my wife, even that which hath given her great joy and pleasure. Yet, I would ask of you if it is fair that I give unto you that which I have toiled to obtain, even for many days have I toiled and labored with my own hands that I might acquire these things. And with my own hands have I fashioned these things into that which bringeth joy to my wife, and which your wives also desire.

99 And ye spend your days in toil by the sweat of your brows for the benefit of all, even the food that we eat and the homes that we live in and the clothes that we wear. And how is it then, that your toil is more important than mine? For behold, ye toil to assure that we live. Yet, what type of life do we live, if we do not have the joy and the pleasure that this life can bring? And ye have beheld that I have provided my wife with that which bringeth her this pleasure and this joy, even beyond that which ye have provided unto your own wives.

100 But I want that ye have the ability to give unto your wives this pleasure and this joy. Therefore, I would that ye should trade with me your labor and that which your labor produceth for that which my labor hath produced, even that which will bring joy unto your wives.

101 And it came to pass that with his words, Beneli convinced the men to give unto him of their labors and of their food and of their clothes. And he caused them that they should build houses for him and fences in which he could mark the land that was his, even that for which he had traded in his dealings with these men.

102 And it came to pass that the gold and the silver of the land became more valuable to the people than their food, and their homes, and their raiment. And Beneli controlled the trading of the gold and the silver, evensomuch that he became very rich among the people and possessed much more than his other brothers and sisters.

103 And many others coveted the things that Beneli had; and they wanted to become rich like unto him. And in this way the children of men began to divide themselves into classes, even into the poor and the rich, or those who had much and those who had little. And those who had little coveted that which the rich possessed. But because gold and silver were so rare and precious among them, these poor could not become like unto the rich. And there were those among the poor who began to steal from the rich. And these justified their actions because they felt that they should have that which the rich kept from them, even their gold and their silver, which they could not find in the land.

104 And thus the children of men began to come under the control of Satan. And he did rage in their hearts and became their God.

105 And Adam labored all of his days to convince them of their errors and to turn them once again to the commandments that he had taught them, which were given unto him by the Lord.

106 And it came to pass that after the death of Abel, Adam called all those who listened to his words and kept the commandments of the Lord. And there were many strong and agile men among them, nevertheless, they had never fought with their brethren, being taught that even anger towards another was not justifiable in the eyes of God.

107 But Adam explained unto them concerning the wickedness and corruption of those among them who did not keep the commandments of God; and that these had caused many sorrows to enter in among them, and that if they allowed this wickedness to continue, that it would surely lead to their destruction.

108 And the children of Adam who followed him were not as many as those that followed after the order of Beneli and Cain. Nevertheless, these had the spirit of God among them. And they had not defiled their bodies with the flesh of animals or with food that had been cooked. And these were strong men and had much more stamina and vigor than those who followed Satan.

109 And Adam spoke unto these strong ones who worshipped the Lord and kept his commandments, and said unto them: I would that ye should know that my heart is burdened by the actions of your brothers and sisters who have disregarded the commandments of God and have established their own laws among them.

110 And I have spent many years preaching unto them and counseling with them with a hope that they would see the error of their ways and return again unto God. But my works among them have been in vain. And they have slain my son Abel, who was your beloved brother, and also a prophet of God. And because they have chosen to rid themselves of all those who do not bow down to their form of government and take the oaths and covenants of that secret society among them, I am afraid that they might come among those of us who keep the commandments of God and live according to His word, and destroy us.

111 Therefore, it is my desire that I should speak unto them one last time and ask them in all humility, even with the love that I have for them as their father, that they change their ways and bring peace once again throughout the land.

112 And if it so be that they refuse to listen to my words and give heed unto my counsel, then I am constrained by the spirit of God, yea, even by the spirit of peace and harmony; which is the spirit of God, that I banish them from this land and command them to leave and go back the way in which those came who do not have the pure blood of the bodies that the Father created for the spirits of His children; even those who are now our brothers and our sisters, but who do not have the pure blood.

113 And I would that ye should know, that it mattereth not whether their bodies are of the pure blood or not. For it is the spirit that commandeth the body. And if their spirit is good, then it shall command the body in righteous works. And there are many among us who keep the commandments of God who do not have the pure blood, and many of these are more righteous than those who have the pure blood. Therefore, it mattereth not unto me, nor unto God, which body they possess, for by their works shall they be known.

114 And if the works of your brothers and sisters were righteous, then there would be no need for that which I must command of them, if it so be that they repent and turn to God.

115 And now, I, Moroni, find it necessary that I write that the sons and daughters of Adam had much respect and honor for Adam and for Eve. Yea, even those who did not follow the commandments of God, still did honor their father and their mother.

116 And Adam and Eve were loved and respected above all others upon the land. And I have shown unto you before that Beneli had a great love for his mother Eve. And he did also love his father Adam, but did not that which he was commanded by his father, and this because he was persuaded by Satan, who had possessed the body of him who was his natural father. And the children of Beneli did also honor Adam and Eve, even for many years after the death of Beneli, who was their father and their leader, who had died many years before this time, because of the imperfections and defilement of his body.

117 And it was the desire of Adam to gather all of his children upon the face of the whole land, even all those who were his sons and daughters, and also their sons and daughters. And there were numerous people upon the face of the earth in and around the place where the Lord had planted the garden of Eden, it being the center and also the borders of their land.

118 Now in this day, Adam was five hundred and two years old when he made a proclamation throughout the land that all the people therein should gather themselves together to hear his words. And it had been over five hundred years that the sons and daughters of Adam had gone two by two upon the face of the land and raised up children. Therefore, the lands round and about the borders of the garden of Eden were full of many people.

119 And in the church of God that had been established by Adam there were many wise and righteous leaders, they being direct descendants of Adam and having the Holy Priesthood passed down through the patriarchal order of the sons of Adam.

120 For after the death of Abel, which death had occurred many years before the time of the gathering of the people to listen to the words of Adam, Eve conceived and bore Seth unto Adam.

121 And now I, Moroni, have once again been constrained by the Spirit to give unto you, yea, even those who shall receive this record, a proper accounting of the years and time of Adam. Behold, when Adam was cast out of the garden of Eden he was a grown man who had reached the age of mortality of thirty and three years; and his wife, Eve, was younger in mortal years, she being the age of mortality of eighteen years when she was deceived by Satan and cast out of the garden with her husband. Now this was according to the years of man, for unto God the time of man doth not exist.

122 Now the bodies that were given to Adam and Eve in the beginning were formed like unto those of a man of thirty and three years old, and of a woman of eighteen years old. And these are the ages in mortality when the children of men are fully mature and have reached the pinnacle of strength and vitality. For according to the laws of nature, yea, even according to the laws that we are subjected to during the days of our probation, our bodies reach this pinnacle after thirty and three years for a man and after eighteen years for a woman.

123 And because Adam and Eve were given perfect mortal bodies that were not defiled by the forbidden things from which God had commanded them to abstain, they lived for many years. And at the age of the pinnacle of health and strength to which they grew, their bodies remained in this state for many years. For this reason, those who carried within them undefiled blood lived for hundreds of years, whereas those who had defiled their blood with the things that had been forbidden, began to die after the pinnacle of their mortality was reached. And in a matter of a few years, they who had defiled their bodies began to grow old and lose the strength and vitality that they had experienced at this pinnacle.

124 And those who had eaten the flesh of other animals and cooked their food, thus destroying the vital nutrients that nature hath provided for their health and strength; and also those who had mixed their blood with the blood of other animals that were not given the same bodies that were given to Adam and Eve; yea, even those whose bodies had been possessed by Lucifer and his followers for many years; yea, even these did not reach the age of longevity with which the pure sons and daughters of Adam and Eve were blessed.

125 And this was also the wise purpose of the Lord. For the Lord knew that the sons and daughters of Adam and Eve would begin to follow the enticings of Satan and turn against the commandments that he had given unto them. And since there are always upon the earth those who disobey the laws of God and follow the enticings of Satan; yea their numbers being exceedingly greater than those who keep His commandments; therefore, in the beginning God assured a balance of righteousness so that the righteous would not be overwhelmed by the wicked.

126 And the [years] of Adam were eighty and two when he begot Cain. And two years after the birth of Cain did Eve conceive and give birth to Abel. And Abel was thirty and three years old when he began his ministry in the church of God. And he taught in the church for five years and preached many things unto his brothers and sisters. And his father placed him over the flocks of the field, even those flocks that were raised for the sacrifices that they performed according to the commandments of God. And when he was thirty and eight years old, his brother Cain slew him.

127 And now I, Moroni, would that ye should know somewhat more concerning the jealousy that Cain had towards his younger brother Abel. For behold, Adam had given each of his sons the work that each of them should do according to each of their abilities and their strengths. And Cain was much stronger than Abel, he having received of his father a body that was exceedingly stronger than the bodies of most other men.

128 And Adam saw the strength of Cain and blessed him and put him over the work that was done in the fields, even the tilling and the planting and the harvesting of the fruits and the plants that the people harvested for food.

129 And even at a young age, Cain became an expert at his trade and demonstrated great skill in his ability to produce food for the people, evensomuch that he produced an abundance of food, and was known throughout the land for his husbandry.

130 But his brother Abel was short of stature and weak in the strength of his hands, evensomuch that he did not contribute to the physical tasks that were required of the men to produce and harvest the food that the house of Adam needed for sustenance. Therefore, Adam assigned Abel to tend the flocks.

131 And he became exceedingly proficient in organizing and caring for the flocks and preparing them for that which they were being raised. And they were being raised exclusively for a sacrifice unto God, as they had been commanded by Him, this being in similitude of the law of sacrifice that was given to Adam and Eve in the Holy Endowment.

132 And it came to pass that Cain did not understand why the works of his hands were not acceptable unto God as a sacrifice like unto those of his brother Abel. And Cain brought forth and placed the works of his hands on the altar that Adam had commanded to be constructed to perform the law of sacrifice. And when he had done this thing, Adam rebuked his son and commanded him to bring no such offering unto the Lord, except it be that the Lord shall command it.

133 And Adam loved his son and made an attempt to explain to him that the law of sacrifice was symbolic of a law that would be fulfilled without the works of man. And as his offering was the work of the hands of men, and the offering of a beast, that God had created, had nothing consistent with the works of man, then his offering was not consistent with the intent of the symbolism of the law of sacrifice.

134 And Cain became angry with his father and jealous of his brother, and went unto the eldest son of Adam, even Beneli, that he might seek his advice, which advice he took unto himself and did those things that Beneli required of him.

135 And it came to pass that eight years had passed after the murder of Abel. And during these eight years Adam did mourn because of the loss of his son, and he did also morn because of such a terrible thing that had come to pass among his children. For there had never been a murder committed during the days of Adam until that time.

136 And after eight years of mourning the loss of her son Abel, Eve conceived again and gave unto Adam another son. And he called his name, Seth. And the Lord had great compassion upon Adam, and made Seth in an exact likeness of his father, evensomuch that Eve rejoiced therein and knew that the Lord had done this to ease the pain of Adam.

Appendix 2
The Sealed Portion—Adam Teaches the Fullness of the Everlasting Gospel

CHAPTER 18

Adam continues his sermon and counsel to his posterity at Adamondiahman concerning our probationary state. He introduces the law of the gospel. Moroni expounds upon this law and writes of the great apostasy from this law in the latter days, and also of the hypocrisy of the Church of Jesus Christ of Latter-day Saints.

AND now, I, Moroni, continue with the words of Adam that he spoke unto those who were gathered in the valley of Adamondiahman:

2 And when the Mothers of our spirits have raised their children to maturity in the world of our Eternal Parents, then each is ready to determine for itself what kind of happiness that each desireth. For they have experienced the happiness that existeth among those who live in the world in which they were created, in other words, they have experienced the type of life, and the types of things that are done in this world that bring happiness to those therein.

3 And we were taught that these exalted Beings experience a fullness of joy, and because of their joy, they dwell in a state of happiness forever.

4 In order to teach us so that we could understand, our Mothers showed us the fruits of the joy that they experienced. For an example unto us, They would pluck a piece of fruit from off of a tree and show that fruit unto us. And They would describe its shape and its size and the texture of its skin unto us, and allow us to hold the fruit in our hands and feel that of which They describe. But to us, as spirits who did not know the difference between good and bad, or between soft and hard, nor did we know the difference between hunger and the feeling of being satisfied, we did not understand completely the feeling of joy that our Mothers tried to explain unto us.

5 And They would eat the fruit and make the sounds of enjoyment as They tasted the sweetness thereof. And a smile would form upon Their face, and a happy sensation would exude from within Their perfected body. And we could sense the joy that was felt by our Mothers, but we did not understand it.

6 And when They smiled, we could sense the joy of Their smile, but we did not understand what it was that made Them smile in this manner. And when They sang to us, we could hear the words of Their voice and the tenderness of the melody that resonated throughout our spirits, but we could not understand why it should cause us to be joyful. Nevertheless, our Mothers received much joy from singing to us and teaching us to sing. And though there were those among us who could sing the songs and melodies that our Mothers taught unto us, none of us could understand the reason that these brought so much joy to Their hearts.

7 And They would hold us gently next to Them and cry upon us, which crying was caused from the exceeding joy that They felt because of us. Yet, we could not understand the cause of Their tears. And when Their tears would fall upon us, we did not have the capability of determining the wetness thereof.

8 And though we could sense a change in the sensations of our own spiritual body when these tears would touch us, we could not determine for ourselves the meaning of such sensations.

9 And we did not understand the peace and harmony that existed among those who dwelt on this world with our Father and our Mothers. For there were other Fathers and other Mothers that did not pertain unto us and were not part of our eternal family. And there were other spirits there also which were not created from the directions that our Father provided, but were given bodies of their own Eternal Mothers and Fathers. And this world was great and glorious; and it was filled with eternal families of eternal parents creating spirit children.

Appendix 2: *The Sealed Portion*—Adam Teaches the Fullness of the Everlasting Gospel
TSP, Chapter 18

10 And when the work of the Eternal Fathers was complete in one part of the vast expanse of the heavens; yea, even when They had placed Their spirit children on the planets in that part that They had prepared for them, these Fathers would then go to another part and create other worlds for the spirit children that were being born unto the Eternal Mothers that resided in this world.

11 But this peace and harmony and cooperation we did not understand, for we had not experienced anything but that which had always existed there. And we took for granted the greatness and glory of this world in which we were created; and we assumed that all worlds were like unto this one, having not experienced anything different.

12 And now, my beloved children, if it were that we could eat a piece of fruit that is good to the taste and which maketh us happy, why is it that we would not want to continue to partake of this fruit and the joy that it provideth forever? And this is the thing that our Mothers explained unto us.

13 And we could see that the make-up of Their bodies was different than our own. And we could see that unless we had a body like unto Theirs, we could never partake of the fullness of joy of which They partake forever.

14 And it became apparent unto us that not all of us were the same, even that our spirits were very individual with different desires and traits that made us unique in and of ourselves. And we knew that there was also much joy in these differences, yet we did not understand these differences.

15 But as we grew in spirit matter, our Eternal Mothers began to discern our spirits and teach unto us the types of joy that would suit each of us, and bring us the state of happiness that would best fit the make-up of our spirit, and that which would best compliment [*sic*] our personalities and the traits that made us unique in and of ourselves.

16 And they introduced to us the varying states of happiness that exist in the kingdom of God. And from the choices that were presented unto us, we determined for ourselves which state of happiness was that which we desired. And when we arrived at the state of maturity when this self-realization had taken place, then we waited upon the Father to create for us the kingdoms in which we would dwell and experience the state of happiness that we had chosen for ourselves.

17 And now, I, Moroni, shall not repeat all the words of Adam concerning the plan of salvation that was presented unto the children of God when they resided with him as spirits. For this thing hath already been given in this record according to the vision that the brother of Jared received regarding it. And the words of Adam are also from the record of the brother of Jared, in which he saw in vision Adam and his posterity and wrote the things which he saw.

18 But I will continue with the words of Adam as he taught his posterity the law of the gospel as it had been given unto him by the Lord after he was banished from the garden of Eden. And this law was given unto him as a prototype of the laws that govern all the glories of the kingdom of God. And it is this law that teacheth a man and a woman the manner in which they must live to maintain peace and harmony one with another.

19 And it is this law that a spirit must be willing and able to abide by in order for it to be allowed to live forever in one of the glories in the kingdom of God. And if a spirit cannot abide by the law of the gospel, it shall not be allowed to enter the kingdom of God.

20 For if a spirit is one that would create problems with others in the world in which it is placed forever, then there would be problems among those who reside in this world forever. But there are no problems in the kingdom of God, and those who reside therein do not have the capacity to cause these problems, having overcome this propensity during the days of their probation.

21 Therefore, the law of the gospel is the most important law that the children of men can learn during the days of their probation. And it was this law that Jesus taught unto his disciples and unto the people. And it was this law that his disciples were commanded to teach unto the people after he was gone. And it is by the law of the gospel that Jesus taught that all the children of God are saved.

22 And again I say unto you, for this reason Jesus, the Christ, is our Savior, in that he is the giver of this law. And there is nothing that Jesus can do for us that will save us in the kingdom of God, except teach unto us this law, which are the commandments of God. And again I say unto you, that there was nothing that Jesus did for us when he was upon this earth that shall save us, except give us the law of the gospel.

23 And there will be many in the latter days that shall believe that by the blood of Christ we are saved; and that the blood of Christ hath atoned for our sins, and that we must only believe in Christ and we will be saved in the kingdom of God. And in these beliefs many people do err and are being led away from the law of the gospel and are taught the precepts of men.

24 And I say unto those of you who believe these things; yea, even as I have said unto you before, even in this record have I said these things unto you: Ye do not understand the scriptures and have not inquired of the Holy Ghost for an understanding of the atonement and what the Lord intended by this. For the intent of the Lord was to make us one with God, even he commanded us that we should be perfect as our Father in Heaven is perfect.

25 And do ye think that ye can become like unto our Father if ye do not understand the things that the Father doeth? And the Father obeyeth the law of the gospel in all things, and He hath commanded His Son, even Jesus the Christ, to teach us this law that we might learn to live by it. And if we live by the same law by which our Father liveth, then we become one with Him, and then the atonement is fulfilled.

26 And I wish that I could write pleasant words unto you like unto the words of Adam which he gave unto his children in the land of Adamondiahman; for these words feel good to your souls and cause you to feel a spirit of joy and optimism, even that they cause you to weep with exceeding joy because of the things that he hath said unto his children.

27 But I am constrained by the Spirit and commanded by the Lord, that I speak unto you the truth in plainness so that ye might understand and have no more excuse for your unrighteousness and your evil ways, which ways are contrary to the law of the gospel, which I shall allow the words of Adam to teach you in this record. And in the part of this record that was unsealed and came unto you with the record of my father, Mormon, I was commanded by the Lord not to reveal these things unto you in their plainness, but that I should give unto you the similitude and symbolism of these things.

28 And it is my duty towards you as my brothers and my sisters that I teach you these things, even that I might bring you unto repentance and prepare you for that great and dreadful day of the Lord, when he shall return once again to this earth with all those who have been resurrected after him, even the righteous who are ready and willing to obey the law of this gospel of which I have spoken.

29 And why do ye suppose that it is called the great and dreadful day of the Lord? Should it not be a day of comfort and of joy? Should it not be a day of rejoicing in which ye shall feel those special feelings of the mercy of his atoning blood that ye have deceived yourselves into feeling all the days of your probation?

30 Yet, nowhere is it written in the holy scriptures that the day of the Lord shall be filled with the feelings of joy that ye express when ye think about him upon the cross; yea, when ye think of his hands pierced and bleeding to pay the debt of your sins. For behold, he did not pay any debt for your sins. For ye shall pay your own debts. And these debts shall be required of you because ye have failed to keep his commandments and abide by the law of his gospel that he hath given unto you.

31 Thus is the day of the Lord great and dreadful, even full of the wine of the wrath of God, which is poured out without mixture into the cup of his indignation. And ye shall be tormented with fire and brimstone in the presence of the holy angels, and in the presence of the Lamb. And your smoke of your torment shall ascend up forever and ever, and ye shall have no rest day or night. And all these things shall come to pass according to the prophecies of all the holy prophets who have ever been.

32 And what then shall ye think who believe that the Lord hath died for your sins and taken upon himself your debts? What then shall ye think who have felt the false sensations of security and peace that the devil hath caused to come over you when ye look upon the cross of Christ as the way by which ye shall be forgiven for the evil that ye do?

33 Will ye feel this sense of peace and security in his presence, yea even in the presence of the Lamb as it hath been prophesied? I say unto you that ye shall not feel these things, but shall shrink from before him and wish that ye could command the rocks to fall upon you and hide you from the countenance of the Lord.

34 For he shall come down in all of his glory and give unto you once again his gospel, which is the same gospel that he gave unto the Jews, and which ye have written in the Bible which proceedeth forth from the mouth of the Jew. And ye shall also have these same words in the record of my father in that part of this record that was not sealed. And then ye shall once again hear these things from his own mouth. And then ye shall have three testimonies of the word of God. And then shall the law be fulfilled which hath been spoken by the Father that in the words of three I will establish all of my words.

35 But this is not all, for ye shall have my words which shall be given unto you in this part of the record of my father which hath been sealed. And this shall be the final testimony of the gospel of Jesus Christ. And my words shall be plain and simple to understand. And if after reading my words, ye still do not understand the meaning of these things, then ye must remain until ye hear them from the mouth of God himself.

36 And if it so be that ye do not understand and accept this gospel, and live by its precepts as it hath been given unto you in all these testimonies that ye shall receive, then when ye hear it from the mouth of God, ye shall hear it to your condemnation, because ye have chosen, even three times, to disregard His words.

37 And now I write to you in plainness concerning these things. And these things I say unto all the world; for by the things that I say unto you in plainness ye shall be judged in the last day when the Lord cometh in his glory with his holy angels:

38 Behold, all religions, all doctrines, all principles, all beliefs, all scriptures, all writings, all holy men, all holy prophets, all institutions, all churches, all governments, all priesthoods, all laws, all sealings, all ordinances, all sacrifices, all traditions, all customs, yea, even everything that is done upon this earth among the children of men, are of no effect and have no power out of this world. In other words, they mean nothing in the kingdom of God.

39 The only thing that hath any meaning in the kingdom of God is the law of the gospel and the commandments that are given therein.

40 Therefore, if there are any among you who hear these things and keep the law of the gospel, then this person is ready for the resurrection and the eternal kingdom of God. They are those who will not cause any contentions in these kingdoms and shall live forever with those of their likeness in the worlds that the Father hath prepared for us.

41 And if there are any among you who think that ye shall be saved in any other way, even in that ye believe that you need the ordinances and doctrines of a church, then ye do not understand the plainness of my words, and shall be one of those to whom the Lord will say: Many will say to me in that day, Lord, Lord, have we not prophesied in thy name? And in thy name have cast out devils? And in thy name done many wonderful works? And then will I profess unto them, I never knew you, depart from me, ye that work iniquity.

42 And why shall the Lord say this unto them? Because they did not keep the law of the gospel as he was commanded by the Father to give unto them. For the things which he shall command of them, this is the will of the Father.

43 Behold, I have seen the last days, both in my own vision, and also through the words of the brother of Jared of which I am making an abridgment and writing to you at this time. And in those days, there are none, no not one, save it be a few only who are the humble followers of Christ who live by the law of this gospel.

44 And your churches and the leaders of your churches to whom ye look to be taught the will of God mislead you and cause you to err and teach not the law of the gospel as it hath been given unto them through the holy scriptures. And more especially, I speak unto those of you of the church of Jesus Christ, even those of you who call your church after his holy name but not in it.

45 Behold, ye are so centered on your church and the ordinances and functions therein, that ye have very little time and effort to spend obeying the law of the gospel. And ye have been taught by your leaders that these ordinances and these functions are saving ordinances which are necessary for your salvation. And in this ye are deceived and are being led captive by the devil.

46 And the words of Nephi are being fulfilled in you, in which he wrote, saying: And others will he pacify, and lull them away into carnal security, that they will say: All is well in Zion; yea, Zion prospereth, all is well—and thus the devil cheateth their souls, and leadeth them away carefully down to hell.

47 And because your church prospereth exceedingly, yea, even above any other church that is built up among the children of men, ye have become a rich and powerful people in the world. And the money that hath come from this prosperity, that should be going to the poor and the needy, the sick and the afflicted, and those that are imprisoned; yea, ye use this money to build up houses of worship which ye go to on one day a week and which are left empty for the rest of the week when they could be used to help the poor and the needy in their afflictions.

48 And if I could stop from condemning you before God, that ye might repent without searing your souls further with the heat of my words, I would. But I have seen the great temples that ye have caused to be constructed. And these ye have constructed to present the Holy Endowment that hath been explained unto you herein. And they are full of the fine things of the world, evensomuch that ye have received much praise from the world because of them.

49 And ye enter into these temples and think that ye are saviors of men, even that the endowment that ye receive is necessary for your salvation. And even this is not the end of your pride and your abominations before the Lord; for ye also believe that the work of your hands, even the work that ye perform within these temples will save those who are dead, which thing is most abominable before God.

50 Oh, my brethren, ye are those that shall suffer the most in the great and dreadful day of the Lord. Ye shall listen to his words in that day and quickly realize that he did not command that these things be done among the children of men. Ye will realize that the only concern that he hath for the world, is that they live by the law of his gospel, which law ye do not teach in your churches and in your temples.

51 And those who belongeth to your church shall watch in horror as the Lord calleth his own servants from among those who do not belong to your church, yea, even those who do not have the priesthood that ye think ye have. Then what shall ye say at that time of the works that ye have accomplished during the days of your probation? What shall ye think when ye are considered a thing of dross by the Lord, and that he giveth no attention to the glory and greatness of your church?

52 And why is it that ye shall suffer more than those who are not of your church? Yea, why do ye believe that the Lord will hold you accountable for more than he will hold the rest of those who have been deceived by the means of the miracles that Satan hath caused to be wrought among you? I say unto you that ye shall be held more accountable because ye have already two witnesses of the gospel of which I have spoken, even the words of Christ that he gave unto us, which is this gospel.

53 And no other people on earth will have these two testimonies which the Lord hath given unto the children of men. And the Lord will use your pride and your arrogance against you. For in your pride and arrogance, ye think ye are better than the rest of your brothers and sisters in the world, and that ye enjoy a happiness that they do not enjoy. And with this pride, ye send out missionaries to take your message of pride throughout the world.

54 And ye shall carry the record of my father with you, and pretend that ye believe in this record. And ye shall testify unto the world that the fullness of the gospel of Jesus Christ is contained in this record. And in this ye testify correctly, but by so testifying, ye are securing your own damnation. For ye testify of those things that ye do not do. And though the Lord will have exceedingly great mercy for the sinner, he shall condemn and punish the hypocrite.

55 And these words which I write unto you at this time, even in the sealed part of the plates upon which my father and I have written, and which I have been commanded to complete and hide in the earth to come forth in the own due time of the Lord; even these things shall ye reject because they were not given unto you by the leaders of your church, which leaders are all men of the world, which have received the fine things of the world and the praises and honors of men.

56 But these things shall condemn you and shall confound your false doctrines and the traditions that ye have allowed to creep into the foundations of the church that is called after the name of Jesus. For in the beginning, the foundation of your church was given in its purity, and the Lord suffered it to be organized according to the power of the Holy Priesthood and under the direction of the Holy Ghost.

57 But ye shall reject the pure foundation that was given unto you by him who shall receive this record from the place wherein I shall hide it. And because of your wickedness, the world will reject you and shall murder him who hath given these things unto you.

58 But another like unto him shall the Lord raise up to bring the sealed part of this record forth among you. And he shall have power given unto him, even the power of the Holy Spirit, to confound you and preach repentance unto you, and show you the wickedness of your ways.

59 And ye shall become like unto the Jews at Jerusalem who were the murderers of the prophets of old. And ye shall call upon your secret combinations, which combinations ye think are of God, and which ye think are righteous even like unto them of old. Yea, ye shall call upon these to murder this prophet.

60 Yea, ye shall become like the Nephites at the time Samuel the Lamanite was called by the Lord to preach repentance unto them. For when Samuel went forth to speak the truth concerning the wickedness of the church of God that was among them, they wanted to kill him and cast him away from them, so that they might not hear his preaching. But the Lord protected him, even that their bows and their arrows could not hit him.

61 And he who shall bring forth the sealed part of this record shall flee unto the rest of the world for protection, even unto those who are not of your church. And they shall protect him and give him sanctuary until he hath done all that which hath been commanded him by the Lord.

62 For it was the world that was responsible for the death of him that brought forth the portion of this record that was unsealed. And it was the cause of the wickedness of the church of God that caused his death. And now this same church shall seek the death of the prophet of God who shall bring these things forth unto you. And it shall be the world that openeth up its mouth and consumeth the flood of water that is issued forth from the mouth of the serpent that hath control of this church of which I have spoken.

63 Then shall the words of John be fulfilled which he wrote, saying: And when the dragon saw that he was cast unto the earth, he persecuted the woman which brought forth the man child.

64 And to the woman were given two wings of a great eagle, that she might fly unto the wilderness, into her place, where she is nourished for a time, and times, and half a time, from the face of the serpent.

65 And the serpent cast out of his mouth water as a flood after the woman, that he might cause her to be carried away of the flood.

66 And the earth helped the woman, and the earth opened her mouth, and swallowed up the flood which the dragon cast out of his mouth.

67 And the dragon was wroth with the woman, and went to make war with the remnant of her seed, which keep the commandments of God, and have the testimony of Jesus Christ.

68 For behold, the prophets of God have been persecuted by the wicked ever since they were first called to bring the law of the gospel unto the children of men. And a true prophet of God is always persecuted and hated by the world. And this is the thing that I ask of ye that belongeth to this great church in the latter days: Are your leaders hated by the world? Do those who have set themselves up as your prophets receive the afflictions of the prophets of old?

A New American Scripture

69 I say unto you that they do not. And why do they not receive this persecution as a true prophet of God should? Because they are of the world, and they seek the praise of the world more than they seek to teach unto you the law of the gospel.

70 And in the day that ye shall read my words, even in the day when the Lord shall give unto the world the words of the brother of Jared, ye shall see your leaders rise up and condemn this work. And they shall condemn this work because it testifieth against them and bringeth to your attention the truth regarding their wickedness and abominations.

71 And they shall say unto you: Behold, these things are not of the Lord. For the Lord would not give unto you anything except he do so through the authority of the church, which is held in the authority of those who have been called of God to serve in his Holy Priesthood.

72 And they shall speak unto you in kindness and smoothness, and in the gentle natures that ye have become accustomed to hearing their words. But in this same way, did Beneli entice and convince Cain that he should reject the words of Abel and rise up and murder him.

73 And they shall teach unto you their precepts that justify the wickedness of your ways. And they shall justify unto you the need for your churches and your temples and the fine things of the world. And they shall do that which hath been done by all the leaders of religions that are not set up according to the principles and laws of the gospel of Christ.

74 And now, I, Moroni, have shown unto you the wickedness of some of those who profess to be the followers of Christ, but deny the power of Christ, which power can only come by keeping the commandments of his gospel. But the whole world lieth under sin and shall come under severe condemnation, except that the children of men shall repent and turn their hearts towards the gospel that was given unto their fathers. And if they do not do this, then the whole earth will be destroyed at his coming.

75 And this is what was meant by the prophet Malachi, of whom the Lord spake when he visited my fathers in the land of Bountiful. And he said unto them: Remember ye the law of Moses, my servant, which I commanded unto him in Horeb for all Israel, with the statutes and judgments.

76 Behold, I will send you Elijah the prophet before the coming of the dreadful day of the Lord;

77 And he shall turn the heart of the fathers to the children, and the heart of the children to their fathers, lest I come and smite the earth with a curse.

78 And now, I, Moroni, ask of you: What was the law of Moses with it [*sic*] statutes and judgments which the Lord had given unto Moses in the land of Horeb? Yea, even that law that was given unto him upon the mount? I say unto you, it was the law of the gospel, or the words of Christ, who was the giver of this law.

79 And when Moses descended down from upon the mount and witnessed the great wickedness of the children of Israel, he threw down the law and gave unto them a lower law, which was a law of sacrifice and ordinances and rituals that pointed them towards the higher law, or in other words, the law of the gospel.

80 And when Jesus came into the world, he testified unto the people that he had come to fulfill the law which Moses had given unto the children of Israel. And he gave unto them the exact same law, or the exact same gospel, that he had given unto Moses before the rebellion of the children of Israel.

81 And this same law that he gave unto the children of Israel, he did give unto the Jews at Jerusalem. And this same law was given unto my fathers, and this law was also given unto others who are not of the house of Israel, but who dwell upon the earth in other parts that were unknown at the time of my fathers. Yet he had received a commandment of the Father to give these peoples the law of the gospel also. And this he did according to their language and their culture and according to their understanding.

82 And in the last days, the world shall have this gospel preached unto all peoples throughout the world. And it shall be carried unto all the ends of the world until all have heard it according to their own language and their own understanding.

83 And those of you who belong to this great church which is called after the name of Jesus Christ, who believe that it is by your words that the world shall receive these things, I say unto you, that it is because of your pride that ye believe these things. For when this gospel shall come unto you by way of the record of my father, behold, in that day, this same gospel shall already be among many of the peoples of this earth. And because it was given unto them according to their own traditions and customs and understanding, ye shall not recognize it. But if it teacheth the law of the gospel, it is recognized by God.

84 And now I would that all the world should have the words of this gospel and live by the commandments which are given therein, which commandments not only shall save you in the kingdom of God, but shall bring peace and happiness upon the entire earth.

85 And this gospel was taught to the children of Adam in the beginning in such a way that they could not misunderstand that which he spoke. Therefore, I return once again unto the words of Adam, according as they are given by the brother of Jared upon the record that he caused to be written. For they are plain and simple and easy to the understanding of the children of men, and in this way, hath the Lord commanded me to present these things.

CHAPTER 19

Adam explains in plainness the law of the gospel and the commandments of Jesus Christ. Love your neighbor as yourself. He explains the sacredness and importance of fidelity in marriage.

AND Adam continued his teachings, saying: Our Eternal Mothers taught us that we must obey the laws of the kingdom of God in order to ensure that we would be guaranteed the happiness that each of us desired for ourselves.

2 And now, I would that ye should know that these laws were also given unto your mother Eve and me upon our expulsion from the garden of Eden. Behold, these laws are eternal and are the same in the world in which our Eternal Parents reside, as well as in all the kingdoms that exist. And these laws ensure order in the universe; and that the end of these laws, which is happiness, may be realized by all those subjected to these laws.

3 And if ye abide by these laws throughout the days of your probation upon this earth, then ye shall also have peace and order among you here. And for this purpose were they given unto us after we left the garden of Eden.

4 And these laws are based upon one great law which encompasseth all of the commandments that God hath given us. Yea, it encompasseth all of the commandments that shall ever be given unto you and your children forever.

5 And this is the law on which all other commandments are based, that was given unto us by the Lord, even that ye should do unto others what ye would have them do unto you.

6 Now, from this law the Lord hath given us specific instructions, or commandments, that we must follow to accomplish the purpose of this law.

7 For he hath commanded us that we should not be angry one with another; and that we should have a respect for the opinions of each other;

and rejoice in the freedom that we each have to express our own opinion without the fear of repression or anger from another.

8 For this anger can cause us to strike out at our neighbors and harm them for that in which we feel that they have wronged us. And why is it that we feel that they have wronged us? Is it not that they do that which doth not agree with us? And why should we believe that our opinion of that which they think or do, is that which is right? Yea, it might be right for us, but might not be right for our neighbor.

9 And this anger can escalate and cause ye to strike out against your neighbor. Now I say unto you, that this is most abominable before God, even that ye should touch your neighbor without first receiving the permission to do so. For upon doing so, ye have taken away the free agency of your neighbor. For they have the right not to be touched by you, if it so be their desire.

10 And the eternal law that is violated by anger, is the law of free agency, which guaranteeth to each of us the right to act according to the desires of our hearts. And according to this law, ye have the right to become angry with your neighbor if that be your desire, even though your desire would be contrary to the commandments of God. But ye do not have the right to strike out in anger and harm another. For your neighbor did not use his free agency to desire that ye should strike him.

11 Therefore, ye have been commanded to respect one another and give unto each other this worthy respect that each of us deserveth. And ye should not be angry because ye do not understand that which your neighbor doeth with his free agency. For he will be held accountable for that which he doeth, and ye will not be held accountable, therefore, why should ye be angry?

12 And the Lord hath commanded us to have kind thoughts towards each other, and to not be involved in rumors or gossip in any manner concerning another. For if we, with our own eyes, do not see that which our neighbor hath done, then why think ye that ye can trust the words of another to tell you the truth regarding that which they claim they have seen? For that person who is making an account unto you of the actions of another would not do so unless he was angry with another. For what other purpose would there be a reason for rumor and gossip, except to make an account of those actions with which we do not agree?

13 And the Lord hath commanded us to refrain from listening to those who would make a bad account of the actions of another. And he would that we should know, that even if the account of these actions is true, we should respect that this person hath his free agency to act. And he hath commanded us not to become angry when another person useth his free agency to act according to his will.

14 For our Father allowed Lucifer and those that followed after him to act according to the laws of free agency. And He did not become angry with them, but He loved them and blessed them. Nevertheless, He was bound by the eternal laws of heaven in the limit of that which He could do to save them, they having acted according to the law, using their own free agency.

15 And nothing good can come from an angry heart; for he who is angry placeth his spirit in a state of rebellion with his body, and for this reason, the body reacteth to the anger of the spirit, thus causing sickness and poor health.

16 And the Lord hath given this commandment unto us that there might not arise contentions and disputations among us. For where there are contentions and disputations, war soon followeth, and many souls are sent home to the God who gave them life unprepared for the state in which they shall be received.

17 And it hath been with great sadness that I have watched death by the hand of another enter in among you because of the anger of which I have spoken. For even my beloved son Cain did submit to the anger of his heart and murdered his brother Abel. And that day I lost two sons. For it became necessary that I banish my beloved son Cain and his wives and his sons and

daughters from among us, that we might guard ourselves against these terrible things.

18 And I would that ye should know that I counseled with Cain and commanded him that he should repent of the thing which he had done. But his heart was hardened against my words, and he would not give heed to the tenderness of my love for him. And he kept the anger that he felt for his brother inside of him and would not release it from his soul.

19 And the Lord hath commanded us that if we have something amiss between each other, that we should reconcile our differences between ourselves in love, not allowing anger to control us and cause us to hate.

20 And it is also with great sorrow that I was forced to construct prisons among us wherein we could hold those who would not give heed unto the commandments of the Lord, and who could not control their anger. And in these prisons, I have caused that they should be taught and counseled and have shown unto them a greater love than that which they experience without the walls of the prisons, that they might know in what way they should act when they are released from these prisons.

21 For if these are imprisoned because of their anger, and are therefore shown greater examples of anger and hate within prison, then when they are released, they shall be much worse off than when they first entered into prison. Thus have I commanded our prisons to be places of instruction and love and tender feelings, that they who are therein might have an example set for them.

22 And the Lord hath commanded us that we should not return evil for evil, but that we should return good unto all. For this is what we would have others do unto us. For when your neighbor doeth something evil unto you, he doth not believe at the moment that he is doing this thing unto you that his actions are wrong. For if he believed that his actions were wrong at the time that he doeth evil unto you, or if he believed that his actions were evil, then he would not have done this thing unto you.

23 And Satan hath been given power to tempt us and cause us to take that which is good as something that is evil; and likewise he causeth us to take that which is evil as something that is good. And in the moment that our neighbor is enticed to do evil unto us, Satan can tempt him, and cause him to justify this evil thing as a thing that is good at that moment. Nevertheless, Satan doth not have the power to tempt us beyond our ability to resist him, thus making us fully responsible for our own actions.

24 But because of the power of Satan, and the weakness of our neighbor in resisting his enticements, many times our neighbor will do evil unto us believing that it is good. And if it so be that we do evil back to him, even though at the moment we might justify it as that which is good—because of the thing that he hath done unto us—we have disobeyed the commandments of the Lord.

25 And the Lord gave us this commandment, saying: Behold, I say unto you, that ye shall not resist evil, but whosoever shall smite thee on thy right cheek, turn to him the other also.

26 And if any man will sue thee at the law and take away thy coat, let him have thy cloak also. And whosoever shall compel thee to go a mile, go with him twain.

27 For there have been many of you who have come before the judges that I have caused to be set up among you to administer the laws that we have established among us to maintain peace and order. And ye bring unto them grievances against your neighbor. Now, when ye do this ye have already broken the commandments of God in that ye have become angry with your neighbor and have the desire to take the matter of your anger against him before a judge. And in this ye do sin. But this is not the end of your sin, for ye cause him whom you have sued to also sin, because in his anger, he will defend himself before the judge.

28 And no good can come of the grievance between you. But the Lord hath commanded any of you who are taken before a judge by your neighbor who hath a grievance against you, to give unto your neighbor all things that he hath asked of you in his grievance against you. In other words, he hath commanded you to not defend yourself, but to submit to the demands of the grievance.

29 And if ye submit to the demands of the grievance against you, then ye are not angry because of it. And if ye give what is asked of you by your neighbor, then ye have stopped the cause of the anger that your neighbor hath against you.

30 And if ye are struck by your neighbor, and ye return the blow unto him, then ye are angry when ye deliver this blow unto him. And in his anger he will return again and strike you. And then the anger of both of you will rise and cause that ye both shall sin before God, even until ye have committed the most grievous sin before Him, even the sin of murder.

31 Therefore, the Lord hath commanded you to turn the other cheek that your neighbor may strike you again in his anger. But ye shall not be angry and strike back. And when ye have offered both of your cheeks unto him that he may strike them, then the end of his anger might be satisfied and both your lives may be saved.

32 And the Lord hath commanded us, saying: Behold I say unto you, love your enemies, bless them that curse you, do good to them that hate you and pray for them who despitefully use you and persecute you, that ye may be the children of your Father who is in heaven.

33 Now, this commandment which he hath given unto us cannot be given with any more plainness than that which the Lord hath spoken.

34 Behold, we are commanded to love each other, in spite of what might be done unto us. For are we not all brothers and sisters who belong to the same Father who hath created us? And doth not the Father love each of us the same? Yea, I know that the Father loveth each of us the same, for He is no respecter of persons and loveth the sinner like unto the prophet. And he loveth Satan as he loveth each of us, for behold, Satan was our brother in the beginning.

35 And we have been commanded to do good in all situations, and love our enemies as well as our friends. And it is easy to love our friends, for even the most evil among us love their friends and hate their enemies.

36 But a sure judge of the righteousness of a man or woman is not in how they love their friends, but in how they love and treat their enemies. And if there are any among you who hate another, then what reward have ye when ye love your friends? For ye shall be loved also by your friends, and this is your reward. But when ye love your enemies, then they will not return unto you this love, but your reward will be given unto you by God.

37 And now my beloved children, I would that ye should understand that this flesh meaneth nothing before God, but that which is in the flesh is of God. And if ye lose this flesh by obeying the commandments of God, then by losing this flesh ye shall be received by God. But if ye keep this flesh because ye have disobeyed the commandments of God, then ye will not be received by God, but will receive the rewards of the flesh, which rewards are contrary to the happiness of God.

38 And I know that when my son, Cain, confronted his brother, Abel, in the field, his brother did not become angry with him, nor did he fight back to save his life. But in his final words, he blessed his brother Cain and forgave him for that which he was about to do unto him. And my son, Abel, was received by God and given a just reward.

39 And Cain hath received a just recompense for that which he hath done. And his reward was that of the flesh, which flesh became his curse and caused him to lose the happiness that he could have enjoyed among us if he would have obeyed the commandments of God.

40 And if your neighbor riseth up against you to take your life, trust in the commandments of God, and bless your neighbor and do not fight against him. And if ye will do this, ye shall be received by God. And if ye defend yourself and take up arms against your neighbor, then ye shall gain the reward of the flesh.

And this reward shall be the continual hatred and anger that shall exist among you for many generations. And there shall be no peace among you.

41 And I ask of you, Is it not better that ye die without anger at the hand of your enemy and be received by God, than it is to be slain in anger in a war against him? For in one instance ye shall die in righteousness; and in the other ye shall die in your sins. And if ye believe that by your strength ye can slay your enemy before he slayeth you, then ye are preparing the way whereby the war that ye have caused shall be the means of slaying many of your sons and daughters by the hand of the sons and daughters of the enemy that ye have slain.

42 And if ye have hate towards another, ye shall not experience the state of happiness with the Father that He hath promised you after ye are dead. For ye will be in the spirit world with those whom ye have hated. And in that world, ye shall not have the flesh that ye have at this time. And without this flesh, what cause can ye give unto your anger for another? And your anger shall cause you to remain in a state of misery, and without the flesh, ye will be unable to act upon this anger.

43 And ye shall see all of your brothers and sisters and realize that we all share the same Eternal Parents. And ye shall realize that ye have disobeyed the commandments that They have given unto you concerning the way that ye should act towards each other. And do ye think that ye can exist in a state of happiness knowing these things?

44 Therefore hath the Lord given unto us these commandments that we might live together in peace and harmony, one with another, enjoying the wonderful blessings that the Father hath provided for us as His children in His eternal worlds.

45 And if we do not learn these commandments and we are not able to abide by them forever, then we will not be able to dwell in His kingdom. For He alloweth none who do not obey His commandments to enter therein.

46 And He hath commanded us, saying: Verily, verily, I say unto you that ye judge not, that ye be not judged. For with what judgment ye judge, ye shall be judged; and with what measure ye mete, it shall be measured to you again.

47 And why beholdest thou the mote that is in the eye of thy brother, but considerest not the beam that is in thine own eye. Or how wilt thou say to thy brother: Let me pull the mote out of thine eye, and behold, a beam is in thine own eye?

48 Thou hypocrite, first cast the beam out of thine own eye; and then shalt thou see clearly to cast the mote out of the eye of thy brother.

49 Now, this doth not mean that the Lord doth not want us to discern between good and evil and choose the good over the evil and cling to it. But who among us hath the right to determine what is good and what is evil? For unto some what is evil might be good unto others. And to others, what is evil might be good unto some. Therefore, if we must judge the actions of others, we must make a righteous judgment.

50 But I say unto you, my dear children, that it is better that ye do not judge at all, but leave all judgment to our Father, who hath created us all, and hath given us our free agency to choose for ourselves that which is good and that which is evil. And He loveth all of His children, whether their actions be good or whether they be evil, He loveth them the same.

51 For what think ye, that ye are better fathers than our Father in heaven? And if one of your children doeth evil in your judgment, do ye love him less than those of your children that do that which ye judge to be good? And if ye, being evil fathers, desire good for your children, then how much more would our Father, who is righteous, desire good for all of His children?

52 And it is a hard thing that ye should determine what is good and what is evil on your own accord. For ye know not the circumstance in which the action of another hath taken place; and therefore, ye have no way to judge righteously whether or not this action is good or evil. For in one circumstance the action could be good, but in another circumstance it could be evil.

53 And if ye judge an action of another to be evil, and it is actually good, then the condemnation resteth upon your shoulders for the judgment ye have rendered. And if ye judge an action of another to be good, and it is actually evil, then this condemnation also resteth upon your shoulders.

54 For if ye judge the action of another, and ye have determined in yourselves that this action is evil, then ye shall show prejudice and bias against this action, which prejudice and bias cause you to have anger against this person.

55 And with this anger, ye have sealed yourselves up to the prison, or the state of misery in the spirit world of which I have spoken. And if ye find out after death that the action that ye have judged was not an evil action, but a righteous action, then ye will not have the power to reconcile with him whom ye have misjudged in the flesh—because ye are in the spirit—and a recompense for prejudice and bias and anger cannot be given in the spirit world. And ye shall not come out of this prison, or in other words, ye shall remain in this state of misery, until the consequences of your judgment hath ended in the flesh.

56 And now, my children, I shall give unto you an example of that which I have spoken, so that ye shall not be confused in this thing. For I have seen this among you, even this judgment which ye have made of something that is good as being evil, and because of this thing that I have seen, and the judgments ye have made, there is much contention among you, and there will be many of you who shall suffer because of these things in the spirit prison as I have explained it unto you.

57 Behold, there are those among you who have condemned others in that which they eat and drink. Yea, there are those of you who have cursed your neighbors because they eat the flesh of beasts and cook their food, which the eating of flesh and cooking are contrary to the strict laws of health that the Lord hath given unto us. And ye believe that because they eat this flesh and cook their food, that they shall be condemned before God and chastised by Him.

58 And in this thing ye have caused much anger and contention among yourselves. But in this thing ye have judged your neighbors incorrectly, and ye have become angry against them and prejudiced your minds and hearts against them that do these things. And your children see your examples and grow up with this prejudice already in their hearts. And this prejudice turneth them cold towards those who do the things that your children have been taught are evil.

59 And because of this anger and this prejudice towards them, ye have caused those who do these things that ye perceive to be evil, to have anger and prejudice towards you. And they also teach their children this prejudice, which divideth us further into families and factions that have anger one towards another. And in this anger ye are disobeying the commandments of God, and not in that which ye eat.

60 For the laws of health associated with that which we should eat, and that which we should abstain from eating, pertain only to this world and our mortal flesh. And those who use their free agency to disobey the laws of health, receive the recompense for their disobedience in this world. And this recompense is the poor health and diminished strength and the disease and pestilence that causeth them to suffer during the days of their probation. But once they are dead, and have cast off the flesh, that is the end of their punishment, and they will receive no further punishment for that which they have chosen to eat and drink.

61 But those of you that have become angry with them and have hardened your hearts against them because of your prejudice and your bias against the things that ye have judged to be evil, will suffer the recompense of your anger, not only in this life, but in the prison of the next as I have explained it unto you.

62 And when, as a spirit, ye observe that your children and their children, even unto many generations, do carry on the hate and the prejudice that ye have caused because of your misjudgment, then ye shall suffer in this state of misery until the end of the cause of this hate and prejudice that ye have taught unto your children.

63 Therefore, my beloved children, love one another and do good to each other. And I would that ye should know that it doth not matter to the Lord what goeth in the mouth of another according to his free will and choice. But it mattereth to him how ye treat one another, and this is the only thing that mattereth unto him.

64 And I would that ye should remember the things that I have spoken unto you regarding the kingdom of God and the different glories that pertain thereto, which are the glories of happiness that all the children of God shall inherit according to the individual desires of happiness of each.

65 Remember that I have explained unto you that each of us determined before we were born into mortality which of these glories of happiness best suited our own desires of happiness. And this time of probation was the time that we would prove to ourselves that the choice that we have made for ourselves is indeed that which we desire.

66 And since each of our desires of happiness are different, then those things that we believe are good for us, might be things that are evil unto another. And likewise, those things that might be evil for us, might bring happiness to another. And for this reason it would be hard to make a righteous judgment.

67 But the commandments of the Lord that I am giving unto you at this time must be obeyed by all. For they are truly commandments that will bring us the happiness that we all desire. And if another chooseth an action for himself that is not contrary to the commandments of God, even the commandments of His gospel, which are the commandments that I am giving unto you at this time; then that person is justified in this action if it bringeth him joy.

68 And we do not do anything except that we might have joy therein. And the things that we do that do not bring us joy, then we may know for a surety that they are evil to us. And those things that bring us joy, are surely good and righteous to us. But remember again, my beloved children, that what bringeth joy to one person doth not mean that the same joy will be experienced by another.

69 Therefore, I would that ye judge not at all, but let our Lord be the judge of us all. And this is what I have caused to be taught among you, even in the churches that the Lord hath suffered us to establish among us for our sake. Even that all of us shall be brought before the judgment bar of God and be judged according to the commandments that he hath given unto us.

70 And for this reason, I give unto all of you these commandments. And if a commandment is not given by me at this time, then that commandment was not given unto me and your mother Eve by the Lord. And therefore, this commandment cannot be a commandment of God, but is a commandment of men. And if it is a commandment of men, then you will not be held accountable for it at the judgment bar of God.

71 And now I would that ye should beware of the commandments of men, for these commandments of men shall usually lead you away from the commandments of God. Therefore, I speak plainly unto you of those commandments that we have received from the mouth of God.

72 And the Lord commanded us, saying: Thou shalt not commit adultery. And whosoever looketh on a woman, to lust after her, hath committed adultery already in his heart. Behold, I give unto you a commandment, that ye suffer none of these things to enter into your heart.

73 Verily, verily, I say unto you, that whosoever shall put away his wife, saving for the cause of fornication, causeth her to commit adultery; and whoso shall marry her who is divorced, committeth adultery.

74 And now I would that ye should know, that in the garden of Eden the Lord commanded me to cleave unto Eve and become one with her. And I was commanded to care for her and stay at her side all the days of my life. And because she was to be engaged in the bringing forth of children, I was commanded that I should make sure she was provided with those things that she desired to make her happy, and to sustain her life and the lives of our children.

75 And ye are all our children. And ye also know that I have spent all the days of my life in labor to sustain your lives and give unto you those things that make you happy. But in all these things, I have depended upon Eve as my companion, and it is she whom I have been commanded to love and honor. And she hath loved me and honored me all the days of my life, which hath brought me much joy and hath fulfilled my desires of happiness concerning her.

76 But even though I was commanded to love and honor her by the Father, I did not need to be commanded in this thing, for I truly do love her, and it is I that am indebted to the Father because of her.

77 And I have caused to be taught among you that it is not the right of a man to ask that a woman be his wife. For it is the responsibility of a man to live his life honorably, and cause that a woman should desire him. And if the woman hath desired him as her husband, then it is because she believeth that he will fulfill the desires of her happiness.

78 And this is the law of the heavens which I have caused to be taught unto you in mortality, because of the physical strength that a mortal man hath over a woman. For if a man was left to the carnal desires of his heart, then he would force himself upon a woman and cause her to accept him by his brute strength over her. But this thing is most abominable before God, and any man that doeth this thing shall be condemned by God.

79 And again, any man that would do this thing shall not be given the eternal body of a man in the kingdoms of glory that permit this type of body.

And only those spirits that are worthy of this body, and desire it to serve others, shall receive this power in the kingdom of God. And those spirits who desire to be women, in this same glory, shall choose for themselves the man that they would have as a husband. And they shall do this according to their knowledge of this man and his righteousness.

80 And I am saddened that there are many of you, my sons, among us, who have corrupted the law of marriage, as I have caused it to be taught unto you. For ye deceive the women, and pretend to be righteous, and pretend that ye are willing to fulfill her desire of happiness, so that the woman will choose you and desire to make you her husband. And ye lust after her and the dowry that is given and not that ye should serve her and provide for her happiness.

81 And because it is by the free will and choice of a woman to make a man her husband, she is bound by the covenant that she shall make unto him. And through this covenant, she hath obligated herself to this man all the days of her life. And for this reason, a man hath no right to put away his wife, if it so be that he accepteth her desire to make him her husband.

82 And a man shall not be compelled in this world or in the next—in the glory that permitteth eternal unions—to accept the desire of a woman. Nevertheless, in the glory of the kingdom of God where these unions are permitted, there will be only righteous men, and a righteous man shall never deny a desirous woman from being his eternal companion. And they shall only desire this union to serve others, for in this, their blessing and their joy are complete.

83 And ye shall not engage in any sexual relations of any kind, even those actions that lead up to the desire of these relations, unless ye have been chosen by a woman to be her husband. And the woman shall remain pure and untouched by other men until the day that she maketh a decision regarding her choice of a husband.

84 For every woman shall one day be the wife of a husband, if she so chooses. And if it so be that a woman commiteth fornication, or anything like unto it, she shall commit adultery against her future husband. And any man that commiteth fornication, or anything like unto it with another woman, hath committed adultery with the future wife of another man, who the woman hath not yet chosen for herself.

85 And if a woman hath committed fornication, or anything like unto it, and maketh a lie to the man that she is desirous to take unto herself as a husband, and presenteth herself as clean and pure before him, then she can be put away, or divorced from him to whom she made the lie. But if that man be a righteous man, then he shall forgive his wife for the things which she hath done before she made the covenant with him. And her sins will be remembered no more before the Lord. And it will be counted unto the man as righteousness.

86 But if he doth not desire to have her as a wife, he shall be justified before the Lord in a divorcement. And likewise also, shall it be for the woman who hath been lied to by a man.

87 And there shall be no other reason that a divorcement shall be given. For this reason, the daughters of God must be cautious, and prove those whom they would have as their husbands. Yea, they must assure themselves that the man whom they choose as their husband is worthy before God. And ye shall test them and see if they live by the commandments of God, and not by the commandments of men. And if they live by the commandments of God, then ye shall receive from them the happiness that ye desire. But if they live by the commandments of men, then ye shall experience misery and strife in a union with them.

88 And there is a sure test, my beloved daughters, that will help you that ye shall know whether a man followeth the commandments of God, or the commandments of men. For behold, it is the natural desire of all men to engage in fornication, and anything like unto it, whenever they are allowed to do so by a woman. Therefore, if a man attempteth fornication with you, or anything like unto it, then ye shall know that he disregardeth the commandments of God and hath followed the instincts of his own carnal desires. And if it so be that ye still desire this man, then you shall experience the strife of which I have spoken, and in the eternal worlds, your union shall not exist.

89 And it shall be that there are very few men who are righteous and are willing to obey the commandments of God in all things. And ye shall realize that if it so be that you depend on the righteousness of men to give you children, then ye would be barren and childless all the days of your life.

90 And if ye are a righteous woman and are desirous to have children, then ye shall be justified in creating these children with an unrighteous man, if it so be that he is chosen by you because ye cannot find a righteous man among you.

91 And if your desires are righteous, then shall the Lord ease the burden of this strife between you and your unrighteous husband, and shall bring you great joy in your posterity. And if ye remain faithful all the days of your life, even that ye keep all the commandments of the Lord, then shall ye be blessed with the choice of a righteous husband in the kingdom of God, if that so be your desire.

92 But if your husband is unrighteous, and obeyeth not the commandments of the Lord in all things, then are ye justified in a divorcement from him. But in all these things ye shall judge only according to the commandments of God, and not according to the commandments of men. Beware that ye are not deceived by men who put themselves up above you and give you commandments that are not of God.

93 Let no man deceive you, and say unto you that the Lord hath commanded him to take another wife unto himself. For the Lord would never command such a thing. For as it hath been explained unto you, it is the choice of a woman to choose a husband. And if a woman cometh unto you and desireth to take your husband also as her own husband, then ye shall have the decision to take her unto yourself as a sister wife to your husband. But if ye do this thing to your sister, then ye must know that she shall be equal to you in the eyes of your husband.

94 And there shall be no man that shall be given the power and authority to give a woman to another man, neither shall the power be given to any to choose a husband for any woman. But unto some, who are righteous men of God, the Lord suffereth to be given the authority to counsel with the women who find themselves without husbands because of the wickedness of men. And it will be given unto this righteous man to seal this covenant before God.

95 And if any woman taketh a sister wife unto herself for her husband, then it will be counted unto her as righteousness before God. But if she doth not allow another woman to take her righteous husband as her own, then it shall not be counted unto her as unrighteous before God. For the Lord delighteth in the chastity and honor of women.

96 Behold, I have been loyal and faithful to Eve all the days of my life. In honor I sustain her and cherish each moment I am blessed with her presence. I have had no lascivious thoughts, and no lustful desires have entered into my heart all the days of my life. And I am one with her. And because of these things, we enjoy a fullness of happiness in the union within which we have been blessed.

97 And now I say unto you, if ye shall love your spouses as we have loved one another, then ye also shall have this joy, which joy causeth the happiness that we share. And because of this happiness, the Lord hath established this union of a man and a woman, and hath given unto us the commandments pertaining to this union that shall be maintained in righteousness. And because of righteousness, this union shall exist in the kingdom of the Father forever.

CHAPTER 20

Adam continues to explain the gospel and the commandments of Jesus Christ. He explains the evil of money and worldly possessions and gives the commandments pertaining to them. He expounds on and explains the evils of the family unit.

AND the Lord continued his commandments unto us, saying: Lay not up for yourselves treasures on earth, where moth and rust doth corrupt, and thieves break through and steal; but lay up for yourselves treasures in heaven, where neither moth nor rust doth corrupt, and where thieves do not break through nor steal.

2 For where your treasure is, there will your heart be also. And the light of the body is the eye; if, therefore, thine eye be single, thy whole body shall be full of light. But if thine eye be evil, thy whole body shall be full of darkness. If, therefore, the light that is in thee be darkness, how great is that darkness.

3 No man can serve two masters; for either he will hate the one and love the other, or else he will hold to the one and despise the other. Ye cannot serve God and Mammon.

4 And when we received these commandments from the Lord, we did not understand the meaning of them. For we had no desire for any of the treasures of the earth. Yea, we did not know what we should even consider as treasures of the earth. Therefore, we could not lay up for ourselves those things that we did not understand. Nevertheless, we covenanted to obey this commandment without fully understanding it at the time it was given unto us. And this we did, because of our faith in the word of the Lord.

5 And we remembered the words of Satan when he was cast out of the kingdom of the Father, in which he said that he would take the treasures of the earth, and with gold and silver he would buy up great armies of men, and that he would buy up the means of justice and laws that the children of men

would be subjected to through his governments and his religions, and that he would reign with blood and horror upon the earth.

6 And when the Lord gave unto us the Holy Endowment as an instrument to give our children the opportunity to know the plan of salvation that he hath provided for us, we were commanded to demonstrate the great enticement that the treasures of the earth would have upon the souls of the children of God. But even then, we did not fully understand that which was commanded of us.

7 And it was my hope that through my daily administrations among you, and also by the preaching of those who have been given the authority to teach you in the church that the Lord hath suffered to be established among us, that these things might not come to pass among you, in other words, that we might not see the necessity of these commandments.

8 But it was our eldest son Beneli, who first introduced gold and silver among us and deceived his other brothers and sisters, and taught them that these things were precious things of the earth. And as ye have these many years developed a system of money, which is based on these things which ye believe are precious, these commandments have become necessary and vital to our salvation and happiness.

9 For ye have used these things to form inequalities among you. And ye began to covet those things of your neighbor that ye do not possess, which things are not the things of God, and have nothing to do with your eternal salvation. Yea, these things also have nothing to do with the sustaining of your lives upon this earth.

10 For who among you can eat gold and silver and obtain nourishment from them? And can ye form them into raiment that can shield your flesh from the ill effects of the laws of nature? And who among you can find use for them in the construction of your houses in which ye live? Yea, what use do these things have unto you, except to deceive you, and give unto you a means whereby ye might disobey the commandments of God?

11 Behold, in the beginning I taught unto you the law of consecration, which is the law of the Lord pertaining to all of the children of God, and the means whereby all of us receive that which we are in need of, according to our individual needs. And by this law, we existed in peace and harmony with each other, having food and raiment and houses to satisfy the needs of all.

12 And there were no poor or rich among us. For how can there be poor, if there are no rich? And how can one man be considered rich, if he hath only that which he needeth, like unto all those whose needs are also filled? And what purpose would a man gain, if he owned more than that which he needed to sustain his life? The only purpose would be so that he could consume the excess of that which he possesseth on the pride of his heart. And it is this pride in his heart that alloweth him to consider himself rich.

13 And when the pride of his heart hath consumed him, in that he spendeth his days counting his abundance and thinking up ways in which he can increase this abundance, then doth the light which entereth his eye causeth his whole body to be full of darkness. Yea, the obscurity of the darkness within him overcometh any light that he once possessed.

14 And we were commanded from the beginning to work by the sweat of our brow in order to eat the food that would bring us nourishment. And the commandment did not say, that we shall live by the sweat of the brow of our brother, but it said, by the sweat of our own brow.

15 And there are those of you who are rich and have justified your laziness because ye think that ye can take advantage of another because of his words. Or in other words, because he is not as intelligent as you. But this I say unto you, I am equally as intelligent as any of you, and I have worked by the sweat of my own brow all the days of my life. And your mother Eve hath worked along with me at my side. And we are not rich, nor do we have more than that which we need.

16 And because ye have placed value upon gold and silver and other things that ye have made precious among you, ye have caused much misery to come to pass among you. For in the beginning there was no need of a commandment that thou shalt not steal. For everything was provided for and offered free to all without a price. And there were no prices or worth affixed to anything upon this earth.

17 But now ye have placed value upon each other, even that the worth of a man and his trade hath a price. And in this, not only do ye sin in the treatment of each other, but ye sin against God, who hath commanded us to love one another and do unto each other what we would have others do unto us.

18 Now, what man among you would want others to consider you of less value than that value which they consider of themselves? And who among you would want to be known for your little value? And what of those that carry the buckets of our waste and bury them outside of our cities, that we should not behold our waste and cause our cities to stink? Of what value do these have unto us?

19 I say unto you, that I would rather live in a clean city that is unburdened by our waste, than I would in a city, where those therein wear fine linens and clothing where moths make their own waste thereon. And we value the dressmaker and the cobbler more than we value he who carrieth our waste from among us. Yet, if we had not the dressmaker and the cobbler among us, we could make our own clothes, though not finely made as they might be, but sufficient for our needs.

20 And if there were none to carry forth our waste from among us, then our cities would begin to stink and we would suffer because of their absence. So I say unto you, which of these should be of more value unto us?

21 And those of you who think that your intelligence should be rewarded at a higher value than the work of those that till our fields and harvest the foods that we eat; yea, what think ye, if they became intelligent like unto yourselves, and thought themselves above the sweat that produceth this food? What then would ye eat?

22 Behold, your intelligence cometh from your deceptions and the advantage that ye have taken of others because of their words. For ye have convinced those who carry forth the waste, and also those who bring forth the fruits of the field, that your gold and your silver are most precious and are desirous to possess. And because of your many words and your deceptions, those who work by the sweat of their brow to support you depend on you for this gold and this silver that they might live.

23 And ye have taken that which they produce and have convinced them who have produced it that its worth is less than the worth that ye know it to be. And then in your deception, ye take that which ye have purchased for little, and sell it for much, so that ye might get gain in this profit and add to the abundance that ye already have.

24 And ye enter into covenants with each other that ye might control those who work by the sweat of their brow to support you. And ye have used your gold and your silver to buy protection for your evil plans; and to hire those who make laws and ordinances. And these laws and ordinances assure that ye might continue to get gain without the consequences of the law to interfere with you.

25 And once ye have established these laws among you, ye use these laws to justify your actions. And before long, your whole body shall be full of darkness, according to the words of the Lord, and Oh, how great is that darkness.

26 I would that ye would take away the gold and the silver from among you, so that Satan can have no more power over you. For if the things of this earth have no value to you, except that it be to sustain your lives and give you joy therein, then shall ye begin to lay up for yourselves treasures in heaven, where neither moth nor rust doth corrupt, and where thieves do not break through and steal.

A New American Scripture

27 And if ye had all things in common, like it was in the beginning; yea, even like unto the church that we have established for your instruction, then there would be no thieves, because there would not be anything to steal. And if the things of the earth had no value, then why would ye keep unto yourself more than what ye needed to sustain your lives?

28 And ye are beginning to establish borders and fences among you. And how do ye think that ye can do these things and comply with the commandments of God? Behold, the earth is not ours to own, for we will soon die and leave it to another and take none of it with us. Then what is the cause in which ye think ye are justified in the ownership of land, which doth not belong to you?

29 And if it doth not belong to you, then ye are thieves who claim it as your own. And if ye are thieves who have claimed it as your own, then ye give the right unto others to enter in among you and take that which is not yours to have. And this will be the cause of much war and contention among you. And with these wars and this contention cometh the anger that the Lord hath commanded us not to have in our hearts.

30 And this desire to own that which is not yours hath caused you to divide yourself throughout the land into families and communities. And when ye have thus divided yourselves, ye cause your thoughts to center on your families instead of on all people, who are your brothers and your sisters. And this family unit shall be the cause of much heartache and contention among you.

31 For ye have begun to believe that your families are more important than the rest of your brothers and sisters, who are your neighbors. And because ye believe this, ye shall concentrate all of your efforts on acquiring the things of the world to care for your family in the flesh. And your children shall become selfish and centered in themselves because of the example of the things that ye have shown unto them.

32 And they shall begin to think that they have no other brothers and sisters, except those with whom they share the same parents. And they shall begin to believe that their family unit is better than that of their neighbor, and that they should put their own family and its needs above the needs of their neighbor.

33 And this belief shall cause pride to overcome them; and they shall begin to think of themselves above all others who do not belong to their own family. And because of this pride, family shall fight against family for the land that ye have divided amongst yourselves for the purpose of providing for the needs of your own family.

34 And ye shall believe that your needs are greater than the needs of your neighbors. And ye shall withhold your substance from your neighbors, and justify the withholding of your substance, because ye believe that if ye give unto them, ye shall not have enough for your family.

35 And because of this family unit in which ye have divided yourselves, ye shall begin to put even more value upon your own lives in comparison to the lives of your neighbors. And ye shall strive to be rich and have more than others. And in your desire to be rich, ye shall make many of your brothers and your sisters—yea, even your brothers and your sisters before God—poor.

36 And ye shall begin to teach your children to focus their lives on learning the ways of the world, that they might get gain therein, and receive the honors and praises of men for the gain that they have received. And your children shall begin to search for gold and silver, and for fine linens, and all the fine things of the world. And they shall make these things their idols, for they shall fall down before them and worship them, in that their hearts and desires are continually focused upon them.

37 And ye have already begun to teach your children that these family units are sanctioned by God, and that it is the most important unit among you. And ye believe that the things that ye have acquired of the world are the blessings of God, and that He hath given you these things because of your righteousness in your families.

38 But I say unto you, these family units are an abomination before God. Behold, they divide the children of God against each other and cause the spirit of God to withdraw itself from you. And when the spirit of God hath withdrawn itself from among you, then ye are left unto yourselves. And when ye are left unto yourselves, Satan beginneth to have power over you.

39 And when Satan hath power over your hearts, he beginneth to convince you that that which is evil and of him, is good, and that which is good and of God, is evil. And in this way he misleadeth you and lulleth you away into carnal security, carefully leading your souls away from God and down to hell.

40 And this hell is not a place where ye shall go after this life, for all of us will return to the spirit world from whence we came. But this hell is a state of being which is either on this earth, or in the spirit world.

41 And it is easy to tell whether or not a thing is from God, or if it is from Satan. For the things of God shall lead you to do the will of God. And when ye do the will of God, then ye are happy. And if ye are not happy, then ye are not doing the will of God. And Satan will allow you to rejoice in your wickedness for a time, but he will not stand by you for long. And when he turneth his back on you, ye shall no longer remain happy in the evil thing that ye are doing.

42 And I know that ye do rejoice in the concept of your family unit, and that ye rejoice in your children, and your spouses, and in the things of this world that ye have accumulated to support them in their needs. And because ye find joy therein, ye believe that these things must be from God. But I say unto you, that these things are not from God. And if ye continue in these things, or in other words, the division of yourselves into separate family units, ye shall reap the recompense of this sin.

43 For once ye have divided yourselves into families, then ye shall divide yourselves into communities of families; and once ye have divided yourselves into communities of families, then ye shall divide yourselves into countries and nations. And ye shall place borders around the lands of your nations, and cause that any that enter into the borders of your nations to be bound by the laws which ye have set for this nation, which laws are based on the things that ye have taught your children in the family units that ye have created.

44 And in your desire to protect your families and those things in which ye believe, which things ye have convinced yourself are from God, ye shall raise up armies and means of force that shall protect the borders of your lands; and ye shall cause to be killed any whom ye believe shall threaten the family units that ye have set up among yourselves.

45 And in anger shall nation rise against nation. And ye shall have diverse wars and contentions among you. And these wars and these contentions shall be caused because ye think in and of yourselves that ye are more righteous than those of other nations. And these other nations are also created by family units, which believe differently than you do, and which also think that the beliefs of their families are more righteous than yours.

46 And ye shall follow the leaders of these nations, and they shall lead you into battle against your brothers and sisters. And ye shall kill them in anger. And they, in recompense for what ye have done unto them, shall kill you. And if it so be that they are a nation of people who do not have the strength to kill you, then their children and the children of their children, even for many generations, shall wait until the time that they are strong enough to rise up against you, and then they shall make war against you because of the things that ye have done unto their families.

47 And ye shall begin to follow the doctrine and commandments of men, and shall cause to be established among you divers religions and priesthoods that conform to the beliefs that ye have taught your children,

which beliefs are contrary to the gospel and the commandments of God that I am giving unto you at this time.

48 And these religions, and these churches, and the leaders that ye follow, shall cause you to hold fast to the family divisions that ye have created for yourselves. And they shall preach gentle words unto you that will keep you lulled away in carnal security, while many of your brothers and sisters who live in other families in other nations beyond the borders of your own, shall suffer because of you.

49 But ye shall not concern yourselves about those in another nation, or in another family, because they are not of your family, and they do not believe the same things that ye believe. And because they do not believe the same things that ye believe, ye shall consider them unworthy of the blessings of God, which blessings ye believe are the things of this world. And ye believe that these blessings of God are your gold and your silver and all of the precious things that ye have accumulated for your family.

50 And then shall the words of Lucifer, which he spoke unto the Father in the beginning, come to pass, in which he said: And with the enmity that thou hast placed between me and the children of men, I will take the treasures of the earth, and with gold and silver I will buy up armies and the means of force and priesthood and religions, and I will reign with blood and horror on this earth.

51 Now, I would that ye should understand what Lucifer meant by this enmity that the Lord hath placed between him and the children of men, which are all of us. For Lucifer had a desire to gain glory for himself. And this is contrary to the first law and principle of the government of the heavens that stateth that this government shall never be self-serving, and it shall never act in and of itself and of its own accord for the sake of its own existence.

52 And the plan that Lucifer had presented to us as spirits was rejected by the majority of us, and was a plan that could not be accepted because of its violation of the eternal laws of heaven that cannot be violated. But there were many of the spirits that desired the things which Lucifer presented unto them. And these followed him and were cut off from the kingdom of God at that time.

53 And they have been with us here upon this earth in the realm of the spirits since the beginning. And Lucifer hath also been here among us. And he tempted Eve, and she gave in to his enticements and disobeyed the commandments of God. But Satan, as he is known among us in mortality, justified that which he had done unto Eve, claiming that it was necessary in order to bring about the mortality of the children of God, as it had been done in other worlds.

54 But Satan did these things of his own accord, and wanted the glory for himself. And he did these things that he might corrupt and possess the bodies that the Father hath created for us.

55 And Satan hath his own kingdom and receiveth his own glory upon this earth among those that follow him and keep his commandments, which are the same commandments and precepts of men. And his kingdom consisteth of all of you who disobey the commandments of God and follow his enticements.

56 And God said unto Lucifer: I will place enmity between thee and the seed of the woman. Thou mayest have power to bruise his heel, but he shall have power to crush thy head.

57 And now, my beloved children, I have caused these things to be taught unto you in the Holy Endowment that ye all have the opportunity to receive. But many of you think this endowment is foolish, and ye do not understand the things that are taught therein. And there are many of you who have received this endowment, but do not ask for understanding and have confused yourselves because of it.

58 And if ye would have inquired of me, I would have revealed unto you all of its meanings, for it is not a secret thing among us and hath been taught openly in the churches that I have caused to be established among you. But many of you do not attend these churches and listen to the words of the leaders, who have been given the authority to teach these things unto you.

59 And ye would not need these leaders or these churches if it were that ye obeyed the commandments of God. And if ye obey the commandments of God, ye shall have the Spirit of God to be with you. And by this same Spirit, ye shall know the truth of all things.

60 But I would that ye should understand these things, and also that ye should understand the commandments of God that ye must live by in order to have the Spirit as your constant companion all the days of your lives. And for this purpose have I gathered you together, even that I might teach these things unto you.

61 And as it is that your feet take you through this life, and make a record, as it were, of all those things that ye do during your life; yea, even that your feet carry you forth unto works of righteousness or works of evil, according to the law of free agency which hath been given unto you; therefore, Satan hath power to bruise your heel, in that he causeth you often to do evil, and bruiseth the works that ye do during the days of your probation.

62 And these bruises can cause you to stumble and walk unsurely in the straight and narrow path that the Father hath prescribed for us and hath directed us to follow. And Satan hath been given power to bruise our heels all the days of our lives.

63 But in the end; yea, when we finally come to an understanding of the righteousness of the Father and the commandments that he hath given unto us; then shall we have power to crush the head of Satan, or in other words, destroy his kingdom with righteousness.

64 And the Lord hath placed enmity between Satan and us. And this enmity that he hath placed between us is the feelings that we receive when we work righteousness, in that we are happy and feel joy. And this enmity is also the feelings that we receive when we do evil, in that we are miserable, where there is an absence of joy, in other words, this enmity is our conscience.

65 And Satan hath taken these feelings, or this enmity, and hath deceived us into thinking that evil is good and good is evil. And he hath accomplished this with gold and silver and the fine things of the earth. And he hath done this with the families in which he hath caused you to divide, so that ye shall hate one another, and put yourselves above others.

66 For when ye are engaged in the pursuit of the things of the world, or Mammon as it hath been called, then ye make that pursuit your God, and it is from this that ye receive your happiness. And ye are happy when ye think on the things that ye own, even your houses, and your clothes and your possessions, and all the things to which ye have given a value that do not sustain your life—even a life that requireth only food, and simple raiment, and a simple shelter to survive.

67 And ye are happy when ye see your families prospering and enjoying the things that ye have provided for them. And ye take no thought of others, for in the happiness of your families ye find your joy.

68 And ye find joy in your religions and your beliefs and in the leaders that teach you the things that ye want to hear, even preaching those things that support you in that which ye believe. And ye shall find happiness and joy in the pride of your nations, and your countries, and the armies, and the means of force that protect you within the borders thereof.

69 And in this way hath Satan used the enmity, that the Lord hath placed between him and us, to deceive us and lull us away into carnal security. And he lulleth us carefully, without our knowing, and leadeth us down into the misery of hell.

70 And I would that ye should know, my beloved children, that any institution that is set up among you that shall be a cause of your disobedience of the commandments of God, shall also cause your destruction.

71 And it is the commandment of the Lord that we should love each other according to the eternal laws of heaven. For it was according to these laws that we were created. And we are all the children of the same Eternal Father. And He hath used these same laws, by which He also liveth, to afford us the opportunity to become like Him and live forever in happiness, according to our desires of happiness.

72 And all of the unions that we create among ourselves, as well as the covenants, contracts, bonds, obligations, oaths, vows, performances, connections, associations, or expectations that we enter into during the days of our probation, have an end when we are dead.

73 And after we are dead, we shall be judged according to the works that we have done, even according to our obedience and conformity to the laws of heaven. And these same laws exist forever in the eternal worlds that have existed long before this mortal state in which we find ourselves. And these same laws shall exist in the eternal worlds after this mortal state, even forever.

74 And all things that are not established by the Lord, according to his word, which word is given according to these eternal laws of heaven, shall be thrown down and shaken and destroyed, and shall not remain after we are dead.

75 And these family units in which ye have divided yourselves are not according to the word of the Lord; and he hath commanded us against such things. Therefore, they are not eternal and shall not last after ye are dead.

76 And what think ye shall come to pass when ye are dead? Do ye think that in the kingdom of the Father we shall be divided into families? Do ye believe that ye shall take the pride which ye feel for your spouses and your children into the kingdom of God, and claim your stake there? I say unto you that ye shall not do any such thing.

77 For those of your own household are also your brothers and your sisters before God. And have ye not heard my words and my teachings concerning the creation and growth of a spirit? Did I not speak clearly unto you, and teach you that there existeth no marriage or families in the kingdom of the Father? For there are no such beings as male spirits or female spirits.

78 Yea, there are those spirits which were given a male body according to the flesh, and there were also those spirits that were given a female body according to the flesh. But in the kingdom of the Father there were no male spirits, neither were there females [*sic*] spirits, but we were all children of the Father, and had not yet determined for ourselves which gender we would take upon ourselves to bring us the happiness that each of us desired.

79 And when we return again to the kingdom of the Father, or in other words, to the spirit world from whence we came, we will return again as spirits without a gender.

80 And after the resurrection, there will be very few among us who will be blessed with the exalted bodies that the Gods possess, which bodies are male and female, and are given according to the eternal laws that govern the Celestial glory in the kingdom of our Father. And these bodies are given for the purposes of creation, and also for the fullness of joy of those who deserve the power that these bodies possess.

81 And I say unto you, that except ye abide by the commandments and laws of God, ye cannot attain to this glory. For strait is the gate, and narrow the way that leadeth unto the exaltation and the power of the continuation of lives, and few there be that find it. And ye do not find it because ye know not God. But if ye receive the commandments of God in the flesh, and abide by them, then shall ye know Him. And if ye know Him, ye shall receive your exaltation, and ye shall be in the same kingdom of glory in which God dwelleth.

82 For behold, this is eternal lives; even that ye might know the only wise and true God, who is our Father.

83 And broad is the way, which leadeth to destruction, and many there be who go in thereat; and this according to the commandments and the words that the Lord hath given unto us.

84 And because Satan hath entered in among us, there shall be many that come in among you in the clothing of sheep, but inwardly are ravening wolves. These shall call themselves prophets of God and set themselves up as your leaders and begin to teach unto you the flattering words that ye would desire of them.

85 And the Lord hath shown unto us the way in which we can judge these who would make such a claim. And I say unto you, that I will show you a sure way that ye might know how to judge a false prophet. For ye shall judge him by his works. And the flatteries of his mouth shall not uncover his unrighteousness. For Satan shall inspire him to speak unto you according to the peace that you have been taught shall be given unto you by the Holy Spirit. And Satan shall mimic this feeling and cause you to believe the words of the false prophet, as if they were the words of God.

86 And ye shall judge all men according to the commandments of God that I am giving to you this day, and which shall be taught unto you in the same likeness and in the same words by all the true prophets of God. And a true prophet of God will not add to or take away from these commandments that I have given unto you, and which I shall continue to give unto you.

87 And I know that God himself, shall come down among those of our posterity in the flesh. And when he is among them, he shall be known as the Son of God. And he shall be the Son of God. But because the Son shall be in the exact likeness of the Father, and shall have the power and authority of the Father, he shall be our God.

88 And he shall also give unto you the commandments that I am giving to you this day, which are the exact commandments that your mother Eve and I received from him after we left the garden of Eden. And these shall be the same words that he shall always speak unto the children of men, regardless in what time period they are given. Whether they be given unto them today, or yesterday, or tomorrow, they are the same.

89 For these commandments are eternal. And if they are eternal, then they are from God, and shall last beyond the days of our probation, even forever.

90 And any of those among you who claim that they are prophets of God, shall teach these things unto you. And again, I say unto you, that they shall not add to or take away from, nor shall they change these commandments in any way. And if they add to, or take away, or cause any of these things to be changed, then ye shall know of a surety that these are not men of God, but are false prophets.

91 And there shall be many false prophets who shall come among you preaching what they claim to be the words and commandments of God. And many of you shall be deceived by their words. And ye shall be deceived because ye do not keep the commandments of God. And many of you shall think that the commandments of God are too hard to keep, and that they do not bring you the joy that ye have been promised.

92 Ye shall say that it is vain to serve God; and what profit is it that we have kept his commandments and have walked mournfully before the Lord all the days of our lives? And we call the proud happy; yea, they that work wickedness are set up, and they who tempt God are even delivered in their time of need.

93 And in this way Satan shall have power over you and lull you away, in that ye will begin to believe that there is no heaven, nor is there a hell, and that there is no Satan, therefore there is no God. And many of you shall say amongst yourselves: Let us eat and drink and be merry, for tomorrow we die, but it shall be well with us.

94 For we will fear God. And by fearing Him, He will justify us in committing a little sin; yea, we can lie a little and take advantage of our neighbor because of his words; and we can dig a pit for our neighbor, so that our own family might not fall therein. And if we do all these things, and tomorrow we die, it shall be well with us. And God will beat us with a few stripes, but in the end, we will be saved in His kingdom.

95 And these things shall be taught unto you by those who are false prophets among you. Therefore, I would that ye should know these things, that ye might not be deceived by them.

96 And do not think that when ye stand before the judgment bar of God that these things will not be known. For ye shall know those things which ye did that were contrary to the commandments of God. But even so, there will be many of you who shall say unto the Father in that day: Oh, Father, have we not prophesied in Thy name, and in Thy name cast out the evil that is among us, and in Thy Holy Name done many wonderful works? Did we not take unto ourselves wives as Thou hast commanded us and brought up unto Thee many children whom we have taught to honor and respect Thee? And in the abundance of that which we took from the earth, did we not dedicate a portion thereof unto Thee?

97 And then will the Father say unto them: Ye did nothing in my Holy Name. For of all the things that I have required of you, ye have done none. For I was hungered and ye gave me no food; and I was thirsty and ye gave me no drink; and I was a stranger and ye took me not in, and was naked and ye clothed me not; I was sick and ye did not attend unto me. And I was imprisoned and ye visited me not.

98 And then ye shall answer the Father, saying: Oh, Father, when did we see Thee hungered, or athirst, or a stranger, or naked, or sick, or in prison, and did not administer unto Thee? And in all these things have we taken care of the needs of our families as Thou hast commanded us.

99 And when they were hungered, we fed them; and when they were thirsty, we gave them to drink; and when they were naked, we clothed them with all manner of fine clothing; and when they were sick, we administered unto their needs; and if any of them were in prison, we visited them.

100 And strangers we were counseled by our leaders to avoid, lest they come in among us and destroy our families and our beliefs.

101 But Oh, Father, when saw we Thee an hungered, or athirst, or a stranger, or naked, or sick, or in prison, and did not minister unto Thee? For had we known Thee, then we would have given all unto Thee, as Thou hast commanded us.

102 And then shall the Father say unto them: Yea, it is because ye did not know me that ye did not recognize me. Verily I say unto you, inasmuch as ye did it not to one of the least of those among you, ye did it not to me.

103 For behold, ye think that those of your own family are they which are the greatest among you. And ye have given these things unto them. But I did not command you to divide yourselves into these families in which ye have placed your priorities. And those who are the least among you are those who are not of your family, but whom I have commanded you to do unto as ye would have them do unto you.

104 And would ye not want that when ye are hungered, or athirst, or a stranger, or naked, or sick, or in prison, that others would attend to your needs, whether they are members of your family or not?

105 Yea, I never knew you, and you never knew me. For if ye had known me, then ye would have known that I am the Father of all, and that ye are all my children. And I have given you a commandment to do unto all of my children, which include the very least among you.

106 And ye have judged the beggar that is one of the least among you, and have denied him your sustenance because ye have said that he hath brought upon himself his own misery, therefore I will stay my hand and will not give unto him of my food, nor impart unto him of my substance that he may not suffer, for his punishments are just, because he hath offended God in his laziness.

107 And how can ye say that this beggar, who is my child, hath offended me, when ye do not know me? Know ye not that the world that I have caused to be created is for all of my children? And do ye not know, that my kingdom is for those who are the least among you?

108 Yea, blessed are the poor in spirit, for theirs is the kingdom of heaven. And blessed are they that mourn, for they shall be comforted. And blessed are the meek, for they shall inherit the earth when I finish my work thereon. And blessed are they which do hunger and thirst after righteousness, for they shall be filled. And blessed are the merciful, for they shall obtain mercy. And blessed are the peacemakers, for they shall be called the children of God. And blessed are the pure in heart, for they shall see God.

109 And these are those who are the least among you. And they are my children and belong to my family, which is the only family that I have ever caused to be organized among you. And because ye did not keep my commandments, ye are not pure in heart. And because ye are not pure in heart, ye shall not see me, neither shall ye know me. Depart from me ye that work iniquity.

110 And Adam continued his words, saying: And now, my beloved children, see that ye learn these commandments which I have given unto you, and also those which I am about to give unto you. And if ye keep these commandments, ye shall have a pure heart, and ye shall know God, and not be cast out of His presence.

FREQUENT REFERENCE

Throughout this book, the phrase "fulness of the everlasting Gospel" is used numerous times (sometimes with the word "fullness" misspelled), often redundantly. The reference comes from Joseph Smith—History 1:34 and refers to the words attributed to Jesus Christ as found in the Bible in Matthew, chapters 5, 6, and 7, which are repeated verbatim in the *unsealed part* of our new American scripture, the *Book of Mormon*, as 3 Nephi, chapters 12, 13, and 14.

On occasion, the phrase will be written as "the fullness of the Gospel of Jesus Christ," or "Jesus' everlasting gospel," or some variation, with all of these phrases referring to the same thing. In sum, this "gospel" provides the foundation of how humans should treat each other. According to the stories told about him, Jesus Christ stated that there was one requirement (commandment) by which all of humanity would be judged: whether or not the poor and needy are cared for. (See NT, Matthew 25:31–46.) In using the *Everlasting Gospel of Jesus Christ* as the main focus in the narrative of our new American scripture, it was the underlying goal and mission of the Real Illuminati® to eliminate poverty from the earth.

ABBREVIATIONS USED IN FOOTNOTES

Books by the Real Illuminati®

BOM	*The Book of Mormon—An Account Written by the Hand of Mormon, Upon Plates Taken from the Plates of Nephi.* Trans. Joseph Smith, Jr. Palmyra: E. B. Grandin, 1830.
SNS	Christopher. *Sacred, not Secret—The [Authorized and] Official Guide In Understanding the LDS Temple Endowment.* Salt Lake City: Worldwide United Publishing, 2008.
THOR	The Real Illuminati®. *The True History of Religion—How Religion Destroys the Human Race and What the Real Illuminati® Has Attempted to do Through Religion to Save the Human Race.* Melba: Worldwide United Publishing, 2019.
TSP	*The Sealed Portion—The Final Testament of Jesus Christ.* Trans. Christopher. San Diego: Worldwide United Publishing, 2004.
JS Bio	Christopher. *Without Disclosing My True Identity—The Authorized and Official Biography of the Mormon Prophet, Joseph Smith, Jr.* Melba: Worldwide United Publishing, 2012.

Books not by the Real Illuminati®

D&C	*The Doctrine and Covenants of The Church of Jesus Christ of Latter-day Saints Containing Revelations Given to Joseph Smith, the Prophet, with Some Additions by his Successors in the Presidency of the Church.* Salt Lake City: The Church of Jesus Christ of Latter-day Saints, 1981.
JSH	*Pearl of Great Price*, Joseph Smith—History.
OT / NT	Old Testament and New Testament, found in *The Holy Bible, Containing the Old and New Testaments, Translated Out of the Original Tongues: and With the Former Translations Diligently Compared and Revised By His Majesty's Special Command.* Authorized King James Version. England. 1611, revised 1629.
PGP	*The Pearl of Great Price: A Selection from the Revelations, Translations, and Narrations of Joseph Smith, First Prophet, Seer, and Revelator to the Church of Jesus Christ of Latter-day Saints.* Salt Lake City: LDS Church, 1976.

WORKS CITED

"5 Basic Necessities of Life." The Humanity Party®. humanityparty.com/5-basic-necessities-of-life.

"2009 Fort Hood shooting." *Wikipedia*. Wikimedia Foundation. 16 May 2021. en.wikipedia.org/wiki/2009_Fort_Hood_shooting.

Abler, Thomas S. "Scalping, Torture, Cannibalism and Rape: An Ethnohistorical Analysis of Conflicting Cultural Values in War." *Anthropologica*. Vol. 34 No. 1. 1992. 3–20. Found online at academia.edu/2573207/Scalping_Torture_Cannibalism_and_Rape_An_Ethnohistorical_Analysis_of_Conflicting_CulturalValues_in_WarAuthor_s_Thomas_S_Abler?auto=download.

"About Us – The Real Illuminati®." The Real Illuminati®. realilluminati.org/about-us.

"Accounts of Joseph Smith's First Vision." Church Historian's Press – The Church of Jesus Christ of Latter-day Saints. josephsmithpapers.org/site/accounts-of-the-first-vision.

"Amendment I," in "The Bill of Rights: A Transcription." National Archives. archives.gov/founding-docs/bill-of-rights-transcript.

"America the Beautiful." *Hymns*. The Church of Jesus Christ of Latter-day Saints, number 338. Found online at "Hymns." *Music Playlist*. Intellectual Reserve, Inc. churchofjesuschrist.org/music/library/hymns?lang=eng.

Anonymous, *Human Reality—Who We Are and Why We Exist!* Melba, ID: Worldwide United Publishing. 2009. realilluminati.org/human-reality.

"Apology," in G.M.A. Grube. *PLATO – Five Dialogues*. Indianapolis/Cambridge: Hackett Publishing Co. 2002. Second Edition revised by John M. Cooper. 21–44. Found online at sas.upenn.edu/~cavitch/pdf-library/Plato_Apology.pdf.

"Arab Spring." *Wikipedia*. Wikimedia Foundation. 21 May 2021. en.wikipedia.org/wiki/Arab_Spring.

"Arguments for presence of Christian interpolations," in "Josephus on Jesus." *Wikipedia*. Wikimedia Foundation. 11 May 2021. en.wikipedia.org/wiki/Josephus_on_Jesus#Arguments_for_presence_of_Christian_interpolations.

"Asenath." *Wikipedia*. Wikimedia Foundation. 9 May 2021. en.wikipedia.org/wiki/Asenath.

"At least 6,070 Black Lives Matter protests and other demonstrations have been held in the past 2,504 days." Elephrame. elephrame.com/textbook/BLM.

Bagley, Will. *Blood of the Prophets: Brigham Young and the Massacre at Mountain Meadows.* Norman, OK: University of Oklahoma Press. 2002. Found online at books.google.gm/books?id=eakce2R_mdkC&lpg=PP1&pg=PP1#v=onepage&q&f=false.

Bassett, Elder W. Mark. "For Our Spiritual Development and Learning." Oct. 2016 General Conference. The Church of Jesus Christ of Latter-day Saints. churchofjesuschrist.org/study/general-conference/2016/10/for-our-spiritual-development-and-learning?lang=eng.

Benson, Ezra Taft. "Fourteen Fundamentals in Following the Prophet." 26 Feb. 1980. Found online at speeches.byu.edu/talks/ezra-taft-benson/fourteen-fundamentals-following-prophet/.

"Biblical Literalist Chronology." *Wikipedia*. Wikimedia Foundation. 24 May 2021. en.wikipedia.org/wiki/Biblical_literalist_chronology.

Bigler, David and Will Bagley. *Innocent Blood: Essential Narratives of the Mountain Meadows Massacre. Kingdom in the West: The Mormons and the American Frontier.* Vol. 12. Norman, OK: The Arthur H. Clark Co. 2008.

"Black Lives Matter." *Wikipedia*. Wikimedia Foundation. 28 May 2021. en.wikipedia.org/wiki/Black_Lives_Matter.

Blue, Ron. "MASONIC TOPICS." 19 Jan. 1993. Edited by George S. Robinson, Jr. *A Page About Masonry*. web.mit.edu/dryfoo/www/Masonry/Misc/more-usa-faq.html.

The Book of Lehi—The Lost 116-Page Manuscript, found in *The Sealed Portion—The Final Testament of Jesus Christ*, 591–633. realilluminati.org/the-book-of-lehi.

The Book of Mormon—An Account Written by the Hand of Mormon, Upon Plates Taken from the Plates of Nephi. Joseph Smith, Jr., Author and Proprietor. Palmyra: E. B. Grandin, 1830. realilluminati.org/the-book-of-mormon.

"Book of Mormon, 1830." The Joseph Smith Papers – Church Historian's Press. josephsmithpapers.org/paper-summary/book-of-mormon-1830/7.

"The Book of Mormon (musical)." *Wikipedia*. Wikimedia Foundation. 28 May 2021. en.wikipedia.org/wiki/The_Book_of_Mormon_(musical).

Burr, Thomas. "Utah gun sales spike amid coronavirus scare." Mar. 24, 2020. *The Salt Lake Tribune*. sltrib.com/news/politics/2020/03/24/utah-gun-sales-spike-amid/.

"capitalism." Macmillan Dictionary. Macmillan Education Limited. macmillandictionary.com/dictionary/american/capitalism#capitalism 3.

"Capitalism - definition and meaning." Market Business News. marketbusinessnews.com/financial-glossary/capitalism-definition/.

"Captain Moroni and the Title of Liberty." YouTube. 26 Dec. 2014. youtu.be/V106VTMRAN4.

Cart, Julie. "Study Finds Utah Leads Nation in Antidepressant Use." 20 Feb. 2002. *Los Angeles Times.* latimes.com/archives/la-xpm-2002-feb-20-mn-28924-story.html.

"Category: Massacres of Native Americans." *Wikipedia.* Wikimedia Foundation. 23 February 2021. en.wikipedia.org/wiki/Category:Massacres_of_Native_Americans.

"Chaplain of the United States House of Representatives." *Wikipedia.* Wikimedia Foundation. 5 May 2021. en.wikipedia.org/wiki/Chaplain_of_the_United_States_House_of_Representatives.

"Chaplain of the United States Senate." *Wikipedia.* Wikimedia Foundation. 13 Feb. 2021. en.wikipedia.org/wiki/Chaplain_of_the_United_States_Senate.

Christopher. *666, The Mark of America—Seat of the Beast: The Apostle John's New Testament Revelation Unfolded.* San Diego: Worldwide United Pub., 2006. Found online at realilluminati.org/666-mark-of-america.

_____. *Sacred, not Secret—The [Authorized and] Official Guide In Understanding the LDS Temple Endowment.* Salt Lake City: Worldwide United Pub., 2008. Found online at realilluminati.org/sacred-not-secret.

_____. *Without Disclosing My True Identity—The Authorized and Official Biography of the Mormon Prophet, Joseph Smith, Jr.* Melba: Worldwide United Pub., 2012. Found online at realilluminati.org/without-disclosing-my-true-identity.

"City Creek Center." *Wikipedia.* Wikimedia Foundation. 26 May 2021. en.wikipedia.org/wiki/City_Creek_Center.

"Civil rights movement," *Wikipedia*, Wikimedia foundation, 27 May 2021, en.wikipedia.org/wiki/Civil_rights_movement.

Clayton, William. "Come, Come, Ye Saints," in *Hymns of The Church of Jesus Christ of Latter-day Saints.* Salt Lake City: The Church of Jesus Christ of Latter-day Saints, 1985. Number 326. Found online at churchofjesuschrist.org/music/library/hymns/come-come-ye-saints?lang=eng.

"Code of Hammurabi." *Wikipedia*. Wikimedia Foundation. 19 May 2021. en.wikipedia.org/wiki/Code_of_Hammurabi.

"Common Sense Is Nothing More Than a Deposit of Prejudices Laid Down in the Mind Before Age Eighteen." 29 Apr. 2014. Quote Investigator. quoteinvestigator.com/2014/04/29/common-sense/.

"Comoro Islands." *Wikipedia*. Wikimedia Foundation. 21 Feb. 2021. en.wikipedia.org/wiki/Comoro_Islands.

Coppins, McKay. "Bloomberg Report Takes Aim At Mormon Church For Online Gun Sales." 6 Feb. 2012. *Buzz Feed News*. Buzz Feed. buzzfeednews.com/article/mckaycoppins/bloomberg-report-takes-aim-at-mormon-church-for-on.

"Copyright Act of 1831." *Wikipedia*. Wikimedia Foundation. 17 Apr. 2021. en.wikipedia.org/wiki/Copyright_Act_of_1831.

"Corresponding Chapters in Editions of the Book of Mormon." The Joseph Smith Papers – Church Historian's Press. josephsmithpapers.org/back/corresponding-chapters-in-editions-of-the-book-of-mormon.

Cowdery, Oliver. "Address." *Latter Day Saints' Messenger and Advocate*. Vol. 1 No. 1 (Oct. 1834), 2. Found online at contentdm.lib.byu.edu/digital/collection/NCMP1820-1846/id/7002.

"Current Apostles Previous Profession." LDSminds. ldsminds.com/current-apostles-previous-profession/.

"Deaths of Tylee Ryan and J. J. Vallow." *Wikipedia*. Wikimedia Foundation. 23 May 2021. en.wikipedia.org/wiki/Deaths_of_Tylee_Ryan_and_J._J._Vallow.

Declaration of Independence. 4 July 1776. Transcript. National Archives. archives.gov/founding-docs/declaration-transcript.

"defraud." *Lexico Dictionaries | English*. Oxford University Press. lexico.com/en/definition/defraud.

Brown, Derren, "Do You Believe In GOD? | Faith and Fear | Derren Brown." YouTube. 16 Jan. 2021, youtu.be/6-xBFjQjFG4.

The Doctrine and Covenants of The Church of Jesus Christ of Latter-day Saints Containing Revelations Given to Joseph Smith, the Prophet, with Some Additions by his Successors in the Presidency of the Church. Salt Lake City: The Church of Jesus Christ of Latter-day Saints, 1981.

Doctrine and Covenants Instructor's Guide. Salt Lake City: The Church of Jesus Christ of Latter-day Saints, 1981. Found online at churchofjesuschrist.org/study/manual/doctrine-and-covenants-instructors-guide-religion-324-325/the-everlasting-covenant-the-fulness-of-the-gospel-lesson-25-sections-66-68?lang=eng.

"Donald Trump photo op at St. John's Church." *Wikipedia*. Wikimedia Foundation. 25 May 2021. en.wikipedia.org/wiki/Donald_Trump_photo_op_at_St._John%27s_Church.

"Dream Mine." *Wikipedia*. Wikimedia Foundation. 20 Dec. 2020. en.m.wikipedia.org/wiki/Dream_Mine.

"Eminent Spirits Appear to Wilford Woodruff." *Joseph Smith Foundation*. 4 Nov. 2020. josephsmithfoundation.org/wiki/eminent-spirits-appear-to-wilford-woodruff.

"Ephraim." *Wikipedia*. Wikimedia Foundation. 21 Apr. 2021. en.wikipedia.org/wiki/Ephraim.

"Emma Smith Bidamon, Nauvoo, IL, to Emma Pilgrim." 27 Mar. 1870. In Clark, John "Translation of Nephite Records." *The Return*. 15 July 1895, 2.

"enmity." *Lexico Dictionaries | English*. Oxford University Press. lexico.com/en/definition/enmity.

"Ethan Smith (clergyman)." *Wikipedia*. Wikimedia Foundation. 3 Apr. 2020. en.wikipedia.org/wiki/Ethan_Smith_(clergyman).

"Family tree," in "Abraham's family tree." *Wikipedia.* Wikimedia Foundation. 13 May 2021. en.wikipedia.org/wiki/Abraham%27s_family_tree#Family_tree.

"First Council of Nicaea." *Wikipedia*. Wikimedia Foundation. 19 May 2021. en.wikipedia.org/wiki/First_Council_of_Nicaea.

"The First Draft," in "Constitution of the United States—A History." National Archives. archives.gov/founding-docs/more-perfect-union.

Fixico, Donald L. "When Native Americans Were Slaughtered in the Name of 'Civilization.'" 2 Mar. 2018. *History.com*. A&E Television Networks. history.com/news/native-americans-genocide-united-states.

"Four-fold Mission of the Church." MormonWiki. 21 Sept. 2020. mormonwiki.com/Four-fold_Mission_of_the_Church.

Garlinghouse, Tom. "Freemasons: Behind the veil of secrecy." July 2020. *Live Science*. Future US. livescience.com/freemasons.html.

Garr, Arnold K. "Joseph Smith: Mayor of Nauvoo." *Mormon Historical Studies*. Vol. 3 No. 1. Spring 2002. 29–46. Found online at ensignpeakfoundation.org/wp-content/uploads/2013/05/MHS3.1Spring2002Garr.pdf.

"George P. Lee." *Wikipedia*. Wikimedia Foundation. 24 Sept. 2020. en.wikipedia.org/wiki/George_P._Lee.

"The Gettysburg Address." 19 Nov. 1863. Abraham Lincoln Online. abrahamlincolnonline.org/lincoln/speeches/gettysburg.htm.

Glader, Paul. "Mormon Church Stockpiled $100 Billion Intended for Charities and Misled LDS Members, Whistleblower Says." 17 Dec. 2019. *Newsweek*. newsweek.com/mormon-church-stockpiled-100-billion-intended-charities-misled-lds-members-whistleblower-says-1477809.

"God Save the King." *Hymns*. The Church of Jesus Christ of Latter-day Saints, number 341. Found online at "Hymns." *Music Playlist*. Intellectual Reserve, Inc. churchofjesuschrist.org/music/library/hymns?lang=eng.

Gould, Skye and Lauren F. Friedman. "Something startling is going on with antidepressant use around the world." 4 Feb. 2016. *Business Insider*. Insider Inc. businessinsider.com/countries-largest-antidepressant-drug-users-2016-2?r=US&IR=T.

"Governor of Utah Territory," in "Brigham Young." *Wikipedia*. Wikimedia Foundation. 26 May 2021. en.wikipedia.org/wiki/Brigham_Young#Governor_of_Utah_Territory.

"Greek mythology." *Wikipedia*. Wikimedia Foundation. 20 Apr. 2021. en.wikipedia.org/wiki/Greek_mythology.

Groat, Joel B. "Joseph Smith's Changing First Vision Accounts." 15 July 2011. Mormons In Transition - Institute for Religious Research. mit.irr.org/joseph-smiths-changing-first-vision-accounts.

Groth, Aimee. "The REAL REASON So Many Mormons Become Executives And Political Leaders." 22 June 2011. *Business Insider*. businessinsider.com/mormon-business-leaders-2011-7.

"Gun History Connected To Church History." *LDS Gunsite*. Reddpublishing. ldsgunsite.blogspot.com/p/john-browning.html.

"Gun laws in Utah." *Wikipedia*. Wikimedia Foundation. 17 May 2021. en.wikipedia.org/wiki/Gun_laws_in_Utah.

"Hammurabi." *Wikipedia*. Wikimedia Foundation. 15 May 2021. en.wikipedia.org/wiki/Hammurabi.

Harden, R. David. "How nations fail: Lessons for America." 27 Oct. 2019. *The Hill* – Capital Hill Publishing Corp. thehill.com/opinion/national-security/467595-how-nations-fail-lessons-for-america.

"Hebrews." *Wikipedia*. Wikimedia Foundation. 6 May 2021. en.wikipedia.org/wiki/Hebrews.

"History, 1838–1856, volume A-1 [23 December 1805–30 August 1834]." Church History Library. Salt Lake City, UT. Found online at josephsmithpapers.org/paper-summary/history-1838-1856-volume-a-1-23-december-1805-30-august-1834/1.

Holmes, David L. "The Founding Fathers, Deism, and Christianity." *Encyclopedia Britannica.* britannica.com/topic/The-Founding-Fathers-Deism-and-Christianity-1272214.

The Holy Bible, Containing the Old and New Testaments, Translated Out of the Original Tongues: and With the Former Translations Diligently Compared and Revised By His Majesty's Special Command. Authorized King James Version. England. 1611, revised 1629.

Horne, Robert. "Reminiscences of the Church in Nauvoo." *Millennial Star.* Vol. 55 No. 36. 4 Sept. 1893. 585. Found online at contentdm.lib.byu.edu/digital/collection/MStar/id/19227.

"How can we become like the 2,000 stripling warriors and Captain Moroni?" *Gospel Lessons for LDS Members Attending Basic Training.* The Church of Jesus Christ of Latter-day Saints. abn.churchofjesuschrist.org/study/manual/gospel-lessons-for-lds-members-attending-basic-training/how-can-we-become-like-the-2000-stripling-warriors-and-captain-moroni?lang=eng.

"Human Reality - A Message to the Youth of the World." Marvelous Work and a Wonder. 21 Oct. 2015. YouTube. youtu.be/z0U3aeUNtck.

The Humanity Party®. (THumP®). 2020. humanityparty.com.

"The Humanity Party® Challenges the United States to End Worldwide Underage Prostitution in One Week!" YouTube. 8 Oct. 2020. youtu.be/vg6-AX8hhJ0.

"The Humanity Party®, in collaboration with a Marvelous Work and a Wonder®, Publishes Memorandum ..." The Humanity Party®. 25 May 2018. humanityparty.com/post/the-humanity-party-in-collaboration-with-a-marvelous-work-and-a-wonder-publishes-memorandum.

"The Humanity Party® introduces their Economic Plan To End Worldwide Poverty – Official Release." YouTube. 14 Dec. 2020. youtu.be/xruLy1LG-f0.

"The Humanity Party® Solves the Israeli - Palestinian Conflict www.HUMANITYPARTY.com." YouTube. 25 Sept. 2017. youtu.be/502SfQ6Mues.

"Hurricane Katrina: Wrath of God?" 5 Oct. 2005. *NBC News.* NBC Universal. nbcnews.com/id/wbna9600878.

"I Am a Child of God." *Hymns.* The Church of Jesus Christ of Latter-day Saints, number 301. Found online at "Hymns." *Music Playlist.* Intellectual Reserve, Inc. churchofjesuschrist.org/music/library/hymns?lang=eng. Written in 1957 by Naomi W. Randall.

"Ida-Holland Audio." *Pearl Publishing, LLC.* pearlpublishing.net/bom/download/Ida-Holland-audio.mp3.

"Ida Smith and The Man From Joe's Bar and Grill," The Real Illuminati®, realilluminati.org/the-man-from-joe-s-bar-and-grill.

"Idle Hands Are the Devil's Workshop." *Wiktionary*. 5 Dec. 2020. en.wiktionary.org/wiki/idle_hands_are_the_devil%27s_workshop.

Imlay, Ashley. "Bill to allow Utahns to carry concealed guns without any permit ignites debate." 22 Jan. 2021. *Deseret News*.deseret.com/utah/2021/1/22/22244734/concealed-carry-bill-gun-rights-legislature-concealed-weapons-ignites-debate-mental-health-crisis.

"Immigration." *Church News*. Intellectual Reserve, Inc. https://newsroom.churchofjesuschrist.org/official-statement/immigration.

"Immigration: Church Issues New Statement." 10 June 2011. The Church of Jesus Christ of Latter-day Saints. newsroom.churchofjesuschrist.org/article/immigration-church-issues-new-statement.

"Jacob." *Wikipedia*. Wikimedia Foundation. 26 May 2021. en.wikipedia.org/wiki/Jacob.

Jaradat, Mya. "Understanding America: Is there a connection between faith and firearms?" 3 Dec. 2020. *Deseret News*. deseret.com/indepth/2020/12/3/21455886/america-faith-firearms-gun-control-gun-rights-gun-violence-evangelical-christian-gun-policy.

Jastrow, Jr., Morris, B. Eerdmans, Marcus Jastrow, and Louis Ginzberg. "Birthright." *Jewish Encyclopedia*. jewishencyclopedia.com/articles/3323-birthright.

"Jefferson Bible." *Wikipedia*. Wikimedia Foundation. 8 May 2021. en.wikipedia.org/wiki/Jefferson_Bible.

Jefferson, Thomas. *Notes on the State of Virginia*. Boston: Lilly and Wait. 1832. Found online at Library of Congress. loc.gov/item/03004902/.

"Judaism," in "Polygamy." *Wikipedia*. Wikimedia Foundation. 27 May 2021. en.wikipedia.org/wiki/Polygamy#Judaism.

"Jewish & LDS (Mormon) Parallels." *Pearl Publishing*. Pearl Publishing, LLC. pearlpublishing.net/tsp/download/JewishLDSParallels.4.4.20.pdf.

"Jews as the Chosen People." *Wikipedia*. Wikimedia Foundation. 18 May 2021. en.wikipedia.org/wiki/Jews_as_the_chosen_people.

"Joseph (Genesis)." *Wikipedia*. Wikimedia Foundation. 24 May 2021. en.wikipedia.org/wiki/Joseph_(Genesis).

"Joseph Smith discourse, July 9, 1843, in Nauvoo, Illinois as reported by Willard Richards." In Hedges, Andrew H., Alex D. Smith, and Brent M. Rogers, eds. *The Joseph Smith Papers, Journals, Volume 3: 1843–1844*. Salt Lake City: Church Historians Press. 2015. 56.

"Josephus on Jesus." *Wikipedia*. Wikimedia Foundation. 11 May 2021. en.wikipedia.org/wiki/Josephus_on_Jesus.

Journal of Discourses. 26 vols. London/Liverpool: Latter Day Saints' Book Depot. 1855–86. jod.mrm.org/10/282.

"Judaism: The Written Law – Torah." *Jewish Virtual Library*. jewishvirtuallibrary.org/the-written-law-torah.

Kennedy, Lesley, et al. "President Trump Declares State of Emergency for COVID-19." 25 Mar. 2020. National Conference of State Legislatures. ncsl.org/ncsl-in-dc/publications-and-resources/president-trump-declares-state-of-emergency-for-covid-19.aspx.

"Killings and aftermath of the Mountain Meadows Massacre." *Wikipedia*. Wikimedia Foundation. 26 Feb. 2021. en.wikipedia.org/wiki/Killings_and_aftermath_of_the_Mountain_Meadows_Massacre.

Kimball, Spencer W. "A Report of My Stewardship." *Ensign*. May 1981. Found online at churchofjesuschrist.org/study/ensign/1981/05/a-report-of-my-stewardship?lang=eng.

"King James Version." *Wikipedia*. Wikimedia Foundation. 24 May 2021. en.wikipedia.org/wiki/King_James_Version.

"Kings & Queens - by Age of Accession to the Throne." *Britroyals*. britroyals.com/ascend.asp.

"Kirtland Safety Society." The Joseph Smith Papers – Church Historian's Press. josephsmithpapers.org/topic/kirtland-safety-society.

"Kirtland Safety Society." *Wikipedia*. Wikimedia Foundation. 22 Apr. 2021. en.wikipedia.org/wiki/Kirtland_Safety_Society.

"Landmark Legislation: Thirteenth, Fourteenth, & Fifteenth Amendments." United States Senate. senate.gov/artandhistory/history/common/generic/CivilWarAmendments.htm.

"Latter Day Saint movement," in "One true church." *Wikipedia*. Wikimedia Foundation. 24 May 2021. en.wikipedia.org/wiki/One_true_church#Latter_Day_Saint_movement.

"Latter Day Saint polygamy in the late-19th century." *Wikipedia*. Wikimedia Foundation. 5 Apr. 2021. en.wikipedia.org/wiki/Latter_Day_Saint_polygamy_in_the_late-19th_century.

"Latter-day Saints" in "Apostasy." *Wikipedia*. Wikimedia Foundation. 14 May 2021. en.wikipedia.org/wiki/Apostasy#Latter-day_Saints.

"The Lee Letters." *Sunstone*. Vol. 13 No. 4. Aug. 1989. 50–5. Found online at sunstonemagazine.com/wp-content/uploads/sbi/issues/072.pdf

"Levant." *Wikipedia*. Wikimedia Foundation. 23 May 2021. en.wikipedia.org/wiki/Levant.

"The Life and Morals of Jesus of Nazareth." *Thomas Jefferson Encyclopedia*. Monticello and the University of Virginia in Charlottesville. monticello.org/site/research-and-collections/life-and-morals-jesus-nazareth.

"Life, Liberty and the pursuit of Happiness." *Wikipedia*. Wikimedia Foundation. 20 May 2021. en.wikipedia.org/wiki/Life,_Liberty_and_the_pursuit_of_Happiness.

Lindsey, Daryl. "Follow the profit: How Mormon culture made Utah a hotbed for multi-level marketers." 8 September 2016. KUTV News. kutv.com/news/local/follow-the-profit-how-mormon-culture-made-utah-a-hotbed-for-multi-level-marketers.

"List of African-American United States representatives." *Wikipedia*. Wikimedia Foundation. 22 May 2021. en.wikipedia.org/wiki/List_of_African-American_United_States_representatives.

"List of African-American United States senators." *Wikipedia*. Wikimedia Foundation. 22 May 2021. en.wikipedia.org/wiki/List_of_African-American_United_States_senators.

"List of Latter Day Saints." *Wikipedia*. Wikimedia Foundation. 8 May 2021. en.wikipedia.org/wiki/List_of_Latter_Day_Saints.

"List of protests against the Vietnam War," *Wikipedia*, Wikimedia Foundation, 18 May 2021, en.wikipedia.org/wiki/List_of_protests_against_the_Vietnam_War.

LiveseySolar. "Head Versus Heart: Why Emotion Is More Powerful than Logic." *LiveseySolar Cataract & Laser Eye Surgery Marketing*. 6 Nov. 2013. LiveseySolar. liveseysolar.com/head-versus-heart-why-emotion-is-more-powerful-than-logic/.

"Lost 116 pages." *Wikipedia*. Wikimedia Foundation. 10 May 2021. en.wikipedia.org/wiki/Lost_116_pages.

Lutz, John Sutton. "Making the Lazy Indian," in *Makuk: a New History of Aboriginal-White Relations*. Vancouver: UBC Press, 2014. 31–47. Found online at web.uvic.ca/stolo/pdf/Lutz%20CHap3%20frm%20Makuk%20(2015_0 8_30%2007_20_22%20UTC).pdf.

MacKay, Michael Hubbard and Gerrit J. Dirkmaat. "Firsthand Witness Accounts of the Translation Process" In *The Coming Forth of the Book of Mormon: A Marvelous Work and a Wonder*, edited by Dennis L. Largey, Andrew H. Hedges, John Hilton III, and Kerry Hull. Provo, UT: Religious Studies Center; Salt Lake City: Deseret Book. 2015. 61–79. Found online at rsc.byu.edu/coming-forth-book-mormon/firsthand-witness-accounts-translation-process.

"The Man From Joe's Bar and Grill," The Real Illuminati®, realilluminati.org/the-man-from-joe-s-bar-and-grill.

"Manasseh (Tribal Patriarch)." *Wikipedia*. Wikimedia Foundation. 26 Nov. 2020. en.wikipedia.org/wiki/Manasseh_(tribal_patriarch).

"Manifest Destiny." *Wikipedia*. Wikimedia Foundation. 12 May 2021. en.wikipedia.org/wiki/Manifest_destiny.

"March for Our Lives." *Wikipedia*. Wikimedia Foundation. 20 May 2021. en.wikipedia.org/wiki/March_for_Our_Lives.

"Memorandum." The Humanity Party® Board of Directors in collaboration with The Marvelous Work and a Wonder®. 25 May 2018. humanityparty.com/memorandum.

"The Missouri Mormon War." Missouri Office of the Secretary of State – Missouri State Library – Missouri State Archives. sos.mo.gov/archives/resources/mormon.asp.

Montague, Zach. "Holding It Aloft, He Incited a Backlash. What Does the Bible Mean to Trump?" 2 June 2020. *The New York Times*. nytimes.com/2020/06/02/us/politics/trump-bible-st-johns.html.

"Mormonism." 5 June 1881. *Kansas City Daily Journal*. 1.

"Mormonism," in "Chosen people." *Wikipedia*. Wikimedia Foundation. 23 May 2021. en.wikipedia.org/wiki/Chosen_people#Mormonism.

"Moroni, Comoros." *Wikipedia*. Wikimedia Foundation. 6 Apr. 2021. en.wikipedia.org/wiki/Moroni,_Comoros.

"Most Republican States 2021." World Population Review. worldpopulationreview.com/state-rankings/most-republican-states.

Murray, Peter Noel. "How Emotions Influence What We Buy." 26 Feb. 2013. *Psychology Today*. Sussex Publishers. psychologytoday.com/us/blog/inside-the-consumer-mind/201302/how-emotions-influence-what-we-buy.

"My Country, 'Tis of Thee." *Hymns*. The Church of Jesus Christ of Latter-day Saints, number 339. Found online at "Hymns." *Music Playlist*. Intellectual Reserve, Inc. churchofjesuschrist.org/music/library/hymns?lang=eng.

"The New Colossus." *Wikipedia.* Wikimedia Foundation. 26 May 2021. en.wikipedia.org/wiki/The_New_Colossus.

"No justice, no peace." *Wikipedia.* Wikimedia Foundation. 26 Apr. 2021. en.wikipedia.org/wiki/No_justice,_no_peace.

Oaks, Dallin H. *The Lord's Way.* Salt Lake City: Deseret Book. 1991.

Oaks, Elder Dallin H. "The Only True and Living Church." The Church of Jesus Christ of Latter-Day Saints. churchofjesuschrist.org/study/new-era/2011/08/the-only-true-and-living-church?lang=eng.

"Oath of a Freeman." *Wikipedia.* Wikimedia Foundation. 18 May 2021. en.wikipedia.org/wiki/Oath_of_a_Freeman.

"The Organization of The Church of Jesus Christ of Latter-day Saints." American Prophet – Timeline. PBS. pbs.org/americanprophet/18300406.html.

Ornelas, Christopher. "The Magician's Oath: A Conversation with Pat Hammond on Magic, Science, and the Wind." *Disclosure: from the end of the line.* May 2021. 16-29. Found online at drachen.org/wp-content/uploads/2012/06/DiscourseIssue12_0.pdf.

Packer, Boyd K. "Scriptures." *Ensign.* Nov. 1982. Found online at churchofjesuschrist.org/study/general-conference/1982/10/scriptures?lang=eng.

The Parallel Book Of Mormon: The 1830, 1837, and 1840 Editions. Introduction by Curt A. Bench. Salt Lake City: Smith-Pettit Foundation, 2008.

Parker, Cameron J. "Cumorah's Cave." *Journal of Book of Mormon Studies.* Vol. 13 No. 1. 2004. 50–7, 170–1. Found online at scholarsarchive.byu.edu/jbms/vol13/iss1/6/.

Partridge, Scott H. "The Failure of the Kirtland Safety Society." *BYU Studies.* Vol.12 No. 4. Summer 1972. 437–54. Found online at byustudies.byu.edu/wp-content/uploads/2020/02/12.4PartridgeFailure-1518c5ab-4202-41eb-84b4-0cc8fce9fc5e.pdf.

"Party affiliation among Mormons." Pew Research Center. pewforum.org/religious-landscape-study/religious-tradition/mormon/party-affiliation/.

The Pearl of Great Price: A Selection from the Revelations, Translations, and Narrations of Joseph Smith, First Prophet, Seer, and Revelator to the Church of Jesus Christ of Latter-day Saints. Salt Lake City: LDS Church, 1976.

Persinger, Dr. Michael, "The God Helmet, Through the Wormhole, Uncut" Vimeo. vimeo.com/144332709.

"The Philosophy of Jesus of Nazareth." *Thomas Jefferson Encyclopedia*. Monticello and the University of Virginia in Charlottesville. monticello.org/site/research-and-collections/philosophy-jesus-nazareth.

Poe, Edgar Allen. "The System of Dr. Tarr and Prof. Fether." Found online at Wikisource, en.wikisource.org/wiki/The System of Doctor Tarr and Professor Fether.

"Press Coverage of Lee's Excommunication Ambivalent." *Sunstone*. Vol. 13 No. 4. Aug. 1989. 47–9. Found online at sunstonemagazine.com/wp-content/uploads/sbi/issues/072.pdf.

"PRIDE." *Lexico Dictionaries | English*. Oxford University Press. lexico.com/en/definition/pride.

"Priesthood Is the Authority to Act in God's Name." *Ensign*. June 2011. churchofjesuschrist.org/study/ensign/2011/06/priesthood-is-the-authority-to-act-in-gods-name?lang=eng.

"Priesthood Principles" *General Handbook: Serving in The Church of Jesus Christ of Latter-Day Saints*. The Church of Jesus Christ of Latter-Day Saints. 2021. abn.churchofjesuschrist.org/study/manual/general-handbook/3-priesthood-principles?lang=eng#p1.

Randal, Henry S. *The Life of Thomas Jefferson*, Vol. 3. New York: Derby & Jackson. 1858. Found online at google.com/books/edition/The Life of Thomas Jefferson/ gbjAAAAMAAJ?hl=en&gbpv=1.

Read, James H. "James Madison," in *The First Amendment Encyclopedia: Presented by the John Seigenthaler Chair of Excellence in First Amendment Studies*. 2009. Middle Tennessee State University. mtsu.edu/first-amendment/article/1220/james-madison.

The Real Illuminati®. *Pentateuch Illuminated: A Five Part Series Introducing A New American Scripture—How and Why the Real Illuminati® Created the Book of Mormon*. Melba: Worldwide United Publishing, 2020. realilluminati.org/pentateuch-illuminated.

——————. *The True History of Religion—How Religion Destroys the Human Race and What the Real Illuminati® Has Attempted to do Through Religion to Save the Human Race*. Melba: Worldwide United Publishing, 2019. realilluminati.org/the-true-history-of-religion.

"Record of the Twelve, 14 February–28 August 1835." The Joseph Smith Papers – The Church of Jesus Christ of Latter-day Saints. josephsmithpapers.org/paper-summary/record-of-the-twelve-14-february-28-august-1835/7.

"Recorded accounts of the vision," in "First Vision." *Wikipedia*. Wikimedia Foundation. 28 May 2021. en.wikipedia.org/wiki/First_Vision#Recorded_accounts_of_the_vision.

Rees, Robert A. and Clifton H. Jolley. "Commentary: Utahns and Mormons need to recalibrate our love of guns." 5 Mar. 2018. *The Salt Lake Tribune*. sltrib.com/opinion/commentary/2018/03/05/commentary-guns-utahns-and-mormons/.

"Religious affiliations of presidents of the United States." *Wikipedia*. Wikimedia Foundation. 23 May 2021. en.wikipedia.org/wiki/Religious_affiliations_of_presidents_of_the_United_States.

"Religious organizations," in "List of wealthiest organizations." *Wikipedia*. Wikimedia Foundation. 24 May 2021. en.wikipedia.org/wiki/Apostasy#Latter-day_Saints.

"Remarks by President Brigham Young, made in the Tabernacle, Great Salt Lake City, November 6, 1863." *Journal of Discourses*, 26 vols. London/Liverpool: Latter Day Saints' Book Depot, 1855–86. Vol. 10. 282–8. Found online at jod.mrm.org/10/282.

Renlund, Elder Dale G. "Infuriating Unfairness." Apr. 2021 General Conference. The Church of Jesus Christ of Latter-day Saints. abn.churchofjesuschrist.org/study/general-conference/2021/04/25renlund?lang=eng.

"Report: Poverty Rate in Gaza Strip Highest Worldwide." 21 Oct. 2019. Asharq Al-Awsat - H H Saudi Research and Marketing LTD. english.aawsat.com/home/article/1954881/report-poverty-rate-gaza-strip-highest-worldwide.

Riess, Jana. "Mormons and guns: It's time to set limits." 24 July 2018. Religion News Service. religionnews.com/2018/07/24/mormons-and-guns-its-time-to-set-limits.

Roberts, B.H. *History of the Church of Jesus Christ of Latter-day Saints*, 7 vols. Salt Lake City: Deseret Book Co., 1902–12.

"Roman mythology." *Wikipedia*. Wikimedia Foundation. 5 May 2021. en.wikipedia.org/wiki/Roman_mythology.

Romney, Marion G. "The Role of Bishops in Welfare Services." Oct. 1977 General Conference. The Church of Jesus Christ of Latter-day Saints. abn.churchofjesuschrist.org/study/general-conference/1977/10/the-role-of-bishops-in-welfare-services?lang=eng,

Sampey, John R. "The Code of Hammurabi and the Laws of Moses." *Baptist Review and Expositor.* 1904. Vol. 1 Issue 2. 233–43. Found online at *SAGE Journals.* journals.sagepub.com/doi/abs/10.1177/003463730400100207?journalCode=raea.

"Saturday's Warrior." *Wikipedia.* Wikimedia Foundation. 16 Apr. 2021. en.wikipedia.org/wiki/Saturday%27s_Warrior.

"School strike for climate." *Wikipedia.* Wikimedia Foundation. 22 May 2021. en.wikipedia.org/wiki/School_strike_for_climate.

"science," *Lexico Dictionaries | English.* Oxford University Press. lexico.com/en/definition/science.

The Sealed Portion—The Final Testament of Jesus Christ. Trans. Christopher. San Diego: Worldwide United Publishing, 2004.

"Seer stone." Church Historians Press – The Church of Jesus Christ of Latter-day Saints. josephsmithpapers.org/topic/seer-stone.

"September 11 attacks." *Wikipedia.* Wikimedia Foundation. 28 May 2021. en.m.wikipedia.org/wiki/September_11_attacks.

"Seven Social Sins." *Wikipedia.* Wikimedia Foundation. 10 Jan. 2021. en.wikipedia.org/wiki/Seven_Social_Sins.

"Since 1982, Subtitle Has Defined Book as 'Another Testament of Jesus Christ.'" 2 Jan. 1988. *Church News.* Intellectual Reserve, Inc. thechurchnews.com/archives/1988-01-02/since-1982-subtitle-has-defined-book-as-another-testament-of-jesus-christ-154250.

Skousen, Royal. "Another Account of Mary Whitmer's Viewing of the Golden Plates: The Interpreter Foundation." *The Interpreter Foundation | Increasing Understanding of Scripture One Article at a Time*, 25 Apr. 2014. journal.interpreterfoundation.org/another-account-of-mary-whitmers-viewing-of-the-golden-plates/.

Smith, Ethan. *View of the Hebrews: Exhibiting the Destruction of Jerusalem; the Certain Restoration of Judah and Israel; the Present State of Judah and Israel; and an Address of the Prophet Isaiah Relative to Their Restoration.* Poultney, VT: Smith & Shute. 1823. Found online at archive.org/details/viewhebrewsexhi00smitgoog/page/n4/mode/2up.

Smith, Joseph Jr., Author and Proprietor. *The Book of Mormon—An Account Written by the Hand of Mormon, Upon Plates Taken from the Plates of Nephi.* Palmyra: E. B. Grandin, 1830. realilluminati.org/the-book-of-mormon.

Smith, Joseph. *Elders' Journal.* July 1838. 42–3. Found online at josephsmithpapers.org/paper-summary/elders-journal-july-1838/10.

Solly, Meilan. "Historical Context," in "158 Resources to Understand Racism In America." 4 June 2020. *Smithsonian Magazine*. smithsonianmag.com/history/158-resources-understanding-systemic-racism-america-180975029/#sectionOne.

Stack, Peggy Fletcher. "How much do top Mormon leaders make? Leaked pay stubs may surprise you." 26 Jan. 2017. *The Salt Lake Tribune*. archive.sltrib.com/article.php?id=4800350&itype=cmsid.

Stack, Peggy Fletcher. "New LDS emphasis: Care for the needy." 9 Dec. 2009. *The Salt Lake Tribune*. archive.sltrib.com/story.php?ref=/lds/ci_13965607.

"The Star-Spangled Banner." *Hymns*. The Church of Jesus Christ of Latter-day Saints, number 340. Found online at "Hymns." *Music Playlist*. Intellectual Reserve, Inc. churchofjesuschrist.org/music/library/hymns?lang=eng.

"The state of Church and State." *AFA Journal*. July 2001. afajournal.org/past-issues/2001/july/the-state-of-church-and-state/.

"The State of Mental Health in America." 2021. Mental Health America. mhanational.org/issues/state-mental-health-america.

"Statue of Liberty, The New Colossus." National Park Service. U.S. Department of the Interior. nps.gov/stli/learn/historyculture/colossus.htm.

Stevenson, Elder Gary E. "Look to the Book, Look to the Lord." Oct. 2016 General Conference. The Church of Jesus Christ of Latter-day Saints. churchofjesuschrist.org/study/general-conference/2016/10/look-to-the-book-look-to-the-lord.

Stevenson, Elder Gary E. "Look to the Book, Look to the Lord." YouTube. 1 Oct. 2016. youtu.be/LHxUcozPcfg.

"Suicide Rate by Country 2021." World Population Review. worldpopulationreview.com/country-rankings/suicide-rate-by-country.

"Sustaining the General Authorities of the Church." *Improvement Era*. June 1945. 354. Found online at archive.org/details/improvementera4806unse/page/n35/mode/2up.

Swaine, Joe, Douglas MacMillan and Michelle Boorstein. "Investigations: Mormon Church has misled members on $100 billion tax-exempt investment fund, whistleblower alleges." 17 Dec. 2019. *The Washington Post*. washingtonpost.com/investigations/mormon-church-has-misled-members-on-100-billion-tax-exempt-investment-fund-whistleblower-alleges/2019/12/16/e3619bd2-2004-11ea-86f3-3b5019d451db_story.html.

Tait, Brittany. "Hundreds Of People Line Up Outside Gun Store In Orem." 9 Jan. 2021. KSL TV – Bonneville International. ksltv.com/452788/hundreds-of-people-line-up-outside-gun-store-in-orem/.

"Testimony of David Whitmer." 15 Nov. 1879. *Saints' Herald.* 341.

"Thomas Jefferson to C. W. F. Dumas." 6 May 1786. National Archives. founders.archives.gov/documents/Jefferson/01-09-02-0389.

"Thomas Jefferson to John Adams." 12 Oct. 1813. National Archives. founders.archives.gov/documents/Adams/99-02-02-6182.

"Thomas Jefferson to John Norvell." 11 June 1807. National Archives. founders.archives.gov/documents/Jefferson/99-01-02-5737.

"Thomas Jefferson to the Republicans of Washington County, Maryland." 31 Mar. 1809. National Archives. founders.archives.gov/documents/Jefferson/03-01-02-0088.

"Thoughts on Lesson Thirty-Eight, by Boyd K. Packer, Ensign August 1975 | Sep. 21, 2005," section titled "Dallin H. Oaks, *The Lord's Way*," LDS Living, 21 Sept 2005. ldsliving.com/Thoughts-on-Lesson-Thirty-Eight/s/5388.

Tienda, Marta and Susana M. Sanchez. "Latin American Immigration to the United States." *Daedalus: Journal of the American Academy of Arts & Sciences.* Vol. 142 No. 3. Summer 2013. 48–64. Found online at amacad.org/sites/default/files/daedalus/downloads/Su2013_Immigration-and-the-Future-of-America.pdf.

"Title Page of the Book of Mormon." The Church of Jesus Christ of Latter-day Saints. churchofjesuschrist.org/study/scriptures/bofm/bofm-title?lang=eng.

"Toddler Besties Share Huge Hug on Sidewalk." Inside Edition. YouTube. 11 Sept 2019. youtu.be/nDQezECAxtQ.

Townsend, Tim. "Missouri remains land of religious promise for Mormons." 20 Sept. 2021. *The Washington Post.* washingtonpost.com/national/on-faith/missouri-remains-land-of-religious-promise-for-mormons/2012/09/20/d40cbbd4-0348-11e2-9132-f2750cd65f97_story.html.

"Transcription Telephone Call – 10:50 am, 12 June 2007, Ida Smith & Jeffrey (Jeff) Holland." *Pearl Publishing, LLC.* pearlpublishing.net/bom/download/HollandTelephoneTranscript.pdf.

True to the Faith: A Gospel Reference. Salt Lake City: The Church of Jesus Christ of Latter-day Saints. 2004. Found online at churchofjesuschrist.org/study/manual/true-to-the-faith/spirit?lang=eng.

"United States Bill of Rights." *Wikipedia.* Wikimedia Foundation. 28 May 2021. en.wikipedia.org/wiki/United_States_Bill_of_Rights.

"Utah v. Lafferty." *Wikipedia.* Wikimedia Foundation. 3 Apr. 2021. en.wikipedia.org/wiki/Utah_v._Lafferty.

Van Dülmen, Richard. *The Society of Enlightenment: the rise of the middle class and Enlightenment culture in Germany.* Polity Press: 1992.

Wan, William. "The coronavirus pandemic is pushing America into a mental health crisis." 4 May 2020. *The Washington Post*. washingtonpost.com/health/2020/05/04/mental-health-coronavirus/.

Weaver, Sarah Jane. "'Mormon' Is Out: Church Releases Statement on How to Refer to the Organization." 16 Aug. 2018. *Church News*. Intellectual Reserve, Inc. churchofjesuschrist.org/church/news/mormon-is-out-church-releases-statement-on-how-to-refer-to-the-organization?lang=eng.

Weaver, Sarah Jane. "Raising Our Hands to Sustain Is Also a Promise to 'Do Our Part.'" 31 Mar. 2018. *Church News*. Intellectual Reserve, Inc. churchofjesuschrist.org/church/news/raising-our-hands-to-sustain-is-also-a-promise-to-do-our-part?lang=eng.

West, Camille. "Age Changes for Youth Progression and Ordination Announced." 14 Dec. 2018. *Church News*. Intellectual Reserve, Inc. https://www.churchofjesuschrist.org/church/news/age-changes-for-youth-progression-and-ordination-announced?lang=eng.

West, Chad. "Legislative Prayer: Historical Tradition and Contemporary Issues." *Utah Law Review*. Vol. 2019 No. 3. 709–34. Found online at dc.law.utah.edu/cgi/viewcontent.cgi?article=1214&context=ulr.

"What are the Five Basic Necessities of Life (FBNL®)." The Humanity Party®. humanityparty.com/5-basic-necessities-of-life.

Whitmer, David. "An Address to All Believers In Christ." Richmond, MO: 1887. Found online at "An Address to All Believers in Christ." Wikisource. Wikimedia Foundation. 19 Jan. 2014. en.wikisource.org/wiki/An_Address_to_All_Believers_in_Christ.

"Why So Many Good Business Leaders Are Mormons." 4 May 2012. The Economist. *Business Insider*. businessinsider.com/why-the-mormon-faith-produces-so-many-good-business-leaders-2012-5.

"Women's liberation movement," *Wikipedia*, Wikimedia Foundation, 9 May 2021, en.wikipedia.org/wiki/Women%27s_liberation_movement.

Woodruff, Wilford. "Discourse by Elder Wilford Woodruff, delivered in the New Tabernacle, Salt Lake City, Sunday Afternoon, September 16, 1877." *Journal of Discourses*, 26 vols. London/Liverpool: Latter Day Saints' Book Depot, 1855–86. Vol.19. 229.

Zinn, Howard. *The People's History of the United States of America*. New York: Harper Perennial Modern Classics, 2005.

Zunes, Stephen, Tom Malthaner, and Richard H. Curtiss. "U.S. Financial Aid To Israel: Figures, Facts, and Impact." Washington Report on Middle Eastern Affairs – American Education Trust. wrmea.org/congress-u.s.-aid-to-israel/u.s.-aid-to-israel-1948-present.html.

ONE RACE,
ONE PEOPLE,
ONE WORLD

THE HUMANITY PARTY®

A NEW WORLD GOVERNMENT
Earth's only hope

HUMANITYPARTY.COM